Housing and Economics
The American Dilemma

The MIT Press
Cambridge, Massachusetts,
and London, England

Housing and Economics
The American Dilemma

Edited by
Michael A. Stegman

Set in Linotype Helvetica by
P&M Typesetting, Inc.
Printed and bound by
Halliday Lithograph Corp.
in the United States
of America

ISBN 0262 19081 8

Library of Congress catalog card
number: 71-128542

Acknowledgments

1.1. "Housing Needs," *Building the American City*, Report of the National Commission on Urban Problems, Washington, 1968, pp. 66–80.

1.2 "The Relationship of Residential Financing and Expenditures on Residential Construction," Sherman J. Maisel, *Proceedings, Conference on Savings and Residential Financing*, Chicago, 1966, pp. 129–140.

1.3. "The Federal Reserve and the Mortgage Market: Some Perspectives on the Crisis of 1966," Jack M. Guttentag, *A Study of Mortgage Credit*, Subcommittee on Housing and Urban Affairs, Committee on Banking and Currency, Washington, May 1967, pp. 392–406.

1.4. "A Review of the Filtering Controversy," *Filtering and Neighborhood Change*, Wallace F. Smith, Research Report 24, Center for Real Estate and Urban Economics, Institute of Urban and Regional Development, University of California, Berkeley, 1966, pp. 1–33.

1.5. "Elimination of Blight and Slums," *Economic Evaluation of Urban Renewal*, Jerome Rothenberg, The Brookings Institution, Washington, 1967, pp. 32–57.

2.1. "Efficiency in the Housing Industry," Leland S. Burns and Frank G. Mittelbach, *A Decent Home, Technical Studies, Volume 2, Housing Costs, Production Efficiency, Finance, Manpower and Land*, Report of the President's Committee on Urban Housing, Washington, 1969, pp. 79–112.

2.2. "Land Planning and the Property Tax," Mason Gaffney, *Journal of the American Institute of Planners* (Vol. 35, No. 3, May 1969), pp. 178–183.

3.1. "A Proposed Methodology for Comparing Federally Assisted Housing Programs," William B. Ross, *Papers and Proceedings of the Seventy-Ninth Annual Meeting of the American Economic Association, American Economic Review* (Vol. LVII, No. 2, May 1967), pp. 91–100.

3.2. "Economic Feasibility Analysis For Urban Renewal Housing Rehabilitation," A. H. Schaaf, *Journal of the American Institute of Planners* (Vol. 35, No. 6, November 1969), pp. 399–404.

3.3. "Rent Supplements and the Subsidy Dilemma," Irving H. Welfeld, *Law and Contemporary Problems, Housing Part II: The Federal Role* (Vol. XXXII, No. 3, School of Law, Duke University, Summer 1967), pp. 465–481.

3.4. "Public Housing or Income Supplements: The Economics of Housing For the Poor," Eugene Smolensky, *Journal of the American Institute of Planners* (Vol. 34, No. 2, March 1968), pp. 94–101.

3.5. "Comment on 'Public Housing or Income Supplements: The Economics of Housing for the Poor,'" Michael A. Stegman, *Journal of the American Institute of Planners* (Vol. 34, No. 3, May 1968), pp. 195–198.

3.6. "Is Public Housing Headed For A Fiscal Crisis?" Albert A. Walsh, *Journal of Housing* (Vol. 26, No. 2, February 1969), pp. 65–71.

3.7. "Facts and Fictions in Urban Renewal," Louis Winnick, *Ends and Means of Urban Renewal*, Papers from the Philadelphia Housing Association's Fiftieth Anniversary Forum, Philadelphia, 1961, pp. 23–35.

3.8. "Home Finance and Housing Quality In Aging Neighborhoods," William G. Grigsby, *The Economic Problems of Housing*, edited by Adela Adam Nevitt, Proceedings of a conference held by the International Economic Association, London, St. Martin's Press, 1967, pp. 105–122.

3.9. "Home Ownership Opportunities for the Poor," Michael A. Stegman *Encyclopedia of Social Work*, National Association of Social Workers, New York, forthcoming.

4.1. "Alternative Futures for the American Ghetto," Anthony Downs, *Daedalus* (Vol. 97, No. 4, Fall 1968), pp. 1331–1378.

4.2. "The Housing Effects of a Guaranteed Annual Income," William G. Grigsby, for the Department of Housing and Urban Development, Washington, 1969, pp. 1–13; 36–62.

4.3. "Major Proposals for Change in Federal Tax Provisions Affecting Urban Housing," *The Federal Income Tax in Relation to Housing,* Richard E. Slitor, Research Report No. 5, for the National Commission on Urban Problems, Washington, 1969, pp. 43–85; 101–113.

4.4 "New York's Housing: A Study in *Immobilisme*," George Sternlieb, *The Public Interest* (No. 16, Summer 1969), pp. 123–138.

Contributors

Leland S. Burns PROFESSOR OF REAL ESTATE AND URBAN LAND ECONOMICS	Graduate School of Business Administration University of California Los Angeles
Anthony Downs SENIOR VICE PRESIDENT, TREASURER AND A MEMBER OF THE BOARD OF DIRECTORS	Real Estate Research Corporation Chicago
Mason Gaffney PROFESSOR OF ECONOMICS	University of Wisconsin Milwaukee Resources for the Future, Inc. Washington
William G. Grigsby PROFESSOR OF CITY AND REGIONAL PLANNING	University of Pennsylvania Philadelphia
Jack M. Guttentag PROFESSOR OF FINANCE	University of Pennsylvania Philadelphia
Sherman J. Maisel MEMBER	Board of Governors of the Federal Reserve System
Frank G. Mittelbach ACTING DIRECTOR	Housing, Real Estate and Urban Land Studies Program Graduate School of Business Administration University of California Los Angeles
William B. Ross DEPUTY UNDER SECRETARY	Department of Housing and Urban Development Washington
Jerome Rothenberg PROFESSOR	Department of Economics Massachusetts Institute of Technology Cambridge
A. H. Schaaf PROFESSOR	School of Business Administration University of California Berkeley
Richard E. Slitor PROFESSOR OF ECONOMICS	University of Massachusetts Amherst
Wallace F. Smith CHAIRMAN	Center for Real Estate and Urban Economics Institute of Urban and Regional Development University of California Berkeley

Eugene Smolensky
PROFESSOR OF ECONOMICS
The University of Wisconsin
Madison

Michael A. Stegman
ASSOCIATE PROFESSOR OF CITY AND REGIONAL PLANNING
University of North Carolina
Chapel Hill

George Sternlieb
PROFESSOR, GRADUATE SCHOOL OF BUSINESS
DIRECTOR, CENTER FOR URBAN SOCIAL SCIENCE RESEARCH
Rutgers, The State University
New Brunswick, New Jersey

Albert A. Walsh
ADMINISTRATOR
Housing and Development Administration
New York City

Irving H. Welfeld
ATTORNEY
Office of General Counsel
Department of Housing and Urban Development
Washington

Louis Winnick
DEPUTY VICE PRESIDENT
DIVISION OF NATIONAL AFFAIRS
OFFICER IN CHARGE
URBAN AND METROPOLITAN DEVELOPMENT
Ford Foundation
New York

Preface

The urgent and deep-seated impulses of students in city planning and related fields to contribute to the solutions of society's most pressing social problems necessitate a reappraisal of traditional educational curricula. As this relates to the study of housing problems, for example, it compels those of us who teach in this area to provide students with some systematic means for viewing and understanding the poverty-low-income housing nexus. We must facilitate their acquisition of a number of analytical and intellectual tools to assist them in translating their bountiful energies into positive, directed actions in the field, and convince them that a proper value orientation is a necessary but not a sufficient condition to permit meaningful participation in a wide range of community-development activities.

In spite of countless books, articles, and related materials focusing on the so-called "urban crisis"—many of which concern housing—none of these recent works have presented penetrating analyses of low-income housing policy. Nor do any assist the interested student in evaluating the rash of "housing solutions" with which current literature is replete. Yet, keener insights into the inherent strengths and weakness of alternative proposals, greater appreciation of the complexities of the phenomena with which they have chosen to deal, and a working knowledge of how to take advantage of existing, albeit imperfect, programmatic options would, in some small way perhaps, lessen increasing student frustration with the real world in which so little progress seems to be made. It is with these thoughts in mind that this book has been compiled.

While there is no single compilation concerned with the economics of low-income housing efforts as they exist, or might possibly emerge, there does exist a relatively large number of recent articles and the like whose collective focus is the cost and related economic implications of rebuilding the residential stock of the urban core—or of alternative housing solutions. It is both interesting and significant to note, however, that the bulk of these papers are not the work of theoretical economists, but of applied economists, methodologists, and others concerned with the course and implementation of low-income housing policy. It is significant because this book represents an initial effort to present an organized analysis of the economics of low-income housing, even though there is today no "pure theory" relevant to many of the important aspects of providing adequate housing for the poor. Thus, if continued progress is to be made toward rationalizing this significant dimension of national housing policy, perhaps it might have to be accomplished primarily through the efforts of those whose pursuits of more adequate analyses are not severely circumscribed by the theoretical limitations of abstract constructs that cannot be applied to real-world economic processes. Too, while most academic economists distinguish between the economic and financial dimensions of low-income housing programs and defer to others the task of inquiring into the nature of the latter, a comprehensive analysis of low-income housing policy must bridge the gap between the two. Perhaps some elaboration on this point is in order.

A practical approach to the problem at hand requires, for example, that not only ought the low-rent public housing program be viewed in the context of economic efficiency and the resultant distributions of costs and benefits but with respect to its financial viability as well. It took more than thirty years of experience with this program before it was officially recognized that the basic formulas under which public housing units are constructed and operated required that most projects would ultimately deteriorate, as costs of operations would continue to rise faster than tenant incomes. The so-called Brooke Amendment to the 1969 Housing Act was directed at this very point.[1]

Similarly, while many economists might refrain from considering the relationships between investments in residential real estate and Federal income tax laws a component of the economics of low-income housing, the 1969 Tax Reform Act is heavy with subsidized-housing implications. At minimum, it is essential that students of housing understand the impacts of depreciation rules, recapture provisions and capital-gains treatment of alternative housing investments and, in general, appreciate how the Internal Revenue Service has given truth to the phrase, in real estate "... profits are losses and losses highly profitable."[2]

The economics of, say, urban renewal cannot in practice be distinguished from the financial implications of declining markets, nor the slum-housing problem from the investment climate in

[1]The Brooke Amendment provided for the use of 75 million dollars in additional federal annual contributions to hold tenant rents at 25 percent of income, enable local authorities to maintain financial solvency, and enable authorities to provide adequate operating and maintenance services and reserve funds. See *Journal of Housing* (Vol. 27, No. 1, January 1970), p. 21.

[2]Phillip M. Stern, *The Great Treasury Raid* (New York: Signet, 1965), p. 140.

the inner city. Comprehension of each of these relationships would have suggested long before it was officially acknowledged that "slum dwellers would not be rehoused on the cleared sites,"[3] and that avaricious slum lords are not the root cause of housing decay.[4] Thus, while financial relationships such as these might be eschewed by many as belonging in the realm of the bookkeeper, to a great extent they are reflective of the stuff and substance of national low-income housing policy.

This book is divided into four parts, with the initial point of entry into the analyses provided by a series of papers that focus on the nature and magnitude of the low-income housing problem, estimation of future housing needs, and on the fundamental processes relevant to an understanding of the market system. With this as general background, the second part concentrates on the peculiar nature of the housing commodity, various components of housing cost, and on the nature of the construction industry. The selections are intended to provide the minimum kinds of insights required for intelligent examination of low-income housing policy or the scrutiny of individual programs.

Part 3 provides both an overview of subsidized housing programs and a varied collection of analytical approaches and methodologies which have been recently applied to the examination and appraisal of specific housing programs or program areas. The concluding section, on the other hand, highlights recent attempts to evaluate alternative proposals *ex ante*, rather than after the fact, and includes selections on a wide range of housing fronts. Here, the reader is challenged to pursue more deeply that which is presented for his consideration and to approach the problems that confront him more creatively and more analytically than he has done previously.

Introducing each of these sections is an essay written by the editor, which is intended to relate individual selections to each other as well as to the overall study of the economics of housing solutions. Also, they were used as vehicles in which to raise questions about specific materials contained in particular selections, to expand upon other materials, and to raise important issues that have not yet been covered adequately in the literature.

[3]Charles Abrams, *The City is The Frontier* (New York: Harper and Row, 1965), pp. 84–85.
[4]See, for example, George Sternlieb, *The Tenement Landlord* (New Brunswick: Urban Studies Center, Rutgers University, 1966).

The editor wishes to acknowledge with gratitude the able assistance of William R. Blosser in the preparation of this volume. Mrs. Margaret Williamson eagerly typed several drafts of the introductory essays, generally oversaw the technical operations of preparing the book, and was instrumental in our successful encounter with most deadlines. Final responsibility for all selections, arrangements, and omissions is the editor's.

Michael A. Stegman
May 1970

1
The Macro and Micro Contexts

Introduction

This book of readings on the economics of low-income housing begins with a series of articles on the housing market. Perhaps the subject could be equally well introduced via an assessment of low-income housing needs or the characteristics of just the low-income market or in some other fashion. There are several compelling reasons, however, for commencing with a broad overview of the market.

First, the existence of what we call a shortage of low-income housing implies that the economy generally and the housing market specifically is not allocating resources to housing production and consumption in a manner consistent with what we might like to see.

Second, every public response to the private market's inability to allocate housing resources consistent with some specified welfare objective has second-order effects on the market. Thus, the existence of publicly owned and operated inventories, the F.H.A. and V.A. mortgage insurance and guarantee programs, and every other existing housing effort has market, price, quality, and occupancy implications for the standing stock of privately owned housing. It is essential that in the formulation of low-income housing policies we be aware of what the market implications might be of not only existing programs but also those that are contemplated.

Third, while most publicly supported housing programs are formulated through political as opposed to market processes, they are frequently designed to evoke particular market responses or alter investment and consumption patterns that would have obtained in the absence of public intervention. For example, the simple decision by a local community to enforce a housing code presents an owner of marginal quality housing units with a set of options different from those he faced before the policy was effected. Whereas before he might have pursued a profit-maximizing objective successfully, he now must choose to minimize his losses by either upgrading to one of many rehabilitation standards or withdrawing his units from the market.[1] The possibility that something seemingly as uncomplex as housing-code enforcement might conceivably result in large-scale abandonments rather than in substantial upgrading or stabilization of the lower quality housing stock represents a compelling reason to understand the arena in which the housing game is played. In short, "... without better market understanding, there is danger that public actions will be frequently blunted in their intended effects, that some of the results may be the reverse of those intended, or that 'side effects' will create new and difficult problems requiring further public attention."[2]

Fourth, it should be noted that the Federal housing policy pendulum has once again swung its full arc, with the result that the private sector is being called upon to participate actively in a wide range of efforts to close the low-income housing gap. Thus, today as never before, government housing programs must not only be palatable philosophically to market-oriented investors, they must also compete successfully in the marketplace for the investment dollar. Therefore, in order for the many housing programs to succeed, their creators, as well as those who will participate in selling them, must possess a much higher level of sophistication of the economics of housing and real estate generally and comprehend the forces at play in the market more fully than those who traditionally relied upon a government owned and operated inventory to ameliorate the housing shortage.

Finally, the low-income housing market, while buffeted by many unique forces, is an integral part of the market at large. In fact, a prior understanding of general market dynamics is often a prerequisite to a full understanding of investment and consumption problems in low-income submarkets. Brief reference to two characteristics of stagnating, low-income submarkets will illustrate this point. In the general housing market, given a particular set of market conditions,

> the landlord will choose a rent level that maximizes the difference between his total costs and total rent receipts. This rent level may be such that only a portion of his apartments will be occupied. If he attempts to fill the vacant units by further rent cuts, he will reduce his total net revenue since any reduction in rent calculated to reduce his vacancies soon must be applied equally to his present tenants.[3]

In the low-income market, vacancies are to be avoided because of the extremely high probability that such units will be vandalized. The pricing policies of inner-city landlords, while designed to maximize the differences between total revenues and costs, are nevertheless products of different market factors. Also, one might expect to find a three-track rental system in the low-income market whereby so-called normal households pay going market rents, stable long-term tenants who pay their rents regularly and care for their units receive discounts, and high-risk households pay premiums for the lowest quality shelter.

In the housing market generally, it is typical for increased costs of doing business to be passed on to housing consumers in the form of higher shelter costs. In the low-income market increased costs of maintenance, insurance, and money, along with the growing risks of vandalism and mounting social and political pressures to "do something about those slums," have all been capitalized into lower property values rather than passed on to consumers in the form of higher housing costs. This explains, in part, the phenomenon of declining values and capital erosion that is occurring in the inner city in spite of what many observers would consider relatively high rent schedules.

In short, the low-income market can be best viewed in relation to the larger housing market because investment capital and other housing resources are highly mobile while the poor typically lack economic and social mobility. Consequently, while "the combination of risk, decreasing profitability, and loss of potential capital gains has substantially restricted the kinds of professional owners who are willing to invest in slum properties,"[4] the bargaining positions of many low-income consumers have either remained unchanged or deteriorated as local markets have grown more active and prosperous.

It is the purpose of this initial section to acquaint the reader with a theoretical view of the macro and micro contexts in which both the aggregate allocation of housing resources and the consumption of dwelling units takes place. At a very general level we know that the annual rate of housing construction in the nation is a complex function of, among other things, household formation, housing preferences, household income, the rate of inventory loss, and the prevailing interest rate. Econometricians debate the precise contribution of each of the previously mentioned variables on the rate of housing production and the extent to which particular variables either lag behind or lead the construction cycle, while we experience crushing credit problems that have sharply reduced national housing output and continue to play havoc with the construction industry.[5] An issue that emerged in the late 1950s, only to become of academic interest a few years thereafter, has once again become of great political significance. Stated simply, should the housing sector continue to be the balance wheel of the economy, or, as Grebler put it in 1960, should "other sectors or industries, presumably of lower social priority, bear the burden of fluctuations if this is necessary for maintaining overall stability or balanced economic growth?"[6] Therefore, it is the role of credit in housing production that characterizes the readings on the macro-market environment.

The issue in its current context is introduced through the Douglas Commission's statement on national housing needs in the coming decade and is developed more fully by Maisel (whose paper was written before the credit crunch of 1966), who suggests that tight-money periods have no impact on underlying demand for housing and thus merely act to defer housing starts from one period to another. Guttentag picks up on the theme and concludes, "there is no evidence to suggest that over a stretch of time long enough to cover both easy and tight money periods, housing output is lower than it would be with stable credit markets," at least within the range of credit fluctuations experienced up to the present.

The relevance of the macro-oriented papers to low-income housing problems is twofold: First, if, as Maisel and Guttentag suggest, over the long cycle demand and output are not affected by intermittent periods of tight money, what might we say about the output of subsidized housing for low- and moderate-income families? As will be discussed at length in the introductory essay in Part 4, Kristof suggests that as many as 300,000 subsidized housing units were not started between 1967 and 1969 because of inflation.[7] Additionally, he indicates that the newest federally subsidized rental program (Section 236) has not been usable in New York State because "prevailing rates of interest require developers to take deep discounts on their mortgages . . . and that there is no way for non-profit sponsors to liquidate this cost while limited-profit sponsors are unwilling to make this additional equity contribution to the project."[8]

Second, the supply of credit is probably related to costs and prices in the construction industry. As a matter of fact Maisel indicates that the general mortgage credit booms and busts we typically go through contribute to the building industry's susceptibility to the so-called ratchet effect. "When starts and demand are booming, costs rise rapidly. When demand falls, costs stay level or rise at a slower pace." That short-run fluctuations in housing starts might contribute to higher costs and a less efficient housing industry can have serious implications for low-income housing policy. In Part 2, we will investigate this subject more fully.

The transition from the macro- to the micro-market context is provided by Wallace Smith's critique of the filtering controversy, which began in 1945 with Ratcliff and has since involved a number of market scholars. Initially defined as changes in occupancy as the housing occupied by one income group becomes available to the next lower income group as a result of a decline in market prices, filtering was considered the normal market process for providing housing for the poor. To eliminate occupied substandard housing, the argument goes, we need only introduce enough new units into the supply at the top of the market. Since Ratcliff, the concept and definition of filtering has been reformulated, redirected, and otherwise altered by a number of theoreticians through a filtering process all their own.

Whether one agrees with Smith that rather than being a market process imbued with welfare objectives, filtering is "simply a change in the allocation of housing units among households of different types," a recent empirical study of the process should help shed some much needed light on the subject.[9] According to Lansing and his colleagues, for every 1,000 new homes constructed, a total of 3,545 moves are generated, less than 10 percent of which are by poor families.[10] With respect to rental units, "of the new occupants, 20% report being in a higher rent interval than was reported by the former tenants, compared to 11% who reported lower rent."[11] Similarly, whereas, 55 percent of all the dwellings in the survey were occupied by people with lower incomes after the move, 25 percent were occupied by people with higher incomes.[12]

As will be discussed more fully in Part 4, the filtering controversy, as it relates to the development of a viable low-income housing strategy, will once again become a topical issue as a number of factors converge to increase the costs, monetary and political, of dealing with the nation's low-income housing problems through direct subsidies to the poor. When the issue reasserts itself, it would be well to remember one last set of statistics provided by Lansing—that the mean value of owner-occupied homes involved in the filtering chains falls from $25,900 at position one to $19,700 for position three and continues to decline slowly for positions four and beyond, stabilizing at $17,300 for positions six and higher.[13] That is, the average values of the last houses released in the filtering chains were in excess of $17,000.

From Smith's paper, which deals with the mechanism through which populations adjust to changes in supply or the supply is reallocated with alterations on the demand side, we proceed next to Rothenburg's entry that focuses on the allocation of local resources to housing, given a particular income distribution. Here, the demand for slum housing is discussed, and some of the factors affecting the supply side of the market are offered as explanations for the existence of slums.

One of the reasons cited by Rothenburg for the perpetuation of slum housing conditions, even though apparently profitable alternatives are available to slum-neighborhood investors, is the existence of market externalities—that is, market factors that affect the value of an individual's property and are beyond his control. A useful device for illustrating the situation in which such investors often find themselves is an adaptation of the "Prisoner's Dilemma" game. In its simplest form the game situation is depicted by a four-call matrix, as in Table 1, the elements of which represent the actual and potential rates of return of two adjacent property owners who have invested in residential properties and have additional capital invested in bonds.

The interpretation of the matrix as presented by Davis and Whinston, who originally applied the game to the problems of urban blight, is as follows:[14]

At present, the average return on both these investments, the property and the corporate bonds considered together, is four percent. Thus if neither owner makes the decision to sell his corporate bonds and makes a new investment in the redevelopment of his property, each will continue to get the four percent average return. This situation is represented by the entries within brackets in the lower right of the matrix . . . On the other hand, if both individuals made the decision to sell their bonds and invest the proceeds in redevelopment of their property, it is assumed that each would obtain an average return of seven percent on his total investment. Therefore, the entry in the upper left of the matrix . . . has seven percent return for each owner.

The other two entries in the

Table 1.

	Owner II	
	Invest	Not Invest
Owner I		
Invest	(.07, .07)	(.03, .10)
Not Invest	(.10, .03)	(.04, .04)

matrix . . . represent the situation when one owner invests and the other does not . . . Consider the entries in the brackets in the lower left corner of the matrix. In this situation, Owner I would have decided to "not invest" and Owner II would have decided to "invest."

Owner I is assumed to obtain some of the benefits from Owner II's investment, the redevelopment contributing something to a "better neighborhood." For example, if the two properties under consideration happened to be apartment buildings, the decision of Owner II to invest might mean that he would demolish his "outdated" apartment building and construct a new one complete with offstreet parking and other amenities. But this would mean that the tenants of Owner I would now have an easier time finding parking spaces on the streets, their children might have the opportunity of associating with the children of the "higher class" people who might be attracted to the modern apartment building, and so forth. All this means that (as soon as leases allow) Owner I can edge up his rents. Thus his return is increased without having to make an additional investment. We assume that his return becomes ten percent in this case, and this figure is appropriately entered in the matrix. Owner II, on the other hand, would find that, since his renters also consider the "neighborhood" (which includes the ill effects of Owner I's "outdated" structure), his level of rents would have to be less than would be the case if his apartment building were in an alternative location. Thus we assume that the return on his total investment (the investment in the now-demolished structure plus the investment in the new structure) falls to three percent. This figure is also appropriately entered in the matrix. For simplicity, the reverse situation, where Owner I decided to invest and Owner II decides not to invest, is taken to be similar.

That the security and profitability of an investment might be a function of market externalities implies that rational investors, acting without collusion, might well refrain from improving their properties even though profitable investment opportunities are available. In this highly simplified game we can surmise that each owner will refrain from improving his property because not only would he improve his situation if his counterpart invests while he does not, but his current return is higher than it would be if he invests while his counterpart does not.

The issue is of direct relevance to low-income housing policy for two reasons. First, we might say that because of externalities or neighborhood effects inner-city investors are locked into the low-income market, unable to take advantage of, say, the latent demand that might exist for another Georgetown or Society Hill. Along this dimension the existence of externalities tends to increase new construction outside of the central city while maintaining the supply of privately owned rental housing available to low-income families within the inner city. On the other hand the same externalities work against any individual, privately initiated efforts to renovate moderately inner-city housing. Unless investors control entire block fronts, or through public intervention all owners are made to upgrade their units, little renovation activity will be forthcoming. In fact, as will be discussed in the final essay, collusion alone is an insufficient incentive to encourage rehabilitation of the low-income stock.

Notes

[1]A. H. Schaaf, "Public Policies in Urban Renewal: An Economic Analysis of Justifications and Effects," *Land Economics* (Vol. XL, No. 1, February 1964), pp. 67–78.
[2]George Sternlieb, *The Tenement Landlord* (Urban Studies Center, Rutgers, The State University, New Brunswick, 1966), p. 3.
[3]*Housing Market Analysis: A Study of Theory and Methods*, Chester Rapkin, Louis Winnick, and David M. Blank (Columbia University, The Institute for Urban Land Use and Housing Studies prepared for the Housing and Home Finance Agency, 1953), pp. 22–23.
[4]George Sternlieb, "Slum Housing: A Functional Analysis," *Urban Analysis: Readings in Housing and Urban Development*, Alfred N. Page and Warren R. Seyfried, editors (Glenview, Illinois, Scott, Foresman and Company, 1970), p. 335.
[5]See, for example, Sherman J. Maisel and Leo Grebler, "Determinants of Residential Construction," Research Study 4 in Commission on Money and Credit, *Impacts of Monetary Policy* (New York, 1962), or Sherman J. Maisel, "A Theory of Fluctuations in Residential Construction Starts," *American Economic Review* (Vol. LII, No. 3, June 1963), pp. 359–383.
[6]Leo Grebler, *Housing Issues in Economic Stabilization Policy* (National Bureau of Economic Research, Occasional Paper 72, New York, 1960), p. 97.
[7]Frank S. Kristof, "Local Urban Development Policy Under Inflation: A Case Study—New York City," paper presented at the meeting of the American Real Estate and Urban Economics Association, New York, December 30, 1969, mimeo; p. 1.
[8]*Ibid.*, p. 3.
[9]John B. Lansing, Charles Wade Clifton, and James N. Morgan, *New Homes and Poor People: A Study of Chains of Moves* (Institute for Social Research, University of Michigan, Ann Arbor, 1969).
[10]*Ibid.*, p. 40.
[11]*Ibid.*, p. 8.
[12]*Ibid.*, p. 45.
[13]*Ibid.* p. 6.
[14]Otto A. Davis and Andrew B. Whinston, "The Economics of Urban Renewal," *Law and Contemporary Problems* (Duke University School of Law, Durham, North Carolina, Urban Renewal: Part II, Vol. 26, No. 1, Winter 1961), pp. 105–117. Reprinted in James Q. Wilson, editor, *Urban Renewal: The Record and The Controversy* (Cambridge, The M.I.T. Press, 1966), pp. 50–67. Quote taken from Wilson, pp. 54–56.

1.1
Housing Needs

One of the most enduring sources of controversy and misunderstanding in urban affairs has been the issue of *housing needs.* At bottom they are, at any moment of time, the needs of the families and other households who do not have what the Congress, in the Housing Act of 1949, called "a decent home and a suitable living environment." Overwhelmingly, these households are among the poor, the near poor, and the lower economic middle class.

Much of the controversy comes on two points: (1) In more concrete terms, what is a *decent* home and what is a *suitable* living environment? (2) What of needs beyond those of the present moment? How many more households will be formed over the coming 5, 10, or 25 years? What will they be able to spend on housing? Where will they want to live? Will internal migration of our physically mobile population result in surpluses of decent housing in some localities and serious shortages in others? How many presently acceptable houses will slide into the substandard category through the ravages of age, neglected maintenance and repair, and shifting land uses in our many growing and ever-changing urban areas?

In other parts of this report, the Commission has tried to come to grips with many of these questions. Here it presents an overview of needs, primarily in quantitative terms, for housing, looking at the present and estimating the future in light of the immediate past. But first, we must call attention to the major handicap in this matter of housing need—the unbelievable inadequacy of the data, which we discuss later in some detail.

The Nation has made a phenomenal record over the last two decades in building housing for the middle and affluent classes, mainly at the edges of the central cities and in the suburbs. The efforts of private enterprise account for most of this construction, but Government policy has provided significant incentives and help through mortgage guarantees, secondary credit facilities, and Federal income tax deductions for interest payments and local property taxes. The intent of Government policy—and its effect—has been to increase substantially the rate of homeownership.

Reprinted from *Building the American City*, Report of the National Commission on Urban Problems to the Congress and to the President of the United States (Washington: Government Printing Office, 1968), Part II, Chapter 1, "Housing Needs," pp. 66–80.

The extent to which Government policy has subsidized the private homeowner is not generally recognized or acknowledged. The homeowner who deducts interest and property taxes as costs in computing his Federal tax return is not required to include the imputed value of rent as a part of his income. This generous but generally unacknowledged Federal subsidy to the affluent or middle-class homeowner needs to be emphasized in view of the self-righteous opposition often expressed toward subsidized housing for the poor.[1]

In contrast to its truly amazing record in housing construction for the upper half of America's income groups, the Nation has made an inexcusably inadequate record in building or upgrading housing for the poor to provide them with decent, standard housing at rents and prices they can afford.

Low-rent public housing built since the 1930s does provide housing for about 2.4 million people and includes an inventory of almost 700,000 units. But today, even by the most liberal calculations, less than 100,000 units a year of all kinds are being built or "made available" under low-rent housing programs—newly constructed public housing, rehabilitation, leased housing units, rent supplements, rent certificates, and other programs. And this small annual total has only been reached in the most recent years.

Even under these programs, the very poor have virtually been excluded. The amounts of subsidy available under the most generous programs often are insufficient to help them. The most needy also are rejected by the administrators of programs and the managers of projects because these poor bring with them so many problems.

It is in part for this reason that a disproportionate share of the units built or made available under public housing in recent years—more than half—has gone to the less troublesome elderly. While not enough is presently built either for them or for other needy groups, families living in poverty have had very little help under existing housing programs.

In addition, with very few exceptions, little has been built for poor families in the large central cities, for much of the small amounts of public housing built for families has gone to middle-sized cities.[2] Further, very few units of three or more bedrooms have been built at all, so that a huge housing gap for the large, poor family exists not only in the larger cities, but nearly everywhere.

Furthermore, over the last decades, Government action through urban renewal, highway programs, demolitions on public housing sites, code enforcement, and other programs has destroyed more housing for the poor than government at all levels has built for them.

Meanwhile, in the past, relocation assistance to persons and businesses displaced through Federal, State, and local public works programs has been inadequate, nonuniform, and for some programs—completely absent.

While public housing, its related programs, and the 221(d) (3) program for moderate-income groups have been of some slight help[3] in meeting the housing needs of the poorer half of the population, urban renewal has essentially been irrelevant to the housing needs of the poor. While the centers of some of our cities have been transformed by urban renewal into attractive business and higher income residential districts with a consequent strengthening of local tax base, very little low-income housing has been built on renewal sites. Fierce arguments may ensue as to whether this was by design or the result of the administration of the program. But few would dispute the fact that to date it has not served to help house the poor.

Finally other provisions of housing and urban legislation by which local agencies have bought and preserved open space, improved some mass transit systems, and built needed community facilities may well have improved the living environment of urban areas, but this benefit is largely general—that is, it is largely unrelated to the critical housing needs of specific segments of the urban population.

These facts make a strong moral case for action to help the most needy now. It justified the passage of the Housing Act of 1968, and, most importantly, it calls for carrying out the goals of the act on schedule.

It should be repeated that this responsibility is based not only on need. It is a moral requirement for the Nation. Having built generously for the most prosperous half of the Nation, and having destroyed more housing for the poor than we have built, we now owe a special effort to provide decent housing for those who have in the past largely been left out.

Today, more than a generation after the Federal Government began to undertake various programs to influence housing production and housing conditions, and decades after improved housing was at least an objective of public regulation by local and State governments, there has been no satisfactory analysis of present housing needs and a similar estimate of probable future needs as guides for housing policy and programs. Aside from the hazards in predicting birth and fertility rates, the *basic facts* for such studies, in reasonable detail and refinement, are not available. In some respects this is the most damning indictment against the public concern, including but by no means limited to governmental concern, with housing in this country.

There are not even good working definitions of a *decent* home and a *suitable* living environment, the supposed anchor points of our national housing goal, used in what statistics are being gathered. Still more elusive, therefore, are the complex questions such as: How many presently acceptable houses will slide into the substandard category through the ravages of age, neglect, and shifting land uses? How many presently substandard houses could be made acceptable through rehabilitation? What is the best balance between public and private investment in housing?

The only reasonably comprehensive data on housing conditions or quality are those of the Bureau of the Census. To say that the available data are inadequate is no adverse criticism of the Bureau, which has worked hard and intelligently on housing. A nationwide, decennial census, however, cannot supply the complete range of facts needed to judge housing quality. The Bureau knows this perfectly well. Its 1960 Census of Housing says,

> The combination of data on condition and plumbing facilities is considered one measure of housing quality. It takes account of the physical characteristics of the unit—the structural condition and the presence of basic plumbing facilities (water supply, toilet facilities, and bathing facilities). Although such factors as light, ventilation, and neighborhood also reflect quality, particularly in urban areas, it is not feasible to measure them in a large scale census enumeration. These elements, however, often are closely associated with condition and plumbing facilities.[4]

The limited role of the large scale census enumeration stems not only from its general focus that omits specific details. Major difficulties include these:

> The term structural condition is confusing. It does not refer to the basic fabric of the building. Rather it looks to "visible defects * * * associated with weather tightness, extent of disrepair, hazards to physical safety of the occupants, and inadequate or makeshift construction."
>
> The Census item of *piped hot water* is misleading because the plumbing facilities are not necessary in the dwelling unit. The proper item is *piped hot water inside the structure*. It may not be in the dwelling unit. And even there, the hot water may be supplied "only at certain times of the day, week, or year."

Omitted items of *light, ventilation, and neighborhood* are crucial to housing quality. Dual egress, in some parts of the country installed heating facilities, size of rooms and dwelling units, also crucial, are left out.

And the census belief in a correlation between those quality items enumerated and those not enumerated is questionable.

The Commission warns against the common tendency to read into the census housing data more than is there. Visible condition of building (which the census classifies as *sound, deteriorating,* and *dilapidated*) and plumbing facilities in combination are indeed, as the Census puts it, "one measure of housing quality," but only one—and a crude one at that. Quite surely it is on the conservative side—that is, it results in a lower estimate of the volume of substandard housing than most reasonable persons would arrive at on the basis of careful local studies. This seems doubly likely for the housing in older, large, central cities and industrial suburbs of metropolitan areas. The census definition amounts to "a nearly weathertight box with pipes in it," and this notion of quality, unfortunately, is hopelessly inadequate.

In short, the hard job of estimating and projecting housing needs is made all but impossible by the ridiculously inadequate data now at hand. Nearly everyone concerned with the subject has known and said this since the first census of housing was published in 1940, more than a quarter of a century ago. Yet these same critics of the data have gone ahead to use, revise, and manipulate these statistics (and often others that are worse) to produce elaborate and rickety structures of partial or misleading facts. Personal guesses and farfetched assumptions with little relation to the actual world around us clutter the housing and urban problems field.

The Commission in its examination of the central city ghettos in every section of the country saw this problem time and again. We saw housing within 1 mile of the White House and the Capitol of the United States which passed the District of Columbia housing code, but which, in the judgment of those who saw it and smelled it, seemed hardly fit to live in. Is this standard housing?

And how is the data related to environment? Commission members saw rehabilitated housing in the blighted areas of St. Louis, New York City, Philadelphia, and Baltimore, among other cities, which met the local code standard. But the housing was surrounded by areas with inadequate city services for their special needs, areas which were deteriorating, or where freeways were scheduled to be built nearby. In many cases these circumstances will make it difficult for the rehabilitated housing to remain in good repair, as was the case in the early Baltimore experiments.

This Commission inspected one housing area where the noxious fumes from a giant chemical company plant nearby led the local housing expert to remark that if such a level of air pollution were found inside a factory, the State would either require gas masks or shut down the plant. But human beings lived in that environment unprotected by local or State law because the company has carved out its separate municipal jurisdiction, thus avoiding both its fiscal and social responsibility to the larger community. Would even a $50,000 house in that environment be "standard" or "decent" housing?

Is a unit correctly defined as standard under available data if the lot next door is littered with garbage; if police protection is limited; if street lights are not provided; if the sidewalk is buckled; if the street is full of potholes; if a liquor store is found on each corner; if sewers are nonexistent or inadequate; if the noise level is excessive; or if a rendering works is found in the block (as is true along the waterfront in the otherwise exclusive Georgetown area of Washington, D.C.)?

The Commission saw large sections of cities where, at the time of our examination, most of the dwellings did not rank very low on the census measures of housing quality but where, nevertheless, insurance companies would not write the usual forms of property insurance, banks and savings and loan associations would not lend on mortgages, and where the FHA would not insure. These areas, in the parlance of the trade, were "red-lined." People there were out of the ball game that has resulted in the improvement of many less needy areas in recent years.

The Commission saw such "standard" housing in virtually every one of the more than two dozen major cities it visited in every part of the United States. Caution is therefore indicated in discussing housing needs, lest the figures available are treated with a respect not due them.

Charting the housing course for urban America requires periodic, reasonably systematic housing inventories in at least all of the larger metropolitan areas of the country, and preferably in the smaller ones and in the independent cities as well. These need not all be full coverage jobs; sampling is possible and proper. They ought, however, to cover all of the items essential to a decent home and a suitable living environment, and they should be carried out uniformly for comparability of one metropolitan area with another. This would overcome many ambiguities and weaknesses of the limited national census enumeration. Also by compiling these local area inventories, much more realistic national estimates could be arrived at. The costs of such inventories would be small in proportion to the capital sums at stake and to their usefulness to housing entrepreneurs, officials, and to the concerned public.

Some 20 years ago the Committee on the Hygiene of Housing of the American Public Health Association developed a reasonably detailed method for measuring housing quality. Its title, "An Appraisal Method for Measuring the Quality of Housing," may have been unfortunate in that *appraisal* implies to some people an estimating of dollar value. Be that as it may, the method was carefully and intelligently put together and deserves equally careful review by those who may have responsibility for plugging the many gaps that now exist in available and useful inventory data on urban housing in this country.

The Commission in this discussion of available facts on urban housing emphatically is *not* saying or implying two things:

It is *not* saying that more data will decide for us what is acceptable housing and what is substandard. All standards, whether in housing or automobiles, require human judgment. "Scientific standards," if anyone wishes to use the term, are simply those based on carefully determined facts rather than on rule-of-thumb or mere opinion. Such facts are indispensable to sound judgment, but they are not a substitute for it.

Neither is the Commission suggesting that no changes be made in housing policy and programs until more adequate data are at hand. Quite the opposite. The need for more decent housing in American cities is so great, so pressing, and so obvious that much larger and more vigorous efforts to meet it are urgently needed. These efforts can and should be started at once, as the Housing Act of 1968 contemplates, using existing tools and programs, plus such modifications and additions as experience to date justifies. If the refinement of housing facts is undertaken promptly, the results would soon be available to light the way for even more effective action toward "a decent home and a suitable living environment for every American family."[5]

The Nationwide Scene

From 1950 through 1959 housing needs for the entire country, according to the author's definition of needs, decreased from 20.5 million units to 15.4 million. This substantial change arose from a decline in the number of substandard units from 17.0 to 11.4 million, and an increase of 0.8 million vacancies in standard units. Crowded households in standard units (those with more than one person per room) actually increased from 2.7 million to 3.9 million units. (See Table 1.)

Note that "substandard units to be removed" includes all units classified by the census as "dilapidated or lacking essential plumbing facilities." Left out of the substandard category are some 4.6 million units that in 1960 had plumbing facilities but were classified by the census as deteriorating (the intermediate category between *sound* and *dilapidated*); i.e., units presumably ripe for rehabilitation. Excluding them further understates the current needs total, as shown by the fact that rehabilitation (under the heading "Upgrading in existing inventory," Table 1, line 23) was recognized as an item that reduced total housing needs by 4 million units in the 1950s.

Also, crowded households in standard units are counted in total needs; crowded households in substandard units are not. This avoids double counting, once for demolition, once for overcrowding. If one family is simply in cramped quarters, this is correct. But it is not correct if overcrowding comes from two or more families doubling up because of poverty, discrimination, or housing shortage; the demolition of such a unit would lead to a need for two or more units. Which of the 2.2 million overcrowded substandard units in 1960 were in which category? The census data, again, are inadequate for making this distinction, so the figures err on the low side.

Strangely, although overcrowding is much more prevalent in substandard than in standard housing, during the 1950s the number of overcrowded, *standard* units *increased* by almost 1.3 million or 47.5 percent, while over the same period overcrowding in *substandard* housing *decreased* by 1.9 million units or 46.8 percent.

This could reflect a preference among some middle- and lower middle-income families, for gadgets over living space. It could be that easy terms induced many young couples to purchase houses that were really beyond their means, so as their families and expenses grew, they had to stay in houses they had out-

Table 1. Estimates of Components of Inventory Change and Changes in Housing Needs for the United States: 1960-89 [In thousands of units]

	Actual	Estimated		
	1950-59	1960-69	1970-79	1980-89
Subject	A	B	C	D
1. Total housing inventory at beginning of the decade	46,137	58,468	69,468	86,618
COMPONENTS OF INVENTORY CHANGE				
2. Units added to housing inventory	16.861	16,900	21,250	23.425
3. New construction	15,003	15,300	19,500	21,525
4. Units added by conversion	807	600	650	700
5. Units added through other sources	1,050	1,000	1,100	1.200
6. Units lost from housing inventory	—4,530	—5,900	—7,100	—8,300
7. Units removed through demolition	—1,933	—2,700	—3,300	—4.000
8. Units lost through mergers	—815	—700	—650	—600
9. Units lost through other means	—1,783	—2,500	—3,150	—3,700
10. Net change in housing inventory which was accounted for by:	12,331	11,000	14,150	15,125
11. Increase in number of households	9,986	9,400	12,300	13.285
12. Change in vacancies	2,345	1,600	1,850	1,840
13. Available for sale or rent	1,411	300	550	550
14. Other vacancies	933	1,300	1,300	1,290
HOUSING NEEDS				
15. Housing needs at beginning of decade	20,530	15,364	10.787	7,706
16. Substandard units to be removed	17,007	11,407	6,883	3,837
17. Crowded households in standard units	2,682	3,957	3,904	3,869
18. Increase in standard available vacancies	841	—	—	—
19. Changes in housing need during decade	—5,166	—4,577	—3,081	—2,021
20. Change in number of substandard units	—5,600	—4,524	—3,046	—1,743
21. Demolitions, mergers, other losses	—3,446	—3,885	—3,380	—2,715
22. Substandard units added during decade	1,886	1,551	1,508	1,382
23. Upgrading in existing inventory	—4,040	—2,190	—1,174	—410
24. Change in crowding in standard units	1,275	—53	—35	—278
25. Change in standard available vacancies	—841	—	—	—
26. Housing need at end of decade	15,364	10,787	7,706	5,685
27. Substandard units to be removed	11,407	6,883	3,837	2,094
28. Crowded households in standard units	3,957	3,904	3,869	3,591
29. Increase in standard available vacancies	—	—	—	—

Source: Frank S. Kristof, "Urban Housing Needs Through the 1980's: An Analysis and Projection," National Commission on Urban Problems, Research Report 10, Washington, 1968, p. 6.

grown. It may also be due to shifts in some substandard housing to the standard category by way of the removal only of "visible defects." This could account for some *decrease* in overcrowded substandard units.

Note also that our need figures require some vacancies: the criterion is 5 percent for owner-occupied houses—"for-sale vacancies." The relatively high level of housing production during the 1950s loosened up the supply as compared with the general shortage in 1950. Thus, according to the data, the housing needs were reduced by some 0.8 million units.

In short, if one puts much credence in the census data as measures or, at least, as indexes of housing quality, the nationwide picture of housing changes during the 1950s is a rosy one. The general housing shortage was wiped out, and the number of "substandard units to be removed" was reduced by almost one-third (32.9 percent). Almost the only disturbing notes were the substantial increase in overcrowding in standard units and the 1.9 million additional units falling into the substandard category. Of course, one also might have some qualms about the 3.4 million units that were demolished or merged. Surely most of these were lived in by lower income families. How did they make out? (Demolition and relocation, however, are taken up later in this report.)

More Roses in the Future?

Before considering the projections of housing needs for the three decades beyond 1960, what characteristics of housing in the 1950s accounted for most of what happened? Are they likely to continue to operate and with similar results?

A major assumption behind the analysis done for the Commission was that the primary force was a high volume of housebuilding in proportion to household formation. The ratio was 1.5 to 1; i.e., three housing units were built for each two additional households formed. During the first years of the 1960s this ratio was about 1.7 to 1, but high mortgage interest rates and rising construction costs in recent years have cut it back. The projections assume that it will be about 1.5 to 1 for the 1960s and, furthermore, that this ratio can be maintained without significant change during the 1970s and 1980s. If so, by 1990 the aggregate national housing need would be only 5.7 million units—a little more than one-third of the 1960 figure. Substandard houses to be removed in 1990 would be only 2.1 million units—less than one-fifth of the 1960 total.

In trying to judge these projections, one ought to look at what lay behind the 1.5-to-1 ratio of the 1950s. Direct building for the poor and near poor was a very minor factor. The overwhelming proportion of the building was by private agencies for buyers and renters further up the income scale. This building volume during the first years of the 1950s was spurred by the substantial remainder of the post-World War II housing shortage. Since then relatively high employment and rising incomes have played a major part. They fueled not only the market for new housing but also were largely responsible for the rehabilitation that corrected the "visible defects" and then raised over 4 million from the substandard to the standard category. Here, too, was a war-induced backlog of work roughly similar to the postwar housing shortage.

Two other factors, however, should not be overlooked. The volume of demolition reached unprecedented proportions—from an estimated average of 11 percent of new housing starts in earlier decades to 25 percent of new starts during the 1950s. Also, easier credit terms on mortgage loans for house purchases probably were a major factor. Lower down payments with longer amortization periods reduced monthly payments, which was called repeatedly to the prospective buyer's attention, but increased his total outlay over the years of purchase, which no one bothered to impress on him. This easing process would seem to be near its limits, short of comparable *new* stimulants to home purchases.

Obviously to maintain the 1.5-to-1 ratio very long would require a substantial removal of housing units from the then-existing supply—the standing stock so-called. Otherwise general overbuilding would result; vacancies would rise substantially and the volume of production would be cut back. In judging projections of housing production, therefore, estimates of removals or losses from the inventory are crucial. Table 1 shows units lost (line 6) as the following percentages of units added (line 2) by decades:

	Percent
1950s	26.9
1960s	34.9
1970s	33.4
1980s	35.4

These are very substantial proportions, particularly those after 1960. Probably few persons who fly over metropolitan areas and see the vast extent of new housing at the peripheries of central cities and on beyond suburbia would believe that for each three of these new houses one other unit has been removed by demolition, merger, or through "other means." Unfortunately the condition of the data on removals is as unsatisfactory as those on housing quality. Without trying to go into much detail on them, one item should be noted.

Line 9 of Table 1, "Units lost through other means"—i.e., other than demolition and merger (the combining of two or more housing units into one)—is a very substantial proportion of the crucially important total of *units lost* or, as sometimes called, *removals* from the housing inventory (line 6). In all four decades *other means* ran a close second to demolitions and accounted for the following proportions of the total lost or removed from the inventory:

	Percent
1980s	39.4
1950s	42.4
1960s	44.4
1970s	44.6

What are these *other means* that have taken so many housing units out of the inventory and may take so many millions more? The breakdown of this category is (1) fire, flood, and other disasters; (2) change of household units into group quarters as the census calls rooming or lodging house, dormitories, and similar structures; (3) change to nonhousing uses (e.g., shops, stores, manufacturing); (4) units closed to occupancy by public agencies or so far deteriorated as to be "unfit for human habitation" (e.g., abandoned buildings in rural areas of declining population and vandalized houses in some urban slum districts); and (5) "units moved from the site."

For none of these subcategories are there firm or reasonably satisfactory figures, so this treatment of units moved is strange. Losses by "moved from site" have been estimated as 540,637 units, 1950–59, or slightly more than 30 percent of total losses or removals by other means than demolition and merger. To offset this "loss" by adding the same units as "moved to the site" is simply figure-juggling. In a *national* inventory a housing unit moved from one lot to another is neither lost nor added. It makes no difference whether the move is to an adjacent lot or to another state. This treatment of moves, however, does have two effects on the estimates prepared for the Commission: (1) it increases somewhat the "units added" figure and, therefore, the ratio of units added to households formed; and (2) it increases the estimated number of units lost, which, as was pointed out, has to be high if anything like the 1.5-to-1 ratio is to be maintained. Fortunately, the figure for units moved during the 1950s was not large enough to distort greatly the numbers given for units lost and added to the inventory, but it was not negligible. It added 13.6 percent to the units lost and 3.3 percent to the units added. No figures are available for moves in the three decades before 1960, but as noted, the estimates for units lost through other means, of which moves are a part, are substantially higher, both in numbers and relatively, than the figures for the 1950s.

The expectation that the 1.5-to-1 ratio can be maintained is only one of several other equally plausible assumptions. It relies essentially on the facts that although from 1900 to 1950 the ratio apparently (based on skimpy data) was about 1 to 1, since 1950 the 1.5-to-1 ratio has been maintained and for some periods exceeded; private and public policies have been developed and applied to achieve a high level of employment and rising personal income with only minor dips or recessions; and similar programs and practices have been followed in housing finance and construction. Now that we have learned how to do it, therefore, what good reason is there for thinking that the 1.5-to-1 ratio would not be maintained? Table 1, based on that probability, shows the estimates of the consequences of continuing this high level of housing production. But the Commission has serious doubts on this score. At crucial points, basic data is alarmingly weak and subject to wide variations in interpretation. We believe the influence during the immediate past of such housing market factors as shortages in both new building and modernization, accumulated during the depression of the 1930s and the war conditions of the 1940s, are underestimated. We doubt that the substantial effects of low down payments and longer amortization periods, although they may well be continued, can be matched by comparable *additional* stimulants in the years just ahead. Finally, we are not overly impressed by the mere fact of 18 years of 1.5 to 1. After all, relatively short-term social trends that have endured much longer than 16 or 18 years have been sharply reversed—including the new housing-to-household formation ratios before 1950.

Although the Commission has doubts about the projections of housing production, and the even more optimistic expectations of reductions in substandard housing, the Commission is making them available and putting down this brief critique of them. They illustrate how the hard job of estimating and projecting housing needs is made all but impossible by the ridiculously inadequate data now at hand. And in many respects, these are the best estimates available.

Despite the inadequacies of the data about housing needs, those of the Census, or the various studies made or used by the Commission, it is interesting that a number of careful students of housing matters have arrived at very close agreement about what to do about meeting the Nation's housing problems.

The Commission's consultant arrived at a proposed 10-year program of about 600,000 units per year under older forms of public assistance in housing as well as the 1 percent interest rate and home-ownership-assistance provisions of the Act of 1968 (which were under consideration by the Congress when Mr. Kristof made his report to the Commission). Of this total, approximately 400,000 units would be new building; 100,000 units rehabilitation; and 100,000 would be "low-rent public housing leasing" —i.e., existing units leased by housing authorities and made available to low-income families at rents within their means. Such a program, according to estimates, would double the rate of housing improvement shown in Table 1 for the 1970s.

The Commission feels with some confidence that this estimate of its effect on the rate of improvement is correct—maybe even understated. Properly spelled out and administered, moreover, it would amount to a direct attack on the worst housing conditions in the country including those in urban and metropolitan areas.

Some reassurance on the need for such a program is given in the testimony earlier in 1968 before the Subcommittee on Housing and Urban Affairs of the Senate Committee on Banking and Currency by Secretary Robert C. Weaver and other representatives of HUD, and by Paul H. Douglas, Chairman of this Commission, who was asked to testify as an individual about 2 months before the Kristof study was available. Analyzing conditions in somewhat different ways and coming up with somewhat differing mixes of the components of the programs, they agree on at least a 10-year program of 500,000 to 600,000 units per year to be provided directly for lower income families. Of course it should be remembered that both Secretary Weaver and Senator Douglas were working with basically the same weak, inadequate data as were the Commission's staff and consultants. Nevertheless the similarity of the results, at least in order of magnitude, would indicate that their conclusions are a reasonable basis for action.

Without analyzing the three proposals here, it is noteworthy that those responsible for them were aware that the plans raise some serious questions that may be put broadly in this way: In the 1970s, the increase in number of households will be high. Yet the birth and fertility rates in this country have been going down since 1957 and now are very substantially reduced. The absolute number of births began to go down in 1962. It is quite possible that in the 1980s the number of new households may decline. If a substantial program of assisted housing for lower income families should tail off at about the same time, would the country be faced with serious overcapacity in building material production and unemployment in the building and allied trades?

Stretching out the increased construction program would cushion any such drop. In estimating the severity of a drop-off at the end of any program representing a substantial average annual increase over a period of years, it should not be forgotten that the annual volume at the end of the period of the program will be substantially more than the average over the period. In other words, the average increase will not be reached in the first years of the period and, therefore, will have to be exceeded later if the annual average over the period is to be attained.

In short, in trying to deal effectively with accumulated housing needs of lower income families in the ways suggested, are we storing up serious trouble for the not-distant future? Clearly this is a complex question. Much of the answer would depend on what kinds of housing units would be built and by whom, as well as on what might be happening around 1980 or thereafter in other parts of the construction industry. The Commission, while urging detailed and careful study of the question, sees one fact in its own and other studies of housing needs that is definitely reassuring on this point. Housing needs estimated previously on the almost-weather-tight-box-with-pipes conception of standard housing *grossly understates needs* as implied by the national goal of a decent home and a suitable living environment. And this is true whether the latter phrase is spelled out in some detail by housing specialists or by the heads of American families trying to better their own and their children's living conditions. Whether the degree of understatement is 50 percent, 100 percent, 200 percent or more, no one knows, now, but few would doubt that it is substantial. When, therefore, a program geared to deal with these rockbottom needs is well under way or substantially completed, the Commission feels certain that all people and agencies concerned with housing production, financing, maintenance, and management will still have more than enough to do in moving ahead toward the goal of a decent home and a suitable living environment. And the Commission would point out that this phrase in the Congress's Declaration of National Housing Policy in the Housing Act of 1949 ends: "for every American family." The last quarter of the twentieth century hopefully would see the most affluent society in the history of mankind deciding that a decent home *should* include adequate facilities for storing, preparing, and serving food and cleaning up afterward, and that a "suitable environment" should include a place near the homes for children to play, other than streets and alleys.

Emphasizing again that total housing needs are actually much greater than the presently available data indicate, some crucial aspects of the national housing need currently may be summarized as follows:

There are about 7 million substandard dwelling units that need to be removed or replaced because they are so dilapidated or lack adequate plumbing.

There are another 4 million standard but overcrowded units. As we have not counted deteriorating housing, and do not double count overcrowding in substandard units, it is fair to estimate a minimum total need of about 11 million units, or about three units out of every 20 in the Nation.

At the present levels of family income and at present rentals and mortgage rates, about a third of the families in the Nation cannot buy or rent decent housing at market rates by paying a reasonable portion of their income for shelter (no more than 20 to 25 percent at most).[6]

Metropolitan Areas

The preceding discussion has had to do with national totals and percentages of housing production, removal, and need as well as changes in them. The Commission, however, is primarily concerned with urban housing and, within that category, particularly with housing in the larger urban concentrations of population—the metropolitan areas. Table 2 shows an estimate of the relative positions of the metropolitan, urban, and rural housing needs in terms of substandard housing (all dilapidated units and all other units lacking plumbing facilities) and overcrowded households (those living at densities of more than one person per room).

The following facts about substandard housing by location in 1960 (based entirely on Census data) stand out:

Table 2. Distribution of Housing Units in the United States by Urban-Rural and Inside-Outside SMSA'S by Quality and by Crowding, 1960 [In thousands of units]

		Inside SMSA'S					
	United States	Total	In central cities	Not in central cities	Outside SMSA'S	Urban	Rural
Quality of all units:							
Total	58,318	36,378	19,617	16,761	21,940	40,757	17,561
Standard	47,727	32,535	17,406	15,130	15,192	36,490	11,238
Substandard	10,591	3,843	2,211	1,631	6,748	4,267	6,323
Percent	100	100	100	100	100	100	100
Standard	82	89	89	90	69	90	64
Substandard	18	11	11	10	31	10	36
Percent of all units	100	62	34	29	38	70	30
Percent of all substandard	100	36	21	15	64	40	60
Person per room:							
Total occupied units	53,024	34,000	18,506	15,494	19,024	38,320	14,704
1.00 or less	46,911	30,479	16,523	13,956	16,432	34,429	12,481
1.01 or more	6,113	3,521	1,983	1,538	2,592	3,891	2,223
Percent	100	100	100	100	100	100	100
1.00 or less	88	90	89	90	86	90	85
1.01 or more	12	10	11	10	14	10	15
Percent of all occupied units	100	64	35	29	36	72	28
Percent of all crowded (1.01 plus)	100	58	32	25	42	64	36

Source: National Commission on Urban Problems, Research Report No. 10, "Urban Housing Needs Through the 1980's," by Frank S. Kristof, p. 28.

	Percent
National total	19
Rural	36
Urban	10
Metropolitan areas	11
Central cities*	11
Suburban	10

*Not the center or the core areas of the big cities, but all the central city of a standard metropolitan statistical area, such as Chicago is to its surrounding urban areas, or as Washington, D.C., is to its Maryland and Virginia suburbs.

Rural housing appears bad, comparatively, in large part because of plumbing differences as compared with urban housing.

The central city and suburban comparison with metropolitan areas seems incredible, but there are several explanations:

The stereotype of the wealthy suburb is misleading. Suburbs which fit the stereotype draw a disproportionate share of public attention. Industrial and low-income suburbs are often not thought of as suburbs by many people.

The rural-urban fringes of metropolitan areas also have their share of poverty and substandard housing.

It overlooks the concentrated needs of housing in inner city areas.

The movement from central cities to suburbs has, for great numbers of people, been a move to better housing. But the Census does not count much of what they left as substandard. Again, the "weathertight box with pipes" definition (light-years removed from the general concept of a decent home in a suitable environment) leads to these anomalous or ludicrous figures.

The definitions and data used in the study led to the finding that housing improved at a virtually identical rate in the central cities and in the Nation as a whole in the 1950s. So from that base, the projection also shows central city housing likely to improve over the next decade on a par with a general improvement.

In their totality, these metropolitan housing needs estimates, like those for the Nation as a whole, project a more favorable picture than the Commission is led to accept. The overly optimistic view does not conform with much of the Commission's research and observation. The Commission is further strengthened in its skepticism because the author of these projections himself lists significant qualifications about the metropolitan housing situation:

First, the criteria of housing quality that were used were blind to the "suitable living environment" aspects of housing. This is a weakness that becomes more serious as the rising incomes and expectations of more and more people combine to make neighborhood or environmental conditions an increasingly important part of their ideas about good housing.

Second, "the housing progress of the past 18 years has been unevenly distributed. Although the housing status of even the lowest income groups has been improved since 1950, the greatest gains have been made in the middle and upper income brackets. Thus the gap in the housing status of the poverty group of the Nation—roughly one-fifth of all households—and the more affluent four-fifths has been widening. . . ."

Third, "an acceleration of the Nation's rate of progress can be accomplished only by focusing on the households of greatest need in the Nation—the poverty and near-poverty groups among whom are concentrated the greatest proportion of housing-deficit families."

Even if the previous estimates and projections given for the Nation and for metropolitan areas could be taken at face value, we deal in the following sections with certain specific housing needs that make the current situation anything but rosy. We will take up in order certain demonstrated relations between poverty and housing, some racial aspects of housing needs, the special problems of large poor families, the widely ignored matter of demolitions of housing (and the accompanying dislocation of families), and the relocation housing problem.

Poverty and Housing

This section draws chiefly on a special Commission study of poverty areas in the 101 metropolitan areas with 1960 population of over 25,000 each.[7] The poverty areas are those marked out by the Bureau of the Census for assembling information for various antipoverty programs. Essentially, poverty areas are made up of those census tracts in the lowest quarter of tracts in each SMSA when all tracts were ranked according to a composite "poverty index" that included not only the percentage of families with incomes under $3,000 according to the 1960 census, but also percentages of four other, often associated, characteristics of families in such areas: (1) children under 18 not living with both parents; (2) males over 25 with less than 8 years of schooling; (3) unskilled males

Table 3. Components of Inventory Change and Changes in Housing Needs for the United States and Inside Central Cities of Standard Metropolitan Statistical Areas, 1950–59 and 1960–69 Estimates [In thousands of units]

	1950–59			1960–69 estimates		
	United States	Inside central cities	Inside central cities as a percent of United States	United States	Inside central cities	Inside central cities as a percent of United States
Beginning of decade:						
Total housing inventory	46,137	16,186	35.1	58,468	18,771	32.1
Occupied units	42,826	15,691	36.6	52,955	17,786	33.6
Persons in occupied units	145,595	49,808	34.2	174,650	53,600	30.6
Persons per occupied units	3.40	3.17	—	3.30	3.04	—
COMPONENTS OF INVENTORY CHANGE						
Units added to housing inventory	16,861	4,061	24.1	16,900	3,921	23.2
New construction	15,003	3,420	22.8	15,300	3,420	22.4
Units added by conversion	807	367	45.5	600	240	40.0
Units added, other sources	1,050	274	26.1	1,000	261	26.1
Units lost from housing inventory	−4,530	−1,476	32.6	−5,900	−1,741	29.5
Units removed through demolition	−1,933	−757	39.2	−2,700	−893	33.1
Units lost through mergers	−815	−347	42.6	−700	−409	58.4
Units lost through other means	−1,783	−372	20.9	−2,500	−439	17.6
Net change in housing inventory which was accounted for by	12,331	2,585	21.0	11,000	2,180	19.8

Increase in number of households	9,986	2,095	21.0	9,400	1,974	21.0
Change in vacancies	2,345	490	20.9	1,600	206	12.9
Available for sale or rent	1,412	418	29.6	300	120	40.0
Other vacancies	933	72	7.7	1,300	86	6.6
HOUSING NEEDS						
Housing need at beginning of decade	20,530	4,658	22.7	15,364	3,279	21.3
Substandard unit to be removed	17,007	3,113	18.3	11,407	1,837	16.1
Crowded households in standard units	2,682	1,251	44.6	3,957	1,442	36.4
Increase in standard available vacancies	841	294	35.0	—	—	—
Changes in housing need during decade	−5,166	−1,379	26.6	−4,577	−1,072	23.4
Change in number of substandard units	−5,600	−1,276	22.8	−4,524	−952	21.0
Demolitions, mergers, other losses	−3,446	−931	27.0	−3,885	−945	24.3
Substandard units added during decade	1,886	256	13.6	1,551	178	11.5
Upgrading in existing inventory	−4,040	−601	14.9	−2,190	−185	8.4
Change in crowding in standard units	1,275	191	15.0	−53	−120	—
Change in standard available vacancies	−841	−294	35.0	—	—	—
Housing need at end of decade	15,364	3,279	21.3	10,787	2,207	20.5
Substandard units to be removed	11,407	1,837	16.1	6,883	885	12.9
Crowded households in standard units	3,957	1,442	36.4	3,904	1,322	33.8
Increase in standard available vacancies						

Source: National Commission on Urban Problems, Research Report No. 10, "Urban Housing Needs Through the 1980's," by Frank S. Kristof.

over 14 in the employed labor force; and (4) substandard housing units or, as they are now sometimes referred to, units "not meeting specified criteria."

Surely few people would have to be convinced that poverty and poor housing are closely linked. A few facts about their relationships, however, are worth noting as a basis for developing a sound national housing strategy.

From 1960 data, $3,000 may be taken as the boundary between the poor and the somewhat better off—what is called the poverty line. Substandard housing is again defined as all dilapidated units plus all deteriorating and sound units lacking one or more essential plumbing facilities. Perhaps the most pertinent facts about poverty and housing are the following:

1. For the whole United States, 19 percent of all housing units were substandard in 1960. Of the units occupied by poor households, 36 percent were substandard.
2. Of all owner-occupied units in the United States, 11 percent were substandard. Of those whose owners were poor, 30 percent were substandard.
3. Of all renter-occupied units in the United States, 23 percent were substandard. Of those whose renters were poor, 42 percent were substandard.
4. For all SMSA's, 11 percent of all housing units were substandard in 1960. Of those units occupied by poor families, 23 percent were substandard.
5. Of all owner-occupied units in SMSA's, 5 percent were substandard: of those whose owners were poor, 14 percent were substandard.
6. Of all renter-occupied units in SMSA's, 16 percent were substandard; of those whose renters were poor, 30 percent were substandard.

Thus in these six key comparisons, the proportions of poor households in substandard housing is about twice the proportion for all households—poor and not poor—in four cases, and almost 3 times in 2 of the comparisons.

Others may be puzzled at first, as was the Commission, that the percentage of the poor in substandard housing does not seem especially high. Only in item No. 3—all poor renters in the United States—did the proportion approach one-half. But, as stressed earlier, the figures are based on a primitive definition of substandard housing; they do not refer to merely poor housing, but only to the rockbottom stratum of utterly unfit housing.

Further, the proportions seem impossible to those who hold the common belief that families usually pay 20 to 25 percent of their income for housing. Many estimates of housing needs are based on this rule of thumb, but it does not hold true. The widespread gap in rent-income ratios by income class is dramatized by the following exceptionally useful information from Mr. Kristof's housing needs study for the Commission:[8]

Of renters with incomes under $2,000 in 1960—
90 percent pay 25 percent or more of income for rent, and of these—
13 percent pay 25 to 35 percent of income for rent.
77 percent pay 35 percent or more of income for rent.

Of renters with incomes between $2,000 and $3,000 in 1960—
63 percent pay 25 percent or more of income for rent, and of these—
31 percent pay 25 to 35 percent of income for rent.
32 percent pay 35 percent or more of income for rent.

Of renters with incomes between $6,000 and $7,000 in 1960—
6 percent pay 25 percent or more for rent.
1 percent pay 35 percent or more for rent.

Of renters with incomes over $8,000 in 1960—
1 percent pay 25 to 35 percent of income for rent.
0.5 percent pay 35 percent or more of income for rent.

Clearly, if many poor households escape rockbottom bad housing, there is little comfort to be drawn from these facts, indicating as they do that such escape can only mean cruelly curtailed expenditures for other basic necessities such as food, clothing, or medical care. (While no comparable figures are available for poor owner-occupiers, presumably those who keep out of substandard quarters also do so at the expense of other necessities.)

What of the districts in metropolitan areas that more or less casual observers and many others have thought contained most of the poor and very poor, as well as most of the bad housing and pathological social conditions? Whether they are labeled slums, badly blighted districts, or whatever, how much of the worst housing is concentrated in them? What are the characteristics of such districts that should influence any attempts to better the housing of their residents? The special census study of housing in poverty areas gives the best perspective on these questions that has been possible to date. What does it show?

First, several sharp contrasts between the poverty areas of the central cities and those of the suburbs should be noted. In the poverty areas of these central cities, the housing density was 100 times as great as in the poverty areas of the suburbs—3,071 units

Table 4. Distribution of Nonwhite Households by Tenure, Quality of Housing, and Family Income Inside SMAS's, for the United States, 1960
[In thousands of households]

	All units		Substandard units		
Family income	Number	Percent	Number	Percent	Percent of income category
Owner households:					
Total	1,224	100	218	100	18
Less than $2,000	252	21	95	44	38
$2,000 to $2,999	126	10	35	16	28
$3,000 or more	846	69	88	40	10
Owner, poverty households	378	33	130	60	34
Renter households:					
Total	2,262	100	765	100	34
Less than $2,000	760	34	360	47	47
$2,000 to $2,999	374	17	139	18	37
$3,000 or more	1,128	50	266	35	24
Renter, poverty households	1,134	50	499	65	44

Source: Kristof, op. cit., p. 36.

per square mile as against 30 units per square mile. Although the central city average undoubtedly is increased markedly by the great bulk and untypically high densities of New York City, these figures do mirror sharply two of the principal and sharply contrasting elements in poverty areas.

In the central cities congestion is the great evil. It makes for acute shortages of open and recreational space, continual crowding in the use of transit and other public facilities, high land prices, and the sense of confinement or containment that gives some support to the label of "ghettos" that has come to be applied to them. Note that in the central cities the average density in nonpoverty areas (1,874) is only 61 percent of that in poverty areas (3,071).

Suburban poverty districts are characterized by scatteration, small and often unsubstantial structures, and a thinness of development that, coupled with the low incomes of the residents, works strongly against adequate community facilities of all kinds —schools, stores, mass transit, churches, etc. Note also that the density figures of nonpoverty areas show a much smaller spread:

central cities, 1,874; suburbs, 90; a ratio of about 20:1. (And the figure for the suburbs is surely low for more or less typical suburban development—watered down by the substandard areas of the rural-urban fringes in many metropolitan areas.)

In the central city poverty areas, 68 percent of the units were rented, and 24.4 percent owner-occupied. Outside the central city, the figures were 53.1 percent owner-occupied, and 36.5 percent rented. The remainder were vacant units.

Of the total number of housing units in the central cities, 33.3 percent were in the poverty areas. The corresponding portion for the suburbs was 10.2 percent.

Second, many of the facts about housing in the poverty areas speak for themselves. Although a third of the housing units in the central cities are found in the poverty areas on less than one-quarter of the land area (23.2 percent), these poverty areas contained

Four out of five of all housing units occupied by nonwhites in these central cities;

Three out of four of the substandard units in these central cities;

Nine out of ten of the substandard units occupied by nonwhites in these central cities;

Over half of the overcrowded units in these central cities;

Five out of six of the overcrowded units occupied by nonwhites in these central cities;

Four out of ten of all housing structures built before 1940 in these central cities, or those which were almost a third of a century old or older; and

Five out of six of all the structures built before 1940 which were lived in by nonwhites in these central cities (Table 4).

These facts are clear evidence of the inadequacy of the figures which show that only 10 or 11 percent of the urban areas, cities, and suburbs of the SMSA's have substandard or over-crowded housing.

These facts show how concentrated the problems really are.

They give some understanding of the outrage of many poverty area residents.

They suggest some of the reasons for (but do not justify) the complacency, indifference, or hostility of many suburban residents to the other man's indignity.

Does bad housing have nothing to do with anger, alienation, frustration, and riots?

Does good housing in the urban ring far from the overcrowding bring to some a certain contentment, misunderstanding, or even at times an intemperate reaction to the just grievances of inner-city residents?

This evidence helps to explain, even if it does not excuse, why one man condones a riot while the other calls for "law and order."

Finally, a summary table from an unpublished sample study by the census in 1965 yields three sets of facts that are pertinent here. The sample was 80,000 households in the same 101 metropolitan areas with 1960 populations of 250,000 or more.[9]

(1) For these sizable metropolitan areas as a group, 28.1 percent of all nonwhite (predominantly Negro) households were below the poverty line; 57.6 percent of all nonwhite households lived in poverty areas; and of those in poverty areas 35 percent were poor. Of all white households in these same SMSA's, 7.9 percent were below the poverty line; 11 percent lived in poverty areas; and of those in poverty areas, 17.3 percent were poor. These percentages, of course, bear out two conditions indicated above: (*a*) The incidence of poverty is much greater among urban nonwhites than among whites; and (*b*) in metropolitan areas poor nonwhites are much more concentrated, geographically, in their patterns of residence than are whites below the poverty line.

(2) Of all poor families in these SMSA's, 67.6 percent were white and 32.3 percent were nonwhite. Of all families in poverty areas in these SMSA's, 58.9 percent were white and 41.1 percent were nonwhite. The more than 2:1 ratio of whites to nonwhites below the poverty line, despite the higher incidence of poverty among nonwhites, is explained, of course, by the rather small proportion of nonwhites in the total population of these areas—11.8 percent, slightly higher than the proportion of nonwhites in the total U.S. population in 1960. The 67.6:32.2 ratio for these 101 SMSA's is similar to the 70:30 ratio often given for the country as a whole.

(3) Rather surprisingly, in these 101 areas, the nonwhite poor—in all parts of the SMSA's, in nonpoverty areas and in poverty areas—had slightly higher median incomes than whites below the poverty line. The percentages: all parts of SMSA's: nonwhite $2,115, white $1,701; nonpoverty areas: nonwhite $2,268, white $1,650; poverty areas: nonwhite $2,053 and white $1,859. This probably can be explained by the fact that some 25 percent of white families below the poverty line are two-person families

whose head is 65 years or older. These are the "aged poor," many of them unemployed or not in the labor force. The corresponding figure for nonwhite poor families is only 8 percent.[10]

Racial Aspects of Housing

Urban Negroes, as a group, are notably poor when compared with whites. Undoubtedly Negro poverty accounts for much of the bad quality of Negro housing. Quite as surely, however, the Negro's difficulties in obtaining decent housing for himself and his family are also the product of racial discrimination on the part of many whites.

In assessing the housing conditions of urban Negroes, is it possible to separate the consequences of Negro poverty from the consequence of racial discrimination? Discrimination alone defies simple analysis, stemming as it does from such a mix of ignorance and fears of whites, and historical practices and attitudes. Similarly, the housing conditions of any sizable social group clearly are the end result of multiple factors or forces. For example, when we separate out family income and race, housing opportunities also are affected by recency and source of immigration, educational level, job skills, value systems of previous group affiliation, physical and mental health, and other personal and social conditions which influence the degree and rate at which either black or white people get their feet on the ground in urban localities. The varying degrees and rates of adjustment or socialization, in turn, are almost certain to be reflected in the quality of people's housing, whatever their color. For many of these conditioning influences we have no measures whatever; for some we have inadequate and often misleading measures or indices. So the more specific one attempts to be on such matters, the more risky are dogmatic claims.

With this warning the Commission presents some crude data that indicate answers to certain questions about the linkage between poor housing and racial discrimination:

(1) In metropolitan areas in 1960, 23.5 percent of all poverty households, white and nonwhite, lived in substandard housing (by the definition of substandard we are forced to use).

(2) In the same areas in the same year, 18.9 percent of white households below the poverty line lived in substandard housing.

(3) In the same areas in the same year, 41.6 percent of nonwhite households below the poverty line lived in substandard housing.

(4) In other words, within the poverty category, the proportion of Negroes and other nonwhites in substandard housing was more

than twice the proportion among whites. Race, therefore, seems to be a significant factor in bad housing.
(5) Although of much less significance because of the spread of the income group, the proportions of those *above* the poverty line but in substandard housing in metropolitan areas may signify little: all households, white and nonwhite—5.4 percent; white—4.4 percent; nonwhite—17.9 percent.
(6) Of all substandard units in metropolitan areas, 69.4 percent were lived in by whites; 30.6 percent were lived in by nonwhites. Here again, as in the poverty figures, the substantially higher incidence of bad housing among nonwhites is more than offset by the almost 9-to-1 ratio of whites to nonwhites in metropolitan populations. The task of replacing substandard units with decent homes is not limited to any one racial or ethnic group.

The conclusion that such striking differences are the consequence of racial discrimination against nonwhites is almost unavoidable. Without any doubt this end result—excessively bad housing—is the most significant aspect of the question. It is not, however, all of it.

In nearly all of the cities it visited, the Commission noted the low level of municipal housekeeping in low-income housing

Table 5. Distribution of Nonwhite Households by Tenure, Quality of Housing, and Family Income for the United States, 1960 [In thousands of households]

	All units		Substandard units		
Family income	Number	Percent	Number	Percent	Percent of income category
Owner households:					
Total	1,974	100	727	100	37
Less than $2,000	641	32	410	56	64
$2,000 to $2,999	247	13	118	16	43
$3,000 or more	1,085	55	199	27	18
Owner poverty households	888	45	528	72	59
Rental households:					
Total	3,171	100	1,537	100	43
Less than $2,000	1,341	42	893	58	67
$2,000 to $2,999	526	17	265	17	50
$3,000 or more	1,304	41	379	25	29
Renter poverty households	1,867	59	1,158	75	62

Source: Kristof, op. cit., p. 34.

districts—dirty streets and rubbish-filled gutters; littered alleys; broken sidewalks; smashed curbs; the infrequent playgrounds, typically with broken equipment and covered with all manner of filth; signs of poor storm water drainage; broken windows and sashes in school buildings; etc. Almost always, to be sure, these evidences of deterioration in public facilities were matched or exceeded by poor upkeep and maintenance of housing and other private structures, with the exception of some church buildings and an occasional shop or industrial building. These conditions not only add to the unattractiveness of these districts but in extreme forms contribute to a genuinely unhealthy living environment—certainly not one that anyone in his right mind would call *suitable* for a decent home. Yet these characteristics of low-income neighborhoods lend effective, if specious, plausibility to the view of some that housing improvement in low-income areas is a hopeless undertaking.

The Commission cannot say with certainty whether such conditions are markedly worse in predominantly white or in nonwhite areas of similar economic status. Some observers, however, do allege that almost as soon as nonwhites move into a district in considerable numbers, both municipal departments and many landlords begin to cut back on essential upkeep and repairs. Where this occurs, it would constitute a type of "discrimination by neglect," which, of course, differs materially from the customary form that works to segregate nonwhites and curtail their freedom of housing choice.

Municipal officials often reply to charges of neglect that much of the condition complained about is primarily the fault of the residents of these districts. The best housekeeper may be helpless if the other members of a large family do not do their part. So why try, particularly when a city is in a continuous financial bind?

The Commission, rather than assessing relative blame, strongly suspects that the process resulting in these disgraceful conditions is circular; the actions or lack of action by one party (whether tenant, landlord, or municipality) encourage similar neglect by the other two. Municipal officials should attempt to break this truly vicious circle, by undertaking vigorous programs to improve low-income housing neighborhoods, giving many residents of these areas reason for hope and self-respecting environment for every American family.

Notes

[1]Alvin L. Schorr, "National Community and Housing Policy," *Social Service Review*, Vol. XXXIX, No. 4 (Chicago: University of Chicago Press, December 1965).

[2]New York and Chicago are among the most notable exceptions.

[3]Instituted under the 1961 Housing Act, the 221 (d) (3) program has only begun to achieve its housing construction goals in the last few years.

[4]Frank S. Kristof, *Urban Housing Needs Through the 1980's*, Research Report No. 10, National Commission on Urban Problems, 1968.

[5]*Ibid.* See also, Nathaniel Keith, *Housing America's Low- and Moderate-Income Families*, Research Report No. 7; George Schermer, *More Than Shelter*, Research Report No. 8; Allen D. Manvel, *Housing Conditions in Urban Poverty Areas*, Research Report No. 9: Walter Smart, Walter Rybeck, and Howard E. Shuman, *The Large Poor Family—A Housing Gap,* Research Report No. 4; and unpublished staff study by Paul H. Douglas, Ellen Kelly, and William F. Glacken on housing demolitions.

[6]Many live in standard housing because they pay a disproportionate share of their income for shelter. Some may have inherited a home. Older people may have their homes paid for. Younger people may double up. As a consequence, the gap between one of six houses which are substandard or overcrowded, from the supply side, and the fact that slightly more than half the families can afford standard housing when looked at from the demand side, is considerably narrowed. Our judgment is that the 11-million figure, both because of demand and quality factors, underestimates our housing need.

For a good discussion of the problem in addition to the Kristof study, see Appendix A, pp. 1344–1349, Vol. 2, "Hearings on Urban Development Legislation of 1968," Subcommittee on Housing and Urban Affairs, Committee on Banking and Currency, United States Senate.

[7]Allen D. Manvel, *Housing Conditions in Urban Poverty Areas*, Research Report No. 9, National Commission on Urban Problems, 1968.

[8]Kristof, op. cit., pp. 61–63.

[9]*U.S. Statistical Abstract*, 1967. Table 485, p. 340.

[10]*Social and Economic Conditions of Negroes in the U.S.*, October 1967, p. 23.

1.2

The Relationship of Residential Financing and Expenditures on Residential Construction

Sherman J. Maisel

Studies of mortgage credit, on the whole, indicate that changes in credit terms influence residential construction expenditures. Some influences of changed credit are effective primarily in the short run, while others cause the long-run trend of spending on housing to vary.

The descriptions of the channels by which credit alters expenditures, however, vary greatly from one study to another. Many works show a correlation between credit and expenditures, but they fail to demonstrate a logical channel of causation. Frequently they include an implicit method of transmission from credit to building which can be shown to be incomplete or false.

It seems to me that most of the studies have not had a decent structure to explain the relationship between credit and construction which they believe exists. In other words, they have failed to show why mortgage credit changes the amount of construction. I think it is critical to have such a structure. Frequently implications and analysis concerning policy are wrong because people do not look at the true underlying relationships. What I want to do is not to argue the magnitude of the relationship between credit and building but to attempt to show what the structure is and the ways in which relationships occur. What is needed is a simple model which can show the causal relationships between credit movements and building volume. With such a model we can analyze the potential effect on construction of changes in the money market.

Credit's impact appears in three different channels. Chart 1 indicates how volatile housing starts have been in the short run in the post-war period. Other studies show that there is clearly a relationship between changes in the amount of credit and fluctuations in housing starts. However, observation of the chart and these studies tell us nothing about whether credit really changes the underlying demand and, if so, how. Note the line indicating demand in Chart 1. This measure of demand shows very little relationship with credit or any other major variable.

If there is no movement in underlying demand caused by credit,

Reprinted with the permission of The United States Savings and Loan League, 1965 Proceedings, *Conference on Savings and Residential Financing* (Chicago, 1966), pp. 129–140.

Chart 1. Housing Starts, Final Demand, and Changes in Housing Inventories in the United States
(Quarterly Estimate of Annual Rates, 1950–1965)

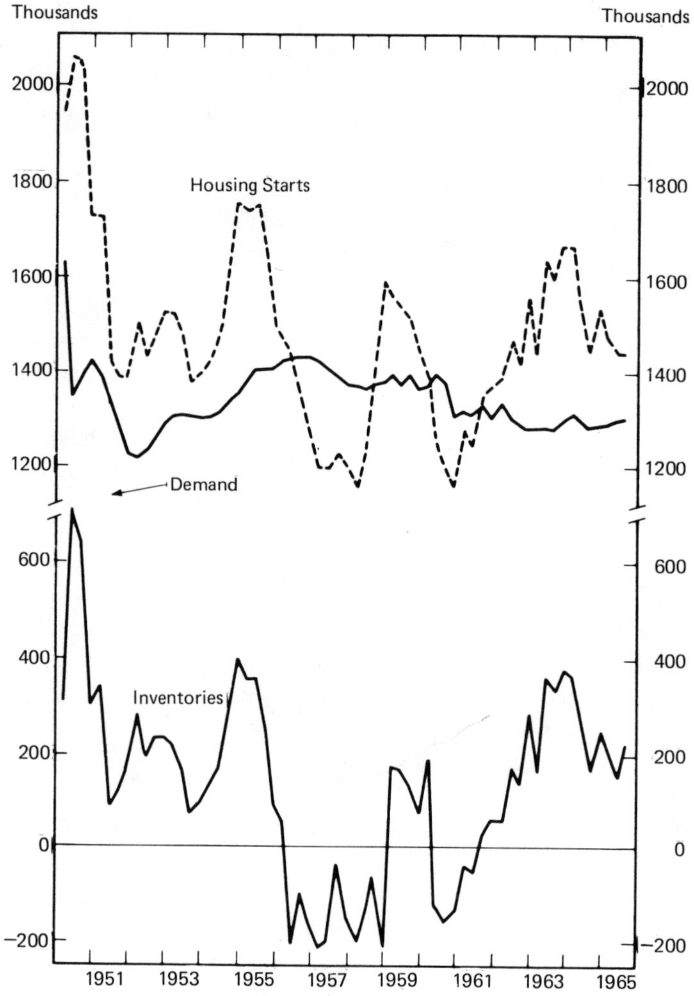

then what the chart shows is simply starts being shifted from one period to another. Such shifts may be extremely important, but much of the discussion in the press makes it appear that when you change credit, you are changing the actual number of houses started over some longer period. This I think may be incorrect.

There is no evidence thus far that changes in the amount of

credit have any great impact upon the number of houses started over any five- or ten-year period. That is one point I want to stress.

The second point I want to make is that credit probably does influence the size of houses and the amount spent per house. Credit has both a long-run and a short-run impact on such spending. While the amount of credit does affect the amount the average family spends on a house, the relationship is somewhat trickier than most people recognize. The analysis of this relationship has usually been too simple.

A third point that is almost entirely neglected in normal discussions is that credit probably influences repairs and alterations. As time goes on and as the housing stock becomes older, it is fairly clear that such expenditures will become a larger share of production of construction in the housing field.

The total value of dwelling units started in any period will vary with the first and second types of movement. Thus, the value of new housing alters either because the number of units started fluctuates or because the average value moves. When movements in alterations and replacements are added to the value of changes in new construction, we can find the complete influence of credit.

Influence of Credit Terms on Expenditures per Unit

Initially, I want to consider the second of these effects—how credit influences the value of individual units. Again, three channels of causation exist in this sphere.

Changing loan-to-value ratios or, conversely, the amounts of down payments, may enable some additional families to purchase houses. Other buyers may pick a larger and more expensive house. Since owner families spend more for housing than renters and since expenditures are directly related to the amount of the purchase, lower down payments that cause these changes lead to a higher allocation of consumer funds to the housing market. Total dwelling expenditures are increased at the expense of a family's spending on other goods or its savings.

The second impact of easier mortgage terms is to increase housing directly at the expense of saving. This point is one on which the literature says very little, but it is important. Many people fail to recognize that a mortgage contract is similar to a life insurance contract. It contains both an expenditure part and a saving part. A good deal of the mortgage amortization payment goes to saving rather than to expenditure.

When people make their decisions as to what sort of a house to buy, they do this in terms of the financial cost which is based on the period of amortization and the interest rate. They frequently pay but slight attention to the real costs.

When mortgage amortization terms are changed, they do not change the real costs. Real costs stay as a given percentage of the value of the house. What changes in mortgage terms do is to cause a basic movement in the rate of household saving. An easing in mortgage terms means that more money is being spent on the consumption of housing at the expense of saving. The amount of saving is decreased, and the amount of expenditure is increased. If you tighten mortgage terms, you have the opposite effect. The person is forced to save more.

Finally, movements in credit terms may alter the real cost of units. Because mortgage terms influence the supply and demand curves for construction, they may lead to an actual shift in the underlying cost structure. Since housing expenditures probably are inelastic with respect to price, higher real costs mean more direct expenditures.

Adding together all these forces, it appears clear that, if credit tightens, families can spend less in real terms on their houses. The average expenditure per unit of new construction will fall. With easier credit the opposite influence is felt. Throughout most of the postwar period, a gradual easing of down payments and amortization periods has been combined with an increase in interest rates and fees. The net effect has been to raise somewhat the average value of the unit that a family with a given income can afford. This increase in real expenditures with easier mortgage terms is probably the major long-run influence of credit on housing.

Influence of Credit Terms on Housing Starts

We come to the second question, the fluctuation in the number of starts. The chart indicates a tremendous amount of volatility in housing starts. The fluctuations in the number of starts resulting from credit have had a far greater short-run impact on construction expenditures than have any of the other forces. The year-to-year movements in the number of starts have been among the most volatile parts of the postwar economy.

How has shifting credit altered starts? Many people seem to have assumed that movements in credit have caused starts to fluctuate by altering the underlying demand for dwellings. I disagree with this analysis. The ultimate demand for additional houses must come either through more household formations or through the more rapid replacement of existing units. I can find no evidence either in theory or in the statistics to show that credit has had any basic effect, even in the short run, on this underlying demand.

This does not mean, however, that credit does not have an influence on starts. It does, and its impact may be large. But the influence arises from alterations in the number of units held in the unoccupied inventory rather than from changes in real demand.

This inventory consists of two parts: (1) units under construction and (2) vacant units available for rent or sale.

In the short run, very significant movements do occur in the inventory of units under construction. If we assume that units are under construction for an average period of six months, we find that in several years from 150,000 to 200,000 of the changes in the level of starts can be accounted for purely by movements in the inventory under construction.

The other part of the inventory is the unoccupied or vacant units in the housing stock. We know that we have a very complex type of housing market. We have new units; these may be rental units or new units for sale. We have old units for sale and for rent. Transfers occur from the single-family ownership market to the single-family rental market. All sorts of geographical diffusions exist.

As credit alters, particular parts of the housing stock may temporarily appear to be better buys. As a result, a movement of households may occur from rental to new single-family units. Some households may move out of one type of rental unit into another. Large changes in the flow of families may increase the number of vacant units.

Given the lack of basic information in individual housing markets, the added vacancies may react only slowly to lower the level of starts. If, as a result of credit changes, one part of this market becomes more active, there may be a flow out of others into the more active part. It will take quite some time for this shifting to be recognized. Since the housing market is basically a micro market that is completely atomistic, it takes a good deal of time for anybody to recognize what is happening. Therefore there is a decided lag between the time that a vacancy appears and the time that a market readjustment occurs.

The result of shifting credit is to raise the number of units going into the unoccupied inventory. While over time these added vacancies will cause starts to fall, there may be a long lag between the two actions. As a result, starts will at first be temporarily high, while later they will be below basic demand.

This variation in the vacant inventory may be even greater if it is increased through surges of optimistic or pessimistic expectations on the part of builders and developers. It is this type of movement, with credit alterations leading to shifts in occupancy followed by changes in expectations, that we seem to have been experiencing in recent years. While credit moves start only in temporary bursts around the stabler level of basic demand, these spurts have a drastic impact on the gross national product.

Long-Run Demand for Housing Starts

Table 1 shows rather rough estimates of the basic underlying demand for private housing starts. The estimates cover the periods 1950–1959, 1960–1964, and 1965–1969. We note that, in the earliest period, household formation was relatively high, averaging approximately 980,000 units per year. Thus far in this decade, household formation has averaged approximately 130,000 lower. New households in the remainder of this decade should fall between the two previous levels.

The item "Net removals" will strike many people as being rather high. In day-to-day discussions, most stress is placed on households as a basic factor leading to housing starts. We note,

Table 1. Estimates of Long-Run Demand for Private Housing Starts (Estimated Annual Averages)

	Net household formation	+	Net removals	=	Underlying demand
1950–1959	980,000	+	400,000	=	1,380,000
1960–1964	850,000	+	485,000	=	1,335,000
1965–1969*	950,000	+	520,000	=	1,470,000

	Underlying demand	+	Change in inventory under const.	+	Available vacancies	=	Housing starts
1950–1959	1,380,000		− 20,000	+	120,000	=	1,480,000
1960–1964	1,335,000		+ 5,000	+	100,000	=	1,440,000
1965–1969*	1,470,000			+	75,000	=	1,545,000

*Projected

however, that removals consistently have been more than 40 percent, and thus far in this decade they apparently have approximated 57 percent of household formation, or 37 percent of basic demand.

"Net removals," as defined here, is a tremendously heterogeneous component. It includes removals from the normal stock because of demolitions and losses through fire and flood, as well as units built for seasonal purposes or second homes. Demand from these sources is offset by households which move into trailers, motels, or publicly constructed units and which, therefore, do not enter the private house building market.

In addition, the removal figures are extremely rough because they are not measured directly. They are estimated by the residual which remains when all other movements are accounted for. As a result, they accumulate all other errors.

Most important, however, is the fact that the growing number of removals has tended to maintain the level of underlying demand. For the rest of this decade the total removals are projected as considerably higher than in the past decade.

The second half of Table 1 shows the relationship between actual starts and underlying demand. Since 1950, on the average, the total inventory has risen 100,000 units per year. This is somewhat higher than would be considered a normal rate of increase in vacancies. It appears that available vacancies could grow at a rate equivalent to 8 percent or 9 percent of new household formation without the new vacancies appearing abnormal. If we assume that vacancies will approach this normal level and that they will not continue to increase as rapidly as in the past, then we find that nearly all the growth in households and replacements expected for the remainder of the decade will be offset by the fall in the accumulation of vacancies.

Short-Run Movements in Housing Starts

The previous table showed that the decade averages for both underlying demand and new starts did not vary greatly. On the other hand, if we look at the starts series for single years, we see that both positive and negative swings of 300,000 to 500,000 starts in a single year are not at all unusual (see Chart 1). Just in this past year (January 1964 to January 1965) we had a drop in the annual rate of construction of over 300,000 units. How can we account for these sharp changes so different from the long-run trends?

I believe that the proper way of looking at short-run fluctuations in housing starts is to consider them as a form of inventory cycle. Basic demand moves slowly. It depends primarily on population forces, the condition of the housing stock, and certain exogenous forces such as floods, road building, and government housing policy. Changes in income and credit have some, but minor, influences on this underlying demand.

On the other hand, as shown in Chart 1, the number of new units going into inventories, of both units under construction and available vacancies, gyrates violently. The forces which set off these movements include credit changes, builders' expectations, and altering ratios between rental income and construction costs. The extent of the movements is dominated by technological and market forces. We know from general theory that inventory movements tend to be large, cumulative, self-reinforcing, but also self-reversing.

The path of the inventory fluctuations depends partly on time lags established by information flows, that is, how fast the market learns about and reacts to changing vacancy and cost rates, and partly on physical factors such as the period to build and sell or rent new units.

Movements in Demand and Inventories

The logic of this belief that short-run housing cycles can most usefully be analyzed as a form of inventory cycle is clear when we examine the basic forces at work in the market.

1. First, let us look at household formation. This is primarily a demographic factor. Our adult population is growing larger. This leads to more family formations. While there has been an upward trend in the movements of adults forming households, it does not appear to have varied greatly from year to year. There is no evidence that the rate of this formation varies with credit terms. We have tested various possible relationships between changes in credit and household formation, and none appear significant.

On the other hand, the rate does appear to be affected somewhat by changes in unemployment. We know that household formation was extremely low during the Great Depression. It fell even during the mild recessions of the postwar period. Furthermore, there is some indication that recently marriages among the lowest age groups have been delayed because of the high incidence of unemployment in this sphere.

2. There is practically no theory as to why net removals might vary in the short run. In fact, we are not certain that they do. Our data thus far are too poor to show any year-to-year fluctuations in this very significant part of demand. One of our great national statistical needs is for better information in this sphere if we are to improve our analysis of the housing market.

3. Since the underlying demand does not appear to alter greatly, it is clear that the basic short-run fluctuations must be caused by sharp movements in builders' and developers' willingness to start houses. The reasons for these sharp movements appear fairly evident. We are all aware of how rapidly changes in expectations can take place. In some years everyone is convinced that houses will sell like hot cakes and that every new apartment unit will rent rapidly. When this turns out not to be true, drops in expectations become sharp.

Credit also appears to play an important role in this market. At times, builders and developers may find it very difficult to obtain loans. The price of construction credit, because of discounts and fees, can rise from a real annual interest rate of 8 percent to one of 20 percent to 25 percent rather rapidly. At other times, lenders seem to be far more eager to make loans. There have been numerous times in the past when builders or developers have been able to "mortgage out"; that is, they have received more funds from the lenders than they actually have paid for the construction process. Clearly, under such circumstances many builders are only too willing to start new units.

But, beyond this, there probably is a clear case of what in general terms is called "credit rationing." The developer's ability to mortgage out will change with the general availability of credit. Among developers a general theory prevails that nobody should ever build investment property with any of his own money. Therefore the amount of building of investment property undertaken may be primarily a question of whether developers can or cannot get 100 percent financing from a lender. There was recently a case in San Francisco where the developer got 130 percent rather easily. It is claimed that he had to give 20 percent back to the lender, but it was still well worth his while to go ahead and build whether or not there were any prospects for success.

One of the big factors in the credit picture is whether there is so much money in the lending institutions that the builder is certain that he can get all the money he needs without any investment, or whether money is tight and he has to "scrounge up" a little money in front of the mortgage.

Thus, there are two sides to this credit influence: (1) the actual change in the cost of money to the borrower; and (2), probably as important, the availability of money to the prospective borrower.

Beyond this influence of credit on starts there is an important, purely technical factor. It is similar to that discussed in connection with other inventory cycles. Because a house takes time to build, it does not influence the supply of new houses for six months or a year after it is started. For high-rise apartments, it may take two or three years to get onto the market.

Impact of Vacancies on the Market

In addition to movements in the inventory under construction, there may be a movement of people out of used houses into new houses. Vacancies develop. The length of time it takes for the vacancy information to get back to the new housing market may be considerable. After the vacancies appear, there must be cuts in rents and cuts in the prices of the existing stock before it becomes uneconomic to build new houses. There is a long time lag. Clearly, there also may be very different lags from market to market.

I have been predicting that housing starts would be lower this year. This is based on an assumption that completions will start to exceed basic demand. Vacancies must be rising, or houses are disappearing somewhere that we do not know about. As a result of this rise in vacancies, I conclude that lenders are going to be warier to whom they lend. Builders and promoters will be more careful about starting new houses.

But it is hard to say exactly when such effects will be felt because of the very different time lags. In the single-family new house market, the lag tends to be very short because a great deal of this building is done on a mass basis. The builder is given a commitment by the lender, but the commitment limits the number of unsold houses under construction. When the limit is passed, the builder may not start any more. He has to cut the rate of starts to his rate of sales. Under such conditions there is almost an immediate impact on the start of houses as soon as the rate of sale of new houses begins to fall. Because of this fact, the actual unsold inventory of new single-family houses is fairly small. It runs between 1 percent and 2 percent of the total stock of houses.

With respect to apartment houses, the impact of vacancies may be much slower. The assumption frequently is made that it is going to take five months to a year to get a new structure fully rented anyway, therefore nobody can be sure during this time whether vacancies in the market result from overbuilding. Also developers and lenders may rationalize that the vacancies exist because the particular development was bad, and they claim that the next one will be good. There is a normal 8 percent to 10 percent vacancy rate in rental units; as a result, there must be a much longer time lag in getting information back from the rental market to where it influences the start of new apartment houses.

Furthermore, the housing market is subdivided into numerous parts by both type and region. This means that even as vacancies are developing in one sector, starts may still be continuing in other places. There may be an extremely long time lag before vacancies in older apartment houses influence the starts of new single-family units. The influence works its way through an altered relationship between rents and new house prices, and this may take a long time to achieve.

Changes in credit and vacancies working through the market alter builders' and developers' profits. Construction remains an extremely risky business. A developer may make a killing or may, nearly as easily, go broke. Changes in their profits and their expectations plus the technical forces of time to build lead to the rapid movements in inventories and in starts.

Long-Run Effects of Changed Credit

Almost all the discussions of credit and housing have been concerned with these short-run fluctuations. While these are significant because of their impact on the GNP and on those engaged in the construction, real estate, and financing industries, the actual long-run influences may be more important. What are these long-run forces?

In the first place, changing credit terms influence tenure or the ownership of homes. As down payments have decreased, many people who otherwise would not have been able to afford their own homes have bought. This usually has meant a rise in their standard of housing. In addition, it is probable that, at least in this country, living in a home one owns is economically more efficient than rental.

This means that one of the significant long-run impacts of credit is on the type of unit in which we dwell. Because single-family financing has been easier in this country, we have tended to stress this type of unit. In contrast, in many parts of western Europe, financing has been simpler for apartment houses, and as a result multifamily buildings are built far more efficiently than single-family homes.

It also is true that credit may influence the amount and type of rental units. Through lowering the cost of financing, more and better apartments have been made possible.

As we have noted, there is no indication that credit has any impact on the basic number of units demanded in the long run. It may, however, influence cost and prices in the construction industry. Thus, it may increase the amount spent from both the demand and supply sides. The building industry seems to be particularly subject to the well-known "ratchet" effect. When starts and demand are booming, costs rise rapidly. When demand falls, costs stay level or rise at a slower pace. As a result, many people believe that the short-run fluctuations in starts lead to a higher level of costs and a less efficient industry than would exist if demand followed a stabler path.

It seems clear that, as with all problems, we still have a great deal to learn about the impact of mortgage credit on construction. I do believe, however, that the type of model outlined in this paper gives a great deal of insight into the type of relationships which exist. With more facts, we should have a still better picture of what is happening and can be expected to happen in this very critical market.

1.3

The Federal Reserve and the Mortgage Market: Some Perspectives on the "Crisis" of 1966

Jack M. Guttentag

Introduction

The Federal Reserve As A Housing Credit Agency

The events of 1966 confirmed a trend that has been in the works for many years: the gradual conversion of the Federal Reserve System into the dominant housing credit agency of the Federal Government. The System's role as the major housing credit agency has two dimensions. First, more than ever before, the Federal Reserve now determines the total volume of credit available for housing, and therefore the total volume of residential construction. Second, the Federal Reserve has become the de facto, if not the de jure, lender of last resort for the savings and loan industry.

The conversion of the Federal Reserve into the dominant housing credit agency is the direct outgrowth of the persistent erosion in the liquidity position of nonfinancial business, households, and financial institutions. As liquidity has declined, so has the capacity of the economy to generate additional loanable funds through the activation of previously idle money balances. Although the financial mechanism for generating additional credit from a given stock of money grows increasingly efficient, the essential ingredient of excess funds has become scarce.[1]

With the decline in idle balances, the Federal Reserve has greater control than ever before of the total supply of loanable funds. But the mortgage credit sector accounts for a large share of the total, while being a relatively weak competitor when funds are scarce. Hence, the System's increasing control over the total supply of loanable funds has implied increasing control over the volume of residential mortgage credit.

The emergence of the Federal Reserve as the lender of last resort for the savings and loan industry also reflects the general erosion of liquidity. The savings and loan industry was among the first sectors to use up the excess liquidity accumulated

Reprinted from *A Study of Mortgage Credit*, Subcommittee on Housing and Urban Affairs, Committee on Banking and Currency, U.S. Senate (Washington, May 1967), pp. 392–406.

during World War II and the early postwar years. By 1950, associations had stopped liquidating Government securities, and the industry became dependent on the Federal Home Loan Bank System to meet unusual liquidity pressures. The Federal Home Loan Bank System, however, is not a money-creating agency. Despite its powerful position in the market, it has assured access to existing idle balances only under fair-weather conditions, when the associations are not likely to suffer extraordinary withdrawals. The erosion of excess liquidity has not only increased the potential for such withdrawals but also the possibility of disorganization in financial markets. If the two occur together, as they threatened to do for a brief time last fall, the Federal Home Loan Bank System cannot function as a lender of last resort to the savings and loan industry, and the task falls on the Federal Reserve.

This development was given implicit recognition by Congress last September when it authorized the Federal Reserve to purchase or sell securities of any Federal agency, including of course obligations of the Federal Home Loan Bank System. It was given explicit recognition the same month by the Board of Governors which for the first time authorized the Federal Reserve banks to open the discount window "in unusual and exigent circumstances" to savings and loan associations in mutual savings banks.[2]

It is important to distinguish the two problem areas noted above. The Federal Reserve System's new last resort responsibilities came to a focus during the brief period of very severe market stringency in the fall. This was the first incident of its kind since the 1930s, it lasted a very short time, and the remedial measures employed by the Federal Reserve[3] were adequate to the task. Similar measures should continue to be adequate in the future, with one proviso. The proviso is that the System retain authority to purchase Federal home loan bank obligations, which is now scheduled to lapse in September 1967. I would urge the Congress to make this authority permanent, since the problem for which it is needed, by its very nature, can develop with dramatic suddenness. It would not be prudent to assume that Congress could always act with the necessary promptness in the event of an emergency. Other than this, I will have nothing to say on the System's new last resort responsibilities.

In contrast, the influence of a tight money policy on the residential mortgage and construction markets is not a new problem at all, and solutions, if any are needed, are quite elusive. The rest of the paper will be devoted to this problem.

The Short View and the Long

Every period of tight money since 1951 has resulted in a decline in homebuilding and in complaints by builders and other adversely affected groups. It has been alleged that tight money has hit residential construction with unreasonable (and discriminatory) severity. Some economists have agreed, and argue that the reduced level of construction resulted in a needless loss of output. Political pressures have arisen to "do something for housing." These pressures were pronounced in 1956–57 when tight money lasted a long time; they were not severe in 1959, because, although the mortgage market became even tighter than in 1957, tightness did not last very long. In 1966, the mortgage market became tighter than it has ever been, the drop in homebuilding was more precipitous, and the political pressures reached a new crescendo. These pressures tend to create a myopic framework which focuses strictly on the short-run burden of tight money on the residential sector. Even the Federal Reserve, once rather aloof on problems of "discriminatory effect," has become extremely sensitive to the short-run plight of the homebuilding industry.[4]

Yet this is an inadequate perspective on which to base proposals for institutional change. Credit tightness in 1966 should be viewed as one phase of a countercyclical monetary policy which involves alternating periods of credit restraint and ease. I will assume my function to be that of assessing the costs and benefits of such a policy, to the housing sector and to the community, over a stretch of time long enough for its full effects to be realized.

Costs and Benefits

Promotion of Stabilization Objectives

The sensitivity of the residential sector to changes in credit conditions has helped the Federal Reserve make a substantial contribution to our overall stabilization objectives. In brief, countercyclical variability in the supply of mortgage credit arising from countercyclical monetary policy has had the effect of shifting a large part of new construction to periods when overall competitive demands on resources have been relatively light. This has necessarily imposed a curtailment of construction during periods when other demands on resources were exceptionally heavy, as in 1966. The benefits to the community as a whole from such compensatory shifts in construction from one period to another are well understood, and I will not attempt any elaboration here. In my view, these benefits are substantial and extend beyond the residential sector. Any costs, in contrast, are concentrated in that sector.

The Problem of Equity: Are Home Buyers Disadvantaged?

Perhaps the most widely stressed problem arising from tight money is the alleged inequity to home buyers, whose demands must be deferred or scaled down because credit is not available, and to home sellers who find themselves unable to market their homes except perhaps by making unanticipated price concessions or paying "points." Commercial interests in the housing and mortgage industries usually act as proxy for home buyers and sellers in reporting these injustices. The point has been overdone.

The decline in the availability of mortgage credit during periods of tight money reflects essentially a displacement of mortgage credit demands by business credit demands under conditions where the Federal Reserve System sharply limits growth in the total supply of credit.[5] The demand for business credit is highly volatile, and during a period of economic expansion it rises sharply in order to finance growing investment outlays. The basic demand for mortgage credit, in contrast, is based on more stable factors such as household formation and income trends over fairly long periods. Thus, in good part, the displacement of mortgage borrowing reflects simply a shift of credit to the business sector where demand is (temporarily) stronger. Such shifts in response to demand are an integral and normal aspect of a well-functioning market system. Unless these shifts generate some misallocation in the flow of real resources, there is no reason to view them as inequitable to the sector losing funds.

It is true that in the competition for the limited available supply of funds the mortgage sector is at a disadvantage. For a number of reasons mortgage borrowers are more sensitive to the higher interest rates generated by the competition for funds, and they are more subject to non-interest-rate credit rationing than is business. (Large firms in particular can usually obtain credit at a price, either from the capital markets or from commercial banks with whom they have a line of credit.) But, against this, one must set the fact that much of the time home buyers can borrow at very advantageous terms, because of a variety of direct and indirect Federal aids. I am referring to the Federal mortgage underwriting programs and to the array of special privileges granted home financing institutions. One can indeed view the impact of tight money on the residential sector as merely the temporary removal of such privileges in the interest of overall economic stability. This was very clearly the case in the tight money periods of 1951–53, 1956–57, and 1959, when virtually the entire contraction in mortgage lending and construction was in the FHA and VA sectors; conventionally financed activity was hardly affected. In 1966 much of the contraction was in the (conventional) savings and loan sector, which is largely locked into mortgages by public policy and which is the recipient of a wide variety of Federal aids (such as share insurance, favorable tax treatment, and borrowing facilities of the Federal Home Loan Bank System). These aids have been important features in the industry's fantastic growth over the period since World War II, and a brief slowdown hardly smacks of injustice.

In any case, one cannot validly assess the equity of countercyclical monetary policy to home buyers by restricting attention to periods of tight money. Prior to 1966 home buyers were faced with five years of relatively easy money. Taking a perspective long enough to cover both periods, it is not at all clear that home buyers as a group are disadvantaged on net balance by being displaced in the market during periods of tight money and invited back in periods of easy money. This pattern does cause inconvenience to some buyers who are forced to wait, but it also causes more home buyers to borrow when interest rates are low than when interest rates are high. Similar considerations apply, although less directly, to renters.

Housing Output: Is There Any Significant Loss?

It is clear that the volume of residential construction is reduced during a period of tight money, but again, tight-money periods alone provide inadequate perspective. The housing conditions of the American people are determined largely by the size and condition of the existing housing stock, and a decline in the net addition to the stock over a year or two has little effect on the availability of units to persons on the move. Thus, the recent decline in housing starts, amounting to about 500,000 dwelling units per year, can be compared to a housing stock of perhaps 65 million units, of which at least 2 million are vacant and available for sale or rent. Housing goals must be met over the long pull, and it makes very little difference whether new units are added this year or next.

The relevant question, then, is whether less housing is produced under countercyclical monetary policy over a stretch of time long enough to cover periods of ease as well as restraint—in contrast to a policy that maintains more credit conditions over the same time horizon.

Perhaps a prima facie case could be made that the Federal Reserve did reduce the flow of resources into housing over the period 1951–61, which included more years of tight money than of easy money. While housing construction fluctuated during this period in response to swings in credit conditions, every expansion was cut short by a shift to tighter money. However, the prolonged stretch of easy money during 1961–65 virtually obliterates this argument. Housing construction was given an opportunity to run its course during this period; for the first time since World War II, an expansion in construction apparently peaked out from lack of basic final demand rather than from tight money.[6] The 1964 peak in construction preceded a tightening in mortgage credit by about 16 months.[7]

Thus, considering the entire period since 1951, there is no reason to believe that the Federal Reserve caused housing output to be any lower than it would have been if there had been no cyclical gyrations in credit conditions. This is subject to the proviso that instability in housing construction did not reduce output indirectly by raising costs, a possibility considered later in this article.

It could be argued, of course, that if the Federal Reserve maintained easy credit all the time, the average level of construction would be higher.[8] This is not a relevant alternative, however, unless one postulates the drastic tightening in fiscal policy required to prevent inflation when monetary policy is chronically easy. The Federal Reserve might prefer a tighter fiscal policy that would permit an easier monetary policy, they may even urge it, but in the last analysis, the System must accept fiscal policy as it is and adapt monetary policy to it. And fiscal policy has not been tight enough to permit a continuously easy monetary policy without generating excessive inflation.

Construction Efficiency: Is It Reduced By Instability?

I discussed the impact of instability on efficiency in an earlier study, and since no work has been done on the problem since, I will be forgiven for quoting myself.

> It could be argued that cyclical instability in residential construction reduces the technical efficiency of the construction industry. I am not aware, however, of any serious effort to demonstrate this. Maisel, who has made the most careful investigation of the problem of efficiency and inefficiency in construction, does not offer any judgment with respect to the probable impact of instability. Pending more evidence, the writer's inclination is to discount it as negligible. . . . The grounds for this judgment are as follows:
>
> 1. Factors arising out of the localization of the market and the spatial requirements of construction are the real deterrents to greater efficiency in the construction industry.
> 2. To the extent that stability bears on efficiency, it is stability in local areas that is relevant rather than stability in the aggregate. An increase in aggregate stability through the moderation of credit swings would not necessarily have a significant influence on stability in local areas, which is heavily influenced by shifting patterns of demand.
> 3. Cyclical swings in residential construction are only one type of instability to which the industry is subject. Seasonal swings, which are dictated largely by the weather and by consumer buying patterns, also are quite sharp; for the Nation as a whole, such swings are of about the same amplitude as recent short cycles. And long cycles in residential construction, which are related mainly to fluctuations in basic housing demand, have had a much greater amplitude than recent short cycles.[9]

It is, of course, possible that a reduction in shortrun instability would improve efficiency, even while other sources of instability remain. But how this would occur has yet to be shown. The Federal Reserve, as the major housing credit agency of the Federal Government, should be urged to investigate the problem further.

Although it is not clear that instability reduces construction efficiency, the countercyclical pattern of instability does have one clear cost-reducing implication: it implies that a larger proportion of residential construction takes place when upward cost pressures are least intense. Tight money forces a curtailment in housing construction during periods when upward cost pressures are most intense. This was very clearly the case in 1966, as shown in the table (col. 3).[10] In this respect, the contribution

Construction expenditures, costs, and unemployment, selected quarters

	Expenditures (billions)		Residential costs (Boeckh)* (1957–59 = 100)	Unemployment rate, private construction (percent)
Quarter	Residential (1)	Nonresidential (2)	(3)	(4)
4th, 1960 (trough in residential expenditures)	$20.7	$16.8	104.1	14.7
			(.5)	
1st, 1964 (peak in residential expenditures)	27.5	18.7	110.3	11.3
			(.9)	
1st, 1966 (peak in nonresidential expenditures)	27.4	26.8	117.6	7.5
			(1.8)	
2d, 1966	26.8	26.0	119.4	7.5
			(1.6)	
3d, 1966	24.0	25.7	121.0	8.1
			(1.2)	
4th, 1966	21.0	25.7	122.2	9.1

*Figures in parentheses show the change per quarter between periods.
Source: BLS, Department of Commerce.

made by the residential sector to general stabilization objectives is also advantageous to the residential sector.

Resource Immobility and Unemployment: Can Resources Be Transferred Out of the Housing Sector As Fast As Credit?

There is another way in which instability in residential construction could reduce efficiency, raise costs, and thereby curtail output. If sharp swings in mortgage credit availability and residential outlays were not accompanied by corresponding movements of resources into and out of the residential sector, the industry would suffer labor shortages during periods of expansion and heavy unemployment during periods of contraction; average unemployment levels and labor costs would be relatively high.

Although more intensive research is needed on this question also, the available evidence suggests that resources move fairly easily between residential and other types of construction. Fluctuations in total construction have been much less pronounced than fluctuations in residential construction alone. Materials used in home construction are by and large the same materials used in commercial and industrial construction (as well as in many lines of manufacturing). The pattern of changes in unemployment in total construction suggests the movement of labor back and forth in substantial volume between residential and other types of construction.[11]

The experience of recent years, shown in the table, illustrates these points. The peaking of residential construction in early 1964 was coincident with the beginning of an exceptionally marked expansion in nonresidential construction. As a result, total unemployment in private construction, which had declined during the 1960–64 period of expansion in residential construction, fell even more rapidly in the two subsequent years of stability in residential construction.

It is true that the marked tightening in monetary policy in 1966 occurred after total construction had leveled out and after the unemployment rate in construction had stopped declining. Yet inflationary pressures in the economy generally were most intense in 1966, as indicated by the fact that the rapid rise in residential construction costs continued through the year.

Shifts of resources between the different categories of construction are not, of course, without cost. It might be argued that the relatively high average level of unemployment, which appears to be a structural characteristic of the construction industry,[12] is a consequence of constant resource shifts. Whether unemployment could be reduced by stabilizing aggregate residential construction, however, is highly problematical for the reasons indicated: only one of many causes of resource shifts would be affected.

Summary of Costs and Benefits

Allowing residential construction to suffer the burdens of tight money, alternating with the pleasures of easy money, while contributing to our overall stabilization objectives, does not necessarily impose a net burden on the residential sector. The favorable consequences are clear: home buyers are pressed to borrow most heavily when interest rates are low, and builders are pressed to build when upward cost pressures are least pronounced. As against this, some home buyers and sellers suffer inconvenience from being forced to wait. Other unfavorable consequences, however, have yet to be demonstrated. There is no evidence to suggest that over a stretch of time long enough to cover both easy money and tight money periods, housing output is lower than it would be with stable credit markets. There is little indication that cyclical instability in housing construction reduces technical efficiency in the homebuilding industry or raises average unemployment levels in the industry. The evidence is not conclusive on any of these points, and it may be that instability does have such consequences, but it seems to me that the burden of proof to demonstrate this is on those who would introduce costly institutional changes.

Concluding Comment

The main points of this paper may be summarized as follows:

(*a*) Cyclical instability in residential construction, arising from countercyclical monetary policy has made a net contribution to our economic stabilization objectives.

(*b*) Shortrun instability in residential construction implies both benefits and costs to the residential sector; where the net balance lies is not clear. Home buyers are pressed to borrow most heavily when interest rates are low, and builders are forced to build when upward cost pressures are least pronounced. As against this, some home buyers and sellers suffer inconvenience from being forced to wait. Other unfavorable consequences, however, have yet to be demonstrated.

(*c*) If we nevertheless wish to avoid sharp swings in the availability of mortgage credit, the best method is to adopt a more flexible fiscal policy, thus eliminating the need for sharp changes in monetary policy. This could best be accomplished by delegating to the administration limited authority to vary income tax rates. Selective credit controls are a poor alternative which would be more costly to impose and maintain, and considerably less effective.

(*d*) Changes in mortgage credit institutions of the types customarily proposed would not appreciably moderate the effects of tight money on the residential sector. Such changes have little potential for expanding the total supply of loanable funds, which we would not want in any case because it would undercut the effectiveness of monetary policy. Changes in mortgage credit institutions would not succeed either in diverting any significant amount of credit from low-priority sectors; that is, from the nonfinancial corporate sector, whose enlarged credit demands are mainly responsible for stringency in capital markets during periods of monetary restraint, or from consumer borrowers. The sectors from which credit might be diverted are necessarily those with a weak position in credit markets, akin to that of the residential sector; in general, these sectors have high social priorities which rival that of housing.

Since changes in mortgage credit institutions are not likely to have much utility in moderating the effects of tight money, heavy weight should be given to efficiency considerations; that is, to the question of whether a given change increases or reduces the capacity of institutions to produce mortgage credit at the lowest possible cost, and to direct credit into areas where it is most needed. It is unlikely that the stabilizing feature of any institutional change would be substantial enough to warrant its adoption if efficiency was reduced. Conversely, a given reform may be desirable if it has some stabilizing tendency, however small, assuming its effect on efficiency is positive or neutral. The efficiency implications of a variety of proposals will be considered in the major study of the savings and loan industry and related institutions authorized by the Congress last year.

Notes

[1]A number of economists have argued, although not recently, that excess elasticity in the supply of loanable funds is a structural characteristic of the American economy. Warren Smith, for example, noted that

With a complex financial system such as ours, when the monetary authorities change the money supply, a number of reactions tend to occur which weaken the effects of the action on aggregate demand by inducing changes in holdings of idle cash balances and corresponding changes in monetary velocity. This tendency is especially troublesome in the case of restrictive policy designed to deal with inflation. ("On the Effectiveness of Monetary Policy," American Economic Review, September 1956, p. 361)

This view fails to distinguish two essential conditions for excess elasticity. These are (*a*) well-organized and efficient machinery for the transfer of funds throughout the economy, and (*b*) excess liquidity positions of economic decisionmaking units. The first condition may be considered an institutional characteristic of the American economy, but the second is not. As liquidity is drained away—that is, as idle funds are drawn into use—elasticity necessarily declines, no matter how smoothly the financial machinery is working.

[2]This provides an interesting perspective on the increasingly rapid pace at which new ideas are becoming obsolete. It was only a few years ago that some well-known economists were arguing that nonbank financial intermediaries could subvert the effectiveness of restrictive monetary policy by pulling funds away from banks. The 1966 experience suggests, in contrast, that deposit-type intermediaries may create problems when the central bank is following a policy of restraint by losing funds to banks in such large volume that last-resort aid may be needed.

[3]In addition to opening the discount window to savings institutions on a stand-by basis and obtaining authority to acquire Federal home loan bank obligations, the Federal Reserve restricted the ability of banks to pull funds from savings institutions, directly by reducing time deposit ceiling rates under regulation Q, and indirectly through certain selective measures designed to limit bank lending to business. These selective measures are discussed later in this paper.

[4]The System can hardly remain aloof when the President of the United States remarks that "[in 1966] housing bore a disproportionate part of the burden of needed restraint" (in his 1967 Economic Report, p. 20).
[5]For a more detailed analysis, see my "The Short Cycle in Residential Construction," American Economic Review, June 1961, pp. 292–293.
[6]The theory underlying this analysis can be summarized as follows:
(1) Changing credit conditions affect mainly the timing of construction activity rather than basic demand, which is relatively stable in the short run. Hence, credit-induced fluctuations in starts cause fluctuations in unsold inventories of new homes or vacancies or both.
(2) If there are no demand backlogs, a credit-induced change in starts thus has a self-limiting tendency. For example, if credit conditions ease sharply, and then stabilize at some level, the rise in starts generated by the shift would at some point level off or reverse itself, due to the increasingly unfavorable technical market situation faced by builders.
(3) Prior to 1961, this self-limiting mechanism was inoperative because accumulated demand backlogs made construction insensitive to changes in vacancies and unsold inventory. Under these conditions, changes in the availability of credit determined the configuration of the housing cycle. By about 1960 or 1961, however, the backlog of housing demand inherited from World War II and the great depression had been depleted. One component of the backlog, consisting of married couples living "unwillingly" in someone else's household, was largely gone by 1950. A second component, a deficit in the vacancy reserve, was depleted about 1960 when the upward trend in the vacancy ratio leveled out. Thus, by 1960 or thereabouts, basic housing demand was on a current basis. Thus, the way was finally clear for expansion in housing to peak out on its own, rather than from the emergence of tight money.
[7]The evidence is not conclusive, however, because the peaking in construction occurred after the mortgage market stabilized (about May 1963). It is possible that construction might have risen further if the mortgage market had eased further. No very appreciable decline occurred following the peak, furthermore, until the mortgage market began to tighten in late 1965. The relative stability of starts at about 1.5 million units between the first quarter of 1964 and the third quarter of 1965, during which period mortgage market conditions were remarkably stable, suggests that this may not be far from the current supportable volume of basic demand.
[8]The extent to which construction would be higher is not clear. Over the long run the number of dwelling units constructed is determined largely by household formation, which is not sensitive to credit conditions. (See Sherman Maisel, "Fluctuations in Residential Construction Starts," *American Economic Review*, June 1963, p. 376.) However, a prolonged stretch of easy credit might have a small effect on the vacancy level, the demolition rate, and the average value per dwelling unit. These effects have never been adequately researched.
[9]Jack M. Guttentag, "The Federal National Mortgage Association." Research Study Two, in *Federal Credit Agencies*, Commission on Money and Credit, Prentice-Hall, 1963, p. 88.
[10]This point is weakened by the upward trend in costs. The residential costs indexes have risen during periods of economic expansion, while they have not declined much during recession periods. Because of the way they are constructed, however, the cost indexes understate the extent of cyclical declines. See Murray Foss, "How Rigid Are Construc-

tion Costs During Recessions?" *The Journal of Business*, July 1961, pp. 374–83.

[11]No data are available on unemployment in residential construction alone.

[12]During the Korean War the unemployment rate fell to 5 or 6 percent. After Korea, the rate ranged generally from 10 to 17 percent, until late in 1965. Since then the rate has been in the 7- to 10-percent range.

1.4 Filtering and Neighborhood Change

Wallace F. Smith

A Review of the Filtering Controversy

"Filtering" is an indirect process for meeting the housing demand of a lower-income group. When new quality housing is produced for higher-income households, houses given up by these households become available to the lower-income group. Though it is a "well-recognized phenomenon,"[1] filtering provides an issue of public policy which has long commanded the attention of housing economists—whether or not it is fundamentally desirable that low-income housing needs be met in this way. The answer to this question can affect the character and pattern of cities, and hence the forecasts of demand for every existing residential neighborhood. In this section we show that the filtering concept and the questions it provokes have played important roles in the development of urban analytical technique, shifting this from a cartographic approach to more rigorous matrix analysis.

The filtering issue today can be traced to an empirical study made during the 1930s by Homer Hoyt.[2] That study offered a concept which would explain and predict the location within a city of certain types of residential uses—the so-called "sector theory." The theory, in turn, implied a succession of occupancy in dwellings originally built for higher-income families. Thus filtering was the dynamic element in the sector theory.

Hoyt's entire study has been subjected to much criticism by other urban economists. In such an important field criticism was nearly inevitable because of the manner in which the sector theory was originally put forward. Hoyt's study called attention to a number of variables affecting the character and evolution of residential neighborhoods, variables such as the distribution of income in the community as a whole, the community's rate of growth and changes in its composition, the quality level of new construction, and, of course, the spatial distribution of socio-economic groups and of construction activity. Having identified these variables, however, Hoyt failed to present an operational framework in which they might be integrated. He provided only a generalized historical description with vague suggestions about the interrelation among the variables.

Reprinted with the permission of The Center for Real Estate and Urban Economics, Institute of Urban and Regional Development, University of California, Berkeley, *Filtering and Neighborhood Change*, Research Report 24, by Wallace F. Smith, pp. 1–33.

Another failing of the original Hoyt study was that it raised policy questions without analyzing their broad implications. The study can be criticized on this score because the work was done for a public agency and was thus to influence public policy. This gave critics of the sector theory even more reason to quarrel with Hoyt and to view his theory as a *justification* of the historical pattern of urban development, a pattern which to many persons seemed undesirable. Rightly or wrongly, Hoyt was soon accused of espousing as "ideal" a form of urban development which he had actually merely described.

Both of these defects in Hoyt's sector theory—the nonoperational nature of his concepts and his avoidance of implied policy questions—could be remedied by creating a model of competitive equilibrium. With a theoretical structure for translating any given set of demand and supply conditions into an equilibrium pattern of residential neighborhoods, the implications of policy or other exogenous changes can be worked out.

The present study is an effort to provide and to illustrate just such an analytical framework as a more flexible tool for both forecasting and policy formulation than the sector theory. First, however, we should explore the sector theory and some of its criticisms and developments in some amount of detail.

The Sector Theory

Hoyt's essential notion was that, as a city grows, the fashionable residential district moves outward from the center, always in the same direction. Obsolete houses left behind by the well-to-do become occupied by the poor, particularly the recent immigrants, so that the wedge-shaped path taken by the high-income group contains both extremes in the income spectrum. This sector is the most vital, the most active, and the most troublesome. Middle-income families group themselves about the well-to-do, hoping that some of the status of the fashionable areas will rub off on them.

The study in which the sector theory was first presented provided a number of specific rules which seemed to determine the direction which fashionable residential development would take. It moves toward high ground, for example, along the best transportation routes, and avoids "dead ends" which would impede further outward movement. Preexisting commercial nuclei may exert a pull on high-income residential development, and real estate promoters may succeed in bending the normal direction of this growth.

These points constitute the sector theory "proper." In Hoyt's original study, however, there are at least two other major components. He discusses and illustrates the impact of the community's rate of growth upon the pattern of neighborhood change: ". . . the rapidity of population growth is one of the most important determinants of the differences in the speed with which high-grade neighborhoods move to new locations."[3]

The other major component of Hoyt's neighborhood study is a series of qualifications by which he seeks to offset the inflexibility and the simplification of his model. For example, he explains that "The rate of neighborhood change may vary even between cities growing in population at the same rate. The component elements of the added population are of extreme importance."[4] Thus, if there were a great wave of poor immigrants, the cast-off mansions of the rich would not suffice to house them; the predetermined pattern of movement within the city would have to be altered in some unspecified way. In this portion of his study Hoyt seems to anticipate, if not to satisfy, some of his later critics.

Firey's Cultural Ecology

Hoyt's simplified and "deterministic" description of residential patterns was attacked by Walter Firey in his book *Land Use in Central Boston.*[5] Firey, a sociologist, found the sector theory inadequate as an explanation for the irregular pattern of residential settlement in the Boston area. He wrote, "The spatial distribution of upper class families is apparently more variable than the Burgess-Hoyt theories appreciate. Whatever forces are responsible for it must be sought in less simple and tangible factors than those of inevitable radial extension or inevitable ringlike expansion."[6]

Chief among the "less simple and tangible factors" were "spatially referred values," according to Firey, meaning that cultural attachments could confound the neat determinism of the sector theory. Fashionable districts might spring up wherever an atmosphere of gentility was once centered, and then such districts might persist in or recover such character again and again, long after the sector theory would have moved them into new suburban tracts. Cultural cohesion among low-income minority (especially immigrant) groups might account for their clustering in the slums, rather than a need for hand-me-down housing. The filtering mechanism seemed to Firey too much apart from human volition and noneconomic motivations.

Perhaps the most imaginative part of Firey's work is his suggestion of a grand balancing of several objectives from among several cultural groups, within the limited confines of the metropolis. We read,

> . . . there is always a problem of allocating space. In such allocation there must always be a *proportionalization of ends* [emphasis Firey's]. This arises out of the fact that every community has a multiplicity of component ends, and not merely one or a few ends. Hence it becomes necessary to achieve a certain "balance of sacrifices" in order that every component end of the community will in some degree be attained.[7]

The further exposition of this idea is rather badly bungled by Firey, but it is not too difficult to read into it an appeal for the development of some mathematical programming technique by which the resources of the community, both real and cultural, may be divided among groups of the population in some optimal way.

Filtering as a Source of Low-Income Housing

The concept of filtering certainly antedates Hoyt's study of residential neighborhoods. For example, a British government report in 1929 contained this statement:

> When post-war building began, it was hoped that there might be a gradual movement of the working-class population of the slums into better houses. This might occur in two ways, either the slum dweller might go direct into a new house, or a process of "filtering up" might occur under which the slum dweller would move from the slum into a better pre-war house, the tenant of which would, in his turn, move into a new house. Both of these processes have, of course, occurred, but on a disappointingly small scale.[8]

By making the filtering process an essential element in his model of residential dynamics, Hoyt implicitly raised an important policy issue. If public policy seeks to raise housing standards among low-income groups, must it—or should it—work through the filtering process? From the standpoint of housing welfare, is the filtering process desirable? Is it even inevitable?

It seems clear that Hoyt originally had no intention of grappling with this issue. In reply to criticism on the filtering issue as it affects low-income housing, he said, ". . . the purpose of the study was economic, and any appraiser who mixes economic and 'social' factors, or ability to pay and need, will make a hash of both economics and social welfare."[9]

Yet the policy issue was there, the more emphatically because Rodwin could charge that Hoyt's sector theory was developed as a policy tool, to be applied by and through the Federal

Housing Administration. The charge is contained in these words:

Perhaps Hoyt may not have intended it as such, but there is a strong emphasis in the study in favor of preserving the better neighborhoods rather than improving the poorer ones. That suspicion is further supported by the fact that the study was made for the Federal Housing Administration whose interest and experience to date have been primarily to protect its insured loans and which has shown little interest in other points of view.[10]

As a reflection on Hoyt's qualifications or his method of attack, this remark by Rodwin seems to misfire. An objective, empirical review of urban development cannot be said to be "in favor of" one course of public action as opposed to some other. Hoyt did not even attempt to justify his sector theory as a normative description of ideal competitive allocation.

There is validity to the point raised by Rodwin, however, in the sense that if the normal market process—i.e., filtering down of older houses—appears to provide only inadequate dwellings for the lower-income population, perhaps somewhat stronger and more direct measures are required. The argument, as developed with particular force by Ratcliff in his *Urban Land Economics*,[11] seems to have evolved in the following way:

1. It is perceived that housing markets usually build new dwellings chiefly for the well-to-do; older dwellings filter down to lower-income families—i.e., Hoyt's empirical generalization is accepted.
2. A social judgment is made that housing of low-income families is deficient. It is proposed to subsidize the construction of new dwellings for them.
3. Some groups—presumably real estate interests—object, pointing out that in the course of time houses now being built will be available to the poor through the filtering process. Hence no interference with the market is required.
4. Welfare-minded economists retort that too great a period of time is involved, since the social pyramid is so narrow at the top and so wide at the bottom. In the great length of time needed to transmit a small volume of new housing to families now ill housed, the filtered units will—in fact must—deteriorate. When they arrive at the lowest income level, they will represent no improvement. Hence direct new construction is required to meet the low-income needs.

The discussion had about reached this point in 1949, which saw the appearance of Ratcliff's book. It was less specifically developed by Ratcliff and Ernest Fisher as early as 1936 when the two reviewed housing programs in Europe.[12] As part of that review the two economists attempted to test the validity of the theory that housing standards may be improved through filtering. They did this by observing the experience of certain European countries, and their conclusion was "... that no evidence has been adduced ... that dependence can be placed on this procedure for a substantial improvement in the housing conditions of the lower-income group. Cures of a more positive nature are demanded."[13]

Their "test" of the theory, however, is unconvincing. In England they observed that between 1920 and 1930 there had been a high rate of building, chiefly for upper-income demand. Concurrently, "... from 25,000 to 35,000 unfit houses were demolished ..." and "... a total of 5,943,462 dwellings were repaired. ..."[14] Further, "The 1931 census indicates a definite improvement in the extent of overcrowding in the preceding decade. The average number of persons per occupied house dropped from 4.85 in 1921 to 4.38 in 1931."[15] On the other hand, the doubling rate was unchanged at 1.21 families per occupied house; the average size of families, clearly, had decreased.[16]

In Holland it was noted that construction volume had been stimulated by government aid. A government official was quoted: "Owing to the numerous unoccupied dwellings and the general fall in rents, many flats of inferior standard have fallen empty and will be difficult to let."[17] However, the reviewers conjectured that migration back to rural areas could account for some of the vacancy of low-rent dwellings.

The principal "test" of the filtering theory in the Fisher-Ratcliff study turns out to be a theoretical one. With the aid of an abbreviate frequency distribution of dwellings in England and Wales by rent, the authors point out that to supply 10 percent of the lowest group with better dwellings through the filtering process the housing stock at the highest level would have to grow by 45 percent, because the number of units in the former group is 4-½ times that of the latter. The authors considered such a volume of building to be unlikely: "... if the producers of housing are well informed of the demand situation, there will be no overproduction in any grade of housing, and no surplus will be created."[18] This argument is repeated with only minor embellishments in Ratcliff's 1949 book.[19]

This theoretical argument, that any "surplus" of housing would curtail new construction, could leave the sector theory without its mainspring and would seem to contradict Ratcliff's candid admission that filtering is a "well recognized phenomenon."[20] All new construction for a population already housed is necessarily redundant in a physical sense, but not in an economic sense. But the "no surplus" idea has a more fundamental flaw. A *subsidized* filtering process can indeed provide the requisite surpluses which will permit upgrading of low-income housing. Ratcliff (in particular) has made it appear that to achieve improvement in housing standards the choice is between an unsubsidized market filtering process and a subsidized public housing program. He has said, "Filtering cannot be forced."[21] This seems to overlook the fact that public policy can, and often does, stimulate the filtering process. There is the FHA, the Home Loan Bank Board, The Federal Savings and Loan Insurance Corporation, and the legion of freeway builders to lure the relatively well-to-do to suburban areas of new housing, leaving older homes to families of relatively lower income. More direct inducements to accelerate filtering are also possible. Perhaps Ratcliff meant to say that filtering cannot be forced *without some public subsidy or other effort*, though it is difficult to imagine how a market process can be "forced" to accelerate *except* by a public program.

Because of this theoretical lapse Ratcliff (and Fisher) cannot be said to have provided the sector theory with a normative test. They were obviously arguing ex parte for public housing, obscuring rather than creating a set of equilibrium relationships.

Rodwin and the Issue of a Competitive Market

Of course, it is not obvious from Hoyt's work that the filtering process or the working out of the sector theory reflects an efficient, competitive allocation of urban resources by the private market. Perhaps the historical regularities which permitted Hoyt to develop his generalized descriptions of urban development stem from more or less universal imperfections in the housing market. If this be the case, the sector theory is robbed of its usefulness as a benchmark of ideal behavior or as an instrument of policy.

Rodwin makes almost this charge in his extensive evaluation of the sector theory which appeared in 1950. He says,

> Throughout the analysis, Hoyt has been dealing with the operation of a relatively laissez-faire competitive economy.
>
> Real estate, however, is a notorious and oft cited example of just such market imperfections. Housing, in particular, reflects an additional complication because its long production period and durability contribute to serious and prolonged marketing errors and maladjustments.[22]

But is the urban housing market so imperfectly competitive? Rodwin mentions the following conditions for "ideal" market performance:[23]

"perfect knowledge and mobility"—but the entire brokerage profession (which some would claim to be overpopulated) and a major portion of newspaper lineage are devoted to the dissemination of knowledge; as for mobility, Hoyt's empirical observations are very largely a documentation of population movement.

"maximization of profit, many buyers and sellers, free entry and departure of productive factors"—but there can be little dispute that these conditions exist in one of the most atomistic of all commodity markets.

"homogenous products"—but product homogeneity is a requirement of two-dimensional *analysis*, not of optimal resource allocation. It is the function, after all, of an economic system to allocate resources among an essentially infinite range of heterogenous products. The defect of analytical equipment ought not to be attributed to a type of product which is inherently heterogenous, but Rodwin does so.

There are two other critical estimates of the market process in Rodwin's essay. As noted above, he calls attention to the durability of housing as an impediment to efficient market adjustments. Here he rather spectacularly misses the point of the filtering discussion and the sector theory; the movement of population through the housing stock is the competitive market's way of making use of a durable but deteriorating inventory. This is surely the import of Hoyt's bold generalizations. Rodwin presumably would not see in the used car market, or in the markets for used machine tools, passenger airplanes, or household appliances a culpable market organization; why then for used houses? It is the nature of the product to go through a succession of less affluent or less particular users; there is nothing necessarily "imperfect" about the process of handing things down.

Lastly, Rodwin calls attention to the fact that land uses which are determined solely by private market considerations can give rise to notorious external diseconomies or "social costs." Factories produce smoke, and automobiles produce congestion. There are sins of neglect, too: "To compete in the urban land and housing market, uses must be income producing and rather high at that. Uses like playgrounds, parks and good minimum standard housing for low-income groups cannot or at any rate have not been adequately served under such a mechanism."[24] The need for public remedies for such conditions clearly is a value judgment on Rodwin's part, with which one may agree or disagree. Valid or not, however, the point hardly reflects on the sector theory or the filtering concept as a description of the urban market. One cannot blame a market for acting like a market.

Rodwin's low estimate of the housing market's performance—in which many other economists, planners, and urbanists generally concur—is not based upon a convincing demonstration that this particular market is ineffectively organized. Nor does Rodwin's disillusion with the marketplace make the sector theory seem less capable of predicting how the clockwork of the marketplace will tick. Rodwin's complaint is fundamentally with social attitudes, not with the sector theory. His intuition that the filtering process somehow harms low-income people cannot be supported with the analytical tools at his command. It remains an intuition.

Grigsby's Empirical Method

With the publication in 1963 of William Grigsby's *Housing Markets and Public Policy*, the sector theory's cartographic representation of housing market interactions gave way to a matrix approach.[25] Though he concedes that his new formulation is "tentative and exploratory,"[26] Grigsby examines and describes promising new tools for urban analysis. He deals explicitly with the concept of filtering, pointing out that ". . . filtering is, in a sense, the subject of the entire book since, broadly speaking, it is the principal dynamic feature of the housing market."[27] The analytical portions of the book, then, can be construed as a new treatment of the filtering question.

How to define filtering, particularly for purpose of empirical measurement, has been a persistent problem, and Grigsby provides a good review of alternative definitions. The "traditional" definition is Ratcliff's: "This process (filtering) . . . is described most simply as the changing of occupancy as the housing that is occupied by one income group becomes available to the next lower income group as a result of decline in market price, i.e., in sales price or rent value."[28] This definition has been found to be unsatisfactory in practice.[29]

The specific objection to Ratcliff's definition is that it speaks of changes in both *occupancy* (i.e., income level of occupants) and *vaule*, as though the two were necessarily related. But in practice one may fall while the other changes in different degree, or different direction, or remains the same.

A reformulation was provided by Fisher and Winnick.[30] "Filtering is defined as a change over time in the position of a given dwelling unit or group of dwelling units within the distribution of housing rents and prices in the community as a whole."

Thus, they chose to measure filtering in terms of changes in relative value rather than in terms of incomes of occupants.

Grigsby, who generally seems to prefer the Fisher-Winnick reformulation, suggests still another concept—that of filtering as an improvement in real housing standards among low-income families. That is, filtering would be said to occur only if low-income housing standards have been raised.[31] He says,

> Such a definition would hold that filtering (changes in house prices and rents) must be measured while holding income, quality, and space per person constant, or in more relaxed form, that filtering occurs only when value declines more rapidly than quality so that families can obtain either higher quality and more space at the same price, or the same quality and space at a lower price than formerly.[32]

This welfare concept of filtering does not play a role in Grigsby's stimulating discussion of market mechanisms. It is not consistent with his expressed belief that filtering is "the principal dynamic feature of the housing market,"[33] for the market may not in fact produce welfare effects.

The welfare issue seems to reduce to this: *optimum use* of given resources should not be confused with *improvement* in the supply or quality of those resources. In the traditional economic jargon, Rodwin, Ratcliff, and others have failed to distinguish the problem of allocation from that of growth. Optimization in the use of a durable good requires shifting it about among different classes of users as its relative usefulness declines or rises. The shifting-about, in itself, affects welfare only as it is an efficient or an inefficient reallocation. Other market circumstances being unchanged, filtering in response to deterioration of the housing stock could well leave aggregate and individual housing welfare unchanged.

If filtering is to be understood as a basic pattern of market behavior, then it must be defined as a response to any change in conditions of supply or demand—in the number or types of households or in their incomes, in the physical quality of the stock or any portion of it, or in construction of particular kinds of new units. The response must be measured in terms of occupancy of particular houses or neighborhoods by some different class of households.

This is still not a completely precise formulation; such is not required, for the data available to the student of a particular market will usually force him to adopt some workable definition. The important point is that the welfare question is best left either to deliberately contrived (and controlled) empirical tests (unlikely without massive financial support), or to careful deductive reasoning based on an operational model and realistic market data. The former is not yet available. The following chapter of the present study presents a hypothetical example of the latter.

If filtering is thought of simply as a change in the allocation of housing units among households of different types, the method of analysis most appropriate to this concept would clearly involve a *matrix* of relationships among submarkets. This is precisely the formulation which Grigsby develops in his analytical chapters. Defining a set of submarkets in the Philadelphia metropolitan area, he illustrates flows among these submarkets on the basis of unpublished National Housing Inventory data and certain assumptions about the "second choices" which different households would make if their actual location were not available to them. The object is to provide a "matrix expressing relative degrees of substitutability among submarkets. . . ."[34]

Such a matrix is potentially capable of predicting market responses—i.e., shifts among submarkets, or filtering—which would result from certain essentially exogenous changes in market conditions, such as alterations in the characteristics of dwelling units. The matrix form permits an analyst to give appropriate attention to the *indirect* links between submarkets which might not be directly substitutable; thus, "Bargain house prices in Area A might be completely ignored by potential home buyers in Area C if the latter area were too far distant. These prices might, however, attract a segment of the market from Area B to Area A. This shift might in turn create values in B which would serve to capture a segment of the potential in C.[35] In this way the entire housing market is seen to be interconnected.

Later portions of the Grigsby book examine issues of new residential construction volume, maintenance of residential structures, and residential renewal. The intention is to make use of the matrix concepts developed in earlier chapters, but the effort is not successful. Grigsby discusses the manner in which the existing stock of houses acts to discourage new construction, the extent to which expenditures on maintenance of the quality of the existing stock (as an alternative to new construction) are justified, and the renewal strategy which will get the best response from the private market.

The problem is that Grigsby's matrix model is not operational (nor does he claim that it is). It cannot simulate market responses to, say, redevelopment of a central slum area, or to development of a suburban middle-income tract. Hence his conclusions with respect to new construction, maintenance, and renewal do not flow out of the model.

Summary

The sector theory has been transformed into a matrix. Conceptually the matrix should be able to provide answers to welfare-type questions such as those having to do with the housing standards of low-income families as affected by subsidized or unsubsidized filtering, by renewal, or public housing. It may also prove to be a much more precise tool for forecasts of construction activity and neighborhood change.

The sector theory was an empirical generalization which described the experience of many cities approximately but of no cities exactly. It generalized from events that were conditioned on certain social structures, technologies, and public policies; wherever or whenever these things differ from those which Hoyt observed, his implied forecasts of neighborhood changes are invalidated. The very agency which commissioned Hoyt's study has been as instrumental as any other single force in changing those conditions.

The sector theory was never intended, explicitly, to answer the welfare questions which so concerned its critics. But those questions must be answered, as public resources in increasing volume are being directed toward improvement in housing standards. A more flexible means of describing competitive market interactions, particularly in response to alternative hypothetical public programs, was clearly needed.

The basic source of confusion over filtering stems from this close association of welfare issues with patterns of movement in an unregulated private market. This confusion would be heightened by a *definition* of filtering—i.e., of the basic dynamic force—in terms of achievement of a welfare aim.

In a mixed economy, the most effective model for all purposes is one which generates private market responses to all manner of exogenous forces, such as mortgage insurance, rising real incomes, shifts in tastes, public housing, population growth, increased property taxes, or earthquakes. As we are interested in changes in the use made of specific neighborhoods, the model must be considerably disaggregated. Then the impact of any proposed welfare program can be traced through each neighborhood in the community, and its real effect on housing welfare assessed.

A Theory of Filtering

The sector theory, the concept of filtering as a "well recognized phenomenon," and Grigsby's matrix approach all represent efforts to read either logic or predictability into the observed pattern of occupancy of an urban area's housing stock. The pattern can be studied in terms of household characteristics (especially income) vis-a-vis housing characteristics (such as quality or age of the structure, or location). Low-income households seem usually to inhabit older, less adequate, centrally located dwellings. New residential construction, by implication, is concentrated at higher price or income levels and at the fringes of the urban area. From what underlying economic circumstances do these patterns arise? How might the pattern be affected by some change in those circumstances? The filtering discussion has succeeded in raising these questions, but not in providing satisfactory answers.

In the previous section a review of the filtering controversy pointed toward the need for some analytical technique which would represent the process of matching households to elements of the housing stock. Hoyt's cartographic technique is both inflexible and, on many critical points, ill-defined. Grigsby's approach was not developed into operational form. We are unable to say what adjustment in the pattern of occupancy will occur from changes in the income distribution of households, for example, from an abnormal rate of in-migration, from a specific type of housing subsidy plan, or from other changes in market supply or demand conditions.

In this section we offer a very simplified but operational model of the matrix type which suggests that such questions do have determinate answers. This model is in terms of the "assignment problem" of recent operations research literature. It involves a hypothetical community consisting initially of an equal number of households and housing units; the households differ with respect to income (or ability to pay for housing in general), while the housing units differ with respect to desirability. We ask of this model several questions which have real world counterparts and for which the model is able to provide at least partial and qualified answers. These are the questions:

1. Given the two-sided differentiation of households and housing units, what pattern of occupancy—of assignment or matching of families with houses—will a free market tend to produce?
2. How will this pattern change if there is a change in the income distribution of the community?
3. If the community remains unchanged in size (number of households), what will be the quality of new houses when depreciation of the stock requires some replacement building?
4. When such replacement building occurs, what pattern of changes in occupancy of the housing stock will accompany it?
5. If the community increases in size, what price level of housing will be constructed?

The model is dependent upon several assumptions which must be borne in mind in conjunction with the effort to find answers to these questions. These assumptions imply important qualifications to the conclusions reached and indicate the imperfect state to which the assignment model technique for housing market analysis is as yet developed.

The Assumptions

The hypothetical community consists of five families, differing as to income but not otherwise, and five houses differing as to quality. Adopting a yardstick of value, which might be the monthly rent or rental equivalent, we need to make assumptions regarding the amount each family would be willing to offer for each of the houses, since each family is a potential occupant of any dwelling. That is, for purposes of simplification we do not consider independent submarkets (apartments vs. one-family homes, for example).

The first step in deciding how these rent offers would differ for different families and for the several houses is illustrated by Figure 1. In this table the vertical columns represent the houses, A, B, C, D, and E. A is the lowest quality dwelling, B the second lowest, etc., and we assume all families rank these houses in the same order. The horizontal rows represent families 1, 2, 3, 4, and 5, with family 1 being the one with least income, family 2 having the second lowest income, etc.

There is some lowest amount of rent that would be offered for any house by any family, and this amount can be designated L. It is the differences from L which will determine the pattern of occupancy rather than the value of L itself, so this value does not need to be specified.

The first figure shows that family 1 would offer $5 more for B than for A, $10 more for C than for A, and so on.[36] Thus, rent offers increase with house *quality*. Figure 1 also shows that for a given house, such as A, rent offers rise with *income*. Family 2 would offer $10 more for A than family 1 would offer. Family 3 would offer $20 more than family 1 for house A, etc.

If we were to complete the table of rent offers with only this information, we would enter in each cell the sum of the amounts at the top of its column and at the left of its row. For example, this would make family 2's offer for house B equal to L+15, family 3's offer for house B equal to L+25, etc. This, however, would imply an assumption which seems unrealistic. It would say that family 2, with a higher income than family 1, would pay no greater premium to have house B rather than house A. The income elasticity of demand for quality would be zero.

One might expect, however, that one step up in quality, from house A to house B, would be worth more to the higher income family. This accords with the notion that housing space itself is a necessity but extra housing quality is a luxury, the consumption of which increases with income.

To represent this income elasticity of demand for quality, Figure 2 shows some assumed increments for each of the cells outside row 1 and column A. Each step up the *income* ladder brings an increase of $1 in the rent offer; each step up the *quality* ladder also brings a $1 increase. There is no necessary reason for these $1 amounts to be the same; the argument is unchanged so long as the effects of both income and quality are always positive.

Figure 3 then adds these several assumptions together. The *market demand matrix* consists of amounts of L plus some increment for income and/or quality. The amount offered by family 2 for house B is L + 10 + 5 + 1 or L + 16. The amount offered for house C by family 3 is L + 20 + 10 + 4 or L + 34, etc.

The Optimal Assignment

We may now answer the question, which pattern of occupancy will produce the maximum aggregate of rent offers? This maximum sum should be realized by a well-organized competitive market of mobile families and is optimal in this restricted sense.

It can be proved that any assignment—i.e., pattern of occupancy—not lying on the main diagonal of this matrix is non-optimal; the aggregate of rent offers could be increased by rearranging the pattern in a specific way.[37] Figure 4 illustrates one such

Figure 1. Effects of Income Change and House Quality on Lowest Rent Offer

	Houses				
Families	A	B	C	D	E
1	L	+5	+10	+15	+20
2	+10				
3	+20				
4	+30				
5	+40				

Figure 2. Effects of Income Elasticity of Demand for Quality

	Houses				
Families	A	B	C	D	E
1					
2		+1	+2	+3	+4
3		+2	+4	+6	+8
4		+3	+6	+9	+12
5		+4	+8	+12	+16

Figure 3. Market Demand Matrix

	Houses				
Families	A	B	C	D	E
1	L	+5	+10	+15	+20
2	+10	+16	+22	+28	+34
3	+20	+27	+34	+41	+48
4	+30	+38	+46	+54	+62
5	+40	+49	+58	+67	+76

non-optimal assignment. The circles indicate the pattern of occupancy; family 1 lives in house C, family 2 in A, family 3 in E, family 4 in B and family 5 in D. Referring to the market demand matrix (Figure 3) it can be seen that the aggregate of rents offered for units actually occupied under this arrangement comes to L + 173.

We note, however, that by switching family 1 to house A, and the family initially occupying A to the house initially occupied by family 1, we decrease the aggregate of rent offers by $10 and increase it by $12, for a net gain of $2. We could then switch families 2 and 4 for a further gain of $2. So long as any pair of families is not "located" along the main diagonal of this matrix, a profitable switch is possible. When they are all on the diagonal, any switch means a greater loss than gain. The optimal assignment, represented by Figure 5, has an aggregate rent offer of L + 180. No other assignment of these families to this supply of houses can add to a greater sum.

Response to a Change in Market Conditions

Our simulation model has now produced a not-too-surprising result. The less desirable houses are occupied by the lower-income families. It is important to point out that this result has nothing to do with the *cost* of building such houses, for at the outset of the problem the five houses were assumed to be already in existence. Their cost, in an economic sense, was nil. In the short run, any commodity which is fixed in supply will be priced and utilized without regard to its cost of production, which by that time is a "sunk" cost.

The real usefulness of the model is yet to be demonstrated. The diagonal assignment is only a starting point from which patterns of *response to changes* in market conditions can be derived. Suppose, for example, that the income composition of the five-family community is changed, so that there is no longer a family 5 with its high income, but there are two families at level 1. If we substitute in the market demand matrix a row 1′ for 5 (and rearrange the rows so that the higher income families are in lower rows), we know that once again the optimal assignment will be along the diagonal. This will require some shifting about of the families, however, with the exception of family 1, who can remain undisturbed. Figure 6 shows the outcome of this "filtering" response to the change in income composition.

The response consists of having family 1′ occupy house B, after family 2 moves from B to C, family 3 moves from C to D, and family 4 moves from D to E. The new aggregate rent offer, L + 130, is less than before, reflecting the loss of a high-income family. Note that the decrease of $50 in this value is less than would have been realized if the new family, 1′, had moved into the house vacated by family 5. That loss would have been $76 to $20, or $56. The filtering process has improved by $6 the resale value, in a sense, of house E. It is interesting to note that while the aggregate situation is improved by this filtering activity, the rent offers for houses B, C, and D, as well as E, are now lower than before; they have "filtered down." Yet families 2, 3, and 4 now occupy better quality houses; they have "filtered up."

Figure 4. Nonoptimal Assignment

	Houses				
Families	A	B	C	D	E
1	←	———	——0		
2	0——	———	→		
3					0
4		0			
5				0	

Figure 5. Optimal Assignment

	Houses				
Families	A	B	C	D	E
1	0				
2		0			
3			0		
4				0	
5					0

Figure 6. Effect of Change in Income Distribution

Families	A	B	C	D	E
1	0				
1′		0			
2		———	→0		
3			———	→0	
4				———	→0

The net result is, in this hypothetical situation, a gain of $6 through filtering; if actions within the community successfully fend off value decline for houses B, C, and D, this net gain will not be realized.

The Implied Values of Houses

The "assignment" model, despite its hypothetical nature, may thus assist in forecasting neighborhood changes. If the assumptions made in developing this model correspond to real market conditions in a specific community, the model will not only point to patterns of change which specific new circumstances are likely to produce, it will also "explain" why those changes in the use of the housing inventory take place. This helps to avoid the common mistake of thinking that the housing market is irrational, or imperfect, and therefore in need of public control simply because the logic underlying its performance is difficult to see. On the other hand, if we are fairly sure what the pattern of rent offers in the community for its housing stock looks like, and we observe a pattern of movement or occupancy not in accord with the simulation model, we can with greater justice criticize the operation of the market and perhaps discover realistic remedies.

The usefulness of the assignment model approach goes beyond forecasts of changes within the existing inventory of houses. The model provides a means whereby the type of new construction which the market requires, as the community grows or as the original stock of houses depreciates, can be predicted. The essential tool for this purpose is an indication from the model of the "economic value" of a specific type of new house, which value can then be compared with its construction cost. "Economic value" in this context refers to the effect of an additional house on the aggregate of rent offers. (Of course, if the rent offers are thought of as monthly amounts, they would have to be capitalized in some way to obtain present value.) Thus, going back to our original market demand matrix, with five families occupying a total of five houses, what would be the effect on aggregate rent offers if an additional house were added? For example, suppose that another house exactly like D were added to the supply. After all profitable shifting about of families among the enlarged housing supply had been completed, how much would the aggregate of rent offers have increased? This situation is illustrated in Figure 7.

We note that family 3 would move into house D′, family 2 into C, and family 1 into B; house A would be left vacant. By referring to Figure 3, the market demand matrix, all the plus and minus effects on the aggregate rent offer can be determined. The net result is an increase of $18.

If the added house were like C rather than D, the aggregate rent offer would increase by $11 rather than $18. Completing this process for all of the original types of houses yields Table 1. The values rise from $0 for A′ to $26 for E′; all these values are dependent on the many assumptions made concerning the pattern of rent offers embodied in the market demand matrix and the mobility of the several families.

Table 1, then, provides indicators of the economic value of the various types of new houses which may be added to the supply. The fact that value rises with quality stems from the assumptions about market conditions. Cost of construction has not yet been brought into the picture.

The "normal market" assumptions are also responsible for the most significant feature of the list of values in Table 1. In such a market higher-income households offer greater premiums for housing quality than lower-income households offer. The function relating value to quality is *convex*; that is, it increases by increasing amounts. A *cost* function, relating the cost of construction to the quality of the dwelling which is built may be linear, convex, or concave. Unless it has more convexity than the value function, efficient new construction will never occur in the middle quality range.

This is illustrated in Figure 8. Here the economic value figures from Table 1 are plotted: the convexity of the curve can be noted. Three different types of cost functions are also shown; X is a linear relation between cost and quality, Y is a convex relation in which cost rises faster than quality, and Z is a concave relation with costs rising less rapidly than quality. All three cost curves are shown lying well above the value curve; if such is the case, no new construction will be justified. The cost curve,

Figure 7. Effect of Adding House D′

	Houses					
Families	A	B	C	D′	D	E
1	——————→	0				
2		——————→	0			
3			——————→	0		
4					0	
5						0

Table 1. Change in Aggregate Value When One House is Added

House Added	
A′	+0
B′	+5
C′	+11
D′	+18
E′	+26

whichever shape it has, must for some reason fall until it touches the value curve; the quality level at which the curves first touch is then the quality level for new construction which the market requires.

If the community in question does not increase in population, new housing demand will be of the replacement variety, a response to the gradual deterioration or obsolescence of the stock of houses. This loss of desirability will encourage households to offer premiums for newly constructed houses; the premiums being offered will increase as time goes by. For example, more would be offered for a new unit E′ than for E, if the latter unit has depreciated. In other terms, there is a *latent* matrix of demand for *new* units of the several qualities. These premiums, due to the wearing out of the original stock, can be represented in relation to values derived from the initial matrix for existing units by a downward shift of the cost function for new construction. Part of the cost of the new construction will be covered by this premium.

As the cost curve shifts downward, the quality level at which it first touches the value curve depends on the shape of the cost curve. If the latter is linear or concave (as X or Z in Figure 8), replacement construction will usually take the form of the highest quality of dwellings. If the cost function is sharply concave (as Y in Figure 8), construction may occur at a middle quality level.

We have no information from which to draw the cost function linear, concave, or convex; in fact its shape may well vary among communities and over time. The important observation is that for most of the range of *possible* shapes of the cost curve, new construction would be economically warranted for replacement only when it is at the upper end of the quality spectrum *in our model*, given the assumptions regarding a "normal market" and in the absence of any submarkets.

This says something about the quality level of new construction in a static community, in which the only demand pressure for new houses is a result of deterioration or obsolescence of the old units. What of a community which is growing in population? The same technique allows comments as to the quality level of new construction in this case, too. Under this condition, however, the economic value of an additional house will differ from the value derived in the previous case. Instead of there being a surplus of houses when one unit is created, there will be a

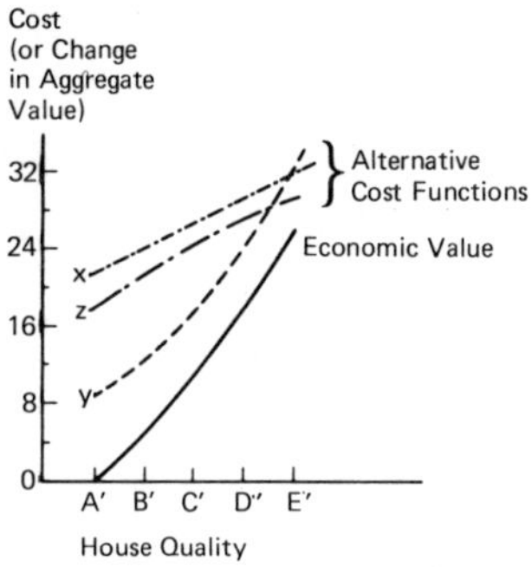

Figure 8. Selecting Quality Level for New Construction—Replacement Case

positive deficiency of houses until another is supplied, in the community which expands by one family.

The economic value of a house under conditions of scarcity can be determined from our market demand matrix by *removing* one house at a time from the five-house stock and computing the effect on aggregate rent offers. Again, the filtering process is assumed to operate sufficiently so as to make optimum use of the now inadequate housing stock, as is illustrated in Figure 9. When house D is removed, family 4 moves into house C, family 3 into house B, family 2 into house A, and family 1 is left, initially, without a dwelling. Thus, wherever the scarcity arises, whether by the in-migration of a well-to-do family, a poor family, or a middle-income family, the tendency in this model is to force out the lowest rent-payer, whoever that may be.

New economic values may now be derived for each of the original types of houses under the condition of absolute scarcity. If house D is removed, the aggregate rent offer will diminish by L + $21. If it is A that is removed, the loss will be just L dollars. In Table 2 all the economic values under conditions of scarcity are presented.

Figure 10 compares the new function relating value and quality to a single illustrative cost function. It is to be noted that in this case the value function does not start from zero for a house of type A, but from the value L. Initially we let the cost function lie entirely above the value function, with no new construction being warranted.

Family 1, however, requires housing of some sort. Its minimum demand is for simple housing space—the bare necessities for which it previously offered L. Now that there is an absolute

Figure 9. Effect of Removing House D

	Houses			
Families	A	B	C	E
1	←———			
2	0←———			
3		0←———		
4			0←———	
5				0

Table 2. Change in Aggregate Value When One House is Removed

House Removed	
A	−L
B	−(L + 6)
C	−(L + 13)
D	−(L + 21)
E	−(L + 30)

shortage of housing space, this family—and all the others as well—must offer more than L. The value curve must shift upward until it touches the cost curve, permitting some type of new dwelling to be constructed.

The value curve may simply move vertically upward, but there is reason to believe this will not be the case. As higher-income families find the price of housing space rising, their real incomes are reduced; they cannot afford to be quite so choosy now about housing quality. As a result, quality premiums associated with higher incomes, such as were assumed in Figure 2, will very likely diminish. The value curve will thus not simply move upward; it will tilt toward a flatter position as it does so. This is shown by the EV and EV′ lines in Figure 10.

With the type of cost function shown in Figure 10, the first contact of the value and cost curves occurs at the lowest quality level; the new house which is needed to meet the demands of an enlarged community will thus be of minimum permissible cost.

It is of course possible that the value curve will move upward more rapidly than it flattens, in which case high-quality new construction would be the answer. The chances for middle-quality construction appear slim, however.[38]

One interesting point about this new construction response is that the quality level of the home which is constructed bears no necessary relation to the income level of the family which migrates into this community. So long as the filtering effect takes place, the increase in demand operates, in this model, to produce any new dwelling so that the enlarged community may be housed. But the income level of the added family is not significant in determining which kind of new dwelling will be built.

Locational Significance

If it is possible to anticipate the quality level of new housing construction within a community, it follows that the location of new residential building activity can also be forecast more readily. High-quality dwellings may reclaim areas in the central area of the community, particularly if they stem from replacement demand which will leave the lowest quality part of the housing supply vacant. Alternatively, high-quality building may take place in the suburban fringe, in which case it would be directed toward sites which contribute to the appeal of expensive homes—view locations or areas with special amenities such as parks, pleasant atmosphere, or country clubs nearby.

If the economic need is for relatively low-quality new homes, however, central sites will probably be unavailable, as this type of home-building is likely to occur when residential facilities are scarce. Then the construction will occur in suburban tracts large enough to provide economies of scale by which costs may be reduced as much as technology allows, but situated in districts which do not command premiums for amenities. The

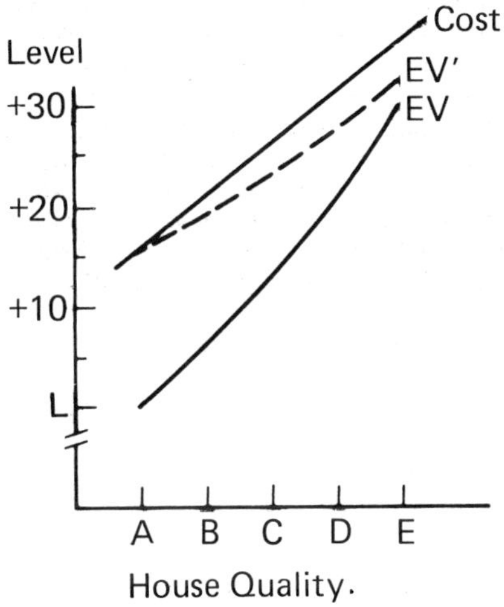

Figure 10. Selecting Quality Level for New Construction—Growth Case

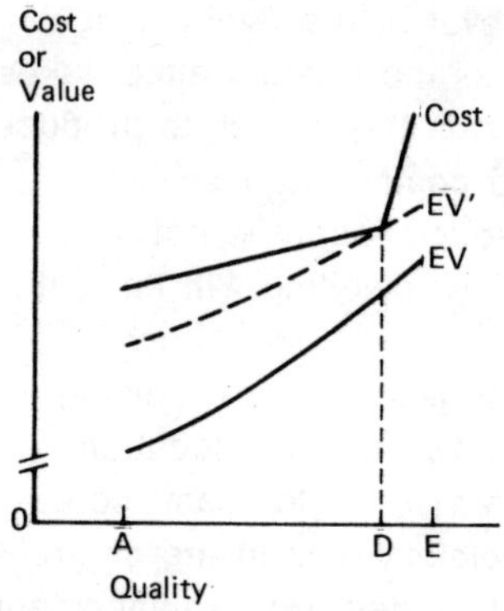

Figure 11. Replacement Demand—Excluding Luxury Dwellings

amenity areas would be on reserve for later high-quality replacement demand.

The assignment model, hypothetical though it is, thus offers interesting suggestions for the rationale behind neighborhood filtering, the quality and price level of newly constructed homes, and the location of residential building activities.

Notes

[1]The phrase is Ratcliff's. Richard U. Ratcliff, *Urban Land Economics* (New York: McGraw-Hill, 1949), p. 321.

[2]Homer Hoyt, *The Structure and Growth of Residential Neighborhoods in American Cities* (Washington, D. C.: Government Printing Office, 1939). Hoyt's "Sector Theory" was not the first effort to present a systematic description of the way an urban community evolves, but it has served as a focal point for much subsequent discussion of the subject. The sector concept itself builds upon the earlier notion that socioeconomic classes group themselves about the center of the city in a series of concentric rings, an idea so colorfully put forth by Burgess in 1925. To this only vaguely dynamic description Hoyt added at least three things—extensive empirical documentation, a rudimentary socioeconomic rationalization for the patterns observed, and the important refinement of directional growth. By the time Hoyt had redone the concentric-circle concept of E. W. Burgess, it can be said that the first "model" of urban development had been created.

See: *The City*, R. E. Park, editor (Chicago, Illinois: University of Chicago Press, 1925), Chapter II.

[3]Hoyt, *op. cit.*, p. 84.

[4]Hoyt, *op. cit.*, p. 88.

[5]Walter Firey, *Land Use in Central Boston* (Boston: Harvard University Press, 1947).

[6]*Ibid.*, p. 55.

[7]*Ibid.*, p. 326.

[8]"A Policy for the Slums," report of a special committee of the National Housing and Town Planning Council (London: P. S. King and Son, Ltd., 1929), p. 16. (Quoted in *European Housing Policy and Practice*, by

Ernest M. Fisher and Richard U. Ratcliff, Federal Housing Administration, 1936, p. 61.)
[9]Homer Hoyt, "Residential Sectors Revisited," *The Appraisal Journal* (October, 1950).
[10]Lloyd Rodwin, "The Theory of Residential Growth and Structure," *The Appraisal Journal* (July 1950).
[11]Ratcliff, *op. cit.* (see especially Chapter 11).
[12]Ernest M. Fisher and Richard U. Ratcliff, *op. cit.* (especially Part IX).
[13]*Ibid.*, p. 66.
[14]*Ibid.*, p. 60.
[15]*Ibid.*, p. 60.
[16]*Ibid.*, p. 61.
[17]*Ibid.*, p. 65.
[18]*Ibid.*, p. 64.
[19]Ratcliff, *Urban Land Economics*, pp. 321–334.
[20]*Ibid.*, p. 321.
[21]*Ibid.*, p. 322. In his book Ratcliff himself contradicts the earlier "no surplus" idea. On page 332 he says, "It has been demonstrated here that filtering cannot take place except in the presence of a surplus."
[22]Rodwin, *op. cit.*
[23]Rodwin, *op. cit.*
[24]Rodwin, *op. cit.*
[25]William Grigsby, *Housing Markets and Public Policy* (Philadelphia: University of Pennsylvania Press, 1963).
[26]*Ibid.*, p. 28.
[27]*Ibid.*, p. 99.
[28]Ratcliff, *Urban Land Economics*, pp. 321–322.
[29]For example, Grebler in his empirical study of New York's lower east side writes, "Commonly accepted notions of the operation of the filtering process are found to be ambiguous and inadequate when subjected to an empirical test, and a reformulation of the theory of filtering, which lends itself to verification, is suggested." Leo Grebler, *Housing Market Behavior in a Declining Area* (New York: Columbia University Press, 1952), p. 17.
[30]Ernest M. Fisher and Louis Winnick, "A Reformulation of the 'Filtering' Concept," in *Social Policy and Social Research in Housing*, Robert K. Merton, ed. (New York: Association Press, 1951). Though Grebler's book (*op. cit.*) was published in 1952, it was available to Fisher and Winnick earlier and is referred to by them.
[31]Grigsby, *op. cit.*, p. 95 ff.
[32]*Ibid.*, p. 97.
[33]*Ibid.*, p. 99.
[34]Grigsby, *op. cit.*, p. 50.
[35]Grigsby, *op. cit.*, pp. 34–35.
[36]Figure I omits "L" from each box but one, since it is the same for all.
[37]A generalized proof is offered in Appendix A.
[38]If house E represents a very luxurious dwelling outside the ordinary market range, a kink in the cost curve could induce the construction of house D to meet this demand, as in Figure 11.

1.5

Elimination of Blight and Slums

Jerome Rothenberg

The Nature of Blight and Slums

What is the purpose of the federal urban renewal program? Possibly the major target of the program is to eliminate "blight and slums." There are at least two ambiguities in this objective, one associated with the meaning of "blight" and "slum," the other with the purpose to be achieved by their elimination.

"Blight" and "slum" are not rigorously defined in the federal statutes, nor in most discussions of the subject. The conventional meanings are in terms of the physical characteristics of dwellings in relation to their occupancy. The closest to an official definition is found in the Housing Act of 1937: " 'Slum' means 'any area where dwellings predominate which, by reason of dilapidation, over-crowding, faulty arrangement or design, lack of ventilation, light, or sanitation facilities, or any combination of these factors, are detrimental to safety, health or morals.' "[1] To use more recent terminology, the dwellings do not provide housing that is "decent, safe, and sanitary." Slum dwellings are usually filthy and vermin-infested and are fire hazards. "Dilapidation," in the above definition, has been given content by the Census Bureau in the 1950 Census as follows: "A dwelling unit should be reported as dilapidated if, because of either deterioration or inadequate original construction, it is below the generally accepted minimum standard for housing and should be torn down, extensively repaired or rebuilt."[2] This usage would certainly seem to be ambiguous for measurement purposes; yet the Census Bureau has apparently used it successfully.[3]

"Blight" is not ordinarily sharply distinguished from "slum." It often refers simply to the process, stage, or state that characterizes a slum but is more general in that it can apply to single structures as well as to clusters. It is more frequently applied to nonresidential structures than is the term "slum." Another difference is that "blight" sometimes is used to indicate the process by which property becomes substandard. So property may exhibit different degrees of blight, whereas the cluster of structures in a slum exhibits well-advanced stages of blight.

Reprinted with the permission of The Brookings Institution, *Economic Evaluation of Urban Renewal*, Jerome Rothenberg, The Brookings Institution (Washington, 1967), Chapter III, "Elimination of Blight and Slums," pp. 32–57.

These definitions are based essentially on conventional judgment—judgment about what kind of housing is decent or safe or sanitary. Sometimes this is supplemented by a criterion that is more operational, the criterion of "standard" versus "substandard" housing. This criterion was formulated by the Census Bureau for the 1940 Census. A dwelling unit is defined as "substandard" if "it is in need of major repairs, or lack[s] a private bath, or private indoor toilet, or running water."[4] The first part of this definition is highly judgmental (as it turns out, more variably so than the later-defined "dilapidated"), and the remainder has been characterized as a criterion of architectural obsolescence rather than of disrepair.[5] Houses that are hampered today because they are of older architectural fashion and standards may in all other respects be in good condition.

Ambiguity about the definition of slums is bothersome but not decisive. Slums do exist, and most observers would agree on the classification of areas into slums and non-slums. Ambiguity introduces slippage into the consensus and makes fuzzy the enumeration of the critical dimensions of the problem.

Slums and Resource Allocation

Under the definitions so far, slum and blight refer to poor housing—housing of low quality.[6] In addition, overcrowding means that the per capita accommodations are small. In this sense they refer also to housing of low quantity. It is not surprising that slums are typically inhabited by poor families.

The "Demand" for Slums

What if these low-income families, given their poverty, want low-quality housing as part of a utility-maximizing pattern of expenditure? What if, given such a demand and considering the conditions of supply for housing, the continued existence of a stock of low-grade housing is part of an optimal overall use of resources? Then a policy goal of eliminating low-grade housing can yield benefits only if some further goal will thereby be facilitated.

Slum removal in itself can yield social benefits only if at least one of the following is true: low-income groups do not demand low-grade housing because of their small budgets; or demand and supply conditions together do not make low-grade housing an efficient resource use; or slums are something more than simply low-grade housing—that is, either they are themselves something more, or they have unintended consequences not easily controlled by consumers and others. Therefore the question must be raised whether slums can be said to be part of an optimal (given an assumed pattern of poverty) equilibrium situation. This must be investigated in some detail to put into better perspective the arguments of those who, on the one hand, assert that the housing market can in effect "do everything" if left undisturbed and those who, on the other, say that it can in effect "do nothing" unless radically disturbed.

If there is poverty, this means that some people are living a "substandard" way of life. Such a way of life must necessarily contain some "substandard" elements—perhaps inadequate food, or clothing, or recreation, or shelter, or various combinations of these. Poor housing may easily be seen as an effective way to economize desperately scarce purchasing power. Moreover, it may be the easiest sacrifice to make. Hunger and cold are immediate pains and are barriers against holding gainful employment in a way that dirty, old, overcrowded living quarters are not. The "decency" of housing rests on conventional value premises that vary widely among groups with different economic, ethnic, and urban-rural backgrounds, and with differences in other dimensions of culture. Urban slums are occupied disproportionately by first-generation immigrant families; many of these migrated away from housing conditions so bad that the urban slum represented an improvement.

Thus, on the demand side it is conceivable that low-grade occupancy is part of the preferred expenditure pattern for many impoverished families. If these families nonetheless dislike such occupancy, and if the general public dislikes it for them as well, then the problem here is not slums but poverty. Subject to what determines the supply response of the housing industry (discussed below), one could argue that the eradication of poverty would eradicate slum occupancy, and indeed that "artificially" destroying particular slums without making an attack on poverty would not eradicate slum occupancy, since other slums would be created elsewhere. But the eradication of slum occupancy by dealing with poverty would be simply a symptom or a by-product of the improvement in the overall standard of living of poor people. The overall improvement is accounted as the benefit of the program. The slum elimination should not be accorded any additional benefits.[7]

Factors Affecting Supply

The supply function for housing is influenced heavily by the durability of residential structures and the relative ease with which quality changes in either direction can be incorporated in existing structures. At any one time the marginal cost of providing some conventional unit of given quality of housing service during the next accounting period from the existing stock of housing is typically considerably less than from a newly built structure. Further, the difference in expected present value of net returns between an existing structure in tolerably good condition and a comparable new structure almost always favors the former—considering relative quality of service and its value, the cost of incorporating quality changes, remaining expected lifetime, and expected maintenance cost, and counting acquisition cost as zero for the former. It rarely pays to build new housing explicitly to replace parts of the existing housing stock that are in at least fairly good condition.[8] New construction usually functions to expand the size of the overall stock. Where dwelling units are retired from the existing stock to offset the effect of new construction on size of stock, this retirement does not occur in the same part of the market that is primarily affected by the new construction. Rather, retirements come mostly from the low end of the stock—the dilapidated, lowest-quality structures. In any one year new construction forms only a small percentage of the total stock and is typically fashioned to the housing demands of middle-income and upper middle-income consumers. Public housing is a well-known exception, but of course it is not part of the private market response; even as an exception, moreover, it is a very small part of new construction.

Housing accommodations for lower-income households are typically made available by converting dwellings from use by higher-income households. This is known as "filtering."[9] Sometimes, the conversion requires more or less extensive physical alteration of the structure—as, for example, the installation of new partitions and walls and additional plumbing and electrical wiring if more occupants are to inhabit the same area. Sometimes conversion requires no physical change at all, but involves the amount and kinds of services that the property owner provides his tenants. Where conversion consists simply in a transfer of home ownership, no change in capital or services is involved at all. Since mobility within the housing market is apt to be greater at higher levels of income than at lower levels,[10] filtering is initiated largely by middle-income and higher-income groups releasing their present accommodations in favor of newly constructured dwellings. Conversion occurs via changes in vacancy rates and relative prices. Thus, the housing stock gradually passes downward from one income group to a lower one. The private housing industry has generally not found it profitable to construct new dwellings for the lower-income groups in competition with the existing stock filtering down.

Thus a stock of typically old, worn housing, cut up in the process of downward conversion in order to decrease the size of the dwelling unit, is the type of accommodation that the housing industry provides to the poor. Unless one can show that such housing is still above the slum level, or that, while at slum level, the supply response reflects externalities that are not heeded in the market, one is led to the position that inferior housing for the poor may well be an equilibrium situation representing optimal resource use. In such a case, a policy devoted to direct eradication of slums produces no benefits on that score at all. It does so only if other goals are simultaneously met in the program.

Suboptimality of Slum Housing: Market Externalities

In the analysis so far, slums and blight have been treated as though they referred simply to housing in a late stage of filtering —an orderly equilibrium market response to normal demand and supply forces. But *is* this what was described above as blight and slums? Low quality, low quantity is one problem; dilapidation, filth, and unsafe and unsanitary conditions may well be another. There are a number of reasons for believing that slums are not an optimizing response to normal market forces.

There are at least three respects in which slums may represent suboptimal resource use: (1) There are important "neighborhood effect" externalities in land use. These are likely to be especially significant in slum areas. (2) The profitability incentives to produce the particular type of low-quality housing that characterizes slums rest upon market biases that are either ethically disapproved or are the inadvertent result of public policies. (3) The functioning of slums entails the creation of important social costs that are externalities to the people involved.

Neighborhood Effects

There are important externalities in the nature of housing services and hence in the value of the property that provides them.[11] The housing consumed by a household consists not only in occupancy of a specific dwelling but also in the location of the dwelling and its neighborhood. The neighborhood consists of other residential dwellings, of commercial and industrial establishments, of public services like schools, street lighting, and police protection, of recreational and cultural amenities, and, perhaps most of all, of people. Consider the simple model presented in Davis and Whinston.[12] The quality of the housing services associated with a particular dwelling depends on the character of the dwelling and the amount of maintenance and repair devoted to it; also on the character of dwellings in the neighborhood, together with their state of maintenance-repair. For each of the *n* pieces of property comprising the neighborhood, the owner obtains the highest return if his property is undermaintained while all or most others are well maintained. He gets a smaller return if his, as well as all or most of the others, is well maintained, less if his and all or most others are poorly maintained, and least if his is well maintained while all or most others are poorly maintained. This is the payoff matrix of the "Prisoner's Dilemma" type of strategic game. Each owner has an incentive to let his property be undermaintained while others maintain their property well. But the very generality of this incentive means that it cannot be realized. All property will tend to be undermaintained. Yet this outcome is less satisfactory to all owners than the only other attainable outcome, namely high maintenance for all. The latter could not be attained by atomistic behavior, since each owner singly would shy away from high maintenance. But it is an outcome that all could agree to bring about simultaneously. That is, each could agree to it contingent on everyone else's agreeing to it.

Private Response to Externalities

The private market could achieve an optimal response in the face of these externalities by either of two means: (1) by voluntary agreements among property owners to coordinate their behavior so as to achieve mutually satisfactory results; (2) by an integration of resource decisions over neighborhoods through large-scale private assembly of land. Both means are likely to be inadequately used, however. Voluntary agreements of the sort envisaged are difficult to bring into being and even more difficult to maintain successfully. Often quite a large number of property owners is involved in any externality. It is an extremely onerous task to get voluntary agreement from enough of them to make a difference in the market. More important though, in order for such an agreement to be successful, some enforcement mechanism is needed, since without it each individual has an incentive to pretend to be abiding by the agreement in order to induce compliance by others and then to violate it by undermaintaining his property. Widespread violations are likely to result.

The integration of resource decisions through land assembly also faces obstacles. The large number of property owners who must be dealt with imposes very costly bargaining burdens on a would-be private assembler. The process of assembly is a sequence of bilateral monopoly confrontations, with each potential seller eager to squeeze out the full amount of profit to be obtained from the assembler's integrated decision making. The result for the latter is a very high cost in both time and money—a formidable obstacle when the number of necessary transactions is large.

Thus, the important externality of neighborhood means that the outcome arrived at by atomistic choice will typically be suboptimal, in the sense that nonatomistic coordinated choice would make all owners better off than when they are acting atomistically.

The notion of this type of externality is deemed so important by Davis and Whinston that they base their entire analysis of urban renewal on it and indeed redefine "blight" in terms of it. "Blight is said to exist whenever (1) strictly individual action does not result in redevelopment, (2) the coordination of decision making via some means would result in redevelopment, and (3) the sum of benefits from renewal could exceed the sum of costs."[13] Moreover, blight is sharply distinguished from slums. Slums are characterized by physical attributes, blight is a process of suboptimal land use. Under their analysis some slums need not reflect blight—they may represent optimal resource use. On the other hand, areas that are not slums may be blighted. To eradicate slums that are not blighted produces no benefits in terms of aggregate national product.

This analysis substantially complicates the discussion up to now. The immediate policy goal of the urban renewal program being the elimination of blight and slums, the two have been dealt with as near synonyms and in recognizably physical terms. If blight is the evil to be tackled and it bears no particular relation to slums, why are slums relevant at all? The problem of blight under this conception stems from the existence of externalities (in production and consumption)—the influence of the neighborhood. But this is a very general kind of influence and may be supposed to affect property in all areas. Moreover, neighborhood effects may not everywhere be such that low maintenance is suboptimal. There may well be situations where high maintenance is suboptimal. Is the market any better able to adjust land uses to the complicated pattern of such externalities in upper-income areas than it is in lower-income areas? At first glance, it would seem that one would have to be willing to say that sub-optimal land use can occur anywhere, at any level, in any direction, and to any extent, depending only on accident; and that one would apply the term "blight" to only those areas whose misallocation could be corrected at smaller "redevelopment" cost than the degree of misallocation.

It should be made clear that land misuse can take many forms: undermaintenance *or* overmaintenance; or the very character of the housing services, such as single versus multiple occupancy dwellings, high-rise versus walkup apartment buildings, attached versus detached structures, etc.; or even the residential-commercial-industrial use mix. The very diversity of these misuse patterns seems to push residential slums further into the background.

Social Action and Slums

Yet there is a special correlation between this type of market suboptimality and slum areas. Neighborhood effects are generally recognized, and special social mechanisms have been devised to minimize their adverse consequences. Building codes, health codes, and zoning are examples of measures that seek to moderate some of the worst effects of land-use externalities. They set lower limits on housing quality to avoid the sheer physical dangers of fire and disease; they forbid a degree of heterogeneity of use that would have significant nuisance value; and through residential zoning, they stipulate quality and quantity minima above that of avoiding physical inconvenience to preserve a desired homogeneity of social status. It should be noted that most of these involve setting lower limits but never upper limits. Overmaintenance and "inappropriate" upward conversion are not controlled by zoning and building codes.[14] Undermaintenance and downward conversion are the objects of control.

While the scope and enforcement of these control instruments vary widely, there is much in the planning and renewal literature that suggests that zoning and building codes are less effective for low-quality areas than for high-quality areas.[15] There are a number of reasons for this. First, slum homeowners are likely to have low incomes. But depreciation on their old dwellings makes necessary substantial maintenance expenses, sometimes major repairs. Their own resources are likely to be too meager, and their efforts to borrow from private sources are almost invariably frustrated. Loans through conventional channels are very nearly unobtainable. When they can be obtained, interest rates are likely to be quite high,[16] thus cutting down the demand. The credit available for housing in these areas is typically undercover financing at very high interest rates for dealers in speculative housing. This encourages not maintenance but conversion of dwellings to slum use.[17]

Second, the situation is somewhat the same for landlords. Low-income rentals often involve tenants who have only slight stakes in the community, often recently migrated from rural, culturally different societies, with little appreciation of the necessary disciplines involved in urban living. Their occupancy is very likely to accelerate markedly the depreciation of their dwelling units. Again adequate maintenance is likely to be very expensive, and, when major repairs are needed, it is likely to be thwarted by the unavailability of credit. Thus, the rapid, even accelerated, depreciation of property makes upkeep onerous. This is enough to induce some homeowners to skimp on maintenance and to risk code violations. For landlords it provides a temptation to skimp; but this temptation is not enough to provoke violation, if to do so would mean weakening their market position *vis-à-vis* tenants. But tenants in these poor areas are likely to have very low bargaining power in the market. They have little wealth, little mobility, highly inadequate knowledge of alternatives, and—as is disproportionately true in slums—they are discriminated against in housing as in employment, education, and political influence. Their alternatives are meager. Finally, they have often migrated to the urban area from an even poorer environment, so that the building code standards are apt to seem to them like high standards and not absolute minima. In short, they do not often either notice, or complain of, or take effective action against poor maintenance and code violations.[18] The uneven political as well as economic contest between landlord and tenant makes code enforcement politically unpopular. In addition, it is unusually expensive in a high-density area, where improvement can be forced legally in many instances only by the costly, cumbersome process of the city taking over property from impecunious or dishonest owners, sometimes evicting poor tenants in the process. The frequent result is widespread lack of code enforcement.

Thus, the kind of misallocation of resources dealt with by Davis and Whinston *is* likely to have unusually heavy incidence in slum areas. Slums are likely to represent suboptimal land use.

Biases in the Profitability of Slum Creation

Slums do not simply happen. They represent a pattern of resource use that is man made. They are produced because they are profitable. It is argued here that this profitability stems partly from a kind of market situation that is not "normally approved" but rather generally desired by the electorate to be publicly rectified. It also stems partly from certain existing public policies, which are also capable of correction. Thus, the profitability of slums is not inevitable, nor does it rest on market forces that are ethically neutral. In a special sense it can be said that it is "socially inadvertent."

Slums are produced both intensively and extensively. Intensive production means converting property to lower and lower use and then, for lowest uses, to lower and lower quality levels of service. Extensive production means extending the spatial boundaries of slum concentrations. The two often go hand in hand. The most important kinds of intensive production are to convert dwellings to increasingly overcrowded occupancy and to allow the state of the property to deteriorate progressively.

To say that slums are profitable to produce is not to say that all property owners get excess returns. It means rather that high rewards are available to "innovators," and, initiative having already been taken, it pays others to follow suit, sometimes against their personal preferences. Profitable opportunities exist, and the dynamics of contagion through neighborhood effects magnifies the drift. There are profitable opportunities because of the characteristics of the demand for inferior housing and because of legal and financial policies.

The Effect of Demand

On the demand side urban slums have historically been occupied by those who are in the lowest income groups. As was argued they have typically been recent immigrants into the area and members of what were at that time minority groups. They have often come to the area in large, concentrated numbers and have been poor. They have been seriously uninformed about housing alternatives and too poor to seek such information. They have been self-conscious about their differences from the rest of the urban community and have therefore been anxious to live in close proximity with members of their own group. They have been largely ignorant of their civil rights, of their rights as tenants, and of the housing code and other aspects of the law.

Such groups would have poor economic leverage on these grounds alone. On top of these bargaining disabilities, however, the rest of the community has often imposed the artificial disability of discrimination. This has become especially onerous in the present generation, when the Negro is preponderantly the slum dweller. The problem of slums is not at present solely a problem of race, but the fact that the Negro disproportionately inhabits the slums aggravates the problem. Discrimination against Negroes in employment and housing has been especially severe. In housing it takes the form of segregation.[19] Large areas of the city are effectively closed to Negro occupants, even when they are able and willing to pay the stipulated rents or acquisition costs.

As a result of all this, there is, especially under tight housing conditions, a strong uninformed, highly inelastic[20] demand for low-quality housing in concentrated areas. Expansion of the quantity supplied most profitably comes from conversion to overcrowding. Moreover, the owners, instead of making up the higher cost of accelerated depreciation by increasing rents, make it up in a less noticeable way by neglecting to maintain the property up to legally required standards. Thus, conversion to slum use often increases revenues without increasing costs and may even actually decrease costs. It is not at all unusual for property to be run down profitably to a state where the cost of bringing the structure up to the legally required minimum level exceeds the value of the property. The property in this sense has *negative* social value.[21]

Slum profitability stemming from these demand characteristics is a dynamic phenomenon. It does not represent a permanent source of surplus. The supply of housing is quite competitive, and the relative shortages that especially favor slum creation tend gradually to be made up. But the high durability of structures, the substantial lead time required for new construction, and discrimination combine to keep the relevant housing stock limited for significant periods of time, although conversions of existing stock down to slum use do partly offset this. A gradually decreasing profitability of slum ownership as the supply increases relative to demand tends to diminish further downward conversions. Besides, longer-run trends in population and construction can moderate slum creation over time.

But such moderation is not equivalent to reversal. It is easier to create dwellings suitable to slum occupancy than to "uncreate" them. One reason is an asymmetry in the functioning of neighborhood effects. The existence of spots of low-quality occupancy in an otherwise higher-quality neighborhood is more likely to depress occupancy levels downward than is the existence of high-quality occupancy spots in an otherwise low-quality area to raise levels. This is because the minority spots are a nuisance calling for majority adjustment in the former situation but not in the latter. Thus, any incentive on the part of property owners to enhance the competitive attractiveness of their slum units when the market loosens tends to take the form of price cuts rather than extensive physical upgrading or outright replacement. Moreover, the attempt to offset these neighborhood effects by elaborate private redevelopment and large-scale simultaneous replacement tends to be discouraged by the very heavy transaction and bargaining costs of large-scale land assembly. Thus, overcrowding often takes place in periods of tight housing, especially when substantial in-migration of minority groups is taking place. Subsequently, in periods when housing is much looser, higher-quality housing options come from other areas (predominantly through filtering), and the slum area experiences not an upgrading but simply a higher vacancy rate and lower rental levels. Slum occupancy decreases, but slum property remains (except where vacancy becomes so great as to warrant abandonment). In sum, while slum-creating forces are sporadic, their effects are asymmetric: once formed, slum structures tend to persist. Indeed, there are additional forces, to be mentioned, that help induce slum owners to keep their property in existence longer than the age and condition of the property would ordinarily warrant.

This dynamic impetus to slum creation may be likened to the profitability from fraud and adulteration in ordinary markets, since both depend to some extent on consumer ignorance and other disabilities. In the latter kind of situation the market response is not considered to be the product of "normally approved" market forces. The consumer is considered to be "unfairly" disadvantaged, and government action is typically called upon to offset the disadvantage. To the extent that such protection is not yet forthcoming, the market outcome is "socially inadvertent." And slum creation too has this element of "social inadvertency."

The Social Costs of Slums

It was indicated above that the existence of slums and hence their eradication could well have far-reaching effects on living patterns in the city. For many years the existence of slums has been alleged to generate important social evils:[22] physical, psychological, and health hazards to inhabitants and passers-by, and heavy resource costs to inhabitants of the rest of the city. These ills are believed to be due not only to the low quality of each dwelling in the slum, but perhaps more to the heavy clustering of a relatively homogeneous poor population in poor housing. The concentration generates serious enough external diseconomies to produce the alleged ills. The diagnosis in much of this literature is as follows:

1. Slum dwellings are likely to be fire traps, significantly increasing the likelihood and extent of fire damage.

2. Given overcrowding, filth, and inadequate sanitary facilities, slum areas are likely to be a health menace, increasing the frequency and severity of illness for both inhabitants and outsiders (through contagion). Insofar as slum dwellers receive subsidized medical care, moreover, some of these costs are borne by the general taxpayer. Additional costs are borne at large through the effect of illness on the overall productivity of the economic system.

3. Slums breed crime. Admittedly, crime stems partly from poverty. But slum living itself adds to the incidence of crime. Overcrowding and lack of privacy—especially in the context of general economic deprivation—tend to generate lack of respect for the individual and frustration over the constant obtrusion of others. Human teeming aggravates many kinds of externalities. This is amplified because the individual is surrounded by a pattern of life and values in the slums that contrasts greatly with the dominant values of the broader culture. Opportunities for crime and recruitment into criminal subcultures are aided by the closeness and swarming of life.

4. Slums generate personality difficulties. For example, beyond poverty, slums can create subcultures of despair, or bitterness, or violence, because the degree of overcrowding makes it possible

to obtain a critical mass for many such movements. Many of these groupings of mutual dependency result in vicious circles: the surrounding examples provoke and support a collapse of socially functional aspiration levels; the outside culture with its achievement orientation is too far away. Recent social science emphasizes the effect of the environment of culture on the socialization of the individual. Inevitably the ethos of the slum becomes a significant part of personality development and hinders many in their attempts in later life to join the dominant culture of the society.

These are examples of the costs alleged to stem from slums, though their existence is by no means generally agreed upon.

For the present, it must be emphasized that these claims are not contravened by evidence that the housing is actually chosen by its residents or that the behavior giving rise to the alleged "social costs" is deliberately engaged in. For example, the causative patterns that are said to be operating are often extremely subtle and difficult for direct participants to observe. For another, many of the processes involve significant external effects. Each individual may or may not be disadvantaged by his own action; but it imposes disturbances on others considerably greater than any disturbance to himself. This general type of relationship can be seen in the following example. An additional motorist entering a congested highway adds to the total congestion. He thus inconveniences himself slightly by his own action. But the sum of the discomfort he adds to all others is a large multiple of this. Similarly, most of the discomfort he feels is the result of the action of others. So it is also in slum living.

A final pattern involved here is that the individual is caught in a dynamic circle of interaction with others—a vicious circle. At each step he takes what seems to be the best possible action for him, given admittedly poor circumstances. The similar choices of each under the same circumstances in fact worsen the circumstances and thus call for further action on the part of each. This carries the progressive deterioration of the living environment further and further. Each is trapped into a marginal response that assumes the environment to be beyond his own power to change. No one can break the pattern as a whole. Thus, the overall pattern is unwanted by all or most, yet the marginal response which unalterably contributes to this pattern is deliberately chosen. The situation is suboptimal.

Summary

To a degree, slums provide a type of commodity that is desired by poor households—low-quality, low-quantity housing. As a first approximation, slums represent an economically efficient way to produce this commodity. Elimination of slums by large-scale demolition would interfere with this warranted response of the market. It would generate not benefits, but costs on balance, even if none of the costs of elimination are considered.

Slum elimination can be considered to produce gross benefits only if slums represent an inefficient market response. It has been argued here that substantial externalities and "artificial," socially questionable incentives in the housing market tend to bring about the particular type of land use known as a slum in contradistinction to simply low-cost housing. Therefore, the slum may not be an efficient market response after all. Moreover, the existence of a slum, however brought about, may engender important social costs to society at large. For these reasons the elimination of slums could well produce gross benefits. The desirability of eliminating them is measured, of course, by comparing these benefits with the real costs of bringing them about. The redevelopment type of project under the urban renewal program is one way of eliminating slums. One of the fruits of this long analysis, however, has been to cast light on the reasons why slum elimination might bring benefits, and therefore on the sources of suboptimality in slum land use. The advantage of this procedure is that it helps to specify an alternative, or set of alternatives, to redevelopment for eliminating the sources of inefficiency in slums. Such alternative policies would either prevent slums from forming, or help them to be transformed, or aid in mitigating whatever social ills they generate. Thus, rehabilitation, spot clearance, code enforcement, credit and tax policies, and income supplements to the poor, may also contribute in producing benefits of this sort.

Notes

[1]Sections 2 and 3. Cited in Jay Rumney, "The Social Costs of Slums," *Journal of Social Issues*, Vol. VII, Nos. 1–2, 1951, p. 69.

[2]U.S. Bureau of the Census, *The 1950 Enumerator's Manual.* Cited in Rumney, *op. cit.*, pp. 75–76.

[3]*Ibid.*

[4]*Ibid.*, p. 75.

[5]Scott Greer, *Urban Renewal and American Cities: the Dilemma of Democratic Intervention* (Bobbs-Merrill, 1965).

[6]The discussion at this point is confined to residential renewal. Some of the analysis will be relevant to nonresidential blight as well.
[7]Later analysis in this book suggests that this is not the whole story. (See pp. 39 ff.)
[8]Housing in tolerably good condition is likely to be directly replaced only if dramatic changes in land use are involved—for example, if a few single family dwellings are to be replaced by a large high-rise structure.
[9]This discussion depends heavily on William G. Grigsby, *Housing Markets and Public Policy* (University of Pennsylvania Press, 1963), Chaps. 2–3. The concept of "filtering" is controversial. For an extensive analysis, see *ibid.*
[10]It should be noted, however, that the wealthiest families are probably more fixed in domicile than any other group, including the poorest. The probability is a function of upward social mobility and dissatisfaction, as well as of wealth and insecurity; so there is a mixture of motives operating on any income class.
[11]This contention is widespread and has been current for some time. Two recent works make this the cornerstone of a theory of urban renewal: Otto A. Davis, "A Pure Theory of Urban Renewal," *Land Economics* (May 1960), pp. 220–26; Otto A. Davis and Andrew B. Whinston, "The Economics of Urban Renewal," *Law and Contemporary Problems,* Vol. 26 (Winter 1961), pp. 105–17.
[12]*Op. cit.*, pp. 106–12.
[13]*Op. cit.*, pp. 111–12.
[14]However, it will be argued that such upward conversion, while by assumption a more expensive use of the land than is warranted, may well mean significant external economies to the rest of the community—that is, heterogeneity introduced through selective upward conversion can result in community benefits that heterogeneity through selective downward conversion may not.
[15]See, for example, Charles S. Rhyne, "The Workable Program—A Challenge for Community Improvement," *Law and Contemporary Problems*, Vol. 25 (Autumn 1960), pp. 685–704.
[16]Jane Jacobs, *The Death and Life of Great American Cities* (Random House, 1961), Chap. 16.
[17]*Ibid.*
[18]Of course, what may be tolerable housing, from the point of view of both individual and group, in rural areas may be intolerable in a city, because it creates externalities. The individual does not see its effects on third parties who have no power to affect the terms of the transaction. This will be discussed at considerable length.
[19]Interestingly, there has been more housing segregation in northern than in southern cities. This does not imply that there has been more prejudice in the North. In the North, segregation by housing has been the only way that social, political, and educational segregation could be maintained. In the South, segregation was long maintained by custom and by law.
[20]Inelastic because of a paucity of known, feasible alternatives.
[21]Irving Dagen and Edward C. Cody, "Property, *et al.* v. Nuisance, *et al.,*" *Law and Contemporary Problems*, Vol, 26 (Winter 1961), pp. 70–84. Compare this with other treatments of the profitability of slums: Chester Rapkin, *The Real Estate Market in an Urban Renewal Area* (New York City Planning Commission, 1959), p. 120; Metropolitan Housing and Planning Council of Chicago, *The Road Back—The Slums* (Chicago,

1954); August Nakagawa, "Profitability of Slums," *Synthesis* (April 1957), p. 45.

[22]A partial bibliography will be found at the end of this chapter. As a counter to some of this literature, see John Seeley, "The Slum: Its Nature, Use and Users," *Journal of American Institute of Planners* (1959).

2
The Components of Housing Costs

Introduction

The urgent need to break through housing production and cost barriers has been recognized at the highest levels of American government. Reaffirming the Kerner Commission's call for an "unprecedented national effort to produce six million low and moderate income units by 1973," President Johnson called upon the private sector to "bring to home-building its skill and resources and the methods of modern technology so that houses can be built faster, less expensively and more efficiently than ever before." With increasing emphasis being placed on the private sector to contribute to a national housing solution, an emphasis that is continuing under the Nixon administration, the American home building industry is facing the greatest challenge in its history. Its capacity to meet this challenge is doubted by many, and the belief is more widespread than ever that the industry has steadfastly refused to take advantage of technologic advances that could revolutionize production processes and drastically reduce the cost of housing.

The primary purpose of this section is to explore the housing production process and the components of housing cost, both economic and institutional. While neither of the papers included in the section deals directly with the economics of low-income housing production, the interrelationship of the deficit of low-income housing and high housing costs ought to be clear. On the one hand, any significant reduction in the cost of new construction, when coupled with a substantial increase in annual output, would ultimately reduce housing costs throughout the full range of quality in the privately held stock. Similarly, with respect to housing subsidies, a given level of expenditure will support more housing units if construction costs are lower, or at least permit higher quality levels to be achieved within present cost schedules.

My own view, however, of relying upon substantial reductions in the costs of construction as a solution to the nation's housing dilemma is somewhat less sanguine than that implied by many housing analysts. I suggest that by placing this problem within the framework of a macroeconomic model formulated for other purposes by Baumol, we can indicate why we ought not count too heavily upon a greater reliance on off-site fabrication to reduce substantially the costs of new construction.[1]

A Macroeconomic Theory of Unbalanced Growth

The economic theory underlying Baumol's model is based on the proposition that one can dichotomize all economic activities: "technologically progressive activities in which innovation, capital accumula tion and economies of large scale all make for a cumulative rise in output per man hour and activities which, by their very nature, permit only sporadic increases in productivity."[2] According to the theory, industries do not fall into one or the other sector merely by chance; rather, the basis of the dichotomy lies in the technological structure of the industries themselves. Cumulative rises in output per man hour are possible in those industries in which "labor is primarily an incidental requisite for the attainment of the final product, whereas, in those industries in which labor is, at least in part, an end product in itself, productivity will remain relatively constant."[3] An example of the former might be the manufacture of television sets, while a classic prototype of the latter would be any one of the performing arts.

A second proposition, that "wages in the two sectors go up and down together," serves as a linkage between productivity and costs throughout the entire spectrum of economic activity.[4] In other words, the long-run spatial and interindustry mobility of the labor force ensures a correspondence in the direction of wages within progressive and nonprogressive industries.

If these two propositions are quantified, it can be demonstrated that "if productivity per man hour rises cumulatively in one sector relative to its rate of growth elsewhere in the economy, while wages rise commensurately in all areas, then relative costs in the nonprogressive sectors must inevitably rise, *and these costs will rise cumulatively and without limit*" [emphasis Baumol's].[5]

Application to the Construction Industry

Having briefly summarized the essential elements of Baumol's economic theory, and having indicated that the sector of the economy into which any particular activity falls is not a matter of chance, we must ask, to which of the two sectors does the production of residential shelter belong? Most critics of the construction industry would argue that the housebuilding industry was "out-to-lunch" during the industrial revolution and that if any economic activity rightfully belongs in the nonprogressive sector, *it* surely does. The most serious problem with such an assertion is the policy implication that one might draw from it; namely, that if we could encourage greater use of mass production techniques, we could substantially lower the costs of new construction.

Such a proposition is fine as far as it goes. Unfortunately, however, the housebuilding industry is probably not as archaic and anachronistic as many would like to believe. The unique and complex nature of the housing commodity is such that by increasing the productivity of the on-site labor involved in building homes in the more traditional manner, or by replacing on-site labor with more productive, off-site labor, the costs of new construction would not be appreciably lowered. Nor, for that matter, could anything less than a complete and totally unanticipated breakthrough in the development and use of new building materials meaningfully reduce the cost of housing.

It would be unwise to expect to lower housing cost through the industrialization of the housebuilding process, which is taken here to mean a reduction in the proportion of on-site labor costs to total building costs, because the existing construction industry is currently far more industrialized than one might think. It has been estimated by the Department of Labor, for example, that only about one-third of all labor costs that go into the construction of a house can be attributed to on-site labor.[6] Thus, if we were to reduce the unit cost of on-site labor by as much as 25 percent, a feat that would be phenomenal, we would only be reducing the total cost of labor by 8 percent and the total cost of new construction by proportionately less, since labor is but a single component of building cost.

Table 1 shows the distribution of the builders' construction

Table 1. Percent Distribution of On-Site Wages, Materials, and Other Costs, Including Improved Land, for Single-Family Dwelling, 1968

Expenditure Class	Percent of Builder-Cost
On-Site Wages	19
Materials and Equipment	36
Profit, Overhead	14
Improved Land	25
Miscellaneous	6
Total	100

Source: Report of the President's Committee on Urban Housing, *A Decent Home* (Washington, U.S.G.P.O., 1969), p. 118.

cost dollar among such expenditure classes as on-site labor, materials, profits, and so forth. If, as the table indicates, on-site wages account for only about 19 percent of the total cost of a new single-family dwelling, then by reducing that component of construction cost by one-half, the cost of the finished house could be lowered by only about 9 percent.

Thus, the dilemma confronting the construction industry can be summarized in Table 2. Here, we see the index of wholesale prices of building materials and an index of union hourly wage rates for the period 1950–1967. Even though it indicates that wages approximately doubled during the period, while the wholesale cost of materials increased by only 27 percent, the fact that on-site labor contributes less than one-fifth to the final building cost of a house sets an upper limit on the extent to which an exchange of off-site for on-site labor can contribute to the production of less expensive dwellings.

Construction Cost and New Building Materials

If a shift to a more industrialized housebuilding process that makes use of the same basic materials currently used in residential construction will not significantly reduce the cost of

Table 2. General Indicators of Construction Costs and On-Site Wages 1950–1967 (1950 = 100)

Year	Index of Wholesale Prices of Materials Used in Construction	Index of Union Hourly Wage Rates: All Construction Trades
1950	100	100
1952	108	113
1954	110	124
1956	119	134
1958	119	147
1960	122	154
1962	118	174
1964	120	185
1966	125	201
1967	127	213

All figures as of July 1.
Source: Report of the President's Committee on Urban Housing, Technical Studies, Vol. II (Washington, U.S.G.P.O., 1969), p. 45.

housing, what about possible breakthroughs in the development and application of new building materials as a path to cost reduction? Here, too, we face major difficulties. This time the problem derives from the rich array of materials and components that go into the typical dwelling unit, no single element of which accounts for a truly significant component of building costs. As indicated in Table 3, the average single-family house constructed in 1962 consumed $482.20 in materials for every $1,000 of building cost, exclusive of land. Of the eleven materials categories included in the table, lumber and lumber products ranked the highest, accounting for approximately 40 percent of the total cost of materials.

Assuming that a synthetic material should become available as an alternative to lumber, possessing all of its desirable attributes but costing only one-third as much, how great a reduction in the cost of housing might we expect? Such a materials breakthrough would reduce the cost of materials from $482.20 per $1,000 of building to $317.10, or by 27 percent. But, since *all* building materials account for only 36 percent of the cost of a house and lot, a 27 percent reduction in materials costs only results in a 10 percent reduction in the total cost of housing. By developing costless substitutes

Table 3. Cost of Selected Material Components for Each $1,000 of Construction Price of Surveyed Private One-Family Houses for the Nation, 1962

Selected Products and Product Groups	Cost
All Products	$482.20
Lumber and Lumber Products	193.10
Stone, Clay, and Glass Products	115.30
Metal Products (except plumbing and heating)	52.80
Plumbing Products	26.80
Heating and Ventilating Equipment	19.60
Electrical Equipment Fixtures and Wire	16.50
Fixed House Equipment (ovens, ranges, etc.)	13.70
Petroleum Products (asphalt shingles, etc.)	11.10
Paints and Other Chemicals	10.30
Construction Equipment (depreciation)	9.80
All Other Categories	13.30

Source: *Housing Facts and Trends*, House and Home, McGraw-Hill/Dodge, New York, 1965: p. 77.

for asphalt shingles, paint, ovens, ranges, and refrigerators in addition to the wood substitute, housing costs would be lowered by no more than a total of 15 percent.

In short, a dwelling unit is unlike a television set or other such commodity that might benefit from a single scientific advance, such as the development of the transistor, or from an individual production breakthrough. Too, many diverse elements and components go into the residential package, each accounting for only a small portion of total cost.

Another dimension of the "cost of housing" issue that is worth noting concerns the relationship between construction costs and housing quality. To what extent do rising costs reflect inflationary trends in the construction industry and higher real costs, and to what extent are they reflective of higher quality? While not a great deal has been written on this aspect of the problem, the Kaiser Committee did note in its final report that "a comparison of the Census Price Index and Boeckh Index with the Average Sales Prices suggests that much of the increase in the average price of single-family homes between 1963 and 1967 was due to quality increases."[7]

In the judgment of the Kaiser Committee, reductions in construction costs can be brought about by improved management techniques in the industry itself as well as through increasing reliance on off-site fabrication. Such efforts, however, can reasonably be expected to bring about no more than a 10 percent reduction in building cost, which can, of course, be completely wiped out by continued increases in land costs, which have doubled since 1956, or further increases in the cost of money, which is currently at a historical peak. While the development of entirely new building systems utilizing new materials, tools, equipment, and labor skills might yield substantial cost savings, it is concluded in a supporting study undertaken for the Kaiser Committee that "the likelihood of finding an all new system . . . is not very good."[8]

Looking at the two study commissions, one would have to conclude that the Kaiser Committee, on the whole, is more satisfied with the technologic advances of the post-World War II construction industry than is the Douglas Commission. At one point, the final report of the former suggests that "While the construction industry still lags somewhat behind manufacturing . . . , it had an annual growth rate of 2.3% in output per employee from 1947–65 . . . (and) there is evidence too that the construction industry has been more responsive to post-war changes in prices of inputs than has the manufacturing sector."

Despite such analyses, the political strength of the systems building advocates seems to be increasing at an increasing rate. For this reason I have selected for this section of the book an article by Burns and Mittelbach that attempts to ". . . assess the productive and distributive efficiency of the housing industry; the effects of certain factors which may adversely affect efficiency and the pace of innovation; and finally, the effect of such factors on the cost of housing." Their analysis, broader than my own, distinguishes between those housing costs that represent "resource waste" and those that "generate external economies to the benefit of the larger society . . . or create internal economies for the benefit of the housing consumer." The latter costs are resource redistributing inasmuch as some higher initial investments in better quality housing may minimize recurrent maintenance costs over time, while resource-wasting costs "increase prices without affecting quality or increasing consumer utility." It is this latter category of housing costs that, according to the authors, must be brought under control if we are to "produce more housing at lower cost without sacrifice of quality." In essence, they suggest that the problems are even greater than my earlier analysis indicated because some possible means of reducing construction costs merely represent tradeoffs between reduced capital costs and increased, recurrent, maintenance costs.

"Operation Breakthrough," Interest and Taxes

In recent months the ardent supporters of the building systems strategy have consolidated their strength behind the Nixon Administration's efforts to improve the entire process of producing and delivering houses. Dubbed "Operation Breakthrough," the Administration's program is designed to "utilize modern techniques of production, marketing and management to provide housing for all income levels through a partnership of labor, consumers, private enterprise and local, State and Federal Governments."[9] Essentially, it is predicated on the notion that if large-scale builders are guaranteed markets for their mass-produced products, they can more fully utilize existing technologic capabilities and realize substantial economies of scale. "Breakthrough" is therefore aimed at aggregating local markets through Federal acquisition of sites, supporting the development of innovative building systems through direct subsidies to giant corporations and consortia, and guaranteeing markets through federal subsidies to consumers or through sale of completed units to public bodies such as local housing authorities.

There are three reasons why the program seems to have generated so much enthusiasm in spite of the odds against the production of substantially cheaper housing: Breakthrough is consistent with the American ethic that says the assembly line can do anything; it provides an opportunity for defense- and space-oriented industries to capture a larger share of the nation's housing budget at a time when defense and space budgets are being bitterly contested and possibly reduced; and finally, the program is designed to encourage the production of better and less expensive housing for all income groups and not just for those families unable to afford decent housing.[10] As a program aimed at helping "middle America," its political appeal is substantially greater than it would be if it were billed as a new attack on the nation's low-income housing problem.

It is even possible that if Breakthrough were to succeed in producing better quality housing at somewhat lower costs, the poor would be unlikely beneficiaries because the ultimate savings, when translated into reductions in monthly rents and carrying costs, would be negligible. This would be the case because about 40 percent of average monthly housing costs are consumed by mortgage interest and local real property tax payments, neither of which is directly related to the technologic aspects of the costs of construction. While Maisel and Guttentag indicated in the previous chapter that short-run increases in the cost of money have no long-run effects on the demand for new housing, this does not mean that the costs of money and local property taxes are not factors that prevent many low- and moderate-income families from entering the new construction market and the ownership market, in general. After all, if, say 6 percent mortgages are sufficiently costly to keep a group of housing consumers out of the market for new construction, then surely a short-run increase of interest rates to 9 percent will have no further impact on that same group of consumers.

While the importance of financing will be discussed further in an article on low-income ownership in Part 3, and the impacts of inflation on the development of a low-income housing strategy will be dealt with in Part 4, it might be appropriate to devote the final paragraphs of this essay to the real estate tax and low-income housing.

It is generally estimated that real estate taxes add as much as 25 percent to monthly housing expenses. Another way of assessing its relative magnitude is to view it as a sales or excise tax on housing. At a 3 percent effective tax rate, the present value of the annual tax payments due over the life of a typical dwelling, discounted at 6 percent, is in excess of 50 percent of the initial value of the house. Moreover, not only is the tax extremely regressive, consuming about 8.5 percent of the incomes of families below \$2,000, while taking only 1.4 percent of the incomes of those with earnings exceeding \$15,000,[11] but according to prevailing incidence theory, ". . . owners of rental property confronting an inelastic demand . . . will raise rents . . .; other landlords will suffer reduced net earnings; and over time, the deterrent to new investment will shrink the supply of rental housing and raise its price."[12]

With the conventional wisdom supporting the view that the property tax on land and improvements has a long-run detrimental impact on investment in new construction and on property maintenance, there is, once again, growing interest in and support for converting the tax to one on site value only. Because of the renewed popularity of the land tax which, according to the Douglas Commission, would not only "stem the upward spiral of urban land costs but might be expected to (1) make feasible some housing and other construction that would not be economic, and (2) reduce present incentives for speculative holding of urban and urban-fringe land in vacant or underutilized form,"[13] I have included in this section of the book an article on planning and the land-value tax.

Gaffney's paper begins with the recognition that the value of privately owned land in the United States approximately doubled between 1956 and 1966, from 269 billion to 523 billion in current dollars,[14] and that a tax on land values is one means by which a government can recapture a portion of the socially induced increments in land value, while having a beneficial effect on the spatial pattern of urban development in the community. While his paper is aimed at describing how the new system might operate, he does not discuss the distributive effects of a land tax, the impacts of the tax with respect to the incomes of property owners, nor the potential effects of the tax on the quality of low-income housing.

Assuming a site-value tax was introduced that was pegged to yield the same revenue as the old tax on land and improvements, a redistribution of tax burdens would occur among land uses and property owners. In fact, any property for which the ratio of improvement value to site value exceeded that for the community as a whole would pay less under the new system.[15] Conversely, "the tax on any property with an improvement-value-to-site-value ratio less than the average for the entire city would pay more under the new scheme than under the old."[16] Table 4 presents a hypothetical example of the tax burdens associated with five properties with widely varying improvement-to-site-value ratios under the existing and land-value tax systems. In this example, site values are assumed to be equal; the ad valorem tax on site and improvements is assumed to be $25 per $1,000 of land and improvements; the site-value tax is $100 per $1,000 of assessed valuation of site only, a rate that would produce from the properties in question total tax revenues identical with those yielded by the existing tax system.[17]

As illustrated in the Table, the last two properties, each with improvement-value-to-site-value ratios below the city-wide average, incur higher liabilities under a land tax, whereas the initial three properties, whose improvement-to-site-value ratios are above average, pay lower taxes under the new scheme. Thus, at first glance one desirable "housing" effect of a site-value tax might be a shifting of the tax burden away from residential land uses that typically exhibit high improvement-to-site-value ratios. Similarly, a spatial redistribution of the tax burden might also occur as more outlying land would be taxed less than the more expensive land in and near the core of the city.

Such seemingly desirable effects of the land tax might be shortlived, however, as we inquire into the impacts of a land tax with respect to income. If one is willing to accept the assumption that there is a close correlation between property value and income of the owner, it can be demonstrated that a land-value tax would be much more regressive than the existing, regressive tax on land and improvements. This would be so if the ratio of improvement value to site value were lower for lower value properties. This might be frequently the case since lower value residential properties in which the poor live are typically close to the core on valuable land. Thus, whereas under the existing tax system the effective rate does not vary with the value of the property, under a land tax the two vary inversely. Going back to Table 4, the effective tax rates for each of the properties under the old system was 2.5 percent. Under the new system, the effective rate is 1.7 percent for the first property and 5.0 percent for the fifth property. In short, low-income, owner-residents near the core might expect to have their taxes substantially increased under a land tax; also, renters might find one of several other possible outcomes: first, the buildings they are living in might not be able to absorb higher taxes, in which case a change in land use might occur, with a consequent decline in the quantity of low-income housing available. Second, since the tax could not be passed on to the low-income tenant, it would be capitalized into lower property values, which would contribute further to a reduction in maintenance outlays and housing quality. This latter possibility is of particular importance because,

Table 4

Properties	I	II	III	IV	V	Total
Assessed Value:						
Improvements	$15,000	$12,000	$ 9,000	$6,000	$3,000	$45,000
Site	3,000	3,000	3,000	3,000	3,000	15,000
	$18,000	$15,000	$12,000	$9,000	$6,000	$60,000
Improvement-Value-to-Site-Value Ratio	5:1	4:1	3:1	2:1	1:1	3:1
Old Tax	$450	$375	$300	$225	$150	$1,500
New Tax	$300	$300	$300	$300	$300	$1,500

Source: "Real Property Taxation and Urban Development: A Research Proposal," prepared for the Office of Development Coordinator, City of Philadelphia, by Morton S. Baratz, Bryn Mawr College, 1962, p. 7.

as will be discussed in the final chapter, existing marginal quality, rental housing already bears a disproportionately high burden under the existing tax system. Neither of these possibilities is desirable from a low-income housing standpoint, in spite of the so-called benefits of a land-value tax.

Notes

[1]William J. Baumol, "Macroeconomics of Unbalanced Growth," *The American Economic Review* (Vol. LVII, No. 3, June 1967), pp. 415–426.
[2]*Ibid.*, pp. 415–416.
[3]*Ibid.*, p. 416.
[4]*Ibid.*, p. 417.
[5]*Ibid.*, p. 419.
[6]*The State of the Art of Prefabrication in the Construction Industry,* Batelle Memorial Institute (Columbus, 1967), p. 8.
[7]*A Decent Home*, Report of the President's Committee on Urban Housing (Washington: Government Printing Office, 1968), p. 120.
[8]Ralph J. Johnson, "Housing Technology and Housing Costs," *Technical Studies, Volume II, The Report of the President's Committee on Urban Housing* (Washington: Government Printing Office, 1968), p. 59.
[9]HUD News, June 11, 1969, p. 1.
[10]See, *House and Home* (Vol. 37, No. 2, February 1970), pp. 51–69.
[11]For a more detailed discussion of the impacts of the tax, see *Impact of the Property Tax: Its Economic Implications for Urban Problems*, by Dick Netzer, supplied by the National Commission on Urban Problems to the Joint Economic Committee, Congress of the United States (Washington: Government Printing Office, 1968), p. 19.
[12]*Building the American City*, Report of the National Commission on Urban Problems to the Congress and to the President of the United States (Washington: Government Printing Office, 1969), p. 390.
[13]*Ibid.*, p. 390.
[14]*Ibid.*, p. 384.
[15]"Real-Property Taxation and Urban Development: A Research Proposal," prepared for the Office of Development Coordinator, City of Philadelphia, by Morton S. Baratz, Bryn Mawr College, 1962, p. 7. See also *Property Taxation and Urban Development*, Mary Rawson, Urban Land Institute, Research Monograph 4 (Washington, 1961).
[16]"Real Property Taxation and Urban Development," *op. cit.*, p. 7.
[17]*Ibid.*

2.1
Efficiency in the Housing Industry

Leland S. Burns
and Frank G. Mittelbach

Introduction

Probably more attention has been focused on the cost of housing than on the cost of any other durable or nondurable good. Two related reasons—the magnitude of housing expenditures in consumer budgets and the universal complaint that housing cost too much—at least partially account for this concern. Ignoring the deeper issue of how-much-is-too-much, the alleged expensiveness of housing has inhibited solutions to the world's shelter problems. Even in affluent societies, the relatively high cost of house construction may be responsible for urban blight, slums, and the syndrome of evils attributed to over-crowding and dilapidation.

Not only has housing always been expensive, but historically the cost of the product has risen more rapidly than the prices of most other consumer goods. The popular literature is filled with charges that the construction industry is inefficient and that it consciously inhibits cost-saving innovations. In fact, housing price increases are often alleged to have outstripped those of nearly all other major items of the family budget. (102, 183)* Of further concern is the assertion, which also finds general support in the literature, that output per worker in the construction industry has lagged behind price increases. The causes of the price increases are not fully understood. The assumed inefficiency of the industry may well be exaggerated; for, given the constraints within which the industry operates, construction may be as efficient as possible. If it is true of the *residential* construction industry as well, then today's homebuyer is getting less for his housing dollar than yesterday's homebuyer. As Charles Abrams notes, "Of all the commodities that have been touched by the industrial revolutions, the house has remained the most impervious to change." (125)

The construction and operating costs of housing have varied not only over time but over area as well. Cost and price indexes

Reprinted from "Efficiency in the Housing Industry," by Leland S. Burns and Frank G. Mittelbach, prepared for the President's Committee on Urban Housing, *The Report of the President's Committee on Urban Housing, Technical Studies, Vol. II, Housing Costs, Production Efficiency, Finance, Manpower, Land* (Washington, Government Printing Office, 1969), pp. 79–112.

*Throughout this paper, sources of information are indicated by numbers in parentheses referring to items listed in the bibliography.

indicate that equivalent shelter sells at different prices in different cities. The same generalization holds for operating costs, as revealed in the intermittent Surveys of Consumer Expenditures.

But what can be done to reduce the cost of housing? Since part of the temporal cost increases and regional cost differentials may result from forces external to the housing industry, steps to reduce costs or equalize them among areas may have to be initiated outside the industry. Some of these efforts are within the realm of public policy. For example, the terms of mortgage credit, which burden household budgets, respond to monetary policy. However, those external forces which are primarily public may be susceptible to policy only at certain levels of government. For example, promulgation and administration of uniform building codes require local initiative, since such codes (like zoning) are powers generally exercised by municipal government.

The purpose of this paper is to assess the productive and distributive efficiency of the housing industry; the effects of certain factors which may adversely affect efficiency and the pace of innovation; and finally, the effect of such factors on the cost of housing. To accomplish this purpose, we have attempted to analyze and synthesize recent contributions to this area of knowledge. Fortunately, there are several studies of the housing industry which, though somewhat dated, serve as a solid base from which to proceed. (41, 23, 52, 74, 24, 61) Thus, the primary purpose is summarization and evaluation of the present "state of the arts," rather than original research. Because of this constricted definition of purpose, it has been far easier to pose questions than to furnish answers.

Moreover, many of the answers are uncertain and, possibly in a few cases, of questionable value. By revealing gaps, this effort should be instructive in guiding further research. But where the evidence is clear, new policy can be articulated and existing policy modified or clarified. We have, however, consciously avoided the temptation to make value judgments or to suggest policy.

The paper is ordered in four principal sections. This introduction sets the stage; first, by considering historically the operating performance of the housebuilding industry and the construction industry of which it is a part; and second, by defining terms and considering housing as an operating subsystem within other systems. The following section identifies factors which affect the price of housing and, possibly, its value as well. Of central concern are those factors either lodged in the public domain or otherwise endogenous to public policy. The third section deals with cost factors by function. The concluding section considers the magnitude of costs ("how much?") and the incidence of costs ("who pays?") and summarizes the whole.

Productivity in Housebuilding

Many of the arguments shaping public opinion state unequivocally that the housebuilding industry is backward and inefficient. Evidence to the contrary is often buried in technical reports which do not receive the same attention.

A short review of industrial performance prefaces this exploration of efficiency in the housebuilding industry. In the process, some priorities and interdependencies are suggested. To illustrate, local programs directed at removing obstacles aimed at cost-reduction through increased industrial efficiency may fail to achieve their ends if simultaneously, through federal programs of massive financial assistance to builders and consumers, the demand for land, labor, and materials is raised. Thus, constraints on homebuilding at the subnational level must be considered within a multilevel context.

The notion that little is being done to improve the efficiency of construction, particularly of homebuilding, is so generally accepted that we must address the subject briefly. Those who allege inefficiency support their argument by referring to two major empirical contentions: (1) the disproportionate increase in the costs of housebuilding as compared to other costs, and (2) the small productivity increases in housebuilding as compared to other industries.

A brief examination of productivity in the construction industry, of which housebuilding constitutes a major part, will establish perspective. In his study of sectoral causes of inflation during the 1947–57 decade, Schultze concludes that construction was the single most inflationary sector of the economy. Prices rose over 5 percent annually, on the average. (102, p. 41)
A study supported by the National Bureau of Economic Research, covering approximately the same period, estimates an average annual change in real product of 5.6 percent, of which 2.5 percent resulted from increases in real product per man hour. (5, p. 284)
One commentator on this research notes further that "construction productivity lagged considerably behind the average for the economy and even behind total services." (142, p. 406)

A study confined to a shorter period of the years 1948–52 reports annual changes in real output per man-hour at about 4 percent. (63) Domar *et al.* estimate the average annual change in productivity at about 2 percent. (145, p. 36) The most recent study, which criticizes some earlier efforts, is more optimistic. In his investigation of productivity and price trends, Dacy challenges the validity of commonly used construction price indexes, which, in his estimation, have "grossly overstated the construction price rise, with the attendant effect that almost every economist who has dealt with construction as a sector has understated productivity." (142, p. 411) According to his calculation, average productivity over the 1947–63 period increased roughly 3 percent annually, and the real output increased nearly 5 percent. (142, p. 408) Residential construction, however, represents only about 40 percent of total construction. Consequently, the inefficiencies noted for total construction may not apply to residential construction. However, it has been alleged that the inefficiencies may indeed result from the residential component in total construction. (185, p. 19)

Synthesizing data from a number of sources, Foote *et al.* claim that rising costs must "be placed at the very center of any explanation of why consumer demand for housing has been less than proportionate to the rise in real income, and why housing appears to be a continuing problem for America and indeed for every industrial country." (35, p. 14) Over the long run, wages in the building trades and costs of building materials have risen much more rapidly than wholesale and consumer prices. Since movements in building costs and home prices are closely correlated, the rising costs have been transformed into higher prices for the consumer. Foote *et al.* speculate that "apparently gains in productivity, which are responsible for keeping the increase in consumer prices well below the increase in factory wage rates, have been nearly totally lacking in housebuilding." (35, p. 16) This is considered to be the result of forces "deeply imbedded in the technology of building," rather than of featherbedding or other restrictive practices. (35, p. 16)

The position is supported by Myerson *et al.*, who estimate increases in productivity of the housebuilding industry at about 1.5 percent, which is below the annual rate of increase for the economy as a whole. (84, pp. 131–132) These conclusions are corroborated by the findings of other observers. According to Kaplan's estimates, output per man-hour in contract construction increased 2.2 percent annually between 1947 and 1956, as compared to 3.6 percent in manufacturing. (60, p. 39) Since Kaplan asserts that productivity in selected nonresidential components of contract construction, such as roadbuilding and engineering construction, have risen at rates well above the rate for the industry, he strongly implies that the increase in productivity in homebuilding is less than it should be. Although lack of complete data prevents pinpointing the precise amount, indirect evidence provided by the close correlation between building cost and changes in house price suggests a low increase in productivity in housebuilding. These pessimistic findings have been challenged in recent years.

In its survey covering the years 1960–1964, the National Association of Home Builders (NAHB) concludes that rising prices for new homes are associated with rising land costs rather than with construction costs. Drawing on information for 23 cities and adjusting for variations in type and size of house, materials used, and different specifications, it was shown that in 1964 it cost "20 cents less per square foot to build the *same house* (our italics) than was the case five years ago." (182) How can one reconcile this estimate with others which have pointed to rapidly rising building costs and home prices? The clue lies in the italicized words. Today's product has changed drastically and is probably superior to that of yesterday: the house is larger and is equipped with many features unknown only a few years ago. The important differences in the size and composition of the product may be ignored in aggregate analyses. If one holds the product constant and considers only modest homes, as is the case in the NAHB survey, the cost changes are far less dramatic and, in fact, may disappear altogether.

On the other hand, several detailed indexes, including those prepared by Boeckh, the *Engineering News Record*, and the U.S. Department of Commerce, have revealed rising costs of material, building, and construction. This brings the cost of house production into sharper focus.

If we examine the mass produced modest sized homes whose basic structural characteristics have remained essentially unchanged, we find that productivity increases of substantial but indeterminate magnitude have characterized the recent history of housebuilding. But this finding fails to consider the changing character of both the market and the product. The cost of producing today's larger and otherwise superior housing probably has risen disproportionately to costs in other sectors of the economy. The use of price indexes for houses placed on the market may seem to be unrealistic, but it must be recognized that products of other industries also have been improved over the years. This fact complicates the problem. The issue is far more than a matter of whether building operations are efficient or not; it involves the difficulty in recent years of marketing new houses at prices which match buyers' incomes. This includes the whole range of participants in the housing market—producers, distributors, consumers, and public agencies—whose decisions affect the operation of the "system."

The Housing Industry as a System

The standing stock of housing may be classified according to a variety of qualifications: type of dwelling unit, tenure status of occupants, value or rent class, quality or condition, location within or among areas, and so on. (47) Since it is a flow as well as a stock, the industry which produces housing for consumption may be viewed as a process subject to its own structure. The process, which includes the production of building sites and the consumption of real property, as well as the production of the stock itself, extends from the time when land ripens for eventual development to the time when the unit finally is removed from the inventory. Throughout this extended period, costs are incurred which, at some point in the process, affect the cost and the price of housing.

The process is diagrammed in some detail in Table 1. Three broad time intervals are relevant. The first major interval, the production phase, extends from the time that potentially developable land is identified, through preparation of the site for construction, and through the construction period, until the housing unit is completed and ready for marketing. The building industry is operative during the preparation and construction stages. The distribution, second phase, repeats throughout the useful lifetime of the structure. The third phase, consumption of the property during occupancy, concludes with the termination of the good's economic or physical life.

During this lengthy period, which may embrace a century or more, a complex of activities is performed by a variety of entrepreneurs. Those involved at some stage in the process include land speculators, subdividers, engineers of many types, architects and designers, mortgage lenders, contractors and

Table 1. The Housing Market: Activities and Institutional Factors Affecting the Production, and Consumption of Housing

Function		Production			Distribution	Consumption and Redistribution
General Activity		Site identification	Site preparation	Construction	Completion and sale of dwelling	Occupancy and resales
Specific Activities		Raw land speculation and turnover	Financing Raw land purchase Subdivision Engineering, grading, excavation Utility and transport system installation	Designing Financing Contracting and subcontracting Purchase of factor inputs	Listing Promotion Negotiation Closing Financing Title searching Deed recording	Listing Promotion Negotiation Closing Financing and refinancing Title searching Deed recording
Possible Institutional Factors	Primarily Public or Quasi-Public (level)	Transfer taxes (local) Recording systems (local) Zoning (local) Subdivision regulations (local, state)	Zoning (local) Subdivision regulations (local, state) Utility standards (state) Usury laws (state)	Utility standards (state) Building codes (local) Building fees (local) Construction licensing (local, state) Transport restrictions (federal) Usury laws (state)	Transfer taxes (local) Recording systems (local) Limits on lending areas (state, federal) Usury laws (state)	Transfer taxes (local) Recording systems (local) Limits on lending areas (state, federal) Property taxes (local) Usury laws (state)
	Primarily Private	Title insurance	Insurance standards	Insurance standards Monopolistic practices among architects and designers mortgage lenders materials suppliers Restrictive work rules	Title insurance Monopolistic practices among realty agents financers lawyers Lender's fees Closing fees	Monopolistic practices among realty agents financers lawyers Title insurance Lender's fees Closing fees
Time (approx.)		indefinite	3 months	6 months	1 month	60 years

subcontractors, real estate agents, lawyers, public servants in broad variety, plus the host of general craftsmen and specialists who will eventually alter or repair the structure.

Equally as important are the many factors affecting price or cost which are often without visible effect on the final product. We label these "institutional factors" and divide them between those lodged primarily in the public domain and those pertaining to the private sector. It is well to note in passing that the distinction is somewhat arbitrary. A public utility, privately owned but regulated in the public interest, is the classic example of quasi-public enterprise. Each of the following factors may also be regarded as a possible inhibitor of innovation.

Production Phase. The production function in the housing system embraces three general activities: identification of the site, preparation of the site for building, and construction of the dwelling unit.

1. Site Identification. This phase covers an indefinite time interval extending to the point in time when raw land is ripe for development. During this period, land is turned over by speculators ambitious to develop "someday" or to resell to potential developers at a profit. If each temporary landholder's ambitions are realized, the price rises with successive transfers.

In addition to increasing speculative profits, each transfer involves a host of institutional factors which raise the cost. Local taxing authorities levy transfer taxes and charge recording fees. More subtle are the effects of zoning regulations. If the amount of land zoned for a given use is short of demand, for example, the price will increase. A fee is commanded for title search and another for title guaranty.

The list of cost items is recursive rather than one-shot. Moreover, they are additive if sellers succeed in passing them along to buyers. If so, they are reflected in the transaction price. In the extreme case—where the sellers' power dominates throughout the chain of transfers—all costs incurred during the site identification phase are included in the price paid by the developer.

2. Site Preparation. Site development involves a large number of individuals such as lenders, subdividers, and engineers, as well as the private and public officials charged with the responsibility for establishing and enforcing zoning laws, standards governing the capacity and installation of utility and transport systems, and standards for insurance underwriting. The subdivider's ability to shift these costs depends on the character of the market in which he operates and on his bargaining power in that market, as we shall see.

3. Construction. The housebuilding industry embraces those firms whose operations are primarily concerned with the construction of shelter space. Defined in this way, the group of firms comprises a subindustry within the housing industry. However, it is well to recognize, as others have (24), that members of this sizable industry, or more precisely *sub*-industry, are highly diverse and may defy any general description. Consequently, the incidence of costs (and frequently their size) varies with the character of the economic units embraced by the industry and its many components.

A more detailed description of the complex construction industry will be given later in this report. Broadly enumerated, however, the functions performed, in addition to actual erection of dwelling units, are designing, financing, contracting, and subcontracting. As in the preceding stage, standards established by utility and insurance companies are still relevant. In addition, the builder must involve himself with building permits and licenses in nearly every community in which he does business.

His costs may be influenced by those from whom he purchases services or materials: architects, construction workers, mortgage lenders, building materials dealers or producers. The bargaining position of each of these entrepreneurs will determine the extent to which he is able to influence the price of his services or products.

The relative bargaining position of each supplier of inputs to the housing package will be given more detailed consideration later in this section. Suffice it to say here that restrictive or collusive practices engaged in by these venders, if indeed they exist, jack up housing prices. As mere examples, collusion in the setting of fees might exist among those providing business services to the industry; organized labor may set wages at higher levels than the competitive rate, as has been alleged, or restrict output and resist cost-reducing innovations; mortgage lenders may either turn down loan applications or restrict the terms of credit; acting singly or in concert, materials suppliers operating in monopolistic markets may demand higher than competitive prices. At every stage of the production process, members of the construction industry and those supplying materials and services are subject to public policies and regulations which influence supply costs and prices. Materials must meet established standards of performance or specification. Building permits must be obtained, and so on. These rules and regulations tend to have a cumulative effect on the final price of the product unless absorbed in lower returns by some of the participants.

Because of linkages in the production of inputs to residential construction, tracing through the relationships and estimating any one supplier's degree of price control is exceedingly complex. We have already referred to the possibility that, under certain circumstances, sellers of raw land may consistently pass on costs with successive sales.

The process is similar for the suppliers of each of the other inputs, but with additional complications. Consider the complex of links in the distribution chain between petroleum and the completed dwelling unit. Tracing through the U.S. input-output table of 1958 (151), we find that 13¢ of every residential construction dollar is spent for lumber and wood products. In turn, every dollar of lumber produced requires expenditures of 5.1¢ for transportation and warehousing, among other inputs to the lumber industry. Similarly, a dollar's output of transportation and warehousing requires purchases of refined petroleum amounting to 4.4¢ and so on.

Each of these suppliers may engage in restrictive practices which inflate the price of the final product when it reaches the consumer. A truly comprehensive study of cost influences on residential construction would require examining the market structure and pricing policies not only of those industries supplying *direct* inputs to construction (such as lumber), but also of those intermediaries linked somewhere in the production process by their *indirect* supplies (such as petroleum). Given the scope of this effort, our focus will be on those factors affecting prices of direct inputs: construction labor, major building materials and equipment suppliers, and mortgage financers.

Distribution Phase. The second of the three major stages involves marketing the completed unit. Specific steps normally taken include listing the property with real estate agents; promotion of the property; negotiation with prospective buyers; and (when a ready and able purchaser consents) the actual transfer of title. Two public requirements—transfer taxes and recording—are repeated at this stage. A title search, probably involving title insurance, will usually be undertaken again. Still another cost-inducing requirement may be identified. Market area restrictions imposed on regulated mortgage lenders—to the extent that they limit operations to a geographical market which is less than optimal in scope—will increase operating costs. If the costs are shifted, they will be reflected ultimately in the terms of credit. In addition, closing fees may be charged by lenders as a device for raising the effective return on borrowed capital, particularly during tight money periods.

Possible collusive practices by agents who assist buyers and sellers in closing arrangements cause potential price increases. In addition, the fees charged for services rendered by realty agents, lawyers, and mortgage lenders—even when collusion is not involved—may inflate the cost of the property through higher transaction costs.

Consumption and Redistribution Phase. For most consumer goods, both durable and nondurable, the final demand is by the ultimate consumer. This is not entirely true of housing, for very rarely will the initial purchaser of a house outlive the product. The first occupant will resell after perhaps five years to another demander who will "consume" another five years of the product's lifetime and then move on. Over a lifetime of 60 years, a house might shelter a dozen different consumers and their families. The durability of the product has important implications, for the element of production cost represents only a portion of the total costs relevant to any consideration of housing costs. The recurrent costs—operating and transfer charges—are no less pertinent.

With the inclusion of property taxes, the same potentially cost-increasing institutional factors apply. Also, with each transfer, the same specific activities are repeated. Unless the house is replaced earlier, it is removed from the inventory at the end of its useful life.

Market Structure and Power

As we have emphasized, the residential construction industry is made up of a potpourri of economic units—individuals, firms, and industries. This heterogeneity suggests that the housing market is really a collection of submarkets each one of which may be unique in comparison to any other. A prerequisite to understanding the magnitude and incidence of institutionally induced costs is to identify and classify the types of markets, and to assess the degrees of market power.

The types of submarkets within the housing market are revealed most clearly in terms of extremes. One extreme is represented by the competitive firm, industry, or market. The other extreme is the monopolistic firm, industry, or market. No economic unit embraced by the housing market is a pure case of one or the other, but the extremes are useful reference points for analysis. Some units will be more competitive in character than others, and, tautologically, some will operate more monopolistically than others. Their rank in the intermediate range between extremes very largely determines the degree to which they can influence prices and shift costs.

In classifying economic units supplying goods and services to house production, one can examine either the characteristics of the firms themselves or their historical performance in the market. If, for example, many firms sell undifferentiated products, it is presumed that the industry satisfies the conditions of the pure competition model; for, no matter how much is offered to the market by any one firm, the large number of firms ensure that the price will remain unaffected. The real world examples of perfectly competitive economic units are rare. In the absence of government price support programs the best examples would be drawn from the agricultural industry, wheat being the classic example. No supplier of inputs to construction—even the timber industry—fully satisfies these strict criteria.

Monopoly, the opposite extreme, is characterized by a single producer-seller who exercises considerable control over price. It is customary to note that there are no good substitutes for monopolistically supplied goods and services. The relevant examples in the housing industry are utilities which, if free of government control, would establish rates and prices monopolistically. There are other factor inputs which approximate the monopolistic model in certain respects. For example, each parcel of land is uniquely sited and immovable. Yet, because there are almost always equally attractive alternatives, few (if any) sites can be regarded as perfect monopolies.

Monopolies—or more correctly, monopsonies—exist when all production of a single type is sold to a single purchaser. As would be expected, there are few cases approaching monopsony in the housing industry. If the construction industry represents a single buyer market, prices will be heavily influenced by the purchaser. Given, however, the large number of firms in the construction industry and their diverse compositions, it is highly unlikely that they classify as a monopsony in the true meaning of the term.

Although the strict sense is also violated when the term "monopoly" is applied to institutional restrictions in the public domain, there are comparable pricing effects. The services of zoning and subdivision controls, for example, are not sold. Yet, since the price of the product they affect may be raised, the results are the same as if the services had been "purchased" from a monopolist. Moreover, the "purchaser" has little control over these costs. Thus, in the crudest sense, by enacting and enforcing policies affecting private sector costs, the government operates as a form of monopoly.

Since the housing industry is characterized by tight interdependencies among producers, any monopolistic producer of an intermediate product in the processing chain may influence prices for the final demander. This holds true even if all processers, save the one monopolist, are perfectly competitive.

Midway between extremes lies the "never-never land" of imperfect, or monopolistic, competition. Difficult to define precisely, the class embraces nearly all firms and industries. Unlike the pure cases of perfect competition or monopoly, these firms exercise some control over prices and produce goods and service inputs for residential construction, which are differentiated to some extent. If licensing requirements, for example, increase the contractor's cost of doing business, all, or a portion of, the higher costs may be passed on to his customer. The degree to which costs can be shifted to buyers depends on the seller's degree of market control. Technically, the more inelastic the demand for his goods or services, the more likely that he will shift the higher costs, and the less reluctant the customer will be to accept the higher prices. Thus, a measure of ability to shift costs is the elasticity of demand for the producer's output, or the position he occupies in the spectrum of market types ranging from pure competition to monopoly.

Closely related to cost magnitude and incidence is the issue of factor proportions. The degree of market control is of less consequence for a minor input than for a major one. The distinction between relative magnitude of factor proportions and bargaining power is clarified by the following matrix, in which each element would contain those firms in the housing industry classified on the two dimensions:

Table 2. Housing Cost Matrix

Cost Magnitude	Bargaining Power: Important	Bargaining Power: Unimportant
Important	II	IU
Unimportant	UI	UU

Producers who exercise considerable bargaining power and who supply major inputs (II in the matrix) are those whose pricing policies have the greatest effect on housing costs. Their counterparts in the matrix (UU) enjoy little bargaining power and supply relatively small shares of total inputs. The two remaining groups of firms occupy positions of intermediate importance. Consider a case involving two suppliers: A produces negligible inputs amounting to, say, $200 of the cost of the typical housing unit, but exercises a monopoly position; B's inputs, sold competitively, are of major importance, say, $2,000 in total cost. In our classification scheme, A would be found listed in the lower left corner (UI) and B would appear in the upper right section (IU). While higher costs of operation may be passed on more easily by A than B, A would have to increase the supply price by 10 percent before it could equal a one percent increase in B's price. In our earlier example illustrating linkages, a minor supplier in the chain of intermediate producers may enjoy superior bargaining position, but his output, like A's, represents a negligible proportion of the bill of goods. Moreover, his control of the market will be diluted to the extent that he supplies goods to a variety of different buyers. In light of existing evidence, we will attempt some very rough approximations of the importance of bargaining power and cost magnitude for the economic units involved in the housing market.

Just as the distribution of costs shifts with differential price increases and with factor substitution, so the bargaining strength of economic units shifts over time as market conditions change. Following tradition, the construction market can be classified at any moment in time either as a buyer's or as a seller's market. (123, p. 256)

A buyers' market has a large number of properties available to the existing number of purchasers. The buyers dominate the market, and, with no shortage of housing units for sale, prices decline, or at least do not increase. The anxious seller is somewhat at the mercy of a handful of prospective bidders for his property and, in order to complete the sale, will agree to assume the burden of transfer costs (and perhaps additional costs representing losses on the capital he has invested in his home).

A sellers' market, on the other hand, is characterized by a shortage of dwellings relative to the number of buyers ready and able to purchase. Bargaining position favors the seller who, given the sluggishness of housebuilding in response to a demand increase, can expect a higher price for his property. Faced with relatively few dwellings from which to choose, the prospective buyer either pays the larger sum or postpones his decision to purchase. Presumably built into the seller's higher price are the costs of transfer, plus other costs incurred during his occupancy, such as property taxes, and possibly a capital gain. The purchaser, who bears these costs, is in fact dealing in a market which approximates monopoly; for he exercises little control over the market price.

Thus, since a large scale speculative contractor with little competition may exercise considerable power in a community, he may be described most correctly as monopolistic in his pricing behavior. But with a market glut, the same builder becomes competitive and, given a substantial investment in unsold inventory, assumes costs himself or even accepts offers at prices which fail fully to cover costs. Thus, the static classification is tempered by prevailing market conditions.

The Structure of Costs

We have already demonstrated that the magnitude and incidence of costs, as reflected in price, depend on market structure (do firms and industries tend toward competition or monopoly?) and on market power (does a buyer's or seller's market govern?). The types of costs involved in the housing industry require further explanation.

Contrary to popular notion, many of the costs commonly regarded as wasteful merely result in shifts of resources over time, among either the sectors of the economy or the items of the budget. Certain costs will not be reflected in price, as we have seen. Some costs reflect change in the level of output, while others are fairly insensitive to scale of operation. Certain costs are necessary adjuncts to investment. Others appear as increments in value to the homeowner or as deferred cost savings. Still other private costs generate social benefits to the community.

To establish order, consider a broad classification of costs by cause and effect. Costs structured by cause include those which change with shifts in scale of operation and those which represent a reward for risk-taking. Costs classified by effect include those with externalities or benefits accruing to society rather than directly to the investor, those which create added value to the consumer, and those which are wasteful.

Costs by Cause. Two types of cost shifts must be identified: first, those which cause an upward or downward shift in the operating costs of a firm or industry without changing the distribution of costs at various levels of output; and secondly, those which do not disturb the level of costs, but whose behavior changes at different levels of output.

Technically, the first type refers to a change in the level of costs, as described by the firm's or industry's average or marginal cost curves, without altering the slopes of those curves. Thus, operating costs increase or decrease despite the level of output. The same amount must be paid for each unit of output, as there are no quantity discounts. Examples are transfer taxes and producer's costs, such as building permit and deed-recording fees. Regardless of whether a contractor builds one or a thousand units, the same unit cost applies. Since such costs vary with scale of output, their effect on the shape of the average cost curve is neutral; they merely shift it upward. For sectors where most costs per unit of output are the same despite size of output, no cost savings will result from changing scale of operation. The savings and loan business furnishes an example, as we shall see.

The shape of cost curves is influenced by "quantity discounts" which differ over scale and consequently generate economies or diseconomies. In housebuilding, costs influencing scale may be dichotomized as "on-site" or "off-site." The former involve production diseconomies or economies; the latter involve management and financing economies and diseconomies. Since the costs of installing utilities and other physical infrastructure are highly responsive to scale differences, economies are obtained with increasing scale of development. Although the fees paid for licenses are only a small component of total costs, they encourage contractors to distribute these fixed costs over as many units of output as possible. Hence, such fees encourage increased scale of operation. Most of the costs of building respond to differences in scale. Consequently, builders' costs will decline over a certain range of production levels. Beyond that range, as diseconomies are realized, costs will increase.

Off-site costs generating scale economies include management and financing operations. As a general rule, the larger the builder, the smaller the administrative staff required per unit of output. Actual—not nominal—fees paid to realty agents, lawyers, and designers normally are based on sliding scales. An architect may charge for only a half dozen floor plans which, with minor variations, become the designs for a tract of several hundred homes. Lawyers, particularly if on retainer, are not likely to base their charges on the firm's level of output; hence their fixed fees decline per unit of output as output increases. Realty agents will usually settle for lower commissions if they have the exclusive rights to market all the homes in a large tract.

Other costs, such as those involving conformance with building codes, are hybrids with both fixed and variable elements. For example, a materials-based code may increase costs at all levels of production by an across-the-board specification of materials for which quantity discounts are not given. In other cases (probably the majority), the code may require materials which shift average costs upward, but which steepen the slope of the curve if discounts are offered for quantity purchases. Lack of knowledge about different sets of codes in regions with multiple political jurisdictions tends to inhibit builders from expanding their markets into new territory. In this fashion, fractionalized codes are likely to cause scale diseconomies which restrict the firm's level of production to less than optimal size. Codes of this type lead to a form of resource waste.

A second class of resource-wasting costs are the "profits" demanded by entrepreneurs in risky ventures. Studies of the business cycle generally agree that the periodicity is tighter and the amplitude is greater for the residential construction cycle than for most other cycles. (44, 155) Much of the instability results from the definition of housing as a tool, rather than as a target, of stabilization policy. (154) As a result, swings in the level of new housebuilding have been frequent and pronounced. Given attendant uncertainty, investors are reluctant to enter the market unless a reward is given for assuming higher than average risks. Other things equal, the larger the scale, the higher the rate of return on investment demanded. This is consistent with the findings of a recent statistical study demonstrating that the amplitude of cycles and profit rates are closely correlated in West European nations and the U.S. (56). It follows that a substantial element in profits is payment for risks and uncertainty. The same would be true of the highly cyclical residential construction industry. According to one industry study, large house-building firms earn over twice the overhead and profits of small firms. If all the difference can be attributed to difference in willingness to bear risk, rather than economies of scale, and if the risk element for which higher returns were demanded could be eliminated, then an amazing sum of nearly $900 could be saved in the cost of an $8,750 home! (74, p. 190)

A more careful consideration of the sources of different classes of costs follows in the description of major organizational components of the housing industry.

Costs by Effect. Costs, described in terms of potentially positive effects, are no less elusive of classification. We refer specifically to a pair of broad classes: (a) costs incurred to prevent or reduce external diseconomies or to generate external economies, and (b) costs which lead to internal economies or accretions to the value of the housing product. The dimension of time, while relevant to each broad type of costs considered so far, is most important here. Both types of effect-classified costs primarily involve resource redistribution (or transfers) rather than resource waste. This is important, for rarely have studies of construction costs recognized the additional betterment resulting from additional costs of certain types. As we shall see, complaints about the "high cost of housing" are frequently misdirected, since many costs are directly or indirectly resource creating or resource redistributing. Rather than resource waste, the result is redistribution among sectors, consumer budget items, and over time (costs incurred today may be saved tomorrow).

The earliest efforts to rid cities of slums by "reforming" housing have recognized that good or bad housing affects the larger society for better or worse. But the return to the investor is likely to be minor compared to the more illusive social benefits. Samuelson was one of the first economists to articulate this phenomenon in economic terms: "Urban land use and city planning is just shot with external economies and diseconomies. It is there that you need programs and precisely there that the oldest theories of government have always said that free play of market forces will not work too well." (100)

The high ratio of externalities to direct returns, somewhat unique to housing, discourages investment in all but those items which generate returns directly to the investor. As an example, the profit-motivated land developer or builder will not include facilities offering amenities to the community-at-large unless, by so doing, his returns on investment increase. In the absence of restrictions, he will be tempted to build the structure which maximizes his profit and only indirectly concern himself with the effect on occupants or their neighbors. A principal obstacle to private urban renewal is that the lion's share of benefits usually accrues to the surrounding neighborhood and its inhabitants, rather than to the investor. Exercises of the public power such as codes and zoning are justified in protecting both the community-at-large and the supposedly naive home purchaser or occupant from investors unconcerned about the general welfare. The higher costs resulting from these exercises of police power often result in increased utility or higher value and are not necessarily wasteful.

Internalities, the counterpart of externalities, refers to rates of return as reflected in investor's profits or consumer's utility. The cheapest house of all is no house at all. But no house has neither utility nor value. Additional costs, except those identified as wasteful, add to the value of the dwelling and to consumer satisfaction. Building codes again furnish an example. Adherence to a stricter code may be costly; yet, to the extent that the additional costs are reflected in value, they are not wasted. However, codes specified too strictly and providing no additional utility may add nothing either to the useful life of the structure or to reduced maintenance over its life.

This begs the question of the relationship between capital initially invested in the dwelling, as revealed in structural quality, and operating charges required to maintain the structure over its life. Since tighter codes may affect capital costs but save later maintenance costs, a superior house today means lower maintenance expenses tomorrow. The relevant, yet unstudied, question is whether the greater initial costs of building a more rigidly specified home are less than the present value of the costs saved from lower maintenance over the unit's life. To the extent that recurring costs are saved, higher costs induced by tighter codes cannot be regarded as necessarily wasteful. If, indeed, there is an inverse relationship between capital in place and the discounted value of operating charges, building codes can favorably alter the time structure of costs.

Other shifts, or "trade-offs," are also relevant. If costs of housing increase and nonhousing costs decrease equally as consumers shift budget shares among expenditure categories, no change in welfare may occur. The hypothesis that households substitute space utility for accessibility is well documented. (4) Given the fact that unit land costs rise with increased access to markets and other activity centers, households may choose to pay higher prices for closer locations in order to save transport costs. The result is a substitution of a stock expenditure (land costs) for a flow expenditure (transport costs). Since land is a cost ingredient of residential property, housing costs increase and transport costs decrease. If the present value of the flow equals the capital value of the stock, there has been no change in the household's aggregate budget position or in its cost of living, but merely a shift among expenditure categories within the budget. Consequently, it is inappropriate to assume categorically that housing cost increases lead to lower living levels. The assumption can be substantiated only if evidence confirms that the housing cost increases did not result in decreased costs elsewhere. Other shifts may take the form of altering the distribution of housing by class. As we illustrate subsequently, codes may act to increase the average quality of the housing stock only by increasing the supply of more expensive housing.

Summary. If our considerations concerned the cost of only one class of housing—such as low-cost housing for low-income families without reference to the quality of the product—we would be concerned with minimizing nearly all costs regardless of type, since stretching construction dollars over the maximum number of dwelling units would be the major criterion. Since this paper considers the quality of housing, it is useful to distinguish those costs resulting either in increased value of the unit and greater utility to the occupant, in lower recurring costs over the lifetime of the property, or in shifts by consumers between housing and nonhousing budget items. Unless one views housing myopically as an ultimate end in itself, the focus of public policy should not be on these costs, which are likely to benefit consumer welfare, particularly in the long run. Rather, policy should concern itself with reducing or eliminating wasteful costs.

In outline we have distinguished two broad classes: (1) costs by cause, and (2) costs by effect. Costs by cause either shift cost curves of producers of housing inputs or change the slopes of their cost curves. Some examples of costs do both, i.e., raise cost curves and alter their slope.

Cutting across these classes are resource-wasting costs which increase price without improving the quality of the product or consumer utility. Resource waste, to the extent that it can be identified, should receive the major attention of policy-makers seeking ways of producing more housing at lower cost without sacrifice of quality. Costs by effect are divided into two broad categories: those which generate external economies to the benefit of the larger society, and those which create internal economies for the benefit of the housing consumer. Costs of the two subgroups tend to be resource redistributing rather than resource wasting. Redistribution takes place, in the first case, between the community-at-large and the occupant and, in the second case, among budget items when trade-offs are made by consumers. As one example of a shift over time within the housing budget item, consumers may invest initially in a better quality dwelling to economize on recurring maintenance costs. Tradeoffs also occur between housing and nonhousing budget items, as when consumers choose to pay more for location to save commuting; housing costs are higher but transportation costs are saved. Any effort to reduce costs which result in resource transfer or waste must take full account of derivative effects on welfare. For example, a policy encouraging dispersal in order to take advantage of cheaper land at the urban periphery must recognize that the savings in housing costs may be more than offset by higher transportation costs, and the *net* effect of the two events may be a reduction in the level of welfare.

Nature and Evolution of Institutional Factors Affecting Efficiency

The institutional factors most commonly suspected as cost-inducing and innovation-inhibiting are zoning, subdivision regulations, building and related codes, and property taxes. Consequently, major emphasis in the discussion is placed on these elements. (The factor of commission paid to realty agents is considered in the next section.) Since "hard" evidence is scanty or nonexistent for most other factors, and since their effect on costs and innovation is probably less pronounced, our treatment of these is sketchy. They include standards set by insurance and utility companies, transfer fees including title insurance premiums, limits on lending areas, and usury laws.

Definition and Evolution of Factors

Zoning. Urban historians generally date the origin of zoning, and of building regulations in general, to 2000–1800 B.C. with the codification of Hammurabi's rules of justice. The true antecedents of zoning regulations are numerous building regulations at the time communities began their experimentation with limiting of land uses.

Disposition of its vast land resources has been the concern of considerable legislation of the United States dating from the earliest days of independence. A multitude of enactments starting with the Congress of the Confederation—the first of which provided that specified areas be used as a revenue source for education—extended through the nineteenth century and concerned the use of rural rather than urban space. In fact, one quarter of all Congressional legislation at the outbreak of the Civil War dealt with the question of disposing of government-owned rural land. With the dwindling supply of these holdings, attention shifted from disposition to conservation, a movement which peaked in intensity and color during the Theodore Roosevelt administration. But it was not until later that public attention focused on the urban land question.

Because of its uncertain legality, most early urban zoning efforts were spasmodic. Around the turn of the century, Boston and Los Angeles passed laws limiting the height of new structures. With the blessing of the courts, Los Angeles declared in 1909 that all the land outside its central business district was limited to residential uses, excluding laundries and brickyards. (38, p. 87) New York City followed several years later with the first comprehensive zoning ordinance. The famous case, *Village of Euclid, Ohio v. Ambler Realty Company* (272 U.S. 363, November 22, 1926) was a significant milestone in the evolution of "the regulation by districts under the police power of the height, bulk, and use of buildings, the use of land, and the density of population," as zoning regulations were defined by the author of the New York ordinance. (9) This affirmed the rights of local governing bodies, in Justice Sutherland's words, to "restrict the use and occupation of private lands in communities." Shortly thereafter, the definition of local governing bodies, previously restricted to municipal governments, was broadened to include counties in legislation passed in Wisconsin.

Zoning, as it is construed today, controls the use and development of the land, the bulk, height, and area covered by buildings, and the density of population. Although zoning was enacted originally to prevent nuisances, its purpose broadened over the years to include (a) conserving the value of property, (b) assuring orderly community growth, and (c) safeguarding the general public welfare. (122, p. 363) One of the fundamentals of zoning is that certain classes of land uses in close proximity are incompatible. By dividing the community into reasonably uniform districts or zones, incompatible uses can be reduced or eliminated. A major distinction between zoning and building codes is that uniformity in the former applies only to the particular zones established; whereas in the latter case the regulations are uniform throughout the community. (122) As will be shown, this distinction is important in assessing economic impact.

Building and Related Codes. Major enactments affecting the construction of residential housing were introduced in the nineteenth century, concurrent with the advent of the industrial revolution in America and the attendant evils of company housing. The regulations, aimed principally at residential structures rather than commercial or industrial structures, prescribed minima for light, air, and lot coverage. The slum reform movement in the United States, particularly in New York City (chronicled in detail by Lubove [69]), resulted in enactment of Model Tenement Laws and a series of later laws dealing with the physical structure of housing. For various reasons, such legislation generally went unenforced, though rarely unnoticed.

Building regulations have proliferated in detail and coverage in the years since. Until fairly recently, codes were as variegated as the communities for which they were written. The differences are breaking down slowly as many communities have adopted "model" codes. These codes protect "the public against faulty design or construction of buildings. The building codes must insure that occupants, adjoining property and neighborhoods, and passers-by are protected from the erection of structures that are likely to collapse or lead to unhealthy or unsanitary conditions. Building codes must also prohibit conditions conductive to both individual and collective fire hazards." (2, p. 11)

Since it would be economically impossible to protect the public against any and all contingencies, building codes must be reasonable and, as a minimum criterion, the benefits they generate should exceed their costs. To insist that structures withstand major earthquakes in areas where they are unlikely to occur would be unreasonable. It is the definition of reasonableness that causes much of the controversy over building codes.

While building codes apply prospectively to new construction, housing codes deal with the conservation and rehabilitation of the existing inventory of housing. "Housing codes prescribe regulatory measures for the maintenance, occupancy and supplied facilities of structures and are concerned primarily with health, safety, and sanitation requirements of buildings after they have been constructed. But certain housing code requirements may indirectly influence the design and construction of new buildings as well." (156)

Housing codes, to the extent that they compel standards of occupancy, maintenance, repair, and replacement of integral parts of structures, will incorporate, by reference or otherwise, provisions of other codes and ordinances. In fact, these other codes may very well comprise the backbone of the housing codes. (55)

In addition to building and housing codes, states and municipalities have promulgated special provisions which can be broadly classified as mechanical codes. These relate to specific features and well-defined equipment in structures, including plumbing, electrical and elevator systems.

Subdivision Regulations. Subdivision regulations establish the standards and conditions under which land can be broken up into parcels prior to development or improvement. They specify the kinds of facilities or services required by the prospective users of the land as well as the general public.

The original requirements in subdivision regulations, concerned primarily with streets, have been expanded over the years to include a large number of other community facilities, such as street lighting, sewage disposal and water systems, street signs, and sidewalks. Also, many areas require dedication of land for schools and parks in subdivisions.

In some respects, subdivision regulations resemble building codes. For example, they are written for the entire community rather than for individual parcels. In other respects, they represent an addendum to zoning for individual neighborhoods. As has been stated, "the primary objective of subdivision control is to assure that the land subdivided will constitute a permanent asset to the community, and will provide the maximum degree of health, comfort, convenience, and beauty consistent with true economy." (122, p. 437)

Property Taxation. The antecedents of the contemporary property tax are deeply imbedded in history. Rooted in feudalism, the tax on land and other property forms constituted a major source of government revenue until other types of wealth were recognized. Although British and European customs broadly influenced the American system of general property taxes, the system was largely indigenous to this country. (57, p. 19) In the context of general taxes the device found its rationale in ability to pay. Ability to pay supposedly was measured by real and personal property holdings. (86, p. 75)

Throughout the last century, property taxes generated the bulk of state and local revenues. Despite this dependence, however, studies of tax administration undertaken in the late nineteenth century uncovered substantial evidence of abuse and evasion, particularly with respect to non-real estate tax items. Ely was particularly opposed to property taxes, claiming they had never worked well "in the entire civilized world." (34, p. 143) He nevertheless admitted that property was a necessary revenue source for local finance. Still, "it ought not in any American city to exceed one percent of the true selling value of the property." (34, p. 145) Clearly, the dictum has not been observed.

Since the turn of the century, income and other nonproperty taxes have replaced the realty tax as the principal revenue source of most states. However, real property still remains the source of most municipal revenue, notwithstanding the fact that the tax is generally considered discriminatory. Eckstein contends that "In our present tax systems, the property tax based on arbitrary, local assessments of value is probably the most uncertain tax, and for this reason leads to a great deal of friction, substantial inequity among property-owners, a reduction of investment in buildings, and no doubt, to some corruption." (32, p. 54)

Effect of Major Factors on Efficiency

Although they are not the only tools available to local government for influencing patterns on the land, zoning, subdivision ordinances, building and related codes, and property taxes are the chief instruments for constraining or enhancing private market developments. In principle, these exercises of police power attempt to improve or protect the welfare of the community-at-large. They also affect the costs of housing and the efficiency of the market.

In a sense, these regulations may be viewed as a means to protect the users, owners, and occupants of the properties affected and to economize on long-run costs. A subdivision regulation requiring the installation of paved streets and sewer lines prior to the development and construction of improvements imposes costs on consumers who might wish either to defer them or even to avoid them altogether. However, it may be more costly to defer the installation of these facilities until after the tract has been built up. By incurring costs in earlier stages and by taking advantage of larger-scale production economies, the ordinance may reduce consumers' costs over the long run.

Moreover, the regulations may reduce or eliminate external diseconomies. While a building code protects owners or occupants from a poorly constructed building, it is also intended to protect neighboring properties and the public against hazards to health and safety. Theoretically, the regulation internalizes these diseconomies; that is, it makes the individual responsible for their creation. Building codes, for example, will raise the costs of construction and usually the prices paid in the market. But apart from protecting present or future consumers from their own ignorance, they should do no more than to shift the cost burden of diseconomies to the responsible individual. In practice, the theory is frequently violated. As one observer testifies, "The main thing that planners don't know about zoning is this: Planners do not know, or at least they act as if they do not know, that their kind of zoning is virtually a myth, at least a great rarity. By the planner's kind of zoning, I mean zoning for everybody's welfare, zoning which implements a plan for the sound development of the entire community—as opposed to zoning for the mere protection of each private piece of property. . . ." (140, p. 197)

Technically, the goal of such restrictions is to raise the level of community welfare and to approximate what in economic terms is called "Pareto Optimality"; that is, the regulations and policies should benefit everyone in the community (or if only some gain, then none should lose). Furthermore, with externalities resulting from certain market actions, it may be possible for the gainers to compensate the losers and still be better off than before. If compensation is not a practical alternative, the reduction of external diseconomies will still be a preferred position in many cases. We shall return to this subject shortly.

Suffice it to say that, so long as social controls impose costs on housing which in the long run reduce external diseconomies, the claim that they burden market participants excessively is somewhat weakened. This is in sharp contrast to regulations which raise housing costs for a large number of persons, but benefit only a privileged few. A building code which prohibits the introduction of cost-saving innovations benefits only a few individuals with vested interests and clearly conflicts with the outlined principles.

Given the extraordinary complexities of regulations on land utilization and buildings, it is often a matter of judgment to separate those rules which appear to raise costs and waste resources from others which reduce or eliminate externalities or protect consumers by merely shifting resources. Moreover, those who are only indirectly affected may not be fully aware of the implications of the regulations or may be reluctant to submit their views to public debate. These problems are clarified by examining the regulations separately.

Zoning. In recent years the conception of zoning has been the subject of criticism. There is a growing concern that the notion of the public welfare has been interpreted too narrowly in one sense and too broadly in another. Moreover, it has become quite clear that the intended effect of zoning and the market realities diverge sharply. Since research on the economic impact of zoning is limited to analyses of a few cases, it is impossible to apply the conclusions to the entire nation.

1. Effect on externalities. Challenging traditional welfare economics, Coase gives a new perspective on the efficacy of zoning and similar types of controls. Using the example of a factory which, through smoke emission, has deleterious effects on neighboring properties, he asserts, "The conclusions to which this kind of analysis seems to have led most economists are that it would be desirable to make the owner of the factory liable for the damage caused to those injured by the smoke, or alternatively liable for the damage caused to those injured by the smoke, or alternatively, to place a tax on the factory owner . . . ," or finally to exclude the factory from residential districts (and presumably from other areas in which the emission would have harmful effects on others). "It is my contention that the suggested courses of action are inappropriate, in that they lead to results which are not necessarily, or even usually, desirable." (138, p. 1, emphasis added) Coase's argument rests on the notion that since property owners' rights are also factors of production, the segregation of land uses may reduce social product, unless the damage done to those ostensibly creating the external diseconomies is also reckoned. But he does not deny the appropriateness of government interference in cases where barriers exist to market transactions. If no barriers exist, government's role is to define property rights and to let the market determine the use of property. Zoning restrictions fail to recognize the reciprocal character of externalities. To illustrate, apartment houses would not be obnoxious to residents of single family homes if it were not for the presence of the latter. Relegating apartment houses to less favorable locations will disadvantage landlords and tenants. In consequence, the relevant question is which of the two uses should be allowed to harm the other. How can we avoid the serious harm? With respect to zoning, Coase says, "I need not devote much space to discussing the similar error involved in the suggestion that smoke producing factories should, by means of zoning regulations, be removed from the districts in which the smoke causes harmful effects. When the change in the location of the factory results in a reduction in production, this obviously needs to be taken into account and weighed against the harm which would result from the factory remaining in that location. The aim of such regulation should not be to eliminate smoke pollution, but rather to secure the optimum amount of smoke pollution, this being the amount which will maximize production." (138, p. 42)

Therefore, if maximum social product is a goal of public policy apart from ethical and moral considerations, zoning ordinances may defeat the very purposes they are trying to accomplish. To argue that relegating particular land uses to separate districts is unlikely to affect output, is to say that location is irrelevant to the success or failure of enterprises.

One of the few empirical economic analyses of a zoning change illustrates the argument. In an attempt to reduce traffic congestion resulting from parking on the street, the city of Oakland revised a zoning ordinance to require a parking space for every apartment unit built after 1961. (105, pp. 103–125) Superficially, the revision may appear to involve shifting a public cost (traffic congestion) to the investor in multifamily dwellings. The contention probably reflects the reasoning of many planners and the residents in the adjacent area. The empirical analysis of the aftereffects reveals the complex chain reaction that resulted from a seemingly minor zoning revision: density of apartment units per acre declined, larger lots were used, median land costs rose ten cents per square foot, apartment unit costs increased by $583, and profit margins of both builders and landlords dropped. Although construction costs per square foot declined because of the construction of less costly space for garages, the building costs per apartment unit rose from $6,613 to $7,805 because of the construction of larger units. On the plus side, competition became keener and market efficiency improved. On the minus side, with the lower density developments, the market rent structure shifted upward as investors sought to recapture higher costs. Thus, resources shifted away from the low-cost, low-rent sector, which had the greatest need for expansion. (105)

These findings, although localized, raise a host of issues relevant to cost inducement arising from institutional factors. First, should zoning ordinances reduce the profitability of developers? It would seem reasonable to contend that, with lower profitability, producers are stimulated to greater efficiency. But, if industry is efficient, marginal producers are usually eliminated and output is reduced. This is a cost which in some form will also be shared by society. Which does society prefer: more traffic congestion and more housing, or less of both? Unfortunately, this kind of choice is often not clear to decision-makers immersed in legal and technical detail and too concerned with reconciling the interests of the community power structure.

Secondly, should zoning ordinances stimulate construction of larger, more expensive dwellings to the detriment of poorer population groups? Many communities, especially if suburban, would answer "yes." While their reasons are clear, they find little economic support. What are the reasons? As two astute observers note, some reasons are debated publicly, and others are only whispered. (127) First, suburban homeowners argue that multifamily dwellings place a heavy burden on the public sector, leading to a property tax increase. Secondly, dense development cuts off air and light. Thirdly, rental units are "the slums of tomorrow." Fourthly, multifamily neighborhoods reduce property values. And finally, they will destroy the character of the community. Actually, there is but little evidence that apartments increase school costs or place any exceptional strain on community facilities, except perhaps in older established areas. If anything, the contrary seems to be true. Families with children typically demand single family homes. With higher density installation, the maintenance of community facilities is likely to be lower than for single family homes. Proper zoning and design can minimize the nuisance effect of further intensive land utilization. The belief that multifamily units are quick to blight is difficult to reconcile with landlord entrepreneurship. With normal vacancies, unless landlords maintain their property, the rentability of their units is reduced. Property values around apartments tend to be high because of expectations for additional intensive land utilization. Finally, the fear that the character of the community will be jeopardized is purely a matter of esthetics on which it is difficult to find agreement.

Some of the real reasons for zoning out higher intensity land uses are not stated publicly. There is often the concern that such housing will attract lower class tenants, although it can be shown that there is not necessarily a relationship between social class and propensity for apartment living. Similarly, the fear exists that the population in these units will be unstable or that minority groups will be attracted.

What are the economic consequences of this type of reasoning? First, much of it is based on some assumed external diseconomy connected with a particular land use for which a market exists in the community. Many of the supposed diseconomies are pure fantasies which have no basis in fact. Even if one grants that some external diseconomies result from the introduction of new land uses into suburban communities, this neglects the problem of the harm to the larger society which is eliminated. As shown, the maintenance of "high standards" in zoning and exclusionary tactics tend to reduce the supply of new housing and to raise prices or rents, especially for those least able to pay. Moreover, locating new housing in less advantageous locations tends to increase transportation costs to places of work and elsewhere.

The issue of apartment housing in suburban communities is neatly summarized by this statement: "If the segregation of dwelling types can no longer be justified under the rubrics of "health, safety and morals," then what is the nature of the "general welfare" by which the enshrinement of the detached dwelling is validated? It may be appropriate to join this latter question with the reminder that the police power was not designed as a cardinal principle, but as a limitation on the primary right of the owner of property to use his property as he sees fit. Unless the developer's use will have a demonstrable and adverse impact upon the general welfare, the police power should not come into play. . . ." (127, pp. 1040–1091)

At least part of the inefficiencies resulting from zoning are traceable to an excessively narrow definition of the general welfare. Cities and towns organized as separate political entities are prone to view the scope of general welfare as coincident with their political boundaries. That the larger urban region is a highly interdependent mechanism tends to be ignored. In the process, little recognition is given to the possibility that the behavior of the communities, and especially those in the suburbs, acting without reference to surrounding territories, can undermine private market operations and even the general welfare of the region.

Zoning, of course, represents only one of a variety of means utilized by communities to fend off imaginary and real problems, and its importance should not be overestimated. However, it should be emphasized that the very problems which zoning and other regulatory devices intend to avoid often appear under a different guise. Tactics employed by suburban governments for maintaining an exclusive character aggravate the housing problems of the central cities. (8) The ensuing conflicts in the central cities generate costs to society of substantial magnitude.

In another sense, the general welfare in regard to zoning is interpreted too broadly. At one time zoning and other land use controls were seen as applications of the police power for arbitrating disputes between competitors in markets where property rights were ill-defined. This view is slowly giving way to the position which holds that the land market is subservient to the public interest. One observer remarks that "Today the attitude of the courts appears to have shifted. The general welfare of the community is now considered to stand independent of the safety and health of individuals." (114, pp. 23–24) The shift has permitted the introduction of zoning ordinances with provisions of social controls where benefits are ill-defined or illusory. Regulations tend to be increasingly protective of low density single-family residential developments at the expense of higher density developments and nonresidential land uses. (114)

In view of these remarks one might assume that the urban public is unaware of the economic implications of zoning. Such an assumption, however, is not necessary for understanding why zoning ordinances usually are adopted. As Davis has shown, given certain assumptions about the body politic, ". . . it seems reasonable to suppose that those who favor zoning will almost always outnumber those who oppose it in any metropolitan area. However, the existence of those who would oppose zoning or the assured lack of unanimity among the populace suggests that zoning cannot be said to move a municipality toward the Pareto optimality frontier in urban property." (143, pp. 374–386)

The reasoning is complex. It involves, first, the perception of external diseconomies imposed on groups in the community, and secondly, the possibility of enjoying indirect pecuniary external economies by imposing external diseconomies on others. Since losses (external diseconomies) are direct and gains (pecuniary external economies) indirect and prospective, more weight will be placed on the former than the latter. If true, renters and property owners who consider their parcel fully developed and who are concerned over possible losses will tend to approve of zoning and outvote those groups whose property is undeveloped or others who desire to develop property in its most profitable manner. The results of this process are, of course, at the very heart of the problem we are addressing, i.e., the restrictive standards and the limited opportunity for land use development or change.

The arguments up to this point have assumed that zoning ordinances are binding. In practice this is not always the case. Zoning administrators are aware of market pressures in making their decisions. The need for interaction between physically incompatible activities will usually dictate change. The exclusive single-family residential suburb with its "clean" research and development industries also demands maids, janitors, and low paid clerks. Unless such workers can find housing within reasonable proximity to places of employment, the costs of acquiring their services will be high. Therefore, efforts are made to accommodate these groups.

2. Cost implications. If zoning tends to be reasonably flexible and in accord with long-run market demand, it may still be regarded as a means for reducing the uncertainty of property owners, and the costs associated with it. Owners of land and buildings are protected against abrupt and unexpected neighborhood change, as zoning provides a smoother transition. If the goal be reasonable stability, then it must be determined whether it necessitates the development and administration of comprehensive zoning ordinances to spell out the provisions of land utilization. Land uses tend to cluster together through the market mechanism. Moreover, devices such as deed restrictions, which are available in the private market, do prevent abrupt and undesired change. With deed restrictions sanctioned by the general public, but without zoning, Houston, Texas, does not appear to differ markedly in its physical appearance, efficiency, and amenities from other American cities. One observer of zoning in the United States reached the conclusion that "... while municipal zoning appears to have enormous potential for regulating urban change, in actuality it has only marginal effects on land values and amenity, and almost negligible effects on the distribution of space users in the city." (114, p. 61). If this evaluation is correct, then the minimum direct cost of zoning in the United States is equivalent to the total cost of developing and administering zoning ordinances in areas where they exist.

3. An example: minimum lot size zoning. It needs to be recognized that zoning includes a multitude of regulatory devices varying greatly in detail among communities. If the previous remarks are not to be considered a glib indictment of regulations whose economic impact has not been studied comprehensively, it may be well to look at minimum lot zoning as one facet of the larger problem.

Planners, attorneys, and others have become increasingly concerned that suburban communities specify minimum lot sizes far larger than reasonable norms. One-, two-, or three-acre lot minima are not uncommon and have been upheld by the courts. (160) What are the economic consequences of this type of restriction?

A Massachusetts study shows that the increases in housing costs resulting from large lot zoning are not as substantial as might be assumed. (81) Frontage requirements and the number and character of improvements are more important determinants of costs than lot size. Assuming uniform raw land cost, a one-acre lot was found to cost 30 percent more—not four times more—than a one-quarter acre lot, raising costs on a $20,000 home by 4 percent. A four-acre lot is but 50 percent more costly than a one-acre lot and increases costs by 9 percent for the total package. The less than proportional cost increases are due to the fact that certain on-site costs in lot development are fixed, regardless of lot size. Usually, large lots tend to be relatively deep, and the average width/depth ratio which might range from say 0.60 to 0.85 for smaller lots would range between 0.48 and 0.70 in larger lots. Thus, with scale economies, off-site improvements do not rise sharply with lot size. However, it is asserted that lot costs would become prohibitive where high standards for lot improvements accompany wide frontage requirements. The research suggests that substantial economies might be obtained if, with large lots, standards are adjusted and improvements waived. For instance, streets might be narrower, so that storm sewers and sidewalks could be eliminated. Whether or not these adjustments are made is another matter. But the study does suggest that alternatives are open; that is, an apparently strict standard governing one aspect of development may well accompany a somewhat lower standard for other aspects.

While the Massachusetts analysis indicates that lot costs do not rise linearly with lot size, the range of lot sizes considered may well have little relevance to families purchasing modest homes. There are reasons to believe that as lot size increases from 6,000 to 10,000 square feet, costs rise more rapidly per 1,000 square feet than in the range above 10,000 square feet.

According to a study in Minneapolis and St. Paul in 1962, development costs for a lot measuring 7,200 (60 × 120) square feet averaged $2,873 compared to $3,335 for a 10,800 (80 × 135) square foot lot and $4,059 for a 15,000 (100 × 150) square foot lot. (113) Increasing the smallest lot size by 3,600 square feet raises total costs only $462 or $128 per additional 1,000 square feet. The difference of $724 between the middle-sized and the large lot represents only $172 per 1,000 additional square feet. The cost increments with size are modest compared to the homeowner's total investment in land and improvements. Requiring families to purchase 1,000 square feet more than they desire would represent only about one percent of the total costs of a typical house priced at $15,000.

Zoning ordinances specifying large lot size minima tend to force buyers out of the market, but the aggregate demand for land depends on the elasticities of supply and demand schedules. Lot size minima also favor development of more peripheral, less expensive land. As development disperses, the costs of commuting rise. Therefore, with a traditionally strong appetite for land, it is likely that minima contribute to rising costs of land and transportation. Although lack of empirical data prevents precise conclusions on any of these issues, it seems reasonable to conclude that a considerable gap exists between the intent of the ordinances and the realities of the market.

The large variety of lot sizes preferred by the public is revealed in research published recently by the Survey Research Center at the University of Michigan. (65) The study indicates that lot sizes in single-family homes have been rising gradually. Sizes for houses built prior to 1940 were generally less than one-fifth of an acre whereas, since 1940, lots on the average approximated one-fifth of an acre or more. Since space demands tend to increase with family income, it cannot be inferred that increasing lot sizes are associated with stricter standards alone. On the contrary, these increases probably reflect demand for more land by those with higher incomes. Generally, more people feel that their lots are too small rather than too large. This is not unexpected since budgetary constraints prevent people from purchasing the preferred amount of land. It is worthy of note, however, that the ideal lot size is not very large and ranges somewhere between 3/10 and 5/10 of an acre. The chief objection from those who feel their lot is too large is the amount of maintenance required; whereas those who feel they are too small express more diverse reasoning related to space and privacy. Given an upper limit to desired lot size, zoning ordinances must continually be studied to determine how closely they match the public's preference.

4. Summary. In light of the variations in zoning regulations of different communities it is impossible to apply the conclusions to the whole nation. Moreover, these ordinances are continually in revision and, on the whole, appear to have become more strict over time. These changes partially reflect the preferences of community leaders who are convinced that the ordinances will accomplish certain desired objectives. In many cases, since the standards set are those which would be met in the market anyhow, the ordinance involves no constraint of the private decision. In other cases, the ordinances reflect either mistaken notions of general welfare or conflicts between adjacent metropolitan communities. Considerations of municipal costs and revenues are of paramount importance in establishing the provisions although, as has been shown repeatedly, optimization in the public sector—too often interpreted narrowly as minimization of public costs—is only one of a number of goals to be attained. (71) The criterion that zoning must enhance the development of land uses with a high tax revenue potential (placing limited demand for services on the community) is subject to criticism, particularly when combined with preconceived notions as to which land uses are desirable and which are not. In the process, the goals of the metropolitan area, the region, and the nation are sacrificed to home rule.

Finally, one of the fundamental assumptions of zoning and other land use controls is that homes are protected against external diseconomies generated by other land uses. This assumption is based on the premise that nonresidential land uses should bear responsibility for, and costs of, actual or perceived deleterious effects to single-family homes. The premise ignores the fact that homeowners are also workers in offices and factories or employers of others who might live in apartment housing. By reducing or eliminating the deleterious effects on single-family homes, inefficiencies in production or location may be created which eventually affect homeowners. Thus, the costs of zoning should not be calculated in terms of direct housing costs alone, as it may take the form of higher costs for other goods and services.

Building and Related Codes

1. Contrasts to other factors. A major difference between zoning and building codes is that uniformity applies in the former only to specific districts; whereas in the latter the ordinances apply to the community as a whole. The producer or consumer who finds that a zoning ordinance requires him to develop or purchase more land than he wishes has the opportunity of moving either to a less restricted zone or, within a particular zone, to areas where land costs are lower. But building codes involving costly features cannot as easily be avoided. The only escape is either to move to another area where the production of new housing is less constrained, to economize on other features of the home, or not to build at all.

In principle, codes share the objectives of zoning ordinances. Both seek to improve the general welfare of the community. In contrast to zoning, however, greater emphasis is placed on protection of occupants against potential hazards of the property. Zoning emphasizes the externalities associated with the property or its occupants and their effect on the community. But by specifying that materials must meet certain standards, codes attempt to protect the occupant, the passer-by, and the neighboring property and its occupants from the possibility that the building will collapse or catch fire. Certainly, such considerations are also present in zoning, but the variation in standards by districts is evidence that protection of neighbors is the crucial difference. Thus, it would be difficult to convince a property owner that, for his own good, the home he intends to build should be set back from the sidewalks, when he knows that in high density apartment areas this provision does not apply.

Moreover, the public interest which prompts the controls on building involves more tangible issues than does zoning. The damage to people and property when a building collapses or burns can be assessed with some precision. The experiences of the past provide guidelines for a continual reevaluation and revision of building codes. This tends to make the building codes sound more reasonable than the zoning ordinances. To illustrate, the public more readily accepts regulations constraining the use of certain materials in buildings in areas with high fire hazards than regulations which limit densities.

Moreover, a degree of reciprocity is present in building codes which appears to be lacking in zoning ordinances. Because a strong building code applies to all buildings, a property owner feels protected from the hazards of neighboring properties, just as his neighbors are protected from him. This, of course, assumes that building codes do not discriminate between types of properties. In many cases this assumption is invalid. A code which is archaic in its provisions for multifamily units but not for single-family homes will encourage low density investment, since it will be relatively cheaper to build homes than apartments.

The building codes assume that the general public, when it purchases or rents housing, is not technically trained to evaluate potential dangers to health and safety. Thus, codes protect the public from its own ignorance. The assumption has merit, but even with building codes and building inspection during the course of construction, faults appear which impose costs on owners and occupants. It is equally correct to say that building codes as a form of risk transfer preclude the opportunity for self-insurance by owners and occupants. In other words, leaving aside questions of externalities, building codes often incorporate standards to obviate those events which have a low probability of occurrence. But owners might prefer either to assume such risks themselves or to insure against them. A sharp divergence could exist between the higher costs of constructing buildings according to the codes to meet a specific risk and the lower costs of insuring. If costs of compliance with a building code exceed costs of insurance, the building code may be considered unduly restrictive. Thus, codes share the weaknesses of other regulations in that their uniform application prohibits certain transactions in the market which would bring consumers closer to optimality, as they perceive it. As such, they inhibit resource redistribution and restrict consumer sovereignty.

In another sense, building codes may substitute for insurance. Higher insurance rates are likely to be charged in areas where building codes are less restrictive. Thus, the higher construction costs of conforming to tighter codes may be compensated by lower insurance costs over the long run. In reality, little faith can be placed in this argument. The National Board of Fire Underwriters grades cities and towns by assigning deficiency points up to a limit of 5,000. A maximum of 200 points, or only 4 percent of the total, are assignable to "building laws." With ten risk classes, holding other things constant, a city with poor building codes at worst could be rated one class lower. (72) The rating scheme indicates that fire insurers are much more concerned with the quality of the water supply and the fire department. Consequently, the relative weights in the fire rating scheme suggest that code quality is a poor risk substitute for fire insurance, but that the quality of those public services affecting fire riskiness are rather good substitutes for codes. At the margin, then, the costs associated with strengthening codes to reduce fire risks must be considered in light of the alternative cost of strengthening other community services which have similar goals.

Building codes applied to new construction may be regarded analogously as a form of preventive medicine; whereas fire protection has both curative as well as preventive characteristics. Society continually must choose between measures which reduce the risk of occurrence of a disastrous event and measures for dealing with the event should it occur. At the extremes, the choice might be between constructing fireproof structures and placing a fire engine in front of every house. Both extremes are patently absurd. However, in allocating resources between prevention and cure, considerations of whether costs appear in private or public accounts are largely irrelevant. The relevant consideration is the relation between imputed gains and imputed losses from each possible course of action. The question of whether gains or losses are public or private is not so much a matter of efficiency, but one of resource redistribution.

Clearly, building codes involve sacrifices of consumer sovereignty. They frequently provide little opportunity for deferring costs to the post-construction period. By improving construction quality, building codes require capital costs today which otherwise would be paid tomorrow for repairs, replacement, insurance, fire protection, and so on. This is not to suggest that consumers would always prefer to defer costs to the future, but to indicate that building codes limit choice and in the process may impose costs which are not directly or immediately measurable.

Externalities apply to building codes as well as to zoning but with less force. In theory, codes are designed to protect passers-by, neighbors, and occupants other than owners from the hazards of unsafe and unsound construction. The imperfection of building codes as instruments for attaining this goal is illustrated by the fact that property owners usually carry insurance against liability. Little heed is paid to the real possibility that high standards of construction inhibit investment in new buildings. If codes raise costs, then some producers and investors leave the market. Which is the more serious problem, reducing hazards to others, or increasing the volume of new housing? To argue that these are not alternatives and that housing production can be expanded as buildings standards are raised violates the principle of limited resources. In the long run, progress can be made on both fronts; but, over shorter periods, priorities are necessary. Moreover, the higher costs of tighter codes burden not only producers and consumers, but also those forced out of the market. Costs in the form of reduced housing consumption and related side-effects could well exceed the costs of a slight increase in risk to neighbors, passers-by, and occupants, if the provision of codes were relaxed.

Much of the discussion of building codes circumvents the issue of resource allocation and ignores budget constraints. It is generally assumed that, should codes raise supply costs, consumers must pay more for housing. However, unless the cost impact is so small that, when spread over the life of the investment, it becomes infinitesimal, aggregate housing investment will be reduced. Furthermore, those remaining in the housing market will seek means to cut costs within the limits of the code, for example, by reducing their space consumption. Moreover, housing costs increase relatively to other types of goods and services. With limited incomes, consumers will shift preferences. In raising standards for new construction, the relative attractiveness of older homes increases, thus slowing up the rate of removal of old structures from the inventory and reducing the average quality of the stock. These propositions relate to the full spectrum of institutional or other impediments, as well as building codes, which tend to raise costs of new housing. It is with building codes, however, that the cost effects are most prominent, if indeed it is true that they are restrictive and raise costs substantially.

2. Cost implications. The arguments of those who have examined building codes and found them to be restrictive take several forms. It is contended that, by not permitting the utilization of the most advanced technical knowledge in construction, codes unnecessarily raise input costs which are passed on to consumers. Building inspection requirements limit the opportunities for prefabrication, a process which applies mass production methods. Lack of uniformity among localities inhibits scale economies and reduces competition, since some entrepreneurs hesitate to enter local markets with unfamiliar codes.

The theme of these arguments is that the provisions and administration of the codes are wasteful of resources. The premise underlying this statement is that code provisions are in fact enforced. However, this is not always true. Reference to the code alone is not *prima facie* evidence that the marketplace is burdened. A study of Portland, Maine, emphasizes the point: "The elements which distinguish Portland from the surrounding communities and 'competing' cities, and which may, in some cases, increase costs, are the enforcement and administration of the code. Portland enforces its code; many other communities do not." (68)

One possible inference to be drawn is that opposition and criticism of codes arises primarily when code officials go by the book. Also, lack of knowledge about enforcement places obstacles in the way of accurately assessing cost impacts. However, this reservation has not inhibited studies seeking estimates of cost effects.

From his in-depth study of housebuilding in the San Francisco Bay Area, Maisel concludes, "In summary, in houses built in the localities where the uniform codes applied without changes—

Table 3. Material and Construction Techniques Prohibited by Local Codes

Percent of Localities Prohibiting	Material and Construction Method
62	2 × 4 studs on 24″ centers for nonbearing partitions
60	Gypsum drywall interior finish on 24″ stud spacing
48	Concrete posts and grade beams as foundation walls
36	⅜″ gypsum drywall interior finish on 16″ stud spacing
27	Elimination of corner bracing when using plywood or fiber board sheathing on 16″ stud spacing
26	Wood roofing material (such as red cedar shingles or shakes)
22	Concrete floor slab-on-grade construction
20	Factory-built chimney and flue lining
15	Roof trusses on 24″ centers

Source: National Association of Home Builders, Building Code Requirement Survey, 2nd Edition (Washington: 1963).

some 33 percent of the total number built in the area—no inefficiency could be charged to the restriction of codes. Fifty percent had their costs raised by less than one percent for the typical house through code alterations. Even in the case of the final 15 to 20 percent, where greater code restrictions were in force, the increased costs did not run more than 3 percent above the uniform code areas." (74, p. 249) The final estimate was that "less than one percent of the money spent for housebuilding was attributable to known code inefficiencies." (74, p. 250) Maisel acknowledged that improvements in national uniform codes might have been made where efficiency would not be assessed.

A round table conference of experts, convened by *House and Home* in 1958, claimed that if ten wasteful practices could be eliminated, at least $1,000 would be saved in the cost of the average house. The savings would amount to $1 billion annually for the nation. (161) The estimate, which ranged between 5 and 7½ percent of total house cost, substantially exceeds that of Maisel. The *House and Home* estimate may be criticized for assuming that the inefficiencies attributable to codes are present in every community. In other words, no consideration appeared to be given to the fact that one or more restrictive provisions might be present, but not necessarily all ten.

A more recent *House and Home* survey of home building technology is less critical of institutional factors. "Contrary to the opinion of many in the home building industry, these traditional whipping boys (building codes and labor practices) are not the most serious barriers to technological progress. The record shows that any innovation that really saves money without impairing quality will be accepted by codes and labor—eventually." (162, pp. 92–93) It is argued that the reasons for the slow change in codes are related to the following items: (a) innovations are costly to incorporate and must produce major benefits before they are accepted by the industry; (b) there exists a general resistance to change, as the whole industry is geared to traditional methods of production; (c) the old building system of wood frame faced with skins on a masonry foundation still is relatively cheap, easy, and flexible.

A survey of builders in the Detroit metropolitan area revealed that variations in building codes affected costs ranging between an average minimum of about 4 percent to an average maximum of about 11 percent. Some estimates were as high as 20 percent. However, the high estimates apparently included noncode constraints such as zoning, building permit fees, and special assessments. It was asserted that "a builder may lump together all these costs, along with those actually arising out of building codes and their enforcement, and may think of the total as the measure of building cost differential produced by local building regulation standards." (95, pp. 10–11) These elements presumably also affected the high estimates of code influence on selling price which ranged between 3.5 and 9 percent.

A recent NAHB study covering 1,200 U.S. communities identifies areas which prohibit certain material and construction techniques (Table 2). Not surprisingly, the study shows that prohibitions are not uniformly distributed. Making some gross assumptions, it is possible to estimate roughly the cost impact of the provisions assumed to be unnecessarily restrictive. First, suppose that the prohibitions are randomly distributed among communities and are not necessarily concentrated in areas with a higher or lower than average proportion of total home building activity. Secondly, assume that labor and material costs are uniform per unit of input and remain unaffected by codes. The added cost of any individual prohibition on a house in which labor and materials amount to $10,000, multiplied by the proportion of communities that have the prohibition, yields an estimate of the average cost added. The existence of all prohibitions would add $600 to $700 to the cost of labor and materials. However, taking into account variations in the relative role of the provisions in the communities, costs on the average would be raised $200 to $300. Since labor and materials represent from 40 to 50 percent of the final price, such a house might sell for $20,000 to $25,000. The results are fairly obvious. On the average, between one and two percent of the housing price is atttributable to restrictive building codes—an average very close to Maisel's estimate. While admittedly crude, the calculations are illustrative. Mechanical codes are other restrictive provisions which should be added to the list.

In addition to building codes many states and localities have promulgated mechanical codes covering items such as plumbing, electrical systems, boilers, and elevators. Also, proprietary mechanical codes have been developed as models which have been adopted widely. The two most prominent examples are the *National Plumbing Code*, jointly sponsored by the American Public Health Association and the American Society of Mechanical Engineers, and the *National Electrical Code* of the American Insurance Association. The NAHB survey of 1965 showed that some versions of the National Plumbing Code and the National Electrical Code ("as is" or with local modifications) applies to 49 and 88 percent, respectively, of the 868 communities studied (89). Relatively few of the communities, however, have adopted these specialized codes without change. In other words, national standards have not entirely resolved the problem of obtaining uniformity.

As with building codes, restrictive provisions for plumbing and electrical systems do not apply to all communities. The cost impact of these provisions, therefore, must be considered by reference to their importance in home building across the nation and the opportunities they provide for achieving savings in residential construction. This can be understood by examining provisions applying to specific types of materials.

NAHB notes, for example, that nearly all communities (86 percent) prohibit the use of plastic pipes. But whether plastic plumbing offers substantial savings in costs appears to be a matter of debate. A brief discussion of the subject in *House and Home*, December 1965, had the following headings: "Plastic plumbing is beginning to gain acceptance, but its price is still too high." (162, p. 102) One of the reasons cited for the high cost was that fittings appeared to be quite expensive; but it was expected that with wider acceptance and higher rates of production costs would be reduced considerably. Also, questions have arisen as to whether chemicals used in solvents for welding such pipes are safe enough to come into contact with water used for human consumption. Eventually, such problems may be resolved, but a blanket indictment of codes which do not permit plastic plumbing at this time would be incorrect in light of some uncertainties relating to health, safety, and cost. The lack of acceptance of plastic plumbing may be partially attributed to fears of new competition by producers of conventional plumbing. Code officials will be under considerable pressure from different directions to revise or not to revise the codes. Their conservatism in this matter must be understood in light of the variety of considerations which influence their behavior and should not be attributed to lack of understanding of the problem.

Among other code provisions which might yield savings, the NAHB suggests the following: (a) 3″ building drain and vent —kitchen, bath back to back (57 percent); (b) omission of drum trap on tub drain (46 percent); (c) bituminized-fiber pipe for house sewer (68 percent); (d) off-site plumbing tree fabrication (44 percent); (e) single stack vent for all traps less than 3′6″ (39 percent); (f) nonmetallic cable (14 percent); and (g) rigid conduit in basement and crawl space (79 percent). The percentages in brackets indicate the proportion of the communities which do not allow these provisions.

By assuming that the provisions are randomly distributed and by taking account of their varying role in communities, costs could be trimmed by $150 to $250, if houses were built in accordance with the recommended changes. Adding these to the estimates of savings for reducing the rigidities in building codes amounts to $350 to $550. Depending on the final selling price, which will be influenced substantially by costs other than building, the estimates represent from 1.5 to 3 percent of the price of an average house.

Eliminating restrictions could imply a decrease in calculated overhead, profit, and financing costs, as well as in costs of production. Even if our estimates were entirely wrong and the cost impact of the restrictive provisions cited were higher than calculated, the conclusion is inescapable. Since certain restrictive building and mechanical code provisions do not apply with equal force to every community, it cannot be said with certainty that substantial savings would accrue by removing unreasonable restrictions. This conclusion leaves aside broader questions relating to the efficiency of codes discussed earlier. Still, much can be gained in efficiency by updating and revising codes. Many communities could be identified where codes limit the construction of low cost housing. (8) This does not change the more general conclusion, however, that removing restrictive provisions *per se* is unlikely to have a substantial bearing on the production of less costly housing for the nation as a whole.

3. Code standardization. It is comparatively easy to identify specific provisions in codes, which, if removed, would conserve construction dollars. However, in examining variations in codes across communities and the implications of lack of uniformity for efficiency, precise magnitudes are difficult to obtain. Competition within industry would be improved by a uniform building code applied to the whole nation with variations reflecting only differences in local conditions, such as climate, fire hazards, earthquake, and public health. Prefabrication and preassembly of component parts also would be facilitated. To the extent that economies of scale are attainable in the industry, firms would grow in size and efficiency. Also, uniformity would avoid the market distortions resulting from the gravitation of the industry to communities with less restrictive ordinances. These are among the potential advantages of a national code.

Several surveys have been made showing the diversity in building codes throughout the United States. Four model codes are used in approximately 58 percent of the communities with a population of 10,000 or more. One estimate suggests that these four codes serve communities with populations totaling one hundred million people and account for 70 percent of all construction in the nation. The *Uniform Building Code* is used in over 400 communities, primarily in California, but covers more than half the states in the nation. The *National Building Code* has been adopted by 337 communities located in 34 states but concentrated in the midwest, the east, and the south. The *Southern Building Code* has been adopted by 196 cities in 13 states with greatest frequency in southern states. The *Basic Building Code* applies in 182 communities in 20 states principally in the East and Midwest. Another 14 percent of the communities have adopted the eight state codes, and 1½ percent have given support to four other uniform codes. Finally, 23 percent of the communities have promulgated independent local codes. (130)

Clearly, particular model codes are favored in certain regions, but judging from the number of states in which the model codes are found, exact boundaries are ambiguous. The four major model codes have much in common, but vary in detail. More important is the fact that when, after proper testing and analysis, a revision in the model code is approved, these changes are not necessarily adopted by the local communities. Also, many communities amend the model codes themselves. Consequently, it would be an error to assume that the adoption of a model code by a community necessarily applies to all of its provisions. This is apart from any variations in interpretation of the code by local building officials or in their enforcement.

Over the years, much thought has been directed to standardizing building codes. Approaches to attain uniformity vary. It has been suggested that one uniform code for the nation be developed by an independent body. Others prefer uniformity to grow out of the coordination of the various model code groups. These efforts have not been universally well received. Some suppliers are concerned that, if one code were to be adopted nationwide, the demand for their goods and services might be curtailed. Municipal bodies fear that local sovereignty, particularly the power to establish building rules, would be sacrificed. Yet, despite the difficulties and conflicts, it seems reasonable to assume that standardization will be realized eventually.

Among the claimed benefits of a widely adopted uniform building code are the following:

1. Elimination of arbitrary restrictions which add unnecessarily to the cost of construction and the price to the buyer.
2. Stimulation of initiative and innovation on the part of material suppliers and builders by reducing the cost and delay involved in securing wide approval.
3. Improvement of the legal climate for codes by relieving inspection officers of conflicting responsibility for the promulgation as well as the enforcement of codes.
4. Assistance to code-promulgation bodies having limited access to technical guidance in resisting the prejudicial influence of self-service voluntary advisors and in securing the benefits of technically sound conclusions embodied in a uniform code.
5. Reduction of the difficulty in combining and harmonizing most advantageous standards originating in different industry groups; these would be brought into proper relationship in a uniform code.
6. Reduction of the cost and the local technical requirements

for maintaining and servicing a code that would be kept abreast of the demands of a modern building industry.
7. Facilitation of the regional training and qualification of local inspectors needed for rational (as distinct from arbitrary) interpretation of a code. (66)

A nationally accepted code would probably encourage innovation. A particular innovation would find a wider market in the future than under present conditions, which stipulate that acceptance be received from the several model code groups, states, and local authorities. If economies are present in large scale production of materials, variation in codes would no longer restrict the breadth of markets. However, the claims may be exaggerated. The responsibilities falling upon a national code promulgation body would be of such substantial magnitude that inertia is certain to result. Costs would never be entirely uniform, as regional differences would have to be taken into consideration. But costs could be reduced, since analysis, interpretation, and diffusion of technical information would tend to be more organized.

Uniform codes would remove many existing constraints on the production and prefabrication of off-site component parts, processes in which mass production techniques necessitate uniformity in standards. Even if long distance transportation costs of component and prefabricated units reduced the competitive advantage from mass production, uniformity of codes at local or regional levels would still be beneficial. The question is whether a uniform national code is necessary to achieve uniformity in codes at these levels.

Bulky components and prefabricated units produced on a massive scale at central points may be less costly, but they are still subject to high transportation costs over long distances. Thus, a national code would not necessarily be accompanied by mass production of components and prefabricated units in a few places. Yet, it could reduce the need for local inspection. With national standards, inspection and certification might be undertaken at the production points rather than at construction sites, thus avoiding situations where components or prefabricated units must be disassembled for inspection after they have been shipped from central production points.

Apart from transportation costs, the variability of the construction cycle militates against mass off-site production of parts and units. With enormous fluctuations in demand, manufacturers are reluctant to invest heavily in fixed plants and in equipment by which true scale economies are obtained. Unless greater stability in homebuilding is realized, it is difficult to see how a nationally uniform code could alone encourage mass production methods which are common in industries where demand is less volatile. This element is frequently forgotten by those who point to other nations where greater progress appears to have been made in prefabrication techniques. (177) The costs of gearing up for high volume production and the attendant risk that this volume cannot be stabilized probably is as serious a barrier to mass production as the heterogeneity of codes. This is not to suggest that uniformity is undesirable or unnecessary, but rather to indicate that uniformity in codes alone is not the magic wand to suddenly transform homebuilding into a highly efficient industry.

Housing Codes

1. Scope. Housing codes provide for prevention as well as cure. They establish standards in housing which must be met in order to conserve housing quality. More often, however, they are used as a means of rejuvenating housing and neighborhoods and of inducing rehabilitation or the removal of blighted units from the inventory. As a consequence, they may be viewed as one of several tools for renewing our cities. Through code enforcement programs, an effort is made to improve the quality of the housing inventory as well as of ancillary facilities. Usually, programs of code enforcement are combined with related activities, as for example, financial and other assistance to owners for upgrading properties and improvement of public facilities.

The very fact that special programs of code enforcement are implemented indicates that conservation and rehabilitation of existing housing is not always undertaken on a sustained basis, and that regulations tend to be spotty. Guandalo, looking at the problem some years ago, expressed this idea in the following manner: "The effectiveness of a housing code depends upon its contents and its enforcement. A housing code with adequate standards must be implemented with firm and vigorous enforcement to insure proper results. In many cities, the enforcement of housing codes has been inadequate and fraught with difficulties. Typical of the enforcement problems are the lack of sufficient staff and funds." (156)

Comprehensive housing codes bringing together under one ordinance the variety of measures regulating the standing stock of housing have been promulgated in larger cities. Model housing codes have also found wide acceptance. However, the large number of communities without comprehensive housing codes either regulate housing by reference to other codes or do not regulate at all, except in response to complaints. Roughly estimated, perhaps up to one-third of the population in communities with building codes also is covered by housing codes.

2. Cost implications. Since housing codes most likely affect properties which are actually substandard or which are in the process of becoming substandard, the provisions usually apply to low rent or low priced housing. Housing codes are thus selective. Some have suggested that they be revised and, as is the case with zoning, be geared to standards in particular neighborhoods. Since they mainly affect the lower income groups which have few or no housing alternatives available, codes may raise housing quality at the expense of imposing burdens on the populations least able to bear them. If a code enforcement program seeks to upgrade a whole neighborhood, it is likely to cause old housing units to be demolished and replaced by new units with higher rents. While the goal is rehabilitation, the actual effect is rebuilding and reduction of the stock of low rent or low priced housing. With a reduced supply, rents and prices tend to rise disproportionately for the lower income groups.

If redevelopment is not a practical alternative for property owners who see little opportunity for raising rents by refurbishing their structures, housing code enforcement may still be an effective tool for raising housing quality. The alternatives to abiding by the codes are closing the building, or demolishing it and earning no rents at all. A reduced income will be preferred by property owners to no income. If, as has been contended at various times, large profits are earned from dilapidated slum properties, the effect of code enforcement may be borne largely by landlords. Grigsby has stated forcefully, "Continuous compliance with local codes would in most cases probably reduce values by forcing up expenditures without altering expected or current revenues." (47, p. 310) Grigsby grants, however, that the duration of the income stream of landlords might be lengthened, but believes that in most cases this is improbable. In situations where landlords cannot shift costs to tenants, the cost impact on renters is of course minimal. Where owners are also occupants, the costs cannot be shifted except at the time of sale when they may be capitalized into value.

Housing codes, like other types of codes and ordinances, raise the complex problem of separating those cost inducing provisions which increase value and quality from other provisions which are wasteful and add nothing to utility. Many of the restrictive practices are not embodied in the housing codes themselves but must be sought in other codes which apply when components of existing structures are repaired, altered, or replaced. Enforcement procedures will determine the size of investment required to refurbish the dwelling, and considerable debate will center on the level of housing quality to be achieved—the minimum standard expressed in the housing code, a standard established by a renewal plan or some other standard. (83) Given the possibility that costs resulting from code enforcement, whether restrictive or not, may or may not be passed on to tenants, the impact on housing costs is not at all clear. We incline to the position, however, that housing code enforcement tends to be relatively flexible in its standards. It seems reasonable to assume, therefore, the restrictive character of the codes is less an issue than the more general problem of whether owners or occupants can carry the cost of repair and replacement.

If the housing codes and inspectors tend to emphasize replacement rather than repair, the costs of rehabilitation will increase considerably. Specificity on these points is often lacking in the codes and their enforcement procedures. As a result, the costs incurred by property owners will be determined by individual inspectors, and not necessarily by widely accepted standards. (83)

Because many courts and enforcement officers are concerned with the impact of their actions on the supply of housing for low income groups, they are often reluctant to press for the elimination of code violations. Penalties for violations are often light. Because of these factors, housing codes rarely influence housing costs substantially, except perhaps for groups at the bottom of the housing market.

Subdivision Regulations. Subdivision regulations are closely linked to zoning ordinances and building codes, although their historical antecedents differ somewhat. (27, 48) Their origins are traceable to the power of communities and states to develop public rights-of-way. The power to regulate private developments with streets and roads which eventually would be dedicated to the community and become public highways or roads, represented a logical extension of the communities' power to purchase land for the same purpose. In contrast to comprehensive zoning based on a general plan with use districts designated well in advance of development, subdivision regulations concern "the growth of particular sites by prohibiting the subdivision of land until the plan of such subdivision was approved and, ordinarily, recorded." (27, p. 189) Zoning ordinances have been adapted in many communities to make provision for planned residential unit developments, which often imply mixing land uses. In the process, zoning and subdivision regulations have come much closer together. Dissatisfaction with uniform district zoning has led to "flexible zoning" and the control of development of land use and activities at particular sites similar to subdivision regulations.

1. Contrasts to other factors. Compared to zoning, subdivision regulations appear to be more sensitive to external economies and diseconomies, and who will bear them. (48, pp. 190–192) This may result in part from the fact that subdivision regulations, unless reasonable, can and have been interpreted as a form of compulsory taking of the land without proper compensation. In zoning, where the costs and benefits are much more uncertain, the tendency has been to bow in the direction of the "community interest" even when this interest has proven to be exceedingly narrow. As Haar has stated, "With respect to subdivision controls, this appears to mean that the conditions imposed should be justifiable by some approximation to a calculus of social costing." (48, p. 191) He is quick to point out, however, that broader questions may also enter into the interpretations.

From the economic point of view, concern with allocation and imputation of costs and benefits in subdivisions probably has prevented some excesses in the power to regulate, although the criteria of efficiency which guide the decision-making process are not necessarily appropriate. As one might expect, conflicts between new residential subdivisions and the rest of the community center on questions of cost allocation. For instance, which costs are attributable to the subdivision and which are chargeable to the municipality? This conflict has touched off a tug-of-war between the interested parties. For example, the requirement to reserve land for a park in a subdivision poses questions as to whether benefits accrue only to the occupants of the project, to the larger society, or to both, as well as to who should pay for it. The answers reflect the ease with which the costs and benefits can be measured, in contrast to zoning where effects are elusive and difficult to measure. A requirement to reserve land might involve partial compensation to the developer by the community. Charging either the subdivider or the occupants with the full cost of a public park would probably represent an external economy to the larger community; yet, if it were totally charged to the larger community, it would be an external diseconomy. As has been shown earlier, the criterion should not be to eliminate externalities but to optimize social product.

In some respects, the economic effects of subdivision regulations approximate those of zoning regulations. In other respects, they are closer to building codes. The requirement for wider streets, for example, in turn requires more land to achieve a given level of lot production. If the regulations are burdensome and raise costs, subdividers will shift to less accessible areas where land costs are lower and, in the process, increase occupants' transportation costs. However, sensitivity to transport cost increases may be less than to higher costs of land and housing. This effect or "trade-off" approximates that of zoning. Alternatively, requirements specifying the quality and type of street surfacing would apply regardless of where the subdivision is located in the community. In this case costs could not be reduced by shifting to cheaper land. These provisions are more akin to building codes. An ordinance increasing street widths has a dual impact on costs. The amount of land available for housing on a given site decreases and, since the streets presumably must be surfaced, the input costs to attain the specified width rise. However, right-of-way requirements may vary in relation to area of streets, sidewalks, and gutters—which also must be surfaced.

2. Standardization. There is little agreement on the appropriate width for streets in subdivisions. The problem is far from trivial, since streets absorb anywhere from 25 to 35 percent of the area of a subdivision. Excessive street requirements are wasteful of land and other resources. The variability in specifying street widths suggests resource waste. In reviewing the subject some years ago, the Housing and Home Finance Agency had this to say: "There are no uniform right-of-way widths and street cross sections equally applicable to all urban, suburban, and rural communities. Each community should consider this problem of street width standards from the point of view of its own experience and local conditions. However, 80 to 120 feet may be considered reasonable for arterial streets, and 60 feet for collector streets, 60 feet for minor streets for row houses and apartments, 50 feet for minor streets for other residences, and 40 feet for marginal access streets." (54)

A recent survey of subdivision ordinances in 33 cities and four counties in the Puget Sound region disclosed extraordinary variations in local street regulations. (28) For major arterials and highways, the minimum right-of-way ranged from 60 to 100 feet. Forty-eight percent of the areas imposed a standard of 80 feet and another 32 percent had a minimum of 100 feet. For collector streets, right-of-way minima varied between 50 and 80 feet with a mode of 60 feet applying in roughly one-half of the communities. For access streets, the most frequently used standard was 60 feet, but the minimum varied from 40 to 60 feet. Some of the communities established standards for streets by reference to a general plan; some stated a minimum for any street to be built which might be increased subject to study by the various authorities; and some used other methods. Without more information on unique local conditions one cannot argue that the most stringent provisions are unduly restrictive. However, the pronounced lack of uniformity in classification and definition of streets which apparently existed appeared to create some hardships.

In view of the diversity in regulatory provisions prevailing in one region alone, it seems safe to assume that lack of uniformity, with resultant waste of resources, characterizes subdivision ordinances throughout the nation. Moreover, there is surprisingly little agreement on what the appropriate standards should be. For example, many planners and traffic engineers would grant that a right-of-way of about 50 feet is adequate for access streets in single-family residential neighborhoods, but would probably prefer 60 feet as the mode. Homebuilders have taken the position that a 50-foot width is appropriate in these areas. (87) But, it has also been argued that a 26-foot width of the street pavement is adequate in single-family areas. A survey by the League of Wisconsin Municipalities showed that "only 21 percent of the cities studied required roadways of less than 30 feet; 41 percent required 30 feet; and 38 percent required widths above this figure." (87) According to the Puget Sound survey, space requirements for paving access streets ranged from 24 to 36 feet (excluding parking lanes) with a mode of 28 feet.

The National Association of Home Builders suggests that excessive standards in roadways result from,

1. A lack of understanding of, or sympathy with, modern subdivision design wherein street location, alignment, and widths are designed with relation to the use to which they are put, and the character and extent of the abutting land uses which they serve.
2. Adherence to the obsolete theory that every street should be designed to become a traffic street eventually—"just in case."
3. Insistence on the continuous alignment and continuity of minor streets as well as major thoroughfares.
4. Lack of recognition of the effect which the provision for off-street parking (in the form of individual drives and similar facilities) has on the width needed for local access. (87)

The NAHB also calls attention to another cost of excessive widths, namely the continuing cost of repairs, maintenance, and resurfacing, which ranges from 38 to 54 percent higher than needed. Thus the consequences of street width provisions, which are excessive, bear directly on total land requirements for housing, the costs of building streets, and finally, on future maintenance and repair. Clearly, the amount of land allocated for streets is also a function of the frontage requirements usually spelled out in zoning ordinances and the permissible lengths of blocks. High minimum requirements for frontages and prohibitions against reasonably long blocks will add considerably to the costs of streets and utilities.

3. Cost implications. Given the diversity and interdependence of the regulatory devices applying to subdivisions, the cost effects of excessively strict provisions are difficult to identify. However, Kelly notes that in subdivisions "typical extra cost per lot of $1,500 might include $600 for concrete streets, $400 for lots an extra 10 feet in width, and $500 for curbs, sidewalks, and storm sewers." (61, p. 326) These estimates were prepared in 1958 and might easily have doubled in size over the intervening years.

An incisive analysis supported by the Urban Land Institute (ULI) offers some important insights into the cost effects of varying subdivision regulations and zoning. (92) These regulations influence both the theoretical maximum number of lots per acre as well as the costs of improving the lots.

Lot size emerges as the single important determinant of lot yield per acre. With 60′ × 125′ (7,500 sq. ft.) lots, block lengths of 1,200 feet, and interior and collector streets with rights-of-way of 50 and 60 feet respectively, the maximum lot yield per acre is 4.61. Reducing lot size to 50′ × 120′ (6,000 sq. ft.), increases the lot yield per acre to 5.72. If lot size remained 7,500 sq. ft., but frontage requirements were increased from 60′ to 70′, lot yield per acre would decrease from 4.61 to 4.46, a decline of slightly over 3 percent. Larger frontage, therefore, does not increase land consumption substantially in order to produce the same number of lots. However, the implications for lot improvement costs are more substantial since the area in streets serving the lots is now greater.

Based on certain assumptions about unit cost lot improvement and standards, the ULI estimates total cost of a 60′ × 125′ lot at $1,065. Raising frontages to 70′ and maintaining lot size adds about $155 or 15 percent to the cost of improvement. If we consider also the cost of raw land and assume that an acre could be purchased for $5,000, the imputed final lot costs rise from $2,150 to $2,340, an increase of approximately 9 percent attributable solely to increased frontage.

If the length of blocks is reduced from 1,200 to 600 feet and other elements are held constant, the final lot costs rise from $2,150 to $2,453 or about 14 percent. Similarly, if standards for the quality of street pavements are increased from a two-inch rock and oil, four-inch base (assumed in the illustration) to six inches, cement concrete increases lot costs by $237 or 16 percent.

The study reveals a number of other features which, if standards were made more rigorous, would reduce lot yield per acre and/or increase improvement costs. Increasing pavement width on interior streets from 50 to 60 feet would decrease maximum lot yield 3 percent. Depending on the type and quality of street pavement in front of a 60′ × 125′ lot, an increase of one foot in street pavement width would add anywhere from $6 to $15 to the costs per lot. Similar kinds of calculations can be made for standards for curbs and gutters, alleys, sidewalks, manholes, utilities, and other such items. Clearly, standards profoundly affect land and lot costs. While this analysis does not determine which of the standards are excessive or simply wasteful of resources, it indicates that standards must continually be examined in terms of their cost impact. Generalizations, however, are difficult, since topography and the shape of the land parcels to be subdivided, among other things, also affect both the attainment of high lot yields per acre and the costs of improving the lots.

That subdivision costs have indeed risen sharply is illustrated in a study of the San Francisco Bay Area. (73) FHA lot costs nearly tripled between 1950 and 1962, rising from $1,300 to $3,850. Approximately $720 of the increase could be attributed to the cost and quality of development. In other words, holding constant lot size and raw land costs, lot costs would still have risen by about 55 percent in this period due to the increased costs of preparing land for development. Construction costs increased more modestly during these years, and there is more than a strong assumption that rising community standards contributed to higher subdivision costs—unless one assumes the changes were determined primarily by consumers' desires for better quality land developments.

Knowledge that subdivision costs have risen disproportionately in relation to other prices, as is also the case for building and raw land costs, does not solve the problem of identifying the influence of restrictive and unnecessary provisions. A case study by the NAHB is illustrative. In a particular subdivision, the costs of improving the land (including labor and materials, taxes, overhead, and interest, but excluding raw land acquisition costs) was estimated at approximately $185,000. The local jurisdiction proposed adding three specifications:

1. fire hydrants placed every 300 feet, whereas previously specification called for spacing from 900 to 1,200 feet;
2. enameled street signs on steel posts embedded in concrete; and
3. a resurvey of the lots after completion of the houses, with steel pins placed on all lot corners.

These items would sum to additional costs of $8,000, or 3.5 percent, for each of the 121 lots. Expressed as a percentage of the proposed selling price of the houses, the cost increment would represent slightly over ½ of 1 percent.

Of course, imposition of the additional specifications may be regarded as appropriate and modest with only a minor impact on final house prices. However, if one reflects that these provisions represent only a few of a multitude of standards which have increased steadily in number over the last few years, then the scope of the problem is placed in perspective. In the example cited, if street signs had not been included at the time of subdividing, occupants of the homes might have requested them from the jurisdiction later, causing the costs to be diffused throughout the community. However, many of the standards in subdivisions shape the patterns on the land for years to come, and adjustments cannot be made without incurring extraordinary expense. What may appear to be an excessive requirement for the width of rights-of-way if families own one auto might be inadequate for families with two or more cars. The standards, therefore, must be examined not only in light of present conditions, but also in relation to future prospects. Again, today's capital costs may be lower than the present values of tomorrow's.

4. Effects on innovation. One means by which developers have sought to deal with rising costs and standards is to get away from conventional subdivisions with freestanding houses on their own lots fronting on streets. The grouping or clustering of houses, townhouse schemes, and other advanced types of design programs achieve considerable savings in land and subdivision costs and in the final prices for homes. Generally, these schemes tend to increase the density of population and dwellings per acre. At perhaps some slight sacrifice in livability immediately around the home itself, planned unit developments, as they are frequently called, offer many amenities by increasing land in common space over that available in the conventional subdivision. Since technical discussions on subdivision costs usually compare a conventional, low-density subdivision with higher-density cluster or group housing, no accurate estimates of the cost impact can be made. (120, 88) Perhaps savings in development costs can be obtained by clustering and increasing common space, as contrasted to traditional lotting without changing density. But the evidence is not entirely clear. Should greater efficiency be possible, then it will be pertinent to ask if local subdivision or zoning ordinances allow for modern design. Certainly, ordinances which do not permit some of the new design techniques should be reexamined.

In this consideration of more common space in housing projects, the incidence of benefits and costs comes to the forefront again. If common areas paid for by residents are open to the public, external diseconomies are created for residents and external economies created for the rest of the community. Permission for clustering or group housing, therefore, might not necessarily present any advantages to the project residents. This is not to deny that cluster or group housing may generate amenities not present in the conventional subdivision. However, this is a different matter which, if pursued, would lead to the slippery topic of consumer preferences.

Few American communities point with pride at the shotgun subdivisions of yesterday which blight many of our cities. Large numbers of 20-foot frontage lots developed during a time when subdivision and zoning regulations were weak or lacking, and when the automobile was less important, remain to impede land use succession. Most agree that greater foresight on the part of developers and the community might have prevented the problems these subdivisions present today. What may be regarded as restrictive standards in the present market on the one hand can also be viewed as investment in the future. It is equally true that investments which primarily benefit future generations must be undertaken at the expense of the present generation. If subdivision and other standards in land development are excessively high in order to provide for the future, then housing consumption today will be curtailed. The trade-off between current and future consumption is clearly relevant and provides a research subject pregnant with policy implications.

Weighing the benefits to the public in both the short and long run against the capital costs to land developers and consumers is a key problem in setting minimum standards. One authority states categorically that "It has been found that compliance with minimum standards with respect to street grading and the installation of water mains and sanitary sewers often may increase the total home cost as much as 20 percent." (11) If correct, the social goal of building low cost housing may not be realized. Which is the greater loss: low cost construction today, or high quality subdivisions which will stand the test of time? Recent experiences suggest that these goals conflict and that to believe both can be attained simultaneously is patently naive.

Property Taxes

1. Magnitude. Few governments today expend tax revenues solely for the carrying out of regulatory or housekeeping functions. A multitude of other purposes are served by taxes in general and by property taxes in particular. Among them are wealth redistribution and the public provision of services at costs lower than they can be provided privately. The property tax, as the single most important source of revenue for local governments, finances educational services, police and fire protection, public housing, sewage and sanitation services, welfare services and poverty programs, and a host of other municipal programs. Yet the taxpayer most likely sees taxes as a burden devoid of benefit. As Morton notes, "The burden of the tax is offset by many benefits to the community necessary and desirable to enhance the well-being of its citizens. To consider a tax merely as a cost without regard to the good that it provides is so partial and prejudicial that it might bring harmful results, such as the oft-recurring demand for tax reduction heedless of its consequences to municipal finance." (86, p. 74) Consequently, to argue, as others have, that taxes lower consumption levels and reduce the value of property by reducing its earnings is not wholly correct. For example, with particular reference to the low-income population,

> First, taxes raise the cost of housing to the occupants and simply put a significant part of the existing housing stock beyond the reach of many in the low-income population. For example, take a large urban family with an income of $4,000. The maximum tolerable rent for such a family . . . might be said to be 30 percent of income, or $100 a month. Assume that the prevailing level of property taxes is 25 percent of rents in that city. Were property taxes on housing eliminated, this family could afford to rent an apartment now renting for $133 a month, without exceeding the 30 percent rent/income ratio, an apartment which is now out of reach. Second, high property taxes discourage consumption of and investment in housing in general, by the entire population. There is ample evidence that consumers will buy more and better housing if its price is lower, just as they do with regard to most other objects of consumption. (173, p. 122)

Critics of the tax are wont to assume that nonproperty tax sources can be substituted to pay for the services now provided by property tax revenues. So long as there is a parity between the cost of public services rendered to property and the cost of those services paid through the property tax, the effect on property values is likely to be neutral. If a given quality of services is provided by the public sector at lower cost because of economies of large scale, the property owner gets more for his tax dollar than if he procured the same services privately. Given balanced municipal budgets, plus the fact that services must be supplied in a given quantity or quality, other tax sources—for example, taxes on income—must be found as substitutes. True, the burden then falls on income in general rather than on housing, but the householder's welfare remains the same as before. Implicit in this reasoning is the efficient provision of services. To the extent that inefficiency exists—the whole tax dollar is not returned to the taxpayer in the form of services—the tax represents resource waste. Determining the magnitude of this waste would clearly involve estimates of governmental efficiency—a courageous undertaking, but one outside our scope.

Property tax revenues to local governments amount to $25 billion annually. (173, p. 123) In some cities, the property tax is not only the major source of revenue but the near-exclusive source; as it is, for example, in Milwaukee, Boston, Minneapolis, St. Paul, Indianapolis, Newark, and cities in Texas. (173, p. 128) Increases in property taxes provided nearly half of the increase in general revenues of state and local government, and nearly all of the increase in local government revenues, between 1953 and 1963. In absolutes, property tax revenues more than doubled in amount during this recent decade. Per capita collections grew from $8.92 in 1902 to more than $100 in 1962, an average annual growth rate of about 4 percent over the 60-year period. However, relative to Gross National Product, collections are the same today as they were a half century ago, though less than they were during the 1920s and 1930s. In 1913, state and local property taxes were 3.3 percent of GNP; in 1962, 3.4 percent. In 1922 and 1932, the fractions were 4.5 and 7.7 percent respectively. (184, Table 1)

Property taxes account for a substantial share of housing expenditures. Taxes amounted to 17 percent of actual before-tax cash outlays for housing in 1960. However, the variation among regions was substantial. The fractions ranged from a low of 10 percent in the South to 24 percent in the Northeast. (173, pp. 118–19) The magnitude of these variations is even more surprising when one recalls that housing, like food, is generally regarded as one of the basics of life. In this respect, Netzer observes, "It is simply inconceivable that, if we were starting to develop a tax system from scratch, we would single out housing for extraordinarily high levels of consumption taxation. More likely, we would exempt housing entirely from taxation, just as many states exempt food from the sales tax." (173, p. 121)

How can property taxes be lowered? The answer is easy if one accepts total substitution of nonproperty bases for taxation, thus shifting the tax burden from housing in whole or in part. Workable alternatives include full Federal financing of local public services (particularly of poverty-linked services, as Netzer suggests, 173, p. 129), Federal general purpose grants, greater reliance on user charges for services which are suited to this type of pricing, or, obviously, increased reliance on non-property revenue sources such as municipal income and sales taxes. Netzer alleges that these devices, if made operational, could reduce property taxes in large central cities by over one-half. (173, p. 129)

Each alternative to the property tax still represents a burden on family incomes. Conceivably, the decrease in property tax burden would be offset by an increase in nonproperty taxes. The relevant question is a modification of that posed originally: how can property taxes be reduced without also reducing welfare levels or levels of local public services?

Accepting the conventional wisdom, we may assume that non-property sources could be tapped to relieve the burden on property, keeping in mind that no effect on welfare is calculated. An example developed by Netzer serves as a base: "In 1964–65, the 42 largest city governments other than New York obtained 33 percent of their tax revenues from non-property taxes. For the city of Los Angeles, the figure was 44 percent; if all 42 cities matched the Los Angeles proportion, their property taxes could have been reduced by nearly one-eighth." (173, p. 128) Under Netzer's proposal, taxes would drop from their current level of 17 percent of actual housing expenditures to approximately 15 percent. The reduction is minimal, for the Los Angeles ratio between property and nonproperty revenue sources is not the lowest. If the balance could be tipped even further in the direction of nonproperty sources, savings to property would be even more impressive. The estimate is thus conservative. Moreover, if we can be content with the assumption that the reduction would not be offset by a compensatory increase in non-property taxes, the homeowner could utilize the cost saving for improving his housing status, for purchasing other consumer items, or for saving. Finally, we might note that the variations in property versus nonproperty tax mix suggests that cities are not quite as constrained in their revenue sources as is commonly assumed.

2. Incidence. Tracing the incidence of the property taxes is a tricky exercise. Scholars on the subject fail to agree on what parties bear the real burden. As Simon notes in his early but important review of thought on the tax, "It is a curious fact that, although there has been common agreement among two genera-

tions of economists as to the fundamentals of tax incidence theory, no consensus has been reached with respect to the incidence of a tax on urban real property." (180, p. 416)
Yet, after completing his own survey of published theorizing, which included a detailed analysis of each explanation, he concludes that "seven different cases can be distinguished which give different results for the incidence of the tax" and each case is equipped with its own set of assumptions. (180, p. 428) Consequently, in each case, choice of assumptions governs the result.

Morton is more definite in his treatment of the subject. (86) Incidence depends, he argues, on market conditions. Given a buyers' market, incidence is on current property owners. In a sellers' market, taxes may be passed along to buyers. Stated somewhat differently, "During a period of rising incomes and heavy demand for rental space, a tax on housing can be readily passed on to the renter; during depression, it may be absorbed by the landlord in reduced profits." (86, p. 114)

In contrast to these disputes, substantial agreement appears to exist on the incidence of taxes on occupants *vis-a-vis* owners of the property prior to construction. As Netzer has argued, the burden rests in substantial part upon housing consumers, regardless of their type of tenancy. The chief exception, he reasons, "is that owners of rental property cannot shift the burden of that portion of the tax which falls on the land underlying their buildings." (173, p. 118) But there are other forms of tax shift as well.

Another dimension of incidence is that of its burden according to income class. On this point there is substantial agreement. The property tax is regressive; that is, it bears more heavily on low income groups than on high. The empirical evidence is startling. Survey Research Center data shows that U.S. families with incomes below $1,000 in 1959 paid nearly 6 percent of income as residential property taxes. In comparison, families earning $10,000 and over in the same year paid less than 2 percent for taxes. (85, Tables 19–1 and 19–6) Calculations developed by Netzer and reported in his comprehensive study of the property tax support the generalization. (91, Ch. III)

Two reasons for regressivity are standard. First, assessors tend to value higher priced dwellings at lower fractions of market value because of their heterogeneity. Secondly, housing expenditures have a relatively low income elasticity. Families in the $10,000 to $15,000 bracket spent less than twice as much for rent in 1960 as did families with incomes below $2,000. (91, p. 40)

While the cost incidence of property taxes is regressive, the benefits financed by taxes are selective. As Netzer points out, "The property tax as an institution is no mean contributor to income redistribution from the richer to the poorer income groups." (91, p. 42)

*Bibliography

Books, Monographs

2. Advisory Commission on Intergovernmental Relations. *Building Codes: A Program for Intergovernmental Reform*, Report A-28. (Washington: U.S. Government Printing Office, 1966).

4. Alonso, William. *Location and Land Use*. (Cambridge: Harvard University Press, 1964).

5. Alterman, Jack, and Eva E. Jacobs. "Output, Input and Productivity Measurement," *Estimates of Real Product in the United States by Industrial Sector*, 1947–1955. (Princeton: National Bureau of Economic Research, Princeton University Press, 1961).

8. Banfield, Edward C., and Morton Grodzins. *Government and Housing in Metropolitan Areas*. (New York: McGraw-Hill Book Company, Inc., 1958).

23. Colean, Miles L. *American Housing*. (New York: The Twentieth Century Fund, 1949).

24. Colean, Miles L., and Robinson Newcomb. *Stabilizing Construction.* (New York: McGraw-Hill Book Company, 1952).

27. Craig, David. "Regulation and Purchase: Two Governmental Ways to Attain Planned Land Use," in *Law and Land*. Charles M. Haar (ed.). (Cambridge: Harvard University Press and The M.I.T. Press, 1964).

28. Darbyshire, Ralph. *A Survey of Subdivision Ordinances*. (Seattle: Puget Sound Governmental Conference and Puget Sound Regional Planning Council, 1967).

32. Eckstein, Otto. *Public Finance*. (Englewood Cliffs: Prentice-Hall, Inc., 1964).

34. Ely, Richard T. *Taxation in American States and Cities*. (New York, 1888).

35. Foote, Nelson N., Janet Abu-Lughod, Mary Mix Foley, and Louis Winnick. *Housing Choices and Housing Constraints*. (New York: McGraw-Hill Book Co., 1960).

38. Gaffney, Mason. "Containment Policies for Urban Sprawl," in E. L. Stauber (ed.) *Approaches to the Study of Urbanization*. (Lawrence: University of Kansas Press, 1964).

41. Gillies, James and Frank Mittelbach. *Management in the Light Construction Industry: A Study of Contractors in Southern California.* (Los Angeles: Real Estate Research Program, University of California, 1962).

44. Grebler, Leo, David M. Blank, and Louis Winnick. *Capital Formation in Residential Real Estate: Trends and Prospects*. (Princeton: Princeton University Press and National Bureau of Economic Research, 1956).

47. Grigsby, William G. *Housing Markets and Public Policy*. (Philadelphia: University of Pennsylvania Press, 1963).

48. Haar, Charles M. "The Social Control of Urban Space" in *Cities and Space*. (Baltimore: The Johns Hopkins Press, 1963).

52. Herzog, John P. *The Dynamics of Large-Scale Housebuilding.* (Berkeley: Real Estate Research Program, Institute of Business and Economic Research, University of California, 1963).

54. Housing and Home Finance Agency. *Suggested Land Subdivision Regulations*. (Washington: U.S. Government Printing Office, 1962).

*Only those sources cited in this selection were included in the bibliography. A full list of citations can be found in the original essay.

55. International Conference of Building Officials. *Uniform Housing Code.* (Pasadena: The authors, 1964).

56. Iwema, R. *The Business Cycle, Structure and Economic Growth.* Unpublished report of the Netherlands Economic Institute, Rotterdam, 1968.

57. Jensen, Jens Peter. *Property Taxation in the United States.* (Chicago: University of Chicago Press, 1931).

60. Kaplan, Lawrence Jay. *Factors Affecting Productivity in the Homebuilding Industry*, Ph.D. dissertation. (New York: Faculty of Political Science, Columbia University, 1958).

61. Kelly, Burnham, and others. *Design and Production of Houses.* (New York: McGraw-Hill Book Co., 1959).

63. Kendrick, John W. *Productivity Trends in the United States.* (Princeton: National Bureau of Economic Research, Princeton University Press, 1961).

65. Lansing, John B. *Residential Location and Urban Mobility.* (Ann Arbor: Survey Research Center, The University of Michigan, 1966).

66. La Que, Frances L., Chairman of Panel, *Report of the Panel on Engineering and Commodity Standards of the Commerce Technical Advisory Board to the Assistant Secretary for Science and Technology, U.S. Department of Commerce.* (Washington: U.S. Department of Commerce, National Bureau of Standards, Institute for Applied Technology, February 2, 1965), PB 166 811.

68. Little, Arthur D., Inc., *The Building Code of Portland, Maine.* Report to the City Council of Portland, Maine, 1960.

69. Lubove, Roy. *The Progressives and the Slums.* (Pittsburgh: University of Pittsburgh Press, 1962).

71. Mace, Ruth L. *Municipal Cost-Revenue Analysis.* (Chapel Hill: Institute of Government, University of North Carolina, 1961).

72. Magee, John H. *General Insurance.* (Homewood, Ill.: Richard D. Irwin, 1961). 6th Edition.

73. Maisel, Sherman J. "Background Information on Costs of Land for Single Family Housing," *Appendix to the Report on Housing in California.* (Sacramento: Governor's Advisory Commission on Housing Problems, 1963).

74. Maisel, Sherman J. *Housebuilding in Transition.* (Berkeley and Los Angeles: University of California Press, 1953).

81. Massachusetts Department of Commerce and the Urban and Regional Studies Section, M.I.T., *The Effects of Large Lot Size on Residential Development.* (Washington: Urban Land Institute, 1958), Technical Bulletin No. 32.

83. McFarland, M. Carter. "Residential Rehabilitation," *Essays in Urban Land Economics.* (Los Angeles: Real Estate Research Program, University of California, 1966).

84. Meyerson, Martin, *et al. Housing, People, and Cities.* (New York: McGraw-Hill Book Co., 1962).

85. Morgan, James N., Martin H. David, Wilbur J. Cohen, and Harvey E. Brazer. *Income and Welfare in the United States.* (New York: McGraw-Hill Book Co., 1962).

86. Morton, Walter A. *Housing Taxation.* (Madison: University of Wisconsin Press, 1955).

87. National Association of Home Builders. *Homebuilders Manual for Land Development*. (Washington: The authors, 1958), 2nd Revised Edition

89. National Association of Home Builders. *Model Building Codes:* 1965. (Washington: National Association of Home Builders, 1966), mimeographed.

91. Netzer, Dick. *Economics of the Property Tax*. (Washington: The Brookings Institution, 1966).

95. Public Administration Service. *Study of Local Building Codes and Their Administration in the Southeast Michigan Six-County Region.* (Detroit: Metropolitan Fund, Inc., 1966).

100. Samuelson, Paul A. "The Dilemmas of Housing" in Burnham Kelly (ed.) *Housing and Economic Development*. (Cambridge: Massachusetts Institute of Technology, 1953).

102. Schultze, Charles L. *Prices, Costs, and Output for the Post War Decade*: 1947–1957. (New York: Committee for Economic Development, 1959).

105. Smith, Wallace F. *The Low Rise Speculative Apartment*. (Berkeley: Center for Real Estate and Urban Economics, University of California, 1964).

114. Ukeles, J. B. *The Consequences of Municipal Zoning*. (Washington: Urban Land Institute, 1964).

120. Urban Land Institute and National Association of Home Builders. *New Approaches to Residential Land Development*. (Washington: Urban Land Institute, 1961), Technical Bulletin No. 40.

122. Webster, Donald H. *Urban Planning and Municipal Public Policy.* (New York: Harper & Brothers, 1958).

123. Weimer, Arthur M., and Homer Hoyt. *Real Estate*. (New York: Ronald Press Company, 1966), 5th Edition.

Articles

125. Abrams, Charles. "Housing in the Year 2000," Paper delivered at the annual meetings of the American Institute of Planners, Washington, D.C. (August 1, 1967).

127. Babcock, Richard F., and Fred P. Bosselman. "Suburban Zoning and the Apartment Boom," *The University of Pennsylvania Law Review,* Vol. III (1963).

130. Blaha, William J. "Do Our Building Codes Need Modernizing," *Concrete Products* (May 1966).

138. Coase, R. H. "The Problem of Social Cost," *The Journal of Law & Economics*, Vol. III (October 1960).

140. Craig, David W. "What the Planner Doesn't Know About Zoning," *Planning 1960* (1960).

142. Dacy, Douglas C. "Productivity and Price Trends in Construction Since 1947," *Review of Economics and Statistics*, Vol. XLVII, No. 4 (November 1965).

143. Davis, Otto. "Economic Elements in Municipal Zoning Decisions," *Land Economics*, Vol. XXXIX, No. 4 (November 1963).

145. Domar, E. D., Scott H. Eddie, Paul M. Hohenberg, Michael D. Intrilligator, and Ichizp Miyamoto. "Economic Growth and Productivity in the United States, Canada, United Kingdom, Germany, and Japan in the Post-War Period," *Review of Economics and Statistics*, Vol. XLVI (February 1964).

151. Frumkin, Norman. "Construction Activity in the 1958 Input-Output Study," *Survey of Current Business* (May 1965).

154. Grebler, Leo. "Criteria for Appraising Governmental Housing Programs," *American Economic Review*, Vol. L (May 1960).

155. Grebler, Leo. "The Role of Residential Capital Formation in Postwar Business Cycles," *Proceedings, Conference on Savings and Residential Financing* (1959).

156. Guandolo, Joseph. "Housing Codes in Urban Renewal," *The George Washington Law Review* (October 1956).

160. Hodza, Richard. "The Constitutionality of Minimum Sizes for Buildings and Lots," *Intramural Law Review of New York University School of Law*, Vol. 15, No. 2 (January 1960).

161. *House and Home* (July 1958). *House and Home* (August 1958).

162. *House and Home* (December 1965).

173. Netzer, Dick. "Needed Reforms in Housing Tax Policies," unpublished paper.

177. Rothenstein, Guy G. "European Pre-Fab Techniques: Will They Answer United States Cost, Quality, Production Requirements?" *Journal of Housing* (August–September 1966).

180. Simon, Herbert A. "The Incidence of a Tax on Urban Real Property," *Quarterly Journal of Economics*, Vol. LVII, No. 3 (May 1943); reprinted in R. A. Musgrave and C. S. Shoup (eds.), *Readings in the Economics of Taxation* (1959).

183. *Survey of Current Business*, various issues.

184. Ukockis, James R. "State and Local Property Taxation," *Monthly Review*, Federal Reserve Bank of Kansas City (February 1968).

185. Watkins, Arthur M. "Why Homes Cost Too Much," *The Saturday Evening Post* (September 21, 1963).

2.2

Land Planning and the Property Tax

Mason Gaffney

Land planners concern themselves with the relations among the uses to which independent private owners put their land. These private owners mostly seek to maximize their individual net welfare after taxes. Since taxes are a large fraction of all costs, after-tax welfare is quite different from before-tax welfare. So public land planners seeking to influence private landowners must perforce be tax planners.

Land planners generally have been tax planners in at least a passive sense: their expectation of private response to public initiative has been based on experience, which in turn reflects landowners' tax avoidance. Some planners have grumbled at individual tax avoidance, as though it were immoral and should go away—not a very realistic approach. Others have sweepingly condemned the entire market mechanism—a "rush to judgment" that might be tempered when we consider to what extent the malfunction of the market results from avoidance of ineptly imposed tax costs. Still others have supported land underassessment to relieve the pressure to develop suburban land—without, I believe, adequately considering that unused land lies among used parcels and disrupts their symbiotic interactions, which are the heart of public land planning and the essence of urban civilization. Yet others have foundered by expecting private landowners to respond to, and fill in, the empty niches in grand plans much more rapidly than the Great American Land Speculator is wont to do.

To be most effective, land planners must become positive tax planners. Collectively, they need to support national reform of the income tax as it bears on land development. Our theme here is what they can do locally through property tax laws and assessment procedures. Tax reform can help the market help the planner. What is good for the market is generally good for planning. Land planning amends and guides the market—it is not at war with the market. On the contrary, effective public land planning presupposes a well-oiled land market.

Planners and the Land Market

The planner, through his influence on zoning, street layout, and other public constraints, presents each landowner with a

Reprinted by permission of the *Journal of the American Institute of Planners* (Vol. 35, No. 3, May 1969), pp. 178–183.

sort of environmental challenge: he hopes the landowner will respond constructively. The planner provides avenues of linkage by which landowners may relate to one another: he hopes they will use those avenues. The market motivates them.

On the whole, the highest use of a site is that which most relates to and complements uses on other sites. This is what cities are all about. Planners are often preoccupied with minimizing conflicts between neighbors, which calls for minor departures from the most lucrative use; but conflicts must not blind us to the overriding value of symbiosis among neighbors. This is the first concern of land planning; it is also the first concern of the self-helping landowner. The worst nuisance a central landowner can commit is passive withdrawal of his land from the life of the city—right where it gets in everyone's way. The market, if he listens, tells him to participate instead. Taxation may be used to nudge the market a little this way or that, but the first concern of tax reform is to unleash the market to do its constructive work.

Capital and people compactly grouped, and with good mutual access provided by quality planning, interact synergistically to produce a large surplus above cost. The whole is greater than the sum of its parts: that is "synergism." Planning and the market work together to maximize synergism.

Another function of the land market is in the development of new areas, or redevelopment when new uses succeed old, to synchronize interdependent private investments that interact synergistically to produce a total community. Thus as a city expands, high land values at the perimeter put simultaneous pressure on all owners there to convert to urban use. Were this mechanism in good working order, planners could extend city services to compact increments of land, initially sizing utility lines and streets for ultimate demand, secure in the knowledge that the ultimate demand would be there in short order. Private builders could orient their plans to a more certain future, minimizing transition costs of, for example, shifting from wells and septic tanks to public water and sewers. Every private improvement could be less self-sufficient and more oriented to the prospect of a total community.

But the market is not in good working order. Taxation intercedes in every land use decision. Every piece of land is periodically mobile among uses—when there is some "sacrament" in its life, such as demolition and construction, sale, subdivision, or assembly. It is then in press among competing buyers, uses, densities, timings, parcel sizes, and so on. In every such press, taxation biases the choice in favor of the lighter taxed use. The real estate tax on building thus always favors old over new; gas stations over apartments; junk yards over factories; parking lots over parking structures; high income residences over low (high income residences are usually less intensive because of larger lots in neighborhoods of higher land value); billboards over offices; unused over improved land; waiting over acting. This bias has half destroyed the market as an arbiter among competing land uses, and an agency promoting urban synergism. It has lowered the density, retarded renewal, and broken up integral linkages of the central city, fostering in their place random scattering of new buildings at the outskirts. It has so far impaired the city's function of linking small independent industrial firms as to bear large responsibility for today's galloping merger movement in which a key word is—synergism! Firms seek through merger and vertical integration the access to services, labor, and supplies which in a well-ordered city they could get from independent firms through the market.

Tax Base Redefinition

I do not propose that we eliminate taxes. The public needs money. I do submit that it is not necessary for real estate taxes to impair the market. The method is to modify the definition of the tax base.

It is not new that we can foster a particular thing by subsidizing it, or just leaving it alone when other things are taxed. It *is* new to note there is a way to tax something and not damage it. We can even tax something and, by taxing, foster and promote it.

Tax capital and you drive it away; tax land and you drive it into use. The technique is to redefine the real estate tax base as land value alone. Value at any time is what the land if bare would sell for. It is value in the best alternative use, the economists' "opportunity cost." It is independent of present use or ownership. It changes year by year, usually gradually as demands and neighborhoods change, or as anticipated public improvements, long since foreseen and discounted into values, are completed. It is very dependent on the things that planners plan and is in large part the product of good planning and implementation of planning—Alfred Marshall called it "the public value of land," in reference to its origin. A proper assessment of land changes in step with the outside determinants, ignoring the specific response that individual landowners make to the environmental challenge. They are taxed not for improving their opportunities, but for having and holding them; not for what they do themselves, but for the good things that planners do for them.

Private Renewal Problems

The real estate tax modified in this way would help planners with many problems that now seem intractable and foreboding. I will focus on one, the problem of slow urban renewal. Few would deny that the market has failed to renew our cities fast enough. For this the real estate tax, bearing differentially on new buildings, must shoulder much of the blame.

The economical time for an individual to clear and renew land is when the current cash flow from existing or "defender" use ceases to yield a fair return on the "scrap value" of the site in the most eligible succeeding use (the "challenger"). This scrap value is the present value of future income less the present value of future costs.[1]

The land-based tax is neutral in this decision, because it is unmoved by renewal: it is the same on the defender as the challenger. The building-based tax is unneutral because it rockets upward when new succeeds old. It weakens the challenger vis-à-vis the defender, by the amount of tax increase. Not only is the new building valued higher than the old: often assessors seize this occasion to reassess the land upward, adding to the bias against renewal.

The general qualitative direction of the bias is clear—I have said that before. Quantitatively, the number of years during which building taxes retard site renewal depends, among other things, on how the cash flow from old buildings drops off. If it plummets steeply, then renewal dates are preordained by nontax factors, and tax policy is unimportant. If it tails off gradually, a substantial tax bias against new buildings retards the renewal of each site regarded individually; and of neighborhoods and school districts even more, as the nonrenewal of each site robs neighboring sites of their renewability and suppresses competition from new buildings which would pull tenants from old defenders.

A number of time series showing historical income experience of commercial buildings have been compiled and published by Leo Grebler, Fred Case, and Louis Winnick.[2] I have deflated them for price level changes.[3] They are much affected by cycles of depression and war. The general time pattern and period of dropoff is clear enough, however. Real income from old buildings dwindles away slowly over many decades, in spite of depreciation and obsolescence. There is no sharp cutoff, no predestined date of demolition determined by technology or taste. Even when an old building has gone vacant, it may come back. After World War II, real income of many buildings rose sharply.

Another source of data is the Institute of Real Estate Management "Experience Exchange" among members of the N.A.R.E.B. In 1967, their 1,069 respondents reported on operating ratios (total expenses including real estate taxes divided by total actual collections) for apartment buildings classified by age groups. For elevator apartments the ratio rose gently from 45 percent for 1961–66 birthdays to 59 percent for all buildings over 47 years old, that is, pre-1920.[4] For low-rise apartments it was from 41 percent to 58 percent; for garden apartments from 40 percent to 48 percent. In other words, almost half the gross collections from old apartments represents net income to the owner. A powerful factor helping hold down these operating ratios is that real estate tax expenses keep falling as a building ages.

Measured in years, therefore, the fiscal deterrent to urban renewal—the threat of increased taxes on new buildings—retards by decades renewal of the individual urban site. I could give you a precise number of years, using Milwaukee's present real tax rate of 4.0 percent; but it would be a false precision, since it would be based on the individual site in isolation. Let us look at the extended effects on neighborhoods.

New Building Impacts

The renewal of one site speeds the renewal of nearby sites in at least three ways. First, it raises the renewal or challenger value of nearby land. One new building gives heart to potential builders of others, who naturally prefer new buildings for neighbors. Slum environs can virtually destroy the renewal value of land—a problem often noted. One or a few sound new buildings as inspiration can support supplementary and complementary renewal roundabout. The new GM building on 5th Avenue is reported by *Fortune* to have doubled floorspace rentals across the street. Once a new neighborhood or city or region gets well started, renewal snowballs because people like to locate near their customers, contacts, suppliers, workers, and friends.

This, of course, raises the negative possibility that new buildings strengthen adjacent defender values as well as challenger values. There are frequent complaints that successful urban renewal projects, for example, raise the cost of nearby land for the next project. However, these higher land "costs" are merely *asking* prices and may be based on higher anticipated challenger values, plus the knowledge that federal funds are on tap to buy. They do not in general represent higher defender cash flow nearly as much as challenger values.

The reason is that new buildings pull tenants from old, in general weakening defenders. This is the second way that renewal reinforces itself. It is especially true when the new buildings are at higher density than what they replace—something which building taxes also discourage—and represent net new supply. Where tenants have a choice they move to newer quarters. The oldest defender filters down to be demolished. Its successor then pulls tenants from others, repeating the cycle. In the right conditions the reverberations from one new structure resound through several rounds of induced renewal.

Milwaukee's progress during the last eight years represents the ramifying effects that may flow from one new building. Through a series of historical accidents and legal technicalities, Wisconsin had an assessment freeze law that proved unconstitutional after being used essentially just once, in 1960, for the Marine Plaza—a high rise office and bank building. It was the first downtown building of consequence in thirty years. It pulled tenants from other buildings, forcing a wave of remodeling and renewal, still in progress, which has changed the face of downtown Milwaukee. By general account, this one new competitor set off the chain reaction. There is a multiplier the like of which few other economic processes approach. Perhaps the time was unusually ripe, but that is mere hypothesis. The facts are there, and they speak volumes.

It is not that this one stroke alone was enough. The ripples are dying out, long before the job is done, but the point is if one original cause can ramify so far, even though every induced new building was fully taxed, twenty original causes would transform a city, if every induced new building were to be tax free.

A third way that renewal reinforces itself is through the higher income that it brings. Renewal means capital inflow, construction payrolls, material sales, new jobs, and so on. This pushes up local income levels. Now new buildings are "superior goods." The higher the local income, the greater the premium paid for new over old floor space, and the stronger are challengers relative to defenders.

So neighborhood and aggregate effects multiply the good done by each new building; conversely, of course, they multiply the damage from the present tax policy, which defers renewal.

But neighborhood effects are not the whole of the story of multiplied effects from taxing challengers more than defenders. Consider that most building is done on borrowed money. We live in a world of credit ratings, cash flows, front money, cash squeezes, and leverage—matters basic in business school but too often under-weighed in economic analysis. A tax on new buildings, coupled with low taxes on old, weakens the credit of challengers and strengthens that of defenders. It adds to challengers' needs for front money and reduces defenders' needs for any money at all.

A tax on new buildings is at its maximum in the early years, the time of tightest cash squeeze. A high property tax rate today may take 30 percent of gross income from a new building. If other expenses take 30 percent, that is three-sevenths of the net operating income. If the entrepreneur is highly leveraged —and today, that is standard—most of the rest of net operating income goes to debt service. The net cash remaining for the entrepreneur then, especially during the early cash squeeze, is doubly leveraged, so a small rise in building taxes can wipe him out.

His credit rating in turn is leveraged by the prospects for his equity position. It is a familiar fact that a small rise of mortgage rates causes a large drop in building. Loanable funds rush out of building, not just because borrowers balk at higher rates, but because lenders lower everyone's credit rating because of lower equity income. Real estate taxes on new buildings add to costs in the same way as interest rates—that is, they are a fixed percent of value. A 3-percent-of-true-value property tax rate hits new building with the impact of a rise of mortgage rates from 4 percent to 7 percent; except that the real estate tax is worse because the tax rate applies to the whole value, while mortgage rates apply only to the debt. The tax not only defers renewal by its simple direct impact, but additionally by its leveraged effect on entrepreneur net cash flow and thence on credit ratings.

So it is powerful medicine to convert the real estate tax base to the site value basis. My current study comparing challenger and defender values in Milwaukee County is finding that a small rise of challenger values over defender values would cause 20 percent of the central city area to be renewed forthwith; and that the large change resulting from a full exemption of buildings from real estate tax would cause some 50 percent to be renewed—*if* the labor and money could be found to do it. Again, these results would be magnified by consideration of the neighborhood effects previously described.

They would be magnified again by consideration of the positive effect of cash squeeze on defenders. So far I have written only of exempting new buildings, but the land basis of real estate taxation does more than that. It raises taxes on defenders. The result is a potent cash squeeze effect. Today's real estate tax puts the squeeze on buildings. The proposed land tax puts it on defenders, holdouts, and preemptors of land.

So powerful is the medicine that, once it is understood, opposition may be expected, not from those who say it will not work, but from those who fear it will work too well: destroy historical antiquities, flood the market, jeopardize collateral values, lower rents, change the character of neighborhoods, sacrifice tradition to progress, overstimulate the economy, encourage immigration, spoil the labor, change voting patterns, weaken old ethnic ties, and generally frighten those who dislike change and abundance. There is also a concern for the welfare cases who inhabit old buildings and may have relocation problems. This is not the place to answer all those points; nor is this the place to answer those who would not have us do any good thing locally without first tracing its possible effects on the equilibrium of the whole world. They should reread *Candide*. But I do have a few words of conciliation and challenge for planners who might be concerned that the proposal to unleash the full force of the free market is also a proposal to substitute the market for planners.

Challenges for Planners

The unleashed market can solve some problems that now divert planners. It can bring urban renewal; group complementary land uses; promote low income housing; contain sprawl; attract an economic base; and weed out the worst generators of fiscal net deficits—old buildings. But on the whole, the land tax proposal implies more need for planners. Indeed, it gives planning so much more force and leadership as to make one ask whether planners are prepared to meet the challenge. Let us enumerate the ways that land value taxation supports and presupposes good public planning.

1. It gives planners a positive tool for influencing private land use, where now they largely have powers to say "Nay." When they designate an area for development, direct routes and utilities in it, and zone it for new use—up go land taxes, cash-squeezing the landowner into early attention to his new opportunities. Further, since high-use zoning is exploited quickly, there need be no great surplus scattered about, as it is today. It remains tight and retains its power to shape land use. This is also true for advantageous locations along public roads—which incidentally cost much more to produce than zoning, and if they are produced in surplus because half are unexploited (again as today), they require the most egregious waste of public capital.

Some may even regard land taxation as a form of tyranny by planners over landowners. But note the limits to the planner's power. He does not direct a landowner to put his land to a specific use. Nor is there usually just one "highest and best" use of a given site, to which every landowner will be forced. Thriving cities are not characterized by monoculture and monotony, but by variety, constant change, and complementation. Whatever is the highest use in a neighborhood, say elevator apartments, is supplied in abundance until the need for another one is no greater than the need for some complement like a grocery store or parking structure. At any time an equilibrium generally prevails and affords each landowner several options. Within limits he may "do his own thing."

The land tax does not turn the planner into an overcentralized administrator or petty tyrant dictating specifics when he should be delegating authority. Rather, it sets a generalized performance standard, cutting off options beyond a certain degree of slothfulness and disregard for the public cost of giving land its latent value, but leaving wide latitude for individual discretion.

2. The land tax gives public investment great leverage over private investment. Today it is the reverse. Within limits, public roads, regulated utilities, the mailman, and school bus will follow you wherever you choose to locate. The regional planning commission uses traffic counts to plan bigger roads, following the lead of private emigres. These outreaching roads often seem to follow wealth and power.

The land tax lets public planners take the initiative—if they will. The city extends roads and sewers a reasonable way and then raises taxes on the land. The cash squeeze says, "Bring me roofs to match my roadways."

We have seen that individual buildings in new neighborhoods need synchronization because of synergistic interdependence. When the community of small independent entrepreneurs lacks synchronization, it is hard put to compete with giant developers of integrated centers and whole towns, who centrally control entire new communities. To compete, the public needs a community synchronizer. This the land tax affords. The planner does not try to play every instrument in the orchestra, but the land tax lets him set the tempo.

But how this puts the conductor on his mettle! The man with the baton had better set the right beat, for everyone knows who he is. From an objective view of administration, of course, that is very good. It may give stage fright to a profession still a stranger to the podium. Are planners ready?

3. The land tax gives planners some leverage over tax assessors. Now, assessors are preoccupied assessing building values. Then, they would assess site potential, the thing planners play such a role in determining.

4. Synchronized expansion lets planners plan for open space. Today, open space is a transitory by-product of land speculation. In transition zones we undersize parks because there is so much open land and so few people. The private open space cannot be entered and supplies only visual amenities, and often not even that. When the landowner is ready for cash, the space is closed and a new load, often an overload, thrown on public land.

The land tax system lets transition be quick and orderly. Knowing the ultimate density, the planner can provide parks in optimal measured amounts and sizes so that settlement is not crowded, but unsprawled. By using tax pressure to assure early compact use of land between open spaces, he justifies the investment in open land and relieves the pressure to invade it. The public planner can work open space into an integrated pattern, just as large private developers can (and sometimes do) now.

With such power in hand, planners might even retain economists to measure the benefits and costs of open space. It is high time we introduce rational management and optimization into a topic now too freighted with hoarding, alarmism, sentimentality, camouflaged race prejudice, opportunistic tax-dodging, and uncritical nature worship.

5. The land tax system shortens the period between site renewals. Every site renewal is another occasion to plan, and to plan ambitiously, excitingly, not just for rehabilitation but from the ground up. The public planner can go further. He can synchronize demolitions and replot the ground itself, something we had better get around to more often if our older city layouts are to avoid utter obsolescence.

6. The land tax system helps free planners from the constraint of "French equity." I allude to the concept of equity, characteristically French, that every man's share of land should be made equal, regardless of social cost, that the object of the institution of property is not good land use but distributive equity. In city planning, that means what you do for Jacques' land you must also do for Pierre's.

Efficiency, on the other hand, calls for neighborhood specialization and differentiation, with high values for some and low for others. The land tax uses the fiscal and monetary mechanism to compensate the losers from the gains of the winners. Those who get the high unit values also get the high tax bills—*not* because of what they do for themselves, but for what the city planner does for them. Thus liberated from the tyranny of pettiness, the planners can relocate things and maximize net urban welfare on a much grander scale than now.

Equally important, the land tax gives city councils a better chance to be honest. Lincoln Steffens once remarked that the troublemaker in the Garden of Eden was not Eve, nor yet the serpent—but the apple! Taxing land values serves to dehydrate the apples of unearned increment which city councils dispense; and for which land developers vie when they contribute to campaigns, lobby, and otherwise influence officials. Keying the land tax to the provision of value-creating public works tempers the landowner's appetite by having him pay for his apples. The planner can now put priorities in the capital budget with a clearer conscience and less fear of pressure.

7. Finally, the land tax system leads to demand for a greater variety of community facilities because it gives people better mutual access. It reduces the self-sufficiency of individual landowners. It obviates vertical integration by individual firms. It increases interdependence. It fosters more linkages of all kinds: social, commercial, industrial, political, cultural. It puts more

load on the linkage mechanism—the sector of the city that planners plan.

To be sure, it greatly shortens the linkage network because orderly, unsprawled settlement lets people live closer, reducing the travel required for any given degree of linkage. Furthermore, it untaxes elevators and utility cores in private buildings and so lets private capital develop the third dimension of the linkage network, reducing the need for public capital. But the public capital released from lengthening the street grid and the planning talent liberated from this single-minded preoccupation have higher and varied uses. They can replan interior areas and central lines; clean up air and water; perfect mass transit; sewer septic-tank suburbs and enlarge inadequate central lines; relocate buildings and lines to maximize synergistic gains from linkages; build a community house, a central mall and plaza, a Tivoli Gardens, a trade fair, an auditorium, stadium, art center, zoo, gymnasium, pool, theatre, marina, museum, library, playgrounds, park facilities, and so on without end.

Reviewing these seven challenges for planners, I must plead innocent of plotting their obsolescence and disemployment. Rather, I am moved to ask, with the Joseph Schlitz Brewing Company, "How much boldness can you handle?"

Notes

Author's Note: *This is a revised version of a workshop paper presented at the 1968 Conference of the American Institute of Planners in Pittsburgh.*

[1]For more detail on this see my "Property Taxes and the Frequency of Urban Renewal," *Proceedings* of the 57th National Tax Conference, Pittsburgh, Pennsylvania, September 14–17, 1967, pp. 272–85.

[2]Leo Grebler, *Experience in Urban Real Estate Investment* (New York: Columbia University Press, 1955); Fred Case, *Los Angeles Real Estate; A Study of Investment Experience* (Los Angeles: Real Estate Research Program, Graduate School of Business Administration, Division of Research, University of California, 1960); and Louis Winnick, *Rental Housing: Opportunities for Private Investment* (New York: McGraw-Hill, 1958).

[3]My study of the detail and trend adjustments will be published next spring.

[4]Institute of Real Estate Management, *Apartment Building Income Expense Analysis* (Chicago: IREM of the NAREB, 1967).

3
Evaluating Housing Programs

Introduction

At the same time that more and more students of housing are questioning the specific objectives of particular housing programs, inquiring into their viability and evaluating their relative efficiencies in meeting intended purposes, there is occurring a backlash against this type of analysis. The reaction has been born of a massive guilt feeling owing to our apparent lack of progress in the low-income housing area and the feeling that any serious effort to evaluate what we have been doing and where we might go will only result in a programmatic slowdown, which we can ill afford. Thus, the nation is admonished by Senator Douglas's National Commission on Urban Problems not to scrutinize too carefully their recommended program because estimating "... cost-benefit ratios of the programs we suggest are mere bickering in light of our need for a real political commitment to solve our problems."[1]

While the ultimate barrier to overcome in the struggle to solve the housing problem might well be political in nature, it is not clear: that we actually know how to allocate wisely what limited housing resources we have; the extent to which the nation ought to be concentrating on expansion of the supply rather than maintenance of the existing stock; or, for that matter, even what demographic groups are getting how much and for what reasons. Nothing could impede a substantial rate of progress more strongly than wasteful, internally inconsistent or misdirected efforts. And yet, for some time we have had the analytic capacity to delve more deeply into the effectiveness of various housing programs than we have been doing; the interest, however, has been lacking. Recently, there has occurred a confluence of interests and abilities, with the result that we are learning a great deal about existing housing efforts and building a basis upon which emerging programs might be evaluated *ex ante* rather than after the fact. The purpose of this section of the book is to provide a representative sample of recent efforts to evaluate a wide range of existing housing programs.

A Note On Efficiency

"The very idea of measuring the economic benefit of some programs against others in the intangible area of 'human investment' tends to stump those who try it," noted the Douglas Commission as it wiped its hands of the troublesome task of recommending trade-offs within and among particular program areas.[2] In like fashion, others dismiss the potential utility of assessing the relative efficiency levels of housing subsidy programs, even though by efficiency one means only "a desire to achieve a specific objective at minimum cost, or conversely, the achievement of the maximum possible amount of a desired object for a given investment of resources."[3] Thus, in and of itself, the concept of efficiency does not imply a lack of concern for intangibles, or for that matter, that unquantifiable goals are inferior. "No more is implied than that, if efficiency is desired, an attempt should be made wherever possible to define the objectives . . . in terms that are amenable to measurement and rigorous analysis."[4]

A Further Note on the Relationships Between Goals and Constraints

At the same time, one must not become entrapped by the false belief that a pure efficiency criterion is the most appropriate guide to program evaluation. Strictly speaking, the most efficient subsidy program might provide financial incentives to the well-to-do, if our unconstrained objective is tc obtain the maximum number of housing units per dollar of assistance. That is, the objective function might be stated in terms which include a number of constraints which reflect purposes of particular housing programs that are "secondary," that is, housing-related or nonhousing in nature. Satisfaction of constraints that are determined by these objectives could be a condition placed upon the attainment of the primary objective. Thus, if in addition to providing a particular client group with decent housing, a program is intended to redistribute income, stabilize the market, stimulate private investment, increase the community tax base, or to strengthen individual and family life, then one's evaluation of that program must take into consideration the fact that satisfying any one of these objectives might well increase the subsidy constraint required to produce a given number of dwelling units. A brief digression at this point on the public housing program might serve to illustrate how we frequently fail to distinguish between the purpose and effectiveness of housing programs and fail to recognize, as well, how program goals, constraints, and costs are interrelated.

In a recent study George Schermer concluded that

". . . from the viewpoint of strengthening individual and family life, most public housing is tragically deficient."[5] Clearly, what Schermer is saying is that the program has been *ineffective* along particular social dimensions and not that its *purposes* have not been served adequately. Few would dispute the proposition that, as a means of delivering safe and sanitary housing to the poor at prices they can afford, the public housing program has served its intended purpose more effectively than any other existing low-income housing program. The apparent confusion between the two terms, which is not limited to public housing, is at least partly responsible for the program's present political difficulties. What is called for, of course, is a redefinition of the intended purposes of the program to include the delivery of the requisite social and related nonhousing services required by many families who occupy public housing. Were this to be accomplished, we might surely expect program costs to increase sharply as we place additional constraints upon the achievement of what was previously a pure housing objective.

In our failure to grasp more fully the several dimensions of the low-income housing problem and how housing and nonhousing needs are related, we have developed tools of intervention that are too narrow and, hence, costly and self-defeating. Although the Congress may increase the construction cost ceiling on public housing units to $25,000, it will typically not fund the bundle of housing-related programs aimed at serving the needs of public housing tenants. As a result the public investment in the construction of the units is all but wasted as the institution of public housing is loathed by broad segments of our population, including increasing numbers of low-income residents. If, however, the housing were viewed as serving one need, and the bundle of tenant services were viewed as serving related, but essential, needs, so that the one could not be provided without the other, the resulting marginal increases in unit costs would make the public investment in the physical structures worthwhile. If, under a more broadly conceived concept of public housing, budgetary cutbacks were required for one reason or another, it would make no sense to maintain a given level of housing production while slashing supportive services. Instead, fewer units ought to be produced, with the flow of services to the ultimate tenants maintained at a high level.

Nevertheless, it is indeed necessary and proper to inquire into the economic costs of providing subsidized housing to low-income consumers, as well as into the viability of the financial mechanisms that lie at the heart of various programs. The Smolensky-Stegman exchange in this section of the book, for example, focuses on the actual costs of public housing and rehabilitation programs, while Walsh highlights the dilemmas confronting local housing authorities as a result of the anachronistic formulas under which public housing is financed. As he indicates, in New York City, since 1952, unit operating expenses in public housing have increased by 125 percent, while tenant incomes rose by only 65 percent and average rents by 72 percent. And, with monthly operating costs of the typical public housing unit in excess of $83 a month, not only is the program in trouble in terms of remaining financially solvent, but such statistics raise additional questions about other aspects of low-income housing policy. Not the least of these questions is, if increased operating costs of public housing units have outstripped the rise in tenant incomes so steeply over the past fifteen years, what are the quality implications for the low-rent, privately owned stock in the inner city, where increased operating costs cannot be passed on to the low-income consumer? More will be said about this in the following section of the book.

Low-Income Housing and Social Policy

Two distinct, but related, issues are raised by this discussion. First, the need to identify the desired outputs of housing programs is, perhaps, among the most important unfinished tasks in the housing-evaluation area. Ross' proposed methodology for evaluating HUD programs, which appears in this section of the book, concerns this matter. Second, we must begin to view the housing problem of low-income families as one dimension of the multifaceted problem of poverty and the allocation of housing resources as an instrument of social policy. It seems essential that we learn more about the kinds of families who are most likely to experience housing problems; the specific nature of the kinds of housing problems from which they suffer; the ways in which particular nonhousing or housing-related problems are likely to minimize the success of solving their problems through direct housing measures; and finally, how some housing problems might

Housing Problem—Population Matrix

Types of Low-Income Families Experiencing Housing Problems	Dimensions of the Low-Income Housing Problem											
	A	B	C	D	E	F	G	H	I	J	K	L
1												
2												
3												
4												
5												
6												
7												
8												
9												

Key

Families

1. Blacks
2. Large families, especially female-headed
3. Welfare families
4. Families experiencing interruptions in income
5. Families with particularly high nonhousing expenses
6. Single males
7. Mentally or physically handicapped
8. Families who are bad tenants either because of irregularity of rent payments, failure to keep quarters reasonably clean, or abusive behavior
9. Recent immigrants with no credit rating, etc.

Problems

A. Lack of adequate quality, including equipment and services
B. Lack of adequate space
C. Lack of adequate furnishings
D. Poor neighborhood environment
E. Excessive housing costs relative to income
F. Excessive housing costs relative to quality, space, and neighborhood environment
G. Lack of tenure choice
H. Lack of locational choice
I. Racial discrimination
J. Involuntary mobility
K. Stigmatizing way in which housing services are provided
L. Lack of housing-related services, e.g., meals, for the partially handicapped

be best dealt with indirectly through nonhousing means.

Grigsby, for example, has identified twelve dimensions of the housing problems of low-income, urban families and a typology consisting of nine problems typically associated with occupancy in substandard housing.[6] While each of the arrays contain overlapping elements, we might for illustrative purposes, combine them into a "housing problem-population matrix," as depicted.

By refining the matrix and relating household characteristics and disabilities to various dimensions of the low-income housing problem, we might ultimately hope to achieve a more effective basis for program intervention. It is safe to say that few, if any, of these factors have been satisfactorily explored by those who have proposed solutions to our housing problem. "In a sense," according to Grigsby, "rather than looking at the problem first and then seeking tools to solve it, [housing experts] . . . have accumulated a kit of tools which they are trying to fit and refit to a changing problem."[7] It might be useful to show that by distinguishing among the various dimensions of the problem, and relating them to population groups, various forms of program intervention are suggested.

Many low-income families who suffer from excessive housing costs relative to income (element e), occupy standard, if modest quality, housing. To a great extent, the problem here is low income, *per se*, and a reasonable mode of intervention in the short run, income or rent supplements. Appropriate forms of long-run intervention would, of course, depend upon the particular characteristics of the families in question. For other, poorer families who reside in substandard housing, the cost of which is not excessive relative to space and quality, some form of income transfer might also be sufficient to enable them to improve their housing circumstances. The problem of excessive housing costs relative, not to income, but to quality, space, and neighborhood environment (element f), however, is experienced by different subgroups for different reasons and might call for other forms of market intervention.

In a study of the dynamics of the inner-city rental market in Baltimore, it was found that a pool of so-called high risk families were generally relegated, not only to poor quality housing, but to that housing whose rents were excessive relative to the dimensions noted.[8] In terms of the matrix, we might say that subgroups 2, 7, 8, and 9 would have the highest probabilities of experiencing this problem. Moreover, families who experience interruptions in income and, as a result, become delinquent in their rents too frequently might be forced to vacate higher quality housing and ultimately join the high risk pool.

The important point here is that low income *per se* might not be at the root of this kind of housing problem. According to the Baltimore study, between 10 and 15 percent of the inner-city tenants fall into the "bad tenant" category (element 8) for one reason or another, and as often as not their housing problems were compounded, if not caused by, domestic difficulties. Not only would income or rent supplements alone not deal adequately with their problems, but were their landlords provided assistance to improve their units, they would probably screen their tenants more carefully so that the high risk families would be reallocated within the stock, relegated once again to the poorest quality housing.

Low-Income Housing Resources
What we ought to be seeking is both an enlargement and a refinement of our abilities to maximize the impact of scarce housing resources as they relate to reducing the incidence of poverty and to evaluate the contributions of individual housing programs as they relate to our overall antipoverty effort, as implied earlier. The quantity of available housing resources is no small matter. In this regard, it is of little comfort to report that, in 1962,

> the Federal Government spent $820 million to subsidize housing for poor people—roughly 20% of the population. For the uppermost 20% of the population (with incomes over $9,000), the subsidy was $1.7 billion. Thus, a family in the uppermost fifth received about twice as much on the average as a poor family . . . The two programs that express the national conscience in housing—public assistance and public housing —together manage to raise poor families to per capita equality with the income tax subsidy that goes to all the rest. No more than that is accomplished.[9]

The fact that these figures refer to 1962 should not mislead us into thinking that things have been much brighter in recent times because "From fiscal 1962 through 1967, $356.3 billion was spent for national defense, $33.2 billion for stabilizing farm prices and income, $24.2 billion for space exploration, and $22.2 billion for Federal highway construction. In contrast, $8.1 billion was budgeted for all programs under Housing and Urban Renewal, and only $1.25 billion for Federal housing subsidies."[10]

In more specific program terms, "the nation in thirty years of public housing built fewer units than Congress, back in 1949, said were needed in the immediate next six years."[11] Running totals of our low-income housing progress to date, including fiscal 1968, are as follows:[12]

Completed public housing (since 1949)	667,000
Completed rent supplement (since 1965)	3,000
Completed "221(d) (3)" units (since 1965)	52,000
Completed rehabilitated units	75,000
Completed elderly "section 202" units	21,000
Total	818,000

Against this spotty record of performance and in recognition of the fact that HUD, in business only since 1965, is an accumulation of separate bureaucracies created over the years rather than a coherent organization capable of developing and implementing a viable housing, if not urban, strategy, the Nixon Administration is in the process of redefining the responsibilities of the department's constituent components. Under the proposed reorganization, for the first time housing production and housing management responsibilities would be separated, with the former activity placed under the direction of the Federal Housing Administrator who would become the Assistant Secretary for Housing Production and Mortgage Credit.[13] Management responsibilities are to be assigned to an Assistant Secretary for Renewal and Housing Management, while the old Housing Assistance and Renewal Assistance Administrations are to be eliminated.

One might rightly question the wisdom of entrusting FHA with the responsibility of leading this nation's low-income housing effort in the 1970s and beyond, in view of its inherent conservative tendencies. In effect, the late Senator Robert Kennedy raised this same point in his testimony supporting S.2100, a tax incentive approach to the production of new housing for the poor:[14]

> . . . the bill establishes a new Low Income Housing Administration within the Department of Housing and Urban Development. Assignment of this program to the Federal Housing Administration would be neither appropriate nor effective. FHA's primary interest is in the construction of single-family homes for middle income families. But the personnel and procedures developed to deal with the suburbs are not well suited to the rapid processing of applications for the construction of multiple-dwelling units for low income families.

Yet, it must be recognized that it was conceived in an environment of scarcity, intended to buy more performance per dollar of assistance through reorganization, as opposed to enlarging the size of the pie allocated to housing.

While new construction is not the sole route to improving the housing circumstances of the poor, the Douglas Commission, recognizing the need to enlarge the annual output of subsidized new units, offered, "... along with its national call to arms, a package of recommendations which, if adopted, would not necessarily guarantee the authorization and appropriations for the requisite number of subsidized dwelling units, but which would raise the political costs for the nation's chief executive and local government officials of not achieving national housing goals:"[15]

Four of the recommendations concern the Executive Branch: (1) An annual Presidential housing message that would parallel the budget message, the state of the union address, and the economic report, specifying housing construction goals for the year ahead; (2) A mechanism ... "in the executive branch to insure that when basic economic decisions are made, their effects on housing construction and housing construction goals be clearly and deliberately considered," as well as requirements that government agencies, such as the Federal Reserve Board, the Treasury, and others, be compelled to spell out what "effects any major changes in economic policy would have on the successful building of the number of housing units set by the President in his annual housing construction message"; (3) A capital budget for housing at the national level in order that "direct federal grants for the construction of low and moderate income housing can be amortized over an extended period of time rather than having to be written off as immediate costs in the year expended"; and (4) A procedure for authorizing and appropriating federal housing funds for a period of three years in recognition of the lead time necessary to develop low and moderate income housing in communities.

In the final section of this book, we will return to the relationship between housing goals and housing standards.

Notes

[1] *Building the American City*, Report of the National Commission on Urban Problems to the Congress and the President of the United States (Washington: Government Printing Office, 1969), p. 25.

[2] *Ibid.*, p. 25.

[3] Robert W. Rafuse, Jr., "The Efficiency of Conditional Grants-in-Aid," *Revenue Sharing and Its Alternatives: What Future for Fiscal Federalism?*, prepared for the Subcommittee on Fiscal Policy of the Joint Economic Committee, Congress of the United States, Volume II, *Range of Alternatives for Fiscal Federalism* (Washington: Government Printing Office, 1967), p. 1053.

[4] *Ibid.*, p. 1054.

[5] George Schermer, *More Than Shelter*, Prepared for the Consideration of the National Commission on Urban Problems, Research Report No. 8 (Washington: Government Printing Office, 1968), p. VII.

[6] William G. Grigsby, Mimeographed outline for seminar on housing, Fall 1969, University of

Pennsylvania, Department of City and Regional Planning, p. 1.
[7]William G. Grigsby, "Housing Aspects of Poverty," mimeographed memorandum, University of Pennsylvania, 1965.
[8]University of Pennsylvania and Morgan State College, under contract with the Office of Economic Opportunity.
[9]Cited in *Building the American City, op. cit.*, p. 57.
[10]*A Decent Home*, The Report of the President's Committee on Urban Housing (Washington: Government Printing Office, 1968) p. 9.
[11]*Building the American City, op. cit.*, p. 13.
[12]*Ibid.*, p. 13.
[13]*House and Home* (Vol. 37, No. 1, January 1970), p. 5.
[14]Statement of Honorable Robert F. Kennedy, presented at Hearings Before the Committee on Finance, United States Senate, Ninetieth Congress, First Session, on S.2100, Tax Incentives to Encourage Housing in Urban Poverty Areas (Washington, September 1967), p. 71.
[15]Michael A. Stegman, "Kaiser, Douglas and Kerner on Low-Income Housing Policy," *Journal of the American Institute of Planners* (Vol. XXXV, No. 6, November 1969), p. 426.

3.1

A Proposed Methodology for Comparing Federally Assisted Housing Programs

William B. Ross

Sheerly by coincidence, the launching of the new Federal Department of Housing and Urban Development followed shortly on the heels of the new presidential directive[1] for increased formal emphasis on more precise identification of national goals and on more systematic analysis of alternative means of reaching them most effectively. From the beginning, there have been no illusions either that the desired objective of effective public administration was a new one or that all the sought-after improvement in the precision and quality of analysis would be achieved overnight—or in a single year—or in a single administration.

The urgency of the presidential instruction was clearly of the "let us begin" variety. But the full burden falls on individual agencies to translate into their own operational setting an analytic approach long pioneered—but still conceded to be in the development stage[2]—in the analysis of defense goals and alternatives. The launching of so many simultaneous diverse efforts—without benefit of the extensive developmental work which preceded the formal Defense Department system—has inevitably resulted in analysis ranging from the uneven to the unsatisfactory and, often, to the unproduced. Each agency making this effort faces its own particular version of generalized national goals supported by broad individual program objectives leading to loosely related program activities on which voluminous records are kept on everything but how the program activities support the program objectives and lead specifically and measurably to the fulfillment of concrete national goals.

When everything depends on everything else, it is not immediately clear whether better analysis can be started most effectively: at better specification of national goals; at clearer development of relationships between overall program objectives and national goals; at testing of the relationships between specific program activities and program objectives; or at development of better data on any or all of the preceding relationships?

The present paper is, at best, a progress report on how one analytic staff in one agency is attempting to approach one

Reprinted from *Papers and Proceedings of the Seventy-Ninth Annual Meeting of the American Economic Association, American Economic Review* (Vol. LVII, No. 2, May 1967), pp. 91–100, with the permission of the American Economic Association and William B. Ross.

specific policy problem cycle. The aim of the paper is to describe what we believe to be useful analytic methodology for the federal decision-maker; we try to be explicit about the stages of analysis in which we choose to defer concentration while presenting for critical review those tentative proposals which now appear to us both to be relevant and to lead in useful directions.

Federal Goals in Housing

Since 1949, the nation has had the expressed goal "of a decent home and a suitable living environment for every American family. . . ."[3] The directness, simplicity, grandeur, and scope of this expression have been the envy of presidential speechwriters and of legislative draftsmen ever since. None has topped it, and most have sensed the futility of even trying.

But the process of refining this broad goal into operational terms—even setting aside for present purposes the phrase "a suitable living environment"—is neither direct nor unambiguous. Certainly, the refinement process must consider the broad variety of action programs enacted under the "decent home" banner. Not all of the relevant programs are the responsibility of the Department of Housing and Urban Development, but even those that are represent a diversity which we feel incapable of encompassing altogether within a single analytic framework.

For initial clarity, we have chosen somewhat arbitrarily to subdivide HUD's housing programs between those which appear to fit most logically under the phrase "to facilitate effective private housing market mechanisms" as distinguished from programs whose ultimate purposes appear to include overt assistance in the provision of housing at below-market costs. This dichotomy is neither a clean one nor of indefinite value. But, for the present, we find it to be a useful distinction.

The "assisted" housing programs are not themselves by any means a homogeneous group. Interpretation and interpolation of recorded legislative histories, inductive reasoning from obvious relationships, and even interrogation of participants in the legislative process all have a part in trying to identify just what unique combination of contributions a particular program was (and is) expected to make toward the overall decent home goal.

Essentially, each well-established federal activity has been the product of a unique, continued exercise in group dynamics involving interaction between (1) proposers of legislation (executive and legislative); (2) subcommittees, full committees, and leadership groups in the legislative process; (3) executive branch program administrators; (4) executive and legislative participants in the budgetary process; and (5) the "target group" of individuals or institutions. The net programmatic result has both the strengths and the weaknesses of the processes of democracy; above all, however, it means that single-dimensional measurement and single-criteria evaluation and even single-disciplinary study are inadequate—or even misleading.

The unraveling of the mixture of motivations and goals is the most difficult and the most critical part of analytic efforts—and, potentially, the most productive. But, the complexity of these patterns means that analysis cannot start at a logical beginning of clear identification of unambiguous goals and proceed in orderly, martial fashion to conclusions. The program grouping with which this paper deals is merely one special case of this problem.

At this stage, for example, we do not find it useful to insist on a direct separation of the income-redistribution goals of housing assistance programs from the developmental goals—both economic and social—of providing more housing of socially acceptable quality for various population groups. Yet, we cannot ignore the existence of "low" income groups too "poor" to be aided directly through existing housing assistance mechanisms. The evidence of constraints on the utility of functional programs for income-maintenance objectives requires more careful delineation of objectives/means relationships but cannot be regarded as a prima facie case for abandonment.

The Concept of Output

In the past, it would have been relevant, or even necessary, to debate at length whether the "outputs" of housing assistance programs should be quantified in "goods" terms (e.g., units produced) or "services" terms (e.g., unit months of occupancy). This dilemma appears to us to have been resolved by increased reliance on upgrading of existing substandard housing units and by the initiation of new assistance methods which involve temporary support of units for varying periods of time. Thus, for the present, at least, we find it necessary to use output concepts of the flow-of-service in order to compare those programs which we now administer, let alone the infinite varieties of alternative assistance devices which could be considered.

Again, the choice is a tentative one, and the probabilities are high that we will, for some parts of the analysis, need to return to production or "goods" output measurements. For either choice, considerably more thought will need to be given to the "standard-substandard" concepts and definitions.

"Housing Assistance" Programs

Any listing of federal "programs" is tentative and subject to expansion or contraction as analysis focuses, at one stage, on relevant characteristics which require separate consideration of distinctions within an administratively cohesive program or, at another stage, on characteristics which blur the distinctions between programs administered by totally different organizations or agencies.

With these reservations, we consider that seven administratively separate programs constitute the "assisted housing" category:

1. Low-rent public housing (including new construction; acquisition of new units; acquisition of existing units, with or without rehabilitation; and leasing of existing units).
2. Rent supplements with mortgage insurance (with or without federal acquisition of the insured mortgage).
3. Direct loans at below-market interest rates for rental housing for the elderly and handicapped.
4. Below-market interest rate loans to higher educational institutions for housing and related facilities (including faculty housing and married student apartments).
5. Insured mortgages at below-market interest rates coupled with federal acquisition of the insured mortgage.
6. Below-market interest rate loans for rehabilitation of owner-occupied dwellings in urban renewal areas.
7. Partial grants to low-income homeowners in urban renewal areas for rehabilitation.

Economic Characteristics of "Assisted Housing" Programs

While this group of programs has the common economic characteristic that the housing for some period of time is provided to the occupant at less than the private market costs, the significant differences within the group may be categorized, tentatively, as (1) differences in degree (level or proportion) of assistance; (2) differences in time pattern of gross and net federal outlay or cost; (3) differences in time pattern of benefits; (4) differences in the physical unit provided; (5) differences in total costs of the unit provided.

For purposes of this paper, it is necessary only to describe the range of these differences rather than the full array of them.

The degree of assistance can be as high as a partial contribution to operating costs plus the full capital costs of building new units as represented by the maximum annual federal contribution under low-rent public housing; it can be as low as a small fraction of the cost of a fix-up job as in the owner-occupant rehabilitation assistance programs. It may be as fixed as the maximum dollar limit for rehabilitation grants; it may be as indeterminate as the rent supplement payment which depends more on the future incomes of the tenants than it does on initial construction costs.

The time pattern of net federal outlays or cost can be as simple and as short as the one-check disbursement of a rehabilitation grant; it can be as long as the fifty-year maximum repayment period on a college dormitory loan; it can be as complex as the forty years of annually calculated net federal contributions to a low-rent public housing project plus the estimated federal loss on tax-exemption of the bonds sold to finance the project.

The time pattern of benefits can last as long as the housing unit stands in many cases; it could change or even terminate at the first annual tenant income reexamination of a rent supplement project; it can be linked to specific time periods as in the case of public housing leased units; or a residual part of it could be capitalized into the net selling price of a unit rehabilitated with grant assistance when the property subsequently changes hands.

The physical units provided show large distinctions within each program group as well as between them—even when reduced from "structures" to "dwelling unit" terms. The range can be from the sleeping/study room shared by two or four college students to the multibedroom apartment for a large family in public housing or a rent supplement project.

Over and above the unit cost differences attributable to differences in average unit size, there are other major cost factors of great policy relevance. Quality of construction standards are among the most significant of these. Quality standards of size, equipment, and allowable amenities are administratively established pursuant to general legislative standards or guidance (e.g., "not be of elaborate or extravagant design or materials")[4] and thus differ most between programs which have been administered separately. The scope of "related facilities" included can also be significant as when a public housing project includes community rooms for recreational or social services activities. Equal size and quality units can be provided in large- or small-scale projects or in single units with greatly differing production costs. And, highly significantly, local land values and construction costs for the same product can differ within the nation by nearly 100 percent.

Relevant Policy Issues

Given a going concern which carries on, among its activities, a series of related programs with this range of diversity, the policy questions most frequently raised are likely to be along these lines: What changes, if any, ought to be made in the multitude of administratively established constraints? What alternative devices could be proposed to better serve all or part of the objectives of this program group? And, most of all, what should be the incremental change in the relative proportions in which these related—and sometimes complementary—programs should be offered in the next annual budget?

The first of these questions is literally always relevant. The others become pressing on at least an annual cycle and become increasingly intense in those years in which a program exhausts its previously authorized time or money limits and must, in effect, have its option renewed. In each such policy question, varying degrees of partial goal reexamination and refinement are necessarily involved, but the complex nature of the composite goal mixture seldom permits abstract, total goals formulation except in the context of a policy issue along one of these lines.

At this stage of development, our approach to the assisted housing program group focuses on the income redistribution (housing cost savings to tenants) aspects which are their most common denominator but not necessarily the dominant goal of any one program nor of equal weights in the goal mix as between programs.

Measuring "Costs"

For present purposes, we believe it appropriate to measure "costs" of the assisted housing programs in terms of net federal payments, although more sophisticated measures may become more useful at later stages of analysis; e.g., in dealing with macroeconomic aspects of national housing investments. Our federal cost measure cannot, however, be restricted solely to direct outlays and recoveries of the Department. The nature of financing mechanisms used in this program group requires consideration of interest costs (only parts of which may be reflected in the agency's books) and the effects of exemption from federal income taxes. These factors are considered not for the sheer joy of complicating the analysis but solely out of the necessity that they be taken into account in reducing the disparate programs to a meaningful common basis.

The consideration of interest costs is present in another form when we attempt to make comparisons between the disparate time patterns of disbursement and repayment possible within this program grouping. Discounted present values are an obvious device for handling this problem, and the use of federal borrowing rates is an equally obvious first approximation of an appropriate rate of discount when we are comparing alternative federal methods of spending money to achieve the same or related ends. Again, more complex discount rate concepts, e.g., taxpayer's marginal value of consumption foregone, are only appropriate in the analysis of more aggregative aspects of the housing problem.

Measuring "Benefits"

Isolating the income-redistributional results of the housing assistance programs can be regarded as a first approximation of one aspect of the "benefits" of these programs, although we will most certainly want subsequently to look at the pattern of "savings" against the beneficiary income patterns to make a judgment on how well the income-redistributional results correspond to public goals. Initially, we may assume that the assisted tenants are those for whom income benefits are intended to accrue.

While the rents (or monthly housing costs for owner-occupants) of the units aided under the various programs are determinable, we need a base concept against which to compare these rents. Comparison with rents paid by the tenants in their previous housing has immediate but superficial attractiveness. It suffers from the defect that varying quality, size, and location of the previous unit make this comparison unreliable at best.

A better concept—which both avoids the uncertainty-of-previous-condition problem and adapts to the variety of factors influencing unit costs—is that of "private market housing of comparable quality." This standard has considerable flexibility in analysis and appears to be useful for a wide variety of comparisons, provided one keeps in mind the weakness of its implicit assumption that the tenant would have chosen housing of this size, quality, location, etc.

At its simplest stage, this standard can be applied to analysis of the pure cost differences to the federal government involved in its choices of financial devices. This can be accomplished by applying the financial assistance parameters of each program in turn to a standard housing unit to determine the variations in net federal cost and net rent savings yielded by each of them. This assumes that the unit would have cost the same to construct and would have served the same tenants under each of the programs compared.

The next stage would involve the assumption that private construction cost of the comparable unit would have equaled that experienced by the assisted unit. By holding unit costs constant and applying the financial parameters of the going private mortgage market (regular FHA mortgage insurance terms and conditions may be useful for this purpose), we may approximate the net rental savings to tenants for each of the programs in turn.

Since, in either case, these rental savings accrue over an extended period of time, they must also be aggregated in some way to compare the relative "rental savings per dollar of federal cost" efficiencies of the various programs. Because these savings are effectively felt by the recipients as the (reduced) rent becomes due, the temptation is very strong to ignore discount factors and simply add the savings over the period in which they are expected to occur even though the costs would be aggregated on a discounted basis. The natural compulsion toward symmetry and reversibility in analysis argues otherwise. In addition, it may be useful in evaluating income-redistributional effects of programs to consider the stream of benefits as equivalent to a stream of cash payments. Thus, by discounting rental savings also at the federal borrowing rate, we have automatically calculated the present value of a stream of payments which can be compared with the present value of the pattern of federal costs incurred to yield that income benefit through an indirect (or multiple-goal) device.

Subsequent relaxation of the "equality-of-cost" assumption will be feasible through successive stages of architectural-engineering analyses of the products of each assistance program to approximate more accurately the private reproduction costs of assisted units. As sufficient operating and maintenance cost data become available, it will also be possible and desirable to put overall construction and operating costs on comparable bases to evaluate differences in total life ("systems"?) costs resulting from differences in construction standards as between programs.

In any event, the relative values of private "rental savings per dollar of federal cost" among the various federal assisted housing programs provide one benefit-cost ranking—one that measures the income redistribution benefit. We may term the highest benefit-to-cost ratio "the income redistribution optimum."

In addition to the income redistribution effects, there are other aspects of the effects of assisted housing programs requiring equal attention, in their turn, such as the unit output/cost optimum or "most bang for the buck" target.

Over and above direct financial cost/benefit comparisons, there are differential benefits associated with the separate housing assistance programs in terms of how each program contributes or fails to contribute to the strategy of providing rebirth to dying cities or critical improvements to decaying neighborhoods.

In short, if we were to give to the poor—through a negative income tax or some alternative device—the dollar equivalent of the income benefits they receive through these housing programs, we would still face the problem of saving our cities and neighborhoods; and this effort, too, would have its very substantial money cost.

Thus, should we identify two alternative housing programs which are comparable in their income redistribution benefits (or comparable in cost to the federal government), but one makes a notable contribution to urban redevelopment or neighborhood improvement and the other does not, then clearly the one making the dual contribution is to be preferred on efficiency grounds.

Accordingly, we would next want to identify the nonquantifiable environmental impacts of the alternative housing solutions and the long-term versus short-term implications. By and large, this would consist of identifying the favorable and unfavorable consequences worthy of note for each relevant housing alternative, including implications with regard to meeting other urban objectives such as the creation of sound neighborhoods and economically viable cities. We would also assess the relative significance of these factors, considering such things as the relationship to overall area needs in terms of roads, facilities, and commercial establishments; the impact on the neighborhood subculture; the hostility or acceptance of nearby residents; the ease of assembling suitable real estate; the probable timing; and the number of persons affected, etc. This could culminate in the creation of a table of descriptive summary data along the following lines: housing alternative; cost disadvantage (over least total cost solution); unfavorable environmental consequences; favorable environmental consequences; significance of consequences.

The final stages of this approach to an optimum solution would consist of a new ranking from "most preferred" to "least preferred" which considers both housing cost/benefit factors and environmental consequences. The theoretical optimum at this stage may be defined as one of the following: (1) the "least total cost" alternative whose net environmental disadvantages are not sufficient to offset its cost advantage over higher cost alternatives, or (2) the alternative whose net favorable environmental consequences provide the most significant offset (nonquantitative judgmental offset) to its cost disadvantage. We will call this approximation the "environmental optimum."

The suggested handling of nonquantitative data is not a mechanical or arithmetic one, and it does not yield a numeric solution. For that reason, it will be unsatisfactory to some. We are all familiar with the horse and rabbit stew problem implicit in any decision involving both quantitative and nonquantitative data. However, we believe that this approach provides the opportunity to quantify everything that can be quantified in a practical situation and to compare systematically alternative packages of concomitant net benefits associated with each alternative as offsets to cost factors.

The President has placed strong emphasis on the careful definition of program objectives and on careful analysis of alternative means for achieving these objectives efficiently. At the federal level, the general strategy in housing and urban development programs will almost certainly be (1) to encourage efforts by local governments to identify and pursue the most efficient local solutions, (2) to develop national data and analyses which identify the most effective overall programs and administrative practices, and (3) to seek expansion of these efficient programs and general and broad application of creative new approaches. We invite your attention to these matters and seek constructive suggestions on the analytical methods we have outlined.

Notes

[1]President's Memorandum to Heads of Departments and Agencies, Aug. 25, 1965; U.S. Bureau of the Budget, Bulletin No. 66–3, Oct. 12, 1965, and Supplement to Bulletin No. 66–3, Feb. 21, 1966.

[2]Alain C. Enthoven, "Introduction," *A Modern Design for Defense Decision: A McNamara-Hitch-Enthoven Anthology* (Washington, Industrial College of the Armed Forces, 1966), p. 7.

[3]Declaration of National Housing Policy, Section 2, Housing Act of 1949 (Public Law 171, 81st Cong.; 63 Stat. 413).

[4]Section 401(a), Housing Act of 1950 (Public Law 475, 81st Cong.; 64 Stat. 48).

3.2

Economic Feasibility Analysis for Urban Renewal Housing Rehabilitation

A. H. Schaaf

This paper focuses on the economic feasibility of housing rehabilitation as compared with replacement or redevelopment. We assume that public policy calls for the elimination of "substandard" units, however defined, and that the only relevant question is how best to achieve this goal. The two alternative approaches are to fix up a unit—rehabilitation—or to tear it down and replace it with a new unit—redevelopment. Both approaches fall under the broader heading of renewal.

The Objective of Efficient Resource Utilization

To cast our approach in a realistic setting, perhaps we can think of it as applying to a Public Housing Authority that is endeavoring to raise housing standards in a given area. The Authority can buy up substandard units and then either rehabilitate them or tear them down and replace them with new units. Which should it do?

In answering this question, we appraise the feasibility of rehabilitation strictly and solely from the standpoint of achieving the most economical and efficient use of resources, that is, the housing stock and the resources used up in construction, demolition, and maintenance activities. Considerations such as the personal income tax treatment of rehabilitation and new construction expenditures, while of great importance to a private investor making a rehabilitation or replacement decision, do not concern us. In our global, public context, such taxes are simply transfers and are important only as policy tools used to stimulate or discourage certain types of investment and entrepreneurship. They do not represent a resource use, and we are interested here only in the feasibility of rehabilitation as a way of providing a *specific amount of housing improvement with the least expenditure of human and nonhuman resources.*

In focusing purely on the objective of efficient utilization of resources, we are avoiding problems of dislocation, relocation, and rationing units after renewal. However, to use again the Public Housing Authority example, we may assume that each occupying household prior to renewal will be the postrenewal oc-

Reprinted by permission of the *Journal of the American Institute of Planners* (Vol. XXXV, No. 6, November 1969), pp. 399–404.

cupant of the identical renewed unit. The price he pays to occupy the unit will be determined by his ability to pay rather than the Authority's acquisition and renewal cost. In the case of owner-occupied units, we see the Authority buying the owner-occupant's house, renewing it, and selling it back to him with contractual payments based on his ability to pay.

The Profitability Criterion

Considered solely as a private investment decision, the feasibility of residential rehabilitation, both absolutely and in comparison with redevelopment, would be determined by its profitability. The investment would be made only if the expected returns were competitively sufficient to justify the investment, and the answer to the question of rehabilitation versus redevelopment would depend on which action promised the greater profit. Insofar as private costs and gains coincide with those of society, the profitability criterion would result in an optimum utilization of the resources in question. This is, of course, the major and time-honored way in which this question is solved in a free market economy.

Our problem, however, cannot be solved by addressing ourselves solely to the task of determining rehabilitation and redevelopment costs, cash flows, residuals, and discount rates—the ingredients of the private investment decision. By and large, we are dealing with situations in which neither course of action is profitable. There may, of course, be instances in which better market analysis would reveal profitable rehabilitation or redevelopment opportunities that were not being acted upon. Similarly, public action may be on such a broad scale that entire areas are changed, new markets are tapped, and no project losses are experienced. However, our objective is to improve aggregate housing conditions to a point above that achieved without public action. Subsidies rather than profits must ordinarily be relied upon to produce this result.

This is not to say that we will not take account of private profitability criteria. As we shall see, they are still important to feasibility analysis even if subsidies are required. However, in much of the literature on rehabilitation the implication has been that its usefulness and generality have been overlooked due to a lack of appreciation of profitable opportunities. This argument has sometimes led to the conclusion that unless rehabilitation is profitable it cannot be used and that redevelopment is then the only remaining course of action.

It is important to see that this conclusion is quite incorrect. Rehabilitation and redevelopment are equally well-suited for subsidization, and the absence of private profitability is no reason for rejection of either. Regardless of profitability, either may be "feasible" as a means of implementing public policies aimed at improving housing conditions through subsidization of an increased volume of residential construction. In our analysis, the best and therefore most "feasible" method is simply the one with the greatest output per unit of input.

The Comparative Cost Approach

The rehabilitation versus redevelopment question can be, and often is, resolved on the basis of least-cost. This criterion is particularly appealing in that it reduces to a minimum the immediate problem of cost absorption. Housing is improved at the lowest possible cost and with the least impact upon rents and prices, thus minimizing the chances of occupant dislocation. However, it is clear that sole reliance on least-cost as the determinant of the renewal method is insufficient since attention must also be directed to the nature and longevity of the housing improvement that is achieved.

In a 1960 study, *Economic Aspects of Urban Renewal*, a modified least-cost approach was employed.[1] The first step consisted of establishing a single standard to which every property in the area was to be renewed. Either rehabilitation or redevelopment was then stipulated depending upon which was the cheapest method of achieving the given standard. The crucial element in this methodology was acceptance of a uniform standard to be achieved either by rehabilitation or redevelopment. Specialized conditions and objectives, partly of a pragmatic nature, made this procedure acceptable for the purposes of this earlier study. However, the specification of the renewal standard is really a crucial part of the problem involved in any comparison of the two renewal methods. Much of what we attempt here is in effect aimed at determining the "best" renewal standard.

In *Economics of Housing*, Lionel Needleman expands the comparative cost approach by noting that future maintenance costs and the economic life of the renewed structure must also be considered.[2] That is, not only may redevelopment and rehabilitation costs differ but, after renewal, the economic life of the structure and the level of maintenance costs may vary depending upon whether rehabilitation or redevelopment has been used as the means of renewal. These observations lead to a formulation of the problem which states that rehabilitation is the preferred method if redevelopment costs exceed the sum of rehabilitation costs plus the present value of the next renewal cost outlay plus the present value of the annual difference in the maintenance costs of a rehabilitated structure compared with a new one.[3] That is, rehabilitation is preferred if

$$C > \left[R + M\frac{1 - (1 + i)^{-n}}{i} + \frac{C}{(1 + i)^{n}} \right] \tag{1}$$

where C = new construction cost,
R = rehabilitation cost,
M = annual savings in maintenance costs with a new structure rather than a rehabilitated one,
n = life of present structure following rehabilitation, and
i = discount rate.

The formulation contained in (1) recognizes relevant cost-comparison variables in addition to the replacement and rehabilitation cost outlays themselves. It also illustrates the point that the feasibility of rehabilitation as compared to replacement is greater the higher interest rates are and the more the rehabilitation work increases the structure's life and postpones the time when replacement must be made. That is, rehabilitation's feasibility is directly related to i and n. However, the construction formulated in (1) contains one error and, more importantly, ignores a number of complicating factors that should be considered in an appraisal of rehabilitation's feasibility.

Shortcomings of the Formulation

The error in (1) concerns the term $C/(1 + i)^n$. The term is used to measure the present value of the amount that will have to be available to replace the structure when rehabilitation's effects have played out. Ignoring M, the formulation contained in (1) implies that the owner would be indifferent between rehabilitation and replacement if $C = [R + C/(1 + i)^n]$. This is not true, however. If he replaces now, he will have a structure n years old in n years, whereas if he rehabilitates and invests the amount $C/(1 + i)^n$, he will have an amount equal to the cost of a *new* structure in n years.

Thus the proper comparison is between C and $[R+C\ (1\text{-}nr)/(1+i)^n]$, where r denotes the annual depreciation rate of the new structure (using straight-line depreciation). We may correctly say (still ignoring M) that the owner is indifferent between rehabilitation and redevelopment if $C=[R+C\ (1\text{-}nr)/(1+i)^n]$ because in either case he will have an income-producing structure for n years and an asset worth the depreciated value of a new structure at the end of n years. If $C>[R+C\ (1\text{-}nr)/(1+i)^n]$, he will rehabilitate and vice versa.

Although this revision corrects the error in the discounted C term, we should note that the use of the C term also represents a limitation in the model. In effect, the model compares the desirability of constructing a new building today with that of rehabilitating the existing building now and constructing the new building n years from now. In the next section we shall formulate a more general model that will also include the possibility of successive future rehabilitation investments, that is, it will not necessarily use C but rather the "most feasible" cost magnitude in n years (or perhaps a series of them) in the discounted cost term. It is well to note here, however, that the investment analysis in any event would still be limited to a period equal to the length of life of the new building; this is another result of adding the depreciation factor (r) to the discounted cost term.

The major shortcoming of the formulation in (1) is that it completely ignores the problem of defining and determining the "best" renewal standard. In effect, there is just one renewal standard, and it is achieved by single-valued outlays for R or C. However, different standards of both rehabilitation and new construction are obviously possible and, thus, different values of R and C. Further, as R and C vary, M and n will also vary. That is, R varies directly with n and inversely with M while C and M vary directly.

Another closely related shortcoming of the formulation in (1) is that it gives no consideration to the possibility that a new structure may provide a higher level of shelter amenities than a rehabilitated one. (The reverse might be true in some cases of "prestige" rehabilitation.) Although the postrenewal occupants would not be paying market prices and the public authority does not seek to make a profit, the best use of resources will prevail if we incorporate some measure of relative levels of shelter amenities into our decision. This is necessary in order to ensure that the renewal expenditure achieves the greatest "bundle" of housing at the lowest possible cost.

Although data may be scarce and unreliable, the best, and probably only, way to handle this problem is to use rent differences to measure differences in amenity levels. By examining the rents of comparable units, we would try to estimate the rents (or imputed rents in the case of owner-occupied units) that the rehabilitated units will bring on the open market. We would similarly estimate the rental value of comparable new units. Then we would add to (1) (as corrected for the C term) a term denoting the present value of future differences in the rent levels of new and rehabilitated structures.

Let
D = differences in the annual rental income of a new structure and a rehabilitated structure.
Rehabilitation is preferred if

$$C > \left[R + M\frac{1-(1+i)^{-n}}{i} + \frac{C(1-nr)}{(1+i)^{n}} + D\frac{1-(1+i)^{-n}}{i} \right] \qquad (2)$$

The formulation in (2) provides the basic model for our analysis of rehabilitation's feasibility. Before we proceed to examine this model in more detail, however, note must be taken of still another factor in rehabilitation analysis that has not yet been considered. Rehabilitation is obviously an infeasible course if major land use changes are indicated for the area. Such changes would include both transfers from residential to nonresidential

Table 1. Characteristics of Five Renewal Standards

Renewal standard	Renewal cost	Structure life (years)	Expected average annual future maintenance cost	Expected average annual market rental value
Code compliance	$ 8,000	10	$2,000	$3,600
Structural repair	28,000	40	1,400	3,600
Modernization	40,000	40	1,000	6,720
Prestige	80,000	40	1,000	8,640
New	100,000	50	800	9,600

uses and major increases in residential densities. Although this problem could be incorporated in (2) within the *D* term, it is probably best to handle the problem as one of overall area analysis.[4] This is the approach adopted in the discussion that follows.

Determining the Optimum Renewal Standard

In order to clarify the concepts developed to this point and indicate the problems that remain unresolved, a simple numerical example is useful. This will illustrate how the model expressed in (2) might be used in an actual renewal area study. It will also show why this model cannot determine the optimum standard of renewal and what must be done in order to determine such a standard.

In this example, we assume an apartment house containing four two-bedroom units with numerous code deficiencies. Following purchase by the local Housing Authority, investigations of the structure and the local rental market are made. It is concluded that the replacement cost of the structure is $100,000 and that the new apartments would rent for $200 a month. Four levels of rehabilitation are also studied with cost estimates and rental values as shown in Table 1. An assumed interest rate of 6 percent is employed in the calculations.[5] After compiling these data, we begin investigation of rehabilitation's feasibility and determination of the optimum renewal standard using the model formulated in (2). Rehabilitation is feasible for any standard if

$$C > \left[R + M\frac{1-(1+i)^{-n}}{i} + \frac{C(1-nr)}{(1+i)^{n}} + D\frac{1-(1+i)^{-n}}{i} \right].$$

The optimum level of rehabilitation is the one that maximizes *Y* when

$$Y = C - \left[R + M\frac{1-(1+i)^{-n}}{i} + \frac{C(1-nr)}{(1+i)^{n}} + D\frac{1-(1+i)^{-n}}{i} \right].$$

The feasibility analysis of each rehabilitation level is as follows:

1. Code Compliance feasibility analysis:

$$Y_1 = \$100{,}000 - \left[\$8{,}000 + \$1{,}200\frac{1-1.06^{-10}}{.06} + \frac{\$100{,}000(1-.20)}{1.06^{10}} + \$6{,}000\frac{1-1.06^{-10}}{.06} \right]$$

$$= \$100{,}000 - [\$8{,}000 + \$8{,}892 + \$44{,}600 + \$44{,}160]$$
$$= -\$5{,}652.$$

2. Structural Repair feasibility analysis:

$$Y_2 = \$100{,}000 - \left[\$28{,}000 + \$600\frac{1-1.06^{-40}}{.06} + \frac{\$100{,}000(1-.80)}{1.06^{40}} + \$6{,}000\frac{1-1.06^{-40}}{.06} \right]$$

$$= \$100{,}000 - [\$28{,}000 + \$9{,}300 + \$1{,}900 + \$93{,}000]$$
$$= -\$32{,}200.$$

3. Modernization feasibility analysis:

$$Y_2 = \$100{,}000 - \left[\$40{,}000 + \$200\frac{1-1.06^{-40}}{.06} + \frac{\$100{,}000(1-.80)}{1.06^{40}} + \$2{,}880\frac{1-1.06^{-40}}{.06} \right]$$

$$= \$100{,}000 - [\$40{,}000 + \$3{,}100 + \$1{,}900 + \$44{,}640]$$
$$= \$10{,}360.$$

4. Prestige Rehabilitation feasibility analysis:

$$Y_4 = \$100{,}000 - \left[\$80{,}000 + \$200\frac{1-1.06^{-40}}{.06} + \frac{\$100{,}000(1-.80)}{1.06^{40}} + \$960\frac{1-1.06^{-40}}{.06} \right]$$

$$= \$100{,}000 - [\$80{,}000 + \$3{,}100 + \$1{,}900 + \$14{,}880]$$
$$= \$120.$$

Results and Limitations of the Feasibility Analysis

As shown by the feasibility calculations relating to each renewal standard, the model indicates that both modernization and prestige rehabilitation are feasible (preferable to new construction) and that modernization is the economically most efficient standard. Similarly, the least efficient course of action would appear to be to meet code standards and repair the structure but not attempt any modernization of the units.

These results, however, are not complete. As noted earlier in our discussion of the C term, the model operates under the assumption that new construction is the renewal action that will be undertaken when the effects of the renewal action adopted now have played out—in n years. In actuality, future renewal investments of any kind could be made. Perhaps the most efficient action is rehabilitation to the code compliance standard three times and then new construction. Similarly, we might consider the possibility of code compliance once and then modernization in ten years, or prestige rehabilitation and then code compliance in forty years, and so on.

It is not possible to represent all of the alternative investment situations in one generalized formulation. The model in (2) remains the basic framework for comparing immediate new construction with the various situations involving rehabilitation. However, three types of changes or additions must be made in the basic model in order to adapt it for use in all possible circumstances. After explaining the nature of these changes, we shall illustrate them in a final numerical example, which should suffice to indicate the exact way in which any investment situation is to be handled.

The three types of changes and additions are as follows:

1. The length of life and corresponding depreciation rate associated with each renewal standard must be identified. We will do so in the form of subscripts. Thus, if subscript 1 denotes the code compliance standard then R_1 is the cost of code compliance, n_1 is the life of the structure rehabilitated to code compliance levels, and r_1 is the straight line depreciation rate associated with n_1, or $100/n_1$ percent.

2. All investment situations should continue to be limited to periods equal to the length of the new structure's life. Accordingly, any future renewal investment with a life extending beyond such period must be depreciated so that only that part of the renewed structure's life that will be used up in the period under consideration is counted as a cost item. This is, of course, the same procedure that we followed when we depreciated the future new construction term in (2). However, as we shall see in the example below, a slightly different treatment is required when new construction is no longer the final or residual renewal investment that is made.

3. If a new future rehabilitation investment is of a different type

than the one immediately preceding it, D and M will change. In this event, the new levels of D and M must be treated as annuities beginning at the time the new investment is made and continuing for the life of the new investment or to the end of the total investment period (the life of a new structure), whichever is less. The values of such annuities are then discounted back to the present time and used as cost-comparison items just as in (2). We must also use subscripts to identify D and M with their corresponding renewal standards.

A single numerical example should demonstrate the method of incorporating these changes in the basic model formulated in (2). In this example we investigate the feasibility of rehabilitating the structure to the code compliance standard three times over and then rehabilitating to the modernization standard. The feasibility analysis of this situation requires solving the following:

$$C - \left[R_1 + \frac{R_1}{(1+i)^{n_1}} + \frac{R_1}{(1+i)^{2n_1}} + \frac{R_3(r_3(n_c - 3n_1))}{(1+i)^{3n_1}} + M_1 \frac{1-(1+i)^{-3n_1}}{i} + D_1 \frac{1-(1+i)^{-3n_1}}{i} + \frac{M_3 \dfrac{1-(1+i)^{-(n_c-3n_1)}}{i}}{(1+i)^{3n_1}} + \frac{D_3 \dfrac{1-(1+i)^{-(n_c-3n_1)}}{i}}{(1+i)^{3n_1}} \right] \qquad (3)$$

where

R_1 = cost of code compliance,
R_3 = cost of modernization,
C = cost of new construction,
n_1 = life of structure rehabilitated to the code compliance standard,
n_2 = life of structure rehabilitated to the modernization standard,
$r_3 = \dfrac{100}{n_3}$ percent,
n_c = life of new structure,
M_1 = difference in maintenance costs between a new structure and one rehabilitated to the code compliance standard,
D_1 = difference in rent levels between a new structure and one rehabilitated to the code compliance standard,
M_3 = difference in maintenance costs between a new structure and one rehabilitated to the modernization standard, and
D_3 = difference in rent levels between a new structure and one rehabilitated to the modernization standard.

Using the values of our earlier numerical example, the solution of (3) is as follows:

$$\$100{,}000 - \Bigg[\$8{,}000 + \frac{\$8{,}000}{1.06^{10}} + \frac{\$8{,}000}{1.06^{20}} + \frac{\$40{,}000\,(.025\,(50-30))}{1.06^{30}} + \$1{,}200\,\frac{1-1.06^{-30}}{.06} + \$6{,}000\,\frac{1-1.06^{-30}}{.06} + \frac{\$200\,\frac{1-1.06^{-(50-30)}}{.06}}{1.06^{30}} + \frac{\$2{,}880\,\frac{1-1.06^{-(50-30)}}{.06}}{1.06^{30}} \Bigg]$$

$$= \$100{,}000 - [\$8{,}000 + \$4{,}525 + \$2{,}492 + \$3{,}486 + \$16{,}524 + \$82{,}620 + \$399 + \$5{,}947]$$

$$= -\$23{,}993.$$

This formulation compares new construction cost with the sum of code compliance cost, the present values of the cost of code compliance ten and twenty years from now, the present value of that part of modernization cost thirty years hence that will be used up during the life span of a new structure (with an annual, straight-line, depreciation rate of .025 stemming from the forty-year life of the modernized structure, one-half of the modernization investment will have been used up in the twenty years that follow the thirtieth year of the fifty-year life span of the new structure), the present values of the annual maintenance cost and rent differences for the next thirty years between a new building and one rehabilitated to the code compliance standard, and the present values of the annual maintenance cost and rent differences between a new building and one rehabilitated to the modernization standard, such differences to obtain for a twenty-year period beginning thirty years from now. In this example, this particular pattern of rehabilitation investment is not feasible. As always, rehabilitation is feasible if the total cost of any investment situation involving rehabilitation is less than the cost of immediate new construction. The optimum standard of rehabilitation is the combination that maximizes such cost difference. If no combination has a total cost less than that required for new construction, the latter is the optimum standard.

Area Analysis Procedure

In order to apply the concepts developed here, the following methodology is suggested in any given renewal area:

1. As a first step, it must be determined that no major areawide changes in land uses or residential densities are desirable since, as already noted, rehabilitation in such circumstances is infeasible virtually by definition. Such a determination should be made by considering the renewal area's place in the general plan of the entire city or metropolitan area. Due attention should also be paid to the market forces at work. The rehabilitation feasibility analysis should be undertaken only if it has been determined that the area in question would and should remain residential at about the same density for the foreseeable future.

The brevity of our discussion of this problem belies both its importance and its complexity. However, we may plead that, in one sense, such questions lie beyond the scope of our analysis here. As stated initially, our interest in this study is in the housing stock and construction resources. In effect, we are viewing residential structures purely as capital assets with no regard to their position in space. This is not to deny that the location of the structures is an important element in determining their most efficient utilization, however; this is a separate problem.

2. Having decided that rehabilitation is a possible choice for at least some of the structures in the area, the various renewal standards must be established and fully specified. The five used in our numerical example are indicative, but others are no doubt possible. The two limiting cases would ordinarily consist of minimum code compliance and new construction. For example, the level of the latter might approximate that of public housing units and would include the cost of clearance as well as the cost of the new building. Perhaps only a third standard, involving modernization and long-term structural renovation, would be necessary. It is desirable, of course, to limit as much as possible the number of alternate standards to minimize the number of investment situations that must be quantified and compared.

3. When the various renewal standards have been specified, the costs of meeting these standards can be estimated for each study property. Similarly, field investigation would be used to produce estimates of the differences between the new construction standard and each of the various rehabilitation standards in terms of maintenance costs and rent levels. Comparisons can then be made between immediate new construction and all of the

other possible investment situations as illustrated by (2) and (3). The most efficient investment situation involving rehabilitation would be the situation that is lowest in cost as compared with immediate new construction. If none is lower, of course, immediate clearance and new construction is indicated.

For purposes of preliminary area analysis, perhaps only a few representative structures might be studied. This would be particularly appropriate if the structures in the area are relatively homogeneous. Such a survey would indicate whether the area should be generally considered suitable for rehabilitation or redevelopment.

If rehabilitation is decided upon as a general approach, the formulation developed here could then be used in the detailed study of each individual structure. In this way both the feasibility and the optimum standard of rehabilitation would be determined for all the structures in the area. In some cases, of course, clearance might be indicated. However, in all cases, the housing "cost-output" ratio would be maximized and the best utilization of housing resources would be achieved.

Notes

[1]A. H. Schaaf, *Economic Aspects of Urban Renewal: Theory, Policy, and Area Analysis* (Berkeley: Real Estate Research Program, Institute of Business and Economic Research, University of California, 1960), chap. 2.

[2]Lionel Needleman, *The Economics of Housing* (London: Staples Press, 1965), pp. 200 ff.

[3]The arithmetic of present value calculations is illustrated by the numerical illustration in the next section.

[4]It should be noted, however, that the previously mentioned "scale" effects that may stem from renewal of a large contiguous area would be incorporated in the formulation in (2). With *either* rehabilitation or redevelopment, larger increases in postrenewal rental values could occur as the area being improved increased in size.

[5]The interest rate in our model represents the opportunity cost of the capital resources used in the housing improvement that results from public policy. The long-term Treasury bond yield with some upward adjustment to reflect corporate income taxes is probably the best approximation of this rate, but there are many issues involved here which cannot be examined within the space limitations of this article. For a good recent treatment of this question and a reference source to much of the literature on the subject, see William J. Baumol, "On the Social Rate of Discount," *American Economic Review*, LVIII (September 1968), 788–802.

3.3

Rent Supplements and the Subsidy Dilemma: The Equity of a Selective Subsidy System

Irving H. Welfeld

The issues are rarely right against wrong in
the law, but rather right against right.

For the ultimate issues veiled by time and mystery, in law as in life,
the most meaningful answer may be the question.
—Paul Freund[1]

I pray to the God within me that He will give me the strength to ask
Him the right questions.
—A Transylvanian Beadle[2]

Introduction

With existing technology, private enterprise unaided cannot meet the needs of the millions of low-income families living in substandard housing. Without a carrot of high caloric content the building industry is unable—in an era in which development costs are rising faster than the personal income of the poor—to produce an adequate supply of housing for families with incomes below the median.[3] As the Senate Committee on Banking and Currency has noted,[4]

> Since the end of World War II, there has been a remarkable increase in new housing production. The accelerated production pace can be attributed in large part to the energy and resourcefulness of American private enterprise, and it has redounded to the benefit of the Nation.
>
> It has become increasingly clear to the committee, however, that lower income families have not been able to participate fully in the benefits of this great burst of new housing production.
>
> . . . .
>
> There are almost 8 million American families who still live in sub-standard housing. The great majority of these families are below the income level needed to afford decent housing.

To fulfill an unredeemed pledge to these eight million families the administration brought forth a new incentive to the home-building industry—the rent supplement. Paradoxically, although few disagreed with the premise that a subsidy was necessary, and even fewer disagreed with the fact that we were a goodly distance away from fulfilling the pledge the nation made in 1949 to provide "a decent home and a suitable living environment for every American family,"[5] the proposal immediately became embroiled in controversy.

Reprinted with permission from a symposium, "Housing, Part II: The Federal Role," appearing in *Law and Contemporary Problems* (Vol. 32, No. 3, Summer 1967), published by the Duke University School of Law Durham, North Carolina

At the heart of the controversy was what we would call the subsidy dilemma. Can an effective program be devised which is fair vis-à-vis nonrecipients of the subsidy? Thus the main issue was neither the income floor nor the income ceiling, neither the rent income ratio nor the payment formula, neither the construction standard nor the workable program proviso, but, rather, the fundamental clash between two values—the need to fulfill the pledge to the poor and the need to be fair to the overwhelming majority of nonrecipients.

The first part of this article will trace the history of the proposal from its introduction into Congress[6] through its final passage, initial funding, and first days of life. The second part will show how the substantial changes which occurred in the legislative journey—changes which radically transformed the program—illustrate in rather sharp relief the subsidy dilemma.

The Legislative History

The Administration Proposal

The initial administration proposal[7] authorized the Administrator of the Housing and Home Finance Agency[8] to undertake a program of rent supplement payments to help make certain private housing available to certain lower income families.

The recipients of the supplements would be landlords who satisfied two criteria:[9] (1) that they were nongovernmental; and (2) that they were either nonprofit, limited dividend, or cooperative entities. The type of housing eligible for supplements also had to satisfy two criteria:[10] (1) it had to be new or rehabilitated; and (2) the construction or rehabilitation had to be financed with a mortgage loan insured by the Federal Housing Administration (FHA) under the section 221(d) (3)[11] market-interest-rate mortgage insurance program for low and moderate income families.

The subsidy would be on the behalf of a tenant who satisfied two criteria:[12] (1) he had to have an income below the amount required to obtain standard privately owned housing but above the amount necessary to obtain admission to public housing; and (2) he had to be (a) displaced by governmental action, (b) elderly, (c) physically handicapped, or (d) occupying substandard housing.

The amount of the payment was subject to two limitations:[13] (1) it could not exceed the amount by which the rent of the unit exceeded 20 percent of the tenant's income (25 percent in situations in which the tenant was given an option to purchase the unit[14]); and (2) it could not exceed the estimated amount of subsidy payable under the public housing program for a comparable unit.

The location of the unit was governed by local planning and zoning requirements. However, rent supplement housing was not limited to communities which had enacted a workable program for community improvement—a requirement of other federal housing and urban renewal programs.[15]

The size of the program requested was large. Authorization was sought for the appropriation of $50 million in the first year with increases of $50 million in the three following years—to a total of $200 million per annum in the fourth year of the program.[16]

Committee Action

House Committee. On May 21, 1965, after public hearings,[17] the House committee considering the bill reported out[18] a new bill[19] that contained a number of important modifications.

The bill altered the first of the qualifying tests for tenant eligibility. In order to be eligible, a tenant was now required to be one who, through the expenditure of 25 percent of his income, was unable to obtain standard private housing, whether or not his income was above or below the level necessary to obtain admission to public housing.[20] The provision dealing with the amount of the payment was altered by (1) limiting the payment to the amount by which the rent of the unit exceeded 25 percent (formerly 20 percent) of the tenant's income and (2) eliminating the requirement that the rent supplement payment not exceed the subsidy payable under the public housing program.[21]

No changes were made with respect to the qualifications of the recipients, the type of housing, the location of the housing, or the size of the program.

Senate Committee. On June 28, 1965, after public hearings,[22] the Senate committee considering the bill also reported out[23] a new bill[24] containing a number of important modifications.

The type of housing eligible was broadened by allowing 10 percent of the appropriations to be used as an experiment[25] in housing financed under the section 221(d) (3) below-market-interest-rate program,[26] the section 231 program of mortgage insurance for the elderly,[27] and the section 202 program of direct loans for the elderly,[28] subject to an additional limitation that the number of units in any such project receiving the benefit of rent supplements was limited to 20 percent of the total.[29] The Senate bill also altered the first of the qualifying tests for tenant eligibility. In order to be eligible, a tenant must now have an income below the maximum amount that could be established for occupancy in public housing.[30]

The Senate committee also modified the provision dealing with the amount of the payment[31] in exactly the same fashion as had the House committee. No changes were made with respect to the qualifications of the recipients, the location of the housing, or the size of the program.

House Floor Action

After debate on the bill,[32] and after a roll call vote in which the rent supplement narrowly survived a motion to recommit,[33] the House bill was passed on June 30, 1965.[34] The major changes were the adoption of the Senate bill's provision limiting tenant eligibility to individuals and families with incomes below the maximum amount that could be established for occupancy in public housing[35] and the reduction of the size of the program by 25 percent by limiting the authorization to $30 million upon enactment, with cumulative increases of $35 million for fiscal 1967, $40 million for fiscal 1968, and $45 million for fiscal 1969.[36]

Senate Floor Action

The Senate passed its version of the bill on July 15, 1965.[37] A number of amendments had been accepted after lengthy debate.[38]

The major changes were (1) the imposition of a new limitation as to the housing that would qualify, that is, housing whose cost of operation was not in excess of the cost of operation of similar housing,[39] (2) the broadening of the class of qualified tenants to include persons (meeting the income qualifications) whose dwellings were extensively damaged or destroyed in a disaster area,[40] and (3) the reduction of the size of the program by 25 percent (to the same level as the House).[41]

The major differences between the House and Senate bills related to the type of housing and the type of tenant that was eligible. The Senate bill (1) allowed, as an experiment, a limited number of below-market and elderly projects to be used, (2) limited the operating costs, and (3) extended the class of eligible tenants to include disaster victims. The House bill had no comparable provisions.

Conference Report

The Conference Committee accepted the Senate's amendments

with respect to the broadening of the class of qualified tenants (disaster victims) and the limiting of the operating costs of rent supplement housing.[42]

The experimental program in the Senate bill was also accepted but revised by requiring that 50 percent of the units that received the benefits of the rent supplement be in 221(d) (3) below-market-interest-rate projects, and removing the 20 percent limitation on the number of units in a project that could receive rent supplements (except for properties financed with loans under section 202 of the Housing Act of 1959 on or before the date of enactment of the bill).[43]

The Conference Report was approved by the Senate by a voice vote on July 26[44] and by the House on July 27 by a vote of 251 to 168.[45] The rent supplement program was signed into law on August 10, 1965.[46]

The Appropriations Fight

First Round. On August 26, 1965, the President requested the full $30 million authorization for rent supplements.[47] After hearings,[48] the Supplemental Appropriation Bill, 1966,[49] was reported out by the House Appropriations Committee on October 13, 1965.[50] The bill reduced the first year's authorization from $30 million to $6 million and limited the location of the housing to areas which had workable programs or in which the rent supplement program had been officially approved by the local community.[51] After debate,[52] the entire appropriation for rent supplements was deleted by the House on October 19, 1965, by a vote of 184 to 162.[53]

The Supplemental Appropriation Bill, 1966, was also reported out, after hearings,[54] by the Senate committee on October 19, 1965.[55] The bill[56] reduced the authorization from $30 million to $12 million. No requirement with regard to local approval was contained in the Senate bill. The bill was approved by the Senate[57] after it rejected two motions, one to delete the rent supplement appropriation provision entirely,[58] and a second to reduce the appropriation to $6 million.[59]

The House-Senate Conference denied any funds for rent supplements but appropriated $450,000 for the preparation of plans and criteria for implementing the program.[60]

Second Round. On February 11, 1966, the President again requested the full $30 million authorization for rent supplements.[61] After hearings,[62] the Second Supplemental Appropriations Bill, 1966,[63] was reported out by the House Appropriations Committee on March 25, 1966.[64] The bill reduced the first year's authorization from $30 million to $12 million and again included the workable program or local approval proviso.[65] The House, after debate,[66] approved the bill on March 29, 1966.[67]

After hearings,[68] the Senate committee eliminated the rent supplement appropriation from the bill.[69] The full Senate, however, overruled the Appropriations Committee and accepted the House version of the bill (by a narrow vote of 46–45) on April 27, 1966.[70]

The bill was signed by the President on May 13, 1966.[71]

Administrative Sequel

May of 1966 also saw the issuance of the administrative regulations which put flesh on the statutory skeleton.

The main changes contained in the administrative regulations and instructions[72] dealt with the housing and the tenants who were eligible for the rent supplement program and with the amount of the payment. Thus, (1) a limitation on the amount of rent that could be charged for a unit was imposed,[73] (2) the maximum income (in order to qualify) was reduced from the maximum permitted for *occupancy* in a public housing project in the area to the maximum permitted for *admission* of *regular* tenants in a public housing project in the area,[74] (3) a limitation as to the amount of assets which a tenant could have and still qualify was imposed,[75] and (4) a limitation on the amount of the supplement that any tenant could receive was imposed (it could not exceed 70 percent or be less than 10 percent of the rent for the unit).[76]

Table 1 summarizes the main differences between the original administrative proposal and the Rent Supplement Program as passed by Congress, signed by the President, and administered by the Federal Housing Commissioner.

The Subsidy Dilemma

The Need for Volume

"One needs only his eyes, his nose, and a willingness to walk through the slums of America's great cities to be aware that we are many leagues away from the goal of tolerable housing for all Americans."[77] The administration, through the use of the rent supplement proposal, attempted to take a giant stride toward the goal. As the Senate committee which held hearings on the proposal stated,[78]

Table 1. Rent Supplement Program—Summary of Major Provisions

Original Proposal	Operating Program
1. Qualified Owners Nonprofit and limited dividend corporations, and cooperatives	Same
2. Eligible Housing FHA Section 221(d) (3) market-interest-rate housing	Limitation placed on operating costs and rents. Program broadened, now includes: A. F.H.A. Section 221(d) (3) market-interest-rate housing B. Experimental Program—10% of payments authorized by appropriations acts. (1) 5%—F.H.A. Section 221(d) (3) below-market-interest-rate housing projects approved for mortgage insurance after August 10, 1965. (2) 5%—Housing for the elderly projects (a) Section 202 of the Housing Act of 1959—Projects approved before and after August 10, 1965. Provided that no more than 20% of the dwelling in a property financed on or before August 10, 1965 may receive supplements. (b) Section 231 of the National Act—Projects whose mortgages have been finally endorsed for mortgage insurance, after August 10, 1965.
3. Eligible Tenants Individuals or families whose incomes are such that they are unable to obtain standard housing at a rental which is equal to or less than 1/5 of their income, and who are 1. occupying substandard housing 2. displaced by governmental action, or 3. elderly or handicapped.	A. Individuals or families who have incomes that do not exceed the maximum amount that can be established for admission of regular tenants in public housing law, and who are 1. Same 2. Same 3. Same 4. victims of disaster after April 1, 1965. B. Limitation on assets of tenants

Table 1. Rent Supplement Program (Continued)

Original Proposal	Operating Program
4. Amount of Payment	
A. Could not exceed difference between 1/5 of income and rent	A. Could not exceed difference between 1/4 of income and rent.
B. Could not exceed public housing annual contribution	B. could not be more than 70% of rent or less than 10%.
5. Location of Unit	
Workable program required only in community which had had a program,	Workable program or local approval required in all communities.
6. Financing	
Authorization to enter into contracts for up to $200 million in supplement payments during initial four years.	Initial appropriation of $12 million

A number of existing Federal and State housing programs have been of significant value in helping low-income families to obtain standard housing. However, as helpful as these programs have been, they reach only a very small part of the total number of these families. Of the approximately 1.6 million housing starts last year, only a small proportion were units assisted under Federal or State programs designed to help low-income families.

. . . .

Sixteen years ago, Congress and the American people pledged themselves to—"the realization as soon as feasible of the goal of a decent home and a suitable living environment for every American family."

This is our national housing objective. Commendable strides have been made toward achieving that objective, but for too many American families the pledge remains unredeemed. The committee recognizes that to redeem this pledge requires a comprehensive housing program that will provide a substantial volume of housing designed to serve families of low income. The committee has concluded that housing for lower income families can be produced in sufficient supply only through enlisting the experience and resources of private enterprise.

The conclusions reached by the committee with respect to using the resources of private enterprise rested on something more substantial than a prejudice either in favor of private enterprise or against government bureaucracy.

Senator Douglas. One more question and then I will yield.

. . . [Y]ou propose your low-rent public housing program and you say it will not meet all of the needs, but it represents our best estimate of what can be done. Now what is it that prevents us from doing more?

Mr. Weaver. The absorbitive capacity of this program, the availability of sites, the approval of programs at the local level, and these types of problems. These are the things.

. . . .

Mr. Weaver. It isn't a matter of bureaucratic hours or a matter of lack of interest. It is a matter of the fact in order to get public housing you have to go through many steps, and even in the city of Chicago, as you know very well, the Chicago Housing Authority would like to do a great deal more, but it has difficulty with sites and this has nothing to do with the efficiency of the Chicago Housing Authority.[79]

Thus, the main reason for rejection of public housing was that it could not serve as a vehicle for a large-volume housing program. As the Senate report summed up the issue,[80]

Valuable as the public housing program is and has been however, it cannot by itself fully meet the housing needs of low-income families. The current waiting list for low rent units has already reached 500,000 families. It is a harsh fact that in recent years the program has been unable to stimulate the construction of more than 30,000 new low rent units a year. There is clearly a pressing need for new programs in addition to this basic tool for low-income housing.

The choice of private enterprise vehicles also revolved around the theme of volume. The 221(d) (3) below-market-interest-rate program—a program characterized by the administration as successful[81]—was available. Although the interest rate applicable to the program was 3⅞ percent and as such too high to reach the "rich poor" range which the administration sought to reach, one would have thought that a variant of that program would have been the logical choice.

Senator Sparkman. I introduced a bill by request that would have provided for further flexibility in the rate, lowering it down, if necessary, even to zero. That would make available housing units for families much lower in the income levels. Have you seen that bill?

Mr. Weaver. Yes, sir. I would say this: We have looked at this very carefully and we have found that even if you had a zero rate of interest, which is kind of hard for me, as a practical person, to conceive of getting, you would not be able to go down as low in the income groups as you can with the administration's rent supplementation program.[82]

This answer went unchallenged. However, it does seem to be but a partial answer since (1) the initial rent supplement proposal did not seek to reach the lowest income groups, and (2) it fails to explain why a program which combined rent supplements and below-market interest was not chosen. It would seem logical and cheaper for the government to take advantage of its credit position and "piggyback" a subsidy on a below-market interest rate rather than to create a program in which a substantial portion of the subsidy is used to reduce a rent based on market-rate interest.

The need for volume seemed to have been again the key to the rejection of this approach—albeit indirect:

Senator Proxmire. I am concerned also about the temptation that every administration has, when we decide to lease post offices instead of buying them, the impact on the budget in the year you lease is smaller, but over the years it is much bigger, I am convinced.

Isn't it true also with the rent supplement program, the budget will be less in the first year, but over the years it will cost more.

Mr. Weaver. I would say it will not be as great as many people would assume, because the amount of subsidy would decline each year.

On the other hand, I would say that the figures would indicate that the total impact, the total cost on a lower interest rate is less than on a rent supplement.[83]

. . . .

Mrs. Sullivan. . . .

. . . .

As I understand it, the proposal is that the mortgage financing the construction, which would be FHA insured, would carry a market interest rate. In other words, the capital to finance these projects would come from private markets and the only cost to the Government would be the subsidy payments paid over time to eligible tenants in the housing. That is correct, is it not?

Mr. Weaver. Yes, and it reflects, of course, the extremely favorable mortgage market we have now as far as the flow of funds is concerned.

Mrs. Sullivan. In other words, I have a suspicion that one of the reasons you were able to "sell" your programs to the Budget Bureau was because of the fact that this program would have a minimum initial impact on the Federal annual budget in contrast to section 221(d) (3) below-market-interest-rate mortgages, for example, where the whole cost of the mortgage is an immediate charge to the budget the minute FNMA buys it. I would like your comments on that.

Mr. Weaver. Two things. Obviously, it did not hurt the program with the Bureau of the Budget, and I think certainly the President has a concern for this and I think the Congress has, too. It has merit.[84]

To illustrate: the administration proposed a program that would finance 500,000 new units in a four-year period. The budgetary impact of such a program (on the assumption of a $400 per unit subsidy) would be comparatively small—$50 million—even in the first year of full operation. In contrast, the impact of a below-market-interest-rate program would have been massive. Since the ultimate source of the funds for (d) (3) was assumed to be the U.S. Treasury, the federal budget would reflect the full amount of the mortgage loan. Thus, in the first year of a (d) (3) oriented program in which 125,000 units are projected with an average mortgage of $10,000, the budget "outlay" would be $1.25 billion, although the actual cost (assuming the interest rate charged to the mortgagor was a full 2 percent below the Treasury's borrowing cost) would be $25 million.[85]

The main thrust of the administration's proposal was the necessity for creating a mechanism that would provide a rapid increase in the supply of standard housing within budgetary and cost limitations. In light of this objective, the rent supplement program held another advantage—namely, the payment was keyed to need. Unlike a fixed interest program in which fine tuning is impossible, the amount of the subsidy could be reduced as income rose. The program, thus, had the economic advantage of (a) not wasting a full subsidy on persons who needed only a partial subsidy, and (b) assuming a rise in the income of the tenants, a reduction in the cost of the program, or an expansion of the program with no increase in cost. There was also the sociological advantage of its being unnecessary to evict families whose income had risen above the point of need, thus (a) encouraging housing in which families of different income groups would live together,[86] and (b) eliminating one of the major sore points of public housing—the disincentive to economic advancement produced by a program in which eviction was the mark of economic success.

Such features of the program as the imposition of the income floor and the elimination of the workable program requirement may seem at first glance to be unrelated to the administration's aim to achieve the greatest bang for the budgetary buck, but upon closer examination it becomes clear that they are crucial components. To the extent a person on the bottom of the income scale requires a greater subsidy input per housing unit, the total volume of units must be reduced. To the extent outlying areas are used, lower land costs and lower construction costs (the predominant type of project in such areas being wood-frame construction) would result in rent levels which require a lesser subsidy input per housing unit, thus enabling an increased volume of units.

In conclusion, given a treasury whose resources are finite, the administration's aim was to achieve the largest possible program (using available homebuilding resources) with the smallest budgetary impact.

The Need for Equity

Whereas, the administration was concerned with fulfilling the nation's housing objectives, Congress was concerned with the fairness of the new program to nonrecipients, both poor and rich.

Thus the income floor was an immediate target of attack. As a politicoeconomist stated during the congressional hearing,[87] "But there is a grave question raised here as to whether when there are vast unmet needs of people with incomes of below $2,000 or $3,000 a year, you then ought to launch a new program to help people who are above the poverty level?"

Congress reacted to this argument by striking the economic floor. The program thus avoided the rocks of Scylla by throwing overboard some valuable cargo—housing units.[88] However, having avoided one hazard, the proposal immediately found itself in the whirlpool of Charybdis—the implications of a program which provides better housing for the poor, at a subsidized rent, than is available for a large number of more successful (and possibly harder working) citizens who must pay the full economic rent. A policy of taxing Peter to provide housing for Paul, who would otherwise have to live in squalor, may rest on sweet virtue. A policy of taxing Peter to provide better housing than his own for Paul is a bitter pill.

Can this unappealing prospect be avoided? And if it can, what are the costs? These two questions will be considered in light of the legislative history of the rent supplement proposal.

The administration was aware of the problem and limited the categories of poor that this program would serve. Thus the qualification for tenancy included not only low income but also being in a category that few would begrudge—the handicapped, the elderly, the displaced, and subsequently the disaster victim. The occupant of substandard housing may not qualify as deserving, but at least he has served his time in squalor.

Congress added an additional requirement—tangible evidence of the occupant's deservedness. One of the earliest amendments required the occupant to pay an extra 5 percent of his income for his new housing. A representative of the American Bankers Association gave the following explanation why this was needed:[89]

What we are saying, Senator, is that since it is generally agreed that a person may spend around 20 percent of his income, gross income, on rent, especially in that group, that income group, that the rent supplements should be based on the criteria of need.

Well, now, if a person has to pay 22 percent of his income on rent, *well, it is a little more than perhaps he should to get his housing*, but it doesn't clearly establish need. But if he had to go as high as 25 percent, it would seem that this is substantially higher than an accepted criteria, so that then supplements would be more logical.

Not only does the occupant thereby show effort but he also guarantees that in order to obtain the good housing he is willing to sacrifice luxuries (or necessities).[90] There will be no shiny new cars outside of rent supplement projects.

Is the conflict real? Must a housing subsidy give the poor better housing than is available to higher income neighbors? Theoretically perhaps not, that is, if there is a surplus of standard housing. However, the premise of the problem and the program is a shortage of standard units.

Can the quality of the housing to be given to the subsidized tenant be limited? Must we build "penthouses for the poor"? Limiting the housing to existing structures has the obvious advantages in this regard in that a "used" house is unlikely to be as good as a new house. Thus it should not be surprising that, although the Housing and Urban Development Act of 1965 contained two new housing subsidy programs, the rent supplement program geared to new construction stirred waves, but the provision granting public housing authorities the power to lease low rent housing in private accommodations scarcely caused a ripple.[91] Nevertheless, although a useful tool in areas in which vacancies in standard housing exists or where rehabilitation of substandard housing is economically feasible, the leasing program does not show any promise of redeeming the pledge to the poor.

Can anything be done to avoid the difficulty if we are forced to rely on new construction? If new construction is a necessary evil, it at least can be restricted to the most basic shelter requirements. The amenities (both structural and environmental) of new housing can be limited.

There are, however, severe economic and urban development constraints in following this course. The building must be of sufficient quality to serve a market for at least the life of the mortgage (forty years). It must, therefore, if it is not to be funcionally obsolete many years prior to its attaining physical obsolescence,[92] include certain facilities which were yesterday's (and possibly today's) luxuries.[93] The dangers of false economy go beyond the structure itself. If the model tenements of the nineteenth and early twentieth centuries are the building blocks of today's slums, the overly modest projects of today may be cornerstones of the slums of tomorrow.

The location of the housing can be channeled so as to limit the environmental amenity. A building of superior quality to house the poor does not offend one's sense of equity if it is placed in an inferior neighborhood.[94] If Peter has to pay for Paul's housing, he need not be forced to live next to Paul. The sentiment was put in its universal form by a novelist—"Generally my fellow townspeople, though they would help the poor, were not particularly fond of them."[95] Or as a Congressman put the issue a bit more bluntly,[96]

> I think the time has come to call a spade a spade....
>
> When the rent subsidy program was before Congress some of us said the purpose of the bill was to force integration of better class neighborhoods. This was denied by the sponsors....
>
> Let me read from a Federal Housing Administration letter, MF Letter No. 63 to all insuring office directors and multifamily housing representatives under date of September 28, 1965:
>
> "Important criteria with regard to approval of a rent supplement project will include full consideration of its contribution to assisting in integrating income groups and furthering the legal requirements and objectives of equal opportunity in housing."
>
> That is in the regulations, in the instructions to those housing officials who will be spending this $6 million, and they are told the first consideration of the rent subsidy program is integrating economic groups and furthering the objectives of equal opportunity in housing. Under this implementation of the program, private homeownership in America is doomed because a man cannot protect the value of his property nor the desirability of his neighborhood.

Must we, therefore, place the home in a less than suitable environment? If one man's home can be his castle, another man's home may be his prison. As another Congressman viewed the issue,[97]

> We can see no reason why private builders should be forced to obtain local approval for rent supplement projects, which are in essence an "FHA for the poor."
>
> ...The local veto rider, if it should become law, will be used to confine rent supplement housing to the areas in which the families entitled to rent supplements already live, thus frustrating the clear intent of the Congress. The problems of our cities will never be resolved if we establish walls or immovable curtains beyond which the poor and elderly cannot go to find decent housing.

Conclusion

The fate of the rent supplement program illustrates that the inability to fulfill the nation's pledge to millions of low-income families living in substandard housing rests on something more than the failure to enlist private enterprise in the task. Rent supplements were proposed and were necessary because public housing could not produce the necessary volume. However, the introduction of new players did not change the rules of the game. The limitations imposed by Congress assure that private enterprise, even though subsidized, will also fail to produce the necessary volume to achieve the nation's housing goal.[98] Both the thirty-year history of the public housing program and the brief history of the rent supplement program illustrate the paradoxical effect of the subsidy dilemma—the creation of powerful instruments whose use has to be restricted because of their capacity to achieve the very goal for which they were designed.

The most promising solution to the dilemma may be the elimination of the need for a subsidy either by lowering development costs or by raising income levels of the poor. It may not, therefore, be a coincidence that 1966 saw major action on both of these fronts. Legislation was enacted to apply technological advances to housing,[99] and a conference was convened whose purpose was the ultimate development of new technologies to enable the upgrading of our physical environment to modern standards at feasible cost levels.[100] The model cities program was also enacted[101]—a program whose premise is that "bricks and mortar" will not renew our cities as long as millions of poor and disadvantaged Americans lack the training and opportunity to participate fully in our nation's life.[102]

Notes

[1]Johnson, *Prof. Freund's 'Avuncular Qualities' Help Students Pit Right Against Right*, Harvard Law Record, March 23, 1967, at 2, 12.

[2]E. Wiesel, Night 16 (1960).

[3]*See generally* J. McMurray, Ways and Means of Providing Housing for Families Unable to Afford Rentals or Mortgage Payments Necessary for Adequate Housing (1960) (an independent study financed by the National Association of Home Builders); Welfeld, *The Condominium and Median-Income Housing*, 31 Fordham L. Rev. 457, 477–80 (1963).

[4]S. Rep. No. 378, 89th Cong., 1st Sess. 3 (1965).

[5]Housing Act of 1949, § 2, 42 U.S.C. § 1441 (1964).

[6]No attempt is being made to trace the rent supplement proposal itself or any of its components to specific persons or groups. "[T]he American political structure puts so heavy a premium on diffusion of decision-making power that it is difficult to determine the relationship between the desires of particular persons and groups and what eventually emerges as effective government policy. After all, the drum beater may be credited, or blamed, for the cloudburst, but whether he is responsible is another matter." Greenberg, *The Myth of the Scientific Elite*, Public Interest, Fall 1965, at 51, 53. *See also* Foard & Fefferman, *Federal Urban Renewal Legislation*, 25 Law & Contemp. Prob. 635, 636 n.4 (1960).

[7]S. 1354, 89th Cong., 1st Sess. § § 101–05 (1965); H.R. 5840, 89th Cong., 1st Sess. § § 101–05 (1965) (Special Provisions for Disadvantaged Persons, Title I, Housing and Urban Development Act of 1965).
[8]The immediate predecessor of the Secretary of Housing and Urban Development.
[9]S. 1354, *supra* note 7, § 101(b).
[10]*Id.*
[11]National Housing Act, 12 U.S.C. § 1715*l*(d) (3) (1964), *as amended,* (Supp. II, 1965–66).
[12]S. 1354, *supra* note 7, § 101(c).
[13]*Id.* § 101(d).
[14]*Id.* § 101(f).
[15]Housing Act of 1949, § 101(c), 42 U.S.C. § 1451(c) (1964), *as amended,* (Supp. II, 1965–66).
[16]S. 1354, *supra* note 7, § 101(a).
[17]*Hearings on the Housing and Urban Development Act of 1965 Before the Subcomm. on Housing of the House Comm. on Banking and Currency,* 89th Cong., 1st Sess., pts. 1 & 2 (1965) [hereinafter cited as *House Hearings*].
[18]H.R. Rep. No. 365, 89th Cong., 1st Sess. (1965); House Comm. on Banking and Currency, 89th Cong., 1st Sess., Correction of Misleading and False Statements Concerning Rent Supplement Program Made in Minority Report on the Housing and Urban Development Act of 1965—H.R. 7984 (Comm. Print 1965).
[19]H.R. 7984, 89th Cong., 1st Sess. (1965).
[20]*Id.* § 101(c).
[21]*Id.* § 101(d).
[22]*Hearings on S. 1354 Before the Subcomm. on Housing of the Senate Comm. on Banking and Currency*, 89th Cong., 1st Sess. (1965) [hereinafter cited as *Senate Hearings*].
[23]S. Rep. No. 378, 89th Cong., 1st Sess. (1965).
[24]S. 2213, 89th Cong., 1st Sess. (1965).
[25]*Id.* § 101(d) (3).
[26]National Housing Act, 12 U.S.C. § 1715*l*(d) (3) (1964), *as amended,* (Supp. II, 1965–66).
[27]National Housing Act, 12 U.S.C. § 1715v (1964), *as amended*, (Supp. II, 1965–66).
[28]Housing Act of 1959, 12 U.S.C. § 1701q (1964), *as amended,* (Supp. II, 1965–66).
[29]S. 2213, *supra* note 24, § 101(d) (2).
[30]*Id.* § 101(c) (1).
[31]*Id.* § 101(e).
[32]111 Cong. Rec. 14,327–51 (daily ed. June 28, 1965); 111 Cong. Rec. 14,588–622 (daily ed. June 29, 1965); 111 Cong. Rec. 14,669–714 (daily ed. June 30, 1965).
[33]111 Cong. Rec. 14,711–13 (daily ed. June 30, 1965).
[34]*Id.* at 14,713–14.
[35]*See id.* at 14,669–82.
[36]*See id.*
[37]111 Cong. Rec. 16,350 (daily ed. July 15, 1965).
[38]111 Cong. Rec. 16,132, 16,137–42, 16,149–90 (daily ed. July 14, 1965); 111 Cong. Rec. 16,295–304, 16,308–23, 16,325–50 (daily ed. July 15, 1965).
[39]111 Cong. Rec. 16,171 (daily ed. July 14, 1965).
[40]*Id.* at 16,161–62.
[41]111 Cong. Rec. 16,323, 16,325–27 (daily ed. July 15, 1965).

[42]H.R. Rep. No. 679, 89th Cong., 1st Sess. 63 (1965).
[43]*Id.*
[44]111 Cong. Rec. 17,630–37 (daily ed. July 26, 1965).
[45]111 Cong. Rec. 17,743–51 (daily ed. July 27, 1965).
[46]12 U.S.C. § 1701s (Supp. II, 1965–66).
[47]H.R. Doc. No. 278, 89th Cong., 1st Sess. (1965).
[48]*Hearings on the Supplemental Appropriation Bill, 1966, Before Subcomms. of the House Comm. on Appropriations*, 89th Cong., 1st Sess., pts. 1–3 (1965).
[49]H.R. 11588, 89th Cong., 1st Sess. (1965).
[50]H.R. Rep. No. 1162, 89th Cong., 1st Sess. (1965).
[51]H.R. 11588, *supra* note 49, ch. 4. H.R. Rep. No. 1162, *supra* note 50, at 12–13. The question as to whether the proviso was legislation on an appropriations bill was debated. However, the Chair ruled that since the proviso was negative in character it was only a limitation and not legislation. 111 Cong. Rec. 26,033–34 (daily ed. Oct. 14, 1965).
[52]111 Cong. Rec. 26,008–45 (daily ed. Oct. 14, 1965).
[53]*Id.* at 26,045–46.
[54]*Hearings on Supplemental Appropriations for 1966 Before Subcomms. of the Senate Comm. on Appropriations*, 89th Cong., 1st Sess. (1965).
[55]S. Rep. No. 912, 89th Cong., 1st Sess. (1965).
[56]H.R. 11588 (in the Senate), 89th Cong., 1st Sess. (1965).
[57]111 Cong. Rec. 26,584, 26,587–631, 26,781 (daily ed. Oct. 20, 1965).
[58]*Id.* at 26,604.
[59]*Id.* at 26,607.
[60]H.R. Rep. No. 1198, 89th Cong., 1st Sess. 4–5 (1965).
[61]H.R. Doc. No. 380, 89th Cong., 2d Sess. (1966).
[62]*Hearings on the Second Supplemental Appropriation Bill, 1966, Before Subcomms. of the House Comm. on Appropriations*, 89th Cong. 2d Sess. (1966).
[63]H.R. 14012, 89th Cong., 2d Sess. (1966).
[64]H.R. Rep. No. 1349, 89th Cong., 2d Sess. (1966).
[65]H.R. 14012, *supra* note 63, ch. 4.
[66]112 Cong. Rec. 6708–69 (daily ed. March 29, 1966).
[67]*Id.* at 6768–69.
[68]*Hearings on the Second Supplemental Appropriation Bill, Fiscal Year 1966, Before the Senate Comm. on Appropriations*, 89th Cong., 2d Sess. (1966).
[69]S. Rep. No. 1137, 89th Cong., 2d Sess. 8–9 (1966).
[70]112 Cong. Rec. 8651–83 (daily ed. April 27, 1966).
[71]Act of May 13, 1966, Pub. L. No. 89–426, 80 Stat. 141.
[72]It should be noted that the regulations, to the extent they changed the plain meaning of the legislation, were codifying the stormy legislative history. They can in effect be deemed the price the administration had to pay to get the program funded. *See* notes 73–75 *infra.*
[73]U.S. Federal Housing Administration, Dep't of Housing and Urban Development, Rent Supplement Program Public Information Guide and Instruction Handbook 5 (1966).

"As a further means of assuring that the program services low-income families in accordance with the congressional intent, the Secretary will establish in each locality maximum per unit rentals which will cover construction costs and maximum mortgage limits based on project prototypes of modest design and cost." *Hearings, supra* note 62, at 273 (a portion of the administration statement placed in the record).
[74]Rent Supplement Program, *supra* note 73, at 10.

"[F]or initial qualification and eligibility, the income limits will be the same as or below the limits that exist now for public housing. . . ." *Hearings, supra* note 62, at 271 (testimony of Secretary Weaver).

[75]24 C.F.R. § 5.20 (1967).

Mr. Evins. Mr. Secretary, let us clear upon the record on one thing, a very crucial and important point. . . . This appropriation got into difficulty last October because some members read from tentative regulations . . . that individuals with assets or income up to $25,000 would be eligible. That is not the case. That is not the situation and it was not intended by the law. . . .

Secretary Weaver. Yes, sir.

Mr. Evins. Your statement is that the asset limitation . . . will be $2,000 except in the case of the elderly, where it will be $5,000. This is correct?

Secretary Weaver. Yes, sir.

Hearings, supra note 62, at 271.

[76]24 C.F.R. § 5.25 (1967).

[77]R. Vernon, The Myth and Reality of Our Urban Problems 46 (1966).

[78]S. Rep. No. 378, *supra* note 4, at 3.

[79]*Senate Hearings, supra* note 22, at 23–24.

[80]S. Rep. No. 378, *supra* note 4, at 5.

[81]*Senate Hearings, supra* note 22, at 6.

[82]*Id.* at 17.

[83]*Id.* at 32–33.

[84]*House Hearings, supra* note 17, pt. 2, 32 233–34.

[85]At the present time the distinction between the rent supplement program and the below-market-interest-rate program with regard to budget impact and cost is in the main academic. Section 102 of the Housing and Urban Development Act of 1965 made it possible for the Federal National Mortgage Association (FNMA) to include the (d) (3) mortgages in its portfolio in its arrangements for pooling mortgages and selling participations. The act did this by authorizing appropriations to reimburse FNMA for the amount of the discount the private market would require to purchase a participation which included below-market-interest-rate mortgages. This eliminated the adverse budgetary impact of (d) (3) mortgages at the cost of the savings the government achieved by using its credit resources to purchase and then to hold the mortgage.

[86]*See* H.R. Doc. No. 99, 89th Cong., 1st Sess. 8 (1965).

[87]*Senate Hearings, supra* note 22, at 18 (Senator Douglas).

[88]The argument was made that by increasing the amount to be paid by tenants from 20% to 25% of income, the lowering of the income ceiling by Congress did not affect volume. *See* 111 Cong. Rec. 16,059 (daily ed. July 13, 1965) (statement by Senator Douglas). In response it should be noted (1) that the administration proposal originally contemplated supporting 500,000 units at an annual cost of $200 million. Secretary Weaver, however, in testimony seeking appropriations after the income limit was dropped, estimated that 250,000 units would be supported by an appropriation of $150 million—a one-third decrease in the number of units per dollar of expenditure. *Hearings, supra* note 62, at 267; (2) that lowering of the ceiling defeated the purpose of economic integration which was strongly favored by Senator Douglas. *See* 111 Cong. Rec. 16,060 (daily ed. July 13, 1965); and (3) it is this paper's contention that increasing volume was not the prime motive (or even a motive) for raising the tenant's payment from 20% to 25% of his income. This point is discussed in the text *infra.*

[89]*Senate Hearings, supra* note 22, at 379 (Kurt Flexner, Deputy Manager, American Bankers Association). (Emphasis added.)

[90]*See generally* on the rent-income ratio, Rapkin, *Rent-Income Ratio,*

in Urban Housing 168 (W. L. C. Wheaton, G. Milgram, & M. E. Meyerson eds. 1966).

[91]42 U.S.C. § 1421b (Supp. II, 1965–66). This provision, especially in regard to the location of the units, can stir calm waters. *See generally* W. L. Miller, The Fifteenth Ward and the Great Society 99–111 (1966), for the experience of a New England city.

[92]"All rent supplement projects must be of modest design and suitable to the market and the location proposed. Swimming pools, two bathrooms per unit, air conditioning, and similar items will not be permitted. Projects should incorporate good design principles and not have features that will contribute to premature obsolescence." Rent Supplement Program, *supra* note 73, at 2.

[93]"*Design Factors Plague Rent Supplement Program.* The NAHB Rent Supplement Task Force was told . . . that builders refuse to design down proposed rent supplement projects, and for this reason a number of projects have either been canceled or postponed." NAHB Compendium Bull., Dec. 1966, at 3.

[94]An architecturally striking public housing development has failed to attract a single white family in spite of strenuous activities by the local housing authority. *See* Dixon, *Goldberg's Variation on Chicago Public Housing*, Architectural Forum, Nov. 1966, at 25.

[95]E. Wiesel, Night 15 (1960).

[96]111 Cong. Rec. 26,019 (daily ed. Oct. 14, 1965) (remarks of Congressman Martin).

[97]112 Cong. Rec. 8667 (daily ed. April 27, 1966) (statement of Senator Clark).

[98]The problems and criticisms which have plagued public housing—(1) site selections; (2) segregation of low-income families; (3) increasing non-white occupancy; (4) income limits which are criticized as being too high and too low; (5) inadequacy of the program; (6) detailed federal supervision; (7) poor design; (8) high development costs—are all applicable to the rent supplement program. *See generally* U.S. Housing and Home Finance Agency, Views on Public Housing 153–59 (1960).

[99]Demonstration Cities and Metropolitan Development Act of 1966, § 1010, 42 U.S.C. § 3372 (Supp. II, 1965–66).

[100]*See* U.S. Dep't of Housing and Urban Development, Science and the City (1967) (a report on the Summer Study on Science and Urban Development in June 1966 in Woods Hole, Mass., sponsored by the Department of Housing Urban Development). For the problems even in such a worthwhile endeavor,

"Yesterday Haggerty [President of the AFL-CIO Building and Construction Trades Department], clearly tiffed at a report . . . issued after a HUD-sponsored conference, hit back at charges that the craft unions block progress and resist changes that could mean faster and cheaper construction." White, *Ribicoff Jabs HUD on Slum Advisers*, The Washington Post, April 19, 1967, at A2, col. 3. "*High Court Backs Right to Strike Over Automation, Decides, 5–4, Unions May Enforce Contract Ban on Prefabricated Items, . . . Justices Agree Law Allows Carpenters to Walk Out in Fight to Save Jobs*," N.Y. Times, April 18, 1967, at 1, col. 1 (Headlines.)

[101]Demonstration Cities and Metropolitan Development Act of 1966, tit. 1, 42 U.S.C.A. §§ 1453, 3301–13 (Pamphlet, Feb. 1967).

[102]For the problems and possibly the dilemmas one again needs only to read the newspapers.

"His name is Jackson, Ernest Jackson. Ernest is something of a celebrity. He's the one-thousandth graduate of the Kilmer Job Corps Center in New Jersey to be placed. Ernest now earns over $200 a week. Not bad for a fellow who dropped out of school in the 11th grade. At Kilmer, a lot of young men are being changed from untrained dropouts to skilled craftsmen." Otten, *New Allies for L.B.J.*, The Wall Street Journal, April 19, 1967, at 1, col. 6. *But see* Semple, *U.S. Finds Only 1% On Welfare Lists Are Employable*, N.Y. Times, April 20, 1967, at 1, col. 1.

3.4

Public Housing or Income Supplements: The Economics of Housing for the Poor

Eugene Smolensky

Extensive reconsideration of the nation's urban welfare programs is just ahead. It is a responsibility of the Office of Economic Opportunity. It is an inevitable outcome of the creation of a million-dollar academic institute for the study of antipoverty programs at the University of Wisconsin. It is the natural reaction to the enactment of Medicare as well as to the flood of other new programs of the Great Society. It is being anticipated by the widespread attention afforded proposals to supplement or supplant those existing welfare programs that provide income-in-kind with programs that give cash, such as the negative income tax and guaranteed minimum income.

One place to begin this reevaluation is with the public housing program, which has been uniquely embattled since its inception: "the public housing program has been executed under conditions of sustained congressional harassment which are unusual in federal experience. Few other federal programs which have survived have enjoyed such a militant, well-organized and powerful congressional opposition."[1] Congressional criticism is now no less than ever and the enthusiasm of its intellectual supporters, its clientele, and its bureaucracy has melted away.[2] Nor could the timing for evaluation be more propitious: in the next year HUD must show that it intends an imaginative reconsideration of its areas of responsibility or it will find the pressures emanating from Senators Kennedy and Percy terribly oppressive and any new momentum the lift to cabinet level has generated will be dissipated.

One of several questions that must eventually be directed at public housing will be posed and quite tentatively answered here. The issue arises directly out of these characteristics of the current program.

1. The major purpose is to reduce the number of families in substandard dwellings.[3]

2. To achieve this goal,

a. families are being voluntarily induced to choose standard housing by subsidizing rents;

Reprinted by permission of the *Journal of the American Institute of Planners* (Vol. XXXIV, No. 2, March 1968), pp. 94–101.

b. the standard housing utilized comes from an expansion of the low-rent housing stock, mainly by building new units under public auspices; and
c. nonsubsidized families are not made to consume worse housing in the process.[4]

Therefore it is pertinent to ask if a larger number of low-income families could be induced to occupy standard housing without making any low-income families consume poorer housing if the funds currently devoted to public housing construction were spent in some other way. Would there be fewer families living in substandard housing if current practices were revised so as to rely upon either direct unrestricted cash subsidies or conditional income supplements to enable low-income families to pay higher rents? Would property owners respond by trying to satisfy the resulting increased demand for better housing?[5]

There are many ways to reduce the number of families living in substandard housing. The law can be used to penalize the owners of substandard dwellings. Condemnation and code enforcement have not been used effectively, however, at least in part because landlords can pass the largest share of the costs of improvements forward to the tenants even when enforcement is directed at the landlords.

There are essentially three routes by which to induce the poor to vacate their substandard housing voluntarily. The accepted procedure has been to build some dwelling units and ration them among the eligible according to a variety of criteria including willingness and ability to pay. At the other extreme, cash grants to be used any way the recipient chooses could be given, since some part of any increment in income would flow into greater expenditure upon housing. With the increased demand for standard housing, some property owners would upgrade their property. Both of these approaches, therefore, rely, at least in part, upon increasing the supply of standard housing in the relevant rental range, although the latter route also increases the feasible rent range for low-income families. A third alternative, which lies between these and which has been employed with increasing frequency, is to provide families with income supplements on the condition that the extra income be used entirely for rent. To evaluate these alternatives to public housing it is necessary to calculate the subsidy that has been provided to the tenants of public projects.

Quantifying the Subsidy in Public Housing

The subsidy that will be measured here is the amount of money, which if it were paid annually to the tenants of public housing for as long as the housing units stand, would leave the total cost of the program to the nation unchanged.

The rationale of the procedure for empirically using this definition of the subsidy is somewhat complex and is best approached indirectly. In a fully employed economy, a decision on the part of the government to construct a public housing unit implies that some other activity cannot be undertaken. Assume that the foregone activity in the private sector is to construct an apartment house. Now a profit-maximizing entrepreneur who chooses to invest in a new apartment house expects that, over the lifetime of the structure, he will earn at least as much as he could earn on any other investment of the same risk; that is, he expects to earn at least what he could earn if he lent the same sum at the market rate of interest appropriate to this risk category. His intended investment must pass the following test:

$$V \leq \sum_{t=1}^{n} \frac{(R_t)}{(1+X)^t}$$

where the right hand term represents the stream of rents minus maintenance and related expenses (R_t), over the life of the building (n), discounted at the appropriate rate of interest (X), and the left hand term, V, is the initial cost of the structure.

When the government commissions a public housing unit, it must expect to generate at least the same amount of satisfaction as a private builder (or any other entrepreneur contemplating projects of the same risk) could have generated. If public housing yields less utility to consumers per dollar of expenditures than private housing, the social welfare of the nation would have been higher had the government abstained from construction. Not that the government must receive its return in cash payments, that is, net rental income, as must the private builder. Indeed, implicit in the government's decision to commission a project must be the belief that the social benefit exceeds the private benefit, which is expressed in the rents that occupants pay. If this were not so, private entrepreneurs could presumably do as well for the national well-being as the government.[6] If the investment is socially justified, the combined rent plus subsidy must also, with due account for the compound interest that could have been earned in alternative investments, equal the cost of building. For the government the test becomes:

$$V \leq \sum_{t=1}^{n} \frac{(R_t + S_t)}{(1+X)^t} \qquad (1)$$

where S_t is the implicit subsidy. Solving for S_t when equation (1) is treated as an equality yields the annual rent subsidy implicit in employing resources in public housing.

We turn now to estimating S_t empirically. Each term of equation (1) will be discussed in turn. The estimate is confined to the public housing subsidy implicit in Public Law 171, the Housing Act of 1949, and its subsequent amendments. For all practical purposes, the calculation can begin with housing units that became available during calendar year 1952.[7]

Rents net of operating costs, R_t ("residual receipts" in the terminology of the Public Housing Authority) have fluctuated widely around a sharply declining trend. Since residual receipts cannot fall below zero for local housing authorities and since operating costs rise as the public housing stock ages and as prices and incomes rise, rents are periodically raised. After a short initial period of high net rents because of atypically low operating costs, residual receipts tend to go through a cycle, jumping up every few years when a general rise in rents is necessary to keep residual receipts from disappearing altogether (see Fig. 1). Given the very long expected life of the projects, no better or more appropriate estimate is feasible therefore than the average for all public housing units during the most recent three-year period ($2.54 per month per unit), even though there was a short period when residual receipts were considerably higher.

Between February 1952 and December 1964, some 360,000 dwelling units were completed[8] at a cost of about 4.81 billion dollars (1965 prices). The average cost per dwelling unit (V_t), therefore, was $13,400 in fourth quarter 1965 prices.[9]

The rate of interest actually paid by the local housing authorities on their long-term bonds is not the appropriate social discount rate, for it embodies a federal subsidy. Interest earned on housing authority bonds is exempt from the federal income tax. The required discount rate, as indicated earlier, must be one that will yield the minimum subsidy that would justify shifting resources from the private to the public sector; that is, it must be an appropriate market rate. One such rate for borrowers very similar to the local housing authorities is the yield earned on FHA mortgages bought in the secondary mortgage market. Weighting the average yield in the months when FHA bonds were sold by the dollar volume of bonds sold and striking the average for the years 1952–1964 yielded an average rate (X) of 5.2 percent.[10] The subsidy, therefore, was estimated assuming a social rate of discount of 5 percent.

Public housing structures may stand for a century, but what is relevant is the length of time the initial investment will continue to earn a return. The most common estimate of the period during which capital expenditures for extensive repairs or modernization requiring outside financing could be postponed is forty years. Since the subsidy estimate is quite insensitive to small changes in expected life, the forty-year period was accepted ($n=40$). It was also assumed that the salvage value of the property at the end of forty years would be equal to demolition charges. These are severe assumptions but the subsidy estimate is quite insensitive to variations in them.[11]

Given these assumptions, the average monthly subsidy per dwelling unit (S_t) for PL–171 units over the years from 1952 to

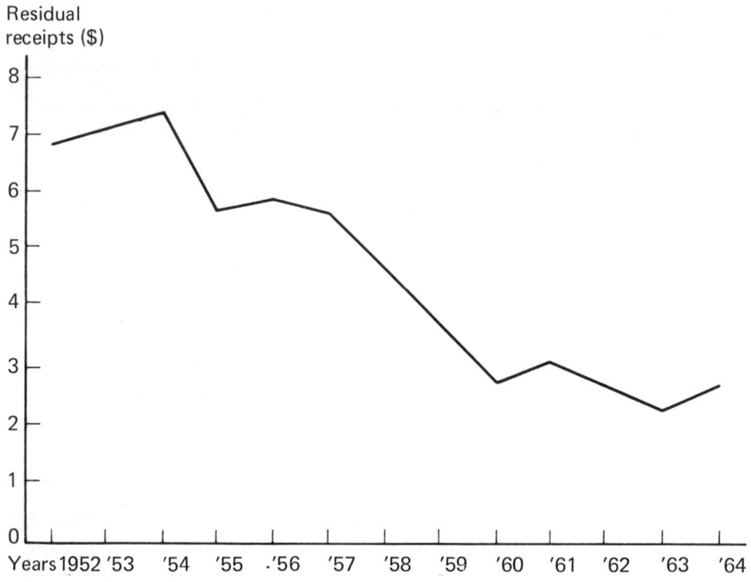

Figure 1. Residual receipts per unit month for locally owned projects: 1952–1964

1964 comes to $62 (in fourth quarter, 1965 prices). Sixty-two dollars is the monthly amount which could have been made available in cash to the successive tenants in average PL–171 units over the forty years from the date when each unit was first occupied without affecting the distribution of the nation's resources between tenants and nontenants. The average rent paid by public housing residents (in 1965 prices) was $47 per month, so that the implicit rent per unit averaged $109 per month; that is, $109 is the rent a private builder would have to charge for units of comparable cost.[12] (Of course, this is not to imply that private builders would ever build units of the same style, in the same places, for the same clientele.)

The subsidy undoubtedly varies considerably among Standard Metropolitan Statistical Areas (SMSA). Adjusting the implicit rent for rent differentials among the twenty largest cities implicit in the Consumer Price Indices raises the combined subsidy plus rental payment total to perhaps $130 per month in Chicago and $120 per month in Washington, D.C., and lowers it in Philadelphia to $100, for example.[13]

What Would an Unrestricted Cash Grant System Achieve?
Suppose the public housing program paid out $62 per month ($745 per year) or less as cash grants without specifying how the money was to be spent. Is it likely that a larger number of families would then come to occupy standard housing than under the existing program? Quite obviously the answer is no. *Every* family receiving the subsidy under the current program occupies standard housing. Given current prices for standard housing and all other goods that the poor buy, and the large proportion of their income already spent upon housing, it would take a very large subsidy indeed to ensure that *every* recipient would consume standard housing. Even at incomes of $5,300 per year, 5 percent of families occupied substandard housing in 1960.

If the current subsidy were given out as an unconditional cash subsidy, the fall in the proportion of families living in substandard housing would be quite modest. The median family income of public housing tenants in 1960 was $2,400 and the subsidy ($660 per year in 1960 prices) would have raised the median to about $3,000. Between these two incomes the proportion of families choosing standard rental housing in Standard Metropolitan Statistical Areas rose by 15 percentage points (from 51 to 66 percent).[14] On the average, 28,000 dwelling units were added by public housing each year, hence 28,000 recipients of the cash subsidy could be assumed. Of these, however, 51 percent would already have occupied standard housing, so that the total net rise in families occupying standard housing would have been roughly 4,200 families ($.15 \times 28{,}000$). Since public housing, however, is by definition standard housing, all of the roughly 13,700 families initially inadequately housed would have been moved to standard housing under the current program, and 14,300 additional standard units would first be vacated and subsequently occupied by families initially occupying substandard housing, assuming rents to be sufficiently flexible, so that all the standard units are fully occupied at the beginning and end of the adjustment period.

The census data indicate, however, that a subsidy of about $500 would have been the most effective unrestricted cash grant. With this smaller subsidy, a smaller percentage of recipients would live in standard housing, but if total federal expenditures on the subsidy are not changed, a larger absolute number of families would receive the subsidy. The larger number of recipients would have more than offset the smaller percentage consuming standard housing. With the smaller cash subsidy per family, about 5,500 families would have vacated substandard housing each year. On the established criteria, the advantage of public housing over a cash grant system remains very large.

The calculations of this section are exceedingly crude, but since refinement would only strengthen the advantage of the existing program, no better estimates have been attempted.[15] It remains only to point out that the criterion by which public housing is being evaluated places no value on the increased satisfaction that recipients would have obtained from being free to choose the most preferred market basket within their means.

Conditional Cash Grants and Rent Supplements

If the goal of public housing is to place the largest number of families in standard housing for a given expenditure level, the Public Housing Program has the crucial advantage of making receipt of the subsidy contingent upon occupying standard housing. Income supplements could, however, be granted only to families who first move into standard housing. If standard housing is more cheaply available from the private sector, such a restricted cash grant would then be superior to the existing program, since a larger number of families would find standard housing at the same total program cost.

Is public housing a relatively expensive solution? Two sources of evidence to be presented in this section suggest that the private sector can provide standard housing more cheaply than the Public Housing Authority. First, it seems probable that the rent plus subsidy in public housing is higher than rent in equivalent private housing. Second, and perhaps more important, both more intensive use of the stock of existing standard housing and the upgrading of substandard housing stand a fair chance of being cheaper approaches than new construction under public auspices to expanding the supply of low-rent standard housing.

From the income limits established by local housing authorities, it can be deduced that the implicit rent in public housing probably exceeds the rent of comparable units in the private market. A definition of the subsidy in public housing, which is different from the one that has been calculated here, is the difference between what the public housing would rent for if it were administered by a private realtor and the rent actually paid. When this conception of the subsidy is estimated, a smaller dollar value results than when the subsidy is calculated from the implied market value of the resources embodied in the Public Housing Authority units. The difference between these two figures measures the extent to which public housing exceeds the cost of comparable private housing.

The subsidy resulting from subtracting rents paid from the market value of equivalent private units has been calculated in the following way by Prescott.[16] The Public Housing Authority requires that maximum rents at admission be no more than 80 percent of private market rents for comparable units in substantial supply,[17] and that tenants pay at least 20 percent of their incomes (adjusted for family size) as rent. Hence, if the upper income limit for tenant eligibility is known for a particular project and if it is assumed that rents are 20 percent of income and rents are 80 percent of *comparable* rents, then the private market rental value of the public housing units can be obtained.[18] Subtracting the realized rents from the market rent of comparable units yields Prescott's subsidy. The (weighted) average of the subsidies obtained by Prescott for six representative public housing projects was $40 per month (1965 prices) in contrast to the $62 per month subsidy obtained earlier when the market value of the resources was calculated. If Prescott's estimates are correct, relying upon the private sector would yield the same housing at no more than 60 percent of the cost of the current program. Alternatively, at the same program cost, instead of housing 28,000 a year, more than 43,000 families could be housed.

This result is critically dependent upon the assumption that the local housing authorities are trying to and can estimate the market value of comparable rental units. More seriously perhaps, the estimate is based upon only six projects that, despite Prescott's efforts, may not be truly representative. The results are suggestive, however, since they rely on the self-perception of the local housing authorities themselves.

The second and somewhat more convincing source of evidence that the private sector can furnish standard housing more cheaply than the public sector is the estimated and actual cost of rehabilitating substandard units. Before turning to that evidence, however, some consideration of the potential role of utilizing available vacant units is required.

One possible source of standard low-rent housing will be from units presently vacant and standard. Annual changes in vacancies among low-rent units is a complex function, which exhibits a pronounced cycle, of demographic variables, the rate of change in the levels and the distribution of income, mortgage rates, and a host of other variables. One can assume, however, that there is unlikely to be any significant number of units which can be drawn upon at the prevailing rent in any period, even the current one in which vacancy rates are at historically high levels.[19] Vacancies relevant to the program may be of the order of 50,000 units, which will allow the program to get under way without an immediate rise in rents, although there are probably many fewer units (particularly in the Northeast and South, where public housing is concentrated and where vacancy rates are below the national average).[20] In the main, however, the stock of standard low-rent housing will have to be increased by rehabilitating substandard units.[21] The upgrading of units is already a major source of annual additions to the stock of standard low-rent units (almost no new housing is built for low-income families by private owners), and the remainder filter down.[22]

A considerable amount of rehabilitation involves previously substandard units. In the period from 1956 to 1960, 77,000 rental units per year were raised from dilapidated to fully standard condition in the SMSA's. An additional 110,000 units per year were raised to standard levels by the improvement of plumbing facilities. These are fairly large numbers when compared with 28,000 new public housing units constructed each year, although only some unknown proportion of these improved units serve low-income families. Furthermore, the supply of units requiring up-grading grows rapidly. Each year about 85,000 units sink into dilapidation, while another 65,000 units become substandard because the plumbing becomes inadequate.[23] The number of units that would be rehabilitated if current rates of spending are maintained would not be a trivial increase. The costs of rehabilitation therefore would be somewhat higher than they now are due to diminishing returns in construction. Costs, however, are not likely to rise sufficiently to justify new construction.

The ideal data with which to appraise the cost and therefore the desirability of substituting conditional income supplements for public housing would be the rehabilitation costs to private owners and the rents charged for substandard units that have been rehabilitated to standard quality for occupancy by low-income families. Such data are not readily available. What limited data are available are associated with public programs, although the widely publicized experiment of the U.S. Gypsum Company meets the ideal requirements.[24] In that project, though rehabilitation costs exceeded $9,000 per dwelling unit, median post-renewal rents are $78 per month, with the company expecting a satisfactory rate of return on its investment. The units in this building are generally quite small, but even with a generous allowance for that fact, the rents are considerably below the rent plus subsidy in public housing in New York City.[25]

Urban renewal experience is a second source of data. It takes two forms: projected rehabilitation costs for spot or neighborhood-wide rehabilitation in urban renewal areas, and the actual costs of rehabilitation in neighborhood-wide renewal programs. Both bodies of data pose difficult problems of interpretation.

The published data on such large neighborhood renewal efforts as the Wooster Square project in New Haven would not be directly relevant even if they were in the appropriate form, which they are not.[26] As the aim is neighborhood renewal, *all* buildings are either upgraded or destroyed, and since as high a level of rehabilitation as possible is coaxed out of the participants, the average costs of rehabilitation are raised above what they would be if the rehabilitation came in response to increased market demand alone. That is, the market would select for rehabilitation only those units that can be improved most cheaply —an outcome that would frustrate some of the objectives of neighborhood renewal. A related factor, which may be working in the opposite direction, is that the renewal agency provides services that lower the cost of renewal to some owners, but these services are in general required primarily to obtain neighborhood-wide compliance. Finally, pre- and postrenewal rents for rehabilitated units and rehabilitation costs per dwelling unit (as opposed to costs per structure) are not published. The prerenewal income levels of the residents suggest an initially higher quality unit than would be involved in an income supplement program, but initial rents in the area were quite low.

It was assumed that rehabilitation would be an acceptable solution only if it required a subsidy of $40 per month or less (as opposed to the implicit subsidy estimated earlier of $62). This was done to be cautious and allow these imperfections in the data to prejudice the case against rehabilitation, and because new units would, in general, be preferable to rehabilitated ones at the same subsidy.

If property owners find they can raise rents by $40 per month, they will be willing to invest up to $4,700 in rehabilitation.[27] Average rehabilitation costs in Wooster Square ran far above this amount, but this was in large part due to the heavy expenditures on owner-occupied single family dwellings where investment considerations were not dominant. Of the sixteen case studies of multiple-dwelling units cited, ten were rehabilitated for under $4,700 per unit.[28] Median rents in the neighborhood rose from $54 per month including heat to $65 per month including heat![29]

The data on anticipated rehabilitation costs are usually in a more usable form for these purposes, but they are anticipated and not realized costs and are probably underestimated. These studies tend to suggest, however, that if housing at code standards is a satisfactory solution then it can be obtained at costs which are trivial when compared with the current subsidy.[30] If completely modernized units are required, however, then there is some doubt. In the excellent study of rehabilitation prospects for Morningside Heights in New York City, for example, complete modernization was found to require postrenewal rents of up to $200 per month per four-room unit. However, for three and possibly four of the nine classes of buildings in the area which were distinguished in the study, postrenewal rents would be well within acceptable limits.[31] The range of rehabilitation costs of these four classes of buildings was from $4,000 to $5,300.

The rent rise permitted by the New York City Rent and Rehabilitation Administration for various improvements is also instructive. New plumbing with new bathroom fixtures warrants about a ten dollar per month rise in rents in high cost multi-dwelling units. Housing in New York has not improved at the same rate as the other major cities.[32] This may be due to inadequate allowances for rental increases after rehabilitation. It would nevertheless seem reasonable to suppose that $15 per month is all that is required to keep a substantial proportion of the 70,000 units that become substandard each year because of inadequate plumbing at standard levels. On the other hand, the New York City rent schedules cast doubt on the feasibility of completely modernizing large numbers of units, unless the U.S. Gypsum experience is quite general and units can be obtained for their land value. New plumbing including new bathtub, sink, and flushometer, a new stove, refrigerator, and kitchen cabinets; electric rewiring including additional outlets, a new heating system; and interior improvements up to code standard will warrant a rent rise of about $42 per month.[33] It might take another ten dollars a month to induce the property owner to tuck point, steam clean, recaulk, and repaint the exterior of his building.[34] Undoubtedly, however, $52 or even $60 per month is less than the implicit subsidy in public housing in New York City by a fair margin.

All that can be deduced from these data is that there is a fair chance that rehabilitation may be a quite feasible alternative to new construction under public auspices. Rehabilitation costs are clearly highly variable, and no conclusive data will be available unless a field test is made. Certain administrative considerations for a field test follow from the preceding discussion and a few additional economic factors.

Administrative Considerations

The number of families that will be induced to choose standard housing depends upon the particular subsidy scheme adopted. Economic considerations alone suggest that the most efficient scheme is to give those families now eligible for public housing a cash subsidy, which the recipient can spend as he wishes so long as he lives in standard housing.[35] A brief examination of existing programs that subsidize rehabilitation mortgages or give rent supplements illustrates why this is so, as these alternatives do not lead to the largest number of families eventually being housed in standard quality units given current program costs.

Subsidizing the interest rate on rehabilitation mortgages (as in the 312 rehabilitation loan program) has two effects. First, it encourages the rehabilitation of houses that would not be profitable otherwise to upgrade. This effect is perfectly consistent with getting as large a number of families as possible in standard housing per dollar of subsidy. The second effect, however, is to encourage a higher level of rehabilitation than would otherwise be profitable. This encourages serving a higher income market,[36] and if the program is to serve to maximize the number of families in standard housing, further administrative controls are required to keep rehabilitation to an acceptable level. Additional administrative controls raise rehabilitation costs and reduce willingness to participate in the program;[37] and hence the 312 program will not induce the largest number of low-income families to choose standard housing at any total program cost.

Rent supplements that pay the owner the difference between a portion of the tenants' income and the fair market value of a standard unit encourage each family to consume as much housing as the local authority will permit. To get the maximum reduction in the number of families in substandard housing, the specified rent limit must be the minimum consistent with the achievement of standard housing. Vigorous searching by FHA[38] or strenuous competition among landlords for the subsidized tenants would be capable of achieving this result. (Of course, only the chance for greater profits will assure vigorous landlord competition.) A restricted cash grant, with any excess of subsidy over rent becoming income to the tenant, assures minimum rents for subsidized standard units consistent with the tastes, family size, and so forth of the participants. It also assures approaching the minimum subsidy per family over time (with the attendant windfalls accruing to the poor), and hence will result in the maximum decline in the number of families in substandard housing, given the total program costs. Finally, it frees the administrator from concern over the quality of rehabilitation, because tenants will be under the obligation to seek new housing if their rehabilitated units fall below standard after they are occupied. This obligation of course exerts pressure on the landlord to do more than a cosmetic job.

Two alternative strategies can be followed while searching out standard units. One is to proceed slowly, waiting for FHA to study exhaustively each local housing market for the minimum feasible subsidy. Alternatively, the program can get under way with a reasonable but fairly arbitrary initial subsidy, and the evidence accumulated from the rental expenditures of the participants will be allowed to influence the size of the subsidy in future periods. Because the market is being tested for a minimum feasible price, the subsidy will become effective more quickly if it starts above and falls toward it. If the housing market must be studied first, benefits to the poor and nonpoor will be delayed (but so will the costs, however). The alternative procedure raises welfare at once, and further, if the subsidy takes the form of a restricted cash grant, any windfalls that result will accrue to the poor.[39]

A Concluding Historical Note

The notion that income supplements ought to be given to the poor to exploit cost savings available from the private sector is at least as old as public housing;[40] only permitting the poor to "keep the change" if any may be novel. That structural improvement of existing buildings is preferable to new construction is also an old idea, but that its prime advantage may be in maximizing the number of families living in safe and sanitary housing has not been generally perceived. One planner, Charles Abrams, has vigorously espoused subsidizing the poor as a means to get the housing stock rehabilitated and the largest number of families in decent housing, and he was opposed a decade and a half ago.[41]

Why has this obvious and simple scheme been avoided in most planning discussions? Part of the explanation undoubtedly lies in the enthusiasm of real estate dealers and builders for some aspects of the idea. Too many planners understand that private vice may be public virtue but will be damned before they'll play that game. Such a position is totally self-defeating in the U.S., for the market will take every decision of the planners as an input into its profit-maximizing calculus. Even Senator Taft, however, rejected income supplements, so there must be other objections too.[42]

Many criticisms reflect earlier characteristics of the housing market. Low levels of construction for two decades accompanied by a massive spatial redistribution of the population preceded the 1949 Act. Now, however, after two decades of expansion and improvement in the housing stock, we appear to be on the downside of the long swing in residential construction. The consequences of perpetually rising income for all segments of the society, along with a once-over decline in income inequality, require a shift of emphasis away from preoccupation with the mechanics of filtering down and toward the ongoing process of upgrading the housing stock.[43] The evidence was already well documented in the National Housing Inventory, but it was apparently overlooked. The unobstructed visibility of discrimination in housing has obscured the rapid rate at which Negroes have been acquiring access to parts of the housing stock that were formerly denied them.[44] The housing subsidy has been misperceived and underestimated. It is the opportunity cost of the resources used, not the interest paid on the bonds, which sets the cost of the program to society, when interest rates are subsidized through tax advantages to holders of the bonds.

There has also been confusion about the administrative costs of such a program. The local administrators ought not to be certifying the quality of housing en masse nor providing the prospective tenants with preexamined lists. Neither ought they to be continuously investigating the income of the subsidized tenants nor the quality of their housing. The census taker probably classifies a house as standard or substandard within fifteen minutes. Must the local housing authority take very much longer? In short, the administrative costs can be less than under the current program.

Some strange sociology was also involved. Charles Abrams has said, "there is a vast spiritual difference between paying the required rent in a government owned building and being on a permanent dole."[45] There is also no reason why rehabilitation must be a tool to revivify the whole city. Isn't it enough if it gets larger numbers of poor families satisfactorily housed?

There is one final possibility—to put the scheme into widespread operation may simply not be feasible. The data presented here are for the U.S. as a whole, but there is no average community in the United States. White backlash, rigid mortgage bankers, bureaucratic torpor, and consumer apathy may be greater than has been allowed for. However, the enormous advantages of income supplements over public housing on sociological and physical planning grounds have been loudly proclaimed in recent years. Only the economics have been in doubt. This paper will not resolve all of those doubts, and for the near future, public housing must continue to be what it has been. But the way is open for vigorous debate and extensive field testing. Even if the results prove the existing program to be the best, the exercise will have been significant for future housing policy.

Notes

[1]W. C. Wheaton, "The Evolution of Federal Housing Programs" (Unpublished Ph.D. thesis, University of Chicago, 1953).

[2]From among the many examples that could be cited see, for example, Charles Abrams, *The City is the Frontier* (New York: Harper & Row, 1965), pp. 265–267, or W. Grigsby, *Housing Markets and Public Policy* (Philadelphia: University of Pennsylvania Press, 1963), pp. 291–292.

[3]Throughout this study, *substandard* will refer to the physical characteristics of dwelling units, in particular to units that are without adequate plumbing or in a dilapidated condition. The local housing authorities are also sensitive to needs arising from the deterioration of surrounding units and overcrowding. No allowance has been made for these other attributes of housing quality in this study.

[4]Public housing raises more general questions of welfare policy which will be ignored because they require a quite different mode of analysis. It seems clear that the program does not have as its purpose to maximize the welfare of the poor, for the program is so obviously inefficient by this criterion that it cannot have been the purpose of its framers. For example, if it were the welfare of the poor that was to be maximized, nothing could be superior to giving the poor the cash equivalent of their subsidy directly. For this reason, the extent to which the poor are made worse off because their taxes are raised by their share of the cost of the public housing program, and the extent to which the poor who do not obtain the public housing subsidy are made to feel worse off because otherwise similar people receive privileges that they do not, will not be considered. Yet there may be an important exception to the text statement. Public housing has required the destruction of substandard housing by statute. Also public housing has often cleared land to build. Both actions have reduced the stock of housing available to the poor and thereby may have raised its price.

[5]Note that as these questions are posed, no value will be placed upon raising housing quality unless the improvement is all the way to standard. Similarly, no value is placed upon improved housing quality beyond standard. As Professor Weisbrod has pointed out to me, the problem of operating from fixed standards which merely dichotomize into satisfactory and unsatisfactory results is ubiquitous, viz. the use of a poverty line.

[6]This must be true even if the aim of the government is to redistribute income toward the lower income groups. Rather than a building program, the government could permit the private sector to use the resources, tax the income that results, and pay out the revenues to the poor. Presumably, the government finds that building achieves its objective more efficiently.

[7]Unless otherwise specified all data are from the *Annual Reports* of the Housing and Home Finance Agency.

[8]*Housing Statistics Annual Data*, Housing and Home Finance Agency, May 1965, p. 74.

[9]The cost figure was derived by adjusting the annual bond sales data to

exclude, whenever possible, sales for other than newly opening units. Sales in December 1964 were also excluded, but the total is probably somewhat high. However, the figure may be somewhat lower than it ought to be because public housing can acquire land through the use of eminent domain. Also, a small part of its land came at subsidized prices from the Urban Renewal Administration. Both these factors can make the cost to the private developer higher than the cost to the local housing authority. The deflator is "the implicit price deflator of new residential construction."

[10]The yield on FHA mortgages was derived from price data in *Urban Development Federal Housing Administration News* on 5¼ percent new home mortgages, 25 year maturity, 10 percent down payment, with prepayment at the end of 12 years. W. Alberts was kind enough to make his calculations for the period through 1960 available to us. Some interpolations were required, which introduced a small amount of error. This is a low estimate of the discount rate, since it measures lenders' as opposed to borrowers' risk. Alternatively, since the bonds will be retired out of general federal revenues, the average return on all invested capital in the private sector may be the appropriate rate. The calculated subsidy is highly sensitive to the interest rate chosen, and the subsidy shown here must be considered a minimum estimate. At a discount rate of 7 percent, for example, the subsidy would rise by almost 30 percent.

[11]For example, if the value of the land at the end of forty years were to exceed the costs of demolition by 15 percent of the initial cost, the subsidy would fall by only 2 percent. That is, only the present value of the salvage value is relevant.

[12]There are two additional factors which must be added to the subsidy but their combined effect is small. First, there are the administrative costs of the program both at the local and federal level. Secondly, there is the difference between the payment in lieu of taxes made by the federal government and the taxes which actually would have been earned on the property. A slight offset may be that labor was valued at its full wage even when unemployment existed.

[13]A test calculation using actual construction and rental data on the Taylor Homes project in Chicago yielded a subsidy of $64. Average rental however in the project was $77 per month so that the implicit rent was $141 per unit month.

[14]Since rental expenditures are best related to permanent (rather than calendar year) income, rental expenditures were taken to be a better measure of permanent income than calendar year revenue as reported in the census. Hence, the effects of the cash subsidy on rental expenditures and the proportion of families in standard housing as implied by those rental expenditures was computed as follows: from the distribution of income within rental classes, the median income was found and associated with the average rent paid in that rental class. Once the rent associated with each income was found, the proportion of families at that rent occupying standard housing was estimated. (*Census of Housing, 1960*, II: "*Metropolitan Housing*," Pt. I, "United States and Divisions," Table B-2, 1–18.) The implicit income elasticity of demand over the range of income $2,000–$3,000 is 0.75.

[15]It has been assumed, for example, that it is sufficient to calculate from averages without taking distributional characteristics into account. These characteristics may strain the assumption that the market price of low-income housing would have been unaffected by withdrawing public housing from the housing stock. In the aggregate, public housing is

in fact so small a part of even the low-income housing markets that this assumption is satisfactory enough, but it may not be true for several selected markets, for instance, the market in Georgia for Negroes with the incomes of Georgia Negro occupants of public housing. However, the result is probably not too far from the truth. In a careful multivariate analysis of South Chicago housing patterns, Muth found, "... the proportion of dwellings which are sub-standard declines by about two-thirds per thousand dollars of income." Further, this is consistent with his intercity estimates; see R. F. Muth, "The Spatial Pattern of Residential Land Use in Cities" (Mimeographed), pp. 11–16.

[16]J. R. Prescott, "The Economics of Public Housing: A Normative Analysis" (Unpublished Ph.D. thes's, Harvard University, 1964).

[17]More precisely, the procedure used by the local housing authority is "To establish a minimum 20 percent gap between the highest admission for rents for public housing development and the lowest rents at which there is a substantial supply of standard private housing. . . ." *The Chicago Housing Authority, Determination of Lowest Private Rents for the City of Chicago*, 1965, cover page. Strictly speaking, therefore, the private housing need not be "equivalent to" or "comparable to" public housing, but if this is not the case the exercise seems totally pointless.

[18]If Y_4 is the annual income limit for families of size i, and R_4 is the rent in the project, and M is the market rental value of the unit, then $.8M = R_4$ and $5R_4 = Y_4$, so that $M = Y_4/4$. Rents do tend to be just slightly more than 20 percent of income on the average. The actual relationship between market rents and public housing rents cannot, however, be independently verified. The low residual receipts of local housing authorities in recent years, however, places pressure on the administrators to keep rents near the 80 percent statutory ceiling. On the other hand, there is pressure upon the local housing authorities not to set income limits too high, and the higher the comparable rent of private units the higher the income limit.

[19]Sherman Maisel, "Fluctuations in Residential Construction Starts," *American Economic Review* (June 1963), p. 375, and U.S. Bureau of the Census, *Current Housing Reports*, Series H-11, No. 43, "Vacant Housing Units in the United States: 1956 to 1965," 1966.

[20]Total vacancies in the U.S. were roughly 2,500,000 units, or about 8 percent of total units in the first quarter of 1966. Vacancy rates have not varied from 7.5 percent more than one standard deviation since 1961. Assuming 7 percent as the equilibrium rate, however, would yield an excess supply of about 300,000 units. Of these about 17 percent would be available for rent at less than $70 per month (Bureau of the Census, "Vacant Housing Units"). In the recent tight money period rental vacancy rates have fallen below 7 percent for the first time since 1959, implying almost no vacancies can be drawn upon without raising rents.

[21]This conclusion is buttressed by noting that despite a continuous ten-year rise in the vacancy rate within the SMSA's, there has been no perceptible tendency for the new construction of rental units to decline (except for the current tight money period).

[22]In the three years from 1957 through 1960, a little over 52,000 units were constructed that were renting in 1960 for under $60 per month (median gross rent in 1960 was $63 per month). In the same period almost 54,000 low-rent public housing units were constructed, so that virtually all of the new units must have been constructed under federal programs. U.S. Bureau of the Census, *U.S. Census of Housing: 1960*, Vol. IV, "Components of Inventory Change—1957 to 1959 Components" (Final Report HC 4), Pt. 2, No. 1, Government Printing Office, Washington, D.C.,

1963, Table 1; and *Housing Statistics* (May 1965), p. 74. During the same period, for renter-occupied units in SMSA's for which the rent in 1956 and 1959 is known, only 260,000 units drifted downward to the $50–$60 rental class, while 300,000 rose into that rental class. 508,000 units were in this rental class at both the beginning and end of the period. Similar results are obtained for the rent class $40–49, although not for the $30–39 class (*Ibid.*, p. 57). Even with generous allowances for the rise in rents during this period, the data suggest that it would be worth further study to determine if while students of low-income housing have been preoccupied with filtering down, filtering up may have been as important.

[23]*Census of Housing, 1960* (Final Report HC 4), *loc. cit.* These numbers are biased downward because no attempt was made to assign a quality level to vacant units in 1960, and only units already in rental use are considered.

[24]U.S. Gypsum Co., New York Rehabilitation Project, *Progress Report.*

[25]M. Carter McFarland and Walter K. Vivrett, eds., *Residential Rehabilitation* (Minneapolis: University of Minnesota, School of Architecture, 1966), chap. 19.

[26]Mary Hommann, *Wooster Square Design* (New Haven: The New Haven Redevelopment Agency, 1965).

[27]Assuming an 8 percent interest rate and a twenty-year life expectancy. The discussion also assumes that a $40 subsidy is also a forty-dollar rise in net rents. This is probably conservative, for upgrading is likely to reduce maintenance costs.

[28]*Ibid.*, chap. 9.

[29]*Ibid.*, p. 65.

[30]It was estimated, for example, that the cost of bringing substandard housing to housing code acceptability in Chicago's Hyde Park would average $410 per dwelling unit, with no unit costing more than $490 per unit. Similar estimates for Morningside Heights in New York City averaged $480 per dwelling unit and did not exceed $78 per room. David Zisook and Zisook Construction Company, *Report on the Feasibility of Rehabilitation*, adjusted to fourth quarter of 1965 prices, and New York State Temporary State Housing Rent Commission, *Prospects for Rehabilitation*, 1960, adjusted to fourth quarter of 1965 prices. These data are probably much too low and suggest that repeated investments will be required to keep the units at minimum code standard. The actual experience in Washington, D.C., has been that units (for large families) were brought to code levels at an average cost of $1,500 per unit. H. Marindin, "Combined Rent Supplement, Rehab-Demonstrations," *Journal of Housing*, No. 5 (May 1966), 256.

[31]The required postrenewal rents for four-room apartments were estimated to be $72, $92, $112, and $128 per month, respectively. *Prospects for Rehabilitation, op. cit.* For the class of building in which the U.S. Gypsum building falls, required postrenewal rents were set at $72, so the results can be accepted as about a 20 percent underestimate.

[32]Beverly Duncan and Philip M. Hauser, *Housing A Metropolis—Chicago* (Glencoe, Illinois: The Free Press, 1960), chap. 2.

[33]*Schedule of Rental Values of the City Rent and Rehabilitation Administration*, April 1, 1964. Adjusting the subsidy for regional price variations would bring New York City estimates within the limits of the subsidy.

[34]*Prospects for Rehabilitation, op. cit.*

[35]It may be worthwhile to point out that the small number of units involved and the custom nature of rehabilitation support the assumption

that rehabilitation can be treated as a constant cost industry and that rents of standard units will not rise, in general, except perhaps for a brief period. Since effective demand and supply of substandard units will be equally affected, rents of substandard housing ought to be unaffected by and large.

[36]Congressional pressure on URA to be "fiscally responsible" will push the program toward improvements of too high a level. Rehabilitation does tend to be viewed as primarily for middle-income families by the housing authorities. *Journal of Housing, loc. cit.*

[37]There is evidence that the 312 program is in fact getting administratively cumbersome, in part for this reason, and that this is reducing the number of borrowers. *See Journal of Housing* (May 1966), p. 250.

[38]Since the number of available units will rise with rents, FHA will be under considerable pressure to "satisfice." The statutory requirement, that the supplement be less than the annual contribution commitment, is likely to be just met. This is certainly the Chicago experience where the rent supplement limit has been set at just about the average public housing subsidy in Chicago, but for elderly tenants who require on the average smaller units. No substantial increase in the number of tenants per program dollar is likely to emerge from this procedure if subsidies tend to be the maximum allowable. Furthermore, tenants of higher income must be preferable because that raises the feasible upper limit to rents, and guarantees the landlord and FHA a higher "caliber" of tenant, as we measure those things.

[39]As an aside, note that the current law discriminates against large families. A large proportion of low-income families who live in substandard housing spend more than 25 percent of their incomes on rent. Those families, assuming an income elasticity of demand for housing of about one, might want to consume units of higher rent and higher quality than they would consume under the rent subsidy plan as now instituted. These families might find the subsidy insufficient to move them to standard housing; they might even feel themselves worse off with the subsidy and therefore refuse to participate in the program. The group most likely to be affected this way are large families, and the program would then discriminate against those families. The upshot well could be that smaller numbers of persons (as opposed to families) are moved to standard housing under the current rent supplement program than under an unrestricted cash grant system.

[40]President's Advisory Committee on Housing, *Appendix 3—Subcommittee for Low Income Families*, p. 323.

[41]Charles Abrams was opposed in his *The Future of Housing*, chap. 19. His support comes in *The City is the Frontier*, pp. 267, 268, as well as in testimony before Congress.

[42]President's Advisory Committee, p. 329.

[43]Increasingly, therefore, public housing has come to serve those outside of the labor force, particularly welfare recipients and the elderly. The welfare program is closest of all existing programs to the program proposed here, but, of course, a substantial increase in cash payment is envisaged.

[44]Not only did one in five Negro families in 1960 occupy a dwelling unit that had been occupied by a white family just three years earlier, but the Negroes were of the same or higher socioeconomic status as the whites they succeeded, and they have maintained or improved their housing accordingly. K. and A. Taeuber, *Negroes in Cities* (Chicago: Aldine Publishing Company, 1965).

[45]C. Abrams, *The Future of Housing, op. cit.*

3.5

Comment on "Public Housing or Income Supplements: The Economics of Housing for the Poor"

Michael A. Stegman

More than twenty years ago, Charles Abrams remarked that the "relationship between housing and the subsidy has been permitted to grow without benefit of maxim or definition" and that "formulation of principles on the subsidy was never more critical than it is today."[1] A recently awakened interest in the subsidy as part of the total costs of housing programs perhaps may be accounted for as one of the spillover effects of Mr. McNamara's cost-effectiveness program within the defense establishment (since the efficiency of various programs cannot be estimated without first estimating the value of the resources that go into each). Another explanation may be that now housing programs, like most other programs with welfare objectives, can be evaluated against various proposals for income supplementation. These have only recently achieved sufficient respectability for consideration as viable alternatives to functional programs with redistributive effects on income.

Smolensky's article, "Public Housing or Income Supplements: The Economics of Housing for the Poor," not only supports Abrams' contention of two decades ago, but more importantly, serves to hammer another nail into the coffin of one of the oldest and most controversial housing programs yet devised; namely, the public housing program. He accomplishes this in two ways. First, he calculates that the average family residing in public housing receives a monthly subsidy equivalent to $62 in cash (which is, most likely, a good deal more than is commonly believed to be the case). Second, he claims the private sector can provide housing more cheaply than the public sector. Hence, a combined private rehabilitation–income supplement program, he concludes, is a more efficient means of providing adequate shelter for poor families who are living in substandard housing.

It is my contention, however, that even if we are to accept his conclusion that "sixty-two dollars is the monthly amount which could have been made available in cash to the successive tenants in average PL 171 units over the forty years from the date when each unit was first occupied without affecting the

Reprinted by permission of the *Journal of the American Institute of Planners* (Vol. XXXIV, No. 3, May 1968), pp. 195–198.

distribution of the nation's resources between tenants and nontenants": (1) recent changes in the public housing program promise to lower the costs of construction; (2) the absolute size of the dollar subsidy is not as significant (within the context of Smolensky's arguments) as is the relative difference between it and the subsidy that would be required under the private rehabilitation–public income supplement package; and (3) the evidence presented in the article with respect to the cost of rehabilitating substandard units in the private sector is incomplete and probably substantially underestimates the magnitude of the real value of the resources that would have to be expended upon such a program. If the latter point is correct, this would imply the necessity of granting larger income supplements to poor families or, at least, increasing the implicit subsidy involved in the combined rehabilitation-income supplement program.

While Smolensky's calculations of the implicit subsidy involved in the construction and operation of typical PL 171 units appear to be quite reasonable, the importance of the discount rate in the determination of the subsidy should be made particularly clear. It should be recognized, for example, that the subsidy is extremely sensitive to variations in the discount rate, and that since there is little agreement on precisely what constitutes an appropriate market rate, a range of implicit subsidies based upon a range of possible discount rates should be provided the reader. At a discount rate of 4 percent, for example, the implicit subsidy would be approximately $54 per month, as opposed to $62; at 6 percent, it would be $71; and, at 8 percent, it would be $91.

Similarly, variations in the capital cost of constructing public housing units influences the magnitude of the subsidy. This point is of particular relevance since it has been estimated that under the recently developed turnkey process which permits the construction of public housing by a private developer, the unit cost of construction can be lowered by as much as 15 percent. If we were to recalculate the implicit subsidy, assuming an average unit cost of, say, $11,400 (15 percent less than the $13,400 unit cost used by Smolensky), the implicit monthly subsidy becomes $42 assuming a 4 percent discount rate; $48 using Smolensky's 5 percent rate, $60 at 6 percent, and $77 at 8 percent.[2]

These points are of major significance in evaluating Smolensky's conclusions: (1) there is no consensus as to the appropriate rate of interest which would justify the shifting of resources from the private to the public sector; (2) recent changes in the public housing program promise to reduce unit costs of construction; and (3) the implicit subsidy is extremely sensitive to changes in both of these. It follows, therefore, that if Smolensky's estimates of the cost of the rehabilitation-income supplement package turn out to be very much on the conservative side, his conclusion as to which of the two programs is the more efficient might be incorrect.

The author's principal argument that "the private sector can furnish standard housing more cheaply than the public sector" is supported by his own calculations and some limited references to the experiences of private enterprise with large-scale rehabilitation efforts. He concludes that "rehabilitation would be an acceptable solution only if it required a subsidy of $40 or less (as opposed to the implicit subsidy estimated earlier at $62)." "This was done," he said, "to be cautious and allow these imperfections in the data to prejudice the case against rehabilitation and because new units would, in general, be preferable to rehabilitated ones at the same subsidy." He went on to state that "if property owners find they can raise rents by $40 per month, they will be willing to invest up to $4,700 in rehabilitation" ($4,700 is the present value of a monthly subsidy of $40, discounted over twenty years, at an interest rate of 8 percent). Since he asserts that statistical evidence exists to indicate that major rehabilitation efforts can be undertaken successfully at less than $4,700 per unit, or at monthly rental increases of $40 or less, he concludes that this is a more efficient means of dealing with the housing problem than is that implied in publicly financed, constructed, and operated housing.

The weaknesses, however, in Smolensky's analysis of the real costs of rehabilitation can be demonstrated by referring to the same project he used to document his case for the efficiency of rehabilitation over public construction; namely, the U.S. Gypsum Company's experiences with its 102nd Street rehabilitation project in New York. Smolensky indicated that "although rehabilitation costs exceeded $9,000 per dwelling unit, median post renewal rents are $78, with the company expecting a satisfactory rate of return on its investment." More recent information indicates, however, that while postrenewal rents do, indeed, average $78 per month, this represents an average increase of $50 per month over the prerenewal rentals, which averaged

$28.[3] If we make the assumption that the income supplement to which Smolensky refers is to be used to maintain postrenewal rents as close to prerenewal rents as possible, then the entire subsidy (and more) would thus be committed to the project. The fact of the matter is, however, that the actual increase in rents and the income supplements that would be necessary to maintain prerenewal families after the rehabilitation effort is completed, does not represent the aggregate real value of the subsidies involved in the U.S. Gypsum project.

Additional information on the project indicates, for example, that the company does not expect to earn a reasonable return on its investment. As a matter of fact, it invested $500,000 of its own money in the $1.6 million project, and now is turning it over at cost to a nonprofit corporation that will finance the purchase with a 221(d) (3) below-market-interest-rate loan.[4] If we assume, for example, that U.S. Gypsum's half million dollar equity investment was tied up for two years during which the project was undertaken, and that the company chose to forego earnings on that amount of money, the earnings foregone surely represent an implicit subsidy that should be added to the real cost of the project. Assuming that the money was tied up for two years and that the company could have invested or otherwise used it to earn, say, 8 percent, then the present value of the equity investment, discounted over two years at 8 percent, represents a subsidy of $71,281 for the two years in question.[5] Since there are 118 units in the project, the annual subsidy for each unit averages $302, or $25 per month.

Moreover, as indicated above, after rehabilitation was completed, the building was turned over, at cost ($1.6 million), to a nonprofit corporation which received a below-market mortgage at an interest rate of 3 percent. Surely, the liberal terms of the mortgage represent an implicit subsidy that should also be taken into consideration in any analysis of the real value of the resources that have gone into this particular rehabilitation effort. If, for example, we assume the mortgage to be for the full project cost of $1.6 million over a twenty-year period, the savings in interest expense alone over a similar mortgage at 6 percent would be $31,104 per year.[6] With 118 units in the project, this comes to an implicit subsidy of $269 per unit per year, or a monthly subsidy of more than $22 per unit. Another way of viewing this subsidy is to discount it back to the present at an appropriate market rate of interest. On this basis, the annual interest subsidy, discounted over twenty years, at an interest rate of 5 percent, has a present value of $388,800.[7] That is, the interest subsidy is equivalent to a lump sum cash subsidy to the nonprofit corporation of more than a quarter of a million dollars.

The Ridge Street Project, undertaken by the Conservation, Rehabilitation, and Renewal Foundation, headed by Roger Starr, is another prominent rehabilitation effort in New York City for which excellent information exists and which can be referred to in support of the contention that many privately initiated rehabilitation efforts involve larger implicit subsidies than are apparent to the casual observer. With $250,000 of Laurence Rockefeller's money, the foundation purchased a 22-unit old law tenement at 92 Ridge Street, New York City. Even with no mortgage payments to reduce the cash flow, Starr concluded that "legal operation of the building (adherence to the building code) was financially impossible."[8] Average monthly rents in the building increased from $23 to nearly $60 (which is, incidentally, within the acceptable range indicated by Smolensky), but it was still not possible to amortize the improvements within a reasonable period of time, even with no interest payments. As a matter of fact, even with the implicit subsidies of an interest-free loan, a twelve-year tax exemption on the value of the improvements, and an abatement on previous real estate taxes, the project could not throw off sufficient cash to make it financially workable. Said Starr,

> With 80 rental rooms in the building it would require an annual net income after all charges and depreciation of $132 per room in order to bring the 8 percent return on Mr. Rockefeller's investment. Three years after rehabilitation, however, net income per rental room does not exceed $67, barely half of the income required to produce an 8 percent free and clear return even with complete tax abatement. This actual net income figure, moreover, does not include a charge for depreciation or a reserve for major repairs.[9]

The evidence above should be sufficient to indicate that "privately initiated" large-scale rehabilitation efforts are more "quasi-public" than private, inasmuch as various forms of public support are usually involved in the acquisition of financing phases of the projects and, thus, involve larger subsidies than are at first apparent.

Smolensky's comparison of the merits of private rehabilitation as opposed to public construction raises some additional questions. It will be recalled that his determination of the $62 monthly subsidy implicit in the public housing program was based on the construction of new dwelling units with forty-year economic lives. His calculation of the subsidies involved in large-scale rehabilitation efforts in the private sector, however, are based on the provision of standard dwelling units with twenty-year economic lives. Thus, we are entitled to ask either or both of the two following questions. First, how much less would be the implicit subsidy involved in the construction and operation of the public housing program if the economic lives of the units were reduced from forty to twenty years? Second, how much larger an initial capital investment would be forthcoming from a private entrepreneur or landlord if he were promised a $40 increase in net monthly rentals for a period of forty, rather than twenty years? That is, how much more would he invest in rehabilitation to extend the economic lives of his dwelling units to forty years? Carrying out the necessary calculations indicates that no entrepreneur would invest more than $5,700 per unit for the opportunity of receiving the $40 monthly subsidy for the full forty-year period (based upon discounting the $40 monthly stream of income an additional twenty years to reflect the extended economic lives of the units, discounted at 8 percent). That is, he would invest no more than an additional $1,000 per unit in order to double the period in which the subsidy would be received. Needless to say, however, present indications would tend to minimize the likelihood that $5,700 unit costs of rehabilitation can produce units that will provide a flow of standard housing services for forty years.

In conclusion, one might say that a close examination of the real value of the resources that must be committed to large-scale, privately initiated rehabilitation efforts might approximate or exceed that attributed to units constructed under PL 171, depending upon the discount rate selected in calculating the subsidy in the latter program. In addition, the major problems with PL 171 housing projects have been largely noneconomic in nature. These problems have alienated many of its liberal and intellectual supporters as well as large segments of its client population, who have serious doubts that it is a viable program to help alleviate the housing problem. It is these noneconomic problems which have taken on major significance in the considerations of whether the program should continue or not, and if so, the form it should take, not the determination of the precise subsidy implicit in the construction and operation of each dwelling unit. The fact that for the first time, however, there is an estimate of the real cost of the program should prove extremely valuable to those concerned with national housing programs. For whether the costs are higher or lower than those involved in other programs, there is now the possibility that we can speak more intelligently about alternative proposals. As indicated, there is also a need to investigate thoroughly the real costs of various rehabilitation efforts. For providing the benchmark analysis that might provide the necessary foothold for such research, Smolensky should be commended.

Notes

[1]Charles Abrams, "The Subsidy and Housing," in *Urban Housing*, edited by Wheaton, Milgram and Meyerson (New York: The Free Press, 1966), p. 365.

[2]Using Smolensky's formula which states that the average cost of a PL 171 unit equals the sum of residual receipts plus the implicit subsidy, discounted back to the present at an appropriate market rate of interest, the different market rates are substituted into the formula while holding constant residual receipts and capital costs.

[3]"Big Business," *Journal of Housing*, No. 4 (May 1967), 212–213.

[4]*Ibid.*

[5]Eight percent of $500,000 is $40,000. The present value of the $40,000 subsidy for the first year, assuming an 8 percent discount rate, is $37,000. For the second year, the present value of the subsidy is lower because money invested today can earn compound interest. The second year subsidy, discounted at 8 percent, has a present value of $34,280. Thus, the combined subsidy over the two-year period has a present value of $71,280.

[6]See note 5.

[7]"Old Building and Low Income Tenants and Profit-seeking Rehabilitation," *Journal of Housing*, No. 1 (January 1967), 28–32.

[8]*House and Home*, XXX, No. 6 (December 1966), 16.

[9]"Old Building and Low Income Tenants and Profit Seeking Rehabilitation," *Journal of Housing*, No. 1 (January 1967), 32.

3.6

Is Public Housing Headed for a Fiscal Crisis?

Albert A. Walsh

The question—"Is Public Housing Heading for a Fiscal Crisis?" must have been framed solely for the sake of rhetoric. Let there be no doubt about it: public housing is not heading for a fiscal crisis; it is already *in* a fiscal crisis. The only question is what will be done about it.

Public housing today is like a traveler confronting a fork in the road leading toward two entirely separate destinations. The choice that is made, the remedy selected to deal with current fiscal ills, will determine the character of the program in the future and even the very income group it will be able to serve.

We can either preserve the present form of the program at the expense of its traditional goal of providing low-rent housing for families of low income; that is, continue its present fiscal structure, with subsidy based on financing costs and rents raised whenever necessary to cover all other expenses. Or we can preserve the goals of public housing and change its form by developing a new subsidy formula that will serve the needs of low-income families, not the debt on the structures they occupy.

If we choose to maintain the status quo, which I might characterize as selecting the fork in the road that leads to the right, I think that we will find that we have embarked on a disastrous detour that leads only to the total failure of the public housing program and eventual abandonment of the goals it has served so well over the past 30 years. Based on our experience in New York City, public housing dwelling units will soon be priced out of the low-income market and a social crisis of major proportions will develop as low-income tenants face the difficult choice of paying a catastrophic proportion of their income for rent—or returning to the slums.

The present system of pegging rents to cover all costs except debt service was reasonable in 1937. The built-in defect of fiscal rigidity was not apparent then, when the terms "low cost" and "low rent" could be, and were, used interchangeably and a favorable balance existed between available and required subsidies. That system would still be feasible today if the economy, the living conditions of the poor, and the needs of

Reprinted from the *Journal of Housing* (Vol. 26, No. 2, February 1969). Publication of the National Association of Housing and Redevelopment Officials, 2600 Virginia Avenue, N.W., Washington, D.C. 20037.

society had all remained unchanged, or if they had changed at the same time, in the same way, and at the same rate. Unfortunately, but realistically, such is never the case in the affairs of men and a reasonably free economy. Thus, at least once each generation, all government-aid formulas need overhauling and updating. It is this overdue updating of the public housing subsidy formula that has brought us to our present perilous state.

From here on, I present only the case of the New York City Housing Authority, which was established in 1934 to undertake a low-rent housing program under the old Public Works Administration. In business from the beginning, it is currently operating almost 67,000 federally aided public housing units, some completed as early as 1937 and some as late as this year. The financial condition of a program of this size, built under the varying conditions of the past 30 years, cannot be expected to present a picture typical of all housing authorities.

If we were operating only our older projects, our position would be worse than it is today, since they have suffered most from the inflationary spiral of operating costs. Conversely, our average figures are modified somewhat by comparatively higher income tenants paying higher rents in recently-opened projects, where we are able to at least break even for the first few years. Some housing authorities may still be in a relatively better position than we are but I know of at least one that is worse off and we are all headed down the same path.

As Chart 1 illustrates, the incomes of public housing tenants in New York City, and consequently the rents they can afford to pay, have not risen in proportion to the general expansion of the economy as reflected in our operating costs. Over the past 15 years, the average of tenant incomes increased 65.1 percent, from $2500 a year to slightly over $4100. During the same period

Chart 1. Percent Increase Since 1952 in Tenant Incomes, Rent Charged, and Routine Operating Expense
New York City Housing Authority Federal Program—November 1968

	Tenant Incomes		Rent Charged		Routine Operating Expenses	
Year	Amount	% Increase	Amount	%	Amount	%
1952	$2,500	0	$37.53	0	$31.36	0
1957	2,840	13.6	47.75	27.2	44.28	41.2
1962	3,400	36.0	57.40	52.9	56.76	81.0
1967	4,127	65.1	64.40	71.6	70.75	125.6

we increased the average rent from $37.53 per apartment per month to $64.40, an increase of 71.6 percent. Obviously, therefore, our tenants are already paying a higher proportion of their income for rent than they did in 1952. Even so, the additional income produced by rent increases did not keep pace with routine operating expenses, which jumped from $31.36 per apartment per month in 1952 to $70.75 in 1967, or an increase of 125.6 percent.

In an expanding economy, not all incomes rise at the same rate. The poor become proportionately poorer. As Chart 2 illustrates, during the past 15 years, the average income of New York City public housing tenants, largely the unskilled and the semi-skilled, rose at a much slower rate than that of our lowest level of housing authority employees. While, as noted above, the average tenant income went up 65.1 percent, the salaries of our blue-collar employees (caretaker, fireman, and maintenance man) went up 103.8 percent, 123.3 percent, and 164.5 percent, respectively. Similarly, the salary of our housing assistant, the bottom job on the management career ladder, charged with the responsibility of day-to-day relations with the tenants, went up 131.4 percent. The salaries of these employees are established as the result of collective bargaining. As one of the city's large employers with about 10,000 employees, the New York City Housing

Chart 2. Trend of Tenant Incomes and Wages of Authority Employees
New York City Housing Authority Federal Program—November 1968

	1952	1957	1962	1967
Tenant Incomes				
Amount	$2,500	$2,840	$3,400	$4,127
% Increase	0	13.6	36.0	65.1
Maintenance Man				
Amount	$3,100	$4,700	$6,400	$8,200
%	0	51.6	106.5	164.5
Caretaker				
Amount	$2,600	$3,200	$3,800	$5,300
%	0	23.1	46.2	103.8
Fireman				
Amount	$3,000	$3,800	$4,800	$6,700
%	0	26.7	60.0	123.3
Housing Assistant				
Amount	$3,500	$4,400	$5,800	$8,100
%	0	25.7	65.7	131.4

Authority must engage in collective bargaining with some 18 unions. The last round of wage increases for the four groups of employees listed on this chart and other employees belonging to the same union, about half of all our employees, increased payroll and related costs by 8.8 million dollars in 1967 and 1968, the two years covered by the contract. We are now in the midst of another round of negotiations with that union, whose current demands, if met, would cost 52 million dollars in additional payroll and fringe benefit costs for 1969 and 1970.

As those from smaller cities undoubtedly know if they have stayed in New York City for even a few days, our notoriously high cost of living is reflected in the salaries we must pay, which are in proportion to the highly competitive condition of the New York labor market and the actual cost of supporting a modest, working class family in that city.

Chart 3, which compares revenues with expenses, and available subsidies with deficits, presents the broad picture of our declining fiscal position during the past 15 years. In 1952, our total revenues, which include non-dwelling rents and income from investments as well as rents paid by tenants, averaged $38.73 per apartment per month, which was considerably in excess of our total operating expenses of $31.93. With debt service at $16.89, the available subsidy was more than enough to meet the op-

Chart 3. Revenue Compared with Expenses, Available Subsidies Compared with Deficits Per Unit Per Month, 1952–1970
New York City Housing Authority Federal Program—November 1968

	1952	1957	1962	1967	1968 (Est.)	1970 (Est.)
Revenue (excluding elderly subsidy)	$38.73	$48.75	$58.95	$66.49	$69.45	$70.45
Total operating expenses	31.93	44.61	57.68	74.38	75.58	89.69
Debt service	16.89	29.59	38.71	50.25	51.84	51.84
Deficit	$10.09	$25.45	$37.44	$58.14	$57.97	$71.08
Contractual subsidy	$16.89	$29.59	$38.71	$50.25	$51.84	$51.84
Elderly subsidy	—	—	.81	3.57	4.04	4.04
Large family, etc., subsidy (est.)	—	—	—	—	—	2.86
Total subsidy available	$16.89	$29.59	$39.52	$53.82	$55.88	$58.74

erating deficit of $10.09, with the result that, under the terms of our annual contributions contracts, the maximum subsidies payable that year had to be reduced by the amount of such surplus income.

Five years later, the situation was worsening. Rents, operating expenses, debt service and subsidies had all gone up and the margin of safety had narrowed. The deficit of $25.45 per apartment per month was only $4.14 less than available subsidies of $29.59. By 1962, the margin had narrowed even further, with a deficit of $37.44 per apartment per month and available subsidies, including the new subsidies for the aged, of $39.52, a differential of only $2.08. By the end of the calendar year 1967, a bleak year indeed, we were in the red $4.32 per apartment per month. In order to pay our bills, this amount, which totaled $3,250,000, had to be withdrawn from reserves, which, by any standard of sound real estate management, were already inadequate.

In order that we not be accused of presenting a fiscal version of *The Perils of Pauline* by ending with our heroine hanging on the cliff, we have projected conservative estimates of the situation at the end of this year and in 1970. The opening of new projects with higher rents, and additional special subsidy income resulting from an increase in the number of apartments for the aged, have pulled us back somewhat, but we're still on the red side of the ledger for 1968, with a deficit of $57.97, available subsidies of $55.88, and $2.09 per apartment per month to be met by withdrawal from reserves.

In 1970, however, we are faced with a disastrous prospect—a deficit of $71.08 per apartment per month as against only $58.74 in combined subsidies for debt service, the aged, and the new subsidies authorized in the 1968 act for large families and especially poor families.

The alternative actions that must be considered are clear—a realistic new subsidy formula or a substantial rent increase to bring in approximately $12.34 per apartment per month.

As Chart 4 illustrates, the federal government's policy with respect to reserves has contributed greatly to this sorry state of affairs. In any business, including the real estate business, the establishment of adequate reserves is absolutely necessary to meet future anticipated costs for the replacement of worn-out equipment and extraordinary repairs, to say nothing of the necessity of having funds available for conservation of the

Chart 4. Revenue Applied to Reduction of Subsidies
and Establishment of Reserves
New York City Housing Authority Federal Program—November 1968

Year	Applied to Reduction of Subsidies	Applied to Reserves
1952	$1,470,000	$ 159,000
1957	1,005,000	382,000
1962	—	1,075,000
1967	—	(−3,250,000)
1968 (Est.)	—	(−1,600,000)
1969 (Est.)	—	(−5,780,000)
1970 (Est.)	—	(−9,565,000)

physical assets and elimination of obsolescence through periodic modernization to keep abreast of current housing standards.

Unfortunately, since the beginning of the public housing program, surplus revenues that might have been set aside against the rainy day that was sure to come, and is now here, have been used each year to reduce the federal subsidy bill. Since we are dealing only with the past 15 years in these charts, we have not shown the $19,600,000 of New York City Housing Authority surplus revenues that have been used to reduce federal subsidies over the life of our program, including $800,000 in cash that one of my predecessors was forced to donate to the federal government some 15 years ago. This is a sad saga: shortchanged every year . . . and one year the victim of a stick-up.

As the chart illustrates, in 1952 we received $1,470,000 less than the authorized federal subsidy and we were allowed to set aside a mere $159,000. Five years later the situation was similar, with contract subsidy reduced by $1,005,000 and only $382,000 set aside for reserves.

By 1962, the cold north winds were figuratively blowing. We collected all of the subsidy authorized under our annual contributions contracts, and we were able to put only $1,075,000 into reserves, approximately one-third of the allowable amount. Five years later, the situation had become really grim; we collected maximum subsidy and invaded our reserves for $3,250,000. We will invade them again in 1968 for at least $1,600,000 and in 1969 for approximately $5,780,000.

The chart shows another anticipated invasion of $9,565,000 in 1970, but that is not quite the full story. That figure represents an anticipated deficit to be met, once again, out of reserves, but since the reserves remaining at the beginning of that year will amount to only $5,127,000, the difference of $4,438,000 represents either total insolvency or the kind of catastrophic rent increase that I mentioned earlier: $12.34 per apartment per month.

The complete inadequacy of the present subsidy formula, as Chart 5 illustrates, is dramatically shown in projects that have been in operation for 25 years or more. In a group of four projects, containing over 8,000 apartments that were built before World War II, the consolidated annual contributions contract provides a subsidy of $13.49 per apartment per month. Fifteen years ago that subsidy represented 31 percent of the total revenue required to meet the cost of operations and debt service. Ten years ago the proportion of costs it met had dropped to 23 percent, five years ago to 19 percent, and last year to only 14 percent.

The conclusion is inescapable: a subsidy formula that is fixed at the time of construction, remains fixed thereafter, and relates only to debt service on bonds sold in the beginning, cannot begin to meet the needs of a public housing program caught in the middle of an inflationary economy.

Chart 6 shows the effect of various additional subsidy authorizations on fiscal solvency as represented by the continuing depletion, and ultimate disappearance, of essential reserves. While adhering rigidly to the fixed subsidy concept in one logic-tight compartment of the federal mind, the Congress has recently provided pittance subsidies for special poverty-stricken groups

Chart 5. Maximum Subsidies as Percent of Total Costs of Operation, Including Debt Service: Four Developments Completed in 1939–1941 New York City Housing Authority Federal Program—November 1968

	1952		1957	
	Per Unit Per Month	%	Per Unit Per Month	%
Total Operating Expense	$30.68	69	$46.03	77
Contractual Subsidy	13.49	31	13.49	23
Total	$44.17	100	$59.52	100

	1962		1967	
	Per Unit Per Month	%	Per Unit Per Month	%
Total Operating Expense	$56.29	81	$83.09	86
Contractual Subsidy	13.49	19	13.49	14
Total	$69.78	100	$96.58	100

Chart 6. Fiscal Solvency: Effect of Various Subsidy Authorizations
New York City Housing Authority Federal Program—November 1968

	1966	1967	1968	1969	1970
Contractual subsidy only	$11,551,900	$ 5,596,500	$(1,114,000)	$(12,224,000)	$(24,919,000)
Additional subsidy for elderly	6,206,800	8,910,500	12,021,000	15,151,000	18,281,000
Sub-total	$17,758,700	$14,507,000	$ 10,907,000	$ 2,927,000	$(6,638,000)
Additional subsidy for large families, etc.	—	—	—	2,200,000	2,200,000
Sub-total	$17,758,700	$14,507,000	$ 10,907,000	$ 5,127,000	$(4,438,000)
Additional subsidy if statutory maximum used	—	—	9,113,000	9,113,000	9,113,000
Total	$17,758,700	$14,507,000	$ 20,020,000	$ 14,240,000	$ 4,675,000

whose worsening financial condition in a period of general prosperity could be ignored no longer. A few years ago the aged and the handicapped were thrown $120 a year and, most recently, the Housing and Urban Development Act of 1968 provided another $120 a year for unusually large and unusually poor families.

These additional subsidies are stopgap measures at best. The special subsidies for the aged enabled us to bolster our declining reserves in 1966 and 1967. Together with an across-the-board rent increase of $3,410,000 spread over two years, the cumulative total of these new funds have enabled us to meet our operating expenses out of reserves. If maximum subsidy payments were geared to the statutory formula, and not to the actual debt service rate specified in assistance contracts, the New York City Housing Authority could receive up to an additional $9,113,000 this year. We would then be able to bring our reserves up to $20,020,000, which is slightly less than the amount recommended by the Housing Assistance Administration for our program and approximately double the actual amount of $10,907,000.

Next year we anticipate the payment of additional subsidies for unusually large and unusually poor families, together with the usual subsidies for the aged. These new funds will postpone total insolvency a while longer but only with another drastic invasion of our reserves. Even if we were to receive subsidies on a statutory, rather than contractual, basis next year, reserves would nonetheless represent a decline over 1968. By 1970, without subsidies based on the statutory maximum, we face a total depletion of all our reserves, even with a substantial rent increase to meet our actual operating expenses.

Chart 7 shows that the discrepancy between average tenant income and the costs rents must meet is expected to widen each

Chart 7. Projected Rents Required
If Current Subsidy Policies Remain Unchanged

	Net Tenant Income (Av.)		Rent Required	
Year	Amount	% Increase Over 1967	Amount	% Increase Over 1967
1967	$4,127	0	$64.40	0
1968	4,292	4	67.43	4.7
1969	4,457	8	75.40	17
1970	4,622	12	80.27	25

year. Until now we have been able to keep a fairly close relationship of rents with tenant incomes. Projecting this relationship through 1970, we find it reasonable to assume an increase in average tenant income of 4 percent each year. However, in order to cover actual costs without further invasion of our already tragically depleted reserves, rents have been increased 4.7 percent this year and, on a cumulative basis, should be increased by 17 percent next year and 25 percent in 1970, the year when there will be insufficient reserves to postpone the inevitable any longer.

First, it seems obvious that early in 1969 the Department of Housing and Urban Development must, somehow, be convinced of the need to exercise the administrative powers it already possesses by increasing subsidy payments from present contractual amounts to statutory maximums. And, if it won't, then we must seek to accomplish this necessary, if limited, fiscal improvement by legislative mandate.

Washington has demonstrated some awareness that the contractual subsidy formula is inadequate to cope with rising costs. Nothing else satisfactorily explains the special subsidies for aged, unusually large, and unusually poor families. Neither the amounts granted, nor the method of payment, have any particular relationship to the special problems involved, nor do they provide any direct benefit to aged, large, or extremely poor families. I also suspect that there is little knowledge of the minimal effect these subsidies have had. We estimate that the most recent addition, for unusually large and unusually poor families, will provide, on a prorated basis, approximately $2.86 per family per month, or only two-thirds of the amount provided by the subsidies for the aged. The total effect of these extra subsidies combined, when we start collecting them fully in 1969, would be a subsidy increase of only slightly more than 10 percent above the amount contracted originally.

This year Washington faced up to rising costs that are pricing the 221(d) (3) program out of the moderate-income market. Sections 235 and 236 of the Housing and Urban Development Act of 1968 authorized subsidies to reduce interest rates to as low as 1 percent. I think our immediate goal should be persuasion, or legislation if that proves to be necessary, to postpone pricing public housing out of the low-income market by paying the maximum statutory subsidy, wherever that is necessary, to meet the increasing operating costs and maintain essential reserves.

Next, we may as well all recognize that the development of a new subsidy formula in time to prevent disastrous rent increases across the country is a responsibility NAHRO must assume. We cannot expect the incoming administration to take on the solution of this problem as priority business unless we are prepared to demonstrate the reason and show the way. And we also cannot expect the new Congress to undertake legislative remedies without a clear understanding that the problem is a general one already affecting many housing authorities to a greater or lesser degree and ultimately affecting all.

Preserving the high goals with which public housing was launched 30 years ago by developing a creative new subsidy formula may be difficult to achieve. But it is a very necessary step, and one to which we should all dedicate ourselves—because we must.

3.7

Facts and Fictions in Urban Renewal

Louis Winnick

The accomplishments to date of publicly sponsored urban renewal are unimpressive, largely because the interval between plan and execution is so awesomely long.

There are many obvious reasons why performance has lagged so badly: insufficient financing; a scarcity of trained personnel; the tooling-up time needed for state and local enabling legislation; the difficulties encountered in establishing operating agencies and administrative procedures. But the most important cause of delay has been the absence of clear-cut urban renewal objectives.

Legislators and administrators understandably become dilatory as they discover that we are not altogether sure what we want to do with our urban renewal programs and that our petitions to Washington seem to be framed more in terms of money than ideas.

The public has not yet given the policy-maker any clear mandates on urban renewal goals or priorities. Virtually every renewal plan is greeted with sharply mixed reactions by the community and, no matter what its content, strong and vocal groups will find fault with the particular location chosen, the type of replacement facilities, the relative proportions of clearance and rehabilitation and, most of all, with the accompanying burden of tenant displacement.

We will debate for many years to come what urban renewal is supposed to do for the city. Is the urban need really a physical improvement program to replace old bricks with new and rehabilitated buildings? Or should our resources go for social programs to correct deficiencies in family behavior? To what extent should urban redevelopment become a device for resettling population, i.e., for exchanging one population group for another at various points in the city in order to achieve a better "mix" of race, income or social desirability? Is urban renewal mainly a housing program or should it freely encompass all types of real estate? Should redevelopment be conceived as slum eradication or as a broader program for land assembly and clearance to overcome the city's greatest lacks—vacant sites and

Reprinted from *Ends and Means of Urban Renewal*, Papers from the Philadelphia Housing Association's Fiftieth Anniversary Forum (Philadelphia, 1961), pp. 23–35; by permission of the Philadelphia Housing Association.

the planned arrangement of buildings? To what degree should renewal be used as a device for strengthening the city's fiscal base by increasing tax revenues and reducing expenditures? Finally, if there can be a "finally" in this catalogue of questions, should the prime mover in renewal be the federal or the local government?

These questions will be settled only by time and public discussion. I would like to intrude on this discussion in the immodest hope of clarifying some of the issues. I suspect, though, that I shall succeed only in provoking still more debate. But, after all, this is the purpose of a forum.

Urban Renewal Versus Urban Redesign

No matter how broadly the concept of urban renewal is drawn, it will still fall short of a true program for urban redesign. By its very nature, urban renewal is confined to neighborhoods of present or impending slum and blight. Which is to say that public intervention in reshaping private land use is largely reserved for the city's weak areas where there can be little or no unaided private investment and is absent in the strong areas where a considerable volume of private construction is taking place.

It would be going too far to say that such an arrangement is topsy-turvy. Yet in many ways it is ironical that the *planned* reconstruction of our cities will take place only where there have been slums; everywhere else the private developer is left virtually to his own devices, subject only to the limited and negative controls of building and zoning ordinances.

The unaided private investor—no matter how enlightened—cannot give us a city in the image we desire. For private redevelopers can seldom assemble sites of optimal size or location. They make do with what they can. Frustrated by multiple titles, by existing leases and stubborn holdouts, by the existing street system and unpurchasable public buildings, they forego their best opportunities for the next best; they design their structures according to the size and shape of the site they are able to get and without much reference to adjacent structures. Private land assembly in the core of the metropolis will always be fortuitous and haphazard and likewise will be its results.

Consider the case in New York City. Since World War II some 40 million square feet of office space and more than 250,000 private dwelling units have been built or started. The buildings vary in design from very good to very bad, density varies from a floor area ratio of 30 to 6, and the structures are spotted about in no clear-cut relation to each other and with none of the "external economies" that could accrue from a large-scale joint planned effort.

Were we to conceive the need of urban areas to be the planned placement of real estate facilities rather than renewal alone, and make much wider use of public assistance in land assembly, whole new possibilities of form and arrangement would be opened up, exemplified by our Rockefeller and Penn Centers. If the municipality were able to offer private redevelopers cleared land at full cost anywhere in the city, most of New York's 40 million square feet of new office space could have been built around six or seven large plazas or landscaped green areas having common underground parking facilities, a more serviceable street pattern, and harmony of form and placement. Similarly, the hundreds of apartment structures built in and around the central ring could have been grouped in more efficient and esthetically satisfying arrangements.

The grouping of buildings is land and cost economizing. It permits the pooling of the small bits of open space required by zoning into truly usable open areas. Grouped buildings also require much less street and parking space per unit of building space. And predetermining the location of structures allows better advance planning—and more efficient utilization—of complementary facilities such as schools, restaurants, stores and transportation.

All of this may seem wild-eyed, particularly coming from one with a healthy respect for free enterprise and a deep skepticism of visionary plans. For what is suggested is massive intervention in the private real estate market, going far beyond our present timorous approach. But genuine city planning on a master scale is not likely to be achieved under the existing rules of private property. The private real estate market works quite inefficiently in altering the physical structure of highly developed cities. The invisible hand cannot lead to correct solutions from the standpoint of the economist or the planner, only to very visible compromises if not downright errors.

Publicly sponsored urban redevelopment may be more, not less, necessary in the non-slum growth areas. For it is in those places where effective demand for new real estate is strongest that the greatest opportunities exist for shaping the city to a preconceived design.

Limitations on Urban Redevelopment

Having just expanded the horizons of urban redevelopment, let me now hastily shorten the perspective.

There is a prevailing tendency to define the scale of the country's urban redevelopment and renewal programs by criteria of need rather than of economic feasibility. As a result, the estimated costs of such programs become astronomical, with some figures ranging as high as $1 trillion. Whether the American economy is capable of supporting such a vast urban investment program, given so many competing claims for the use of resources, I confess I do not know. But I would venture that the future scale of urban redevelopment will be determined much less by needs or available resources than by what we can sell to private occupants. Apart from reuse with public or quasi-public facilities, urban redevelopment cannot proceed any further or faster than markets can be found for the replacement real estate.

How large a market exists in the older cities for large amounts of new building space remains to be seen. The economic disabilities of present cities—as was most recently and forcefully brought out in the Vernon studies of the New York Region[1] —are too great to take for granted a large, not to speak of a limitless, market for new or rehabilitated real estate at rents required by current and future building and operating costs. True, the market can be widened by public aids to reduce rents. But, even with such aids, rents can be lowered only so far; and rent cuts are effective only in the degree to which demand is responsive to price.

Regional and suburban shifts in population and economic activity have been highly unfavorable to the market for real estate in the typical older city. The demand for office space, for example, has become exceedingly selective. In the 1920s and earlier, office construction was quite diffused, reaching into nearly all cities of 50,000 and over. Today, largely as a result of improvements in transportation and communication, a sizable amount of administrative office space is being built in only a handful of cities.

The potential market for new downtown retail facilities is even poorer; disinvestment is more common than new investment.

While industrial reuse has many possibilities in the outer rings of the city, the average industrial plant requires so much land per unit of building space that formidable economic barriers would have to be overcome.

Residential investment, given the favorable demographic trends of the next two decades and the greater ability of housing to command support for public aids, is likely to have a more promising market but only in the larger and more urban cities. We must also remember that as more and more places within a metropolitan region get on the renewal bandwagon they will find themselves competing for the same set of occupants. Estimates of potential demand become inflated because each of a number of communities in a housing market area tends to measure its anticipated housing demand from the same total.

The most reasonable picture one can draw is that the future market for renewal real estate is likely to be quite spotty: very strong in some cities, very weak in others, stronger for certain types of real estate than for others and, in some sections of even the strongest cities, no market at all for any kind of private real estate.

We must continually remind ourselves that the dramatic renewal plans now being drawn in so many cities have yet to meet the stern test of the market. We should not be deluded by the initial rush of private sponsors into renewal. The individual sponsor is concerned with the success of his own venture. He may well fill his new office building, hotel or apartment house, but the real test of long-run economic feasibility is: will the space vacated by his new tenants be filled? Or will there be an overhang of vacancies in existing buildings which can offer powerful competition with respect to rents? Because the capital costs of existing buildings are sunk, rents in such structures can drop to levels just sufficient to meet operating costs. The trend in vacancies and rents of existing buildings, other than those which are woefully obsolete or poorly located, will measure the potential for redevelopment.

In short, large-scale redevelopment must lead to more than a mere redistribution of present occupants. There must be a sizable net expansion in the demand for urban real estate facilities. Only in the latter event can renewal efforts be sustained and continuous. In some cities one can already observe that new facilities have resulted in redistribution rather than expansion.

The new buildings have been tenanted at the expense of vacancies in existing buildings. In other cities the demand for new space depends heavily on civic-minded financial institutions and businessmen who, eager to further local renewal efforts, may sponsor new facilities even when the added cost for space exceeds the gain in convenience or utility. A measure of philanthropy is involved, and no market can long survive on philanthropy.

The scale of redevelopment will be largest in those cities where the underlying demand for space is genuine but cannot be filled because the private market is unable to assemble sites of the right size or location or on a scale sufficient to change neighborhood environment. That is, redevelopment will succeed in urban areas where the impediments to capital investment lie more on the supply side than on the demand side of the market. Redevelopment, therefore, is likely to be most successful in urban centers where real estate markets are already comparatively strong and where the rate of private construction in the inner rings is high. To mention names, redevelopment is likely to fare better in New York than in Newark, in Washington compared to Baltimore, in Chicago rather than Detroit.

One never knows where to draw the line between realism and gloom. But future prospects do not point to the replacement of all or most existing slums by private real estate facilities. In a very large number of cities, particularly smaller cities near major urban centers, the choice will be between limited rehabilitation plus stricter occupancy controls on existing structures or reuse with nonmarket facilities such as public and institutional buildings or even parks. It is in such places that federal Title I aids will be most necescsary.

Title I Versus Urban Redevelopment

I would like to challenge a prevailing notion that publicly sponsored urban redevelopment is either synonymous with Title I or economically possible only with federal aids.[2] As a result of such a view, local redevelopment programs have become almost completely dependent on federal initiative and control. The size and scheduling of our redevelopment programs are left to the vagaries of each session of Congress, to the political coloration of the national administration, and to the rules set forth by the Urban Renewal Administration.

But let us consider the economic realities of urban redevelopment and ask ourselves whether local programs cannot succeed without massive help from Washington. As presently conceived, planned redevelopment seeks to bring about the reuse of slum or blighted areas in two ways: first, by encouraging the exercise of eminent domain for assembly of privately held real estate; second, by making reuse economically feasible through government help to bridge the gap between the acquisition cost of land and its market value in reuse. (For reasons I do not wish to get into here, I will refrain from using that abused word, subsidy.)

Eminent domain is clearly a state and local power to which Title I adds nothing. The real contribution of Title I is financial aid to balance part of the difference between the cost and reuse value of sites, an aid commonly referred to as land writedown. Our redevelopment concepts all seem to be centered on the importance of reducing the selling price of land to private sponsors.

In my judgment, the emphasis on land writedown is unwarranted and has resulted in mistaken policies.

The success of private redevelopment hinges not on land writedown as such but on the rent (or price) per unit of space in the new improvement. Rent must be low enough to attract occupants, so that sufficient income will be generated to meet capital and operating costs, including an adequate return to the investor. Obviously, the final rent (or price) on new or rehabilitated facilities is determined by a large number of costs besides the price paid for the site: architect's fees, building materials, bricklayers, taxes, mortgage funds, janitors, elevator operators and doormen. There is no special quality about the cost of sites that makes it essential for this single component of total costs to become the be-all and end-all of financial aid.

We shall remain confused on the economics of urban redevelopment until we understand that the real objective of government aid is to *bring down the rent (or price) of new private real estate to its market level.* Land writedown is a misnomer for what should be more accurately termed *rent (or price) writedown.*

Clearly, no financial help would be required if the earning power of the new real estate facility (in its recreated environment) were deemed sufficient to pay full capital and operating costs. This is by no means an impossible case; indeed, most urban redevelopment in America has required no public grants-in-aid. Moreover, there are instances in the present Title I program where land costs have been unnecessarily or excessively written down, i.e., the reuse real estate could have commanded a rent sufficient to pay all costs, including the full cost of the site. But in most urban neighborhoods which are deteriorated enough to justify redevelopment, market rent on the reuse real estate is likely to be insufficient to defray full capital and operating costs so that government aid becomes obligatory.

Writedown of land, however, is by no means the most effective, and certainly not the only, way of achieving economic feasibility. The cost of land plays usually but a minor role in rent determination, accounting for 15 percent or less of the monthly rent per unit of space in elevator apartments or office buildings. For example, in New York City an apartment house built on cleared land costing $25 a square foot and financed with an FHA mortgage would, at typical density, require a monthly rent of approximately $50 per room. Of this, less than $6 is attributable to the cost (purchase price and subsequent taxes) of land. Each $5 per square foot in writedown would therefore reduce rent by little more than $1 per room per month. Thus with a $25 (100 per cent) writedown, monthly rent would remain at $44 (actually more since the site would carry more than a zero assessment). Where land can be assembled and cleared for $10 or less per square foot, the effect of land writedown on the rent of high-rise structures at urban densities would be quite negligible.

By contrast, the rent-reducing power of easier credit terms or real estate tax concessions, or a combination of both, is far greater. For example, under a New York City program of low (3½ percent) interest rates plus 50 percent tax abatement, the monthly rent on the above hypothetical project could be reduced to $32.25 per room *without* land writedown. In other words, credit and tax aids would, in this illustration, reduce rents by three times as much as a full land writedown.

The significance of this financial arithmetic cannot be overstated. For it tells us that not only is redevelopment possible by local action but, more important, that tax and credit aids can result in the redevelopment of areas *which are now beyond the reach of Title I*. There are many neighborhoods in every large city, the so-called gray areas outside the core, where land and clearance costs are not excessive, perhaps $8 or less per foot, and where it would be difficult to find a market for apartments renting for more than $18 to $25 per room. In such cases, something more powerful than land writedowns may be needed.

When we recognize that the real purpose of government financial aid is to reduce the rent (or price) of the redevelopment facility rather than the cost of land, and that large rent reductions can be brought about by extending local credit and tax aids to renewal areas, it becomes clear that Title I assistance is neither a necessary nor a sufficient condition for redevelopment. However, none of the foregoing means that the search for federal assistance should be relaxed. For one, not all communities are in a position, politically, to evolve tax-exemption and mortgage loan programs. For another, every city contains neighborhoods where the spread between cost and market rent is so great that there will be a necessity for some form of direct financial grants which, if it so pleases us, can be applied as land writedown.

By adding tax and credit aids to land writedown, the city is provided with a much fuller set of redevelopment tools, three aids instead of one. Each aid could then be used singly or in a wide variety of combinations, depending on the cost-rent factors of every reuse plan. The scope of urban redevelopment programs could thus be expanded well beyond the limits of Title I, and local redevelopment authorities would be enabled to conduct independent programs without the delays and uncertainties that stem from federal controls.

Notes

[1]Hoover, Edgar M., and Vernon, Raymond, *Anatomy of a Metropolis,* Cambridge, 1959.

[2]Title I of the Housing Act of 1949 is the basic federal legislation under which slum clearance or redevelopment programs are carried out.

3.8

Home Finance and Housing Quality In Aging Neighborhoods

William G. Grigsby

Introduction

This paper is directed to the problem of mortgage financing for old, inexpensive, one- and two-family homes that are not competitive with new construction, but are at or above minimum code standards, and to the relationship of this problem to the level of expenditures for the maintenance and improvement of these homes. In American cities, it appears that such structures constitute as much as 15 percent of the total occupied inventory.[1] Moreover, numerous additional dwellings, now in serious violation of local codes, were at some prior time no doubt in this category. The matter of adequate financing for aging sectors of the stock is, therefore, a large component of the total residential finance problem. It is also a subject which American housing policy, in its emphasis on new construction and on rehabilitation programs that operate largely outside normal market mechanisms, has almost completely ignored.

The Quality-Life Expectancy-Financing Issue

That a home financing problem in older neighborhoods does indeed exist is commonly recognized. Yet it might be helpful to give it some dimension in order to focus the subsequent discussion.

In the City of Philadelphia, to cite a situation which is not atypical, mortgage payments required for an old \$8,000 house are not appreciably less than those on a new \$12,000 home. Thus, in the former case, the maximum loan which a buyer can obtain is about \$7,000, at not less than 6 percent, for not over fifteen years, necessitating a down payment of \$1,000 and monthly level payments of \$59.08. By comparison, on the \$12,000 house, it would not be unusual for a mortgage institution to give a thirty-year 5½ percent loan for \$11,000, terms which would result in the same initial cash outlay and monthly charges of only \$62.48 (Table 1). Assuming taxes on the more expensive structure were proportionately greater, though in Philadelphia this is uncertain, the tax differential would be \$8.00. Outlays for maintenance and heat, however, might very well show a reverse

Reprinted by permission of the International Economic Association from *The Economic Problems of Housing*, edited by Adela Adam Nevitt, Proceedings of a conference held by the International Economic Association (London, St. Martin's Press, 1967), pp. 105–122.

relationship, assuming the older house was adequately maintained. Combining financing charges, taxes, and operating costs,

Table 1. Comparison of Typical Monthly Operating Expenses of New and Old Six-Room Single-Family Row Homes, City of Philadelphia, 1964

Monthly Costs	Property A Value—$8,000 Age—50 years	Property B Value—$12,000 Age—New
Financing	$ 59.08*	$ 62.48†
Taxes	16.00‡	24.00‡
Utilities	40.00§	40.00§
Maintenance	15.00‖	15.00‖
Insurance	1.00¶	1.50
Management	—**	—**
Vacancy loss	—††	—††
Interest foregone	—‡‡	—‡‡
Depreciation	—§§	—§§
Total	$131.08	$142.98

*$7,000, 15-year, 6 percent, level payment loan.
†$11,000, 30-year, 5½ percent, level payment loan.
‡$4/100 of assessed value. Assessed value assumed to equal 60 percent of market value. There is some tendency in Philadelphia, however, for the AV/MV ratio to be higher on old, inexpensive homes than on new ones.
§For structures of equal size and similar occupancy, water and electric bills should be about the same. Since newer structures are better insulated, however, and may have more efficient heating units, their fuel bills may be lower. Nevertheless, to avoid controversy, utility payments have been assumed to be equal.
‖Annual maintenance assumed to be 1½ percent of market value of the new home and equal, in absolute terms, on the old structure. Assuming "adequate" maintenance, somehow defined, this expenditure certainly will not be less on the old than on the new, but might very well be more. Again, to avoid argument, equality has been presumed.
¶Assumed to be proportional to market value, though insurance rates are frequently higher in older areas.
**Structures assumed to be owner-occupied, so no management charge unless one is imputed.
††Structures assumed to be owner-occupied.
‡‡This is not an operating expense. The monthly interest loss for the first year on the $1,000 down payment at 4 percent is $3.33. The interest loss in subsequent years depends on the amount of real equity accumulated, which in turn is a function of market trends and the rate at which the mortgage loan is repaid. If lenders have correctly assessed the remaining economic lives of the two buildings and if the mortgage terms accurately reflect these assessments, the amount of accumulated real equities should not differ greatly. One of the points at issue, however, is whether mortgages do, in fact, forecast the future correctly.
§§Unknown until property is transferred. The amount of actual depreciation is frequently obscured by the fact that owners take depreciation, as it were, in the form of alterations, additions, and even some forms of repairs, which actually improve the quality of the structure over what it was originally.

therefore, it seems likely that the monthly outlays for the two houses would differ by less than 10 percent, with virtually all of the difference being due to the tax component. Or looking at the matter somewhat differently, if the $8,000 house could be financed on the same terms as the $12,000 house, monthly mortgage payments would be only $39.76 and total costs correspondingly lower.

On the basis of evidence such as this, some analysts have concluded that the older sectors of the used stock and those who seek to buy homes in these sectors are being discriminated against by private lenders. Such apparently onerous terms are, in fact, said to lead to a shift to absentee ownership, conversions, lower maintenance, and decline in quality—the very consequences which lenders fear and seek to avoid. Their policies seem rational only because they help create the situation which has been prophesied.

Lenders contend on the other hand that (*a*) life expectancy of the older structures does not warrant a longer-term loan; (*b*) the higher risk with respect to both buyer and property warrants a higher down payment; (*c*) the family really is not being discriminated against, for if his home depreciates more slowly than the mortgagee has predicted, he simply accumulates equity faster; (*d*) a lower down payment would mean higher monthly payments which the borrower quite possibly could not afford; (*e*) the comparison in any case is not fair because most new-home buyers make down payments considerably above the minimum required; (*f*) an older, cheaper house can be financed with loans exceeding fifteen years if in good condition and in a good neighborhood; and (*g*) after all, many families do buy old homes despite the more onerous mortgage terms.

Without more information, it is not possible to deal with all of these assertions. It does seem intuitively, however, that lenders may be overcompensating for the extra risks which their experience suggests do exist, and in any case it can be shown that, for one reason or another, payments on homes in the older, lower-quality neighborhoods are excessive. The following section of the paper attempts to demonstrate this proposition and discusses a few of the immediately apparent implications.

Monthly Mortgage Payments and Housing Quality

The widespread existence of similar down payments and monthly mortgage payments on structures having substantially different values does not, in theory, necessarily indicate different mortgage lending policies with respect to either the structures or the individuals acquiring them. In practice, however, it does suggest some problems with respect to the functioning of the housing market which demand attention. Both the theoretical and practical questions can perhaps best be illuminated by a series of illustrations which show how changes in quality and expected economic life of hypothetical residential structures affect monthly payments and market value. First, however, it is necessary to define our terms.

In ordinary usage, housing quality and expected economic life are not mutually exclusive. Higher quality implies longer economic life and vice versa. To simplify the analysis, housing quality is defined here in such a way as to eliminate this relationship. Specifically, it refers only to the *current flow of services* of a residential structure, not to the structure itself. As a consequence, it excludes durability, an attribute which is commonly regarded as one aspect of quality, but which, since it also has to do with the absolute level of services over time, is obviously an element of economic life as well.

To simplify things even further, quality is interpreted here to mean everything that would affect market value except space, expected length of flow of services, financing, real estate taxes, and perceived risks of ownership. Thus it includes not only condition of structure, but accessibility to work and community facilities, quality of surrounding neighborhood, architectural style, modernity of household equipment, and services by the landlord. Because style is included as one of the factors, either a positive or negative shift in the quality of a dwelling could be occasioned by a simple change in tastes which render the unit more or less able to satisfy consumer preferences. Such an assumption would not always be acceptable. For some purposes, it is vital to regard quality and style as quite distinct characteristics. In the present instance, however, lumping the two together reduces the complexity of the discussion without altering the essential points.

Proceeding now to the analysis, imagine first a new $10,000 rental dwelling unit which has a firmly fixed life expectancy of forty years that is known in advance, which does not change in quality either absolutely or relative to the rest of the inventory,[2] and which has zero scrap value. Assume too that there are no real estate taxes, so that the only expense which may vary significantly over the life of the structure is monthly debt service. Assume further that the unit is transferred every five years to an investor who desires the same rate of return and perceives the same risks as the preceding investor; whose credit rating is so high he is able to obtain 100 percent financing for a period equal to the remaining life of the building; and who chooses this financing because he does not desire to accumulate equity over his short period of ownership. Finally, postulate no booms or recessions, or changes in population, income or market knowledge that would affect rates of occupancy or sale prices.

Under these circumstances, where housing quality and investor motivation are constant and where economic life expectancy and all risks are known and invariant, what would be the shape of the depreciation (price) curve for the structure and how would financing terms and monthly payments shift in each succeeding five-year period?

This question is best answered indirectly. It is obvious on the face that monthly rentals[3] on structures providing services of equal quality must be equal, just as differences in quality of services must be reflected in differences in rent. Therefore, if, as assumed here, expenses and desired rate of return are also equal, so then will be monthly mortgage payments regardless of the age of the structure. Working backward, if monthly payments are equal and no real equity is accumulated, the value of the structure at the end of any five-year period will be the unpaid balance of the mortgage outstanding at that time. All of this is shown in Table 2 and Graph A where it may be seen that the depreciation curve is convex to the origin and describes a path precisely equal to that of a curve which would show the rate of accumulation of equity on a forty-year level payment mortgage. Or, in other words, as monthly payments per $1,000 rise with successive decreases in terms of mortgage, the amount of market value which can be supported by constant total mortgage payments declines at an increasing rate.[4]

It can be seen too that the assumption of a fixed life is not necessary to conclusions regarding monthly payments and quality. We can, in fact, generalize as follows: Regardless of age or expected remaining life, residential structures which provide services of equal quality should have equal monthly mortgage payments; and structures supplying services of different quality should have different payments; if all other factors mentioned earlier are equal.[5] If the economic life of one dwelling is longer

Table 2. Value of a Hypothetical Residential Structure over the Various Stages of Its Economic Life, Assuming Constant Quality, Fixed and Predetermined Life Expectancy, and No Accumulation of Equity by Owner*

1 Age of Structure (Years)	2 Monthly Level Mortgage Payment ($)†	3 Term of Mortgage (Years)	4 Interest Rate on Mortgage Loan (%)	5 Monthly Level Payment $1,000 ($)‡	6 Value of Structure Which Mortgage Payments Can support ($)§
0	55	40	6	5.50	10,000
5	55	35	6	5.70	9,650
10	55	30	6	6.00	9,150
15	55	25	6	6.44	8,550
20	55	20	6	7.16	7,670
25	55	15	6	8.44	6,500
30	55	10	6	11.10	4,950
35	55	5	6	19.30	2,850
40	—	—	—	—	0

*See text for complete enumeration of assumptions.
†Remains constant because quality, as defined in text, remains constant.
‡Rises over time, because, with change of ownership each five years as assumed in text, a new mortgage loan with shorter amortization period is created.
§$\frac{\text{Column 2}}{\text{Column 5}} \times \$1{,}000$. Rounded to nearest $50.

than that of another, this fact should be reflected in price, not monthly payments. No matter what combinations or changes in quality and life expectancy one assumes, these theoretical relationships hold.

The next question is: How much would monthly payments and prices be affected by *assumed* differences in quality? To illuminate this matter, a second illustration is presented, this time with a more realistic representation of economic life expectancy of the residential inventory.

Assume a structure which through the first ten years of its existence is expected to have an indefinitely long life; during the next forty-five years, a life expectancy of seventy years from date of construction; and for the remaining years of its existence, an economic life of fifteen more years, regardless of its age.[6] Further, assume somewhat unrealistically that mortgage lenders at any time will grant 100 per cent loans for the full length of the

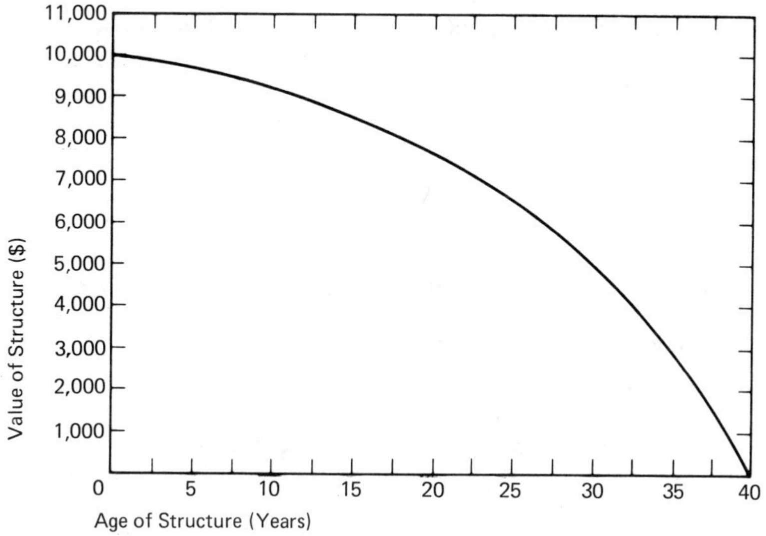

Graph A. Hypothetical Depreciation Curve

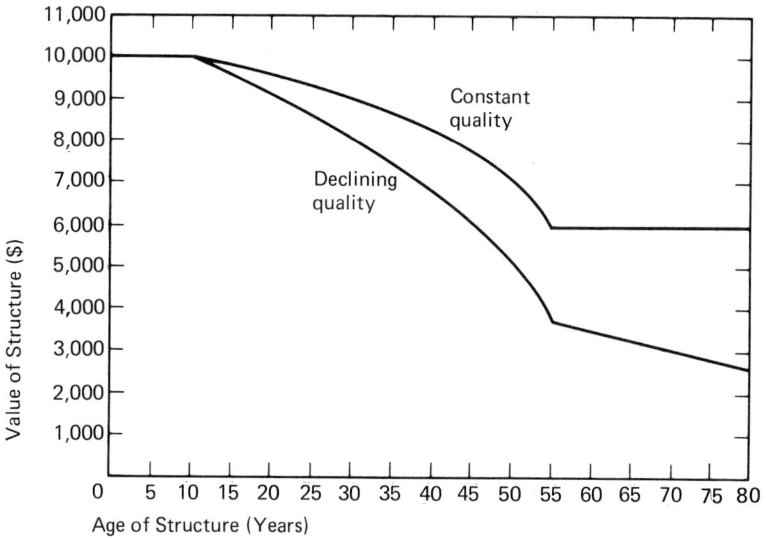

Graph B. Hypothetical Depreciation Curves

remaining anticipated life of the structure.[7] Finally, in order to provide a basis for comparison with situations of declining quality, which is our purpose here, assume initially that quality remains constant throughout the life of the structure.[8] The depreciation curve which results from these assumptions is presented in Graph B (line A) and Table 3 (column 7). Except for the first ten and the final fifteen years, the curve follows a path similar to that shown in Graph A, so needs no further explanation.

Now, to determine the effect of assumed declines in quality on the shape and level of the price curve and on monthly payments at successive points in time, let the level of maintenance, repair, and periodic modernization be such as to yield a rate of deterioration and obsolescence valued in the market at $50 (one-half of one percent of the original value of the structure) per year, after the tenth year. Combined with the effect of decreasing life expectancy on value, this produces an overall average depreciation rate after seventy years of one percent per year (Graph B, line B, and Table 3, column 8) which is not out of line with several empirical studies.[9] The monthly mortgage payments required to finance the purchase of the structure at its various value levels appear in Table 3, column 9.

Comparing columns 7, 8, and 9 in Table 3, it is apparent that the effect of assumed differences in quality on monthly payments and market value for our hypothetical structure do not approximate to reality. For example, in the fiftieth year, a quality difference of only 20 percent $\left(\frac{(50)\ (40)}{10{,}000}\right)$ between old and new structures is associated with a price differential of 50 percent $\left(\frac{10{,}000-5{,}000}{10{,}000}\right)$ and a monthly payment differential of almost 30 percent $\left(\frac{50.00-35.80}{50.00}\right)$. Similarly, at the end of seventy years, a quality differential of only 30 percent results in a price that is fully 70 percent lower and a spread in monthly payments of 50 percent.

By comparison, it will be recalled that typical new $12,000 and old, obsolescing $8,000 structures in Philadelphia have virtually the same monthly mortgage payments (Table 1). The comparison is somewhat misleading, because for these dwellings the quality gap is reflected not only in the $3.40 difference in financing charges, but also, in part at least, in the $8,00 spread in tax payments.[10] That is, if the structures were either not

Table 3. Value of a Hypothetical Residential Structure over the Various Stages of Its Economic Life, Given Certain Assumptions Regarding Original Value, Life Expectancy, Changes in Quality, and Available Financing*

1 Age of Structure (Years)	2 Expected Remaining Life (Years)	3 Monthly Level Mtge. Payment, Constant Quality ($)	4 Term of Mortgage (Years)	5 Interest Rate on Mortgage Loan (%)	6 Monthly Level Payment/ $1,000 ($)	7 Value of Structure, Constant Quality ($)†	8 Value of Structure, Declining Quality ($)‡	9 Monthly Level Mortgage Payment, Declining Quality ($)§
0	Indefinite	50	Unamortized	6	5.00	10,000	10,000	50.00
5	Indefinite	50	Unamortized	6	5.00	10,000	10,000	50.00
10	Indefinite	50	Unamortized	6	5.00	10,000	10,000	50.00
15	55	50	55	6	5.19	9,750	9,500	49.30
20	50	50	50	6	5.26	9,500	9,000	47.30
25	45	50	45	6	5.36	9,300	8,550	45.80
30	40	50	40	6	5.50	9,100	8,100	44.50
35	35	50	35	6	5.70	8,750	7,500	42.80
40	30	50	30	6	6.00	8,350	6,850	41.10
45	25	50	25	6	6.44	7,750	6,000	38.60
50	20	50	20	6	7.16	7,000	5,000	35.80
55	15	50	15	6	8.44	5,950	3,700	31.20
60	15	50	15	6	8.44	5,950	3,450	29.10
65	15	50	15	6	8.44	5,950	3,200	27.00
70	15	50	15	6	8.44	5,950	2,950	24.90

*See text for enumeration of assumptions. See footnotes * and ‡, Table 2, for explanation of columns 3 and 6.

†$\frac{\text{Column 3}}{\text{Column 6}} \times \$1{,}000$. Rounded to nearest $50.

‡Column 7 minus $50 per year for each year of life of structure *after* year 10. Rounded to nearest $50.

§$\frac{\text{Column 8} \times \text{Column 6}}{1{,}000}$ Rounded to nearest ten cents.

taxed at all or taxed on the basis of current rents, the spread in capital values and hence in monthly financing charges might be greater. Even when the full tax load is included, however, the equivalent difference in monthly payments is a mere 15 percent $\left(\frac{59.08+16.00}{62.48+24.00}\right)$, an amount which seems an inadequate reflection of quality differences.

Theory Versus Reality

Although the model just presented fails to approximate the real world, it does describe a market which would probably be superior, from the standpoint of the consumer, to the only one now existing. For this reason, it may be useful to inquire into its underlying assumptions and implications more thoroughly. Are the relationships revealed by the model a consequence of its simplifying constraints, or do they correctly imply defects in the existing real estate market mechanism?

Perhaps the most critical assumption has to do with quality, for which there are no objective measures except those provided by the market itself. Since the functioning of the market is in essence the matter which is in question, we are left without any measure of quality at all, only vague judgments. Nor is there any easy way out of this dilemma. Several of the seemingly obvious ways to identify and measure quality differences turn out on closer inspection to be unacceptable. For example, at first glance it might appear that the true difference between the quality of two structures is equal to the amount of money required to eliminate this difference. Some aspects of quality, however, are not reproducible in an existing structure except at great expense, if at all. Indeed this is a major barrier to unsubsidized rehabilitation efforts. A second possible method for determining differences in quality would be to have a sample of persons visit homes in various price categories and estimate what they, themselves, would be willing to pay for each structure. It seems probable, though, that persons who could afford products appreciably higher in quality than the ones which they were examining, whether these be houses or automobiles or food or clothing, would tend to undervalue the lower quality items. And conversely, that high quality items would tend to be undervalued by persons who could not afford them. Moreover, all observers would be influenced by the prevailing price structure.

There is, moreover, some evidence that differences in quality *are* reflected adequately in the market. Thus, in Philadelphia in 1960, at least 30 percent of the households residing in single-family owner-occupied structures valued at less than $9,000 had reported value-income ratios of 1 to 1 or less, suggesting their ability to acquire much more expensive accommodations. In other words, no matter how the relationship of quality to value and monthly payments in the older, cheaper sections of the stock is viewed by "impartial" observers, a substantial number of families who have actually made a market decision and who have a reasonably wide range of choice are evidently either not aware of any significant distortions or place such a low value on housing quality as to be unresponsive to them.[11]

The second major assumption which may be called into question is not part of the model itself, but is one of the reasons for its construction. This is the implicit suggestion that because quality differences seem to be proportionally greater than monthly mortgage payments, the fault lies in financing practices. It might be argued, however, that unduly high prices, not conservative mortgage terms, explain the apparently excessive monthly payments for old units. Further, that if terms were liberalized, prices might simply rise correspondingly, leaving monthly payments the same.

This line of reasoning fails to consider that if demand is great enough relative to supply consistently to value houses at an excessively high figure, the economic life of these structures must be longer than lenders are ready to admit. Equally important, the argument is tantamount to a claim that financing terms are neutral in their effect on the market. Such is hardly the case. As increasingly conservative mortgage terms on older structures depress prices, they also prevent the accumulation of equities by existing owners, thus limiting potential demand by this group for more expensive units. Moreover, although liberalized mortgage terms would certainly stimulate additional demand from lower income families, this demand by definition would not inflate prices enough to leave monthly payments unchanged. Further, price inflation would certainly affect demand as purchasers with somewhat higher incomes observed a diminishing differential in prices between new and old structures without any change in either quality or economic life expectancy of the latter. Home buyers whose income and asset position is such that they are not dependent upon liberal financing for their acquisitions would be particularly responsive to such a change.[12] The shift of these families upward not only would stimulate new construction, but simultaneously would limit the extent of price inflation in the sectors of the existing stock from which these families came by an amount sufficient to yield some net reduction in monthly payments.

The key point, then, is much more than that financing is not a passive factor, an observation which all would accept. It is that liberalized financing of old, less expensive, used homes should, by providing support from below, stimulate the demand for new construction.

A third and final feature of the model which merits comment has to do with the relationship between financing and depreciation which, for purposes of simplicity, was defined in such a way that owners never accumulated any equity in their homes. In real life, variations in down payments and amortization periods yield differences in real equities among owners which obscure comparisons of monthly payments and housing quality. Where payments appear to be excessive, for example, the owner may be amortizing his loan much faster relative to depreciation than are other owners with whose properties comparisons are being made.[13] To make the model a useful tool for evaluating actual situations, the original constraint with respect to financing must be relaxed to allow for normal differences in lending terms within sectors of the inventory which are of equal quality. With this modification, the conclusion of the model would be that, holding buyer risk constant, differences in quality among structures should be reflected in corresponding differences in monthly payments on the most liberal mortgage loans which can be readily obtained for these structures.

In conclusion, differences in quality among various parts of the residential inventory do not seem to be adequately reflected in prevailing prices and mortgage terms, though the extremely limited evidence that was examined is mixed. Perhaps, if lower quality housing had been included in the analysis, more firm judgments could have been reached. In any case, however, even if one cannot successfully argue that financing practices with respect to older sectors of the stock are discriminatory or irrational, or perverse, it does appear that more liberal mortgage lending policies in these sectors would not only benefit families who seek inexpensive residential accommodations in the existing stock, but would stimulate new construction as well.

Consequences of General Relaxation of Loan Criteria

At the present time, use of liberal mortgage terms to provide better housing in older areas for lower-middle and low-income families is limited almost entirely to designated renewal areas and to structures that are rehabilitated to so-called "long-term" standards.[14] This approach has proven to be slow, cumbersome, and quite inadequate to the task. Although there are a number of areas where striking improvements have been achieved, the rate at which rehabilitation is occurring is discouraging. And an unintended consequence in some instances is the displacement of resident families and the re-occupancy of the improved dwellings by higher income households.

The implications of this situation and of the preceding analysis are that more rapid gains could be achieved by making long-term, low-down-payment loans generally available in areas and for structures which are now denied such financing. Lower income families in large numbers could then move into better accommodations, and part of the savings in monthly payments would in the normal course of events be applied to better maintenance and limited rehabilitation. The visual results would not be so striking as in the case where all the savings which result from refinancing are applied to renovation, but the improvements would be more widespread. This at least would seem to be the argument.

In order to check this reasoning in a preliminary way, a comparison was made of the position of mortgagors under existing versus liberal financing, assuming a general change in mortgage lending policies in old areas (Table 4). Given the assumptions in Table 4, not all of the hoped-for consequences appear to be likely, because about one-half of the reduction in monthly payments due to a longer amortization period is offset by a larger mortgage and by premiums for insurance that would be necessary to attract debt capital. Part of the insurance is an extra benefit as well as an extra cost to the borrower, but it still increases his total cash outlay, if only slightly. Monthly payments on debt, and also taxes, are affected additionally by the rise in prices (in this case assumed to be 5 percent) which more favorable credit terms would engender.[15] The net result is only a modest decline in monthly payments, not enough to have a material effect on maintenance, repairs, and rehabilitation. Indeed, since the principal consequence of the change in credit

Table 4. Comparison of Monthly Operating Expenses for an Old, Six-Room Single-Family Row House, Under Two Different Assumptions as to Financing, City of Philadelphia, 1964

Monthly Costs	I Value—$8,000 15-Year, Level Payment Mortgage, $7,000, 6%	II Value—$8,400* 30-Year, Level Payment Mortgage, $8,000, 5½%
Financing	$ 59.08	$ 44.94
Taxes	16.00†	16.80†
Utilities	40.00‡	40.00‡
Maintenance	15.00§	15.00§
Property insurance	1.00‖	1.00‖
Mortgage insurance	—	3.33¶
Mortgagor insurance	—	1.88**
Total	$131.08	$122.95

*Value of $8,400 assumes that liberal credit increases prices by 5 percent.
†See footnote
§See footnote ‖, Table 1.
‡, Table 1. ‡ See footnote §, Table 1.
¶Assumed to be one-half of 1 percent of outstanding value of mortgage.
**Assumed to be 3 percent of monthly payments on mortgage, taxes, and property insurance.

terms would be a shift in occupancy to families with both lower earnings and fewer liquid assets, unless various carrots and sticks were used to generate higher levels of maintenance and rehabilitation, no increase in this activity would occur except that which owner-occupancy itself would precipitate.[16] And to the extent that improvements did occur, monthly housing costs would rise, because for the lower income immigrants, the leverage of liberal financing would already have been exhausted at the time of purchase.

The principal benefits, then, would accrue not in the areas in which liberalized credit were extended, but to the families who received it.[17] Admittedly, they would probably have to pay higher prices than formerly existed and their mortgage payments would continue over a much longer period of time, but they would also have better housing than before. The difference should be particularly pronounced for families moving into owner-occupancy from marginal rental units where a large portion of their total payment represents a return for entrepreneurial risk and management expense.

In brief, although the lower monthly payments would create a potential for rehabilitation (in Table 4, about $1,000 of improvements could be financed without increasing total payments), upward filtering of families would substantially reduce it. The consequences of extending liberalized mortgage terms widely throughout the older sectors of the housing stock would, therefore, not only be quantitatively different from the effects of credit extension that is tied to rehabilitation, but qualitatively different as well.

Reversing Present Lending Policies

Although, as stated earlier, it cannot be demonstrated that individual mortgagees are unduly cautious with respect to the risks of making loans in lower-quality areas, it does seem possible that for the group as a whole steps could be taken which would lessen the likelihood of severe loss by any single institution and thus provide the basis for a change in lending policies. The federal government has already done much to overcome mortgage finance problems associated with creating new inventory. It now needs comparable procedures to effect a more orderly market for old structures as well.

The most obvious first step would be for lending institutions and the Federal Housing Administration to either abandon or rationalize the concept of economic life as a basis for determining mortgage terms, since its use obscures the nature of the problem to be solved. Each residential structure does indeed have an economic life which is not simply the period of years over which it provides a flow of services, but its value in each of these years. There is, however, virtually no knowledge on which to base estimates of the future economic life of various types of structures or to justify present FHA practices in arriving at estimates of remaining economic life. This fact is reflected in the abysmal predictive record which lenders have amassed. Actually, while they talk generally about economic lives of twenty, thirty, forty, and fifty years for various structures, their policies constitute a statement that they really have no idea as to how to make specific predictions, and, therefore, quite understandably, grant terms that minimize risk of loss either through or in case of foreclosure. Thus, short-term mortgages are granted not where economic life has been shown to be brief, but where risks and uncertainties are greater than average.

This would suggest that a solution to the problem lies in the direction of identifying these uncertainties, protection against which demands a high fee, and converting them to socialized risks which could be handled actuarily for a lesser charge. Among the greater than average uncertainties which mortgage investors in older areas face are the possibility of loss of income by borrowers, diminution in overall demand, lower quality occupancy, neighborhood decline, and ultimate complete and permanent rejection of mortgaged structures by the market.

Extension of mortgage insurance programs to older dwellings would seem to be one obvious approach. It seems apparent, though, that much more is needed to change lending practices, especially since insurance and liberal terms probably would not extend to the lowest levels of the inventory where stabilization is also needed. The problem here is particularly acute, because the increment to new construction which would be supported by better financing in older areas would lead to increased abandonment in some of these areas. Thus, unless care were taken as to where credit terms were liberalized, the prophecy of longer economic life, as implied in these terms, would not, in contrast to the pessimistic prophecies that underlie present lending policies, be even partly self-fulfilling. Rather, it would be self-defeating.

How to identify structures actually nearing the point of retirement and how to treat them are, then, crucial questions. At the moment, government programs, in so far as their effect on these structures is concerned, are almost perverse. For as private new construction and residential renewal are accelerated to expand the supply of housing, there is a corresponding acceleration of abandonments at the bottom, a condition which intensifies investor uncertainty, perpetuates high rates of return and guarantees low levels of maintenance. The potentially favorable effects of faster filtering are in this manner at least partially unrealized. The situation is made worse by the fact that public housing takes primarily "good" families, leaving private enterprise to cope with the maintenance and other difficulties created by problem tenants.

Two proposals which have been offered to improve both mortgage financing practices and housing quality in the lowest sectors of the inventory are, first, a guaranteed retirement price for residential structures, and, second, the assurance that all families can afford to pay enough rent to acquire standard accommodation. Analysis of these possibilities is beyond the scope of this paper, but, to end on a note of hope, their examination by others suggest that perhaps they are less utopian than might initially seem to be the case.[18]

Notes

[1]According to rough calculations by the author, assuming values of one- and two-family rental units in this quality range to be approximately sixty times gross monthly rents.

[2]Thus it is very much like the one-horse shay. The illustration implies that the neighborhood does not change in quality. The neighborhood need not, however, have the same economic life as the house.

[3]Or monthly housing expenses for owner-occupiers.

[4]It might seem on the surface that the depreciation (price) curve should be linear; that is, if quality is constant, the structure should be worth $5,000 after 20 years, $2,500 after 30 years, and so forth. It is necessary, however, to discount the value of future streams of services to arrive at present value. More precisely, value for any year *X* between zero and 40 would be the present value of an annuity for 40 minus *X* years.

[5]Particularly taxes, which, if *ad valorem*, do reflect quality differences, and thus in the real world would have to be included along with monthly mortgage payments in any comparisons.

[6]The assumption of 15 years' life expectancy would seem reasonably consistent with current mortgage practice of not granting loans of over 10 years on old, low-quality structures. At the other end, a presumption of an economic life expectancy of 70 years for new structures may not seem consistent with maximum mortgage loans of 30 years, but mortgage lenders limit the maximum term to 30 years for other reasons.

[7]This is simply to avoid the arithmetic problem of accumulated equity and does not affect the essence of any arguments to follow.

[8]In addition, of course, all the other assumptions presented in connection with the first model also apply.

[9]William Hoad, "Real Estate Prices," unpublished doctoral dissertation, University of Michigan, 1942. Grebler, Blank, and Winnick, *Capital Formation in Residential Real Estate*, National Bureau of Economic Research, Princeton University Press, 1956. Robert W. Hartman, "Demand for the Stock of Non-Farm Housing," unpublished doctoral dissertation, Harvard University, 1964. Hoad, closer to 1 percent, is thought to be more accurate than Grebler *et al.* The loss in value due to deterioration and obsolescence must not be interpreted as equal to the amount of money required to restore the structure to its original quality, particularly when, as in this example, the definition of quality includes neighborhood environment.

[10]Again assuming maintenance expenditures are equal for the two structures, even though higher initial quality could imply less frequent replacement and repair of various parts of the structure.

[11]Or are locked in as a consequence of price declines. This, however, would seem improbable for more than a small proportion of owners.

[12]Ramsay Wood, "Credit Terms and Demand for Residential Construction," *Study of Mortgage Credit*. Committee on Banking and Currency, Subcommittee on Housing, United States Senate, 85th Congress, 2nd Session, United States Government Printing Office, 1958, pp. 87–121.

[13]Indeed, this is one argument which mortgage lenders make in defence of their policies with respect to older dwellings. Even when they err, so the argument goes, in assigning short economic lives to structures that continue in the inventory for many more years, the consequence is simply a more rapid than anticipated accumulation of equity by purchasers. Or in other words, mistakes on the side of caution simply benefit consumers and hence are no cause for concern. The problem with this argument is that it ignores the potential purchasers who are

excluded from the market by undue caution. Consequently, to the extent that apparently excessive required monthly payments on old structures do have the effect of raising the rate of growth of real equities above the average for the total market, this is support for the contention that the payments are in fact too high. As already observed, though, the depressing effect of such policies on prices may tend to retard growth of real equities.

[14]An exception may be New Haven, Connecticut, where the Federal Housing Administration now interprets code and long-term standards as one and the same.

[15]Thus for buyers who can afford the higher down payments and monthly charges, the liberalized credit has undesirable consequences. See Ramsay Wood, *op. cit.* By the same token, however, it brings benefits to sellers, but since most sellers, particularly the absentee owners, probably have higher incomes than the buyers, the price rise is not neutral in its welfare effects. Against this argument, though, must be weighed the possibility that increased construction occasioned by the change in credit will ultimately reduce prices and rents in the lower-quality stock. This aspect of the question has already been discussed.

[16]A possible exception would be existing owners who had already paid off most of their mortgage loans and chose to rehabilitate with funds obtained by refinancing. Without encouragement of such activity, however, there is no reason to expect it to occur at any greater scale than is the case today.

[17]And to the home-building industry, but this point has already been discussed.

[18]Background papers prepared for the Existing Housing Committee and the Finance Committee of the Philadelphia Housing Association by the staff of the Association, 1964.

3.9 Home Ownership Opportunities for the Poor

Michael A. Stegman

"A nation of homeowners, of people who own a real share in their land," said Franklin D. Roosevelt more than a generation ago, "is unconquerable."[1] A more contemporary version of the notion that homeownership contributes to the stability of the nation and to the advancement of its ideals was born of the racial tensions and fiery uprisings from within, which charred the cities in the 1960s. Thus, Lyndon B. Johnson, in his message to the Congress on the crisis of the cities, in 1968, said, "Owning a home can increase responsibility and stake out a man's own place in his community. The man who owns a home has something to be proud of and good reason to protect and preserve it."[2]

However subtly, with respect to national low-income housing policy, we have moved from a perspective which relates universal ownership to such democratic ideals as security and independence, to one which makes home ownership opportunities for the poor a key element of an overall defensive strategy designed to "keep things cool."

It is not the purpose of this paper to pass judgment on the morality of a political option based upon the assertion that "a man won't burn down a house that he owns," although it does seem to pervert a basic democratic ideal. Instead, we will inquire into the potential impact on the low-income housing problem of a major effort to increase dramatically the opportunity of the poor to own their own homes. In so doing, we will first report on the nature and magnitude of the expected population growth in the coming decade, describe housing conditions as the 1960s drew to a close, project them into the 70s, analyze the most important national effort undertaken thus far to bring ownership opportunities within the grasp of the poor and near-poor and conclude that only about 2½ million of the estimated 7½ million house-poor families in the U.S. in 1978 will probably represent potential homeowners, and of this number, a large portion will probably be incapable of assuming the burdens of ownership for one reason or another.

A Decade Hence and Back Again

Looking into the future seven years hence, it has been estimated

Originally prepared for the *Encyclopedia of Social Work* (in press), reprinted by permission of the National Association of Social Workers, Inc.

that the nation's population will increase by more than thirty million to 235 million people.[3] The nonwhite rate of growth will continue to outstrip that of the white so that the decade ending 1978 will show a 25 percent increase for the former and only 15 percent for the latter.[4] As would be expected, such differing growth rates, along with the expected nature of inter- and intra-metropolitan flows will impact heavily in central cities, where in 1978, the white population is expected to have declined in absolute terms by one million, while the nonwhite increase will be around 5 million.[5] The net result of the continuation of these current trends will be nonwhite majorities in several major cities and an overall nonwhite increase in all central cities from the current 20 percent, to 30 percent of the total population.[6] While it is anticipated that there will be continued progress in nonwhite suburbanization during this period, the National Commission on Urban Problems has concluded that

> If Negroes continue moving into the suburbs at the present rate, their projected number will jump from 2.8 to 6.8 million by 1985. But, the number of suburban whites will also more than double from 52 million to 106 million. So additional Negroes will be all but lost in a sea of whites as the proportionate increase will move from only 5 to 6 percent.[7]

Housing Conditions 1968

With this sketchy background, we now focus on the nature and magnitude of the low-income housing problem in the United States in 1968. While the precise nature of the problem depends upon the source from which the information is secured, there is some concensus that there were between 6 and 7 million occupied substandard housing units in the United States in 1968, 4 million of which were structurally sound but lacking adequate plumbing facilities and 2.7 million which were structurally unsound.[8] If the dimension of overcrowding is added to these physical indicators and the overlap netted out, then, more than 11 million families were ill-housed in the United States in 1968.[9]

Although fully three-quarters of the substandard units were occupied by white households in 1968, it would be pure folly to ignore the strong racial implication of the nation's chronic housing problem both historically and at present. For example,

> Between 1950 and 1960, even though the absolute number of substandard units declined, the number of non-white occupied units increased from 1.4 to 1.8 million.[10]
>
> Non-white renter households occupied 32 percent of the nation's substandard rental housing in 1960 although they made up only 16 percent of all rental households.[11]

> Non-white households needed one-third more earnings, irrespective of household size, than whites, to secure standard housing.[12]
>
> If you are poor and non-white and rent, the chances are three out of four that you live in substandard housing.[13]

As implied earlier, the housing-race problem is further protracted by the fact that the nation's central cities are becoming more heavily black as they continue to deteriorate. Thus, not only are the poverty areas of most cities heavily nonwhite, but they are among the oldest, most intensely developed, and least desirable residential areas within most metropolitan areas. In general, they contain one-third of the city's housing stock on one-quarter of the land area, three out of four of the city's substandard housing units, and nine out of ten of the substandard housing units occupied by nonwhite families. Overall, the residential densities of the inner cities' slums and ghettos are 1,000 times those of similarly settled areas in the outlying sections of metropolitan regions.[14]

Projecting to 1978

In 1968, the President's Committee on Urban Housing concluded that

> about 7.8 million American families—1 in every 8—cannot now afford to pay the market price for standard housing that would cost no more than 20 percent of their total incomes . . . assuming no marked changes in current economic trends, national policies and priorities among federal programs . . . in 1978 about 7.5 million families—1 in every 10—would still be unable to afford standard housing.[15]

According to the Committee's studies, the house-poor families of the late 1970s will be predominantly nonwhite (70 percent), with 1 out of every 4 nonwhite families needing housing assistance compared to 1 in every 12 white households. Furthermore, among the house-poor whites, 50 percent will be elderly and 70 percent will be small households of two persons or less.[16] Among the non-whites, only 27 percent are expected to be elderly and 43 percent small, 1- or 2-person households.[17] Thus, we might disaggregate the population that is expected to lack effective demand in the late 1970s as shown in Table 1.

We might expect twice as many nonwhites to need housing assistance as whites, almost 8 times as many large, nonwhite families as white, and while a greater percentage of the needy whites will be small households and elderly, in absolute terms, the nonwhite need will be greater across the board.

Table 1. Race

Size of Household	White # (000's)	White %	Nonwhite # (000's)	Nonwhite %
1, 2 persons	1,800	72	2,200	43
3, 4 persons	450	18	1,300	26
5 persons	100	4	400	9
6 or more persons	150	6	1,100	22
Total	2,500	100	5,000	100

Home Ownership for the Poor: A Look at Section 235

As of this writing, the low-income homeownership program commonly referred to as "Section 235" represents the nation's first serious effort to bring ownership opportunities within the reach of moderate and low-income families. Under Section 235, eligible families are entitled to interest subsidy payments which serve to reduce their monthly mortgage payments. The amount of the subsidy depends upon going F.H.A. interest rates, the size of the mortgage, and the adjusted family income of the eligible families.

With the subsidy, which is paid by F.H.A. to the lender, a family can pay as little as 1 percent interest on its mortgage loan. As family income rises, the subsidy is reduced. It ceases altogether when the family is able to pay the full mortgage interest rate, insurance, and property taxes without exceeding 20 percent of its income.[18]

In order to understand more fully the economics of the program, let us hypothesize that an eligible family is interested in purchasing a new, 3- or 4-bedroom home which sells for $17,500, the maximum mortgage amount available under the program. Assuming no federal subsidy is available, the monthly costs of owning such a home in one of our major cities might be as shown in Table 2.

In attempting to understand how Section 235 operates, it is important to remember that maintenance costs, heat, water, and other utilities are not included in calculating the size of the interest subsidy an eligible family might receive. Yet, of course, such monthly expenditures are as necessary and as recurring, though more variable, as the mortgage cost and certainly must be considered in assessing the costs of owning a home. Let us now consider the financial burden of owning the same home on

Table 2. Monthly Housing Costs

Purchase Price: $17,500	
100 percent F.H.A. Mortgage at 7½ percent + ½ percent	
Mortgage Insurance for 30 Years	
Mortgage Payments	$132.50
Real Estate Taxes*	29.00
Utilities	30.00
Maintenance**	20.00
Hazard Insurance	3.00
Total Monthly Housing Expense	$214.50
Annual Housing Expense	$2,574.00

*Effective Tax Rate of 2 percent of market value
**Average maintenance costs of approximately 1.4 percent of market value

families of different incomes with and without financial assistance like that provided under Section 235.

Table 3, while looking somewhat awesome, simply presents, for each of ten family income groups, ratios of housing expense to income associated with owning our hypothesized home with and without interest subsidies like those available under the Section 235 program, and some related information.[19] By scanning down column 4, for example, one can see that the full economic cost of owning the $17,500 home, under the assumed monthly cost schedule detailed in Table 2, would consume 86 percent of the lowest income groups' resources, 72 percent of the next lowest, down to 31 percent of the adjusted income of families with $8,400 a year. Moving over to column 5, which presents the maximum monthly subsidy for which each income group is eligible, it will be noted that the first four would each receive the same amount, $76.72. This is because their incomes are sufficiently low to make them eligible for the largest subsidy available under the program, namely an amount which would bring their mortgage costs down to a one percent rate of interest. Each of the other subsidies in the table are somewhat lower than the maximum and are based upon the difference between the costs of paying the full mortgage interest rate, property taxes, and insurance, and 20 percent of the adjusted incomes of the families.

Since the interest subsidy program does not take into con-

Table 3. The monthly Cost of Ownership for Selected Family Income Groups With and Without Interest Subsidies

(1) Adjusted Gross Annual Y	(2) Adjusted Gross Monthly Y	(3) 20% Adjusted Gross Monthly Y	(4) % Income Toward Housing Expense Without Section 235 Assistance	(5) Maximum Monthly Housing Subsidy Under Section 235	(6) Monthly Housing Expense with Section 235 Assistance	(7) % Adjusted Gross Y Toward Housing with Section 235 Assistance
$3,000	$250	$ 50	86	$76.72	$137.78	55
3,600	300	60	72	76.72	137.78	46
4,200	350	70	61	76.72	137.78	39
4,800	400	80	54	76.72	137.78	34
5,400	450	90	48	74.50	140.00	31
6,000	500	100	43	64.50	150.00	30
6,600	550	110	39	54.50	160.00	29
7,200	600	120	36	44.50	170.00	28
7,800	650	130	33	34.50	180.00	28
8,400	700	140	31	24.50	190.00	27

sideration maintenance and utility needs, the housing expense/income ratios, after taking interest subsidies into account, are still extremely high for many of the income groups, beginning at 55 percent for the poorest group and ending at 27 percent for those with the highest incomes. In short, as the program is presently construed, few really low-income families will be able to absorb the assisted costs of owning and caring for a home valued at somewhere close to twenty thousand dollars.[20]

The significance of this analysis does not lie in the fact that, as written, Section 235 might not reach the real hard-core housing-poor families. After all, program guidelines, eligibility criteria, and subsidy formulations can be readily altered, although it is of course important that existing program limitations be recognized. Rather, the real significance lies instead in frankly confronting two related problems. On the one hand, an effort must be made to estimate the number, composition, and characteristics of the families who both desire and can cope with the responsibilities associated with owning and maintaining a home, and on the other, we must consider the serious problems involved in finding satisfactory locations and desirable neighborhoods in which to build a sufficient number of subsidized housing units to be sold to low-income families; the latter requirement has proved exceedingly difficult in the several publicly supported housing programs with which we have experience.

To return for a moment to Table 1, we see that approximately four million families needing housing assistance in 1978 will be 1- and 2-person families—hardly potential homeowners. The remaining house-poor families, 3½ million strong, obviously represent a real mixed bag with respect to race, age, family composition, and other social characteristics of importance in assessing the causes of their limited incomes and assumed housing difficulties. Without knowing any more about the estimated 1.2 million families with six or more individuals who will need housing assistance in the coming years, except their size, we might predict that a great many of them will have difficulties in assuming the costs and other burdens associated with homeownership. First, we may fall back on a rich national tradition of failing to consider the extraordinary plight of the large, poor family in subsidized housing programs. As recently as 1968, Senator Douglas reported that in seven major cities investigated, there were 107,000 large families who needed housing assistance, while only 20,000 units with 3 or more bedrooms were available in publicly assisted housing.[21] Because large houses cost more to build, and thus to subsidize, are more costly to heat and maintain, and because large families consume more electricity and water than others, as well as have many more urgent non-housing needs, it is reasonably safe to conclude that many of them will be unable to assume the economic burdens of owning a home under any subsidy program that the Congress is likely to formulate and support.

Second, among the large families, both white and nonwhite, as well as among the smaller house-poor families reflected in Table 1, there is a good possibility that homeownership is not their most sought-after goal. A good many of the 2 million or so women receiving AFDC might not be interested in adding to their already overburdened lives the responsibilities associated with maintaining and repairing their own homes. Moreover, in a study we have conducted of the low-rent housing market in a large central city, we have found some evidence to indicate that many poor families receive rent reductions if they are long-term, stable tenants, or become delinquent in their rents when crises arise, including moving out without notifying their landlords to avoid paying arrears, and are able to make other adjustments in order to survive that they might not be able to make if strapped with thirty-year mortgages.[22] We have also found that many poor families who have rented their houses all of their adult lives are hesitant to accept the responsibilities of maintaining owner-occupied units. In part, this problem derives from the fact that their present units are often in excess of 50 years old and extremely difficult and costly to keep in repair; in part, also, it is a function of never having had the opportunity to own their own homes. In any event, any ownership program aimed at the poor which ignores the issue of home management, repair, and operation will be doomed to costly failure. Homeownership will neither erase the social ills of our society nor reweave families and individuals, so beaten and broken that they cannot cope adequately with the pressures exerted upon them, into the social fabric of our urban culture. To thus imply that universal ownership, or anything close to it, will save our cities is both cruel and deceptive. We have lost faith in existing efforts like public housing and seem willing to chuck it all for the "fee simple" solution—not because public housing does not provide physically sound housing that the poor can afford, or because it is rental housing—but because we have built housing projects that are not fit for people, in neighborhoods that died years before the projects were conceived. Thirty years after the program was created, we awakened to the patronizing and heavy-handed manner in which nonrepresentative boards have executed and administered local efforts throughout the country. Tenure has very little to do with the issue. Yet, there are those who present the case that a new emphasis on ownership will turn the trick.

We cannot wipe the slate clean and begin again. While it makes eminent sense from a public policy standpoint to broaden housing choice and thus increase the options available to families needing housing assistance, we must not be lulled into thinking this will solve the problems of the cities nor those of most of its angry people.

Notes

[1]Quoted in Glen H. Beyer, *Housing and Society* (New York, the Macmillan Company, 1966), p. 249.

[2]"The Crisis of The Cities," The President's Message to the Congress on Urban Programs, February 22, 1968.

[3]The Report of the President's Committee on Urban Housing, *A Decent Home*, Technical Studies, Volume I (U.S.G.P.O., 1969).

[4]*Ibid.*

[5]*Ibid.*

[6]*Ibid.*

[7]Report of the National Commission on Urban Problems, *Building the American City* (Washington, U.S.G.P.O., 1969), p. 5.

[8]*A Decent Home*, Technical Studies, Volume I, *op. cit.*, p. 6.

[9]*Ibid.*, p. 9.

[10]*Report of the National Advisory Commission on Civil Disorders* (New York, Bantam, 1968), p. 457.

[11]*Building the American City, op. cit.*, p. 10.

[12]*A Decent Home*, Technical Studies, Volume I, *op. cit.*, p. 6.

[13]*Building the American City, op. cit.*, p. 9.

[14]*Ibid.*, p. 77.

[15]Report of the President's Committee on Urban Housing, *A Decent Home* (Washington, U.S.G.P.O., 1969), p. 7.

[16]*A Decent Home*, Technical Studies, Volume I, *op. cit.*, p. 7.

[17]*Ibid.*

[18]"Federal Housing Administration's Section 235," *Journal of Housing*, (Volume 26, number 6, June 1969), p. 280.

[19]A somewhat similar analysis of the costs of owning a home under Section 235 was undertaken by Charles Field and Robert Schafer in an article in the *Journal of Urban Law*, June 1969. Adjusted family income refers to the statutory deduction from family income of $300 per minor dependent.

[20]If we calculate the costs of owning a $14,000 house under the program, the housing cost/income ratios range from 49% for the lowest group, 41% for the next lowest, down to 24% for the highest. If the program is to reach the real poor, a way must be found to reclaim the hundreds of thousands of structurally sound units located in central cities that are

in the process of deteriorating. Such units are often available for only a few thousand dollars or less. Whether or not, however, it would be wiser to reclaim them through ownership or investment programs is another question.

[21]*Building the American City, op. cit.*, p. 10.

[22]University of Pennsylvania—Morgan State Evaluation of Baltimore's Anti-poverty Efforts, under a contract with the Office of Economic Opportunity, 1966–1970.

4
On the Horizon

Introduction

As indicated in the introduction to this volume, considering the extent to which many of our inner cities have been torn by riots and lesser disturbances and the apparent importance attached to the lack of decent shelter by ghetto blacks and other minorities, it is no wonder that a great deal of attention is currently being focused on the housing problems and programs of major urban centers. Today, most local administrations have at their disposal a conglomeration of disparate housing programs from which they must shape and implement their housing strategies. Among the familiar program options are urban renewal and redevelopment (including all of its variants such as conservation, rehabilitation, concentrated code enforcement, and the newer Neighborhood Development Program), public housing, nonassisted code enforcement, and such instruments as rent supplements, Section 236 rental housing, and the Section 235 low- and moderate-income ownership programs. Particularly among the larger cities, the options are even greater because of state and/or municipal activity in public housing, middle-income rental programs, and a variety of punitive actions such as those implied in rent withholding, receivership programs, and special housing courts, which are designed to force recalcitrant owners to comply with minimum housing standards.

In a recent study in New York City, for example, it was estimated that there currently exist

> At least 19 programs of government intervention in New York City's housing market, a count that could easily be increased to 24 by separate enumeration of closely related Federal, State and City activities. The forms of intervention include public financing, construction, ownership and operation of housing units; financial assistance to private construction and to privately owned and operated units; regulation of private construction and management of housing, including rent control and maintenance standards, and direct assistance to consumers of housing[1]

In spite of such lengthy arrays, city administrations like New York's remain at the mercy of the dynamics of inner-city housing markets and can do little to alter those tendencies through the manipulation of these program ingredients. Moreover, the problems with implementing many of the existing housing devices are such as to minimize their effective use in the development of any viable strategy to deal effectively with the apparently increasing rate of housing deterioration. Witness, for example,

- more low-rent housing has been demolished than constructed under the provisions of the renewal program;
- the construction of low-rent housing cannot be made economically feasible through the exclusive use of the "land-writedown," the principle upon which the renewal program operates;
- local contributions to low- and moderate-rent housing programs, such as tax abatement, while reducing monthly rents, increase the financial drain of scarce, local tax resources;
- because of extremely tight, low-rent housing submarkets, rigorous code enforcement activities might only be pursued if the desired outcome is to force abandonment, rather than upgrading, of the stock which cannot be rehabilitated economically;
- the "bombed-out" look of many sections of the inner city demonstrates that the renewal program cannot create a market for desired land uses, but is, instead, constrained by the existing pattern of demand and state of the market;
- existing receivership programs, if implemented, lead to the undesirable end of making the city a large-scale holder of uneconomic, substandard housing rather than an agent for change or an efficient rehabilitator of housing;
- the rather slow rate of production among nonprofit sponsors of subsidized housing which, rather than being insulated from the vagaries of the market, seem to be buffeted not only by market forces but are also swept up into major social issues such as those dealing with community control, which threaten to impede their progress even more in the coming years.

Not only is the need for additional housing tools based upon the recognition that existing instruments have failed even to keep abreast of mounting decay, the economic contradictions inherent in some of them, and the insensitivity with which many of them have been administered, but it is even more firmly rooted in the fact that the dynamics of the inner-city market have changed, a point to which we will shortly return.

While one cannot make any judgments about possible alternative futures of the American low-income housing effort without taking great risks of being more in error than not, it is probably fair to reason as Abrams did almost thirty years ago that, while the subsidy is only one aspect of housing policy, "the form it ultimately takes will influence more than housing programs alone."[2] That is to say, the means by which the public purse is opened to both consumers and private investors is affected and influenced by the kind of economic system under which we live. Thus, we might preface our discussion of emerging housing policy by acknowledging the fact that those housing proposals that have been enacted into law over the past two decades were most likely acted upon because they included subsidy arrangements that were capable of garnering widespread political support and of being justified as consistent with the aims and objectives of a free-enterprise economy.[3] Similarly, the extent to which some of the efforts have succeeded in attracting relatively large appropriations over the years is a function of their compatability with the system rather than their efficiency or effectiveness in serving those most in need of government housing assistance. Perhaps another way of saying the same thing is to suggest that past successes have hinged, to a great extent, on the broad basis upon which assistance has been offered; the most effective way of assuring middle-class support for low-income housing subsidies has been to provide assistance to the not-so-poor as well. And, as has been suggested before, an inefficient program that provides *some* housing for the poor is better than an efficient program that can garner no congressional appropriations at all.[4]

Housing and the Subsidy

In the immediate future, attention will most likely continue to focus on the subsidy, its purported beneficiaries, and its broader economic implications —with one major modification. Today, it is commonly acknowledged that those subsidy arrangements most consistent with our usual way of doing things typically are not sufficient to bring prices or rents down to where those most in need of housing assistance might benefit materially from government action. As we look ahead, we might envision contention between advocates of the politically more practical filtering strategy and those supporting a renewed effort to funnel larger direct subsidies to the most ill-housed, with the emerging trend supporting the latter. Keeping in mind that, politically, an "old subsidy is a good subsidy," and the need for reducing prices and rents beyond the provisions of existing programs, while not veering too far from our political and economic mainstream, we might expect to see a continuation of the flow of recommended housing proposals which

reflect attempts to piggy-back existing subsidy programs, each of which contains a politically acceptable subsidy formulation; stress the need to eliminate barriers which prevent the more widespread use of existing subsidy programs such as the elimination of the workable program as a prerequisite for local participation in the public housing and rent supplement programs;[5]

suggest the tying of federal assistance in nonhousing areas to community participation in subsidized housing programs and, in general, increasing pressures on suburban communities to accept greater responsibilities in the low-income housing area;

recommend increasing the financial incentives available to limited dividend sponsors and other private investors in existing housing programs which have never attracted the active interest of the investment community;

urge the Congress to demonstrate that the nation is committed to dealing with the housing problem through the full funding of existing programs.

While the piggy-backing of two or more existing federal assistance efforts can produce housing that the poor can afford—i.e., rent supplements on top of a below-market-interest-rate mortgage—it would seem that subsidies on top of subsidies merely results in the government subsidizing itself, increasing the overhead cost of the program through duplicating administrative procedures, and making the housing assistance function of the Federal Government more, rather than less, complex and burdensome to those in the public and private sectors who might participate. More importantly, perhaps, the nature of our appropriations system can blunt the low-income thrust of such a strategy since sufficient monies must be forthcoming in several program areas if subsidies are to be piggy-backed. Another way of summarizing the problems with such an approach is to suggest that it represents more of a nonpolicy than an affirmative approach to producing a viable low-income housing strategy.

Perhaps, the major barrier to developing an achievable, direct subsidy approach to dealing with the low-income housing problem was raised initially in the preamble to the Housing Act of 1949, and most recently reaffirmed in the 1968 Act. Both pieces of legislation contain national commitments which not only could never be afforded but are most likely not supported by a sufficiently large constituency to be carried out even if more funds were to become available. A conservative estimate of the capital costs of constructing one million public housing units is well over 15 billion dollars, more than seven times the entire budget of the Department of Housing and Urban Development for fiscal year 1969–1970. Yet, and this is the most interesting aspect of the problem, there seems to be little overt interest among low-income housing advocates and our political leaders in modifying the nation's goal of putting every ill-housed family into a new quality house in a good neighborhood in spite of the fact that fewer and fewer superior quality units can be built each year per million dollars of public assistance. As construction costs continue to rise, it seems more, rather than less, likely that the housing program support of the nonpoor will erode more rapidly, as they must not only continue to pay for the programs but increase their contributions to the point where the low-income beneficiaries are living in units whose typical costs exceed the values of their own homes. One inevitable consequence of a policy which is based upon "the undesirable results of a society's trying to require poor urban households to meet housing quality standards which are in reality beyond their capacity, or the society's, to achieve is that it produces more low quality than is necessary."[6] Stated more positively, if we were to accept a more moderate quality standard for publicly assisted new construction as well as in our rehabilitation efforts, perhaps government housing programs would be much more capable of assisting larger numbers of families in real need and more likely to harness broadly based political support across all income groups.

Direct Subsidies Versus a Filtering Approach

It appears likely that unless the economic and political limitations of the direct subsidy approach are recognized and a concerted effort is made to spread existing resources among more, rather than fewer, needy families through the adoption of more realistic housing standards, a modified filtering strategy will emerge as the dominant approach to dealing with the problem in the seventies. Such an approach will stress a "peppering" of financial assistance across income groups with some direct subsidies enabling a limited number of moderately poor families to move into new construction. The likelihood of this latter strategy dominating the seventies is further enhanced by the recent inflationary spiral in which we have become entrapped.

Recently, it was estimated that the effects of general inflation on national housing output during the two years, 1967-1969, was somewhere around 700,000 units.[7] That is, approximately that many new dwellings, including perhaps 300,000 publicly aided housing units, were not produced because of rapidly increasing costs, shortages of investment funds, lagging returns on mortgage instruments, the withdrawal of state and municipal bond issues for lack of bidders and Congressional apprehension to sustain high levels of public assistance to housing in light of what were obviously viewed as more pressing national needs. Not only can the effects of inflation be calculated on the basis of units not produced, but available data on New York City, for example, indicate some of the consequences of inflation on publicly assisted housing that was constructed within the 1967–1969 period:[8]

The impact of a one percent rise in interest costs in the year 1969 for a recently completed Limited Profit Housing Company Project with a (40-year) mortgage of $5,000 per room was $3.55 per room per month (or $16.00 per month for an average sized apartment of 4.5 rooms).

Building construction costs in New York City (as indicated by the Engineering News Record index) have increased by 6.2 percent annually over the past three years, 1966–1969, compared with a 3.4 percent annual increase over the ten-year period, 1956–1966. Construction costs per room for New York City's Limited Profit Housing Companies projects have increased from $2,870 to $3,720 or 30 percent between 1957 and 1967. Since 1967, construction costs for similar projects have been estimated at $4,450 to $5,615 per room. Holding financing costs constant, construction costs in the ten years, 1957–1967, have added $3.10 per room per month in rent while in the three years, 1967–1969, the increase has ranged from $2.90 to $7.60 per room per month. This year's union construction contract settlements for New York City are averaging from $3.00 to $4.00 per hour in increases, the most exorbitant increases in the history of contract settlements. When these settlements are translated into overall construction costs, estimates indicate that they may result in increases of 10 percent per year over the next three years. Further translated into rent per room for Limited Profit Housing Companies, holding all other costs constant (including interest rate at 6.5 percent), this will mean an additional increase in rent of $9.40 per room per month over the contract period.

In summary, Limited Profit Housing Companies that were being priced out at $35 per room per month in 1966, $40 in 1967, and $50 in 1968, currently fall within the range of $55 to $65 per room per month. These figures encompass the combined impact of rising interest rates, construction costs, and operating costs (including the need for security not computed in the earlier history of these projects) and have occurred despite the increase in tax exemption from a maximum of 50 percent to approximately 80 percent.

There are two somewhat related reasons why rising construction costs will ultimately broaden the appeal of a filtering strategy. First, as construction, land, and financing costs continue to increase, larger subsidies are required to house poor families whose money incomes do not increase as rapidly, if at all, as prices. Additionally, alterations in Congressionally invoked construction cost ceilings typically lag far behind changes in market prices in most large urban centers, with the result that public construction of low-income housing grinds to a halt or is slowed significantly. Secondly, and perhaps more importantly, in the face of steeply rising construction costs, a greater proportion of the total population will require some form of financial assistance to move into new construction. Thus, for example, with limited profit housing companies subsidizing new units renting at $65 a room in New York City and limited rent controls recently extended to cover privately constructed new and near-new housing, public attention is beginning to focus more on the housing problems of the nonpoor, with the possible consequent funneling of greater proportions of housing assistance funds to this group as well.

Likely Policy Issues in the Seventies

Regardless of which strategy ultimately dominates future housing policy and the myriad of subsidy proposals that emerge, we are also likely to witness an increasing flow of proposals aimed at enlarging the available resource pool for the financing of urban housing in the coming decade. In fact, as of this writing, the Government National Mortgage Association (GNMA), created in the Housing Act of 1968, was preparing to enter the mortgaged-backed securities business in order to channel additional funds into housing. The 1968 Act gives GNMA the authority to issue securities backed by pools of FHA-insured or VA-guaranteed mortgages that would be attractive to pension funds and trusts which have traditionally shown relatively little interest in straight mortgages.[9] While the mortgage-backed security is expected to be issued in large denominations only and be a suitable investment option to highly capitalized pension funds and the like, we might expect to see similar kinds of proposals aimed at attracting the limited capital of the middle-income consumer. Typically, such proposals might call for the creation of some form of "urban bonds," the proceeds of which would be used for the construction or rehabilitation of housing by nonprofit sponsors. Issued in denominations as small as $500, the bonds would provide a tax-free yield of between 4 percent and 5 percent and additional tax benefits to their holders in the form of a portion of the unused depreciation allowances applicable to the housing that is constructed with the bond revenues. One proponent of this device suggests that an overall after-tax return of more than 8 percent could be realized by a middle-income investor who participates in this program, and that such returns would be sufficient to support and implement a "gigantic master plan for urban redevelopment."[10]

A quite different type of proposal, albeit with a similar objective, is that which calls for the development of gigantic housing corporations which, it is implied, could be the housing industry's new way of retailing its product:[11]

> The Housing Corporation can introduce the continuity of managerial responsibility that the housing business lacks today. The Housing Corporation is a specialized institution organized to buy, build, own, rent, and sell housing. The corporation could, for example, buy well-maintained existing properties for its housing inventory or it could buy rundown properties, refurbish them, and include them in its inventory. It could also build new housing on new or reclaimed land . . . The corporation would enter into contracts with wholesale suppliers of the six discrete ingredients that constitute the housing package. Out of the proceeds from the sale or rent of its housing, the corporation would (1) pay cash or pay a ground rent to suppliers of *land*, (2) pay property taxes to the *community*, (3) pay the suppliers and installers of *building* facilities, (4) pay interest to suppliers of money, and (5) pay suppliers of *management* services, including insurance and title transfer and related real estate tasks. . . .
>
> Corporations can attract equity capital, borrow from lending institutions by mortgaging their assets, raise money to finance their day-to-day operations, collect payments from their customers, pay off investors, and make a profit in the process. Because large sums of long-term capital are so important to housing, the corporate route for raising money has many advantages over its traditional dependence on the "feast-or-famine" mortgage market which characterizes the industry.
>
> The Housing Corporation would tap new money by providing an additional savings opportunity for the consumer. He can acquire an equity in the corporation that supplies the very housing he lives in and begin to build up an estate. The Corporation would offer him a type of tenure that combines, under a single contract, the convenience of renting with the advantage of owning—a combination with special appeal for consumers who want the best of both worlds. The ownership of stock in a Housing Corporation would provide a convenient way for a family to invest in real estate without the complications that owning a specific residential property usually entails.
>
> As far as the consumer is concerned, the Housing Corporation would combine the functions of a builder, realtor, lender, and manager of residential property. In dealing with such a corporation, the con-

sumer would have a wider choice of housing to fit his needs than he has in today's market. After selecting a particular house or apartment, the consumer would make a deposit and sign an agreement obligating him to monthly payments that would include maintenance and utilities. The Corporation would offer him four types of tenure or occupancy agreements to choose from: he can *rent* with or without an option to buy, he can *buy* with or without a guarantee of his investment. A contract to rent without option would require a one percent investment on the consumer's part, or the deposit of the last month's rent in advance; an option to buy would require a 5 percent deposit. To buy without an investment guarantee would require a 10 percent down payment, and to buy with a guarantee would require a minimum investment of 20 percent of the property value.

Another emerging solution path to the problems of decaying housing and deficient environments, which will be the focus of much debate in the 1970s, is the new town. Even though existing legislation provides some assistance to would-be developers of new communities, thus far, we are a nation without a new-towns policy. Recently, however, one HUD official estimated, on the basis of expected population growth and its distribution, a national potential will exist for 272 large, new communities of at least 50,000 population each, by the year 2000.[12] While the bases for a new-towns-type urbanization policy might be "to combat urban sprawl, protect land and water resources, and to provide in a more orderly way for large-scale population growth," others have opted for such a policy thrust as a means of eliminating the ghetto and producing a desegregated society. When viewed in this latter light, one new-towns strategy has been described as containing the following three elements:[13]

1. A massive ten-year program of development of new towns in outlying areas to accommodate the projected Negro and white population growth.
2. The construction in these new towns of some additional 350,000 subsidized housing units each year for ten years, which will allow the ultimate replacement of urban substandard housing and create a temporary housing surplus.
3. The withdrawal of public expenditures for housing subsidies, sewer, water, roads, and mass transportation from ordinary subdivision development and their rechanneling into new towns, thus virtually eliminating the competition of segregated housing development.

Because virtually any new-towns policy must contain a multiple objective function, it is important to devise some means to assess the relative efficiency of the new-towns concept in dealing with the low- and moderate-income housing problem, lest the nation's limited housing assistance budget be unwittingly rechaneled into other high priority areas similar to those indicated. At the heart of any basic analysis of the economic efficiency of a large-scale community building project is a determination of cash flow, which "identifies the rate at which money will have to be made available for investment in the project and, at a later date when sales provide revenues in excess of expenses, the rate at which money will be available for other uses."[14]

One way of measuring the social value of public expenditures in support of new communities that provide adequate housing, employment, and related opportunities for large numbers of low-income and minority households is to strip the new-towns concept of its social objectives and first inquire into the financial feasibility of privately financed, market-oriented, large-scale community developments, and then to proceed to estimate the public subsidies required to make it financially advantageous for them to pursue variously defined social objectives. If, for example, privately financed, market-oriented new communities can be shown to be feasible investment options and the costs of pursuing low-income housing goals are limited to the subsidies required to build the housing, we might conclude that the new-towns device is a relatively "costless" social solution inasmuch as the subsidized housing must be paid for and constructed somewhere. At the other extreme, if it is ultimately determined that the profit-motivated new-towns developer must be heavily subsidized in order to create a purely market-oriented community and that additional public resources must be committed to pursue low-income housing and related goals, we might conclude that the new-towns concept is a rather expensive device for pursuing limited income housing objectives.

This final section includes no readings that are primarily extrapolations of current policy approaches for the simple reason that the reader has been provided sufficient exposure to the current state of the Federal housing assistance system to be able to form his own conclusions about the efficacy of extending and expanding existing programs. I have likewise refrained from including any number of potential entries that ostensibly contain would-be solutions but are either too sketchy in detail or unclear in their logic to provide the reader a sufficient basis for analysis and refinement. Similarly, it would have been quite simple, as any student of housing would quickly admit, to fill these final pages with a veritable buffet of tempting new ideas and tantalizingly fresh proposals since, nowadays, virtually everyone interested and concerned with housing problems seems to know what's wrong and how to make it right again. I concluded, however, that little could be gained from an assemblage of proposals that were sketchy at best and lacking in any reasonable economic rationale at worst.

Rather, my primary objective in this section is to expose the reader to several significant, but undecided, policy issues, while demonstrating the value of rigorous, applied economic and related analyses. After some consideration, I chose to devote this final section to four issues: alternative futures for the American ghetto; the housing effects of a guaranteed annual income; the effects of existing federal income tax laws and proposed alterations on investment in housing; and the dynamics of the inner-city market.

Even though, as Downs suggests, "Americans typically do not attempt to solve social problems by means of behavior patterns that could reasonably be considered strategies . . . strategic thinking about social problems can play a vital role in stimulating social change. . . ." While not purely an economic appraisal of alternative futures, Downs's paper posits five futures for the American ghetto, each of which possesses different racial, spatial, and resource mixes. It is within the broad policy parameters set down in the paper that the remaining selections might be read and evaluated.

As Grigsby indicates in his introduction, "the increasing support for some form of guaranteed annual income for all Americans requires that those who are concerned with housing problems enlarge their frame of reference to consider the effects of such a policy on the housing market generally, on the low income sector of the market in particular, and on the continuing need for existing housing subsidy programs." His exploratory work on the housing effects of the GAI is quite significant, not only because of the conclusions he reaches but because of the manner in which he carries out his analyses. By virtue of disaggregating potential beneficiaries of a politically realistic, prototypical guaranteed income plan, identifying eleven potential market impacts of the GAI, and examining separately the *income effects* of the guarantee from the potential *income stabilizing effects*, he concludes that a guaranteed annual income would have "only a slight impact on the housing market in the short run and that over a longer period of time the effects would also be moderate unless the guarantee were accompanied by other programs." Significantly too, his analyses indicate related policy alternatives that ought be investigated to deal with market problems with which the GAI could not.

Whereas the Grisby selection tends to evaluate particular policy consequences *ex ante,* Slitor's paper on the federal income tax is more an evaluation of the housing effects of *existing* policy, combined with some analyses of several proposals for tax reform. Even though he presents a thorough evaluation of the potential benefits of various tax routes to increasing investment in housing—such as tax credits, limiting total depreciation, or accelerating depreciation write-offs—my reasons for including his paper in this volume are primarily based upon his thorough and concise presentation of the basic effects of income taxes on investment decisions, in general. From my limited observations, I would judge that all too few planners are aware of the tax dimensions of investment and management decisions and proceed in their work as if the tax was neutral with respect to those decisions. It is hoped that Slitor's "short course" sheds some much needed light on this important area.

The volume closes with Sternlieb's paper which, rather than posing a solution to the housing problem, discusses the "strategy of inertia"—the unfortunate results of the conflict between social priorities and market facts. While Sternlieb's setting is New York City, the context of which he speaks is the inner-city market of the seventies, with the glaring contradictions of the luxury "gold coasts," the "zones of abandonment," and "burgher lands," neighborhoods of vastly differing environments in which live the very wealthy, the very poor, and the very comfortable.

The Dynamics of Decay

Of particular interest in this volume are the "zones of abandonment"—large sections of the inner city in which there exists

A situation of dynamic degeneration . . . the peculiar anomaly of high vacancy rates making for even higher vacancy rates in municipalities where the overall housing situation for the poor is one of extreme shortage. The owner response to this phenomenon indicates that the market mechanism has broken down.[15]

Today, there continue to exist tight housing markets in inner cities, as indicated earlier, but the characteristics of such markets are not the same as they were several years ago.

Additional characteristics of today's declining market areas might be as follows:

1. Steadily increasing rates of tax delinquencies, board-ups, and outright abandonments.
2. Gross rents multipliers of existing multifamily dwellings extremely low—in some cases between 1 and 2.0.
3. Disproportionate tax assessments of marginal quality units with respect to their earning capacities.
4. Lack of private participation in most existing subsidy programs and an absence of private equity capital.
5. A general lack of mortgage capital for the purchase of existing one- to four-family buildings and, consequently, a general availability of physically sound structures at prices as low as $2,000, but more commonly in the $3,000 to $6,000 range.
6. General inactivity among professional investors or traders, including a hesitancy to increase personal holdings, a low level of turnover, or both.
7. An increasing tendency for traders to become large-scale landlords through a lack of market for their inventory.
8. An acceptance on the part of large-scale holders of marginal housing to accept paper losses on existing holdings because current cash returns as related to current market value are greater than those available through alternative investment outlets.
9. Increasing difficulty in securing fire and liability insurance on inner-city rental housing.
10. Private owners of one- and two-family homes wishing to sell being forced to sell to professional investors who are able to secure such housing at low prices by paying cash for the purchases; thus, the distribution between owners and renters in many sections of inner cities increasing in favor of the latter.
11. In structures in which annual cash flows are as low as three or four hundred dollars, any large, unanticipated expenditure for repair completely wiping out the profit potential of the affected unit(s) for a period of years.
12. Monthly rentals of many

low-income families being higher than monthly costs that would be required to service reasonable mortgages, if they were available.

13. In the absence of any opportunities for the poor to "purchase" existing inexpensive structures, means of "financing and transferring" houses to the poor devised by investors and local lenders that increase housing costs to the consumer.

14. Continuing neighborhood and environmental deterioration, including low levels of municipal services such as trash collection, street lighting, recreation, etc.

"Between 1965 and 1968 the buildings abandoned or boarded up in New York City alone could have housed the population of a good sized American city like Jersey City—275,000 persons."[16] Such profound changes in market conditions in New York and other cities such as Philadelphia, Detroit, and Boston not only indicate that efforts to build anew cannot possibly keep apace of abandonments and demolitions but also illustrate the fact that the nature of the rights and privileges typically associated with the institution of real property are likewise undergoing major changes in the inner city. At no previous point in our history as a nation has the ownership of real property proved to be such a liability that extramarket and in some cases extralegal means have been devised to rid oneself of ownership of such would-be assets.

Somewhat paradoxically, the heightened demands for neighborhood control of the inner-city housing stock, which one might think absentee owners would gladly agree to under the circumstances, cannot be seriously entertained without the creation of dramatically new legal and financial mechanisms. In the absence of such program packages, hostility between landlord and tenant increases, the use of such political-economic weapons as rent strikes becomes more frequent, housing quality continues to decline, and the city remains powerless to intercede.

Thus, the policy issue of who is to own, manage, and maintain the existing stock of housing in the inner city becomes at least as important as those focusing on how the housing stock is to be expanded and the standards to which we will adhere. Here, however, the field is more wide open since the issue has not been given much creative thought at any level of government. In fact, the Federal Government's failure, heretofore, to consider the breakdown of the market mechanism in the inner city as a major policy issue is implicit in a relatively unnoticed section of the Housing Act of 1968. Section 509 of the Act, which among other things defines eligibility criteria for federal loans and grants to homeowners and tenants under a rehabilitation or concentrated code enforcement program states "... no loan with respect to residential property shall be made under this subsection, to any person whose annual income ... exceeds the limits prescribed for occupants of projects financed with below-market-interest-rate mortgages insured under Section 221(d) (3) of the National Housing Act."[17]

The irony of such a provision is simply that the income position of the private *investor* ought to be one of the least important determinants of the economic feasibility of rehabilitating a dwelling unit or multifamily structure that is being held for investment purposes. The factors that are of direct relevance are those affecting the current state and value of the particular unit under consideration, estimates of current and potential demand for the housing at various levels of quality, cost estimates to rehabilitate the housing to various quality states and any other factors that might affect the economic variables in the investment calculus, such as available financial aids on both the demand and supply sides. He could, under a comprehensive code enforcement or rehabilitation program, minimize his losses, which might result in his electing to meet code standards, rehabilitate to a higher standard, or to withdraw his property from the market.

By restricting financial incentives to resident-owners and low-income investors, the legislation implicitly assumes that investors are nothing more than former owner-residents who view their properties as consumption rather than as capital goods. It assumes that they will choose to upgrade their holdings if only somehow they can scrape up the necessary funds. Nothing could be farther from the truth.

A Break with Existing Policy: The Housing Delivery System

Perhaps, we might summarize this broad program area that is not included in any of the selections in this book as one which is intended to bridge the incremental approach to low-income housing policy discussed earlier, with those which represent clear breaks with existing policy. This program area calls for either the creation of an entirely new administrative institution or new administrative arrangements between existing institutions in the public and private sectors for the multiple purposes of

1. Facilitating the sound maintenance of the existing stock of marginal-quality units in the inner city.

2. Developing a viable mechanism to encourage the exchange of ownership of large quantities of inner-city housing as between investor and individual consumer, investor and investor, investor and city, and investor and neighborhood corporation.

3. Stabilizing particular sections of the inner-city market through the selective purchase, rehabilitation, and resale of residential properties.

4. Performing short-run holding operations in other sections of the inner-city market, which are destined by design for substantial long-run change in land-use pattern.

One might refer to such conglomerations of market supporting activities as efforts to develop comprehensive housing delivery systems. Specifically, what is implied in the term "delivery system" is the creation of a quasi-public organizational entity that has the capacity to rehabilitate a substantial volume of inner-city housing over a sustained period of time, to facilitate sound management through a capacity to assist in maintenance and servicing functions and, in general, to affect positively the inner-city market. While yet untested on any significant scale, the City of Philadelphia, like a few others, developed used-house programs, the purposes of which are to increase the rate of production of public housing, reduce unit costs, integrate public housing into the fabric of the city's lower- and moderate-income neighborhoods, and to stabilize declining market areas. In Philadelphia, the local authority, with the consent of the City, entered into a series of agreements with the Federal Government, permitting it to exercise greater control over the production process:[18]

Scattered site public housing development was a substantial departure from the previously employed single site principle. Prior to the formulation of the Used House Program, the Federal Government—through the Public Housing Administration (now the Housing Assistance Administration of HUD)—had to formally approve each site proposed by a local housing authority for public housing use. In Philadelphia the City Planning Commission also was required to approve each site. The Used House Program permitted the acquisition of undesignated scattered sites, located within broadly established geographical boundaries, approved in advance by the Federal Government, the City Planning Commission, and the City Council.

The Used House Program permitted Philadelphia housing officials the programming flexibility essential to large-scale housing production. The local autonomy embodied in the principle of funding undesignated sites was gradually extended to give the Philadelphia Housing Authority complete control over actual site selection and the administration of the construction and price standards governing the program. For instance, from the inception of the program the Authority alone has been responsible for contract compliance and construction inspection. While initially HUD was represented on a committee responsible for reviewing site offers and rehabilitation proposals, the standardization of site selection procedures, acquisition prices, construction specifications and rehabilitation prices . . . has removed the need for this type of time-consuming, continuous administrative review. Operational decisions are now made at an operating level. HUD control over the program is exercised through administrative reviews every six months or upon the completion of 500 units. Changes in operating procedures have been made as a part of such reviews, or as a part of the periodic negotiations for increasing the Federal funding allocation for the program.

In addition to changes of relationships within the bureaucracy, the program introduced an effective pattern of private enterprise participation in the accomplishment of housing goals for low-income families. The profit potential of large-scale production for a guaranteed market attracted private developers to undertake the entire responsibility for the physical construction activity of the Used House Program and, initially, the site acquisition responsibility as well. The production relationship was established through negotiating rather than bidding contracts and improved upon by the standardized procedures described later in this chapter. . . .

The Needs and the Powers

In order for the new housing development corporations to fulfill their mandates effectively, they must possess broader powers and be capitalized more substantially than the Philadelphia Used-House Program. Using some preliminary findings from some work in progress in Baltimore to illustrate our point, we might indicate three distinct, but related, issues with which such corporations would have to deal as the primary agent for administering the cities' low-income housing policy.[19] The first concerns the lack of coordination between the activities of the growing number of nonprofit housing corporations, the administration of city housing programs, and the investment activities of the inner-city investment community; the second relates to the so-called black tax that must be paid by low-income consumers in order to purchase their own homes in the inner city; and the third revolves around the need to facilitate not only a large-scale exchange of ownership of inner-city property, but the development of new forms of management and maintenance entities as well.

Nonprofit Housing

As is the case in most large urban centers, the activities of Baltimore's OEO-supported, nonprofit housing corporation (Project HOPE) are conducted outside of the mainstream of the city's low-income housing efforts and without reference to the investment activities of the city's professional inner-city landlords and management firms. Organizations like HOPE are typically understaffed, inexperienced in both the dynamics of the inner-city market and the dollars and cents of rehabilitation for low-income families; they conduct small-scale operations and generally produce rehabilitated units at costs substantially above those the immediate neighborhoods and the market can support.

Juxtaposed against these small-scale, but costly, operations, are those of the professional owner-investors who have collectively demonstrated unmatched skills in modest rehabilitation. As private, profit-motivated investors, they cannot afford, especially in today's market, to produce housing at unit costs exceeding $15,000, but they can be encouraged to increase their expenditures on maintenance and renovation if the investment climate is altered. One way of altering it would be to replace the skepticism investor-owners display toward projects such as HOPE and the hostility the HOPEs display toward investor-owners, with a city-directed effort to coordinate the investment programs of the two to the mutual benefit of both investment entities and the city's low-income community.

By taking a broad view of the market, it becomes clear that HOPE's maximum rehab approach might be best directed at abandoned buildings or other strategically located units that existing investor-owners cannot, for one reason or another, deal with, but which threaten the security of their nearby investments. That is, HOPE's limited, high unit cost operation would exert maximum leverage in the market if it served as an anchor for much more widespread privately initiated and financed modest rehabilitation activity. By rebuilding, at or near new construction standards, units that previously lay vacant and vandalized and discouraged existing investors from keeping up their surrounding units, organizations such as Project HOPE could become vital elements in broad-based efforts to improve the housing circumstances of the poor.

The "Black Tax"

"Due to racial inequalities and injustices in this country and in this city, real estate speculators have for years cheated the white and exploited the black communities. . . . It should be understood that while the white seller is cheated . . . it is the black family which is in the terrible position of having to pay $13,000 for a $7,000 house in a neighborhood which is being drained of money and therefore steadily deteriorating."[20]

In Baltimore, as elsewhere, where traditional lending institutions will not finance the sales of moderately priced housing for low-income families, other means are devised to accomplish this end—typically with the result that the poor pay more. While this description of the charge against the real estate speculator may be summarized as buying cheap and selling at a premium, it is likely that the problem is more complex than that. In fact, according to our investigation of the problem in Baltimore we found that[21]

1. When investors buy units, they generally put a good deal of money into their renovation and rehabilitation.
2. Because investors are in one sense middlemen here, they must pay commissions when they buy the houses as well as when one of their people sells the units. Those two commissions must be reflected in the prices paid for the houses.
3. Also, two sets of closing costs must be included in the sales prices—when the investor buys the units and upon their transfer—since low-income consumers have no liquid assets.
4. Taxes and insurance must be paid while the houses are being renovated, which must be reflected in the sales prices.
5. Finally, since the investor typically finances the sales of the units, until consumers can obtain their own financing, if ever, profits might be spread over 15 to 18 years and must be discounted quite highly; also, while face interest rates might be nominal, at least 15 percent of the base price might be typically charged to cover risks of providing capital.

In general, one might find that the magnitude of these elements of cost lead to typical sales at prices approaching 100 percent mark-ups over base acquisition prices. Our preliminary thinking as to whether there is any exploitation here and, if so, who the perpetrators are, is that the poor are being taken advantage of but not primarily by the investors. It seems more a case of a host of institutions, including the city, lending institutions, and others, all contributing to the mark-up required to make these deals go. Here we must look into the possibilities of socializing particular risks, reducing holding costs while the properties are being rehabilitated, and reducing the risks and attendant costs of long-term financing in this sector of the market.

An Exchange of Ownership

Perhaps if it weren't the case that it is becoming increasingly difficult to earn positive cash flows from inner-city housing, more and more large-scale holders want to get out of the business while the smaller and nonprofessional holders can't cope with the management problems, and the demands for black control of the housing stock in black neighborhoods is on the rise, the need for a broadly based housing development corporation would not be as great as it is.[22] In Baltimore, however, it is becoming increasingly clear that no attack on that city's housing problem can be successful unless it includes some provision for transferring the ownership of large segments of the inner-city inventory, including the establishment of new management and maintenance organizations to service the stock under any revised ownership pattern. As a matter of fact, since any widespread, low-income ownership program must involve existing units, the purchasers, if they are to remain in decent housing, will need to be assured of competent, very low cost maintenance assistance, another indication of the need for a quasi-public maintenance pool. When all of these elements are combined, they spell out massive public intervention in the private market, a step all major cities must contemplate in the not-too-distant future.

Conclusions

Some serious thinking about any one of the responsibilities that were suggested as reasonable charges for the proposed corporations will produce a multitude of questions concerning the practicality of the recommendations and the implications of creating such a free-wheeling organization to which the city is a party. Some will claim that it is not possible for a municipality to exercise the freedom of movement of, and to participate in, the full range of activities so characteristic of individual actors in the private sector. Others will assert that, to a limited extent at least, many cities are currently carrying out activities that are similar to those built into the delivery system idea.

Still others will suggest that something on the order of a rent supplement program, under which private investors would be eligible beneficiaries, would be much simpler to implement and would more satisfactorily deal with the inner-city housing problem.

While these and other criticisms of the schematic recommendations made warrant careful consideration, several comments might be in order concerning the need for more positive intervention in the private market at the local level.

First, it makes eminent sense to conceive of municipal involvement in efforts to encourage the continued maintenance and preservation of the existing stock of privately held housing in the inner city. In fact, most local offices of licensing and inspection and other code-enforcement departments are currently engaged in such activities. The problem with such existing arrangements is simply that these offices are without the power to mount anything more than coercive efforts to deal with the problems of substandard housing. These recommendations merely recognize the economic nature of the problem and attempt to provide the necessary powers to influence effectively the investment climate.

Second, while the powers and responsibilities of the proposed corporations might seem too vast and their flexibility too great for any single agency, many local communities are going to be forced, on an *ad hoc* basis, to perform many of the same activities in the years ahead if something is not done to alter the forces operative in the inner-city housing market. It makes more sense to think ahead about how the city might contribute to stabilizing the market while providing greater opportunities to low-income families than it does to wring one's hands over the problems. As tax delinquencies increase, abandonments rise, and investors continue to desert the inner-city market, it will become all too clear that coercive powers and passive participation upon the part of the city will have to give way to vigorous, active participation; cities must ultimately accept major responsibility for altering market conditions.

Third, as private investors continue to encounter mounting difficulties in preserving their capital intact and in maintaining adequate returns, it seems likely that they will welcome the entry of the city into the private market and join with the public sector in an effort to improve the investment climate. Fourth, with increasing emphasis being placed upon the potential role of indigenous, nonprofit development corporations in revitalizing vast sections of ghetto communities, it is reasonable to expect the city to work closely with such entities, to the ultimate benefit of both. With respect to the city, such a working relationship would provide an opportunity for the public sector to maintain a meaningful role in the amorphous program area of community development, which it seems to be losing in light of continuing cries for black control over black neighborhoods. Moreover, by working closely with neighborhood corporations in the formulation of basic policies with respect to the maintenance of the existing stock, the city could facilitate the transfer of housing units to local ownership and control under clearly defined conditions and widespread community support.

From the community's perspective, working closely with the local corporation would be valuable because it could assemble large numbers of low-cost housing units for ultimate transfer, recruit the necessary technical expertise needed to train potential investors and would be ultimately responsible for coordinating city-wide housing policies for a host of housing programs that have significance for ghetto communities. The realistic alternative to such a strategy is the bulldozer approach of which Sternlieb speaks. But, as he also indicates, "Before you can call in the bulldozer, you have to have a notion of what kind of housing you want to put up—and then you have to reconcile this with budgetary and/or market constraints"; thus evolves the strategy of inertia.

Notes

[1]David Dreyfuss and Joan Hendrickson, *A Guide to Government Activities in New York City's Housing Markets*, Memorandum RM-5673-NYC, The Rand Corporation, Santa Monica; November 1968, p. 2.

[2]"The Subsidy and Housing," Charles Abrams, in *Urban Housing,* edited by Wheaton, Milgram and Meyerson (New York, The Free Press, 1966), p. 365; originally appearing in *Journal of Land and Public Utility Economics*, May 1946.

[3]While, the low-rent public housing program serves only the poor and was initially the subject of much contention vis-a-vis the nature of our free-enterprise economy, it was also viewed in the context of a pump-priming device intended to help bring the nation out of a serious depression, adding to its political acceptability.

[4]See "Housing the Urban Poor: The Economics of Various Strategies," Anthony Downs, *The American Economic Review* (Vol. LIX, No. 4, Part I, September 1969), pp. 646–651.

[5]As of this writing, pending housing legislation includes provisions for eliminating the Workable Program requirement for public housing. The 1968 legislation creating Sections 235 and 236 ownership and rental assistance programs do

not require workable programs as prerequisites for program eligibility.
[6]Downs, *op. cit.*, p. 650.
[7]Frank S. Kristof, "Local Urban Development Policy Under Inflation: A Case Study—New York City," presented at the Annual Meeting of the American Real Estate and Urban Economics Association, New York City, December 1969, p. 1.
[8]*Ibid.*, pp. 1–2.
[9]See *House and Home*, "It's Ready! First Mortgage-Backed Security Bowing In" (Vol. 37, No. 1, January 1970), p. 12.
[10]See, for example, "A New Proposal for Financing the Construction of Urban Housing," A Report Presented to the American Management Association, by Alvin E. Gershen, May 1969. Whether sale of the so-called urban bonds to moderate- and middle-income investors would simply reallocate a share of the existing pool of investment capital away from established lending institutions such as Savings and Loans and thus not have any net effect on new construction, or actually would enlarge the size of the resource pool, must be determined.
[11]"The Housing Corporation," William K. Wittausch, in *Urban Land* (Vol. 28, No. 4, April 1969), Urban Land Institute, Washington, pp. 3–4.
[12]"Trends and Projections of Future of Population Growth in the United States, With Special Data On Large Urban Regions and Major Metropolitan Areas, for the Period 1970–2000," Jerome P. Pickard, U. S. Department of Housing and Urban Development, presented to the Ad Hoc Subcommittee on Urban Growth, Committee on Banking and Currency, U.S. House of Representatives, Washington, D.C., July 22, 1969, p. 25.
[13]*Ibid.*, on the latter, see, for example, "An Urban Strategy," by Bernard Weissbourd and Herbert Channick, *The Center Magazine,* Center for the Study of Democratic Institutions (Vol. I, No. 6, September 1968), p. 5.
[14]"Large-Scale Community Development," Paul F. Wendt, *Journal of Finance* (Vol. XXII, No. 2, May 1967), p. 224.
[15]George Sternlieb, "Bulldozer Renewal," *Journal of Housing* (Vol. 25, No. 4, April 1968), p. 181.
[16]"Cities Losing Revenue, Face Safety, Health Hazards in Vacant Building," Associated Press report in *Durham Morning Herald*, Monday, December 1, 1969, Section B, p. 1.
[17]In pending 1969 housing legislation, this clause is amended so that so-called "over-income" individuals will be eligible for Section 312 loans although the legislation directs that *priority* be given to families within 221-d-3 limits.
[18]Christy P. Emerson and Bernard R. Spector, "The Rehabilitation of Houses for Low Income Families: A Volume Production Achievement in Philadelphia," Working Paper No. 15, Institute for Environmental Studies, University of Pennsylvania, Urban Studies Institute, Morgan State College, February 1969 (Mimeo), pp. 10–12.
[19]University of Pennsylvania—Morgan State College, Evacuation of Baltimore's Anti-Poverty Efforts, under contract with the Office of Economic Opportunity, in Progress.
[20]*Edmondson Village Under Seige,* Sampson Green, Reuben Jones, and John Martinez, published by Activists, Inc., Baltimore, Maryland, September 1969, p. 7.
[21]See, Michael A. Stegman, "Slum Housing: Cash Flow, Maintenance and Management," paper presented before the Conference of the American Real Estate and Urban Economic Association, December 1969.
[22]*Ibid.*, pp. 4–11.

4.1 Alternative Futures for the American Ghetto

Anthony Downs

In the past few years, the so-called "ghetto" areas of large American cities have emerged as one of the major focal points of national and local concern. Yet there have been very few attempts to develop a comprehensive, long-run strategy for dealing with the complex forces that have created our explosive ghetto problems.

Historically, the word "ghetto" meant an area in which a certain identifiable group was compelled to live. The word retains this meaning of geographic constraint but now refers to two different kinds of constraining forces. In its *racial* sense, a ghetto is an area to which members of an ethnic minority, particularly Negroes, are residentially restricted by social, economic, and physical pressures from the rest of society. In this meaning, a ghetto can contain wealthy and middle-income residents as well as poor ones. In its *economic* sense, a ghetto is an area in which poor people are compelled to live because they cannot afford better accommodations. In this meaning, a ghetto contains mainly poor people, regardless of race or color.

Considerable confusion arises from failure to distinguish clearly between these different meanings of the word "ghetto." In the remainder of this analysis, I will use the word in its racial sense unless otherwise noted.[1]

The Population of Ghettos

In March 1966, there were 12.5 million nonwhites living in all U.S. central cities, of whom 12.1 million were Negroes. Since the Negroes were highly segregated residentially, this number serves as a good estimate of the 1966 ghetto population in the racial sense. Approximately 39 percent of these racial ghetto residents had incomes below the "poverty level" (the equivalent of $3,300 per year for a four-person household), based upon data for 1964 (the latest available).[2]

On the other hand, in 1964 the total number of persons with incomes below the "poverty level" in all U.S. central cities was about 10.1 million. Approximately 56 percent of these persons were white, and 44 percent were nonwhite.[3] Since there were about 11.3 million nonwhites altogether in central cities in 1964,

Reprinted by permission of *Daedalus, Journal of the American Academy of Arts and Sciences*, Boston, Massachusetts (Vol. 97, No. 4, Fall 1968), pp. 1331–1378.

the ghetto in its purely economic sense contained about 11 percent fewer people than in its racial sense. Moreover, about 4.4 million persons were doubly ghetto residents in 1964—they were central city citizens who were both poor and nonwhite.[4]

No matter which ghetto definition is used, it is clear that the population of ghettos is a small fraction of total U.S. population—less than 7 percent. Moreover, future growth in the ghetto population will be dwarfed by future growth in the suburbs of metropolitan areas, which are predominantly white. From 1960 through 1980, those suburbs will gain about 40.9 million persons.[5] Thus the *growth* of suburban population in this period will be almost twice as large as the *total size* of all U.S. ghettos by 1980.

Any policies designed to cope with the ghetto must recognize that the concentrations of Negro population in our central cities are growing rapidly. In 1950, there were 6.5 million Negroes in central cities. In 1960, there were 9.7 million. This represents an increase of 49.2 percent, or an average of 320,000 persons per year. In the same decade, the white population of central cities went from 45.5 million to 47.7 million, an increase of 2.2 million, or 4.8 percent. However, in the largest central cities, the white population actually declined while the Negro population rose sharply.[6]

Since 1960, the growth of nonwhite population in central cities has continued unabated. White population growth in all those cities taken together has, however, ceased entirely. In 1966, the total Negro population of all central cities was about 12.1 million. This is a gain of 2.4 million since 1960, or about 400,000 persons per year. Thus the *absolute* rate of growth of ghettos per year has gone up to its highest level in history. In contrast, the white population of central cities in 1965 was 46.4 million, or 1.3 million *less* than in 1960. So for all 224 central cities considered as a whole, all population growth now consists of gains in Negro population.[7]

Moreover, nearly all Negro population growth is now occurring in ghettos, rather than in suburbs or rural areas. From 1960 to 1966, 89 percent of all nonwhite population growth was in central cities, and 11 percent was in suburbs. Nonmetropolitan areas (including the rural South) actually *lost* nonwhite population. This indicates that heavy out-migration from rural areas to cities is still continuing to take place.[8]

All evidence points to the conclusion that future nonwhite

population growth will continue to be concentrated in central cities unless major changes in public policies are made. Not one single significant program of any federal, state, or local government is aimed at altering this tendency or is likely to have the unintended effect of doing so.[9] Moreover, although nonwhite fertility rates have declined since 1957 along with white fertility rates, ghetto growth is likely to remain rapid because of continued in-migration, as well as natural increase.

Recent estimates made by the National Advisory Commission on Civil Disorders indicate that the central city Negro population for the whole U.S. will be about 13.6 million in 1970 and could rise to as high as 20.3 million by 1985. These estimates assume continued nonwhite in-migration at about the same rate as prevailed from 1960 to 1966. But even if net in-migration is reduced to zero, the 1985 central city Negro population would be about 17.3 million.[10]

Within individual cities, rapid expansion of segregated ghetto areas will undoubtedly continue. Our 1967 field surveys in Chicago show that about 2.9 city blocks *per week* are shifting from predominantly white to nonwhite occupancy, mainly on the edge of already nonwhite areas. This is somewhat lower than the 3.5 blocks-per-week average from 1960 to 1966, but above the average of 2.6 from 1950 to 1960.[11] If such "peripheral spread" of central-city ghettos continues at nearly the same rate—and there is no present reason to believe it will not—then a number of major central cities will become over 50 percent Negro in total population by 1985. These cities include Chicago, Philadelphia, St. Louis, Detroit, Cleveland, Oakland, Baltimore, New Orleans, Richmond, and Jacksonville. Washington, D.C., Newark, and Gary are already over 50 percent Negro. The proportion of nonwhites in the public school systems in most of these cities now exceeds 50 percent. It will probably be approaching 90 percent by 1985—unless major changes in school programs and districting are adopted before then.[12]

This future growth has critical implications for a great many policy objectives connected with ghettos. For example, it has been suggested that school district boundaries within central cities should be manipulated so as to counteract *de facto* segregation by creating districts in which many Negroes and many whites will jointly reside. This solution is practical over the long run only when there is reasonable stability in the total size of these two groups. But when one group is rapidly expanding in a city where there is no vacant land to build additional housing, then the other group must contract. The only alternative is sharp rises in density which are not occurring. Therefore, as the Negro population expands in such cities, the white population inevitably falls. So possibilities for ending *de facto* segregation in this manner inexorably shrink as time passes. For this and other reasons, no policy toward ghettos can afford to ignore this rapid expansion of the Negro population.

The Complexity of the Ghetto Population and Ghetto Problems

To be accurate, every analysis of ghettos and their problems must avoid two tempting oversimplifications. The first is conceiving of the ghetto population as a single homogeneous group, all of whose members have similar characteristics, attitudes, and desires. Thus, because many ghetto residents are unemployed or "underemployed" in low-paying, transient jobs, it is easy—but false—to think of all ghetto households as plagued by unemployment. Similarly, because some ghetto residents have carried out riots and looting, whites frequently talk as though *all* ghetto dwellers hate whites, are prone to violence, or are likely to behave irresponsibly. Yet all careful studies of recent riots show that only a small minority of ghetto residents participated in any way, a majority disapprove of such activity, and most would like to have more contact with whites and more integration.[13]

In reality, each racial ghetto contains a tremendous variety of persons who exhibit widely differing attitudes toward almost every question. Many are very poor, but just as many are not. Many have radical views—especially young people; many others are quite conservative—especially the older people. Many are "on welfare," but many more are steadily employed.

This diversity means that public policy concerning any given ghetto problem cannot be successful if it is aimed at or based upon the attitudes and desires of only one group of persons affected by that problem. For example, take unemployment. Programs providing job training for young people could, if expanded enough, affect a large proportion of ghetto dwellers. But the inability of many adult ghetto men to obtain and keep steady, well-paying jobs is also a critical ghetto problem.[14] Also, many women with children cannot work because no adequate day-care facilities are available. Thus, public policy concerning every ghetto problem must have many complex facets in order to work well.

A second widely prevalent oversimplification of ghetto problems is concentration of remedial action upon a single substandard condition. For instance, improving the deplorable housing conditions in many slums would not in itself eliminate most of the dehumanizing forces which operate there. In fact, no single category of programs can possibly be adequate to cope with the tangled problems that exist in ghettos. Any effective ghetto improvement strategy must concern itself with at least jobs and employment, education, housing, health, personal safety, crime prevention, and income maintenance for dependent persons. A number of other programs could be added, but I believe these are the most critical.[15]

The Location of New Jobs

Most new employment opportunities are being created in suburban portions of our metropolitan areas, not anywhere near central-city ghettos.[16] Furthermore, this trend is likely to continue indefinitely into the future. It is true that downtown office-space concentrations in a few large cities have created additional jobs near ghettos. But the out-flow of manufacturing and retailing jobs has normally offset this addition significantly—and in many cases has caused a net loss of jobs in central cities.

If we are going to provide jobs for the rapidly expanding ghetto population, particularly jobs that do not call for high levels of skills, we must somehow bring these potential workers closer to the locations of new employment opportunities. This can be done in three ways: by moving job locations so new jobs are created in the ghetto, by moving ghetto residents so they live nearer the new jobs, or by creating better transportation between the ghetto and the locations of new jobs. The first alternative—creating new jobs in the ghetto—will not occur in the future under normal free-market conditions, in my opinion.

That nearly all *new* job opportunities will be located in suburbs does not mean that central cities cannot provide *any* employment to their Negro residents. There are still millions of jobs located in central cities. Just the turnover in workers regarding those jobs will open up a great many potential positions for Negro central-city residents in the future—if employers and other workers cease racial discrimination in their hiring and promotion practices. Nevertheless, as the total number of Negro central-city job-seekers steadily rises, the need to link them with emerging sources of new employment in the suburbs will become more and more urgent as a means of reducing unemployment in Negro neighborhoods.

Recently, a number of proposals have been advanced to create public subsidies or guaranteed profits encouraging free enterprise to locate new jobs in ghettos.[17] It is possible that they might work to some extent if the promised profits are high enough to offset the risks and disadvantages involved. Any ghetto improvement strategy must, however, face the problem of linking up persons who need employment with those firms which can provide it or those public agencies assigned to create it.

The Future "Cost Squeeze" on Local Governments

Traditionally, individual productivity has risen faster in the manufacturing, mining, construction, and agricultural sectors of our economy than in sectors where personal services are dominant—such as finance, insurance, and real estate; retailing; services; and government. The ability to employ larger amounts of capital per worker, coupled with technological change, has caused much larger increases in hourly output-per-worker in the former sectors.

All sectors compete with one another for talent and personnel, and all use many of the same products as basic inputs. This means that wages and salaries in the service-dominated sectors must generally keep up with those in the capital-dominated sectors. This tends to place a "squeeze" on the cost of those activities for which individual productivity is hard to increase.

A recent analysis of the performing arts by economists William Baumol and William Bowen highlighted this type of "cost squeeze" as the major reason why it is so difficult to sustain theaters, opera, symphonies, and ballet companies on a self-supporting basis.[18] A pianist cannot perform Chopin's Minute Waltz in 30 seconds, or spend half as much time learning to play it, to improve efficiency. Yet his salary and the salaries of all the electricians, accompanists, administrators, and others needed for the performing arts are constantly raised to keep their living standards comparable with those of people in the sectors where wage gains can be offset by productivity increases.

Baumol has argued that a similar cost squeeze is one of the reasons why state and local expenditures have risen so fast in the postwar period. They increased 257 percent from 1950 to 1966, as compared to 159 percent for gross national product and 206 percent for federal expenditures.[19] Moreover, Baumol believes that this pressure to increase service-oriented wages and salaries faster then real output-per-man-hour in the service-oriented sectors will generate an even bigger "explosion" of local and state government costs in the future. For one thing, a higher fraction of society is now and will be employed in public activities than ever before. So there is a steady increase in the proportion of persons whose compensation tends to rise faster than their real output. This reflects both rapid automation in nonservice-oriented sectors and an increasing shift of consumer demand toward such services as education, entertainment, and government activities of all types.

The resulting upward pressure on local and state government costs—and tax needs—will undoubtedly be offset to some extent by two forces. The first is greater automation of services themselves through use of computers, closed-circuit TV, duplicating machines, and other devices. The second is the partial substitution of semiskilled and low-skilled assistants for highly skilled professionals. For example, teachers' aids could relieve professional teachers of immense amounts of administration and paperwork, thereby freeing the latter for more effective use of their time.

Nevertheless, the huge growth of suburban population will almost certainly force a continuance of the trend toward rising local and state taxes that has now gone on for twenty years. Similar upward pressure on revenue needs will be felt even more strongly by central-city governments. They will contain ever-higher proportions of low-income residents who need more services per capita than wealthier suburbanites.

This future cost squeeze is important to our analysis because of its impact upon the willingness of suburban taxpayers to help finance any large-scale programs aimed at improving ghetto conditions. Such programs would almost certainly require significant income redistributions from the relatively wealthy suburban population to the relatively poor central-city population. Yet suburbanites will be experiencing steadily rising local and state tax burdens to pay for the services they need themselves.

The "Law of Dominance"

The achievement of stable racial integration of both whites and nonwhites in housing or public schools is a rare phenomenon in large American cities. Contrary to the views of many, this is *not* because whites are unwilling to share schools or residential neighborhoods with nonwhites. A vast majority of whites of all income groups would be willing to send their children to integrated schools or live in integrated neighborhoods, *as long as they were sure that the white group concerned would remain in the majority* in those facilities or areas.

The residential and educational objectives of these whites are not dependent upon their maintaining any kind of "ethnic purity" in their neighborhoods or schools. Rather, those objectives depend upon their maintaining a certain degree of "cultural dominance" therein.[20] That is, these whites—like most other middle-class citizens of any race—want to be sure that the social, cultural, and economic milieu and values of their own group dominate their own residential environment and the educational environment of their children. This desire in turn springs from the typical middle-class belief of all racial groups that everyday life should be primarily a *value-reinforcing* experience for both adults and children, rather than primarily a *value-altering* one. The best way to ensure that this will happen is to isolate partly oneself and one's children in an everyday environment dominated by—but not necessarily exclusively comprised of—other families and children whose social, economic, cultural, and even religious views and attitudes are approximately the same as one's own.

There is no intrinsic reason why race or color should be perceived as a factor relevant to attaining such relative homogeneity. Clearly, race and color have no necessary linkage with the kinds of social, cultural, economic, or religious characteristics and values that can have a true functional impact upon adults and children. Yet I believe a majority of middle-class white Americans still perceive race and color as relevant factors in their assessment of the kind of homogeneity they seek to attain. Moreover, this false perception is reinforced by their lack of everyday experience and contact with Negroes who are, in fact, like them in all important respects. Therefore, in deciding whether a given neighborhood or a given school exhibits the kind of environment in which "their own" traits are and will remain dominant, they consider Negroes as members of "another" group.

It is true that some people want themselves and their children to be immersed in a wide variety of viewpoints, values, and types of people, rather than a relatively homogeneous group.[21] This desire is particularly strong among the intellectuals who dominate the urban planning profession. They are also the strongest supporters of big-city life and the most vitriolic critics of suburbia. Yet I believe their viewpoint—though dominant in recent public discussions of urban problems—is actually shared by only a tiny minority of Americans of any racial group. Almost everyone favors at least some exposure to a wide variety of viewpoints. But experience in our own society and most others shows that the overwhelming majority of middle-class families choose residential locations and schools precisely in order to provide the kind of value-reinforcing experience described. This is why most Jews live in predominantly Jewish neighborhoods, even in suburbs; why Catholic parents continue to support separate school systems; and partly why so few middle-class Negro families have been willing to risk moving to all-white suburbs even where there is almost no threat of any harassment.

However demeaning this phenomenon may be to Negroes, it must be recognized if we are to understand why residential segregation has persisted so strongly in the United States, and what conditions are necessary to create viable racial integration. The expansion of nonwhite residential areas has led to "massive transition" from white to nonwhite occupancy mainly because there has been no mechanism that could assure the whites in any given area that they would remain in the majority after nonwhites once began entering. Normal population turnover causes about 20 percent of the residents of the average U.S. neighborhood to move out every year because of income changes, job transfers, shifts in life-cycle position, or deaths. In order for a neighborhood to retain any given character, the persons who move in to occupy the resulting vacancies must be similar to those who have departed.

But once Negroes begin entering an all-white neighborhood near the ghetto, most other white families become convinced that the area will eventually become all Negro, mainly because this has happened so often before. Hence it is difficult to persuade whites not now living there to move in and occupy vacancies. They are only willing to move into neighborhoods where whites are now the dominant majority and seem likely to remain so. Hence the whites who would otherwise have moved in from elsewhere stop doing so.[22] This means that almost all vacancies are eventually occupied by nonwhites, and the neighborhood inexorably shifts toward a heavy nonwhite majority. Once this happens, the remaining whites also seek to leave, since they do not wish to remain in an area where they have lost their culturally dominant position.

As a result, whites who would be quite satisfied—even delighted—to live in an integrated neighborhood *as members of the majority* are never given the opportunity to do so. Instead, for reasons beyond the control of each individual, they are forced to choose between complete segregation or living in an area heavily dominated by members of what they consider "another group." Given their values, they choose the former.

Many—especially Negroes—may deplore the racially prejudiced desire of most white middle-class citizens to live in neighborhoods and use schools where other white middle-class households are dominant. Nevertheless, this desire seems to be firmly entrenched among most whites at present. Hence public policy cannot ignore this desire if it hopes to be effective. Moreover, this attitude does not preclude the development of racial integration, as long as whites are in the majority and believe they will remain so. The problem is convincing them that their majority status will persist in mixed areas in the face of past experience to the contrary. Even more difficult, the people who must be persuaded are not those now living in a mixed area, but those who must keep moving in from elsewhere to maintain racial balance as vacancies occur through normal population turnover.

Clearly, the dynamic processes related to this "Law of Dominance" are critical to any strategy concerning the future of American ghettos. They are especially relevant to strategies which seek to achieve stable residential or educational integration of whites and nonwhites, instead of the "massive transition" and "massive segregation" which have dominated the spatial patterns of nonwhite population growth in the past twenty years. Such stable integration will occur in most areas only if there is some way to guarantee the white majority that it will remain the "dominant" majority. This implies some form of "quotas" concerning the proportion of nonwhites in the facility or area concerned—even legally supported "quotas."

Unless some such "balancing devices" are *explicitly* used and reinforced by public policies and laws to establish their credibility, whites will continue to withdraw from—or, more crucial, fail to keep entering—any facility or area into which significant numbers of nonwhites are entering. This means a continuation of *de facto* segregation and a reinforcement of the white belief that any nonwhite entry inevitably leads to "massive transition." Even more importantly, it means continued failure to eliminate white perception of race as a critical factor by encouraging whites and nonwhites to live together in conditions of stability. Thus, in my opinion, the only way to destroy the racial prejudice at the root of the "Law of Cultural Dominance" is to shape current public policy in recognition of that "Law" so as to encourage widespread experience that will undermine it.[23]

The Concept of Social Strategy

Americans typically do not attempt to solve social problems by means of behavior patterns that could reasonably be considered "strategies." The concept of strategy implies development of a single comprehensive, long-range plan to cope with some significant social problem. But U.S. decision-making concerning domestic issues is too fragmented and diffused to permit the formulation of any such long-range plan regarding a given problem. Instead, we approach most social problems through a process which has been aptly labeled "disjointed incrementalism."[24] Each decision-maker or actor makes whatever choices seem to him to be most appropriate at that moment, in light of his own interests and his own view of the public welfare. For two reasons, he pays little attention to most of the consequences of his action upon others—especially the long-run consequences. First, no one has the detailed knowledge and foresight necessary to comprehend all those consequences. Second, no one has the time or the energy to negotiate in advance with all others likely to be affected by his actions. So instead he acts "blindly" and waits for those who are hurt to complain or those who are benefited to applaud.

A process of mutual adjustment ensues. Those who are unduly harmed by each decision supposedly recoup their losses by exercising whatever economic, moral, or political powers are available to them. Those who benefit use their powers to encourage more of the same. Presiding over this melee is a set of mainly "reactive" governments and other public agencies. They keep altering the "rules of the game" and their own programs and behavior so as to correct any grievous imbalances that appear.

There is no guarantee that the checks and balances built into this uncoordinated process will effectively counteract every destructive condition or trend that emerges from it. It is certainly possible that each individual will be motivated by the incentives facing him to take actions that, when combined with those taken by others acting in a similar individualistic fashion, will lead to collective disaster.

So far in history, the system has been remarkably effective at avoiding such outcomes. Part of this success undoubtedly results from society's ability to generate in most of its citizens a single set of basic values and even broad policy objectives that exert a cohesive influence on their supposedly individualistic decisions. But another important ingredient in the system's success is the ability of enough significant actors in it to perceive potentially threatening trends in time to formulate and carry out ameliorating policies.

This means they must accurately forecast any potentially dire outcome of current trends. They must also visualize alternative outcomes that would be preferable and are within the capabilities of society. Finally, they must devise policies and programs that will shift individual incentives so one of those alternatives will occur. In some cases, the ongoing trends that threaten society are strongly entrenched in its institutional structure. If so, alternatives that avoid the pending threats may not be attainable without fundamental changes in institutions. Those changes in turn may be possible only if a preponderance of powerful people in society share at least a broad concept of the need for a change and the kinds of objectives motivating it. This concept closely resembles a social strategy. It visualizes a certain desired outcome, implies a wide range of policies by various actors necessary to attain that outcome, and serves as a "hidden coordinator" of seemingly individualistic behavior.

This reasoning implies two conclusions crucial to this analysis. First, strategic thinking about social problems can play a vital role in stimulating social change even where decision-making is dominated by disjointed incrementalism. Second, the alternative outcomes conceived in such thinking can usefully include some which could not be achieved without major changes in existing institutions or values. For example, some of the strategies discussed herein require a highly coordinated set of policy decisions. Such coordination is unlikely to occur in the presently fragmentalized governmental structures of our metropolitan areas unless major changes in the incentives facing these governments are created.

I will therefore formulate several alternative strategies for coping with the problems posed by future ghetto growth, even though carrying out some of them would require a far more consciously coordinated development of social change than has been typical of America in the past.

Formulation of Major Alternative Strategies

Because of the immense complexity of our society, an infinite number of alternative future strategies regarding ghettos could conceivably be designed. But for purposes of practical consideration, this number must be narrowed drastically to a few that highlight the major choices facing us. Selecting these few is inescapably arbitrary—there is no "scientific" way to do it.

I believe, however, that the narrowing of alternative ghetto futures can best be accomplished by focusing upon the major choices relating to the following three questions:

To what extent should future nonwhite population growth be concentrated within the central cities, as it has been in the past twenty years?

To what extent should our whites and nonwhite populations be residentially segregated from each other in the future?

To what extent should society redistribute income to relatively depressed urban areas or population groups in society in a process of "enrichment"?

Each of these questions can be answered with any one of a whole spectrum of responses from one extreme to the other. But for purposes of analysis, I believe we can usefully narrow these answers down to just two points on the spectrum for each question. This allows us to reduce the alternatives to

Degree-of-concentration alternatives:

1. Continue to concentrate nonwhite population growth in central cities or perhaps in a few older suburbs next to central cities. *(Concentration)*

2. Disperse nonwhite population growth widely throughout all parts of metropolitan areas. *(Dispersal)*

Degree-of-segregation alternatives:

1. Continue to cluster whites and nonwhites in residentially segregated neighborhoods (regardless of where they are within the metropolitan area). *(Segregation)*

2. Scatter the nonwhite population, or at least a significant fraction of it, "randomly" among white residential areas to achieve at least partial residential integration. *(Integration)*

Degree-of-enrichment alternatives:

1. Continue to provide relatively low-level welfare, educational, housing, job-training, and other support to the most deprived groups in the population (both those who are incapable of working, such as the vast majority of public-aid recipients, and those who might possibly work but are unemployed because of lack of skills, discrimination, lack of desire, or any other reason). *(Nonenrichment)*

2. Greatly raise the level of support to welfare, educational, housing, job-training, and other programs for the most deprived groups, largely through federally aided programs. *(Enrichment)*

Even narrowing the alternatives in this fashion leaves a logical possibility of eight different combinations. A number of these can, however, be ruled out as internally inconsistent in practice. For example, I believe it is extremely unlikely that any strategy of dispersing the nonwhite population throughout metropolitan areas could be accomplished without provision of substantially greater incentives to both nonwhites (to get them to move) and whites (to increase their willingness to accept large numbers of nonwhite immigrants without strong resistance). Thus no combination of both dispersal and nonenrichment need be considered.

Similarly, in the very long run, concentration of future nonwhite population growth within central cities is probably inconsistent with integration. Many of those cities will become so preponderantly nonwhite that integration within their borders will be impossible. Admittedly, it may take two or more decades for this to occur in some central cities, and it might never occur in others. Nevertheless, some types of integration (such as in the public schools) will become impossible long before that if a concentration policy is followed. For these reasons, I will consider only one special combination containing both concentration and integration. This consists of continued concentration, but a build-up of a gradually expanding inner-city core of fully integrated housing and public facilities created through massive urban renewal. For reasons to be explained, this strategy would require a significant enrichment program too.

This whole process of elimination leaves five basic alternative strategies relevant to future development of ghettos. For convenience, each has been assigned a short name to be used throughout the remainder of this article. These strategies can be summarized as follows:

1. *Present policies:* Concentration—segregation—nonenrichment.

2. *Enrichment only:* Concentration—segregation—enrichment.
3. *Integrated core:* Concentration—integration (in the center only)—enrichment.
4. *Segregated dispersal:* Dispersal—segregation—enrichment.
5. *Integrated dispersal:* Dispersal—integration—enrichment.

Before these strategies are examined in detail, two things about them should be emphasized.

First, they apply to individual metropolitan areas. Therefore, it would be at least theoretically possible to adopt different strategies toward the ghetto in different metropolitan areas. There are, in fact, some convincing reasons why this would be an excellent idea.

Second, these strategies are formed from relatively extreme points on the relevant ranges of possibilities. Hence they could actually be adopted in various mixtures, rather than in the "pure" forms set forth here. This further strengthens the case for using a variety of approaches across the country. For purposes of analysis, however, it is fruitful to examine each of these strategies initially as though it were to be the sole instrument for coping with ghetto problems in all metropolitan areas.

The Present-Policies Strategy

In order to carry out this strategy, we need merely do nothing more than we do now. Even existing federal programs aimed at aiding cities—such as the Model Cities Program—will continue or accelerate concentration, segregation, and nonenrichment, unless those programs are colossally expanded.

I do not wish to imply that present federal and local efforts in the antipoverty program, the public housing program, the urban renewal program, health programs, educational programs, and many others are not of significant benefit to residents of ghettos. They are. Nevertheless, as both recent investigations and recent violence have emphasized, existing programs have succeeded neither in stemming the various adverse trends operating in ghetto areas nor in substantially eliminating the deplorable conditions there. Therefore, the strategy of continuing our present policies and our present level of effort is essentially not going to alter current conditions in ghettos.

This may make it seem silly to label continuation of present policies as a specific antighetto strategy. Yet failure to adopt effective policies is still a strategy. It may not be a successful one, but it nevertheless is an expression of society's current commitment and attitude toward the ghetto.

Thus, if we maintain our current programs and policies, segregated areas of residence in our central cities will continue to expand rapidly and to suffer from all the problems inherent in both racial and economic ghettos.

The Enrichment-Only Strategy

The second fundamental ghetto-future strategy I call "enrichment only." This approach is aimed at dramatically improving the quality of life within the confines of present ghetto areas and those nearby areas into which ghettos will expand in the future if concentration continues. I presume that any such policy would apply to the poverty meaning of ghetto more than the racial one—that is, any enrichment strategy would aim at upgrading the lowest-income and most disadvantaged citizens of our central cities, regardless of race. Nevertheless, a sizable proportion of such persons are nonwhites. Moreover, programs aimed at reducing racial discrimination in employment and in the quality of public services would form an important part of any strategy aimed at upgrading the most deprived groups. So the enrichment-only strategy would still concentrate upon the same areas as if it were to follow a racial policy.

The basic idea underlying the enrichment-only strategy (and part of every other strategy involving enrichment) is to develop federally financed programs that would greatly improve the education, housing, incomes, employment and job-training, and social services received by ghetto residents. This would involve vastly expanding the scale of present programs, changing the nature of many of them because they are now ineffective or would be if operated at a much larger scale, and creating incentives for a much greater participation of private capital in ghetto activities. Such incentives could include tax credits for investments made in designated ghetto areas, wage subsidies (connected with on-the-job training but lasting longer than such training so as to induce employers to hire unskilled ghetto residents), rent or ownership supplements for poor families, enabling them to rent or buy housing created by private capital, and others.[25]

It is important to realize that the enrichment-only strategy would end neither racial segregation nor the concentration of nonwhites in central cities (and some older adjoining suburbs). It would help many Negroes attain middle-class status and thus make it easier for them to leave the ghetto if they wanted to. Undoubtedly many would. But, by making life in central-city ghettos more attractive without creating any strong pressures for integration or dispersal of the nonwhite population, such a policy would increase the in-migration of nonwhites into central cities. This would speed up the expansion of racially segregated areas in central cities, thereby accelerating the process of "massive transition" of whole neighborhoods from white to nonwhite occupancy.

The Integrated-Core Strategy

This strategy is similar to the enrichment-only strategy because both would attempt to upgrade the quality of life in central-city ghettos through massive federally assisted programs. The integrated-core strategy would also seek, however, to eliminate racial segregation in an ever-expanding core of the city by creating a socially, economically, and racially integrated community there. This integrated core would be built up through large-scale urban renewal programs, with the land reuses including scattered-site public housing, middle-income housing suitable for families with children, and high-quality public services—especially schools.

All of these reuses would be based upon "managed integration" —that is, deliberate achievement of a racial balance containing a majority of whites but a significant minority of Negroes. Thus, the integrated-core strategy could be carried out only if deliberate racial discrimination aimed at avoiding *de facto* segregation becomes recognized by the Supreme Court as a legitimate tactic for public agencies. In fact, such recognition will probably be a necessity for any strategy involving a significant degree of integration in public schools, public housing, or even private residential areas. This conclusion was recently recognized by the Chicago Board of Education, its staff, and its consultants, who all recommended the use of quotas in schools located in racially changing neighborhoods to promote stable integration.[26]

The integrated-core strategy essentially represents a compromise between an ideal condition and two harsh realities. The ideal condition is development of a fully integrated society in which whites and Negroes live together harmoniously and the race of each individual is not recognized by anyone as a significant factor in any public or private decisions.

The first harsh reality is that the present desire of most whites to dominate their own environment means that integration can only be achieved through deliberate management and through the willingness of some Negroes to share schools and residences as a minority. The second harsh reality is the assumption that it will be impossible to disperse the massive Negro ghettos of major central cities fast enough to prevent many of those cities from eventually becoming predominantly, or even almost exclusively, Negro in population. The development of predominantly Negro central cities, with high proportions of low-income residents, ringed by predominantly white suburbs with much wealthier residents, might lead to a shattering polarization that would split society along both racial and spatial lines.

This strategy seeks to avoid any such polarization by building an integrated core of white and nonwhites in central cities, including many leaders of both races in politics, business, and civic affairs. Negro leadership will properly assume the dominant position in central-city politics in many major cities after Negroes have become a majority of the municipal electorates there. By that time, integration of leadership within those cities will, it is to be hoped, have become a sufficient reality so that leaders of both races can work together in utilizing the central city's great economic assets, rather than fighting one another for control over them.

Thus, the integrated-core strategy postulates that a significant movement toward racial integration is essential to keep American society from "exploding" as a result of a combined racial-spatial confrontation of central cities vs. suburbs in many large metropolitan areas. It also postulates that development of integration in the suburbs through massive dispersal cannot occur fast enough to avoid such a confrontation. Therefore, integration must be developed on an "inside-out" basis, starting in the core of the central city, rather than in the suburbs.

The Concept of Dispersal

The two dispersal strategies concerning the future of ghettos are both based upon a single key assumption: that the problems of ghettos cannot be solved as long as millions of Negroes, particularly those with low incomes and other significant disadvantages, are required or persuaded to live together in segregated ghetto areas within our central cities. These strategies contend that large numbers of Negroes should be given strong incentives to move voluntarily from central cities into suburban areas, including those in which no Negroes presently reside.

To illustrate what "large numbers" really means, let us postulate one version of dispersal which I call the "constant-size ghetto strategy." This strictly hypothetical strategy aims at stopping the growth of existing central-city ghettos by dispersing enough Negroes from central cities to the suburbs (or to peripheral central-city areas) to offset potential future increases in that growth. Taking the period from 1970 through 1975, estimates made by the National Advisory Commission on Civil Disorders show that the nonwhite population of all U.S. central cities taken as a whole would, in the absence of any dispersal strategy, expand from about 13.6 million to about 15.5 million.[27] Thus, if dispersal of nonwhites were to take place at a scale large enough to keep central-city racial ghettos at their 1970 level during the five subsequent years, there would have to be an outmovement of 1.9 million Negroes into the suburbs. This amounts to 380,000 per year.

From 1950 to 1960, the suburban Negro population of all U.S. metropolitan areas grew a total of only 60,000 per year. In that decade, the white population of suburban portions of our metropolitan areas (the so-called "urban fringe") increased by about 1,720,000 persons per year. Thus, 96.6 percent of all suburban population growth consisted of whites. From 1960 to 1966, the Negro population growth in all suburban areas declined sharply to a rate of 33,300 per year. In fact, there was actually inmigration of Negroes from suburbs to central cities. But the white population in all suburbs went up an average of 1,750,000 per year. Thus the proportion of suburban growth made up of whites climbed to 98.1 percent—an even higher fraction than in the decade from 1950 to 1960.[28] Undoubtedly, some of this white population increase was caused by an exodus of whites from central cities in response to the growth therein. If future Negro population growth in central cities were stopped by a large-scale dispersion policy, then white population growth in the suburbs would be definitely smaller than it was from 1950 through 1966. The size of the resulting decline would depend upon the fraction of white exodus from central cities that occurs in response to Negro growth, as opposed to such other factors as rising incomes, the aging central-city housing stock, and shifts in life-cycle position. If whites leave central cities in a one-to-one ratio with the expansion of Negro population therein, then a cessation of Negro ghetto growth would result in a large drop in white suburban growth. In that case, future suburban population increases would consist of about 23 percent Negroes (based on very rough calculations). This contrasts with proportions of less than 5 percent from 1950 through 1960 and less than 3 percent from 1960 through 1966.

Clearly, such dispersal would represent a radical change in existing trends. Not only would it stop the expansion of Negro ghettos in central cities, but it would also inject a significant Negro population into many presently all-white suburban areas. It is true that policies of dispersal would not necessarily have to be at this large a scale. Dispersal aimed not at stopping ghetto growth, but merely at slowing it down, could be carried out at a much lower scale. Yet even this would represent a marked departure from past U.S. practice.

Such a sharp break with the past would be necessary for any significant dispersal of Negroes. Merely providing the *opportunity* for Negroes to move out of ghettos would, at least in the short run, not result in many moving. Even adoption of a vigorously enforced nationwide open-occupancy law applying to *all* residences would not greatly speed up the present snail's-pace rate of dispersion. Experience in those states that have open-occupancy ordinances decisively proves this conclusion.

Hence, positive incentives for dispersion would have to be created in order to speed up the rate at which Negroes voluntarily move from central cities and settle in suburban areas. (Certainly no policy involving *involuntary* movement of either whites or Negroes should ever be considered.) Such incentives could include rent supplements, ownership supplements, special school-support bonus payments linked to the education of children moving out from ghettos, and other devices which essentially attach a subsidy to a person. Then, when the person moves, he and the community into which he goes get credit for that subsidy. This creates incentives both for him to move and for the community to accept him gladly. Both of the strategies involving dispersal would thus represent radical changes in existing practices.

Segregated vs. Integrated Dispersal

One of the fundamental purposes of any dispersal strategy is providing Negro Americans with real freedom of choice concerning housing and school accommodations. The experience of other ethnic groups indicates that Negroes would exercise that choice in suburban areas in a combination of two ways. Some individual Negro households would become scattered "randomly" in largely white residential areas. But other Negro households —probably a larger number—would voluntarily cluster together. This would create primarily Negro neighborhoods, or even primarily Negro suburban communities. Such a combination of both *scattering* and *clustering* would occur even if Negro households had absolutely no fears of hostility or antagonism from white neighbors. It is unrealistic to suppose, however, that *all* prejudice against Negro neighbors can be eliminated from presently all-white suburbs in the immediate future. As a result, even if a dispersal strategy is carried out, there will still be some external pressure against Negro newcomers. This will encourage an even higher proportion of incoming Negro households to cluster together than would do so in the absence of all fears and antagonism. Moreover, public policies to accomplish dispersion might include deliberate creation of some moderate-sized clusters of Negro families, as in scattered-site public housing developments.

Once all-Negro clusters appear in previously all-white suburbs, there is a high probability that they will turn into "ghetto-lets" or "mini-ghettos." The same forces that produced ghettos in central cities are likely to repeat themselves in suburbs, though in a much less pathological form. Those pressures are rapidly expanding Negro population, the "law of cultural dominance" among whites, and at least some restriction of Negro choice in areas far removed from existing all-Negro neighborhoods. Therefore, once a Negro cluster becomes large enough so that Negro children dominate a local elementary school, the typical phenomenon of white withdrawal from the local residential real estate market is likely to occur. This has already taken place regarding Jews and gentiles in many suburban areas. Thus, any dispersal strategy that does not explicitly aim at preventing segregation too will probably create new segregated neighborhoods in the suburbs.

This new form of *de facto* segregation will, however, have far less damaging effects upon Negroes than existing segregation concentrated in central cities. In the first place, if Negro clusters are deliberately created in almost all parts of the metropolitan area at once, whites will be unable to flee to "completely safe" suburbs without accepting impractically long commuting journeys. This will strongly reduce the white propensity to abandon an area after Negroes begin entering it. Moreover, the presence of some Negroes in all parts of suburbia will also make it far easier for individual Negro families to move into all-white neighborhoods on a scattered basis. Thus any dispersal policy that really disperses Negroes in the suburbs will immediately create an enormous improvement in the real freedom of residential choice enjoyed by individual Negro families. This will be true even if most of those families actually choose to remain in Negro clusters.

Second, any dispersal strategy would presumably be accompanied by strongly enforced open-occupancy laws applying to all housing. At present, these laws do not lead to scattering, but they would in the climate of a dispersal strategy. Then Negro willingness to move into all-white areas would rise sharply, and white antagonism toward such move-ins would drop.

Third, *de facto* residential segregation need not lead to segregated suburban schools. In relatively small communities, such as most suburbs, it is easy to bus students to achieve stable racial balance. Thus, the formation of clustered Negro housing would not have to cause the quality-of-education problems that now exist in central-city ghettos. True, if a given suburb became predominantly Negro, its schools might become quite segregated. In that case, school systems in adjoining suburbs might have to merge or at least work out student exchange procedures with the segregated community in order to counteract segregation. This may be difficult to accomplish (though in the climate of a dispersal strategy, it would be at least thinkable). Hence it is possible that some segregated school systems might appear in suburban areas. But Negro families would still have far more opportunities than they do now to move to areas with integrated schools.

A dispersal strategy that did not succeed in initially placing Negro households in almost all parts of the metropolitan area would be more likely to generate ghetto-lets. Hence, if dispersal tactics call for initially concentrating on dispersion only to a few suburbs, it is quite possible that segregated dispersal would result. This implies that integrated dispersal could be attained in only two ways. Either the initial dispersal strategy must place

Negroes in almost all suburban communities, or specific integration-furthering mechanisms—such as school and residential quotas—must be adopted.

The speculative nature of this discussion illustrates that society needs to do much more thinking about what dispersal really means, how it might be achieved, what alternative forms it might take, and what its consequences would be.

In an article of this length, it is impossible to present an adequate analysis of each of the strategies described. Certain factors will, however, have a crucial influence on which strategy actually prevails.

The Possibility of a Spatial-Racial "Confrontation"

Society's existing policies toward the ghetto are, by definition, those called for by the present policies strategy. Yet there are strong reasons to believe that maintenance of these policies in ghettos is not possible. The striking increase in violence in big-city ghettos is probably related to a combination of higher aspirations, reduced sanctions against the use of violence, and continued deplorable slum conditions. If so, persistence of the present-policies strategy may continue to spawn incidents, riots, and perhaps guerrilla warfare. Then existing local police forces might have to be supplemented with paramilitary forces on continuous alert. Thus, the present-policies strategy might lead to further polarization of whites and Negroes and even to the creation of semimartial law in big cities.

Moreover, when Negroes become the dominant political force in many large central cities, they may understandably demand radical changes in present policies. At the same time, major private capital investment in those cities might virtually cease if white-dominated firms and industries decide the risks of involvement there were too great. In light of recent disorders, this seems very likely. Such withdrawal of private capital has already occurred in almost every single ghetto area in the U.S. Even if private investment continues, big cities containing high proportions of low-income Negroes would need substantial income transfers from the federal government to meet the demands of their electorates for improved services and living conditions.

But by that time, Congress will be more heavily influenced by representatives of the suburban electorate. The suburbs will comprise 41 percent of our total population by 1985, as opposed to 33 percent in 1960. Central cities will decline from 31 percent to 27 percent.[29] Under a present-policies strategy, this influential suburban electorate will be over 95 percent white, whereas the central-city population in all metropolitan areas together will be slightly over 60 percent white. The suburban electorate will be much wealthier than the central-city population, which will consist mainly of Negroes and older whites. Yet even the suburbs will be feeling the squeeze of higher local government costs generated by rising service salaries. Hence the federal government may refuse to approve the massive income transfers from suburbs to central cities that the mayors of the latter will desperately need in order to placate their relatively deprived electorates. After all, many big-city mayors are already beseeching the federal government for massive aid—including Republicans like John Lindsay—and their electorates are not yet dominated by low-income Negroes.

Thus the present-policies strategy, if pursued for any long period of time, might lead to a simultaneous political and economic confrontation in many metropolitan areas. Such a "confrontation" would involve mainly Negro, mainly poor, and fiscally bankrupt larger central cities on the one hand, and mainly white, much wealthier, but highly taxed suburbs on the other hand. Some older suburbs will also have become Negro by that time, but the vast majority of suburbs would still be "lily white." A few metropolitan areas may seek to avoid the political aspects of such a confrontation by shifting to some form of metropolitan government designed to prevent Negroes from gaining political control of central cities. Yet such a move will hardly eliminate the basic segregation and relative poverty generating hostility in the urban Negro population. In fact, it might increase that population's sense of frustration and alienation.

In my opinion, there is a serious question whether American society in its present form could survive such a confrontation. If the Negro population felt itself wrongly "penned in" and discriminated against, as seems likely, many of its members might be driven to supporting the kind of irrational rebellion now being preached by a tiny minority. Considering the level of violence we have encountered already, it is hard to believe that the conditions that might emanate from a prolonged present-policies strategy would not generate much more. Yet the Negro community cannot hope to defeat the white community in a pitched battle. It is out-numbered 9 to 1 in population and vastly more than that in resources. Thus any massive resort to violence by Negroes would probably bring even more massive retaliation by whites. This could lead to a kind of urban *apartheid*, with martial law in cities, enforced residence of Negroes in segregated areas, and a drastic reduction in personal freedom for both groups, especially Negroes.

Such an outcome would obviously violate all American traditions of individual liberty and Constitutional law. It would destroy "the American dream" of freedom and equal opportunity for all. Therefore, to many observers, this result is unthinkable. They believe somehow we would "change things" before it occurred. This must mean that either the present-policies strategy would not lead to the kind of confrontation I have described, or we would abandon that strategy before the confrontation occurred.

Can the Present-Policies Strategy Avoid "Confrontation"?
What outcomes from a present-policies strategy might prevent this kind of confrontation? For one thing, if incomes in the Negro community rise rapidly without any additional programs, the Negro population of central cities may enter the middle class at a fast rate. If so, the Negro electorate that comes to dominate many major central cities politically by 1985 under the present policies strategy may consist largely of stable, well-to-do citizens capable of supporting an effective local government.

To test this possibility, we have done some projections of incomes in the nonwhite population on a rough basis through 1985, assuming a present-policies strategy. These indicate that about two-thirds of the nonwhite population at that time will have incomes *above* the existing poverty level—about the same fraction as at present. Since nonwhites will then form a much larger share of total central-city population, however, the percentage of *total* central-city population below the present poverty level might actually *rise* slightly. It is possible that nonwhite incomes might increase faster than in this forecast. Yet it is almost certain that the substitution of a relatively poor nonwhite group for a middle-income white group in central cities under a status quo strategy will counterbalance likely increases in the incomes of nonwhites.

As a result, the electorate that will exist in major cities when Negroes become a majority will probably be just as poor as it is now (in real-income terms). In contrast, the population in surrounding suburbs will be much wealthier than it is now. Thus, even if nonwhite incomes rise rapidly, there is still likely to be a significant "gap" between central-city and suburban income levels at that time—probably larger than at present.

Yet even under *present* conditions, many large central cities are critically short of revenue. Furthermore, in a generally wealthier society, it is highly probable that most central-city electorates will demand higher-than-existing levels of public service. Finally, the general cost of all government services will have risen sharply because of the productivity trends explained earlier. Hence, future central-city governments will have much higher costs but not much greater resources than they do now. So rising incomes among nonwhites will not remove the fiscal pressure on central-city governments that is a key ingredient in the confrontation described here.

Moreover, the population group most responsible for violence and disturbances in central cities appears to consist of young Negro men between fifteen and twenty-four years of age. A high proportion of these people are unemployed because of lack of skills (many are high school dropouts) and lack of elementary training and motivation. This group will undoubtedly grow larger through natural increase and in-migration. Its problems are not likely to be solved under a status quo strategy. Hence, even if the vast majority of nonwhites in central cities have increasing reason to abhor violence and riots, the *absolute size* of this more alienated group in 1975 will be 40 percent larger than in 1966, and even larger by 1985.[30] This implies that at least part of this group might start actions forcing the kind of confrontation I have described.

Most of the other possible developments under a nonenrichment strategy that would avoid any major confrontation involve abandoning concentration of Negroes in central cities. Thus, some observers argue that members of the Negro middle class will increasingly move out to suburban communities as their incomes rise with no further encouragement from public programs. In this way, Negroes would be following the precedent of other ethnic groups. Up to now, there is no evidence that this has started to occur, even though a large Negro middle class already exists. But if such a pattern did evolve, it would amount to dispersal rather than the concentration implicit in the present-policies strategy.

Can Present Policies Be Sustained?

In any event, there appears to be significant probability—which I subjectively judge to be at least 25 percent and perhaps as high as 75 percent—that the present-policies strategy will prove unsustainable. If adopted, it would probably generate major repercussions that would force it to be abandoned. Society would be compelled either to suspend traditional individual rights and adopt martial law in cities or to institute major programs to improve ghetto conditions or to move toward wider dispersal of the Negro population, or some combination of these. Admittedly, there is no certainty that the present-policies strategy will lead to these outcomes. Nevertheless, I believe the probability that it will is high enough to make this strategy essentially self-defeating. Modern life is too dynamic for the status quo to be preserved for long.

Yet the present-policies strategy is the one society has so far chosen. Almost all current public policies tend to further concentration, segregation, and nonenrichment, as mentioned earlier. The few supposedly anticoncentration devices adopted, such as open-occupancy laws, have proved almost totally ineffective. All we have to do to confirm our choice of this strategy is to continue existing policies. In fact, avoiding this strategy will be difficult, because doing so will require major changes in present attitudes as well as in existing resource allocations.

The "Black Power" Case for the Enrichment-Only Strategy

The enrichment-only strategy is consistent with a current ideology that has come to be called the "Black Power" viewpoint. This viewpoint has been criticized by many, and some of its proponents have misused it to incite violence. Yet it is certainly an intellectually respectable and defensible position containing some persuasive elements.

The Black Power argument states that the Negro American population needs to overcome its feelings of powerlessness and lack of self-respect before it can assume its proper role in society. It can do so only by exerting power over the decisions that directly affect its own members. According to this view, a fully integrated society is not really possible until the Negro minority has developed its own internal strength. Therefore, the ideal society in which race itself is not an important factor can only come much later. It could exist only after Negroes had gained power and self-respect by remaining in concentrated areas over which they could assume political and economic control and direction. Hence this view contends that a future in which central cities become primarily Negro and suburbs almost entirely white would be an advantage rather than a disadvantage.

The Black Power view has several notable strongpoints. First, such assumption of local power would be fully consistent with the behavior of previous nationality groups, such as the Irish in New York and Boston. They, too, came up from the bottom of the social and economic ladder, where they had been insulted and discriminated against. And they did it by gaining political and economic control over the areas in which they lived.

Second, it is unquestionably true that one of the two most important factors providing Negroes with all their recent gains in legal rights and actual welfare has been their own forceful presentation of grievances and demands. (The other factor has been high-level prosperity in the economy in general.) Negro-originated marches, demonstrations, protests, and even riots have had immensely more impact in improving their actual power, income, and opportunities than all the "purely voluntary" actions of whites combined—including those of white liberals.

Third, time is on the side of the Black Power argument if current population growth and location trends continue. As pointed out earlier, Negroes are likely to become a majority of the electorate in many large American cities within the next fifteen years, unless radically new policies are adopted. By giving Negroes political control over these cities, this trend would provide them with a powerful bargaining position in dealing with the rest of society—a tool they now sorely lack.

Fourth, the Black Power viewpoint provides many key ideological supports for Negro self-development. It stresses the need for Negroes to become proud of their color and their history, more conscious of their own strengths. It also focuses their attention on the need for organizing themselves economically and politically. Hence it could provide a focal point for arousing and channeling the largely untapped self-development energies of the Negro American population. One of the greatest difficulties in improving ghettos is discovering effective ways in which the lowest-income and most deprived residents can develop their own capabilities by participating more fully in the decisions and activities that affect them. Such "learning by doing" is, in my opinion, a vital part of the process of bringing deprived people into the mainstream of American society. Insofar as Black Power proponents could develop such mechanisms, they would immensely benefit American society.

There are, however, also significant flaws in the Black Power argument. First, Negroes do not in fact have much power in the U.S. Nor is it clear just how they can obtain power solely through their own efforts, particularly in the near future. Black Power advocates constantly talk about "taking what is rightfully theirs" because they are dissatisfied with what "whitey" is willing to turn over to them voluntarily. They also reject the condescension inherent in whites "giving" Negroes anything, including more power. But what bargaining power can Negroes use to compel whites to yield greater control over the economic and political decisions that affect them?

There are two possible answers. First, they could organize themselves so cohesively that they would become a potent political and economic force through highly disciplined but fully legal action. Examples would be block voting and economic boycotts. So far, nearly all efforts at such internal organization have foundered on the solid rocks of apathy, lack of funds, internal dissension, and disbelief that anything could be accomplished.

Second, Negroes could launch direct action—such as demonstrations and marches—that would morally, economically, or physically threaten the white community. This approach has so far proved to be the most successful. But many Negroes believe it has not improved their situation as fast as is necessary. Hence, there is a tendency to shift the form of threat employed to more and more violent action in order to get faster and more profound results. This tendency need only influence a small minority of Negroes in order to cause a significant escalation of violence. Yet such an escalation might result in massive retaliation by the white community that would worsen the Negroes' position in nearly every way. What is needed is enough of a threat to cause the white community to start changing its own attitudes and allocation of resources in ways far more favorable to Negroes, but not so much of a threat as to cause withdrawal of all white cooperation and sympathy.

This conclusion points up the second flaw in the Black Power case: Ultimately, U.S. Negroes cannot solve their own problems in isolation, because they are fully enmeshed in a society dominated by whites. The solution to Negro problems lies as much in the white community as in the Negro community. This is especially true because whites control the economic resources needed to provide Negroes with meaningful equality of opportunity. Hence, any strategy of action by Negro leaders that totally alienates the white community is doomed to failure.

Yet Black Power advocates are probably correct in arguing that Negroes must develop an ideology that focuses upon self-determination and therefore has some "antiwhite" tinges. They need an "enemy" against which to organize the Negro community. History proves that organization *against* a concrete opponent is far more effective than one *for* some abstract goal. They also need an abrasive ideology that threatens whites enough to open their eyes to the Negroes' plight and their own need to do something significant to improve it. The question is how they can accomplish these goals without going too far and thereby creating violent antiwhite hostility among Negroes and equally violent anti-Negro sentiment among whites.

In the past few years, many Negro Americans—including prominent community leaders—have shifted their sights away from direct racial integration as a goal. Instead they have focused upon other goals more consistent with the Black Power viewpoint. They want better housing, better schools, better jobs, and better personal security within all-Negro areas—and a much stronger Negro voice in controlling all these things. These enrichment-only objectives have apparently eclipsed their desire for greater ability to enter directly into white-dominated portions of the society. This rather dramatic change in values appears to rule out much possibility of Negroes' accepting either dispersal strategy.

In my opinion, the main cause of this shift in objectives is the failure of white society to offer any real hope for large-scale integration. After years of seeking equality under the law, Negro leaders have discovered that even removal of legal barriers is not producing much progress toward a true sharing in the life of white-dominated society. Why should they keep knocking on the door if no one will answer? Why not turn instead to existing all-Negro communities and try to improve conditions there? Indeed, I believe continued white refusal to engage in meaningful, large-scale integration will make it impossible for any self-respecting Negroes to avoid espousing some version of the Black Power viewpoint. Understandably, they will not be able to accept the conclusion that most of the millions of Negroes whom whites force to live racially segregated lives must therefore be condemned to inferior educations, housing, culture, or anything else.

Rather, they will reason, there must be some way to make the quality of life in all-Negro portions of a racially segregated society just as good as it is in the all-white portions. And if equality in terms of the indices of desirability accepted by whites cannot be achieved, then some of these Black Power advocates will be willing to attain at least nominal equality by denouncing those indicators as specious. They will further claim—with some justification—that life in all-white portions of society cannot be any better and may be morally worse because whites suffer from racial blindness.

The reason why this argument is and will be advanced so strongly is certainly understandable. Those who advance it would hardly be human if they were not at least tempted to do so. As long as present white attitudes and behavior persist, adopting any other view amounts to despairing of any chance at equality for most Negroes.

Can the Enrichment-Only Strategy Create "Separate But Equal" Societies?[31]

The Black Power viewpoint essentially argues that racially separate societies in America can provide equal opportunities for all their members if Negroes are able to control their own affairs. Yet there is a great deal of evidence that this argument is false.

Certainly concerning employment, equality of opportunity for Negroes cannot possibly be attained in a segregated labor market. Negroes must be provided with full freedom and equality regarding entry into and advancement within the white-dominated enterprises that are overwhelmingly preponderant in our economy. Only in this way can they have any hope of achieving an occupational equality with whites.

In education, the evidence is far more ambiguous. The recent reports of the Office of Education and the Civil Rights Commission contend that both racial and economic integration are essential to the attainment of educational equality for Negroes.[32] Yet critics of these reports point out that many types of enrichment programs were not tested in the studies conducted by the authors. Unfortunately, most alternative approaches have not yet been tried on a scale large enough to determine whether any of them will work. Yet one conclusion does seem reasonable: Any real improvement in the quality of education in low-income, all-Negro areas will cost a great deal more money than is now being spent there, and perhaps more than is being spent per pupil anywhere.

Thus, society may face a choice between three fundamental alternatives: providing Negroes with good-quality education through massive integration in schools (which would require considerably more spending per pupil than now exists), providing Negroes with good-quality education through large-scale and extremely expensive enrichment programs, or continuing to relegate many Negroes to inferior educations that severely limit their life-time opportunities. The third alternative is what we are now choosing. Whether or not the second choice—improving schools in all-Negro areas—will really work is not yet known. The enrichment alternative is based upon the as-yet-unproven premise that it will.

Regarding housing, the enrichment-only strategy could undoubtedly greatly improve the quantity, variety, and environment of decent housing units available to the disadvantaged population of central cities. Nevertheless, it could not in itself provide Negroes of *any* economic level with the same freedom and range of choice as whites with equal incomes. Clearly, in this field "separate but equal" does not mean *really* equal. Undoubtedly, all-white suburban areas provide a far greater range and variety of housing and environmental settings than can possibly be found in central cities or all-Negro suburbs alone.

Moreover, there is an acute scarcity of vacant land in many of our largest central cities. Therefore, greatly expanding the supply of decent housing for low-income families in those cities at a rapid rate requires creating many new units for them in the suburbs too.

Thus, if society adopts one of the many possible versions of the enrichment-only strategy, it may face the prospect of perpetuating two separate societies—one white and one Negro—similar to those that would develop under the present-policies strategy. If the enrichment programs carried out proved highly effective, then the gap between these two societies in income, education, housing, and other qualities of life would be nowhere near as great as under the present-policies strategy. Hence, the possibility of a potentially catastrophic confrontation between these two societies sometime in the next twenty years would be greatly reduced.

Nevertheless, I do not believe it will really be possible to create two separate societies that are truly equal. Therefore, even if the enrichment-only strategy proved extraordinarily successful at improving the lot of disadvantaged central-city residents of all races and colors (which is by no means a certainty), it would still leave a significant gap in opportunity and achievement between the separate white and Negro societies which would continue to emerge over the next twenty years. This gap would remain a powerful source of tension that might lead to violence, for experience proves that men seeking equality are not placated by even very great absolute progress when they perceive that a signifiant gap remains between themselves and others in society who are not more deserving of success than they. And that would be precisely the situation twenty years from now under the enrichment-only strategy—whether linked to Black Power concepts or not.

Why Dispersal Should Be Seriously Considered

As pointed out earlier, either of the two dispersal strategies would require radical changes in current trends and policies concerning the location of Negro population growth. Moreover, it is likely that massive dispersal would at present be opposed by *both* suburban whites and central-city Negroes. Many of the former would object to an influx of Negroes, and many of the latter prefer living together in a highly urbanized environment. Why should we even consider a strategy that is not only socially disruptive, but likely to please almost nobody?

In my opinion, there are five reasons why we should give enrichment plus dispersal serious consideration. First, future job-creation is going to be primarily in suburban areas, but the unskilled population is going to be more and more concentrated in central-city ghettos unless some dispersion occurs. Such an increasing divergence between where the workers are and where the jobs are will make it ever more difficult to create anything like full employment in decent jobs for ghetto residents. In contrast, if those residents were to move into suburban areas, they would be exposed to more knowledge of job opportunities and would have to make much shorter trips to reach them.

Hence they would have a far better chance of getting decent employment.

Second, the recent U.S. Office of Education and U.S. Civil Rights Commission reports on equality of achievement in education reach a *tentative* conclusion that it is necessary to end the clustering of lower-income Negro students together in segregated schools in order to improve their education significantly.[33] As I understand these reports, they imply that the most significant factor in the quality of education of any student is the atmosphere provided by his home and by his fellow students both in and out of the classroom. When this atmosphere is dominated by members of deprived families, the quality of education is inescapably reduced—at least within the ranges of class size and pupil-teacher ratios that have been tried on a large scale. Therefore, if we are to provide effective educational opportunities for the most deprived groups in our society to improve themselves significantly, we must somehow expose them to members of other social classes in their educational experience. But there are not enough members of the Negro middle class "to go around," so to speak. Hence this means some intermingling of children from the deprived groups with those from not-so-deprived white groups, at least in schools. Because of the difficulties of busing large numbers of students in the hearts of central cities to suburban areas, it makes sense to accomplish this objective through some residential dispersal. This consideration tends to support the integrated-dispersal strategy to some extent, even though these reports have received significant criticism, as noted.

Third, development of an adequate housing supply for low-income and middle-income families and provision of true freedom of choice in housing for Negroes of all income levels will require out-movement of large numbers of both groups from central cities to suburbs. I do not believe that such an out-movement will occur "spontaneously" merely as a result of increasing prosperity among Negroes in central cities. Even the recently passed national open-occupancy law is unlikely to generate it; a program of positive incentives and of actual new construction in suburban areas will be necessary.

Fourth, continued concentration of large numbers of Negroes under relatively impoverished conditions in ghettos may lead to unacceptably high levels of crime and violence in central cities.

The outbreak of riots and disorders in mostly nonwhite areas in our central cities in the past few years is unprecedented in American history. As the report of the National Advisory Commission on Civil Disorders indicates, continuing to concentrate masses of nonwhite population in ghettos dominated by poverty and permeated with an atmosphere of deprivation and hopelessness is likely to perpetuate or intensify these disorders. This could lead to the disastrous outcome already discussed in connection with the present-policies strategy.

Fifth, a continuation of ghetto growth will, over the next three or four decades, produce a society more racially segregated than any in our history. We will have older, blighted central cities occupied by millions of Negroes, and newer, more modern suburban areas occupied almost solely by whites. Prospects for moving from that situation to a truly integrated society in which race is not a factor in key human decisions are not encouraging. In fact, by that time we will be faced with a fantastically more massive dispersal problem than the present one if we really want to achieve a society integrated in more than just words.

Thus, only the two enrichment-plus-dispersal strategies explicitly seek to create a single society rather than accepting our present perpetuation of two separate societies: one white and one Negro. Dispersal would involve specific policies and programs at least starting us toward reversal of the profoundly divisive trend now so evident in our metropolitan areas.

It may seem extraordinarily difficult to begin such a reversal. But however difficult it may be now, it will be vastly more difficult in twenty years if the number of Negroes segregated in central cities is 8 million larger than it is today.

The Difficulty of Gaining Acceptance for Dispersal

I am fully aware that any strategy involving significant dispersal may now seem wholly impractical to responsible politicians and social leaders. The voluntary movement of large numbers of Negroes from ghettos to the suburbs encouraged by federal programs presupposes radical changes in existing attitudes among both suburban whites and central-city Negroes.

In spite of our social mobility, Americans are extremely sensitive to class differentiations. We have deliberately developed class-stratified suburban areas. Residents of each suburb use zoning, tax rates, lot-size requirements, and other devices to exclude persons considered farther down the ladder of social and economic prominence. As each group and each family moves upward in our mobile society, they become very concerned about creating social distance between themselves and those now below them—including those who were once equal to them.

I certainly do not deplore the historic traditions of self-improvement and protection of amenities and privileges that have been won through hard work and perseverance. These traditions should and will continue in some form, because it is proper for successful people to enjoy the fruits of their efforts.

Nevertheless, it is at least possible that the social objective of upgrading the lowest and most deprived groups in our society cannot be accomplished if we simultaneously insist upon excluding those groups from nearly all daily contact with other more fortunate people—as we do now—by maintaining extremely rigid class distinctions by geographic area. Thus, the best dispersal policy might be one that promoted day-to-day interclass and interracial experiences without changing the dominant socio-economic character of the receiving suburban areas. This would allow persons moving out from the inner city to benefit from the existing character of those suburbs. Such a policy implies that the newcomers would comprise a minority in each area into which they move. This means that an integrated-dispersal strategy might ultimately provide the most desirable form of dispersal. It would enable the group that was already there to maintain nearly intact their conception of the proper standards for that community, while sharing the benefits of those standards with others.

Even this change in attitude, however, presupposes a shift in values of profound magnitude among white middle-class Americans. Furthermore, I doubt that most Negroes today want to live in white communities in which they would be relatively isolated from other Negroes. Hence they might prefer a segregated-dispersal strategy, if they were willing to accept dispersal at all. Yet, since most suburban areas are already incorporated into predominantly white communities, where and how could such a strategy be initiated?

Some Tactical Mechanisms for Encouraging Dispersal

Any attempt to achieve dispersal must involve two basic questions: What *mechanisms* can be designed to encourage voluntary out-movement of large numbers of Negroes into the suburbs and their peaceful acceptance and welcome by whites there?

What *incentives* can be developed leading particular groups in society to politically press for—or at least support—employment of those mechanisms?

Let us consider the mechanisms first. Americans have always used one basic approach to get people to overcome inertia and voluntarily make some socially desirable change. It consists of providing a significant economic or other reward for persons who behave in the desired manner. That reward might be free land (as for homesteaders and railroads in the nineteenth century), or tax reductions (as for homeowners or investors in equipment in the past few years), or direct payments (as for farmers), or services and income supplements tied to participation in specific programs (as for users of the G.I. Bill in education).

In the case of dispersion, I believe the system of rewards used should probably have the following characteristics:[34]

1. Advantages should accrue both to the Negro households moving out from central cities and to the suburban households into whose communities the newcomers move.

2. Whenever possible, these advantages should consist of rewards administered under metropolitan-area-wide organizations specifically set up for such a purpose. These organizations could be quasi-private bodies able to cooperate directly with existing local governments and other geographically limited organizations. Hence they would not be metropolitan governments.

3. Advantages to out-moving households might include the following:

The possibility of sending their children to top-quality schools that receive special grants because of participation in programs involving out-moving children.

Home-buying or renting financial aids available only to out-moving families or at least with assigned proportions of their total funding available only to such families.

Top-priority access to special programs concerning employment and on-the-job training in suburban industrial and other firms. In my opinion, such programs might be effectively built around the self-selection principle embodied in the G.I. Bill—that is, eligible persons would be given certificates making those firms who hire them able to receive special benefits to compensate for their lower productivity or training costs. Such benefits might include tax credits or direct payments. The persons receiving these certificates would then make their own choice of employers among firms participating in such programs. This would preserve maximum individual choice among program participants.

4. Advantages to households already living in the receiving areas might include

Special aid to schools receiving children in out-moving Negro families. Such aid should consist of funds linked to the students in such families (as Title I funding under the Elementary and Secondary Education Act is now linked to low-income families). But the per-student amount of aid should greatly exceed the added direct cost of teaching each out-moving student. Hence the school district concerned would have a positive incentive to accept such students because of the financial "bonuses" they would bring with them. Those bonuses could be used to upgrade the entire receiving school or cut locally borne costs therein.

"Bonus" community financing to participating suburban local governments. Again, the payments involved should significantly exceed the added costs of servicing in-coming families, so that each participating community would be able to improve other services too.

Giving higher priority in other federal programs to communities participating in out-movement programs than to those refusing to participate. These related programs could include sewer and water financing, planning aid, and selection as locations for federal installations.

5. Benefits available for out-moving families and receiving areas could be restricted by geographic area to avoid either paying people discriminatorily by race or wasting funds paying families who would move out anyway. A precedent for giving residents of certain neighborhoods special benefits already exists in the urban renewal and model cities programs. Thus, specific ghetto neighborhoods could be designated "origination" areas and largely white suburban communities designated "receiving" areas. Benefits would accrue only to persons moving from the former to the latter or to residents of the latter participating in reception programs.

6. If these programs were part of an integrated-dispersal strategy, they could be linked to quota systems concerning newcomers to each school or community involved. Thus, the special bonus aids would be available only up to a certain fraction of the total school enrollment or residential population of a given receiving community. This restriction would be aimed at retaining in the schools or communities concerned the dominance of the groups originally residing there. It is to be hoped that

the result would be suburban integration rather than a shift of massive neighborhood transition from central cities to suburbs.

These suggestions are highly tentative and exploratory. Yet I hope they at least indicate that practical mechanisms can be created that might achieve a substantial amount of peaceful Negro out-movement—*if* they were adopted in a general atmosphere of social encouragement to dispersal.

Some aspects of the basic approach described may seem terribly unjust. In particular, this approach rewards the advantaged (those already living in suburbs) as well as the disadvantaged (those moving out of deprived areas into suburbs) in order to get the former to accept the latter. Yet that is a key mechanism, one which free enterprise systems have always employed when they seek to attain high-priority ends through voluntary action. Our society abounds with arrangements that provide special economic advantages to those who are already privileged, presumably in order to evoke socially desired behavior from them. Examples are oil depletion allowances, stock option plans for top executives, profitable contracts for defense firms, lower tax rates on capital gains, and subsidy payments to wealthy farmers. I am defending neither the equity nor the effectiveness of these particular examples. Yet they illustrate that we often adopt public policies that pay the rich to undertake behavior which presumably benefits society as a whole.

A second aspect of the approach to dispersal I have described which might seem harsh is that no benefits apparently accrue to disadvantaged persons who fail to move out to the suburbs. As stated earlier, however, I believe dispersal programs should only be undertaken simultaneously with large-scale ghetto enrichment programs. The latter would provide comparable, or even greater, benefits for those "left behind" in central cities—who will undoubtedly comprise the vast majority of Negroes in our metropolitan areas for many years to come.

Developing Political Support for Dispersal

The concept of dispersal will remain nothing but an empty theory unless a significant number of Americans decide their best interests lie in politically supporting specific dispersal mechanisms. It is conceivable that such support might result from a massive "change of heart" among white suburbanites. They might view dispersal as a way to "purge themselves" of the kind of "white racism" which the National Advisory Commission on

Civil Disorders described. I do not think this will occur. In fact, I believe recent urban violence has tended to make white suburbanites more hostile than ever to the idea of having Negroes live next door to them.

Yet, on the other hand, several specific groups in society are beginning to realize that dispersal might benefit them immensely. The motivation of persons in these groups varies widely, from pure moral guilt to sheer self-interest. But almost all significant social change in the United States has occurred because a wide variety of different types of people with diverse motives have formed a coalition to accomplish something. In my opinion, only through that kind of process will any of the basic strategies I have described (except the present-policies strategy) ever be achieved.

I believe the groups favorable to dispersal now (or soon will) include the following:

Suburban industrialists. In many metropolitan areas, they are experiencing acute labor shortages, particularly of unskilled workers. They will soon be willing to provide open and powerful political support for the construction of low-income and moderate-income housing for Negro workers and their families in currently all-white suburbs.

Downtown-oriented retailers, bankers, restaurant operators, hotel operators, and other businessmen in our larger cities. In cities where disorders have penetrated into central business districts (such as Milwaukee and Washington), many former patrons have stopped visiting these areas altogether—especially at night. If disorders in these areas become worse, the impact upon both consumer patronage and future capital investment in big-city downtowns could be catastrophic. Those whose enterprises are "locked in" to such areas will soon realize they must vigorously support both stronger law enforcement and positive programs aimed at alleviating Negro discontent. At first, these programs will consist primarily of ghetto enrichment, but these groups will soon begin to support dispersal too.

Homebuilders. They would benefit from any large-scale programs of housing construction. But the delays and difficulties of carrying out such programs within central cities are much greater than they are on vacant suburban land. Hence they will eventually exert at least low-level support for dispersal if it means large-scale subsidy of privately built homes.

White central-city politicians in large cities. As the populations of their cities shift toward Negro majorities, they will be more and more willing to support some dispersal policies, as well as the enrichment programs they now espouse.

Businessmen in general with plants, offices, or other facilities "locked in" to large central cities. An increasing number of such persons will realize that they will emerge losers from any major "confrontation" between black-dominated central cities and white-dominated suburbs, as described earlier.

Persons of all types whose consciences influence them to accept the National Advisory Commission's conclusion that dispersal of some kind is the only way to avoid perpetuating two separate societies, with the Negro one forever denied equality.

Since these groups now constitute a small minority of Americans, a great many other Americans must change their existing values considerably if large-scale dispersal is ever to occur. Yet the alternatives to such a strategy—especially the one we are now pursuing—could conceivably lead us to equally grave changes in values. For example, if there is an extremely significant increase in violence in Negro ghettos which spills over into all-white areas, the white population might react with harshly repressive measures that would significantly restrict individual freedoms. This, too, would call for a basic shift in our values. But it is a shift which I regard with much more alarm than the one required by a dispersal strategy. In fact, in this age of rapid technological change, it is naive to suppose that there will not be significant alterations in attitudes that we presently take for granted.

The Scale of Efforts Required

The foregoing discussion emphasizes that any strategy likely to have a significant impact upon ghettos will require a very much larger effort than we are now devoting to this problem. Even a "pure" ghetto-enrichment strategy, which does not eliminate or even slow down the growth of the racial ghetto, would require a significantly greater allocation of financial and manpower resources to coping with the problems of the urban poor. A dispersal strategy that addresses itself to breaking up or at least slowing down the growth of the racial ghetto would also require even more profound changes in values and attitudes. Only the first strategy—that of continuing our present activities—requires no immediate change in effort or values. But it may eventually result in significant value changes too—and perhaps far less desirable ones than are required by the other two alternatives.

Thus, there is simply no easy way to cope with this problem. In my opinion, past federal programs and many currently suggested approaches have suffered from the desire to find a cheap solution to what is an extremely expensive problem. The problem is expensive in terms not only of money but also of our national talents and our willingness to change our basic values. In one way or another, we must and will accommodate ourselves to this problem. We cannot evade it.

Creating the Programs and Incentives Necessary to Achieve Any Desired Ghetto Future

Each strategy contains two basic parts: a desired outcome and a set of actions designed to achieve that outcome. I have not placed equal emphasis on these two parts in discussing each of the five strategies concerning ghetto futures. For example, the present-policies strategy as I have described it is essentially a set of actions—the continuation of present policies. Hence it does not emphasize a desired outcome. In fact, I have pointed out several reasons why its outcome might be quite undesirable. Conversely, my discussion of the enrichment-only strategy has focused upon its outcome. Hence I have not made many suggestions about how that outcome might be brought about. Similar emphasis upon the outcome rather than the means of attaining it also marks the discussion of the integrated-core strategy. Even my tentative analysis of how dispersal might be carried out hardly represents a complete blueprint for action.

Any strategy is really just wishful thinking until it links the outcome it envisions with some feasible means of attaining that outcome. This is especially true regarding several of the ghetto futures I have described, since they embody such radical changes in society. They are likely to remain largely fantasies, rather than real alternatives, until specific programs for achieving them can be defined. I have made some program suggestions in connection with dispersal strategies in order to prove that dispersal is not totally unrealistic. The complexity of developing similar suggestions for the other strategies involving social change prevents my attempting to do so here. Nevertheless, there are five basic principles crucial to formulating such programs.

1. No proposed "solution" to ghetto problems that is not

eventually supported by the majority of the white middle class can possibly succeed.[35]

2. The actions designed to bring about any desired outcome must be linked to incentives that will appeal both to the self-interest of all groups concerned and to their consciences. In fact, the most difficult part of implementing any strategy (other than the present-policies strategy) will be providing effective incentives for the relatively well-off white majority. This group must be persuaded to expand many resources, and alter its own traditional behavior, in order to produce outcomes that appear to benefit mainly a small minority of the population. As indicated in the discussion of dispersal, each segment of the white majority (such as business, labor, suburbanites, senior citizens, farmers, and so forth) must be presented with arguments and incentives which appeal specifically to its interests. An example is the argument that business suffers great losses of potential profits and output because of the failure of poor Negroes to engage in high-level consumption and the inability of poorly educated Negro workers to help meet high demands for skilled labor.

3. Any program designed to achieve a given outcome should involve significant action by the private sector. Otherwise, society may relegate ghettos to a position of dependency upon government that is inconsistent with full equality in American life. On the other hand, it is naive to suppose that the private sector can or will bear the huge expense of coping with ghetto problems unaided. Society as a whole must pay the extra costs of on-the-job training programs, new factories located in ghettos, union training of unskilled Negro apprentices, and other actions aimed at helping the unskilled or otherwise "left out" enter the main stream of our economy. These actions must be carried out by nongovernmental organizations, but financed by the government through direct payments, tax credits, or other means.

4. No program involving ghettos can be effective unless it involves a high degree of meaningful participation by ghetto residents and significant exercise of power and authority by them. We must realize that ghettos cannot be drawn into the main stream of American life without some redistribution of authority and power, as well as income, for equality in America means exercise of significant self-determination. Admittedly, lack of skill and experience may cause that exercise to be disorderly, inefficient, and even corrupt at first—as it was among the Irish,

Italians, Jews, and others in the past. Therefore, turning over more power in ghetto areas to local residents may actually cause a short-run decline in the professional quality of government there—whether in schools, the police, or local government in general. Yet it will greatly alter the attitudes of residents toward those institutions and begin to draw them into the real functioning of our society. So it should and must come.

5. The more benefits that most ghetto residents receive through programs aimed at helping them, the more dissatisfied and vocally discontent certain small parts of the ghetto community are likely to become. This makes the problem of persuading the white majority to support large-scale aid programs doubly difficult. It also means that socioeconomic programs will have to be accompanied by greatly enlarged and improved law-enforcement efforts, particularly those in which ghetto leaders themselves play significant roles. Yet emphasis on improving law-enforcement alone, without massively trying to meet the other needs of ghetto residents, will probably prove disastrous. Such one-sided emphasis on "law and order" could easily provoke steadily rising violence shifting in form toward guerrilla warfare. The need to avoid this outcome further emphasizes the importance of relying more and more on ghetto communities to develop their own internal controls of violence, with outside aid, as is consistent with the preceding principle of greater self-determination.

Merely stating these principles emphasizes how far we are from having designed practical programs to achieve most of the outcomes set forth in this article. In my opinion, one of the most important tasks facing us is the formulation and public discussion of the specific ingredients needed for such programs. But even that cannot be done until we have recognized more explicitly the various possible futures of American ghettos and weighed their relative advantages and disadvantages.

At present, most public discussions and thinking about racial and ghetto problems in America suffer from failure to define or even to consider explicit possible long-range outcomes of public policy. This is one reason why such discussion seems so confused, inchoate, and frustrating. I hope that the ideas set forth in this article can serve as a nucleus for more fruitful public discussion of this crucial topic, for the future of American ghettos will determine to a large extent the future of America itself.

Notes

[1]The first draft of this article was written in the early summer of 1967. Subsequently, the author became a consultant to the National Advisory Commission on Civil Disorders. In that capacity, he wrote the rough drafts of several chapters in the Commission's final report. One of these (Chapter 16) contains many of the ideas set forth in this article. Nevertheless, there are sufficient differences between the contents and presentation of Chapter 16 in the Commission's Report and this article to warrant separate publication of the latter. The contents of this article express the thoughts of its author only and do not necessarily represent the views of either the National Advisory Commission on Civil Disorders or Real Estate Research Corporation.

[2]Data from the Social Security Administration.

[3]*Report of the National Advisory Commission on Civil Disorders* (Washington, D.C.; March 1, 1968), p. 127. This document will hereafter be referred to as the *NACCD Report.*

[4]*Ibid.*, pp. 121, 127.

[5]Based upon the Census Bureau's Series D projections of future population—the ones assuming the lowest of the four levels of future fertility used by the Census Bureau. See U.S. Bureau of the Census, *Statistical Abstract of the United States, 1967* (88th Edition; Washington, D.C., 1967), pp. 8–10.

[6]*NACCD Report*, p. 121.

[7]*Ibid.*

[8]*Ibid.*

[9]Open-occupancy legislation appears to be aimed at shifting the location of some future nonwhite growth to presently all-white areas. Experience in those states which have had open-occupancy ordinances for some time indicates, however, that they have little, if any, impact in altering the distribution of nonwhite population growth.

[10]*NACCD Report*, p. 227.

[11]Surveys conducted annually by Real Estate Research Corporation, results unpublished.

[12]*NACCD Report*, p. 216.

[13]See Raymond J. Murphy and James M. Watson, *The Structure of Discontent*, Mimeographed, Los Angeles: University of California at Los Angeles, June 1, 1967.

[14]*NACCD Report*, pp. 123–31.

[15]Specific recommendations concerning these subjects are set forth in the *NACCD Report*, Chapter 17.

[16]See John F. Kain, "The Distribution and Movement of Jobs and Industry," in *The Metropolitan Enigma*, ed. James Q. Wilson (Washington, D.C., 1967).

[17]These include legislative proposals made by Senator Javits, Senator Robert Kennedy, and Senator Percy.

[18]William Baumol and William Bowen, *The Performing Arts: The Economic Dilemma* (New York: 20th Century Fund).

[19]*NACCD Report*, p. 217.

[20]Insofar as I know, this principle was first formulated by my father, James C. Downs, Jr.

[21]Two well-known urban specialists with such views are Jane Jacobs and Victor Gruen. See Jane Jacobs, *The Life and Death of Great American Cities* (New York, 1961), and Victor Gruen, *The Heart of Our Cities* (New York, 1964).

[22]This phenomenon explains why it is so difficult to halt "massive

transition" from white to nonwhite occupancy once it begins. It tends to continue even when whites originally living in the area concerned do not "panic" at all. As long as normal turnover continues to produce vacancies, and only nonwhites fill them, such transition is inescapable. The key persons whose behavior must be affected to stop transition are not the whites living in the area at the outset, but those living scattered elsewhere in the metropolitan area or even other parts of the nation. They are the persons who must move into the areas as vacancies appear in order to maintain racial balance therein. Thus, attempts to organize existing white residents so as to prevent them from fleeing almost always fail to halt transition. Organizers can rarely identify "the whites who aren't there yet," so they cannot influence the decisions of these potential future occupants, and transition continues relentlessly.

[23]The U.S. Supreme Court will soon have to face up to the consequences of this "Law." In order to attack de facto segregation, it must recognize racial discrimination in the form of school quotas as Constitutional. At present, our society cannot achieve integration or end segregation without deliberate and explicit racial discrimination by public authorities. This is true in relation to other public facilities besides schools, including hospitals and housing.

[24]This term and usage were coined by Charles E. Lindblom. See Lindblom and David Braybrooke, *The Strategy of Decision* (New York, 1963).

[25]See the *NACCD Report*, Chapter 17.

[26]See their statements as quoted in the Chicago *Daily News*, August 25, 1967.

[27]*NACCD Report*, p. 227.

[28]*Ibid.*, p. 121.

[29]These figures are based upon the Census Bureau's Series D population projections. If higher fertility projections are used, the suburbs would contain slightly higher proportions of total population in 1985. See the reference cited in footnote 5.

[30]*NACCD Report*, pp. 216–17.

[31]This section of the article was written after Chapter 16 of the *NACCD Report* had been completed and closely parallels the contents of certain parts of that chapter.

[32]See James Coleman *et al.*, *Equality of Educational Opportunity* (Washington, D.C., 1966), and the U.S. Civil Rights Commission, *Racial Isolation in the Public Schools* (Washington, D.C., 1967).

[33]*Ibid.*

[34]Many of the programs described in this section have been recommended by the National Advisory Commission on Civil Disorders. See the *NACCD Report*, Chapter 17.

[35]This fact is recognized by most Negro leaders not committed to zealously militant separatism. For example, see Kenneth Clark, *Dark Ghetto* (New York, 1965), p. 222.

4.2

The Housing Effects of a Guaranteed Annual Income

William G. Grigsby

Introduction

The increasing national support for some form of guaranteed annual income for all Americans requires that those who are concerned with housing problems enlarge their frame of reference to consider the effects of such a policy on housing generally, on the low-income sector of the market in particular, and on the continuing need for existing housing-subsidy programs. While Congress may not pass general "incomes" legislation in the near future, and while a guaranteed income may never be implemented in any of the pure forms which have been suggested by Friedman, Tobin, and others, it does seem likely that the nation will move steadily in the direction of income guarantees for everyone. This movement is currently proceeding, however, with scant knowledge of its possible economic and social consequences. Hence, exploration of the possible effects of a guaranteed income on urban housing serves a dual purpose. It partially tests the income approach to the reduction of poverty generally while examining specific housing impacts. If the guarantee could be shown to have substantial positive effects on the living accommodations of low-income families, the argument for its adoption would obviously be strengthened. On the other hand, if potential favorable effects on housing appear to be marginal, some doubt is cast on the efficacy of the proposal. Additionally, examination of the possible housing effects of the guaranteed income serves to open the door to a broader housing issue which is as important as it is neglected—how to create a quality floor and investment stability at the lower end of the market. Recent experience in inner-city areas attests to the urgency of this problem.

The purpose of this paper, therefore, is to pursue possible relationship between the guaranteed income and housing. It does so largely on intuitive grounds. As the paper progresses, reference will be made to relevant empirical and theoretical studies. The fact is, however, that existing knowledge is insufficient to enable us to reach firm conclusions on most dimensions of the housing-to-guaranteed-income relationship.

Reprinted from *Possible Impacts of the Guaranteed Annual Income on Housing Markets*, prepared for the Department of Housing and Urban Development, by permission of William G. Grigsby, 1969, pp. 1–13; 35–60.

Nature and Organization of the Research Problem

Perhaps the first question to ask is what are the housing effects which *might* flow from a guaranteed income? Once these possible effects have been identified, they can serve as the framework for subsequent analysis. Very generally, eleven potential effects can be postulated:

1. Improvement in the quality of the occupied standing stock,
2. Increase in utilization of space
3. Rise in the rate of new construction
4. Abandonment of some portion of the standing stock
5. Shifts in the intraurban distribution of income (hence, racial) groups
6. Increase in the proportion of owner-occupants and reduction of mortgage foreclosures
7. Rise in prices and rents
8. Shifts in interregional migration patterns
9. Increase in household formation and family stability
10. Shift in the location and type of new construction within metropolitan areas
11. Reduction in involuntary mobility within metropolitan areas

With the exception of number 8, all of these *possible* outcomes depend in part upon a prior change either in family expenditures for housing or in the cost of supplying a given amount of space and quality.[1] In turn, residential expenditures and the cost of providing adequate shelter are potentially affected by both the *rise*, if any, in income that would accompany a guarantee, and the income *stability* which a guarantee would bring.[2] Thus, ideally the analysis of each possible outcome should consider four different situations, as depicted in Figure 1.[3]

Rise in Y	Stability of Y
Increase in housing expenditures	Increase in housing expenditures

Rise in Y	Stability of Y
Change in cost of supplying housing services	Change in cost of supplying housing services

Figure 1

Expressed differently, the analysis of each potential impact must proceed in three stages. First, estimates or assumptions must be made regarding the changes in income flows which the guarantee would bring. Second, these income figures must be translated into likely changes in housing expenditures and in supply costs. Finally, the impacts of the changes in expenditures and costs must be explored.

Each impact cannot always be viewed in isolation, however. Indeed, a major policy concern is that one potential impact—a general upward movement in the price and rent structure—would largely nullify the other impacts. This fact obviously complicates the analysis.

A further complication arises from the fact that the immediate impact of a guaranteed income would vary among families. Some types of families would be helped a great deal relative to their present position while others would be benefited scarcely at all. These differential improvements might correlate with different supply-side submarkets. Thus, *who* gets how much may be very important with respect to likely market impact. It would appear desirable, therefore, first to look at how the guaranteed income might affect different types of families and structures and then develop an aggregate estimate out of the individual submarket analyses.

In brief, then, a thorough analysis of the effects of a guaranteed annual income on housing would have to address itself to eleven possible impacts for perhaps five or more basic family types, and the examination of each of these 55 or more cells would have to proceed in three separate analytical stages. This implies at least 165 separate steps. It seems probable, however, that once certain key dimensions and relationships were pinned down, most of the rest would fall into line. In this hope, the remainder of this paper collapses the inquiry into four major parts: The first part is concerned with specification and analysis of client groups affected by a guaranteed annual income. The next section examines changes in income flows that the guarantee would generate among these groups. In the third section, effects of changing income flows on housing costs and expenditures are explored. Finally, conclusions in each of these three areas are related to the extent possible to the eleven possible impacts listed earlier.

Characteristics of Recipient Groups

As just suggested, the housing impact of a guaranteed annual income may vary considerably, depending on what types of families receive assistance. Consequently, the question which must be raised first is what are the size and characteristics (including housing) of such families. As a beginning, it is useful to distinguish among (a) low-income populations who are beneficiaries under existing income programs; (b) low-income populations who are not beneficiaries under any such programs; (c) non-low-income populations who would fall into a low-income status if benefits which they now receive under current programs were to cease; and (d) non-low-income populations near the poverty line who would benefit if the guarantee program were generous enough to include them.

Low-Income Beneficiaries Under Existing Income-Maintenance Programs

This category includes those who receive one or more of the following forms of assistance: aid to families with dependent children (AFDC), old-age assistance (OAA), aid to the blind (ATB), aid to the permanently and totally disabled (APTD), general public assistance (GA), low-income recipients of veteran's disability benefits, and low-income families who are on social security or receiving unemployment compensation. The five public assistance categories total roughly 6,500,000 individuals in more than 2,000,000 households and absorb almost $5½ billion in public funds, most of which go to families with children and to the aged.[4] The veterans group absorbs another $2 billion; low-income, social security recipients, $9 billion; and low-income persons receiving unemployment compensation, probably over $1 billion.[5] Total benefits received by all these groups combined is nearly $18 billion. Of this amount, between $4 billion and $5 billion probably is channeled into the housing market, constituting housing's largest subsidy program.[6]

The overlap between the welfare population and the other categories listed was not determined. However, very crudely it could be estimated that the low-income population already receiving a guaranteed income of sorts, but one which is not sufficient to raise them out of poverty, includes about one-half of those below the Orshansky poverty line.[7] The gap between an adequate income and the benefits which the various programs actually provide varies widely. Indeed, these programs do close the gap for some of the population.[8] The elderly welfare poor who occupy public housing are one example of families who, in a material sense, are not severely deprived. An unknown portion of the disabled veterans could be similarly classified.

The wide range in overall well-being which is achieved by recipients under the programs is found within as well as among categorical groups. The variations among states and cities are particularly pronounced, with per-person welfare benefits in Mississippi, for example, averaging only one-fourth or one-fifth of the national average. Understandably, therefore, generalizations as to the impact of a shift to a guaranteed income must reflect these differences.

A further analytical complication is the fact that the population which is actually on welfare or receiving unemployment compensation either at a point in time or even over the course of a year does not adequately measure the universe of beneficiaries. This point is readily understood with respect to unemployment beneficiaries who are recognized as a constantly shifting group. By contrast, the welfare population is widely viewed as one that is dominated by a permanent welfare clientele. The truth is somewhat different. Recipients of OAA, APTB, and ATB are permanent recipients, but not those receiving AFDC. In Baltimore, for example, the average length of time open for AFDC cases assisted in November 1966 was 36 months, and for cases that were closed during the month, 20 months. Of 16,000 cases assisted in December 1966, 88 percent had been opened subsequent to December 1960.[9] These figures do not tell the whole story, however. Many families are frequently, even if not continuously, on welfare. Of all AFDC closings in Baltimore in 1960, 65 percent had been reopened by 1963. Of the 1963 closings, 35 percent were reopened within three months. Over a six-year period, it is estimated that as many as 28,000 different families in Baltimore received help through AFDC. This figure is 75 percent greater than that for a single year. More important, nearly all of the 28,000 constituted a permanent population at risk. About 2,000 were continuously on welfare, while as many as 24,000 would appear to have been on-again, off-again, on-again. The remainder received help just once for periods varying all the way from one month to more than five years, but even some of these may appear on the welfare rolls again.

Non-Low-Income Beneficiaries of Guarantee Programs

This group includes that portion of those receiving social security or unemployment compensation or private insurance payments or public assistance or veterans benefits who are so close to the poverty line that they would be in a state of severe deprivation if these programs did not exist. About $10.5 billion in social security, perhaps $0.5 billion in unemployment compensation, and an unknown amount of private insurance funds, welfare payments, and veterans' benefits go to such families, and serve to provide substantial support to the housing market.[10] A minimum estimate of the number of such families is at least six million.[11] The relevance of these families to the present inquiry stems not from the fact that a guaranteed annual income plan might improve their position, since for most of them it would not, but because to some degree their present housing situation represents what conceivably could be achieved for others if a system of universal guarantees were instituted. Comparisons would have to be made with a good deal of caution, however, as this group may differ from the current poor in other significant ways and also because the macro market effects of the guaranteed income are not revealed by intergroup comparisons.

Non-Low-Income, Nonbeneficiaries

Under certain guaranteed income plans, tax rates for families above the poverty line but in the lower half of the income distribution would be reduced to zero or less, depending upon the particular plan. Although some proposals are much more generous in this regard than others, realistically it is extremely doubtful whether Congressional munificence would extend to those who were very far above the line. Nevertheless, the existence of such a group must be kept in mind in any evaluation of possible impacts on the housing market. These families also are of relevance because, as will be discussed later, many of them probably move back and forth across the poverty line.

Uncovered Low-Income Population

Who are the one-half of the poor who do not benefit at all from any guarantee, however inadequate? They consist of three major groups. First are those whose incomes are too high or assets too great to allow them to receive welfare benefits but who are still in poverty according to nearly any reasonable measure. Since the rules on assets, like those on income, are excessively restrictive in most states and since the major asset of many needy families is a home, a shift to a guaranteed income for these families could have direct market repercussions.

Second are all of the needy families and individuals whose incomes and assets fall well below the limits that have been set in their states, but who are not eligible for any of the assistance programs for other reasons. Technically, all persons who meet state residency requirements and whose income is below the welfare standard should qualify for at least one of the guarantee programs. If they are not permanently or totally disabled, or totally blind, or over 65, or can not qualify for AFDC because (in most states) of the presence of both parents in the household, they should be able to receive general public assistance. In practice, however, since general assistance is solely a state and local responsibility, policies regarding grants are often vague, arbitrary, and less than comprehensive. As a consequence, many needy families headed by unemployed or partially employed adults under 65 who have exhausted their unemployment compensation benefits (if any) do not receive help unless their situation is so desperate that the local welfare agency simply cannot turn its back.[12]

The third major needy group that does not now receive any welfare assistance consists of all those persons and families who are eligible for help but for one reason or another do not now receive it. Estimates as to the size of the group vary. Many analysts think it is quite large. For example, Orshansky has calculated that one-half of low-income, female-headed households do not receive AFDC.[13] Presumably, most would be eligible to do so. There are also probably at least some elderly persons who do not draw enough social security to rise above the poverty line, but do not draw OAA either. Further, of the many needy families in which someone works at least part-time, some no doubt could qualify for assistance. The possible reasons why eligible persons do not receive assistance vary from ignorance, to desire to avoid a stigmatizing situation, to bureaucratic barriers, to optimism regarding the future, to a preference for work instead of dependency if earned income is not far below what welfare benefits would be. The fact is, however, that we really do not know the reasons, nor even the size of the group itself.

Having identified various types of client groups that might or might not benefit from an income guarantee, the next crucial question is how are they now housed? Unfortunately, no hard data could be found which relate residential accommodations to any of these population categories or subcategories. It is astonishing that this should be true after more than three decades of serious research into housing problems. It is absolutely fantastic that for one of the largest target groups—the AFDC population—scarcely more than a few casual observations on shelter conditions can be found.

From bits of information, we can piece together part of the picture. A majority of low-income families reside in safe, if not attractive, housing. A large proportion of this group appears to be owner-occupants who acquired their homes during a period in their lives when earnings were higher. Surprisingly, many low-income renters also have decent accommodations. Of special importance is the fact that those renters who lack such quarters frequently pay as much or even more for their shelter than do their better-housed counterparts. This peculiar situation stems from the fact that the low-income sector of the rental market has a three-track system of distribution: families who are good tenants frequently are charged below the market rate to keep them from moving; the ordinary family pays the market rate; and tenants who either are not desirable or who are desirable but are in high-risk categories from the standpoint of the landlord are refused occupancy in good structures entirely. Those in the third track gravitate to less well-maintained buildings, owned by indifferent landlords, where they pay more than the quality of their dwellings would seem to warrant. Among those who are especially disadvantaged in this respect are fatherless families.

A parallel high-risk group of unknown size exists with respect to the owner-occupancy market. It consists of families with wage earners who, because of income fluctuations, are not judged to be suitable mortgage risks even for inexpensive dwellings. Their gross rents are higher than the housing expenses of owner-occupants of comparable dwellings. In many cities, a large inventory of low-priced, renter-occupied, reasonably good-quality, single-family structures would be available to this group if the risk characteristics of both the families *and* the stock itself either improved or were perceived more favorably by lenders.

In the absence of information much beyond what has just been said, many of the inferences which will be made as to possible impacts of the guaranteed annual income on the housing market tend to be speculative.

Income Effects

Turning now to the task of estimating the income effects of a guarantee, we will look first at income *increases* and then at *stabilization*. It goes without saying that these effects will vary depending upon the form and funding of the income plan that is eventually adopted. Since there is no widespread agreement as to form and funding, severe analytical complications arise.

As a first step toward simplification, it may be noted that, although numerous guarantee formulas have been suggested, they can be divided into two basic groups. The first is family allowances, a form of the social-dividend idea which has been in effect for many years in other countries. The allowances are paid to *all* families regardless of income in proportion to the number of children in various age groups. The intention is to shift income to families who are at a critical phase of their life cycle insofar as the relationship of their income to family needs is concerned. The presumed benefits of allowances are, therefore, a more even matching.

Changes in Family Expenditures for Housing

Having assumed that, overall, a modest level of income expansion and a marked increase in income stability for low-income groups would result from a guarantee program, we can now turn to the question of whether these changes would alter demand and supply curves for housing. The fact that the average guarantee will not be great might suggest on the surface that the effect on these curves would, at best, be barely perceptible. It is much too early, however, to accept such a view, given the fact that certain portions of the population may benefit a great deal even though others who already are covered by existing programs would improve their financial situation scarcely at all.

Demand Shifts

Basically, the question here is what is the short-run and long-run income elasticity of demand for housing among the various low-income households who would receive transfer payments under a guarantee program. If this information were known and if new income levels could also be predicted, calculating changes in current rent-income relationships would be a matter of simple arithmetic. There is, however, a great deal of disagreement among the various scholars who have examined income elasticities in this area of consumption as to what a reasonable figure would be. Estimates vary all the way from 0.5 or less to 2.00.[14] And regardless of what estimate is accepted, it is also a fact that variations in income appear to explain very little of the variation in expenditures for housing.[15] Further, none of the studies focuses specifically on low-income populations, and few are based on income data which are refined enough to permit distinctions in behavior among families within the lowest income categories. Still further, they all fail to account for shifting rent-income relationships over time.

Finally, and most important, the findings are really not applicable to the situation being considered here. All of the estimated elasticities obtain only if the income distribution remains constant, whereas a guaranteed income is meant to change the distribution. Stated differently, the behavior of the lowest quintile under a situation of rising incomes for the entire quintile cannot be inferred from the market behavior of the next higher quintile who differ from the poor in many ways other than income. This is especially so when the economic environment that has produced these elasticities, whatever they are, excludes an element which conceivably could be quite instrumental in shaping elasticities—the guaranteed annual income itself.

It would be improper, therefore, to base our calculations here even on the most carefully derived elasticity estimates. Nor would it be legitimate simply to adjust mechanically empirical rent-income and value-income matrices to reflect changes in the level and distribution of incomes that the guaranteed income is expected to bring. Rather, in the absence of satisfactory data, it is necessary to deduce what the elasticities might be, relying where possible on solid pieces of information.

Three separate lines of argument lead to the conclusion that elasticities would be very low, at least in the short run. First, families in the lowest income brackets already pay such high rents relative to income that they deprive themselves seriously in other ways. Aware of this, they are likely to maintain their existing housing situation when their financial condition improves while they attempt to satisfy their other needs. The fact that it is physically easier to buy a few more clothes or groceries or medicines than to move to a new dwelling contributes to this response. Second, as was suggested earlier in the paper, the major effect of the guaranteed annual income may be in eliminating interruptions in the flow of income to families rather than in substantially raising the earnings which these families would receive in a "normal" year. Thus, it could be argued that since it is easier to adjust nonhousing expenditures than to defer outlays for shelter during periods of income decline, if income flows were stabilized, very little of the additional funds which families received would find their way into the residential market. Third, as was argued earlier, the amount by which incomes will be affected, either by stabilization or by a permanent increase, is bound to be limited, and this fact may have some bearing on the income elasticities themselves. To explain, logic alone would suggest that a change in the income elasticity of demand for housing would be a function to some extent of the amount by which income increased over a given period of time. The larger the increase, the more likely that a shift in housing accommodations would be considered; the smaller the rise, the more likely the family would perceive its housing options as relatively unchanged. The latter reaction would be most strong among the very families with which this paper is concerned, since the housing alternatives for most of them are additionally restricted because of race or family composition. Thus, until these families were ready to move anyway, it is conceivable that none of their added income would go into shelter *per se*, although some of it might be allocated to furnishings and utilities.

In the short run, the only possible exception to the conclusion that elasticities would be low, and perhaps an important exception at that, has to do with rent losses which landlords incur when families either skip out or obtain rent forgiveness for a few weeks. These losses are estimated by some landlords to exceed 10 percent of gross rents annually. One of the first effects of a guaranteed annual income would be to increase the possibility that these rents will be collected. Whether this in turn would favorably affect the quality of the housing inventory or would simply result in a recapitalization of assets is a question which will be discussed in the next section.

In the long run, as low-income families made their inevitable moves to new quarters for other reasons, would the impact of the guaranteed income on residential expenditures be any different? More specifically, would the slightly higher and more stable incomes be translated into larger outlays for housing than occurred in the short run? The income increase alone is of doubtful importance, if it is as modest as we have predicted. Stabilization, however, could, by opening up a sector of the low-rent inventory that is now closed to families with poor payment records, have more favorable effects. With a higher quality inventory available to these families at only a slightly higher cost, many of them might raise their sights a bit. Whether the stabilized income alone would cause them to change their spending for housing significantly is doubtful, though income security might occasion a decline in discretionary spending for momentary pleasures, thereby releasing dollars for housing.

Certain other possible longer-run consequences must also be noted. Low-income owner-occupants might take better care of their homes than is now the case. Since in most states public assistance rules regarding assets dissuade many owners from going on welfare in time of financial crisis, this possibility should not be ignored entirely even though it would be difficult to quantify.

Still another way in which the guarantee might increase housing expenditures is via an upward trend in family formation. One is nevertheless forced to conclude, that, overall, the income elasticity of demand for housing under conditions of a guaranteed annual income would be low both in the short and long run.

Accepting the probability that this is so, that the elasticities would not exceed, say 0.4, what increase in housing expenditures could the guaranteed income be expected to bring? Assuming in a given year that 12 million families with an average income of $2,500 and average annual rents of $900 received an average supplement of $750, housing expenditures would increase by $1.3 billion over what they otherwise would have been. Families would raise their expenditures, on the average, from $75 per month to $84. This estimated increase in spending is significant, but it is also misleading. For the reasons mentioned earlier, over a period longer than one year the number of families obtaining benefits would be much larger, probably double the recipient population for any one year, and the average payment, taken as a percentage of a recipient's total income for a two- or three-year period, would be correspondingly less. Thus, if the various assumptions are realistic, and they are meant to be, even though the guaranteed annual income were to cause a rise in housing expenditures of over $1 billion annually, the mean increase per family would be extremely modest.

It was suggested at the outset, however, that the mean figure obscures the fact that certain groups might be given much larger than average increments to income, while others received virtually nothing at all. In the short run, this is almost a truism. Over the longer term, though, it is difficult to visualize that many families, those in the South excepted, would regularly be paid very much more than $700 to $800 over and above what they now may receive. The reasons for this conclusion were elaborated upon in the section on Income Effects.

Before leaving the subject, it may be worth looking briefly at the question of whether any other form of guarantee would result in market responses appreciably different from those which were postulated here. In particular, would family allowances have greater or different impact on demand? If it is assumed that for recipient households the allowances were fairly generous, on the order of $360 per year per child, and thus comparable to the benefits under a negative tax for many of these families, the market consequences still might be somewhat different. Since no type of family is likely to receive very much more income under allowances than under a negative tax, and since many would receive less, and since allowances also score low with respect to income-stabilization, the probable impact on housing expenditures would appear to be negligible.

Supply Shifts

Inadequacy and instability of income lead both directly and indirectly to higher costs of supplying housing services. Risks associated with instability result in higher insurance costs, and higher interest rates and shorter amortization periods for mortgage loans. Instability also translates into more frequent mobility with its attendant effect on tenant behavior, hence on costs of maintenance and rent collection. In addition, it frequently means higher electrical and water bills for the landlord, as unemployed persons stay at home watching television and doing their wash in the sink. In the low-rent market these extra utility costs have more than a trivial impact on net cash return to equity.

Even without instability, low-income confines families to the oldest portions of the stock where maintenance is more expensive, partly because of age of structure alone and partly because funds are lacking to perform the maintenance function properly. Inadequate income combines with instability to turn landlord and tenant into adversaries, both of whom in their fight for survival impose extra costs on themselves and each other.

Some of the higher costs just described are capitalized into lower-market values rather than passed on to the consumer, so gross rents remain much more stable than values as downward filtering occurs. Conversely, if reductions in costs could be achieved, some of these too would be capitalized rather than redound to the benefit of the tenant. It seems probable, however, that both landlord and tenant would be favorably affected if a guaranteed annual income could eliminate some of the unnecessary expense which the conditions of poverty create.

Much depends on the extent to which the guaranteed income can change the objective situation in which landlords and tenants find themselves and on whether this change would alter behavior of all concerned in a positive direction. In this connection, it has frequently been observed, not always correctly, that giving goods, services, or money to the poor does not necessarily improve their behavior patterns. Equally, many unkind words are directed at landlords. Without attempting to predict behavior, it should be stated that a major argument for a guaranteed annual income is that present forms of financial dependency lead to perverse patterns of conduct by recipients and invite identical responses from those with whom they deal. If this is so and if the guaranteed annual income is substantively different from present assistance programs in this respect, then it also has the potential for bringing about certain favorable market consequences which cannot as easily be achieved by several of the major current subsidy programs.

Impacts on Housing

If, as is by now eminently clear, we are uncertain about the effects of the guaranteed annual income on the flow and distribution of income in both the short run and the long run, and if, as is also the case, we are not sure as to how expenditure patterns would shift as a consequence of the changes in income, it may seem somewhat absurd to explore the further question of how the new spending patterns would affect the housing market. To do so may simply be adding another layer of speculation to a structure that is already top-heavy with assumptions. Yet there is some merit in exposing all parts of the structure, however wobbly, to full view. With this goal in mind, the next few pages attempt to bring all of the preceding discussion to bear on the original question of what indeed would be the impact of the guaranteed annual income on housing.

It will be recalled that eleven possible impacts were originally postulated. Each of these will be discussed in turn. The remarks apply, in the main, to metropolitan areas.

Household Formation and Family Stability

Although these two related variables appear near the bottom of our list of eleven possible housing impacts, they may be among those which would be most affected by a guaranteed annual income. And to the extent that this is so, the effect of the guarantee on the other market variables would be correspondingly greater. Hence, it seems appropriate to begin our discussion of specific impacts here.

It is virtually certain that the benefits of any program of income guarantees will have to attach to individuals, not families. Thus, if an adult child living with his parents chose to form a separate household, the subsidy would follow him, in the same manner as social security benefits follow the elderly. And just as social security and private pension plans have contributed to the huge reduction in three-generation households, so too might a guaranteed income encourage low-income youngsters to leave home somewhat earlier than would otherwise be the case. It is even conceivable that children from middle- and upper-income families would be similarly influenced. Although they could no doubt earn incomes high enough to render a guarantee superfluous, many might not immediately choose to do so, but decide instead to move into the adult world of work in several stages of part-time employment. The dimensions of this form of behavior would be counteracted to an unknown degree by the encouragement which a guarantee would give to low-income youngsters desiring to continue their education beyond high school.[16] So the net effect on household formation becomes almost impossible to estimate. Some crude inferences could perhaps be made, however, by studying the household formation patterns of middle- and upper-income males and females in the 16- to 25-year age bracket.

It is improbable that the guaranteed income would increase headship ratios among the elderly, since they already enjoy a level of benefits equal to any which a new formula would provide. The guarantee might, however, substantially change residential behavior patterns among low-income groups in the middle ranges of the age spectrum. Here, despite recent changes, welfare regulations still encourage the separation of couples who have children and who are in financial distress, so that the family can qualify for AFDC. In addition to the obvious adverse effects which this situation has on the emotional well-being of all concerned, it brings with it several unfortunate housing consequences. First, unless the male can live rent-free with a friend or relative, housing expenses for the family rise. Second, landlords who try to maintain their buildings in good condition are reluctant to rent to the very types of households which the separation creates—fatherless families and single males. Third, those landlords who do rent to these households offer inferior accommodations and charge high rents.

Care must be taken not to overestimate the importance of low-income fatherless families in the market. Most such families would probably not be re-united with the absent parent if welfare rules were either replaced by a guaranteed income or amended. This is because for many, the regulations were not the immediate cause of the separation, and for others, the process of separation either involved or has created irreversible forces. One is led to wonder, nevertheless, whether over a longer period of time, a steady flow of income for all families might overcome many of the conditions, other than punitive welfare rules, which contribute to separations. If so, the favorable consequences for the low-income sector of the housing market could be impressive. Even if as few as one-half of the separations were prevented, this reduction would improve the housing opportunities of a large proportion of those who occupy substandard units in many cities.[17]

Interregional Migration

There are two opposing forces at work here. A guaranteed income, particularly if the standards are set nationally, would seem to reduce some of the incentive for persons to move from low-opportunity areas to more thriving labor markets. The individual's current situation would not seem all that bad, nor his short-term prospects elsewhere, all that good. On the other hand, a guaranteed income would eliminate some of the fears and uncertainties of moving. At least, this is the reasoning behind state residency requirements for welfare recipients. Which of the two forces became dominant would depend in part on the level of guarantee. It may be that up to a certain benefit level, the guarantee would enlarge freedom of movement without materially improving the existing living environment, while at a higher level, it would retard migration. Realistically, since it probably would never reach that higher level, it would act primarily to give expression to some of the latent mobility desires already existing among younger persons. Even so, the increase in migration rates would probably be quite modest. This preliminary conclusion needs to be checked, however, against data on current migration patterns, especially since even a small increase in the flow of families to expanding urban centers could aggravate already difficult problems in these areas.

Involuntary Mobility

A recent study sponsored by the Philadelphia Housing Association estimated that approximately 20,000 low-income families in Philadelphia, comprising fully one-quarter of all low-income renters in the city, were forced out of their dwellings in 1966 because they could not pay their rent or because they were judged by the landlord to be undesirable tenants.[18] An additional 5,000 were evicted due to code enforcement and urban renewal. About 10,000 of these households are estimated by the study to be "migratory-problem" families whose various difficulties make it virtually impossible for them to be housed permanently and satisfactorily in the private market. The remaining families were forced to move because of nonpayment of rent. About 300 of these were evicted by the Philadelphia Housing Authority. In interpreting these figures, it must be kept in mind that failure to pay rent often provides landlords with an excuse to get rid of tenants whom they wish to remove for other reasons that are more difficult to prove. If a tenant is satisfactory in other respects, it is clearly more in the "slum" landlord's interest to lose several weeks' rent than to have the property vacant for an indeterminate period or re-reoccupied by a family of unknown character. If a landlord evicts for nonpayment, he either knows he can re-rent the unit quickly, or expects the patterns of nonpayment to persist, or is concerned with other problems which the tenant is creating.

Even with this qualification, the market effects of the inability to pay rent regularly are overwhelming, for inability to pay and negative tenant behavior are causally intertwined. Families that make their first involuntary move purely because of failure to pay rent will find decent units unavailable to them. Forced to accept somewhat inadequate accommodations, hopefully for a temporary period, their behavior patterns with respect to their apartment and landlord begin to deteriorate. This negative trend is reinforced by the disinterest of a landlord who was careless or desperate enough to rent this unit to a questionable tenant in the first place. And soon another eviction may occur. Even if it does not, the feeling of "home," which will cause even a tenant to be meticulous in caring for his apartment, will diminish, and with obvious consequences.

Looking at the process somewhat differently, low-income families who are extremely uncertain about the future and who consciously or subconsciously anticipate an early move, are not likely to be as careful of the landlord's property as would more permanent residents.

The argument, then, is that involuntary mobility, occasioned primarily by interruptions in income or unexpected increases in spending for other purposes, creates and supports a submarket of indifferent and, eventually, undesirable landlords and tenants, which in turn raises the required costs of maintenance and lowers housing quality. Scanty figures for Baltimore suggest that adequate maintenance in this sector of the low-rent market would cost twice as much as is usually allotted for up-keep by responsible inner-city landlords. And these data do not allow for vandalism by evicted tenants or by those who keep a sharp eye out for empty buildings in areas where involuntary mobility is most common.

The extent to which protection of the tenant against loss of income would reduce this problem can only be surmised. At first glance, it would seem that rent supplements would be much more effective in reducing involuntary moves, since existence of an assured flow of income does not by itself mean that the landlord would get his share. Nevertheless, knowledge of the assured flow would cause many landlords to modify their eviction policies. Additionally, the longer run effect of income security on family behavior might be of some significance. The potential favorable impact is, of course, much greater in the standard sector of the inventory than in the already deteriorated portions and is limited by the level of guarantee. This is because families who are now living in lousy quarters and whose prior record denies them access to decent accommodations at any reasonable price will continue to have a lousy attitude even if they no longer have to move so often.

Homeownership

While it is true that an income guarantee would transform many families who have a poor credit record into suitable mortgage risks, the amount of debt which the income could support would not be sufficient to bring most of them into the unsubsidized ownership market. It would, however, vastly enlarge the reservoir of families who could qualify for a below-market-rate loan, especially in cities when there is a large number of old, inexpensive single-family structures in reasonably good condition. Since, however, that reservoir is already quite large, increases in home ownership will be determined by Congressional appropriations for subsidized ownership programs rather than by the income guarantee.

Over the long run, the impact on ownership rates could be more substantial if the guaranteed annual income could protect families from periodic setbacks and thereby provide them a base from which to move to much higher levels of income. If its effects played themselves out in this fashion, the number of potential homeowners would increase and the number of families who would lose their homes through foreclosure would decline. It is not possible, however, to estimate the magnitude of these effects without more data.

Prices and Rents

An increase in prices and rents, holding quality constant, could occur only if housing demand rose sharply in the short run, moving against an inelastic supply. If demand moved upward more gradually, it would be accommodated by an expanding supply of better units, either indirectly through new construction or upgrading of the standing stock. With all its imperfections, even the low-rent sector of the market should respond in this fashion. The question, therefore, is whether a guaranteed annual income would initiate a large and sudden increase in demand. The answer, argued in detail in the previous section of this paper, is no.

Given these conclusions about demand, there might be some reason to hope for modest *decreases* in rents, holding quality constant, as continuity of income reduced the costs of supplying decent housing. This point was elaborated upon earlier in the paper.

New Construction

Prior assumptions regarding the level of the guarantee lead to the conclusion that neither directly nor indirectly would an income guarantee substantially change the volume of new construction. The recipients would simply be too far removed from the new construction market, or from the market for existing units that rent or sell at new construction prices, or even from somewhat less expensive units occupied by families who can afford newly built units, to make their presence felt on home builders. This is in sharp contrast to rent supplements which would, if not tied to specific programs, have a marked impact on housing starts. If the aggregate level of new construction would not be affected, it follows that its composition with respect to tenure, value or rent, and location would also remain relatively unchanged. Hence, we can also dispose of these potential impacts without further consideration.

Intraurban Distribution of Racial and Income Groups

With respect to housing, a desired impact of the guaranteed annual income is the greater market choice which a higher and more stable income would bring. All things considered, however, it would seem reasonable to assume that this choice would be broadened only within approximately the same geographic areas where low-income families now reside. For the income guarantee would not, for most families, move them very far above their present level. Consequently, they would continue to find their housing alternatives largely confined to those areas where low-income families just above the poverty line reside, i.e., the same neighborhoods they are now in.

Abandonment of the Low-Quality Inventory

More thought must be given to this variable. A pure guess would be that in rural areas and small towns the rate of abandonment would accelerate slightly, if, as our reasoning suggests, migration to larger urban areas did in fact modestly increase. For policy purposes, this impact can be regarded as imperceptible, however.

In the core areas of our central cities quite different processes are at work. In the 1950s, abandonments occurred as new construction in excess of family formation permitted upward filtering in the market. More recently, however, abandonments seem to have occurred for other reasons. Vandalism has destroyed standard units, and a deteriorating neighborhood environment has caused reasonably sound structures to be permanently vacated. Strict code enforcement not coupled with subsidy programs has further depleted the usable inventory. The result is a high number of derelict buildings juxtaposed against a low vacancy rate. In this situation, a guaranteed annual income would probably not result in additional boarding-up. To the extent that it helped to stabilize the bottom of the market, it might even retard this activity. Before jumping to this conclusion, however, one must be mindful that there is a complex of other factors at work, only some of which may be susceptible to change through income guarantees.

Housing Quality

This dimension of impact is possibly the most important on our list, and is certainly the one which traditionally is of most concern and interest to housing analysts. It is examined at this late stage of the paper only because much of the prior discussion provides the basis for the conclusions which are reached here.

Ultimately the question of the quality-impact of a guaranteed annual income boils down to this: How much of the housing problem can be explained by low, unstable incomes alone, and how much is due to other factors? As was suggested at the outset of the paper, the answer to this question varies from group to group and market to market. Drawing on all of the facts and assumptions up to this point, the following paragraphs will briefly explore possible consequences in several sectors of the market.

The analysis will depend more on assumption than fact. Originally it had been hoped that data on the housing conditions of various types of low-income families receiving various kinds of transfer payments would yield enough information to permit inferences about the changes which a guaranteed income might bring. For all practical purposes, such data are nonexistent. Census figures are completely inadequate for this purpose, and the occasional analyst who has used them to translate assumed changes in income into new rent and quality distributions is indulging in self-deception. There is too much unexplained variance of income with respect to rent and rent with respect to quality to allow such an approach. Moreover, as suggested earlier, the stabilization feature of a guaranteed income invalidates the procedure.

Perhaps the best way to approach the question is through a process of elimination. First of all, if any improvement in quality occurred, it would be through improvement of the existing stock, since an increase in new construction has been ruled out as a possible impact. Second, the improvement in quality would not occur via substantially higher rates of owner-occupancy and the increased maintenance expenditures which this form of tenure usually brings, since this possibility has also been rejected. Third, among families who are already owner-occupants, levels of maintenance would not be affected significantly, if our assumptions about family expenditures are correct.

The important favorable effects on quality, if any, would occur therefore in the standing stock of rental units. Moreover, they would occur, if they do, largely within existing low-income areas; significant migration out of these areas as a consequence of the guaranteed income has been judged to be unlikely.

Further, if the argument which was presented under "Prices And Rents" is valid, they would not be dampened in a major way by rent increases. Finally, since even among renters a large proportion of low-income families occupies reasonably adequate quarters, the *important* quality effects would have to be among those who are now ill-housed. Although the relevant characteristics of these families are not known, one would suspect that most of them fall into one or more of four overlapping groups: (a) the permanent and intermittently poor rather than those whose incomes have recently fallen for the first time;[19] (b) the universe of families who are frequently on AFDC rolls; (c) families who are not desirable tenants; and (d) tenants who, even though desirable, fall into "high-risk" groups whom responsible landlords avoid. It is of course true that not all of the families in these categories are badly housed. Yet it would seem safe to venture that most of them are. If this is so, we can confine the question of whether the guaranteed income would materially affect housing quality primarily to these families.

Overall, it seems doubtful that the impact on quality would be very great, because of imperfections on the supply side of the market and the inability of a guaranteed income to erase quickly present behavioral patterns on the part of both suppliers and demanders of low-cost housing. Thus although in most cities housing of good quality can be found at rents which are not greatly different from those that are being paid for slum quarters, it will take more than stable or slightly higher incomes to give most of the badly housed families access to the better stock. Barring a weakening market for units of somewhat higher quality, a possibility that is outside the framework of this analysis, the social and market institutions which were created by low and unstable incomes must be changed for upgrading to occur. To put the matter more concretely, if welfare families, who constitute housing's largest subsidy group, are badly housed, it seems unlikely that simply shifting them to another form of income maintenance and extending this form of maintenance to others is going to create vast improvement in the inventory.

Something else has to happen. Earlier, mention was made of a few possible changes which might have a favorable impact on quality, e.g., increase in family stability and reduction of involuntary mobility with their consequent effects on housing choice, landlord-tenant relations, and costs of maintenance. While such possibilities should not be discounted, the full potential of the guaranteed income or any other income plan can be realized only as part of a larger program of change. At the same time, the income guarantee may be just what is necessary to make the various components of the larger program work more effectively.

One such component of direct relevance to housing is code enforcement. To the extent that the guaranteed income permitted minimum housing standards to be more rigorously pursued in slum areas, the impact on the quality of the inventory would be greater than what has previously been suggested. Landlords, instead of having to board-up structures where the code was strictly applied, could pass on the costs of improvements to the tenant. In effect, the income guarantee would approach a rent supplement. The income elasticity of demand for housing would be forced upward by public policy, and the entire increment in shelter expenditures would be channeled into higher quality. Whether the income guarantee would extend the potential of code enforcement beyond what is already possible under existing HUD programs would require more study. A reasonable inference, however, might be that, unless the code-enforcement programs were interjected before spending patterns became adjusted to the guarantee, they could capture very little of the new income. Beyond that, the dilemma of the nonincome market constraints would remain.

One final note. Housing quality is recognized by all to include neighborhood environment, even though the question of what aspects of the environment are relevant and important to housing is elusive and ill-defined. It should be mentioned, therefore, that low-income families are becoming more concerned about neighborhood conditions than about deficiencies in their living accommodations. A recent field survey in Baltimore, for example, revealed that serious dissatisfaction with neighborhood was more prevalent than serious dissatisfaction with home in the ratio of about five to one.[20] This situation reflects the success which has been achieved in upgrading the housing stock; as shelter needs become satisfied, they are replaced by new wants. It is also true, however, that neighborhood deterioration has typically accompanied a general rise in the quality of occupied housing. As rising incomes have caused once middle-class areas to shift to occupancy by lower socioeconomic groups and, in turn, the areas in which these latter families had lived to filter to the more unstable poor and to be partially abandoned, housing conditions have improved for all concerned but not, apparently, the neighborhood environment. While it might be argued that the new surroundings of those who have filtered upward in the market are better than those from which they migrated, this does not seem to be so for those at the bottom. Many of the negative elements of their old environment seem to move with them and to become more exaggerated as institutions which once served both the stable and unstable poor disappear. The guaranteed annual income would do little to alter this situation in the short run. At best it would enable a few families to escape from these conditions, but would leave the environment itself untouched. Over time, however, stabilizing incomes might change behavior patterns of many of the poor and, to the extent that they create their own environment, enable them to improve their surroundings.

Utilization of Space

There are three ways in which a guaranteed annual income might alter the amount and type of housing space which families demand. First, new household formation among young, unrelated individuals might increase. This possibility has already been discussed. The tentative conclusion was that any increase would probably be quite modest. Second, families in which the children or parents had been separated due to economic adversity might become reunited and future separations reduced in number. Such a trend would tend to offset household formation by young persons and to increase, if only slightly, the demand for larger dwellings. Finally, some of the families that were overcrowded would seek larger quarters. Among low-income families, the income elasticity of demand for housing space is apparently greater than it is for quality.[21] In the short run, the supply of large, low-rent units could not accommodate a large increase in demand, but in both the short and long run, a large increase would be unexpected anyway due to the low level of the guarantee.

Concluding Remarks

The general conclusion of this paper is that the guaranteed annual income would have only a slight impact on the housing market in the short run and that over a longer period of time the effects would also be moderate unless the guarantee were accompanied by other programs. This conclusion follows largely from the fact that the level of benefits which the guarantee would bring do not appear to be substantial enough either to change housing expenditures significantly or to reduce market imperfections materially or to solve housing-associated family problems. At some higher level, income redistribution could without any doubt create vast changes in the market, but present guarantee proposals do no more than open the door to this possibility.

Even though most of the arguments in the paper are predicated on the expectation that any program of income maintenance would be modestly funded, they depend also on a host of additional assumptions concerning the effect of the guarantee on labor-force participation rates and the structure of wages; the types of families which would experience an income increase and how much; the housing-preference structure of these families; their existing housing conditions; the effect of income regularity as well as income supplementation on behavior of landlords and tenants; and the dynamics of the low-rent sector of the housing market. Any one of these assumptions could perhaps be seriously challenged, and with it the subsequent threads of the analysis.

The paper was begun in the hope that the assumptions which would be necessary would be fewer in number and of less importance. The basic notion was that, using knowledge of the housing conditions of various categories of families who already benefit in differing degrees from income-maintenance programs, inferences could be drawn about the impact on families to whom similar or superior benefits might be extended. The requisite data, however, proved to be totally lacking. This fact not only weakens the analysis but also raises more important questions concerning the adequacy of the information on which housing policies are now based. It is a common practice for research papers to conclude with a call for more research. Whether these pleas reflect masochistic tendencies, a compulsive thirst for facts, an exaggerated belief in the importance of subjects in which there is a personal interest, or balanced judgment is never clear. It would perhaps be best, therefore, for others to ponder the need to gather the data which were so glaringly absent in this paper. Nevertheless, it should be mentioned that much of the information could be obtained at little extra cost in communities which are experimenting with guaranteed-income plans and by agencies that already administer such programs.

It was almost inevitable that, in thinking about why the guaranteed annual income would not provide much beneficial support for the housing market, possible alternatives came to mind. This last paragraph discusses a few of those which were nurtured if not supported by the study. First, if neither guaranteed incomes nor rent supplements are likely to be funded on an adequate scale, perhaps some sort of rent-insurance scheme could be developed which would cheaply fulfill one of the purposes of both of these other programs. If rent insurance is not feasible, some other method of reducing involuntary moves *must* be developed. Second, the dilemma of the low-income problem family must be met head-on. Families who fit this description probably constitute no more than 10 to 15 percent of the badly housed, but they plant the seeds of deterioration in entire neighborhoods, and they prevent four or five times as many families with similar demographic characteristics from obtaining decent accommodations. They constitute more or less of an invisible skid row that has escaped its confines to poison a larger environment. Present policy is to keep such families out of public housing and penalize, through code enforcement, private landlords who cope unsuccessfully with them. If this problem is to be eradicated, as it must be if the housing problems of a much larger group are to be solved, almost the opposite strategy must be pursued. Third, a solution must be found to the dilemma of families who are reasonably good tenants but who are denied access to adequate housing because responsible landlords view them as high risks.

Policies pinpointed at these three areas, if successful, could greatly magnify the positive effects of the guaranteed annual income as well as of existing housing programs on conditions in the low-income sector of the residential inventory.

Notes

[1]Or in expectations about costs or expenditures.

[2]No. 8 also is a function of the change in inter-regional differences in incomes which a guaranteed income might effect. This possibility will be examined later in the paper.

[3]The diagram is not intended to exclude the possibility of incomes rising and becoming more stable simultaneously. Nor is it intended to imply that the four types of changes will necessarily be significant in all cases.

[4]Projected from 1967 data and assuming that the number of cases that are closed and re-opened in the same year is minimal.

[5]Total unemployment benefits exceeded $2 billion in 1968 and were paid to over 11,000,000 persons (not allowing for cases closed and reopened the same year). While these benefits are broadly available, it is assumed here that they benefited primarily those in the lower half of the in-

come distribution. See Henry J. Aaron "Income Transfer Programs," *Monthly Labor Review*, February 1969. Also Table A–13, p. 108, same issue.

[6]In fact, public assistance alone channels almost five times as much money into the residential inventory as does public housing which, in turn, is several times larger than any other housing assistance program.

[7]Estimates of the poor who benefit from an income program as a proportion of total poor vary, depending on what poverty line is chosen, what income data are used, etc. The estimate of one-half comes from Mollie Orshansky, "How Poverty is Measured," *Monthly Labor Review,* February 1969. According to Orshansky, 10.9 million households were in poverty in 1966; 16 million would have been in poverty had there been no income programs. Thus of 16 million poor households, one-third were pulled above the line; one-third were helped but not enough to rise above the line; and one-third received no help at all. Orshansky's estimates do not include unemployment compensation and may exclude low-income veterans.

[8]Orshansky, *ibid.*, estimates that public assistance raises about one recipient family out of six above the poverty line. Also see note 7.

[9]These estimates and those which follow in this paragraph are from "A Report on Caseload Increase in the Aid to Families with Dependent Children Program, 1960–66," Research Report No. 2, State Department of Public Welfare, State of Maryland, July 1967, pp. 15–16.

[10]The figure for social security payments is from Aaron, *op. cit.*, and the figure for unemployment compensation is guessed from Table A-13, *op. cit.*

[11]Orshansky, *op. cit.*, estimates that in 1966 the number of families who were pulled above the poverty line by public programs alone, and excluding unemployment compensation, was 5.1 million.

[12]Accounts of the new food stamp plan in South Carolina referred to several families in this situation.

[13]The Maryland State Dept. of Welfare has calculated that slightly less than 40 percent of all poor families with children, not just female-headed families, are on AFDC. See "A Report on Caseload Increase. . . ," *op. cit.*, p. 31.

[14]Margaret G. Reid, Housing and Income, Chicago: University of Chicago Press, 1962.

[15]Sherman J. Maisel and Louis Winnick, "Family Housing Expenditures: Elusive Laws and Intrusive Variances," Proceedings of the Conference on Consumption and Savings, University of Pennsylvania, Vol. 1, 1960, pp. 359–392.

[16]With obvious longer term effects on the housing market.

[17]This statement is based on preliminary data from a 1968 household survey in Baltimore, Maryland, by the University of Pennsylvania and Morgan State College.

[18]Lenore E. Berson, "The Dispossessed," Philadelphia Housing Association, Philadelphia (since renamed "The Housing Association of Delaware Valley"), December 1967.

[19]Of course, some of this latter group may join the ranks of the permanent or intermittently poor, but only then would there be a perceptible impact on quality.

[20]1968 Baltimore household survey, *op cit.*

[21]Maisel and Winnick, *op. cit.*

4.3

Major Proposals for Change in Federal Tax Provisions Affecting Urban Housing

Richard E. Slitor

This section analyzes several major tax approaches to urban housing problems, designed to stimulate housing investment, encourage better maintenance or rehabilitation, discourage quick turnover and related deteriorative investment practices, or assist in the enforcement of local housing codes. (Table 6 at the end of this chapter compares the major plans discussed.)

Faster Depreciation

At least until the advent of the investment credit, the standard tax incentive (and financial encouragement) device employed by the Federal Government was some form of accelerated amortization or speedier tax depreciation. Faster tax writeoffs are still advanced as a method of encouraging housing, pollution abatement facilities, industrial development of depressed areas, and the various other risky low-return forms of investment required to accomplish high-priority national objectives. Without attempting to analyze in detail any specific plan, the following discussion examines some of the generic characteristics of the fast depreciation approach to providing financial assistance and incentive for low-cost urban housing.

Accelerated amortization (five-year tax writeoff) was used in World War II and during the Korean War period plus some time thereafter to assist the construction of certified emergency defense facilities.

In 1946, the 150 percent declining balance method of depreciation, hitherto available only under special conditions involving group industrial equipment accounts, was extended by administrative action to buildings with a particular view to assisting multiple-unit residential construction. In the Internal Revenue Code of 1954, the 200 percent declining balance and sum-of-the-years digits formulas were introduced for use on any new depreciable asset acquired or constructed after 1953, with a useful life of three years or more. During the latter part of the 1950s, five-year amortization was allowed on grain storage facilities to help alleviate a shortage of this kind of storage capacity. In 1958, in connection with tax revisions to aid small business, an ad-

Reprinted from *The Federal Income Tax in Relation to Housing*. Research Report No. 5, for the National Commission on Urban Problems (Washington, Government Printing Office, 1969) by Richard E. Slitor.

ditional first-year depreciation allowance was provided equal to 20 percent of the first $10,000 of annual new machinery and equipment acquisitions with a useful life of at least six years. In 1962, shorter depreciation guideline lives were promulgated administratively for all forms of commercial, agricultural, and industrial machinery and equipment and farm buildings, a major objective being to encourage modernization and more dynamic replacement practices. Shorter lives were withheld from nonfarm buildings largely because of the absence of recapture safeguards to prevent wholesale conversion of ordinary income into capital gains through resale of overdepreciated real estate. Current investment proposals in the real estate area also include faster depreciation features such as reduction in useful lives for income tax purposes.[1]

Faster depreciation offers a number of basic tax advantages to the investor:

1. If it is taken in a period of high emergency tax rates, and there is every expectation that the rates will be lower in the future, the accelerated writeoff concentrates deductions in the period when they secure greater tax benefit and serves to neutralize the disincentive effects of the temporary high rates. If rates trend upward, however, the quicker timing of deductions may be disadvantageous to the taxpayer.

2. Faster tax writeoffs enhance the present discounted value of capital recovery allowances, thus increasing the value of the investment or increasing the profitability of a given amount of private capital commitment.

3. Since faster depreciation in effect puts tax-free return of capital further ahead of the payment of tax, it increases after-tax cash flow in the early years, reduces the private commitment accordingly, and thus reduces risk and illiquidity.

4. Depreciation is taken on the entire cost of a depreciated building, and it is taken by the equity owner; with heavily leveraged financing, the value of the faster depreciation (tax deferment, etc.) on a given gross building cost is beneficially concentrated on a much smaller equity investment. This increases the rate of return to the equity owner above the return calculated on the entire building cost without mortgage financing; the increase is of course greater the thinner the equity.

5. The depreciation allowance shelters from tax part or all of the cash income remaining after operating costs, property taxes, and mortgage interest. The larger the depreciation allowance, the

greater the release of earnings for repayment of mortgage principal. Excess deductions creating a tax loss may exempt partnership shares, convert corporate dividends into nontaxable capital distributions, and provide a tax deduction against other income.

6. Speedier depreciation is ordinarily expected to produce merely faster timing of deductions; if the investor keeps the property, he will eventually pay more tax on income from that property to replace the tax he deferred during the fast writeoff period. But if property can be resold at capital gain rates, the faster writeoff, which represents an artificial reduction in book value, is reflected in capital gain; under these circumstances the advantage of *timing* is supplemented with the advantage of *substitution of capital gain* for ordinary tax rates on the deferred income generated by the faster writeoff.

7. Since fast depreciation operates by providing increased deductions, its benefits vary directly with the income level and applicable tax bracket rate of the investor. High-income investors thus benefit more than those in the lower brackets.

Much of the incentive value of accelerated amortization in the World War II and Korean periods depended upon the existence of high corporate and excess profits tax rates during the emergency period. This factor is not present in the present situation in anything approaching the same degree. The adoption of the temporary 10 percent surcharge (or other temporary emergency income taxes) will, however, set up a new advantage for accelerated tax writeoffs by permitting the eligible investor to defer more income from the period of higher rates now and to pay tax on it later at lower rates. This would be in addition to the timing advantage (or the conversion of ordinary income into capital gain) at constant tax rates.

What is the tax incentive value of acceleration, measured in terms of the present discounted value of the depreciation allowances? The Table 1 set of figures illustrates the effect of shortening the tax depreciation life of a building or changing the method of depreciation. Figures are shown for the present discounted value of the entire depreciation deduction, the accompanying tax savings at a 50 percent tax rate, and the tax savings at a 70 percent rate. (The tax saving rate for large corporations would be 48 percent at 1967 rates and 52.8 percent under the 10 percent surcharge proposal; the tax saving rate for the top bracket individual would be 70 percent at 1967 rates and 77 percent for a full year under the 10 percent surcharge plan.)

Table 1. Present Discounted Values of Depreciation Allowances on $1,000 of Building Investment, for Selected Alternative Depreciable Lives and Depreciation Methods (5 Percent Discount Rate)

	Entire deduction	Tax savings at 50%	Tax savings at 70%
Expensing in year of purchase	$1,000.00	$500.00	$700.00
Straight-line depreciation:			
7-year life	867.97	433.99	607.58
10-year life	810.78	405.39	567.55
20-year life	654.27	327.14	457.99
40-year life	450.43	225.22	315.30
50-year life	383.37	191.69	268.36
200 percent declining balance depreciation (with switch to straight-line at optimal point):			
10-year life	857.96	428.98	600.57
20-year life	723.71	361.86	506.60
40-year life	542.50	271.25	379.75
Sum-of-the-years digits depreciation:			
10-year life	869.88	434.94	608.92
20-year life	753.79	376.89	527.65
40-year life	584.94	292.47	409.46

Note: Roughly consistent with the fact of substantially current tax payment, the value of the "depreciation annuity" is calculated as though the first-year allowance is immediately available (no discount); the second year's allowance is available one year hence (one-year discount); the third year's allowance is deferred two years (two-year discount); and so forth.

As the figures in the table show, shortening the depreciable life of a building from 40 to 10 years, for example, would enhance the present discounted value (5 percent discount rate) of the straight-line "depreciation annuity" (tax savings from depreciation allowances) by about $180.17 ($405.39 less $225.22) for the large corporation or individual in the 50 percent bracket and by about $252.25 ($567.55 less $315.30) for the individual in the 70 percent bracket. These amounts would be approximately equivalent in value to a tax credit or tax-free cash grant of 18 percent and 25 percent, respectively, of the building cost.

The table also shows that shortening the depreciable life from 40 to 10 years, but requiring the taxpayer to give up the 200 percent declining balance formula otherwise available with the 40-year life and to employ the straight-line method with the 10-year life, would on balance increase the present discounted value of the depreciation annuity by about $134.14 ($405.39 less $271.25) for the 50 percent bracket taxpayer and by about $187.80 ($567.55 less $379.75) for one in the 70 percent bracket. These amounts would be equivalent to tax credits or tax-free grants of roughly 13 percent or 19 percent, respectively, of the building cost.

To gain some perspective on these magnitudes, one may compare them with the present 7 percent investment credit on machinery and equipment. Or it may be noted that they are several times the value of the advantage gained by using the accelerated depreciation formulas. For example, as shown in the table, in the case of the 50 percent bracket taxpayer the excess of the present discounted value of the 200 percent declining balance allowance over straight-line with a 40-year life is about $46.03 ($271.25 less $225.22) per thousand dollars of building cost; for the 70 percent bracket taxpayer the advantage is about $64.45 ($379.75 less $315.30).

Plans which required additional equity financing (reduced leverage) as the price of the use of the shorter tax lives would of course to that extent reduce the profitability of the faster depreciation relative to the equity capital commitment. The following simplified analysis helps put the values of the present accelerated formulas and shorter depreciable lives for buildings, with or without the accelerated formulas, into perspective with leveraged investment situations:

The value of the advantage of 200 percent declining balance depreciation over straight-line for a 40-year life building is, as we have previously calculated, about $46 per thousand dollars of building cost for the 50 percent bracket taxpayer and $64 for the 70 percent bracket taxpayer. Although only about 4½ percent and 6½ percent, respectively, of the entire building cost, these savings would be 23 percent to 32 percent of a 20 percent equity ($1,000 building cost financed with an 80 percent mortgage). The value of the combined shortening of depreciable life from 40 to 10 years and shift from 200 percent declining balance to straight-line depreciation was calculated at about $134 in the 50 percent bracket and about $188 in the 70 percent bracket. These values amount to 67 percent and 94 percent, respectively, of a 20 percent equity. If they were available, for example, only to the investor with a 50 percent equity, the corresponding percentages would be about 27 percent and 38 percent, only moderately higher than the ratio of existing accelerated formula advantages to a 20 percent equity.

An important consideration in evaluating the incentive force of faster tax writeoffs for housing is that their value depends upon the taxpayer's having income with which to absorb the additional deduction. If the venture is in a corporation, the corporation must have taxable earnings to utilize the additional deductions or be able to pass through the losses to wealthy stockholders. Low-earning, low-income housing ventures may not generate the income to absorb readily a substantial increase in depreciation deductions. Ordinary corporations cannot pass loss deductions through to stockholders. Subchapter S partnership-type treatment permitting such passthrough is not readily available under present law for real estate corporations.[2] In syndicates or partnerships, of course, the excess deductions of the housing project may spill over as pro rata losses to the owners. Unless some such outlet is available, the additional depreciation will run to waste or its tax effect be deferred until such time as the deductions are utilized through net operating loss carryovers. Waiting for the actual tax benefit via a loss carryforward will negate much of the value of the "speedy" writeoff.

It is thus evident that accelerated depreciation, to be effective as a tax incentive device, requires either project earnings or available side income of investors (preferably wealthy) plus appropriate legal organization from the tax standpoint to ensure a tax payoff. In using faster tax writeoffs to beef up otherwise inherently low earnings from housing investment, the government would in effect be saying, "Here is a tax bonus if you can use it; to utilize it effectively you should have income from sources other than the housing investment we want you to make; the bonus will be worth more, the richer you are; ordinary investors may be well advised not to participate." This kind of appeal is limited to a certain investment clientele; its discomforts are obvious from a semantic and tax policy viewpoint.

To explore the capacity of housing ventures to utilize additional depreciation, the figures below assume net operating income before interest, depreciation, or income tax on a $1,000,000 building project (operating on leased land) ranging from 5 to 8 percent of the building investment. Assuming mortgage interest on an 80 percent loan at 2 percentage points below the gross rate of return, we have the results in Table 2:

Table 2. Schematic Comparison of Alternative Levels of Depreciation Deductions with Taxable Earnings Margins in First Year of Operation

($ Thousands)

Net operating income before interest depreciation or income tax		50	60	70	80
Mortgage interest		24	32	40	48
Net income before depreciation		26	28	30	32

Depreciation and taxable income or loss (−) first year for alternative depreciation lives and formulas:

	Depreciation	Taxable income or loss (−)			
SL[a] 50 years	20	6	8	10	12
SL 40 years	25	1	3	5	7
SL 33½ years	30	−4	−2	0	2
SL 25 years	40	−14	−12	−10	−8
SL 20 years	50	−24	−22	−20	−18
SL 10 years	100	−74	−72	−70	−68
150% DB[b] 40 years	37.5	−11.5	−9.5	−7.5	−5.5
150% DB 20 years	75	−49	−47	−45	−43
200% DB 40 years	50	−24	−22	−20	−18
200% DB 20 years	100	−74	−72	−70	−68

[a] SL = straight line
[b] DB = declining balance

If these figures are reasonably representative of earnings results on a low-income housing project, it appears that tax losses would appear if depreciation went much above 2½ percent (40-year life, straight-line). Consequently, to be effective, accelerated depreciation would require either higher project earnings than the level assumed here, other income in the corporation, or the possibility of passthrough of tax losses to owners.

One of the basic objections to the use of accelerated depreciation either by itself or as part of a package (including tax credits, capital gain deferment, or other features) is that it deliberately creates a special kind of real estate tax shelter device—complex, carefully structured to meet sophisticated tax rules, feasible only to the initiated with skilled tax counsel—in the name of ameliorating the slum.

Unless safeguards were adopted, such as full depreciation recapture (or substantial new compensating liberalities were

	Straight line		Double declining balance	
Acceleration from:	40 years		40 years	
To:	20 years	10 years	20 years	10 years
Revenue loss at 50 percent tax rate in the first full year (in $ millions):	$12.5	$37.5	$25.0	$75.0

introduced), the accelerated depreciation approach would lead inevitably to resale as depreciation ran low and (in combination with lower interest deductions) exposed income to tax. Straight-line depreciation with shortened tax lives has a less marked effect in this regard than the declining balance or sum-of-the-years digits formulas, but it is not innocent. To minimize the quick turnover and tenure instability effects and the concomitants of irresponsible ownership and upkeep policies, the fast depreciation approach would probably need to entertain such things as

Exclusive use of straight-line depreciation.

Assistance in refinancing after, say, 10 years.

Restoration of basis after substantial depreciation writeoffs had been taken to permit the process to start over again.

Tax penalties on early sale or on inadequate maintenance.

Any defensible use of faster depreciation techniques is thus driven into the application of more complex, esoteric, and compulsive tax mechanisms leading to results quite different from usual concepts of free enterprise.

The schematic summary above indicates the order of magnitude of revenue lost per $1 billion of eligible construction expenditures under alternative possibilities in the first full year.

As this indicates, the revenue impact depends upon the normal tax life and depreciation method for the housing investment (or the comparable investment it displaces in the economy)[3] and on the extent of the depreciation speedup.

Revenue losses indicated in this schematic presentation would increase cumulatively in subsequent years, assuming continuation of the program. For example, in the simplest type of case, involving an assumed reduction from a 40-year life to a 20-year life or from a 40-year to a 10-year life on the straight-line basis, the revenue losses for the first 10 years would mount as follows for a constant-level program of $1 billion annual eligible construction:

Revenue Impact Calculated at a 50 Percent Tax Rate
(dollars in millions)

Year	40 years to 20 years	40 years to 10 years
1	$ 12.5	$ 37.5
2	25.0	75.0
3	37.5	112.5
4	50.0	150.0
5	62.5	187.5
6	75.0	225.0
7	87.5	262.5
8	100.0	300.0
9	112.5	337.5
10	125.0	375.0

In the switch from 40-year life to 10-year life, straight-line, the maximum annual losses would be reached in year 10 and thereafter decline, unless the program expanded. In the change from 40-year life to 20-year life, the losses would continue to rise until the twentieth year and thereafter decrease, again assuming a constant $1 billion annual investment outlay. The analysis would be more complex in detail for declining balance depreciation, but the general pattern of results would be similar.

It may be noted that the current revenue cost to the government of increasing straight-line depreciation by a reduction from a 40-year life to a 20-year life is about the same for the first year as an interest rate subsidy of two and one-half percentage points on mortgage loans *equal to* the assumed depreciable construction costs. The two and one-half percentage points of depreciation would involve a "net cost" to the government of about 1¼ percent of the investment under a 50 percent average tax rate. An interest rate subsidy would increase taxes by about 50 percent of the additional income reflecting the two and one-half percentage points subsidy leaving a net cost to the government of roughly 1¼ percent of the loan. This cost would mount as the program unfolded over the years, as in the case of the faster tax depreciation plan. Over the longer run, the timing aspects of depreciation speedups may bring compensating revenue gains; this compensation is not present in the case of interest rate subsidies.

The exhaustive analysis and public discussion of the relative merits of accelerated depreciation and the investment credit, in connection with the legislation introducing the credit for machinery and equipment in 1962, turned in considerable part on the question of their comparative impact on investment incentives per dollar of revenue concession. It was concluded that fast depreciation in its various forms (initial writeoffs, shorter tax lives, more concentration of allowances in the early years, etc.) is relatively inefficient as a fiscal device for increasing the profitability of depreciable investments. Short-range revenue losses from fast tax writeoffs were estimated to be larger than for an investment credit which would produce equivalent increases in after-tax rates of return.[4]

Joseph A. Pechman[5] has presented calculations showing that the combined effect of the 7 percent investment credit with the existing 200 percent declining balance depreciation was to increase profitability on a 10-year asset previously earning 10 percent with straight-line depreciation to 12.5 percent—an increase of 25 percent. The investment credit accounted for 60 percent of the increase in the rate of return. Yet, as between the two existing incentive features, rough calculations readily show that the introduction of 200 percent declining depreciation on machinery and equipment would cost more revenue in the second year and considerably more revenue annually than the 7 percent investment credit on the same level of investment in 10-year assets by the third year.[6]

An independent analysis by the Machinery and Allied Products Institute in 1961 (when the then-pending legislation embodied an 8 percent credit rather than the 7 percent figure finally adopted) concluded, among other things, that

> Because it is a direct offset against tax, and does not reduce subsequent depreciation allowances, the proposed 8 percent credit is equivalent to initial writeoffs several times as large. While the equivalence varies with the service life of the assets concerned, for companies subject to the full corporate tax rate it would require at least a *40 percent* writeoff to match the credit in average, or overall terms.[7]

The MAPI analysis also considered the tax and revenue effects of an 8 percent investment credit and a 40 percent initial writeoff (an extreme form of acceleration) assuming a flow of investments in 15-year assets with a 5 percent annual growth rate. This showed that the initial writeoff would lose about two and one-quarter times as much revenue in the first year, more than one and one-half times as much in the fifth year, and about equal amounts in the seventh year, after which revenue losses under the credit would be greater, amounting to about twice as much in the fifteenth year.

The 1961 MAPI study also found that the credit is more favorable to short-lived than to long-lived assets, whereas an initial write-off yields virtually uniform benefits (increased profitability) over the service-life range.[8]

A more recent MAPI study (1964) on the same topic reaches similar conclusions.[9] This study compared the profitability effects of (1) the present 7 percent credit, (2) guideline depreciation assumed to shorten average tax lives by 15 percent, and (3) the general corporate tax rate cut from 52 to 48 percent under the Revenue Act of 1964. The study covered a service-life range from 4 to 25 years. Among its findings: "The beneficial effect of the investment credit is by far the largest; in fact it exceeds the combined benefits of the other two measures. The smallest is from the guideline depreciation system."

In the 25-year asset class—corresponding to the lower end of the normal range of building tax lives—the 1964 MAPI study found that, with all or substantial equity financing, the 7 percent credit was two or two and one-half times as potent in raising profitability (rate of return on original investment) as the guideline depreciation producing a 15 percent shortening of tax life.[10]

In the first year of operation, the investment credit reduced revenues by about $1 billion; guideline depreciation, about $1.5 billion. Some adjustment must be made, however, for the fact that guideline depreciation was available at the start on all existing assets and included extra revenue-losing features such as restoration of fully written-off assets to group accounts; the credit was limited to current acquisitions. Making this adjustment (allowing, say, 10 percent of the guideline revenue cost for current acquisitions) and taking account of the buildup of the impact of faster depreciation on the revenue base as more expenditures are made each year, it appears that guideline depreciation limited to current acquisitions would build up to annual revenue losses on a given level of investment equal to those of the credit in six or seven years (greater revenue losses thereafter) and still have only a fraction of its profitability-bolstering effect.

As the better tax plans in this field now clearly recognize, fast tax depreciation for low-income housing in the inner cities (or housing accessible to the urban poor) would not be an automatic or virtually self-administering scheme. The standards and criteria for acceptability of projects in terms of physical characteristics, location, financing, and rental scales would almost certainly involve exacting regulations, certification procedures, and bureaucratic overhead. In these circumstances, unlike the simpler situation of grain storage facilities in the 1950s or even the emergency defense facilities of the Korean and post-Korean period, fast tax writeoffs could not avoid the trappings and paraphernalia of another government housing program, nor would they tap directly the energies and creativeness of the private sector by the almost automatic operation of built-in incentives of the tax system in its universal contact with private enterprise. As one examines the problems of suitable eligibility criteria for tax writeoffs for low-income urban housing, this use of the tax system appears more and more to be essentially a complex and rather cumbersome substitute for direct expenditures, having selective appeal chiefly for high-income investors. Under these circumstances one wonders

Whether the private investor participants would not in fact be fairly tame captives of a highly elaborate system of governmental prescriptions for method of operating, financing, tenure, rents, resale, etc.

Whether the zest of the private enterprise system for producing a better product and for producing it more efficiently could be effectively linked to the quest for tax savings in lieu of ordinary profits.

Whether the result would not combine the disadvantages of a grant system with those of the indirect use of the tax system to make "backdoor" payments.

Much of this line or argument applies also to investment tax credits for low-income housing, discussed in the next section. Fast tax depreciation, however, is somewhat different since it bestows its benefits from tax deferment and capital gain creation in a more complex manner so that its cost is harder to identify or calculate for later appraisal.

Investment Tax Credits

Fast depreciation postpones tax; investment credits eliminate tax. As we have just seen, various forms of accelerated depreciation have already been used and could be used further to encourage capital investment in housing. Acceleration of capital recovery allowances does not eliminate eventual tax liability with respect to an investment unless fast depreciation is the means for converting ordinary income into lower taxed capital gains or for moving income from a high-tax to a low-tax year;

rather, it postpones the day of tax payment with respect to income from a particular investment and is frequently characterized as an interest-free loan by the government to the investor; more specifically, it can be viewed as a procedure which advances the "annuity of tax savings" inherent in a stream of depreciation deductions in point of time, thus enhancing the value of the tax depreciation annuity. Particularly if a business needs liquid investment funds and operates on the basis of a careful calculation of the timing of cash flows, faster capital recovery allowances make the investment in eligible depreciable assets more attractive. The benefits to recipients may exceed the cost (interest on deferred tax) to the government. It does not require a highly sophisticated view to see an accelerated depreciation plan as a method for pooling risks and advancing capital funds from government revenues for a variety of high-risk, potentially high-return, projects.

The revenue costliness in the short run of the accelerated depreciation method relative to its incentive effect (increased profitability), which was explored at some length here, is understandable in common sense terms when one views it as a procedure by which the government advances interest-free loans (earlier timing of the tax depreciation annuity) in order to give the investor the benefit of the interest gain. The government has to move large capital funds out into industry in order to give it the benefit of the interest on these funds (tax postponement).

This characteristic of accelerated depreciation prompted the Administration in 1961–62 to recommend an investment credit approach as a more efficient, less immediately costly device to bolster after-tax profitability and thus stimulate investment. The investment credit in contrast with accelerated depreciation represents an effort to promote economic growth and modernization in the industrial equipment field by more directly subsidizing new investment by an actual subtraction from tax liability. This technique yields more increase in after-tax profitability per revenue dollar foregone; each dollar of tax concession is reflected in an equal increase in the taxpayer's investment rewards. The faster depreciation method has to advance the investor $100 of postponed tax in order to increase his profitability by the interest savings—$6, $7, $8 or more per year—depending on what the taxpayer's benefit may be considered to be on the $100 interest-free loan.

The current vogue in tax incentives for housing, pollution abatement, and other goals accordingly is to recommend investment credits—either by themselves or sometimes in combination with faster depreciation and other benefits.

The leveraging factor which works wonders in concentrating interest rate-earnings rates differentials and accelerated depreciation tax savings on a thin equity margin would accomplish the same minor miracle for investment tax credits. The potency of an investment credit would indeed be so great on leveraged real estate that a problem would arise of avoiding (1) large disparities in the effective rate of the credit on equity depending on the debt ratio and (2) extreme tax inducements for overleveraging and unsound financial structures.[11]

As was noted in the case of accelerated depreciation, the distribution of tax benefits through the investment credit device to taxpayer beneficiaries who met specific eligibility tests for low-cost housing construction or slum rebuilding would almost certainly necessitate detailed regulations and a certification procedure. The distinction between giving a tax credit on a certified structure or rehabilitation outlay and paying the investor by means of a government check thus becomes tenuous.

The tax credit also normally has to clear several hurdles such as the percentage of tax limitation, a passthrough to stockholder procedure, or a possible unused credit carryover waiting period before it becomes fully effective. In these respects, the tax credit seems inferior to the direct check-writing procedure.

The essence of the investment credit tax device for low-income urban housing would seem therefore to be the back-door approach to the Federal budget, with all the short-circuiting of regular legislative and budgetary checks which that entails. Only to the extent that one could demonstrate that the process of qualifying for the credit on the basis of stipulated eligibility criteria with some accompanying certification procedures was simpler, more objective, more widespread and effective in its appeal than the cash subsidy, could it overcome the basic economic presumption against using the tax system to pay for the accomplishment of specific desired goals.

This discussion up to this point tends to support these viewpoints:

Investment credits are more efficient than faster depreciation if increasing profitability of slum housing investment is the objective.

The application of necessary criteria and certification would seem to make investment credits and direct cash payments almost indistinguishable.

Some of the difficulties in making tax credits fairly and uniformly available to potential investors without contortions of the tax law and business practices argue for the direct cash subsidy route.

The skeptic (as represented by current Treasury and Congressional viewpoints) could well contend that the credit offers only the strategic advantage of avoiding direct confrontation with the budgetary watchdogs—a waning advantage now that guards have been posted at the back entrance.

There are, however, some interesting further questions as to the difference in practical operation of eligibility criteria in conjunction with tax credits as against a direct subsidy. Would the administration of desired standards be as effective under a tax credit system as under a cash or loan subsidy program? Would the separation of certification and the almost automatic "disbursement" of tax credits loosen standards? Would not claimants for widely advertised tax benefits be in position to secure qualification more readily and with less exacting standards than recipients or direct subsidies or preferred loan treatment?

Viewpoints within the Federal Government on policy questions as great as the urban housing problem necessarily vary and often conflict. Priorities and value standards of those concerned with maintaining the integrity and intactness of the revenue system may appear negative in relation to the positive thrust of those seeking stimulus and aid from any source—and from the creative energies of private enterprise in particular—since, despite the high priority attached to the rebuilding of the inner cities, extending an investment credit for slum building would impinge upon the complex of difficult and unresolved issues that surround the present somewhat unsatisfactory state of the tax provisions applicable to real estate investment generally.

The present situation is not entirely a stable one. While housing is favored in some respects, it is shortchanged in others as the previous review in this study spelled out in some detail. The extension of an investment credit and possibly related liberalizations for low-income housing would tend to set a pattern for real estate generally. The present pattern, whatever its implications for the equity and integrity of the tax system, is that of the real estate tax shelter on which much of our finest urban construction depends.

Some better, more comprehensive approach might revise the present treatment of real estate investment to put it on a par with industrial equipment. This could help reduce dependence on the real estate shelter device, with its sensitivity to interest rate differentials and credit availability, and subject to diminishing cash flow over time and resulting quick turnover practices. It might help lessen the diverting appeal of the luxury high-rise apartment and make low-income housing a reasonably attractive investment, particularly with, but possibly even without, differential tax credits. Such an approach would apparently have to look to revised depreciation formulas and a careful scaling of investment credits to holding period and possibly to debt structure.

In the low-income housing field, the rental structure which the tenants can bear at present does not produce a favorable earnings interest rate differential. Subsidized interest rates can help, but there is an inherent problem of profitability adequate to cover risks and attract real estate capital and entrepreneurial talent from the more attractive alternative opportunities.[12]

If the diagnosis is correct that the inherent profitability of adequate nonslum low-income urban housing is too low to attract vigorous investment, even with no income tax at all, the role of investment credits in slum housing is essentially different from its present role in the industrial machinery and equipment field. For the typical manufacturing company, for example, the credit alleviates the 48 percent tax on business income derived from the use of manufacturing facilities. The investment decision continues to rely primarily on the inherent profitability of the manufacturing operation which is merely reduced less than otherwise by the tax, now that the investment credit is available (the credit itself being limited to the first $25,000 of tax liability plus 50 percent of the liability of the business in excess of $25,000). It is true that the present investment credit is not necessarily restricted to the income directly traceable to the particular machinery and equipment on which it is claimed (tax on other income of the business entity or on other income of the individual taxpayer may be offset up to the prescribed dollar and percentage of tax limits), but that is the general purpose and result. The credit cuts down on some of the negative effects of tax rates. The deliberate extension of the credit device under conditions in which (1) tax on other income has to be "dragged in" to get a benefit, and in which (2) only affluent taxpayers with plenty of other income are logical candidates to make the investment, is a substantial change in its intended use. In effect, it makes the credit a kind of negative income tax on the housing income but one which applies to the claimant a means test in reverse.

The discussion here of tax credits then must close with these interrelated expressions of doubt and skepticism:

Is a selective investment credit (which in practice would have to be offset against tax on income other than that generated by the low-income housing itself) the appropriate way for the Federal Government to approach the interrelated problems of building and operating costs, tenant ability to pay, and profitability?

To what extent would the credit have to be supplemented from situation to situation with loan guarantee and interest rate subsidies?

If the other subsidies are essential, could they not be pushed to the point where they deal with the basic problem of cost and profitability without resort to the tax credit device?

Supplementary Allowances for Improvement and Maintenance Expenditures

Another tax approach to low-income housing is one directed at the gradual process of physical and economic deterioration of the housing resources of the core city. With the exodus to the suburbs of middle-class families, accelerated by spreading slums and rising crime rates, deterioration of neighborhoods becomes progressive; if all landlords made an effort toward improvement, deterioration might be halted, but it does not pay any one landlord to maintain or improve his property; private return on investment becomes small, and it is not profitable to maintain and improve since well-kept buildings are difficult to maintain and do not command significantly higher rental income. This is the familiar "downward conversion" or "filtering" process with adverse externalities operating against the preservation of the cities (sometimes likened to the "Prisoner's Dilemma" of game strategy) which creates slums.[13] Only concerted landlord action, for which market forces provide no incentive or mechanism, could reverse the cumulative worsening process and preserve decent neighborhoods.

The supplementary tax allowance approach is designed to provide a tax motivation for the individual landlord to maintain and improve his property so as to break the vicious spiral that otherwise occurs.

As a first basic step under the supplementary allowance plan, depreciation allowances on all residential property[14] would be placed on a more realistic basis; a *50-year-life* and the *straight-line* method on the building structure or shell would be the norms for rental housing. Shorter-lived equipment components of the building might be written off more quickly. This would reduce the attractions of the real estate tax shelter which draws money into luxury high-rise construction, yet it would maintain incentive for initially including and periodically modernizing essential components. The substitution of straight-line for the accelerated formulas on the basic structure would correct the present strong tax motivation for resale of property after 8 or 10 years when optimal tax depreciation begins to run low.

The *supplementary allowance* to be provided for the rental property owner would consist of a deduction against gross income for all expenditures on improvement and maintenance of the property (without regard to present distinctions between repair and maintenance expense and capital-type improvements to be capitalized) up to some specified annual percentage, possibly equal to the depreciation rate, of the capital cost of the structure, with a carryover of unused allowances in excess of the limit in any one year to subsequent years. The possibility of expensing capital improvement elements in housing expenditures for income tax purposes would thus set up a tax inducement for upgrading the older rental housing supply, comparable, for example, to the present privilege of expensing intangible drilling and development expenditures for petroleum.

To reinforce this incentive for capital improvements and extend it also to repair and maintenance which tend to be neglected despite current tax expense deductions, the supplementary allowance plan would include a provision that a portion, say, one-half of the depreciation otherwise computed on old properties, would be contingent upon matching repair and improvement expenditures. This proposal would in effect place $2 of deductions at stake in the landlord's decision to make $1 of expenditures on repair or improvement of older properties. The tax base and revenue concession actually involved would be limited to the expensing of improvements since the plan would also involve a curtailment of ordinary depreciation on older properties which were allowed to deteriorate.

This plan, which is spelled out in more detail with illustrative figures in both the following pages and the concluding section of this study, might have some adverse impact on the selling price of slum properties which under present law derive part of their value from the ability of the landlord to take unreal depreciation. However, this would have no significant effect on the investment in new housing. The "announcement" or decision-influencing incentive effect of the combined expensing and additional depreciation allowance would add to the effective supply of decent older housing and combat the present vicious spiral of deterioration and neglect of repair. If the reduction in the immediately available depreciation for the neglected property did not stimulate better upkeep, it might encourage razing the property to secure the immediate deduction of the remaining depreciable basis as a demolition loss. This would at least pave the way for reconstruction on the site. In effect, this would bring Section 1250 of the Internal Revenue Code, dealing with partial recapture of the excess depreciation component of real estate gain, into line with Section 1245, which provides full recapture at ordinary rates of gain on machinery and equipment sales reflecting depreciation.

Dollar limitations on the expensible improvements (beside limiting the deductions to, say, half the normal depreciation) might be necessary to prevent unintended benefits for very expensive luxury apartment renovation.

How important and effective would be the resulting incentive for repair and improvement of older rental housing?

The expensing of improvements would mean the government would in effect share immediately in a portion of the expenditure geared to the applicable tax rate: 48 percent in the case of a sizeable corporation, 70 percent in the case of a top bracket individual taxpayer, and so forth. While repairs and improvements would be treated alike, and the cash flow effects of the tax writeoff would be identical in either case, the incentive value of the plan would of course be greater for improvements which would otherwise be depreciated over the period of their useful life. The right to additional depreciation on the whole property in matching amounts up to the (illustrative) figure of half the depreciation allowance as normally computed would have the proximate effect of the government's immediately sharing in a still large portion of either repair or improvement outlay—96 percent for a 48 percent tax corporation, 100 percent for an individual in the 50 percent bracket, 140 percent for the investor in the top individual bracket.

As the basis for an illustrative analysis of the comparative treatment of repairs and improvements under the supplementary allowance approach, assume straight-line depreciation at 10 percent to be the present-law alternative to the proposed expensing of improvements; assume further that expenditures for either repair or maintenance qualify the taxpayer under the plan for depreciation allowances otherwise deferred until applied as part of the tax basis in computing ordinary gain or loss on sale of the property 10 years later. What are the tax savings to a 50 percent bracket taxpayer from each type of expenditure under the plan as against not making the expenditure, and how do these results compare with present law?

Case of $1,000 Repairs

(1) Under present law, repairs are deductible and the deduction of $1,000 repairs results in a $500 tax saving, leaving a net out-of-pocket cost to the taxpayer of $500. The plan makes no change in the deductibility of repairs, so that in this respect the supplementary allowance plan provides no new advantage for repair expenditures.

(2) Under present law, the repair outlay would have no direct effect on depreciation (unless it was recognized as lengthening the life of the asset). Under the proposal the repair expenditure would produce $1,000 of immediate depreciation allowances not otherwise available under the plan. These allowances represent no net increase over present law since the plan involves a cutback of normal depreciation in the absence of repairs. Contingent as they are upon repairs, however, these allowances do represent a net increase—or more accurately, an advance in timing—in the deductions available under the plan, an increase attributable to the decision to make repairs. Within the framework of the plan (the decision model which would confront the landlord), the allowances otherwise available would consist of offsets against receipts on resale 10 years hence; these alternative tax savings would have a present discounted value (at 5 percent) of about $307.[15] The net excess of the present discounted value of the depreciation tax saving over that of the alternative

use of tax basis in computing gain or loss on resale would thus be $193 ($500 minus $307).

Case of $1,000 Improvements

(1) Under present law improvements are to be capitalized and written off over their useful life; the plan substitutes an immediate writeoff of the $1,000 improvement outlay with tax savings worth $500 for depreciation allowances having a present discounted value (again, at 5 percent) of about $405.[16] The net advantage under the facts assumed is about $95 ($500 minus $405) in present discounted value.

(2) The improvements, like the repairs, also trigger the additional matching contingent depreciation allowances. These produce a net present discounted value advantage of about $193 ($500 minus $307) as seen above.

The overall net advantage in terms of present discounted value of tax savings from capital allowances would thus be about $288 ($95 plus $193) for $1,000 of improvements, under the assumed facts. In terms of the present discounted value stimulus, the superiority of improvements over repairs would be about $95 per $1,000 of expenditures.

In terms of immediate cash flow, the plan thus produces a large benefit for repair and especially for improvement of eligible older properties. This stimulus would be especially effective for the investor who is short of cash and highly cash-flow conscious. In terms of actual present discounted value of benefits, the concessions offered by the plan are more moderate, indicating of course that the substance of the modification is a rearrangement of the timing of capital recovery allowances on old residential properties.

The phase of the plan which makes depreciation contingent upon matching outlays entails no actual revenue decrease since it deals with depreciation available under present law which would be deferred under the plan unless matched by upkeep dollars. It would produce some revenue gain effects to the extent it reduced (deferred) depreciation in the absence of matching upkeep.

The phase of the plan which permits the immediate writeoff rather than the gradual depreciation of capital improvements would involve a current revenue decrease in proportion to the level of improvement outlays as affected by the plan.

In 1966, total expenditures of owners on residential additions, alterations, maintenance and repairs, and replacements amounted to $11.7 billion, according to preliminary estimates.[17] Of this total $7.9 billion was spent by owner-occupants of either single-family homes or properties containing two to four units (with one unit owner-occupied). The remainder of $3.8 billion (repairs and improvements) was spent by nonresident owners of rental properties of all sizes ranging up to large multiple-unit properties.

Improvement-type outlays accounted for about $6.9 billion of the $11.7 billion total; repairs and maintenance, $4.8 billion. The improvement-type outlays on properties other than one-family owner-occupied homes probably amounted to about $1.8 billion in 1966; of this amount perhaps about $1.3 billion was spent on properties without an owner-occupant.

Assuming (1) that about one-third of the existing improvement-type expenditures would not qualify (because the property had not reached the required elapsed age, say, 30 or 40 years; because the expenditures were made on the owner's living quarters; because per-unit outlays exceeded specified limitations; and for similar reasons) and (2) that the *average* effective tax rate applicable to the deductible amounts was in the vicinity of 25 to 30 percent, the immediate annual revenue decrease resulting from the improvement-expensing feature of the plan would amount to several hundred million dollars at existing expenditure levels. Revenue effects would be greater to the extent that the plan stimulated improvements. Revenue recapture would immediately commence, reflecting the absence of tax basis and future depreciation allowances with respect to the expensed improvements. The rate of recapture would build up year by year so that after 10 years or so the current revenue cost of the plan would be relatively insignificant, except for the possible effects of appreciable growth in the process of upgrading and improvement of old deteriorated properties.

The figures cited as a basis for the above revenue-effect calculations are drawn, as indicated, from preliminary Census data for 1966. An overall summary of residential upkeep and improvement expenditures for 1966 is presented in Table 3.

An analytic summary of final data for 1965 showing the general "anatomy" of repair and improvement expenditures for owner-occupied and rental residential properties—pertinent to the consideration of tax incentive approaches in this area—is presented in Table 4. One of the striking aspects of the picture presented in Table 4 is the difference in per-unit improvement levels for owner-occupied and rental units. Improvement ex-

Table 3. Expenditures by Owners for Upkeep and Improvement of Residential Properties by Size of Property: 1966[a]

(In millions of dollars)

Type of work	All residential properties	Owner-occupants of properties with 1 to 4 housing units	Owner-occupants of properties with 1 housing unit	Other residential properties[b]
All types of work	$11,702	$7,945	$7,127	$3,757
Upkeep				
Maintenance and repairs	4,805	2,380	2,067	2,425
Heating and central air-conditioning	196	106	97	90
Plumbing	470	219	184	252
Roofing	323	199	173	123
Painting	2,122	1,264	1,092	858
Other	1,694	592	521	1,102
Improvement				
Additions, alterations, and replacements	6,897	5,565	5,060	1,332
Additions to residential structures	1,205	995	995	210
Additions and alterations on property outside residential structure	880	730	684	150
Alterations within residential structure	2,898	2,501	2,252	397
Heating and central air-conditioning	381	357	350	24
Plumbing	228	124	113	105
Remodeling	650	526	473	124
Other	1,639	1,495	1,316	144
Replacements	1,913	1,338	1,129	576
Heating and central air-conditioning	409	299	259	110
Plumbing	421	244	204	197
Roofing	428	326	280	102
Other	656	489	386	167

[a]All data are preliminary.

[b]Expenditures by owners of properties with five or more housing units and nonresident owners of one to four housing unit properties.

Source: U.S. Department of Commerce, Bureau of the Census, Release CB 67-121, October 24, 1967.

penditures per unit for single owner-occupied homes were more than two-and-one-half times ($144 versus $57 per unit) those on large multiple-unit properties. Maintenance and repairs, on the other hand, were greater per unit ($90 versus $72) for large multiple-unit rental housing than for the single owner-occupied home.

The practical implementation of a supplementary allowance plan of the type outlined here would need to deal with a number of detailed but important questions of specification, including the treatment of older properties acquired prior to the effective date of the plan, the specific age-of-property qualification, possible limitations on the dollar amount of expenditures per unit, possible eligibility limitations based on the unit rental value, and others. It would seem to be desirable to avoid specific, difficult-to-administer locational rules which might limit the plan to defined property areas and thus exclude helpful generalized effects on the housing supply.

The plan would be kept more manageable and the revenue losses reduced if it were restricted to very old and dilapidated properties, or to expenditures required to bring properties up to minimum code requirements or other specified standards. Dollar and rental value limitations would serve to exclude luxury-type housing from the proposed financial stimulus.

The tax expensing-contingent depreciation treatment would only partially compensate the average slum landlord in the brackets below 50 percent for additional repair and improvement outlays. In tax brackets of 50 percent or above, the taxpayer could obtain immediate tax savings equal to or greater than the outlay, subject to a requirement to repay the portion representing the borrowing of future capital recovery allowances. The extent to which the plan would actually encourage upgrading of older properties would depend also upon related factors: the extent to which the added improvements would be reflected in increased rentals and capital values; the extent to which landlords in poverty areas and elsewhere recognized this potential gain through higher rentals or ultimate resale values (possibly figuring on some similar response on the part of other landlords).

Many variations could be developed on the general theme of the supplementary allowance plan. The basic thrust of this approach is to upgrade old housing and combat the externalities which hinder the economic operation of unfettered market forces

Table 4. Expenditures by Owners for Maintenance and Repairs and for Improvements by Size of Property: Total, Average Per Property, and Average Per Dwelling Unit, 1965

Item	Total	1-family owner-occupied	2-4 unit properties with 1 unit owner-occupied	All other residential properties[a]
Owners' expenditures on residential properties (millions)				
Total	$11,442	$7,033	$717	$3,692
Maintenance and repairs	4,999	2,382	344	2,273
Improvements	6,443	4,651	373	1,419
Average amount per property (dollars)				
Total	253	216	280	367
Maintenance and repairs	109	72	134	226
Improvements	144	144	146	141
Indicated numbers of properties (millions)	45.9	33.3	2.6	10.1
Estimated numbers of dwelling units[b]	64.2	33.3	6.0	25.2
Computed average amount per dwelling unit (dollars)[b]				
Total	178	216	120	147
Maintenance and repairs	78	72	57	90
Improvements	100	144	63	57

[a]Includes all rented and vacant 1-unit properties; all condominium and cooperative units; 2-to-4-unit properties without any owner-occupant; and all 5-unit-plus properties.
[b]Estimated; total includes about 7 million vacant units.
Source: Compiled (and where indicated, estimated) from data in U.S. Department of Commerce, Bureau of the Census, Construction Report, C50-10, Part 1.

in the conversion and utilization of old, lower-grade housing resources.

Other things being equal, a system of special tax encouragement to renovation and rehabilitation of older housing as against the creation of entirely new housing might be open to the accusation that it would produce uneconomic distortions, directing investment into avenues which would not meet the usual tests of optimal efficiency in the use of resources. The basic riposte is that the defects in the existing market mechanism encourage deterioration and disregard both the social costs of slums and the benefits (external to the horizon of the particular landlord) of better upkeep of the housing stock. More adequate upkeep and conservation of the present low-income housing stock may thus represent a better allocation of resources than the undirected market forces would achieve.

Special advantages for investment in old housing improvements could, nevertheless, lead to various uneconomic responses—excessive extension of the useful life of outmoded building shells, preoccupation with rebuilding or expanding older properties that may not meet any realistic definition of low-income housing, neglect of vital new ideas in new construction, extensive tax-subsidized activity in the form of rehabilitating numerous Georgetown-type areas throughout the country for the relatively affluent, and the like. Safeguards and limitations could become complicated and might alter the character of the plan as a relatively automatic, self-operating incentive in the low-income housing area.

Use of Federal Tax Depreciation Rules to Compel Compliance with Local Housing Codes

The facts that

slum landlords make profits,

these profits are in part due to the income tax savings from depreciation allowances on the depreciable cost of the slum property,

tax depreciation is not closely in step with year-to-year falloff in resale value, and

tax depreciation may be claimed no matter how miserable the housing, no matter how rundown the property, and no matter how gross the operator's violation of local housing ordinances

has led to suggestions to use the Federal tax system to help enforce the local housing code or support its purposes.

In its simplest form, this approach would consist of denying depreciation allowances for Federal income tax purposes on any property not in full compliance with the local housing code.[18]

In a variant form, this suggestion would make all depreciation allowances on substandard housing conditional upon the expenditure of equivalent sums for bringing the property up to standard.

What are the stated objectives of such an approach, what is their merit, and what are their chances of attainment through depreciation tax penalties?

One objective is of course to tax the profits from slums or tax the slumlord out of existence. Whether the denial of depreciation and resulting imposition of a kind of gross income tax on slum rents would do more than satisfy natural punitive attitudes toward slum operators is questionable. Some authorities feel this approach would indirectly at least lead to further deterioration because it would discourage ownership of slum property by the relatively good landlords who would find the riskiness of the investment further increased.[19]

Another aim is to "squeeze the water out of inflated slum values making it possible for public authorities, nonprofit sponsors or competent profit-motivated private operators to acquire and rehabilitate the properties or, if that is infeasible, demolish the building and transfer the land to a more appropriate use."[20] This objective could of course be furthered in various other ways, including local taxation of gross rents in substandard properties,[21] and more effective direct enforcement of local housing codes. Bending the Federal income tax structure to this purpose seems cumbersome, and the end result may be to put the property —still in slum condition—into the hands of organizations which for one reason or another are effectively tax-exempt.

Still another related purpose of the punitive depreciation policy approach is to force the bad landlord to become a good one or face the prospect of substantial Federal income tax penalties —or, failing this, to halt a drain on the Federal Treasury. In marginal cases, the threat of loss of Federal tax depreciation allowances and related difficulties with the Federal income tax authorities might induce better maintenance and reconditioning of properties. If this effect were widespread in a deteriorating housing area, it might help in its negative way to reverse the cumulative degenerative process that leads to the worst slums just as the supplementary allowance plan previously discussed would do in a more positive and systematic manner.

If the tax depreciation on a $100,000 structure, for example, is $4,000, its tax saving effect at the general 48 percent corporate rate as of 1967 was $1,920 annually. The prospect of losing this tax benefit, theoretically essential to the Federal tax objective of correctly measuring net income from the property, would spur considerable expenditure to retain the depreciation, provided there were no other way out for the taxpayer.

Depreciable basis, however, is available for calculation of gain or loss as well as for annual depreciation deductions. The first reaction of existing slum property holders might be to sell their properties at a loss, reflecting the present discounted value of the future tax depreciation denied them, taking a Section 1231 ordinary loss deduction. This would normally be equal to a number of years' tax depreciation. The operators could then go back into business with lower capital outlays and continue the essential slum operation: charging relatively high rents for the privilege of crowding undermaintained premises. Without the aid of tax depreciation, the operation in the long run would, it is true, be less profitable since it would not benefit from the prime tax shelter phenomenon: the writeoff of depreciation which does not really materialize at ordinary tax rates and resale of the property at or above original cost subject to capital gains tax rates.

The impact on capital values of slum real estate of the denial of depreciation could be severe. If the depreciation is in reality a pure tax giveaway, with no actual decline in usefulness or value over the entire tenure of the property, the resulting loss of value of the property would in that case be the present discounted value of the withheld depreciation less the present discounted value of the capital gain tax otherwise due on resale.

	At 5 percent discount rate	At 6 percent discount rate
1. Present discounted value of 25-year tax annuity of $1,920[a]	$28,413	$26,017
2. Present discounted value of $25,000 capital gains 25 years hence	7,383	5,825
3. Net loss of capital value from loss of depreciation (1 less 2)	21,030	20,192

[a]Computed as value of sum of $1,920 immediate tax savings in year 1 plus an annuity of $1,920 for 24 years.

Note: Basic values rounded to nearest dollar; net value calculated from rounded figures.

For the $100,000 property using 25-year straight-line depreciation of $4,000 annually, with the prospect of tax savings of $1,920 each year, and a capital gains tax of $25,000 in prospect at the end of the line, the capital value of the loss of depreciation could be calculated, assuming a 25-year holding without depreciation (see preceding page).

A loss of capital value as great as this (in the order of 20 percent) could wipe out slum propertyholders' equities and threaten ability to repay mortgages. Using higher discount rates which might be considered appropriate for the degree of risk involved, the loss of property value would of course be less.

But this is not the whole story. Suppose that some long-range decline in the value of the depreciable structure occurs and that the loss of depreciation is partially replaced with a loss deduction on resale of the property. Suppose, for example, it could be expected that the $100,000 property would be sold after 25 years for $50,000 with a tax deductible loss of $50,000 ($24,000 tax saving at 48 percent) if no depreciation had been allowed. For comparable purposes the present discounted value of the loss of depreciation and the related tax changes could then be calculated (see below).

Some effects similar to those of the denial of depreciation on substandard property could be obtained by

Reducing depreciation to a stringently realistic level, including

	At 5 percent discount rate	At 6 percent discount rate
1. Present discounted value of 25-year tax annuity of $1,920[a]	$28,413	$26,017
2. Present discounted value of $25,000 capital gains tax 25 years hence	7,383	5,825
3. Present discounted value of $24,000 tax savings from $50,000 tax loss on resale	7,087	5,592
4. Net loss of capital value (1 less 2 less 3)	13,943	14,600

[a]Computed as value of sum of $1,920 immediate tax savings in year 1 plus an annuity of $1,920 for 24 years.
Note: Basic values rounded to nearest dollar; net value calculated from rounded figures.

not permitting property to be depreciated below its salvage or probable resale value (this could be done administratively).

Applying full recapture to gains on resale to the extent of prior depreciation along the lines of Section 1245 of the Internal Revenue Code so as to take the repeated cycle of overdepreciation and sale, with systematic ordinary income-capital gain conversion, out of the slum investment picture (this would require legislation and was previously suggested by the Treasury in 1961 and 1963).

Looking at the whole approach from what might reasonably be expected to be the Federal tax policy standpoint, the denial of tax depreciation would seem merely to shift to the Federal tax system and its depreciation rules in particular much of the burden of enforcing penalties for noncompliance with local housing codes. To the extent tax depreciation is grossly unrealistic or favorable in a special way to slum properties because their falloff in value is slower than ordinary buildings, one might argue that some cutback in slum housing depreciation is called for anyway on grounds of uniform measurement of net income. The proposed punitive or enforcement effect to that extent would merely be corrective.

If one examines proposals such as that involving some kind of certification by local housing officials to accompany the Federal tax return claim for depreciation, a few practical administrative realities first need to be taken into account. Under the conditions of inadequate enforcement implicitly assumed, the effectiveness of the proposal would appear to be not much greater than the willingness of local housing code officials to deny Federal tax certification. If housing code violators can resist enforcement or avoid local fines or penalties, one might expect that they would be able to secure certification where substantial Federal tax penalties were at stake. The shift of onus from local housing code officials to the Federal tax collector for code enforcement may be more apparent than real.

Apart from the question of the realism of slum property depreciation, the question of the consistency of tax deductions on substandard property with expressed Federal or state policy might be raised on behalf of this type of proposal. The analogy with illegal business may be instructive. Income from illegal business operations is taxable. The ordinary and necessary expenses of an illegal business are deductible unless contrary to an expressed Federal or state policy or unless the deduction would amount to avoiding the consequences of violating the law.[22] Certain types of payments associated with illegal business activities are not considered essential operating expenses and thus are not deductible: "protection" payments, bribes, blackmail or extortion payments to avoid exposure, etc.[23]

It could be argued that depreciation allowances on a code-violating property are contrary to expressed public policy of providing decent housing for all American families. But Federal administrative practice would encounter serious problems in denying depreciation in properties not in conformity with local housing law, in view of the wide variations that would be encountered in the local housing standards themselves, and in the effectiveness with which they were enforced. Many rural or semirural properties which would fall short of any reasonable standards of health, safety, or comfort doubtless produce rental income and tax depreciation claims. The precedent of denying depreciation for persistent housing code violations would be troublesome in view of the many other health, safety, and regulatory requirements in other fields where more effective local enforcement aided by Federal tax sanctions might be desired.

A variety of other technical and policy questions could be raised against the denial of depreciation which could otherwise be supported by a showing of need for realistic capital recovery. The tax-sanction approach would draw no distinction between the excessive and the realistic tax write-off. Periodic sales of property could establish tax losses if depreciation were denied, unless depreciation were denied and a downward tax basis adjustment required nevertheless, as though depreciation were taken—a harsh penalty indeed. A sample of other questions posed by the tax-sanction approach: Would a year's depreciation be sacrificed because of a minor or temporary housing violation? Would the effective intervention of local housing inspectors in the application of the Federal income tax law lead to bribery and similar abuses where slum operators sought to get certification by illicit methods? Would Federal tax authorities be drawn into the surveillance of slum property operation and certification? Would local governments be entirely happy with a situation in which they assumed the burden and responsibility of housing inspection and the Federal government collected the penalties?

Proposal to Combat Slums by Limiting Total Depreciation on Buildings to a One-Time Write-Off of the Original Cost Plus Capital Improvements

Another "punitive" type of approach to the slum problem, also concerned with the repetitive depreciation cycle, is a plan to deny depreciation on rental housing in excess of the original construction cost plus subsequent capital improvements.[24] To illustrate how such a plan would work, assume a building constructed in 1963 at a cost of $1,000,000 and depreciated for a period of five years under the 200 percent declining balance method on a 40-year life basis. The cumulative total of depreciation taken would amount to about $226,000, and the unrecovered cost or adjusted basis in 1968 would thus be about $774,000. If the property were sold for $1,000,000, the plan would nevertheless limit the new owner to a depreciable basis of $774,000, the unrecovered cost in the hands of the original holder. Present law would allow the purchaser to depreciate his $1,000,000 purchase price using either the straight-line or the 150 percent declining balance method. If the second owner then proceeded to write off the $774,000 on a straight-line basis using a 3 percent rate, he would recover 30 percent of $774,000, or roughly $232,000 in the next 10 years, leaving the unrecovered original cost at about $542,000 ($774,000 minus $232,000). If the second owner then sold the property for $900,000, the plan would nevertheless limit owner No. 3 to a depreciable basis of $542,000, rather than the $900,000 purchase price recognized as the depreciable basis under present law. If after the passage of years and a series of owners, the entire original cost was written off, the depreciable basis thereafter would be zero (unless new capital improvements were made) regardless of the selling price or cost of the property to current investors.

Without going into the details of the operation of such a plan in respect to the measurement of gain or loss on sale of the property (which to some extent determines the severity of the denial of depreciation above the first owner's investment), it is evident that this approach falls in the general category of taxing gross rents in order to tax slums out of existence.

For the original owner who held the property over the long pull, the proposal would apply the income tax in the conventional fashion—first allowing tax-free recovery of the owner's investment and then exposing the entire net earnings to tax after the depreciable base had been fully exhausted. For the original owner who sold the property before his capital was recovered, the plan would also make no change in the present treatment.

For the second and subsequent holders who purchased the property at a price not in excess of the adjusted tax basis in the hands of the previous owner, the plan would also follow present law in permitting write-off of the owner's investment.

For second and subsequent holders who purchased the property for more than its adjusted basis in the hands of the prior owner, the plan would apply a higher effective rate of tax than under present law.

In effect, second and subsequent holders would pay tax on the same taxable income (assuming the same rentals and operating expenses other than depreciation) as if the property had continued to be held by the original investor.

Sale and resale at constant or rising prices would not affect the taxable income under the proposal. Tax-free return of the entire investment of subsequent owners under these conditions not only would not be assured, but actually would be prevented. Tax would be imposed on more than net income by ordinary standards of measuring net returns with reference to the particular owner's investment.

This proposal would tend to reduce the resale value of rental housing property as compared with present law wherever the market value tended to go above the adjusted basis, since the subsequent holders would receive less than the usual present schedule of depreciation. The reduction in value would thus be equal to the present discounted value of the "tax depreciation annuity" presently attached to the amount of step-up in depreciable basis on resale at a gain.

The prospect of reestablishing a higher depreciable basis in line with the purchaser's price is a significant factor in the market valuation. The ability to write off capital appreciation included in the purchaser's cost, possibly on a schedule faster than actual decline of useful value, is another related factor in market valuation. The plan would thus undercut these elements in rental property valuation, turnover, and mortgage financing.

This approach would have a pervasive and depressing effect on real estate investment in any category potentially affected by the plan. This would include new investment, the resale value of which would no longer receive the support it now has under the depreciable tax basis rules. In this respect, despite its anti-slum ingredients, the plan would tend to operate adversely upon the overall housing supply situation.

Slum or deteriorating properties now in existence would continue to operate. Proponents of such a plan would hope, of course, that it would have the salutary effect of bringing home to the deteriorating housing owner that, his resale prospects having been hurt, he must make provision for property replacement out of earnings and must in his long-range interest give effect to the depreciation reserves accumulating on his books.[25]

It is by no means clear, however, that the proposed restrictions would have the psychological effect of predisposing the housing owner to pour more money into the upkeep and improvement of a property the resale value of which has been hit adversely by stringent tax rules. Part of the purpose of capital improvements is to create resale value in excess of the capital expenditures. In the nature of the original cost limitation plan, such additional value would be squeezed by its tax handicaps.

In short, the plan would have a number of interrelated effects, many of which would not be consistent with the desire to combat slums:

1. The restrictions on depreciation and accompanying tax advantages where depreciation may be taken in advance of property decline would reduce resale value, ability to finance, and profitability for housing, not only in the slum or substandard category but also for new investments, unless the proposed rule were limited by some set of criteria to very old and inferior rental housing. Such arbitrary distinctions would be difficult to work out and the dividing line hard to defend.

2. Any weakening of tax incentives for new housing investment would affect adversely the whole housing supply situation. Tighter supplies would put additional demand pressures on inferior housing and strengthen the position of the substandard housing operator. Additional nontax actions would be called on to make up the difference.

3. The restriction would tend to put pressure on substandard housing owners to "milk" their properties even more intensively for at least two reasons:

(a) The natural tendency to try to absorb the additional "gross income" tax due to loss of depreciation by cutting back even further on upkeeping or improvements.

(b) Rational response to the fact that, even though rehabilitation expenditures were themselves deductible either as a current expense or as depreciation on capital improvements, it would be difficult to establish a higher resale value which was not depreciable to the purchaser.

4. The plan would apparently strike its heaviest initial blow at existing owners of rental housing and current investors in new buildings who would be caught between relatively fixed new construction costs and the prospect of the loss of resale value; future buyers of old property would be able to acquire property at lower prices which discounted the nondepreciability of values in excess of the former holder's adjusted basis.

5. Slum operators deprived of their familiar diet of favorable depreciation plus some leveraging would nevertheless tend to become adjusted to the new situation by taking advantage of the depressed prices; operating on a shoestring, they would perhaps be less responsible than before. The situation might indeed appeal to a less desirable type of owner and operator than before, particularly those who had little or no income tax to be concerned with or those who had operating losses elsewhere which they might offset against the taxable income margin created by denial of depreciation.

6. In knocking down old rental property values, the scheme would reduce the cost of urban renewal programs by lowering the price at which the core city slum properties could be acquired by public and nonprofit organizations.

It is obvious that a plan of this technical complexity with the possibility of multiple basis rules (for computing depreciation, for computing gain or loss on exchange, for determining casualty loss, transition provisions, etc.) would create a veritable field day for the alert tax practitioner and the creator of tax gimmicks. The allocation of purchase price between rental housing and other properties acquired in a single transaction and the substitution of leasehold for property sales would be obvious problems. The austere and high-minded purpose of the plan could readily break down in a morass of complexities and long-drawn patch-up legislation.

If it is desired to take the profit out of overdepreciation with its accompaniments—leveraged investment arrangements and capital gain conversion—in the rental housing field, it would seem to be simpler, more effective, and less inconsistent with the whole spirit of the income tax (which measures net income with reference to the situation of the particular taxpayer and his own investment, not the historical investment of other taxpayers) to apply the full-fledged recapture rule[26] to real estate as recommended by the Treasury in the past.

The denial of purchase-price depreciation is designed to halt the instability of ownership and periodic turnover characteristic of the present tax shelter arrangements. But it would tend to push ownership of depreciation-bare property into the hands of (1) low-bracket taxpayers, (2) taxpayers with excess deductions from other sources and operating losses, and (3) tax-exempt institutions.

Property might well rotate among the taxable-type investors as surplus deductions or losses were used up here and reappeared there. The fast-turnover syndrome could thus be replaced by another undesirable type of unstable ownership in which operation of the property in weak or indifferent hands would be less responsible than with the present tax-shelter rules.

Slum property operation would normally continue as long as rentals exceeded out-of-pocket expenses. Values of slum buildings would reflect the discounted present values of the expected quasi-rents, along with their proposed tax disadvantage. The denial of tax depreciation would result in an earlier economic demise of the slum property only in marginal cases. In brief, the reason for this is that the rate of return secured by tax depreciation allowance alone, without any supporting net rental return, on amounts invested in the property in excess of the non-depreciable land value would generally be so low as to represent an inferior use of the site.[27] The presence or absence of tax depreciation itself would not spell the difference for a property with no other return. The slum-destroying impact of the plan would thus seem to have a narrow range, since public condemnation would be expected generally to step in and compel abandonment, demolition, or rebuilding of the property before its continued use literally hung upon the tax depreciation.

Like recapture, the denial of depreciation approach would involve increasing taxes so that it would produce rather than lose revenue in the long run. However, the short-run impact of tax losses on sale of adversely affected property would be unfavorable to the revenues. The long-run revenue gain could, in the broader scheme of things, be available for direct use in upgrading housing resources. However, viewing the plan as a tax device in and of itself, its effect on new housing investment and on rehabilitation expenditures would seem on balance to be negative. Its contribution would be limited to the earlier demolition of the marginal fringe of property clinging to the depreciation advantage, and this effect would not by itself assure positive replacement of the scrapped housing resources.

Urban Rehabilitation Allowances for Owner-Occupants or Investors in Low-Income Housing

Another line of tax approach to the urban housing problem is through provision of special tax incentives for homeowners in blighted areas as well as for investors to maintain their property in good condition or to recondition them.

Tax Aids to Owner-Occupants in Blighted Areas

It has been suggested that (along with denial of depreciation on code-violating rental property, previously discussed) the owner-occupant in designated blighted areas be allowed a personal income tax deduction for all home maintenance expenditures up to some appropriate ceiling amount, such as $1,000 a year.[28] This might be coupled with some generous straight-line depreciation of the home-owner's adjusted basis to further encourage him to remain where he is *after* his property needs no further improvement, since there remains risk in the ownership of property in the neighborhood. These features are designed of course to halt blight and decay, upgrade deteriorated or deterioration-threatened neighborhoods, and stabilize ownership; a major aspect of the stated philosophy of this approach is to get away from "grantsmanship" and reduce the dependence of local governments upon Federal direct assistance in the housing area.

This plan would involve a tax subsidy to maintenance amounting to from 14 percent up to 70 percent (1967 tax rates) of the owner's outlay, depending upon his tax bracket. For low-income residents the tax assistance would be modest. To qualify, of course, the taxpayer would have to be an itemizer. If the proposed deduction caused a switch from the standard deduction to itemization, the loss of unused standard deduction would reduce the net benefit of the maintenance deduction. Some of the revenue concession would go for necessary expenditures which would be made anyway. The positive incentive effect would be greatest for relatively affluent home-owners with the least risk or disinclination to assume risk in spending further sums on maintenance and improvement of their homes; least, for the poor homeowners with the greatest risk. An interesting aspect of the plan is the possibility that it would bring higher-income citizens back into blighted areas to reap the tax rewards of rebuilding and fixing up older dilapidated homes.

The plan would place a considerable premium upon the receipt and retention of an official designation as a blighted area. Pressures would be great to broaden eligible areas into neighborhoods adjoining blighted areas. Once such a designation was made, it would be difficult to remove, particularly if it involved the availability of depreciation on the homeowner's adjusted basis after the particular property in the blighted area is itself brought up to standard.

The depreciation of home costs would produce some highly favorable tax results for homeowners in designated eligible areas. The combined deduction of depreciation at, say, 4 percent on the house and equipment, property tax at, say, 2 percent on the entire fair market value of the house and land, and mortgage interest at, say, 6 percent of the unpaid principal of, say, two-thirds of the property value, would amount to the following on a $20,000 home ($15,000 house and $5,000 land):

Property tax	$ 400
Mortgage interest	800
Depreciation	600
Total annual deduction	$1,800

This would be approximately equivalent to the entire rental of $150 a month ($1,800 a year) on a comparable property.

The effect of these features of the homeowner's tax incentive approach would be appreciable, particularly in the better semi-blighted areas which might qualify. In these areas, existing or potential new homeowners, to be attracted to the suggested allowances, would have sufficient taxable income to respond to tax incentives. A dominant result of this approach might be an influx of new, higher-income owners, and liquidation and exodus of the former residents.

Tax Aids to Investors in Residential Rental Property in Blighted Areas

Extra depreciation or similar deductions have been recommended under tax plans for combating blight for both

Investors in rental property in blighted areas, the allowance to consist of additional depreciation if matched by equivalent repair and improvement outlays (to encourage maintenance and upgrading).

Resident (owner-occupant) investors in rental property in blighted areas, the allowance to consist of some additional allowance presumably based on cost or value of the property (to encourage resident, as against absentee, ownership).

These features involve use of the tax system to pay owners and investors some varying fraction of the cost of maintenance and improvement on blighted-area housing and some varying percentage of the cost or value of their rental property to encourage resident landlords to continue to live there.

The objectives are reasonable, and their costs could be kept moderate because they would be limited to blighted-area expenditures or housing values.[29] The focus of these plans is on resisting deterioration, stabilizing neighborhoods, and conserving or improving the quality of existing housing. This is in contrast with the more ambitious and costly approach of creating tax incentives for housing (low-to-moderate-income or general) in order to ease the whole housing supply situation with some trickle-down to the most necessitous slum dweller.

By strict standards of tax equity, this system of tax allowances would be inequitable since it would result in varying benefits, depending upon the beneficiary's tax status and tax bracket, without regard to need. Some would benefit substantially; others, not at all.

Viewing these concessions as expenditures via the tax system, the critic would be in position to assert that the tax benefits are inefficient: their effective scope would be limited to that of the tax system and variations in benefit would not meet the standards of a rational expenditure program.

Slum dwellers and even blighted-area residents are presumably not in high tax brackets. The incentive effect of this type of allowance would be most potent for the higher bracket investor in the moderately blighted area; the tax rewards would tend to be least for residents of the poorer areas where the monetary and indeed physical risks of continuing to invest and live in the neighborhood are the greatest.

Rehabilitation Tax Write-Off Plan

Still another special-purpose proposal of interest would allow a 20 percent initial write-off and an optional five-year amortization of the remaining 80 percent of eligible expenditures for the rehabilitation of low-income rental housing.[30] The net effect of this proposal would be to permit the deduction of 36 percent (20 percent plus one-fifth of 80 percent) of the eligible outlays in the first year and 16 percent (one-fifth of 80 percent) to be amortized in each of the next four years.

This plan would have a time limit; under the latest formulation studied, eligible expenditures would have to be made prior to 1971.

Expenditures, to be eligible, would have to be made on qualified rental housing meeting certain criteria.[31] Expenditures required to correct a recorded violation of local minimum housing requirements would not qualify for the proposed fast tax write-off. Optional passthrough of the proposed allowances to shareholders of corporations is a feature of the plan as conceived.

Since rentals, financing, and rate of return on investment would be subject to Federal government approval, it is evident that the plan is essentially a technique for using the tax system to pay for the subsidization of what are essentially semipublic housing rehabilitation projects. The scope for creative imaginative effort by the private investor—often cited as an advantage of the tax concession device—would not seem to be particularly enlarged by the plan. Since the tax benefits are mechanical results of a given time schedule for given deductions at given bracket rates, they do not by themselves stimulate either economy or quality in housing.

In light of the pass-through feature, the plan is evidently designed to attract high-bracket individual investors for whom nominally low rates of return based on the approved rental and financing structure would be converted into attractive after-tax rates of return. This conversion would depend upon the quick write-off of the capital outlay against individual rates ranging up to 70 percent.

For 50-to-70-percent-bracket taxpayers each $100 of eligible improvement outlays would produce a series of potential "pass-through" tax deductions and tax benefits, supplemented by a possible return of the amortized investment in the form of capital gain on resale, as shown on the following page.

If the project was increased in value by the amount of the improvement expenditure and the shares in the project sold at a corresponding capital gain after five years, the present discounted value of the stream of tax deduction benefits (plus the $75 after-tax capital gain after five years, but excluding regular operating

	Year 1	2	3	4	5	Total	Proceeds of sale after 5 years*
Tax write-off	36	16	16	16	16	100	—
Tax savings at 70 percent	25.20	11.20	11.20	11.20	11.20	70	75
Tax savings at 50 percent	18	8	8	8	8	50	75

*Capital gain after 25 percent tax after five years, assuming resale at cost.

returns) acquired by each $100 of improvement expenditures would be as follows:[32]

	6 percent discount	5 percent discount
For a 70 percent bracket taxpayer	$120	$124
For a 50 percent bracket taxpayer	$102	$105

In combination with net operating returns this would appear to afford a very substantial incentive for the 70 percent bracket taxpayer. The $120 discounted value (at 6 percent) for the 70 percent bracket taxpayer, for example, indicates that in addition to regular operating returns, the tax write-offs would produce an after-tax yield of 6 percent plus very roughly 4 additional percentage points of return each year (20 divided by 5)—a total of approximately 10 percent annual tax-free return from the tax features alone (including the assumed return after five years of the written-off capital as capital gain). The $102 value for the 50-percent-bracket taxpayer indicates that he would derive slightly more than a 6 percent after-tax return annually from the tax features (again, including the return after five years of the original investment as capital gain) plus regular operating income. For taxpayers in lower brackets, the tax benefits would represent progressively smaller additions to the operating returns.

The present discounted value computations summarized here, however, represent the "gross" tax savings value of the fast tax write-offs. The "net" would be smaller since the rehabilitation expenditures would have some write-off under present law. The net additional incentive the plan would provide would therefore depend upon the excess of the value of the proposed pattern over that of the present law pattern.

Table 5 compares the present discounted value of the fast tax write-off pattern just examined (including recovery of the written-off expenditures after a 25 percent capital gains tax at the end of the write-off period) with comparable values for straight-line write-offs over 10, 20, and 25 years, respectively.

As the comparative discounted value analysis in Table 5 shows, the proposed fast tax write-off package, although valued at about $120, would be worth much less in terms of the net advantage over present law patterns; moreover, only a part (less than half) of the advantages would be due to faster tax write-off per se; most of the calculated overall net advantage would be due to the assumed resale at cost after the write-off period to recover the value created by the written-off rehabilitation expenditures.

The plan has the usual relatively high revenue losing effect per dollar of incentive effect that is characteristic of fast tax write-offs. It has the merit of focusing on the rehabilitation approach to combating deterioration and expanding the supply of adequate low-income housing. The initial write-off plus five-year amortization technique seems to be more costly revenue-wise per

Table 5. Present Discounted Value (at 6 Percent) for a 70-Percent-Bracket Taxpayer Per $100 Rehabilitation Expenditures

	Plan	10 year straight-line	20 year straight-line	25 year straight-line
Tax write-offs	$ 64	$55	$43	$38
Recovery of expenditures after 25 percent capital gains at end of write-off period	56	42	23	17
Total	120	97	66	55
Excess for plan over alternative:				
Tax write-offs	0	9	21	26
Recovery of expenditures after capital gains tax	0	14	33	39
Total	0	23	54	65

dollar of rehabilitation and appears to be less imaginative and efficient for the purpose of combating slums than the supplementary allowance plan examined earlier.

The complexity, range of possible variants, and differences in scope and objective of the various plans discussed here make it difficult to present any very satisfactory comparative evaluation or cost efficiency rating scale. As a reminder to the reader and as a basis for overall appraisal, Table 6 attempts such a summary.

Conclusions and Recommendations

These conclusions and recommendations deal with several aspects of tax impacts upon, and tax approaches to, low-income housing problems:

The various conflicting unneutralities of the present tax system in its application to housing investment and consumption.

The possibilities for improving and rebalancing the existing tax environment for housing in general and low-cost housing in particular.

The merits and demerits of massive tax incentive programs to stimulate and finance the conquest of slums by private initiative.

The problem of intergovernmental fiscal responsibilities toward substandard housing.

The potential, in efforts to halt deterioration and encourage rehabilitation in urban housing areas, of reasonable adjustments in overly rigid and literal-minded features of present tax provisions.

The inherent limitations of the tax instrument for dealing with such a large and complex problem as urban housing needs.

Observations on the Nature of the Problem

The tax laws, like other phases of public policy affecting low-income housing, can be substantially improved:

To increase the supply of low- and moderate-income housing.

To resist the process of progressive deterioration and blight in large urban areas.

To set in motion incentives for active rehabilitation of older properties.

To rebalance the structure of housing construction incentives so as to give needed emphasis to low-income housing needs.

Tax changes alone cannot deal adequately with the Nation's slum housing problem and urban deterioration. They can, however, supplement existing and proposed direct housing programs and thus contribute to a broader-spectrum effort. The housing

Table 6. Comparative Summary Evaluation
of Seven Federal Tax Plans Affecting Urban Housing

	Plan	Major Objective
A	Faster depreciation—new housing	Stimulate new investment in low-income housing
B	Investment credit—new housing	Stimulate both new housing and rehabilitation outlays for low-income urban families
C	Supplementary allowance for maintenance and improvement	Reduce existing accelerated depreciation on housing generally; stimulate maintenance and improvement expenditures
D	Denial of depreciation on substandard housing	Compel conformity with local housing codes
E	Limitation on aggregate depreciation to original historic cost of building	Penalize slum operation—encourage upkeep or demolition
F	Urban rehabilitation allowance for owner-occupants and rental investors in blighted areas	Combat flight—encourage rehabilitation and stable owner occupancy in blighted area
G	Initial write-off plus accelerated amortization for approved rehabilitation expenditures	Stimulate rehabilitation expenditures in approved low-income housing projects

problem of the inner cities is basically a manifestation of both poverty concentration and the understandable failure of the market mechanisms of the private economy to provide low-cost housing consistent with American standards of minimum comfort and decency. The very process of urban renewal, as an organized effort to rebuild core city areas, may have aggravated the immediate low-income housing supply problem by destroying much low or substandard housing for which there was no immediate replacement.

More specifically, one may view the housing problem of the inner cities as a basic manifestation of the underlying economic problem: how to allocate limited means among urgently compet-

Scope of Positive Tax Incentive	Estimate of Cost-Efficiency: Benefits per Revenue Dollar
"Eligible" new low-income rental housing	Relatively low rating in short run; permanent losses largely avoided if recapture is provided and if plan is eventually terminated
Both new units and rehabilitation of low-income rental housing	Higher than accelerated depreciation approach; but plan involves permanent revenue loss, not just deferment
Maintenance and improvement of older residential rental property	Good, especially after allowance for revenue gain component due to curtailment of overly liberal depreciation
Repair and improvements required to conform dilapidated housing with local building codes	No revenue loss—some revenue gain; effectiveness of penalty difficult to estimate—probably low
All rental housing—possibly all tax depreciable construction	Intended revenue gain—but possible short-run loss due to demolitions and sales at loss; effectiveness of penalty doubtful—some adverse effects on new housing investment and rehabilitation outlays
Maintenance and improvement expenditures of both owner-occupants and rental investors in designated blighted areas	Moderate—possibly some unintended effects: changing ownership and higher income beneficiaries
Rehabilitation activities in approved projects	Relatively low—primary appeal to high-income investors

ing wants. At the national budget level, the cost of closing the housing gap through public investment and subsidies to low-income families challenges the Nation's budgetary resources and its willingness to redistribute private incomes. At the family budget level, decent housing costs—including property taxes and an unsubsidized rate of return on investment—exceed what the low-income family can afford to pay.

Since basic housing even of substandard quality and quantity is 25 percent or even 35 percent of typical low-income budgets, solution of the decent housing problem would in itself be a great gain in the alleviation of poverty. However, efforts in this direction involve many difficulties: the technological and logistical ability of industry to supply acceptable housing at lower cost, the ability of families to pay those costs in rent or mortgage payments, and the ability of the metropolitan areas to finance community services without unduly adding to the property tax component of housing expense.

Even with extensive subsidies the rental cost of a new or rehabilitated one-bedroom unit would be substantially more than low-income families in the deteriorated areas could possibly fit into their budgets—in many cases several times more than they could absorb. For large families the gap between decent rental housing and rent-paying ability becomes even greater.

Various measures can be invoked to close the gap:

Increased productivity and income for the slum residents.

New building technology.

Additional subsidies.

Basic redesign of city living with various ends in view, including reduction in the burdensome overhead of the central metropolis.

With this background in mind, it is evident that a realistic view of the role of taxation in contributing to the present problem or its solution suggests that intelligent tax policy can at best only assist or complement a broader program.

Massive Tax Credits for Low-Income Housing Not Recommended

As the earlier discussion makes clear, on balance the case for the tax incentive route to aid slum housing is not persuasive in the present context:

Even if limited to specific forms of low-income housing in designated problem areas, the budgetary commitment would be great.

The Nation could ill afford to relieve a program of this importance and magnitude from the customary budgetary scrutiny and review procedures.

In the present environment of budgetary and resource stringency, there is increasing awareness of the essential equivalence of negative taxes and expenditures although they occupy opposite sides of the Budget.

Specific tax concessions for social purposes are thus increasingly identified as indirect use of public monies.

The pragmatic appeal of the tax incentive route as a means of winning acceptance by avoiding a direct confrontation with the facts of dollar cost and effectiveness has lost force in the more sophisticated framework of modern decision-making.

The newer argument that the tax credit is the simplest way of harnessing the creative energies of private business with minimum government interference does not hold up in the slum housing field because (a) specific standards and government cooperation through finance and guarantees would probably be essential in any event, and (b) low-cost housing can be built by private industry under contract in the same kind of partnership with government that prevails in space exploration and missile production.

Because of the magnitude of the problem of rebuilding and rehabilitating the inner cities,

The size of the effort in any year will have to be tailored closely to economic and budgetary resources.

The timing of housing expenditure will need to be watched closely and coordinated with economic conditions and resource availabilities to acceptable goals without excessive strain and inflationary pressure.

The use of tax credits or similar incentive devices is not suited to this kind of flexible adjustment to prevailing conditions.

Package Tax Reform in the Real Estate Investment Area

The present complex of income tax provisions applicable to investors in housing, along with other real estate, is open to criticism on several basic grounds:

1. The tax incentive for housing construction which the present law affords is a kind of happenstance, a byproduct of (a) heavy debt financing characteristic of real estate investment, and (b) liberal accelerated depreciation formulas designed primarily for industrial facilities. The benefits of acceleration focused on a relatively thin equity margin, with only partial recapture of excess depreciation on resale, produce the phenomenon of the real estate tax shelter—the tax incentive which has promoted much urban construction.

2. The incentive which investors' ingenuity has managed to distill from the present structure is ill-designed for low-income housing activity. There is a stimulus to quick turnover of rental residential property after the cream of accelerated depreciation has been skimmed—undermining stable tenure and concern with the maintenance of long-range values. Moreover, in the competition for real estate tax shelter investment, low-income housing is no match for commercial or office construction and

luxury-type apartment projects, where credit terms and prospects for capital appreciation are more favorable.

3. Much of the present real estate investment incentive and accompanying revenue decrease is squandered indiscriminately on repeated purchases and resales of older properties. While this may help maintain older property values, it is most unlikely that the net stimulus to *new investment* is in proportion to the tax monies foregone.

4. Investment in housing (as well as other forms of construction) is denied the investment credit available since 1962 for investment in industrial machinery and equipment.

In developing a balanced new tax environment helpful to investment in low-income housing, it is desirable to

Seek alignment with a general package of tax reform in the real estate area which would maintain incentives for new housing investment (as well as commercial and industrial construction generally).

Remove the necessity for housing investment to take place under the cover of the real estate shelter write-off and resale cycle.

Eliminate the repetitive series of turnovers of old properties which afford no direct incentive for new investment and lose disproportionate amounts of revenue.

Place investment in housing and other construction on a more equal footing with machinery and equipment investment.

To Accomplish These Objectives, Federal Income Tax Provisions Should Be Modified to Incorporate the Following Set of Interrelated Changes:

Limitation of depreciation on all buildings to a straight-line basis, in order to lessen motives for quick turnover.

Provision of liberalized depreciation guideline lives on buildings, in keeping with the machinery and equipment life system.

Establishment of full recapture rules to backstop the easing of depreciable building lives.

Allowance of an investment tax credit for new construction and major structural rehabilitation, suitably tailored to the building life and to the extent of mortgage financing.[33]

In view of the special risks and deterrents to investment in low-income housing and rehabilitation of older residential properties, such a balanced reform package might well include some type of differential benefit for such outlays, if that is feasible without requiring a highly detailed and selective certification procedure.

This proposed approach would tend to equalize tax incentives—now focused heavily upon luxury and highrise development—and distribute the interest of private enterprise more evenly over the whole housing field. It should also eliminate existing tax incentives toward excessive property turnover. Revenue gains in areas where taxpayer advantages now produce little or no new investment could thus be employed to provide tax benefits for desirable housing construction.

Encouragement of Rental Housing Rehabilitation

The Federal income tax treatment of rehabilitation expenditures rests upon a distinction between deductible repairs and non-deductible (capitalizable) improvements which is ill-suited to the world of substandard housing and the economics of the slum.

It insists, for example, that if the taxpayer in compliance with a city ordinance rewires an entire building, even though the value of the building is not correspondingly increased by this expenditure, it is a permanent improvement to be capitalized and not taken as a deduction for repairs.[34]

In the case of slum properties, expenditures which constitute improvements in the eyes of the tax law represent in reality long overdue repairs accumulated over years of neglect and deterioration. They may be equivalent to a bunching of repairs which would have been deductible currently if made year by year.

The existing tax barriers to rehabilitation expenditures reinforce the underlying economics of "mining" or "milking" of older low-income housing. The rehabilitation expenditures of the particular taxpayer often add little to the current earning power of the property and possibly little to its anticipated resale value. Yet, in addition to failing to qualify for a current income tax deduction, rehabilitation outlays may

Lengthen the estimated useful life of the property and thus reduce depreciation rates and increase exposure to Federal income tax.

Result in a higher local assessment and thereby increase property tax costs which neither the landlord nor tenant (nor owner-occupier in other situations) can very well support.

The risk that rehabilitation will not entirely "pay off" is especially obvious and great for the owner of residential property in congested urban neighborhoods with numerous old properties. It would be especially desirable and logical, accordingly, to focus tax incentives for maintenance and rehabilitation especially upon such housing. The "supplementary allowance" plan detailed earlier would be a suitable instrument for this purpose, and is the basis for the following proposal:

Federal income tax provisions should be modified so as to provide, with regard to rental housing structures that are relatively old (i.e., at least 30, 40, or 50 years), that

1. *Up to some specified annual percentage (perhaps equaling the depreciation rate) of the capital cost of such structures, a current expense deduction be allowed for all expenditures on improvement and rehabilitation (as well as for repairs and maintenance, as presently allowed), with a carryover of unused allowances in excess of the limit in any year to subsequent years; and*
2. *A portion—perhaps one-half—of the depreciation allowable on such property would be contingent upon the taxpayer's making matching expenditures for repair and improvements.*[35]

In order to prevent unintended benefits for renovation of very expensive luxury apartments, it might be necessary to include dollar limits per dwelling unit upon expensible improvements. Appropriate use of this approach would also call for adoption of the changes proposed with regard to depreciable real estate generally—to place all depreciation allowances on a straight-line basis and provide for ultimate recapture at ordinary rather than capital gains rates of "excess depreciation" allowed.

The suggested provision for "expensing" of improvement expenditures on old rental housing property is largely justified as a realistic expense allowance under the economic circumstances of the slum, and would provide a marginal encouragement to rehabilitation. The tax savings from such a current deduction would, however, absorb only a fraction of the cost (22 percent for a small corporation, 48 percent for a large corporation, and percentages ranging from 14 to 70 percent for individuals).

This encouragement would be expanded into a more positive incentive portion of regular depreciation allowances on substandard or deteriorated housing by the second suggested change, with regard to taxpayers' matching expenditures for repair, maintenance, or rehabilitation. The reason for this is that, up to the amount of the depreciation allowance which was conditioned upon matching upkeep or rehabilitation expenditures, the rehabilitation outlay would give rise to a current tax deduction of twice the amount expended.

The resulting immediate current tax savings per dollar of rehabilitation expenditures would be 96 cents for a corporation in the 48 percent bracket and up to $1.40 for an individual investor in rental housing (double the effect of the 70 percent top bracket rate). However, the revenue loss attached to the extra allowance (over and above the expensing of rehabilitation) would be nil even in the short run, since the extra allowance would merely represent depreciation available under the present treatment. There might indeed be some temporary revenue gain from curtailing unreal depreciation on properties already deteriorated to "rock bottom" resale value, on which landlords chose not to undertake better maintenance or rehabilitation.

Whatever offsetting revenue losses occurred would be attributable to a higher level of deductible maintenance and rehabilitation plus the write-off of improvements now required to be capitalized and depreciated over the useful life. This "cost" would be only a fraction of that of equivalent direct Federal outlays for housing renewal.

The conditioning of a portion of depreciation allowances on very old housing properties upon matching upkeep or rehabilitation expenditures is justified since (1) the depreciation concept applied to old dilapidated properties is to a great extent unreal; and (2) full tax-free recovery of capital is provided in any case through loss on sale, razing, or abandonment of the property.

How would this incentive plan work in practice? Suppose an apartment building already 50 years old is acquired at a cost of $100,000. Its remaining useful life is determined to be about 20 years, corresponding to a straight-line rate of 5 percent or a deduction of $5,000 annually. The landlord contemplates improvements involving new wiring and extensive plumbing renewals at a cost of $2,500 a year for the first three years. These amounts would be capitalized and depreciated under present law. Under the plan outlined here, they would be expensed and give rise to immediate deductions of $5,000 a year assuming the one-half of the normal straight-line depreciation was made contingent upon matching upkeep and renewal expenditures. The effect of the plan upon combined tax deductions for depreciation and upkeep in the first year is summarized in Table 7 (assuming use of straight-line depreciation under both present law and the suggested plan).

Comparing actual deductions under the proposal with present law for the first year, we find the information in Table 8.

As Table 8 makes clear, the proposal would

Table 7

	Tax Deduction Under Present Law	Tax Deduction Under Proposal
No rehabilitation	$5,000	$2,500
$2,500 rehabilitation	5,125	7,500
Increase due to rehabilitation	125	5,000

Table 8.

	Present Law	Proposal	Increase or Decrease
No rehabilitation	$5,000	$2,500	$ − 2,500
$2,500 rehabilitation	5,125	7,500	2,375

1. Reduce deductions by $2,500 below present law if there was no rehabilitation.
2. Increase them by $2,375 above present law if there was $2,500 rehabilitation expenditure.
3. Increase them by $5,000 over what they would otherwise be under the plan if there was $2,500 rehabilitation expenditure.

The expensing of rehabilitation outlays plus the effect of contingent depreciation under the supplementary allowance plan would provide an incentive to economical, quick-result upgrading of existing housing. It would tend to halt the process of continuous housing deterioration. It would not reduce the existing supply of housing as more drastic renewal operations may do but should increase the effective supply of adequate housing. The suggested tax changes do minimal violence to realistic standards of income taxation and in some respects increase its realism of income measurement in the substandard housing area.

Adjustment of Availability of Homeowner Tax Advantages

Turning now from the tax treatment of *investors* in housing to the treatment of the *homeowner* and *consumer* of housing, we may consider the potential thrust of housing tax reform with regard to

The existing tax incentives for homeownership under the individual income tax (the exclusion of imputed rental value and allowance of deductions for property taxes and mortgage interest for owner-occupiers).

The prevailing academic view that various undesirable effects—attrition of the tax base, economic distortion toward "over-housing" by middle- and upper-bracket taxpayers, equity discrimination against renters, and tax bias toward labor force immobility that is associated with homeownership—would justify abolition of present income-tax advantages of the homeowner.

The position taken in this study is that homeownership involves important social and economic values which merit tax assistance through the Federal income tax system. These values would be important in ameliorating and correcting the problems of the core cities for several related reasons:

Homeownership encourages social stability and financial responsibility.

It gives the homeowner a financial stake in society with a built-in inflation hedge.

It encourages better maintenance both through reduction of unnecessarily hard usage and through the creation of incentives for long-range upkeep.

It helps eliminate the "alienated tenant" psychology.

It helps reduce the cost of housing, which necessarily includes in the case of rented quarters a substantial rate of return on risk capital in an inherently capital-intensive activity; the homeowner can in effect earn this return on his own commitment rather than having to pay it to a landlord investor.

The present tax benefit provides a potential counterbalance to the heavy local property tax, which discriminates against basic housing consumption.

These considerations are directly pertinent to the problems of the core city. They are for the most part economic in character. It is not a matter of invoking elusive "value judgments," therefore, to urge that the Federal income tax benefits for homeownership be retained. Many of the criticisms of the tax treatment of homeowners as compared with tenants, which are ostensibly concerned with "horizontal inequities" (as between persons at the same income level), are in reality triggered by the "vertical tax differentiation" (as between higher and lower incomes) which results from excessive benefits for wealthy homeowners and the inability of lower-income taxpayers to secure the benefits.

Retention of the basic income tax encouragement to homeownership could be reconciled with appropriate maximum limitations where the present benefits are so large as to go beyond their ordinarily understood objectives. A direct and seemingly simple approach would be to set dollar limits on allowable deductions for residential property tax and home mortgage interest payments. However, such an approach would face some important problems. For example, an attempt to "see through" the use of alternative financial arrangements and deny interest deductions actually related to "sumptuous home" finance would encounter the well-known difficulty of "pairing particular debts and assets."[36] Thus, while such restrictions have an appeal on equity grounds, it may be preferable to leave the delicate task of ironing out excesses or misapplications of the homeowner deductions to comprehensive tax reform. One such possibility could be the minimum-maximum tax approach discussed in recent years.[37]

Homeownership need not, of course, be identified solely with detached single-family houses or diffused exodus to the suburbs. Active programs of encouragement to cooperative housing or condominiums which would provide economical housing for low-income urban residents would assist in placing homeowner status within their reach. If the culture and personal preferences of the slum dwellers require more conventional single homes or row-house construction, new or rehabilitated units of these types could be made available for purchase by them.

Efforts along these lines, obviously, would involve public and private action with respect to housing supply, rather than changes in Federal tax provisions. Moreover, their direct benefit would flow primarily to core city families above the very lowest income level—i.e., those with a potential capacity to shift from renting to homeowner status. Those below this economic level commonly incur little or no individual income tax liability by reason of personal exemptions and standard deduction allowances against their very small incomes. For this part of the population, it would seem clearly necessary to deal with housing needs in other ways than through any revision of the homeowner aspects of individual income taxation.

Tax Factors in Realistic Perspective

The process of exploring the tax environment of urban housing, its consumers, and its owners, almost unavoidably creates an impression of preoccupation with, or overemphasis on, tax impacts and the potentialities of tax changes to the neglect of various nontax factors and alternatives. To dispel any such impression, it is stressed that

The urban housing problem is too complex to be explained

or corrected merely in a simplistic tax dimension; it will not yield readily to simple, automatic tax incentive solutions.

It is theoretically possible for a minor tax adjustment increasing the after-tax return on housing investment by *x* percentage points to elicit additional private capital commitments by some multiple of the revenue concession involved; however, this is unlikely in slum housing, and if it were possible, the same results would be achieved by a comparable subsidy in other forms such as grants or submarket-interest mortgage financing.

The essential economic cost and resource allocation problems involved in paying for subsidizing low-income urban housing is not magically waved away or transmuted by translating the costs into tax concessions, particularly if they are not well-suited to accomplish the precise job demanded to rebuild the inner cities.

A considerable part of the urban housing problem is people, their poverty, their lack of preparation for modern urban living, and as a consequence the conditions of their use of urban housing.

The latter aspect of the housing problem is only remotely related to the tax structure.

One-sided or excessive preoccupation with housing per se, through the tax or other approach, may prove disappointing if the "externalities" or indirect benefits from better housing for the urban poor prove transient or symptom-oriented.

Any elaboration of the points just raised is outside the scope of this study. Nevertheless, they are essential parts of the overall perspective.

Within the immediately relevant perspective, however, is the actuality on which many, if not most, experts seem to agree (and the financial arithmetic bears them out) that

Housing investment is affected basically by interest rates, credit availability, and the possibilities of profitable leveraging.

Tax factors in the last analysis merely supplement the inherent profitability of advantageous leveraging to utilize the differential between estimated gross rates of return and interest costs on a substantial mortgage indebtedness.

There is virtually no barrier to a housing construction project which cannot be surmounted by sufficiently liberal mortgage financing, which at the extreme can (1) provide funds for virtually all construction and acquisition costs, (2) reduce equity capital at risk to minimal amounts, and (3) cut mortgage service charges for interest and principal amortization below prospective rentals.

A reasonable appraisal of tax alternatives need not be diverted by the potentials of unrealistic mortgage financing aids to urban housing construction or rehabilitation. These potentials flow from the capital-intensive and risk-demanding aspects of housing investment. But the lesson for this study seems evident that for greatest effectiveness any tax program to activate private enterprise participation in low-cost housing should be integrated with financing, loan guarantee, or equity capital insurance programs.

Notes

[1]S. 2100, 90th Cong., 1st Sess. (introduced by Senator Kennedy of New York) provides both investment tax credits and reduction in depreciable lives for eligible low-income housing in urban poverty areas. The proposed encouragement would encompass the building of new units and the rehabilitation of existing structures, including demolition costs and site improvements. The investment credits would cover land as well as building costs. Both investment credits and the reduction of depreciable lives would be scaled according to the equity investment percentage so as to benefit the high-equity investor and moderate the tax advantages of leveraging. Both the initial investor and subsequent holders would qualify, but the scale of benefits would be more liberal to the initial investor. For the initial investor, investment credits would range from 3 percent in the case of a 20 percent equity to 30 percent for a 100 percent equity; the reduced service lives for buildings would range from 20 years in the case of a 20 percent equity to 7 years for the 100 percent equity investor. The option to use the shorter tax lives would, however, exclude use of the accelerated depreciation formulas (declining balance and sum-of-the-years digits) so that the net advantage of the shorter depreciation lives, especially on new property, would be less than would otherwise be the case. The proposed legislation also includes a variety of related tax provisions: provisions to enable Subchapter S of the Internal Revenue Code to accomplish the pass-through of the tax benefits of low-income housing project corporations to their shareholders as though they were partnerships; nonrecognition of gain on disposition of low-income housing projects under certain conditions; restoration of depreciable basis to a continuous owner; and certain minimum and maximum holding period rules to encourage continuity of ownership. S. 2100 also includes a variety of other aids to poverty-area housing including more liberal mortgage credit and a property tax abatement plan. See *Tax Incentives to Encourage Housing in Urban Poverty Areas,* Hearings Before the Committee on Finance, U.S. Senate, 90th Cong., 1st Sess., on S. 2100, Sept. 14, 15, and 16, 1967, U.S. Government Printing Office, Washington, 1967.

[2]As we have seen, S. 2100 would modify Subchapter S to make it available to eligible low-income housing projects.

[3]As this parenthetical qualification observes, a full analysis of the revenue effect of a depreciation incentive which reallocates investment needs to take account of the earning and depreciation allowances of the investment which would have occurred in the absence of the incentive.

[4]See, for example, *President's 1961 Tax Recommendations*, Hearings Before the Committee on Ways and Means, House of Representatives, 87th Cong., 1st Sess., Vol. 1, pp. 8 and 24–25.

[5]*Federal Tax Policy*, Studies of Government Finance, The Brookings Institution, Washington: 1967, p. 122.

[6]For $1 billion annual eligible expenditures, a 7 percent credit costs about $70 million each year. Changing the depreciation rate from 10 percent straight-line to 20 percent declining balance costs about 5 percent of $1 billion at a 50 percent average tax rate or $50 million the first year, about 1.6 times that amount or $80 million the second year, and roughly 1.9 times that amount or $95 million in the third year.

[7]George Terborgh, *Incentives to Capital Investment: Two Approaches Compared*, Machinery and Allied Products Institute and Council for Technological Advancement, Washington, 1961, p. 17.

[8]Ibid., p. 16.

[9]George Terborgh, *Incentive Value of the Investment Credit, the Guideline Depreciation System, and the Corporate Rate Reduction*, Machinery and Allied Products Institute and Council for Technological Advancement, Washington, 1964.

[10]Ibid., Charts 1 and 2, pp. 14–15.

[11]S.2100, it will be recalled from the earlier summary, proposes to deal with this problem by scaling the credits in direct proportion to the equity percentage.

[12]Discussions in connection with S.2100, for example, would indicate that low-income housing can only bear 2 percent interest on 80 percent mortgages plus a yield of about 3 percent on equity (far below the yield commensurate with the risks and opportunity costs involved) if costs are to be kept down so as to provide adequate rental units at $70 to $100 a month. The problem is then how to raise the 3 percent basic equity yield to the considerably higher percentage which seems to be required. See *Congressional Record*, U.S. Senate, July 13, 1967, pp. S9594, S9595, and S9597.

[13]See Otto Eckstein, *Public Finance*, 2nd ed., Foundations of Modern Economics Series, Prentice-Hall, Englewood Cliffs, N.J., 1967, p. 47, and Rothenberg, op. cit., pp. 38–40.

[14]And possibly all building construction.

[15]Present value of $500 discounted for 10 years at 5 percent.

[16]Present value of (1) $50 immediately available plus (2) an annuity of $50 for 9 years, at the specified 5 percent per annum discount rate.

[17]See U.S. Department of Commerce, Bureau of the Census, Release CB67-122, October 24, 1967.

[18]As one expert has put it, "Uncle Sam is a principal cause of the phenomenon known as the slumlord . . . no matter how many violations have been lodged, the slumlord may file his depreciation . . . even in an old-law tenement he may take it on an accelerated basis . . . . In a contest between an on-the-premises tenant with meager resources and no access to the conventional lending market and a slumlord with access to all kinds of money markets and a federal tax bonanza to boot, who is going to win?

"I suggest a simple amendment closing the loophole. No more depreciation allowed until and unless the owner can produce a certificate from the local government that the property for which the depreciation is claimed is in full compliance with the codes." Address entitled "Let's Make Rebuilding Cities Simple," by Edwin J. Logue, then Development Administrator, Boston Redevelopment Authority, Lisner Auditorium, George Washington University, Washington, D.C., March 29, 1967 (George Washington University News Release).

[19]Dick Netzer, "Needed Reforms in Housing Tax Policies," Paper prepared for Conference on Housing for the Lower-Income Population, June 1–2, 1967, pp. 34–35.

[20]Logue, previously cited address, p. 17.

[21]This too has been frequently suggested but effectively criticized. See James Hellbrun, *Real Estate Taxes and Urban Housing*, Columbia University Press, 1966, Chs. 7 and 8, cited by Netzer in "Needed Reforms in Housing Tax Policies."

[22]See *Federal Tax Course 1968*, Prentice-Hall, pp. 1812–1813.

[23]Kickbacks, bribes, and similar improper payments to officials or employees of a foreign country, which would be unlawful under U.S. laws if they were applicable, are not deductible even by a legal business under Internal Revenue Code Section 162(c).

[24]Originally advanced by Arthur D. Sporn in "Some Contributions of the Income Tax Law to the Growth and Prevalence of Slums," *Columbia Law Review*, Vol. LIX, No. 7 (November 1959), pp. 1026–1063.

[25]Sporn, op. cit., pp. 1054 ff.

[26]Ordinary rather than capital gain treatment for gain to the extent of prior depreciation taken on the property.

[27]For example, suppose an investor pays $10,000 for a slum property with no net earnings other than the depreciation privileges, $7,500 representing the depreciable building and $2,500 nondepreciable land. Tax depreciation at 4 percent a year (followed by resale at original purchase price subject to capital gain later) would provide a return of substantially less than 1½ percent a year for a taxpayer in a 50 percent bracket. The annual income tax savings of $150 (50 percent of 4 percent × $7,500) would amount to 1½ percent of the $10,000 investment, but partial recapture of the depreciation at even the 25 percent capital gain rate on resale would reduce the effective return well below this figure.

[28]"Let's Make Rebuilding Cities Simple," previously cited address by Edwin J. Logue.

[29]By way of perspective, if 1 million blighted-area residents spent $1,000 each at a tax saving of even 14 percent, the income tax loss on this $1 billion outlay would be $140 million.

[30]Embodied in S.1199, 90th Cong., 1st Sess., introduced by Senator Jacob K. Javits.

[31]Qualification would require that the outlay be certified by the Secretary of Housing and Urban Development to be attributable to fulfilling standards prescribed by him for suitable rental housing for low-income families.

[32]Present discounted value computed as the sum of the first year tax savings undiscounted, and annuity for four years of $11.20 or $8, as the case may be, based on the figures shown in the preceding table, plus the present discounted value of the $75 after-tax proceeds five years later from capital gains reflecting value added to the property by the written-off expenditures.

[33]The details of the "tailoring" of the suggested credit for building are not worked out here, and there is considerable room for differences

of opinion on the exact structure which would best accomplish the purposes of an investment credit for construction. In general, the credit should be designed to accomplish a substantial increase in the after-tax profitability of the investment, with some scaling of the percentage amount according to depreciable life in order to avoid gross non-uniformities between longer-lived and shorter-lived assets as in the case of the present credit for machinery and equipment. Proportionate recapture presumably should apply where the property was sold prior to the lapse of a substantial portion of the depreciable life. The full credit should be available where there was a "normal" percentage, say 75 or 80 percent, of mortgage financing; the credit would be graduated downward where there was a higher percentage of debt financing both to achieve a reasonably uniform impact on profitability and to avoid inducements to artificially high leveraging and unsound financial structures. Since equity capital is relatively scarce and costly, it would be unwise for the proposed credit arrangements to provide particular rewards for 100 percent financing or for financing with mortgages less than the "normal" percentage of the cost of the property.

[34] *Tax Guide for Small Business*, 1968 edition, Internal Revenue Service Publication No. 334, Ch. 11, p. 33.

[35] However, expenditures subject to special treatment under this provision should not qualify for the investment credit previously suggested for construction and rehabilitation expenditure in general.

[36] See, e.g., Goode, *The Individual Income Tax*, p. 160.

[37] The essence of such a plan is to mute interpersonal differentials due to excessive deductions or exempt forms of income. See, for example, the address by Stanley S. Surrey, Assistant Secretary of the Treasury, before the Boston Economic Club, May 15, 1968. Treasury Department release, p. 10.

4.4

New York's Housing: A Study in *Immobilisme*

George Sternlieb

New York is unique among American cities in that it has the greatest potential freedom of choice to define its future. The market realities of all but a handful of our cities are such that they have no alternative to being what they are—the repositories of those who are occupationally bound to them, with a small supplement of free-floating central-city workers, transient intellectuals, and the like. But New York, as the business capital of the world, has the basic capacity substantially to shape itself. No single industry predominates. No single firm is terribly important. The skills of its labor force are, to an extraordinary extent, marketable elsewhere. And new jobs, mainly white collar, are constantly attracting new workers to the city. In the last six months alone, the construction of commercial buildings that will employ upward of 100,000 people was announced. No other American city is in such a constant state of flux and of self-transformation. There is then capacity to change—but is there the will?

Amid all this, more than a million people are on the welfare rolls, and the number is increasing by nearly 12,000 a month. Only the rich can live in New York and still succeed in isolating themselves, at least to some degree, from the very poor. The middle class, lacking the appurtenances of defense—the vacation house, the twenty-four-hour doorman, the access to private schools—is being driven out, though it is still a numerical majority. Housing policy in the city continues to waver between the two sharp crests of demand: the rich and the poor. So, even as New York changes, its housing policy is frozen into a self-defeating, inertial equilibrium.

If the city obeyed only the economic realities, it would seek to maximize the housing opportunities for the well-to-do and middle class: the executives, the mini-executives, the skilled white-collar workers, the young professionals, etc. Such tenants—self-financing, with small families—impose a relatively small burden on the city's budget, while at the same time expand its tax base. With the income derived from this type of housing, the city could then invest in amenities—including subsidized housing—for the poor. But the political folklore of our day inhibits such a traditional exploitation of the housing market's

Reprinted by permission of *The Public Interest* (No. 16, Summer 1969).

potentialities. City planners find their sense of social justice violated by it. Political leaders would risk their necks if they sanctioned it. Consequently, we find the emphasis on a "balanced" housing policy, and especially on the use of new housing developments to "integrate" the economic classes. Such emphasis is given further weight by the fact that the city's land-use controls, tax policies, and the like give the political authorities nearly complete power either to encourage or frustrate major construction programs.

Faced with a conflict between social priorities and market facts, officialdom has resorted to a "strategy" of inertia. A recent proposal, for example, to utilize a substantial segment of the air space over the West Side Highway for high-rise luxury housing bogged down for a number of reasons—not the least of which was the insistence by a variety of pressure groups that at least 25 per cent of the units be given over to the housing of the poor. Because the rich may love the poor but don't like to live too near them, the developer took his chips and went away.[1] More and more frequently, in New York these days, the choice is between no housing and "economically segregated" housing, and the result is no private investment in housing.

The Housing Stock

The growth of New York City as the nation's corporate headquarters has reinforced the divisions of the city's housing stock that have been clearly delineated for more than a generation. When we speak of New York City's housing stock, we speak of essentially three relatively disjointed segments:

1. The Gold Coast

This housing complements the city's growth industry, i.e., white-collar work. A large portion of the participants in this area live outside New York and, therefore, outside the bounds of this discussion. A significant proportion, however, do live inside the city, typically within a small geographical portion, that of Manhattan south of 96th Street. If we exclude the lower east side, some of the remnant tenements awaiting high-rental rehabilitation and/or replacement by high-cost housing, and additionally some of the west side slums that are fast disappearing under the impact of a revitalized Lincoln Square, we behold here a city and a real estate market unto itself.

In character and in type of inhabitant, it is not too dissimilar from the small area of Brooklyn Heights that faces it across the East River. The inhabitants of this area either work in the New Monuments to American Industry or furnish the complementary services required by them, i.e., the physicians, lawyers, accountants. Their location in these limited, discreet areas is in part a reflection of logistics, of proximity to the major employment nodes. But a glance at a subway map of New York would indicate that there are many other equally convenient areas in other sections of the city that have no allure. To the naked eye, there is nothing wrong with these areas except that people with money refuse to live there. The path of Marjorie Morningstar's parents from the elite areas of Jewish Harlem, to the west side towers, and then in all probability to their east side equivalent was a reflection less of the deterioration of the several earlier areas than of the full flourishing of the Morningstar exchequer. The new concentration is largely self-imposed and results in the decline of peripheral elite residential areas.

The concentration in one area has been complicated by the influx of central-city-oriented individuals with money to the city. The latter term, "to the city," does not mean to New York City per se, but rather to a vision of New York seemingly only fulfilled within a small part of its geography. To many people the city begins somewhere around city hall and ends where Harlem begins. Although there are small outposts of revived quarters—for example, Brooklyn Heights and possibly the Park Slope area of Brooklyn—they are limited indeed. The subways still run, surprisingly enough, frequently on time, and the distance from Brooklyn's Bedford-Stuyvesant area to midtown is perhaps no more than fifteen or twenty minutes. But it is a quantum jump in land values, from perhaps no more than \$3 or \$4 a square foot to land that sometimes trades for as much as 100 times that.

In large part, the rich are where they are because the rich are there. Every small-town father, faced with his children's decision to move to New York, reads lurid headlines about crime in the streets and makes their move conditional on their location in an appropriate address, i.e., typically a midtown east side one, with rental support paying the cost of the doorman. It is an area of childless families, of doubled-up young people, of social and economic mobility starting at a relatively high plateau. *In all renter-occupied housing units in Manhattan, 73.5 per cent are occupied by one- and two-person households. Indeed, for the city as a whole, 72.8 per cent of all "new" (built after 1947) rental housing units have no children under eighteen*. Rentals in these new facilities are commonly more than $100 per room.

2. The Residence of the Poor

Within this same municipality live more than one million people on welfare. In addition, it is a fact that the bulk of New York's manufacturing jobs are relatively low-paying. The city, therefore, must house not merely those on welfare but also its working poor. Sometimes, such housing is cheek by jowl with those of the elite groups. The distance between the lower east side tenement and the new high-rise, high-cost apartment houses of the East Village may only be an alleyway. More typical, however, is physical segmentation of the city's housing areas by economic class and/or race.

Harlem still presents a very substantial refuge for many of the poor blacks. But Harlem is a tired, middle-aged community now, with incomes much higher and the proportion of children much lower than in the new "growth areas" for the poor. The largest of these is the Bedford Stuyvesant area of Brooklyn. Sections of the Bronx, too, serve as a refuge for the poor. Indeed, the south Bronx is rapidly becoming an environment whose impact on its inhabitants may be even more deleterious than that of the older slums. The lower east side, with its wall-to-wall, five- and six-story, walk-up, old-law tenements, has partaken of every population shift in the city's history. The current surge is the replacement of Jews by a substantially Puerto Rican and Negro population. But the lower east side is, like Harlem, an area moving gradually into decay. Like Harlem, it is steadily losing population.

3. Burgherland

Uncomfortably sited between these two groups is the largest single element of New York City population, the middle class. New York, by most definitions, is a middle-income city, with 56 percent of its households in the $5,000-to-$15,000-a-year bracket. *Nearly a quarter of the city's population lives in one- and two-family houses, largely concentrated in Brooklyn and Queens*. And the number of Negro and Puerto Rican homeowners in the city went from under 50,000 to over 70,000 from 1950 to 1960; there is every indication that this trend has continued.

The Upper Bronx is lined with the six-story, semidetached, with sections of Brooklyn and Staten Island—the taxi driver, the fireproof, elevated apartment buildings that house—in common dry-cleaning storeowner, the Wall Street clerk, and all the myriad families of the city with incomes and/or occupations and/or folkways that keep them from the suburbs but also keep them from falling into the slum areas. Queens is largely inhabited by the upper-income elements of this same group, with only a small proportion of Negro and Puerto Rican tenancy: a mere quarter of a million out of nearly two million residents. The equivalent figure for Negro and Puerto Rican tenants in Manhattan is 580,000 out of 1,435,000; for Brooklyn, 850,000 out of 2,507,000; for the Bronx, 580,000 out of 1,428,000.

The Changing Definition of Property

Though the fact seems not widely to be recognized, New York City is by far the most sophisticated municipal government in the United States. As such, it provides us with some actual experience of approaches to housing that, in other cities, are still in the discussion stage. Basic to these approaches is the shift of the housing market away from one that, though often nourished by broad-based government financing, was essentially an activity of private industry. The options of private housing decision-making are now so limited by city government as to require a redefinition, a relabeling of the market actualities.

The bundle of rights and privileges we call property is far from immutable. The brief in Frank vs. Maryland 359 U.S. 360 (1959) states the basic fact of broad public interest in real estate perhaps as succinctly as it can be stated: "A man's home may be his castle, but that castle no longer sits on a hill surrounded by a moat. The modern castle is connected to a central water system, a sewerage system, a garbage collection system, and frequently houses on either side."

Real estate, the prototype and foundation of the legal definition of property, is particularly susceptible to social pressures. Inherently, it is uniquely subject to the impact of local laws and prejudices. Unlike most other forms of property, it is immobile: the banks may move their investment elsewhere; when accused of overly high prices, the supermarket operator simply closes the store and bobs up in a more congenial and profitable atmosphere; the credit merchant can always peddle in another jurisdiction. The apartment house, fixed in space, is a much more dependable hostage. I say "apartment house" rather than "house" because it is the multiple-family dwelling, where the votes represented by the tenantry naturally exceed the votes typically under the command of the owner—which is most vulnerable to political pressures. And in New York City 75 percent of families live in multiple-family dwellings, as against a much smaller percentage in other major cities. Indeed, 45 percent of the apartment houses in the United States are located in New York.

In New York City, the functional relationship of the private landlord to the residential real estate market is becoming less significant year by year. The basic rent levels are those set by rent control, which still survives in New York though hardly anywhere else. (Two-thirds of the city's housing stock is under strict control; rent increases in the remaining one-third have also recently been brought under control.)[2] The levels of maintenance, which substantially define the cash outflow from the property, are similarly determined—or at least stringent efforts are made to determine them—through the intervention of code enforcement. The right to choose tenants, and to evict at pleasure, are things of the past, often sighed for by owners but scarcely to be regained.

The erosion of the classic bundle of rights and privileges of property, which is a clear-cut phenomenon everywhere in the United States, is more apparent in New York City because of rent control. There are few other forms of property that the courts have treated as casually. For example: the implicit legalization of rent strikes as a political fact of life; the capacity (in New York today, elsewhere tomorrow) for the city to move into a building that is not properly maintained according to the letter of the law, make repairs, and then bill the landlord for them; the ability of the city to reduce rents, because of violations, to a nominal dollar-a-month; the power to subject the landlord to criminal penalties for mismanagement—all this is fast becoming "normal."

Given these restrictions, the "possession" of residential real estate becomes a most tenuous good. In the better areas of west side Manhattan, for example, there are excellent apartments in large rent-controlled buildings with monthly rents of $20 to $25 per room, or half their open-market value. Owners who wish to sell these buildings frequently find that their best buyers are the present tenants organized as a cooperative. But before the building can be converted into a cooperative, a significant proportion of the tenants must agree. And, because they already enjoy bargain rents, they will only do this if they get a bargain purchase. They often do. The *New York Times* has reported a number of recent instances in which tenants purchased their apartments at the equivalent of $3,000 per room and then promptly resold them for the equivalent of $7,000 per room—that is, at their free market value once the specter of rent control was lifted. In essence, the state, in league with the middle class renter (there are few poor in the category of buildings discussed), has disposed of the middle-class owner's property.

For the assault on real property is not the monopoly of the poor; the middle class, with short-sighted rapacity, has lustfully joined in the game. All of the heretofore uncontrolled housing in the city—typically post-1947 construction—is now rent controlled. Under these circumstances, it is difficult to envision fresh private residential funds flowing into the city. And because high-rise, high-rent housing is one of the more significant elements of the city's ratable structure, this will have a considerable fiscal impact. The net result is that one element of the middle class is subsidized at the expense of another—not to mention the poor who depend on the city's taxes for supporting services.

As a result, we see two markets developing in New York: one subject to the immediacies of the political pressures of the central city, the other much closer to the classic realty market, the suburbs. The fact that private funds and entrepreneurial skill flow to the latter needs no explanation.

As the spectrum of options available to the owner of urban real estate narrows, the function of private ownership is increasingly open to question. When this is complemented by the failure of private construction to add to the housing stock, regardless of the explanations, the principal historical reason for any overall political commitment to private operation goes by the board. And this is what is occurring.

New Housing

It is especially when we turn to new housing construction that it is clear that the basic model of housing activity in the United States—essentially that of private enterprise aided by government financing—has very little relevance to the realities of the urban scene. This is particularly the case with New York. The private new housing market in New York City has ground to a near halt. The levels of rent necessary to make new housing in the city an economically viable proposition are such that, without very definite and specific governmental intervention, they have become prohibitive. In the 1950s, 73 percent of New York's new housing was private and unsubsidized. The ratio is now nearing the 50 percent mark. There is every prospect that this trend will be accentuated in the future.

Why should this be the case? After all, the suburbs are filled with hungry tract-developers, garden-apartment builders, and the like, who rarely even take advantage of FHA financing, and seemingly need little else. I think the answer for New York City—and it is an answer of terrible significance to all major cities—is that there is comparatively little money to be made in residential construction in the central city. New York City still has its Gold Coast, and within that Gold Coast this generalization would not hold true. But once one leaves that area and its pitifully small equivalents in other cities, there is little to attract the developer other than the fast returns secured by a bail-out mortgage. Private builders require extra-large rewards to build in poor areas, where their investment is riskier; such rewards are not now available. And in New York City they face, in addition, a conflict of municipal priorities when they try to build in good areas.

There is nothing more conducive to the generation of inertia than the clash of righteous platitudes. A striking example of this rule is the question of the density of zoning to be permitted in residential areas of New York. Six years ago, with much fanfare, new zoning regulations were promulgated in the city. The group responsible for them pointed to the "inhuman" levels of density that characterized most new residential development, particularly in Manhattan, and further pointed to the disappearance of the low-rise structures which enriched "the human scale" of the city. The new zoning plan adopted to right these wrongs had, as a primary aim, the stabilization of Manhattan's residential densities, while at the same time encouraging development in other boroughs. An enormous rush by the construction industry to develop properties prior to the enforcement of these new requirements flooded the housing market of the city for the several years that followed. This has now come to an end, and with the termination of the old era of intensive development a new age of more appropriate levels of density in housing should be opening. This may be the case but only at the cost of no construction whatsoever.

Despite romantic hopes to the contrary, the development of high-rise luxury apartments outside Manhattan and a few selected areas of Queens has been noticeable only by its absence, and the city's privately financed housing is immobilized.

Despite a fantastically low vacancy rate in luxury buildings (little more than 1 percent), there is next to no new construction underway. Privately financed, full taxpaying new units completed in Manhattan have gone from ninety-three buildings with 13,000 units in 1963 to five last year with 1,154 apartments. It is estimated that no more than fifteen to twenty privately financed multifamily buildings have been completed or are in construction in Manhattan under the new zoning ordinance. Virtually all the completions since 1961 were under the old zoning ordinance.

The demons and villains in this drama are many. Not least among them may be developers who are holding their land rather than building on it, with the hope of being able eventually to secure heavier levels of density (and therefore greater value) from the authorities. The developers' retort to this accusation is quite simple and not without some cogency: given the income-expense ratios of present-day construction, and the levels of density most of Manhattan is subject to, the economic minimum for a building site under the new regulations is approximately three-quarters of an acre in area—as contrasted with a little more than half this area under the old zoning regulations. And the cost of assembling land goes up nearly *geometrically* as the parcel is increased in size. Thus, little new housing, and that ferociously expensive, in only a few choice locations, is constructed.

Has New York City residential development been at an inhuman scale? The question, as phrased, would probably get an affirmative response, particularly from those New Yorkers who are already satisfactorily housed. Is maintaining a lower level of density of development worthwhile, in the face of an acute housing shortage? I suspect that this question would get a more ambivalent answer today. Everyone may be for lower residential density, but few people are actually in favor of a housing shortage.

Some relief from this situation has been sought recently by city hall, which has encouraged the rezoning of three Manhattan areas, at present relatively lightly developed, with low-rise tenements and light-manufacturing lofts. But here, once again, a war cry goes up that the use of this land will reduce the number of relatively unskilled jobs in Manhattan, which are few enough in number as is, and that in addition there will be some dislocation of the poor. Even when the actual level of dislocation involved in the several sites turns out to be minimal, the opponents are not appeased. For permission to erect housing with a high level of density next to low-density poor areas will intensify the pressure to convert those latter areas to more rewarding forms of real estate improvement and will ultimately lead to the displacement of the poor. These last criticisms have been advanced by, among others, an insurgent group within the city planning commission. Predictably, the municipal response has been to take the path of least resistance—to do nothing.

These incidents are significant, not only in and of themselves, but perhaps even more so as an indication of the indecisiveness which municipal policy-making must fall prey to, until it has more clearly defined its role and purpose. In this clash of the "brights"—the young, college-educated city planners, social workers, poverty warriors lured to New York as the locus of "action" from all over the United States—with the natural market tendencies, there are no obvious, clear-cut answers. Any answer will be costly to—and seen as unjust by—a segment of the community. On the other hand, no answer is costly to all and is felt as an injustice by all.

Public Housing—The Nest of Dilemmas

There are only a limited number of satisfactory sites for housing the rich. Middle-class subsidized housing, even with tax-exempt forty-year mortgages and 50 percent tax rebates, costs $50 a room, which strains any middle-class budget. What of public housing for the poor?

Public housing is the apotheosis of all the frustrations inherent in the city's housing problem. To begin with, we have the increase of construction costs clashing with the cost ceiling of federal support problems, despite the "extensions" given to so-called high costs areas. Little can be built in New York City that comes under the federal support standards. But it is much more than this fact that inhibits new public housing in the city. And here again we find a common dilemma that runs through all of the city's housing policies: to maximize the number of units constructed with the limited dollars available or to improve the standards of what is constructed at the cost of reduced construction.

Operating and maintenance costs of public housing must be paid for by the tenantry. The federal contribution is substantially limited to the capital investment. Unless the units are built to be run cheaply, public housing simply is too expensive for the poor. But how can we minimize administrative costs, given the current reaction against "the hideous monoliths" and the current demand for small units on scattered sites? The conflict between providing shelter in bulk as against improving the quality of public housing has no resolution; the cost has been immobility.

The folklore of high-rise public housing that characterized the Robert Moses era of the city has been rejected in recent years. It has been rejected by "enlightened" city planners, "progressive" architects, by the intellectuals, and the *New York Times*. Unfortunately, it turns out to be impossible, under present conditions, to build anything else, or more precisely, to build in sufficient quantity to matter. Vest-pocket public housing makes good architectural news; it also tends to be slow in production, expensive, very difficult to secure sites for, and substantially nonexistent. Did it exist, most of the poor couldn't afford it because the operating costs, and hence the rentals, would be too high.

The fact is that the role of public housing in New York has been completely misunderstood, lost in a sea of rhetoric about regimented living conditions, overly homogeneous tenant groups, the exclusion of natural leaders by artificial income limitations, and so forth. Yet the reality of public housing in New York City is that, historically and up to the present time, it has provided a major source of housing for the working class. It has been able to do this by rigorously avoiding making public housing a form of welfare housing. Historically, New York's public housing has been built for a relatively stable, substantially employed sector of the city's population. As a result, there has been considerable stability of residents. Nearly 10 percent of all the public housing residents in the city have lived in the same unit for more than fifteen years, and an additional 21.2 percent moved into their present units between 1954 and 1959, with 56.5 percent coming in from 1960 to 1966.

This is now in the process of changing. Faced with operating deficits resulting from increased costs, unionization of maintenance workers, and so on, the city's housing authority is in the process of "raising" by 47 percent the rents of the welfare recipients who occupy public housing. The increase is only on paper, of course. In other words, instead of an across-the-board increase in all rents, or an outright subsidy, funds will be juggled out of the welfare budget in the form of increased subsidies to the public housing structure. Because the welfare budget is already said to be inadequate, there is some mystery as to how this is going to accomplish very much. What the recent announcement of this ploy did highlight, however, is the substantial increase in the proportion of welfare recipients living in public housing over the last several years. Currently, one-sixth of public housing units are occupied by people on welfare, and odds are very high that this discovery of a means of increasing rents without increasing them will drive the city, given its increased welfare rolls, to raise that proportion.

"Rehabilitation"

Perhaps something can at least be done to refurbish the city's existing stock of housing. Of the city's rental stock of 2,096,000 occupied rental units, more than a quarter of a million were built before 1902, less than a third since 1929. It would seem that something might be accomplished here. Alas, the simple but sad fact of life is that rehabilitation of central-city housing, with the exception of few special cases, simply hasn't worked. Of the nearly quarter of a million of New York City's dwelling units that are old-law tenements, the bulk are four- or more-story walkups, nearly half are five and six stories. Their classic "dumbbell" shape, with narrow air shafts at the waist, have frustrated every effort at rehabilitation since they were constructed as "model tenements" prior to 1902.

Worth noting are two of the more publicized efforts: the "Instant Rehabilitation" effort and the 102nd Street Project. In the former, a scheme was devised for drilling a hole through the core of a set of old-law tenements (using a specially constructed crane), gutting the center of the structure, and replacing the kitchens and bathrooms with prefabricated utility units lowered by the same crane through the roof—and all this in forty-eight hours! After a year's practice on a building purchased specially for the purpose, with much fanfare, the experiment was initiated. Deducting all the start-up expenses, the end result cost $38 a square foot, *slightly more than the most luxurious of new housing;* all this with the basic problems of vertical transportation, of narrow corridors and inadequate room configurations, relatively untouched!

An equally publicized rehabilitation effort, utilizing more conventional approaches, has been undertaken on West 102nd Street. Originally conceived as a very modest brush, paint-up, fix-up, rehabilitation effort, costing perhaps $3,000 a unit, present costs are substantially over the $13,000-a-unit figure, with an end product that is substantially unsatisfactory.

The anecdotal material surrounding the fate of these two ventures (and others) is voluminous, but titillating as the stories of late contractors, recalcitrant unions, and uncooperative tenant organizations may be, they cannot obscure the basic message: if new housing for the poor costs too much—and in new housing, remember, we have all the efficiencies attendant on mass production and standardization—then rehabilitation of existing structures, which means a much higher level of hand work and individualized expertise, is even more uneconomical.[3]

The inescapable truth is that in housing rehabilitation we have come to the end of our string of platitudes. Though housing authorities keep mumbling ritualistic lip service to the concept, the reality seems much further away than it did just a few years ago.

But there is a further point to be made. If rehabilitation cannot help the poor, it could help the well-to-do. New York City—at least that part of the city sited on Manhattan south of Harlem—has an upper-class housing demand without parallel in the United States. Rehabilitation to service this demand is entirely practicable within the present-day cost context. Yet here, once again, we run into the Hamlet-like inability of the municipal authorities to decide on housing policy because satisfying the housing needs of the rich does mean, to some extent, frustrating the housing demands of the poor.

It is the difficulty in rehousing the dislocatees as a function of renewal and rehabilitation efforts that more than any other single factor inhibits private activity in this sphere. Statutory rights of tenants in New York are without peer in any other major American city. The political realities of the day enable old-law, six-story, walk-up tenements, with average rent rolls of perhaps $40 an apartment, to occupy land that, if cleared, would be worth substantially more than $100 per square foot—or if massively rehabilitated, would have apartments renting for $100 or more a room per month.

Whether in the long run this is good even for the poor, or whether the flow of funds into municipal coffers that housing for the affluent might secure would better serve their purposes, has yet to be thought through.

The Maintenance Problem

The maintenance of housing in New York City is more difficult than in most other municipalities. New York shares with the latter the problems of the poor; of their size of families; of the tensions between minority tenantry and white landlords; of owners faced with a profitless future and unsalable property playing "end game"—attempting to drain their buildings of whatever cash can be secured before abandoning them. But all these are complicated by the tenure characteristics and size of structure unique to New York City.

Three-quarters of all New York City's housing is rental; this contrasts with less than half that figure in Philadelphia, for example. In addition, and much more significant, is the fact of the size of buildings in New York City. More than two-thirds of the rental housing is in buildings with twenty or more units. Indeed, nearly 20 percent of the units are in buildings with one hundred apartment units and over. There are certain efficiencies of scale in the maintenance of such large structures; but there is also a greater vulnerability to the "contamination effect."

In areas with one- and two-family houses, the impact of the problem tenant—the junkie, the whore, the drunkard, the psychotic, the criminal—is minimized. Though he may be a pain in the neck to his neighbors, his effect on them is relatively trivial as contrasted with the potential of the same tenant in a large structure. The drug-addicted tenant, who hacks out the copper pipes or radiators for sale to the local junk dealer, would in most cities usually be inconveniencing perhaps one or two families. In New York City, on the other hand, the odds are high that he may be closing down the housing of ten times that number. It only takes two or three problem tenants to make the living conditions in a 100-family building unbearable. The degree of control over tenants required to maintain large structures, therefore, is very high indeed.

Such control is very difficult to achieve in New York for political reasons. Tenants not only have their rights inscribed in law; they even have lawyers paid by the Office of Economic Opportunity, to defend these rights. Getting rid of the problem tenant is a herculean effort that is rarely even made. The contagion effect on the other tenants is massive. "Why should I try to maintain my apartment when nobody else gives a damn?" So he doesn't. And the building becomes a shambles—very soon, an uninhabitable shambles.

The dynamics of slum development, obviously, are not unique to New York. They are accentuated, however, by the size of structure. And their symbol is the zones of abandonment.

Zones of Abandonment

The jarring incongruity of a very tight housing market occurring simultaneously with the virtual abandonment of literally thousands of residential buildings is one of the paradoxes of our older cities—and especially of New York. Though the precise figure is somewhat controversial, there are in New York today probably somewhere in the vicinity of 5,000 multiple-tenancy buildings, containing at least five or six times that number of apartments, which have been vacated by the tenantry and, to all intents and purposes, abandoned by the owners. These abandoned residential buildings are concentrated in two areas: the bulk of them are in the Brownsville-East New York section of Brooklyn, but there are a fair number in the Williamsburg and Bedford Stuyvesant sections. (The incidence of this phenomenon in Harlem is also increasing.) Many of the buildings are not old-law tenements (i.e., built before 1902) but rather—particularly in the Brownsville-East New York section—are four-story walkups built in the early 1900s to house the flood of first-generation Jews and Italians leaving the squalor of the east side for better housing. The blocks Alfred Kazin described so movingly in *A Walker in the City* are now, many of them, littered with the wreckage of broken and abandoned buildings. Some streets look as if they had been bombed by B-52s.

It is easy to comprehend why these buildings get abandoned. It is less easy to understand why they *remain* abandoned in a period of what everyone agrees to be acute housing shortage. But I would suggest that the reason is that for the first time in our history there is no poor immigrant group—poor, but with a middle-class ethos—to move into the derelict houses: to move into them *and* to maintain them. Indeed, if there had been no agrarian migration across the Mason-Dixon line, and its equivalent from the Caribbean, the incidence of vacated buildings would probably have occurred earlier. Now, the flow of migrants from Puerto Rico into New York has substantially stabilized, and though the movement of Negroes from the South continues, it does so—as best as we can read the evidence—at a reduced rate. Increasingly, the move is to more attractive areas than some of the older cities—to smaller cities, and especially to the suburbs. Despite the exhortations of activists anxious for geographic concentration as a way station toward political power, the Negro and Puerto Rican middle class, and to an increasing extent the working class too, are voting with their feet—away from the central city. And there are no replacements.

The abandoned buildings are abandoned only when they are in dreadful condition. No reasonable observer can make very much of a brief for their continued utilization. But this has always been true, in greater or lesser degree, of bottom-of-the-barrel housing. Ours is a unique turning point in New York history. Given the legislation and climate of opinion which makes up our welfare state, and given the lack of new immigrants, such bottom-of-the-barrel housing no longer has any sound function. People on welfare don't want to live there, and no welfare official would even dream of "dumping" them there. Such housing is beyond the pale in our society.

The particular incidence of abandonment, i.e., where it takes place, and in which structures, is subject to much accidental variation. In some cases, particularly in the Brownsville area, the buildings abandoned are not the worst in the city. The particular reason for the specific choice of building or area is a compound of ownership characteristics, sometimes drug-addiction problems in the neighborhood, of tenant vandalization, and the like. The basic message, however, that comes through all of this anecdotal material is that essentially there is no economic market for these buildings in spite of the fact that the city's poor, its middle class, and its wealthy all suffer from a housing shortage!

The slums of New York are growing at their periphery and dying at their core. At this periphery, older white housing, sustained in fair condition by the relatively advanced age of the inhabitants and their relative childlessness, but systematically undermaintained for a generation, is being submerged by Negro and Puerto Rican emigration from the hard core. Left behind are structures of very marginal value, indeed. The economic—even the humane—logic of the situation would seem to call for the bulldozer. But the political logic of the situation makes this impossible. Before you can call in the bulldozer, you have to have a notion of what kind of housing you want to put up—and then you have to reconcile this with budgetary and/or market constraints. In New York City, such a reconciliation, which will involve hard and often unpopular decisions, seems beyond the power of government.

Notes

[1]At this writing the future of Battery Park City is bogged down in a similar controversy. This proposal would fill the wharf area at the southwestern tip of Manhattan and create ninety acres of new land immediately adjacent to the financial center. In an effort to forestall the inevitable, present plans provide that a third of the 15,000 units to be constructed on the site shall be in subsidized housing for low-and middle-income families. But now political pressure is mounting to subsidize the majority of the site's housing. The argument that, on a fully taxable base, the city's earnings per luxury unit constructed on this site would enable it to build *two* units of subsidized housing elsewhere seems to cut no ice. Forecasting is a dangerous profession. But as in the case of the starving donkey unable to decide between two equally distant trusses of straw, there will, in all probability, be no resolution of this dilemma.

[2]The subject of rent control is far too complex to be discussed in the space available here. Suffice it to say that the Temporary Rent Control Law was passed in 1943, during the war, and has continued on temporarily, if not merrily, ever since—with no end in sight.

Answers to the question of whether rent control in and of itself has generated a misallocation of residential space within the city—of old, childless families continuing to live in large apartments while the relative newcomers, typically the minority groups with children, can find only less desirable or more expensive accommodations—must be somewhat conjectural. Still, something of the sort does seem to have happened.

Based on the 1968 Housing Vacancy Survey conducted by the Census Bureau, there seems little doubt that there is far less turnover in the more desirable rent-controlled facilities (inhabited mainly by whites) than there is in the poor, controlled ones. The city's old-law tenements, five- and 6-story walk-ups typically, with a predominance of poor, minority-group tenantry, would seem to have the greatest degree of turnover, whereas the more modern rent-controlled buildings, particularly those in structures built after 1929, and inhabited by predominantly white and middle- (or even upper-) income groups, show signs of a tenantry that simply doesn't move.

Similarly, a glance at data on persons per room shows that well over 50,000 controlled units of post-1929 construction have one-half or fewer persons per room—a supply more than adequate to rehouse, at densities of only a little more than one person to the room—*all* the families now living in overcrowded old-law tenements. *Indeed, the amount of space, per capita, in rent-controlled housing, is often higher than in non-controlled (including luxury) housing*; 43.5 percent of controlled housing units have .5 or less persons per room whereas for the noncontrolled the equivalent percentage is 35.3 percent.

There is thus every indication that it is not the ethnic minorities of the city, the poor Puerto Ricans and the blacks, who benefit most from rent control, but rather middle-class whites. It should be noted in this context that *barely a fifth of all white households in rent-controlled apartments in the city have children under eighteen*. For blacks the proportion of such families with young children is double that, and among Puerto Ricans it is nearly two-thirds greater.

Could one protect rentals for the poor while abolishing the "free ride" that the middle class now receives from rent control? No one has as yet come up with an answer—perhaps because no one is looking very hard for one. These middle-class people, after all, do represent a lot of votes.

[3]A recent analysis of the economics of rehabilitation by the then-chief of program planning and development for the New York Housing Development Administration summarizes the situation very accurately, if depressingly. In this study, Frank Kristof took a half dozen of the modular forms of New York City housing and subjected each to an analysis of rehabilitation costs. He then matched the latter to the smorgasbord of available federal, state, and municipal programs. As an exercise in frustration, it is unbeatable.

Index